RESTRUCTURING FOR GROWTH

RESTRUCTURING FOR GROWTH

JOHN MICHAELSON

McGraw-Hill

New York   Chicago   San Francisco   Lisbon   London   Madrid   Mexico City
Milan   New Delhi   San Juan   Seoul   Singapore   Sydney   Toronto

The *McGraw·Hill* Companies

Library of Congress Cataloging-in-Publication Data

Michaelson, John C.

Restructuring for growth : alternative financial strategies to increase shareholder value / by John C. Michaelson.

  p. cm.

Includes bibliographical references.

  ISBN 0-07-140229-2 (hardcover : alk. paper)

  1. Corporations—Finance   2. Corporate reorganizations.

3. Subsidiary corporations.   I. Title.

  HG4028.R4 M534 2002

  658.1'6—dc21

2002011265

Exhibits 8–9, 8–10, 17–6, and 17–7 were supplied by FactSet Research Systems Inc., 2002.

Exhibits 4–1, 4–3, 6–2, 7–1, and 8–2 were supplied by the Financier.

Chapter 16 is adapted from "Exit Strategies," by John C. Michaelson, in *Starting Up and Advising an Emerging Massachusetts Business,* Massachusetts Continuing Legal Education, 2002.

1 2 3 4 5 6 7 8 9 0   DOC / DOC   0 9 8 7 6 5 4 3 2

ISBN 0-07-140229-2

This publication is designed to provide accurate and authoritative information in regard to the subject matter covered. It is sold with the understanding that neither the author nor the publisher is engaged in rendering legal, accounting, futures/securities trading, or other professional service. If legal advice or other expert assistance is required, the services of a competent professional person should be sought.

> —*From a Declaration of Principles jointly adopted by a Committee of the American Bar Association and a Committee of Publishers*

McGraw-Hill books are available at special quantity discounts to use as premiums and sales promotions, or for use in corporate training programs. For more information, please write to the Director of Special Sales, Professional Publishing, McGraw-Hill, Two Penn Plaza, New York, NY 10121-2298. Or contact your local bookstore.

To the women I love:
Susan, Anne, Elizabeth, Vera, and Marjorie
And to a great teacher, Raymond H. Parry.

CONTENTS

PREFACE

Subsidiary equity redeployments (SERs) play a major role in current corporate restructurings and in the US equity markets, with equity redeployment IPOs alone accounting for fully 73 percent of the funds raised in U.S. IPOs in 2001, and a similar percentage in the first half of 2002.

Building the value of a subsidiary—and the parent—is a pressing concern for much of corporate America. *Restructuring for Growth* addresses the creation of shareholder value by companies through the redeployment of the equity of a wholly or partially owned subsidiary operation to generate cash, increase focus, improve performance, restructure the balance sheet, and attract investor attention. Beneficiaries of smart redeployment efforts include parent companies, subsidiaries, shareholders, private equity investors, and strategic alliance partners.

The goal of this book is to provide a comprehensive road map which will detail how parent companies can successfully redeploy subsidiary equity to create shareholder value from initial planning through final value realization. We present numerous redeployment strategies, as well as examine the risks and rewards inherent in each strategy. This book also contains case studies that mirror each alternative. In addition, it identifies key action points, including tax, legal, and accounting considerations. Because this book is comprehensive, it can be used as a much-needed decision support tool that will guide readers through the process of achieving successful equity redeployment to create shareholder value.

Before we detail the target audience for this book, let's preview the equity redeployment strategies that we will later examine in depth:

Minority carve-outs

Majority carve-outs

Spin-offs

Two-step spin-offs

Split-offs

Tracking stocks

Private equity partnerships

Strategic partnerships

Exchangeable (convertible) securities

Mergers with a public, or soon to be public, company

I selected these strategies and the examples that accompany them based on experience gained in my current work as president of a fund management company that invests in a wide range of equity securities and my prior work as head of corporate finance at Needham & Company for 10 years. Needham & Company is a leader in structuring and executing SER transactions, and my partners and I were the financial advisor or managing underwriter on many of the examples mentioned in this book. In addition, I queried corporate executives, colleagues, legal and accounting professionals, and even competitors to ensure that the strategies presented in this book are helpful, timely, and appropriate—and meet the needs of the target audience.

Readers will find in this book the tools they need to gain in-depth knowledge of equity redeployment strategies. As such, the book is geared toward parent company executives who want to:

- Increase shareholder value.

- Raise funds for the parent company or a subsidiary.

- Reduce the parent company's outstanding debt.

- Simplify the parent company's corporate or business structure.

- Highlight the hidden equity value in a subsidiary.

- Realize some or all of the value in a subsidiary.

- Provide the resources for the subsidiary to better achieve its business potential.

- Allow the subsidiary to more effectively respond to challenges and changes in its environment.

- Prevent conflicts between the parent and the subsidiary.

- Provide adequate compensation incentives to attract and retain the subsidiary's management.

- Obtain resources and help from strategic partners without an outright acquisition or merger.

Other market segments that will benefit from this book include:

- Subsidiary company executives who want to assess available alternatives or redefine a relationship with the parent

- Executives at potential merger partners seeking an acceptable structure for a combination other than an outright sale

- Venture capitalists considering a partnership with a parent or a subsidiary

- Executives at a corporation looking to form a strategic partnership

- Public stock investors considering an investment in a spin-off, carve-out, tracking stock, or SER merger

- Lawyers, accountants, and consultants advising on strategic alternatives
- Executives in advanced management education programs
- General managers looking to familiarize themselves with the subject

ORGANIZATION AND STRUCTURE OF THIS BOOK

The first section of this book presents an overview of the subsidiary equity redeployment methods along with the general advantages and disadvantages of SERs for the parent and for the subsidiary. This section also looks at the steps to put in place prior to transitioning a subsidiary from a private entity to a public company. Note that there are numerous ways that a company can become public, including spin-offs and mergers. Therefore, this discussion covers all the means to create a public company—not just IPOs.

The second section of this book is its heart and soul, as it details each equity redeployment alternative, including:

- The advantages and disadvantages specific to each alternative
- The mechanics of each alternative
- Case studies of successful and unsuccessful deployments to provide extra insight into each alternative

The chapters in this section also include a discussion of:

- Advance preparation needed for a successful equity redeployment transaction
- Tax, legal, and accounting issues specific to each alternative

The third section of the book takes an in-depth look at how to create a successful public company and how to execute a successful public SER focusing on IPOs. Information about public SERs and IPOs is included in this book for the following reasons:

1. A number of SERs involve subsidiaries becoming public companies through a spin-off or a merger with a public company. Other SERs involve IPOs such as carve-outs. As suggested, many recent IPOs have been used to redeploy equity.

2. Other SER alternatives lay the groundwork for a future public market event, such as mergers with a private company and private equity and strategic partnerships.

3. With many of these SERs, the success of the subsidiary as a public company will determine the value creation of the SER for the shareholders of the parent.

4. The environment in the public markets on Wall Street and in the IPO market has changed dramatically in the past few years. Therefore, even readers who have had considerable exposure to the public markets may wish to know how

to create a successful public company in today's environment, how to execute a successful IPO, and how to succeed as a public company so that they may consider SER alternatives that make use of the public markets.

There is every reason to believe that SERs will continue to play a major role in corporate strategic thinking and the public and private equity capital markets in the years ahead, as corporations respond to intense shareholder pressure for results in a tougher economic and capital markets environment by rethinking many of the acquisitions made in the past five years, adopting a new, leaner business model that focuses on core competencies and makes greater use of alliances and partnerships, and as the special needs of growth operations are increasingly recognized. The growing acceptance of SERs by corporations and investors has opened up many more ways to better meet parent strategic objectives. There are now a number of alternatives to the traditional ones of complete control or complete divestiture.

FOREWORD

John Michaelson and I have been professional friends for 20 years. It is a relationship based on mutual respect and our shared enthusiasm for innovation in the financial world. *Restructuring for Growth* is a scholarly work deserving of a foreword from a leading academic or investment banker. So, I am surprised and quite pleased John asked me, an equities analyst and portfolio manager, to introduce you to this extraordinary book.

More than 30 years ago (my, how time flies when you're having fun), I developed the *private market value* (PMV) approach to equities investing. This approach focused on buying stocks trading at a deep discount to the underlying company's intrinsic, or in my terminology, private market value. Identifying a catalyst, some element of change that would help surface value in a timely fashion, has been critical to the success of the PMV methodology. Catalysts come in many forms, ranging from the simple (improving industry fundamentals, new product introductions, and deregulation) to the more exotic (the use of sophisticated financial tools and strategies to highlight business values and help close the gap between public and private market appraisals).

Through the years, my firm's clients have benefited enormously from our investments in companies utilizing what John Michaelson calls *subsidiary equity redeployment* (SER) strategies. Portfolio companies that have been acquired by other corporations or bought by management and financial partners via leveraged buyouts top the list. However, we have also had great success investing in "stubbs" (stocks left in the public market following LBOs), spin-offs, IPOs of subsidiaries, liquidations, and convertible securities. As chairman and CEO of American Stock Exchange-listed Lynch Interactive Company, Inc. (a spin-off of ASE-listed Lynch Corporation), I have employed several SER strategies to help surface the value of our businesses. These include spin-offs, subsidiary IPOs, and rights offerings for four public companies. I would like to think that in a small way these financial engineering successes helped motivate John to write this book.

Although the financial world is constantly spinning, some principles never change. Corporate managers will always have a dual mandate—to grow the intrinsic value of their companies and take initiatives to ensure that stock price keeps pace with this growth in value. To accomplish this mission, they must embrace new ideas and use new financial tools and strategies—the very things John Michaelson does such a wonderful job presenting throughout this exceptional book. *Restructuring for Growth* should be on every CEO's and CFO's "must read" list.

Mario Gabelli

ACKNOWLEDGMENTS

I have a number of people to thank for this book. Without their help and advice, this book would not have appeared.

First is my senior partner, George Needham, for his support and wise counsel to me for over 16 years at Needham & Company and before that at the First Boston Corporation. I have spent almost my entire professional career working with George. I cannot begin to express my appreciation and gratitude to him for his friendship and loyalty over 20 years. I have not, as far as I remember, ever told this to George. Let me now make up for this omission. Much of the advice in this book reflects what George has taught me. George personifies integrity and trustworthiness, values that are all too rare on Wall Street today.

Second, are my two wonderful editors, Jean Eske and Kelli Christiansen. Jean worked with me tirelessly to ready the manuscript. I am equally as appreciative of her patience and good humor as of her great capability. Jean is a gem. Kelli has overseen the editing, production, and marketing of this book from the beginning. She had the courage to commit to a first-time author and to work with me through the long process of turning an outline into a book. My thanks also to my copy editor, Ginny Carroll, who prepared the manuscript for publication and exhibited great grace in the face of deadlines.

Third is Mario Gabelli, who wrote the foreword to this book. Mario was the first major investor to see the potential of many now great industries including cellular communications, cable television, and entertainment content. He founded a major fund management company and also is a successful industrialist.

A number of my colleagues at Needham & Company contributed to this book. My thanks to my assistant, Eileen Kinsella, for all her help and support on this book as on everything else over the years. We are a team. My thanks also to Stephen Helfeld, who provided help in the preparation of early drafts of this book; my partner John Prior, who had many helpful comments; Thomas Hovore, Esq., who assisted with the chapters on IPOs; Pooyan Medizadeh, who assisted with statistical research; Larry Tarantino, our staff editor, who provided editorial assistance; Rob Wright, who assisted in preparing the materials on ESS Technology; the peerless Dorothy Brand, who, with the help of Caroline Estevez, formatted the exhibits; Professor Charles Wolf, who reviewed the valuation chapter and provided insights on Dell Computer and Palm; Bruce Alexander and Laura Black, who reviewed the sections on the SER activities of TRW; Ray Godfrey, a founder of Needham & Company, who provided guidance on this as he has on so many other projects; Robin Graham, who assisted me in preparing an article on spin-offs that was published in 1995 in *Financier* magazine; and Jan Triolo, who reviewed the chapter on marketing an IPO.

Outside of Needham & Company, I owe great thanks to Barry Dastin, Esq., managing partner of Kaye Scholer LLP, who provided invaluable comments on this text. Barry is the best lawyer with whom I have had the privilege of working. His partner, the renowned entertainment lawyer, Sherri Jeffrey, Esq., assisted me in navigating the contractual aspects of publishing of this book; this was akin to Clarence Darrow cheerfully defending a parking ticket. Thanks also to Jeremy Weitz, Esq., also of Kaye Scholer, who reviewed tax sections of the text; Saul Cohen, Esq., of Proskauer Rose LLP, who reviewed the chapters on IPOs; Eric Swanson, of Ernst & Young, who provided comments on certain tax aspects of SERs; and Robert Blair and James Boyd, of ESS Technology, who reviewed the case study on ESS. My thanks also to all the contributors quoted in the text. Of course, the errors are all my own.

Above all, my special thanks to my beloved wife Susan, and our two daughters Anne and Elizabeth, who have borne the brunt of my effort in writing this book over the past two years and are always first in my heart.

John C. Michaelson
New York

SECTION **I**

SER OVERVIEW

INTRODUCTION

BACKGROUND

Over the past few years there has been a dramatic increase in the number of parent companies using subsidiary equity redeployment SER transactions to create shareholder value. From 1997 to 2002 there were over 250 public SER initial public offerings (IPOs) and spin-offs and a considerably greater number of private SERs. Exhibit I–1 shows that four of the five largest IPOs in the first quarter of 2002 were SER IPOs.[1]

In fact, SERs have dominated IPO activity for the past several years, as Exhibit I–2 shows.

New approaches are being tried by parents to increase shareholder value. SERs play a key role in many of these new strategies. As a result, a whole range of SER options have become an integral part of strategic decisions by large and small U.S. and international corporations.

The primary reasons that more companies are undertaking SERs are discussed in the following sections.

A New Mind-Set About How to Achieve Shareholder Value

In the past, many parent companies viewed control of assets as essential. Now, more and more companies are realizing that bigger is not always better and that, in many cases, separating the parent and a subsidiary will benefit both the parent and the subsidiary and create greater value for shareholders of the parent. Over the past decade a new, leaner business model has emerged which dramatically diverges from the centralized command-and-control model of the past. With this new model a company's success is not based on owning and controlling ever larger asset and

EXHIBIT   I-1

Five Largest U.S. IPOs—First Quarter of 2002

Rank	Type of Transaction	Issuer	Industry	Principal Amount) ($ millions)
1	Carve-out SER	Travelers Property Casualty	Insurance—property & casualty	4,273
2	Carve-out SER	Alcon	Health care products	2,531
3	Tracking stock SER	Carolina Group—Loews	Consumer products—tobacco	1,127
4	Carve-out SER	GameStop	Own, op video game stores	373
5	Traditional IPO	PETCO Animal Supplies	Retail pet food, and supply store	317

Includes underwriters' overallotment
Source: Dealogic

employee resources. Instead, success is measured by creating shareholder value. With this new model, only those resources that are viewed as critical or *core competencies* are kept in-house, and everything else is outsourced or divested. Another element of this new model is entering into strategic partnerships to leverage the core competencies of outside companies. One of the best examples of a

EXHIBIT   I-2

SER IPOs as Percentage of Total Transaction Volume of IPOs

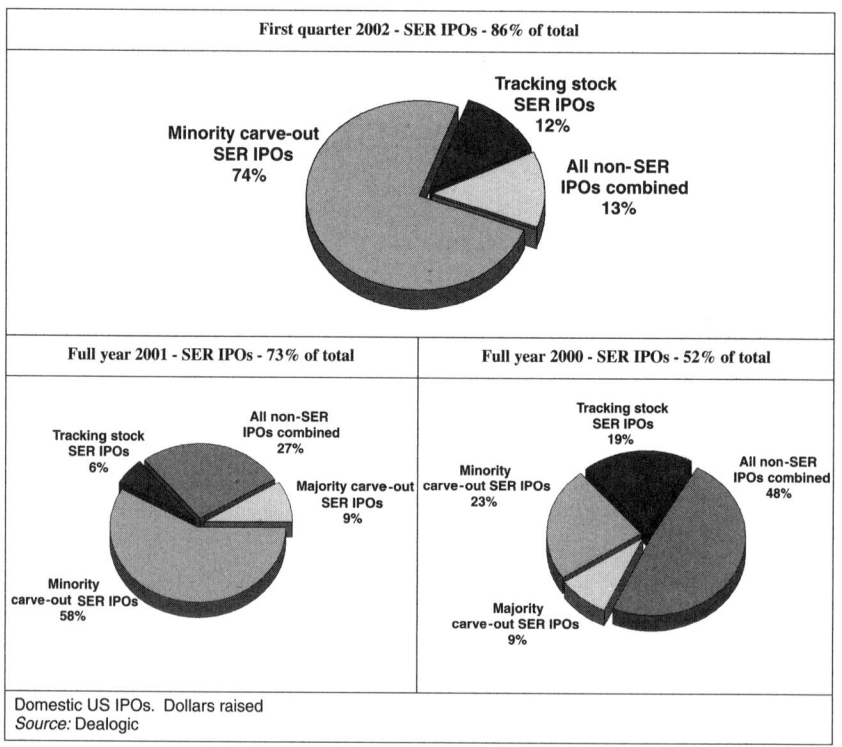

First quarter 2002 - SER IPOs - 86% of total

Tracking stock SER IPOs 12%

Minority carve-out SER IPOs 74%

All non-SER IPOs combined 13%

Full year 2001 - SER IPOs - 73% of total

All non-SER IPOs combined 27%

Tracking stock SER IPOs 6%

Majority carve-out SER IPOs 9%

Minority carve-out SER IPOs 58%

Full year 2000 - SER IPOs - 52% of total

Tracking stock SER IPOs 19%

Minority carve-out SER IPOs 23%

All non-SER IPOs combined 48%

Majority carve-out SER IPOs 9%

Domestic US IPOs. Dollars raised
Source: Dealogic

company structured on this new business model is Dell Computers. Ford Motor Company, once the model for the entire world for vertical integration, spun off its internal components business, Visteon, and is outsourcing many of its other activities. Today, with resources constrained and shareholders impatient, more parent companies are embracing the idea that they do not need to own and control all operations to realize value. Instead, they can create greater shareholder value by redeploying subsidiary equity in ways that benefit all parties and by entering into strategic partnerships in place of acquisitions.

In January 2001, Scios Inc. formed a partnership with Quintiles to commercialize Scios's congestive heart failure drug, Natrecor, in the United States. Quintiles provided a complete sales and marketing effort for Natrecor. This included hiring, training, and deploying a dedicated sales force. It would have taken Natrecor years and great cost to build a comparable sales effort on its own.

The idea that some subsidiaries may prosper best when separated from the parent is now accepted widely. At the same time, despite the relatively depressed state of the private and public equity markets, there has never been a more supportive environment for a subsidiary to succeed as a semi- or totally independent entity.

Demands by Investors and Analysts That Companies Focus on a Core Group of Businesses

In the 1990s growth was richly rewarded by the stock market. This led to an unparalleled merger wave as corporations, aided by high stock prices and easy access to equity and debt capital, made numerous acquisitions and also launched internal operations in many new areas. Many parent companies today own subsidiaries which do not fit with the parent's other operations. This collection of businesses makes it very difficult for investors and research analysts to value the parent company and its subsidiaries. As a result, investors and analysts are placing relentless pressure on parents to simplify corporate structures. In many cases, SERs present a means to achieve these objectives. According to *Business Week,* "After years of merger mania, some of the largest U.S. companies are doing a 180-degree turn. They are spinning off operations to raise badly needed cash, to recast their images as more focused entities or simply because the mergers didn't work."[2]

In 2002 Citigroup carved out Travelers Property Casualty, which it had acquired in 1998. When Citigroup merged with Travelers Insurance in 1998, the purpose of the merger was stated by Citigroup as "cross-marketing and providing better services to clients." According to Citigroup's CEO, the cross-selling synergies "really didn't work well."[3]

Recognition that Some Subsidiaries Will Perform Better When Separated

There is recognition by parents that many noncore subsidiaries are languishing from restricted access to resources, lack of attention from the parent, and an unclear role in the parent's future strategy. Yet, there is also recognition that many of these subsidiaries have favorable long-term prospects.

In the late 1990s, Du Pont divested the majority of its ownership of its subsidiary Du Pont Photomasks in a series of public offerings. Du Pont was not willing to make needed investments in the subsidiary but recognized that the subsidiary would competitively benefit from raising public capital and also from greater independence.

A Response to a Difficult Market for Traditional Divestitures

While for many parents, the preferred method of divestiture is a traditional cash sale at a premium price, the environment for these divestitures has deteriorated. Buyers, too, have low stock prices, pressure to converse cash, and limited access to the credit markets. As well, directors are opposing new acquisitions while existing operations are not robust, and investors are opposing any acquisitions that are not immediately accretive to per-share earnings. SER transactions are increasingly viewed as an alternative to a traditional cash sale that may create greater shareholder value for the parent.

In July 2002, Tyco International completed a majority carve-out of all its stock in its wholly owned subsidiary, CIT Group. This IPO raised $4.6 billion for Tyco in the fourth-largest IPO in U.S. history. Tyco earlier had tried to sell CIT in a traditional cash divestiture but received no acceptable offers.

A Response to Pressure to Restructure Balance Sheets

Many parents are under varying degrees of pressure from shareholders, directors, and creditors to restructure balance sheets. SERs provide a number of means to improve the balance sheet.

In 2001, under pressure to reduce debt, Lucent Technologies exchanged shares in its subsidiary, Agere, for $2.3 billion of parent debt.

A Solid Alternative to Acquisitions

Acquisitions often destroy the shareholder value that they were intended to create. As a result, many companies are looking for alternatives to outright acquisitions. These alternatives include SER options that do not require complete ownership of another company or subsidiary to create value based on win-win relationships.

In 1996 TRW's satellite operation, a defense contractor without commercial market experience, entered into a partnership with RF Micro Devices (RFMD) to commercialize TRW's advanced technology. Instead of acquiring RFMD, TRW acquired 40 percent of RFMD. RFMD maintained its entrepreneurial culture and went on to become a leading vendor in its market. TRW realized over $1 billion from selling its RFMD stock.

SER Track Record of Success

It has not gone unnoticed by corporations and investors that many SER transactions create shareholder value. This book will explore many successful SER examples in great detail. This success is in stark contrast to the highly publicized low success rate for most acquisitions, which currently have the reputation of destroying shareholder value.

A natural result of these successes is a greater level of comfort and familiarity among the parties involved in SER transactions, including private and public equity investors, lawyers and accountants, investment bankers, strategic partners, and creditors. This is demonstrated by the increasing, and substantial, role that SERs play in the public stock markets, as 86 percent of the IPO volume in the first quarter of 2002 was SER-based IPOs.

SERs are a viable means of creating real shareholder value. But, as with many fundamentally sound financial ideas, in the excesses of the late 1990s and 200 SERs were abused. Parents and investment bankers cashed in on market enthusiasms with poorly conceived and executed SERs. There is now a focus again on SERs that create real value.

Empirical Evidence That SERs Create Value

There is a considerable body of empirical literature to document that, in contrast to acquisitions, many SERs create shareholder value for the shareholders of the parent, the subsidiary, and outside investors in the SER. This topic is treated more fully later in the book.

Availability of More SER Alternatives

SERs are not new. For example, the breakup of Standard Oil almost 100 years ago was an SER. What is new is that there are many more SER alternatives than ever before, and these are much more widely accepted. This gives parent companies greater flexibility to create transactions that are beneficial in a myriad of ways. In the past, the primary strategic tools were acquisitions and divestitures. Now, parent companies can choose from many SER options outlined in this book. These create a great deal of flexibility in the relationship between the parent and the subsidiary, and offer a broad middle ground between complete ownership and complete divestiture that was not available in the past.

SUMMARY

This chapter briefly examined the reasons why both small and large companies are increasingly using SERs to create value for parent shareholders. Chapter 1 will review the various types of SER alternatives that are available to parent companies.

CHAPTER 1

SER TYPES, BENEFITS, AND CHALLENGES

INTRODUCTION

Public and private companies are under a great deal of pressure to create—and sustain—shareholder value by increasing both returns on capital and growth rates and the company's stock price or equity value.

The primary reasons for this include unrelenting pressure from shareholders to improve company performance, depressed stock prices, the linkage of management compensation to equity returns, the highly competitive global marketplace, and the willingness of other companies or private equity investors to make less-than-friendly offers for companies with underutilized assets.

No doubt most readers have experienced these pressures and are looking for techniques to increase shareholder value for their companies. Subsidiary equity redeployment (SER) transactions can often accomplish this key objective if planned, timed, and executed correctly. Therefore, this book will detail various SER strategies and examine the advantages and disadvantages of each. In addition, detailed examples of successful—and unsuccessful—SER efforts will be examined in depth. In many instances, the examples also provide details about specific transactions from company executives who actually planned, structured, and deployed them.

This chapter will introduce readers to numerous SER techniques and explain the benefits and challenges inherent in an SER effort. This will lay the groundwork for an in-depth look at the pluses and minuses of individual SER strategies detailed later in the book.

SUBSIDIARY EQUITY REDEPLOYMENT DEFINED

Subsidiary equity redeployment is defined as creating shareholder value through the successful redeployment by the parent of the value partially or fully owned operation or subsidiary. For the convenience of the reader, the ways that parent companies can structure SER strategies to create shareholder value are categorized in the following manner: (1) use the subsidiary's equity, (2) use the parent's equity, and (3) use the combined equity of the parent and the subsidiary. These approaches are detailed as follows.

Using the Subsidiary's Equity

The SER transactions that fit into this category include:

- *Minority carve-outs.* The parent or the subsidiary sells the stock of the subsidiary for cash to private or public investors representing a minority interest in the subsidiary. A minority carve-out can be accomplished through a sale of stock to the public in an IPO or to passive investors in a private offering.

- *Majority carve-outs.* The parent or subsidiary sells the stock of the subsidiary for cash, representing a majority or complete interest in the subsidiary through a sale of stock to the public in an IPO or to passive investors in a private offering.

- *Tax-free spin-offs.* Shareholders of the parent receive a distribution of stock in the subsidiary representing all or a majority of the parent's shares in the subsidiary. Upon the distribution, the parent does not have to pay tax on any gain, and shareholder tax is deferred until the shares are sold.

- *Taxable spin-offs.* Shareholders of the parent receive a distribution of stock in the subsidiary representing all, a majority, or a minority of the parent's shares in the subsidiary. Upon the distribution, taxes may be payable by the parent on any gain and by the shareholders on dividend income.

- *Mergers.* The parent merges the subsidiary with an existing public company or a private company in return for a minority or majority stock position in the combined company.

- *Private equity partnerships.* The parent or the subsidiary sells a minority or majority position in the subsidiary to a value-added and active private equity investor.

- *Strategic partnerships.* The parent or the subsidiary enters into a partnership with another company that includes an equity component to add value to the subsidiary.

Using the Parent's Publicly Traded Equity

Tracking stocks are the only SER transaction that fit into this category. Tracking stocks are a class of parent stock that the parent issues in an IPO or spin-off that tracks the performance of a subsidiary rather than that of the parent as a whole.

A key point about tracking stocks is that, while they are connected to the performance of a subsidiary, they are a class of parent stock, not a separate subsidiary stock.

Using the Publicly Traded Securities of the Parent and the Subsidiary

The SER transactions that fit into this category include:

- *Split-offs.* The parent exchanges subsidiary shares for parent shares, reducing the number of parent shares outstanding, or for parent debt, reducing its indebtedness. In many cases, there are substantial tax benefits to this approach.

- *Exchangeable securities.* The parent issues parent securities exchangeable for shares of the subsidiary or of another public company in which the parent owns a substantial equity position.

As we will see later in this book, many of these SERs can be combined to create value. For example, a carve-out IPO may be combined with a later spin-off in a *two-step spin-off,* a minority carve-out may be turned into a majority carve-out through subsequent sales of stock by the parent or the subsidiary, or a spin-off may be combined with stock or debt split-off.

CREATING A BUSINESS CASE FOR UNDERTAKING AN SER EFFORT

Let's take a closer look at how companies can gain from an appropriate—and well-executed—SER effort.

Increase Returns for the Parent's Shareholders

SER techniques enable a parent company to increase returns for its shareholders by:

- *Creating focused parent companies.* In the 1960s and 1970s, conglomerates were at the height of investor fancy. Today, the empirical evidence is strong that focused companies have a strong advantage over competitors. This results from their ability to focus all their efforts on areas of core competency. SERs enable vertically integrated and diversified companies to free capital tied up in areas of low competitive advantage where it is not contributing to shareholder value.

- *Divesting noncore assets.* SERs provide an opportunity to divest noncore operations, raise cash, and provide parent shareholders with a valuable asset.

- *Increasing investor interest and research sponsorship.* Often investors are not willing to take the time to understand a parent company that operates in many unrelated areas, as this necessitates having to understand the intricacies of each industry. With a few notable exceptions such as GE, investors will heavily discount these parents. SER alternatives can address this problem by creating *pure-play* (meaning industry-specific) companies, resulting in increased investor interest and availability of equity capital at a lower cost. A classic conglomerate, Hanson PLC, recognized this discount and split itself into four focused public companies in 1996, increasing shareholder value.

Investment bank equity research analysts are also specialized and equally unenthusiastic about non-pure-play companies. These analysts are still an important conduit to investors and their coverage can greatly increase the investor interest in a company. As a result, diversified parents and parents with businesses in different growth stages usually have a harder time obtaining coverage from research analysts, reducing the appeal to investors who look to research analysts for information. Varian Associates greatly increased its research coverage when it split into three focused companies (see Chapter 8).

- *Increasing transparency in corporate structures.* Especially in the post-Enron environment there is a premium attached by investors and analysts to simplicity and clarity in corporate structures. SERs are a means to simplify corporate organizations. U.S. Steel recognized the premium on a simple corporate structure when it spun off Marathon Oil in 2002.

- *Unlocking—and advertising—the hidden equity value of a subsidiary.* Parent companies are often not given credit by public stock investors for a highly successful subsidiary in a business unrelated to the parent's primary business or with a growth rate different from that of the parent. Even if investors are aware of the subsidiary, they have no objective means to value it because it is part of the parent. If the value of the subsidiary is significant, the parent may be very undervalued by public stock market investors, increasing the cost of equity capital, disappointing shareholders, and impeding the value of management equity incentives. The parent might also attract the attention of a stock market predator or competitor able to assess the true hidden value. In 2002 TRW had operations in two unrelated businesses: automotive components and defense and satellite electronics. Due to investor focus on the automotive operations and its problems, the very successful electronics operation was not given value in TRW's stock price. Northrop Grumman recognized the value of this gem operation and launched a successful hostile bid for TRW with the announced intent of keeping the defense and satellite operation and divesting the automotive.

- *Attracting a premium-price acquirer for the parent.* Often a potential high-value acquirer will want one major business of a parent but have no interest in its unrelated businesses. An SER may be a means to divest the subsidiary with the highest return to parent shareholders. C-Cube created great value for its shareholders by selling its two distinct businesses, each at a premium price to different buyers.[1]

- *Facilitating acquisitions.* In some cases, an acquisition candidate may be unreceptive to a merger unless it maintains a degree of independence, which can be provided by a tracking stock. When AT&T acquired Comcast, it agreed to issue a tracking stock for Comcast's Liberty Media operation. This facilitated the merger because it met the needs of the controlling shareholder of Comcast for a separate subsidiary to run within AT&T. It also enabled the controlling shareholder to participate directly in the equity value growth of that subsidiary. In other cases, sellers may want to continue to participate in the upside after a sale. When General Motors bought Hughes Aircraft, the seller, the Hughes Institute, wanted to continue to participate in its upside and was issued a tracking stock for that purpose.[2]

- *Realizing hidden value in a parent investment.* The stock market doesn't tend to value a successful investment in another public company owned by the parent. The parent may realize or highlight this value with an SER. The Tribune Company obtained value for its large holding of AOL through issuing an exchangeable note.

- *Retaining an interest in the future of the subsidiary.* The parent may want to cash in on part of the value of a subsidiary, but retain a continuing interest in the subsidiary's future success. An SER can help a parent company meet this objective. The parent may also wish to separate from the subsidiary but continue involvement. Nestlé SA maintained a majority ownership of its Alcon eye care subsidiary after Alcon's 2002 SER.

- *Attracting investor attention.* An SER can create a new—or renewed—interest in a parent that may have underperformed and fallen out of favor with investors. An SER effort signals to these investors that the parent has a newfound commitment to increase shareholder value. Hewlett-Packard was perceived as showing a commitment to shareholder value when it spun off Agilent in 2002.

- *Separating businesses perceived by investors as underperformers.* More often than not, a significant, underperforming subsidiary will drag down the value of the parent company stock disproportionately to its actual impact. An SER enables a parent to separate an underperforming subsidiary from its other businesses, resulting in an increased stock price for the parent. General Signal achieved this when it divested Electroglas through an SER.

- *Reducing the financial strains placed on a parent of a subsidiary.* Often parents will need to invest large amounts of cash to enable a promising subsidiary to succeed. The level of investment may be unacceptable to the parent. Du Pont raised needed capital for its subsidiary Du Pont Photomasks through SERs.

- *Reducing the effect of subsidiary losses on the parent's reported earnings.* For numerous reasons, a promising, but earlier-stage, subsidiary may be accumulating losses that detract from the profitability of the parent's core business. This is an acute problem for a mature parent that is valued by investors based on its earnings. A spin-off or carve-out of the loss-making subsidiary will help bring out the parent's favorable finances to the investor community. Barnes & Noble did this with its barnesandnoble.com operation.[3]

• *Reducing the volatility of parent earnings.* Because investors in mature companies are attracted to stability and predictability in earnings and dividends, investors will punish any activity that puts earnings stability or predictability at risk. An SER can address this problem by separating a subsidiary with unpredictable or cyclical earnings, reducing the parent's earnings volatility. Rockwell did an SER of its semiconductor subsidiary, Conexant, in part because of its earnings cyclicality.

• *Separating out liabilities.* In March 2002, Citigroup carved out Travelers in an IPO with a plan to spin off the remainder to Citigroup's shareholders. One possible reason for the SER, cited in the press though not by Citigroup, was to distance Citigroup from the potential liabilities of Travelers' asbestos claims exposure. Similarly, Goodrich believes that it passed its asbestos liabilities on to EnPro Industries in a spin-off.[4]

• *Overcoming internal opposition to new areas.* Investments in new areas that may transform the parent, at great risk, are often opposed by the managers of existing units who do not wish to see cash diverted to that area. An SER can mitigate these tensions.[5] Cray Computer separated from Cray Research to solve a conflict over development funds for a new supercomputer.

• *Enabling the parent to focus on core operations.* Redeploying the equity of a subsidiary can often free up the management team of the parent company to focus its time and energy on other crucial business activities. This was important to the management of ESS in the spin-off of Vialta.

• *Accommodating differing performance objectives.* Mature businesses have long-standing processes, procedures, attitudes, measurements of performance, and compensation systems geared to established operations. An emerging business with different needs may not flourish under these systems. For this reason, AMR separated the large and mature American Airlines and a promising growth software-based reservation system, Sabre. This also enabled the management of each to focus solely on its own operation.

• *Solving regulatory problems.* Regulatory and antitrust constraints are one of the primary reasons companies separate subsidiaries from the parent through majority carve-outs and spin-offs. One example is the majority carve-out of Balzers-Pfeiffer from Oerlikon-Buhrle in response to antitrust action.

• *Providing a superior alternative to an acquisition.* SER techniques can enable parent companies to obtain many of the benefits of a strategic acquisition while not stifling the smaller acquired company. Instead of acquiring a company, it often makes more sense for the parent and the other company to form a close strategic partnership. In this way, each organization gains resources and talents that were unavailable before the partnership. This was the case with Roche and Genentech. In that case, the entrepreneurial culture of the subsidiary was preserved while the parent received substantial benefit.

Increase the Value of a Subsidiary

SER techniques can enable a parent company to increase the value of a subsidiary by:

- *Enhancing the subsidiary's ability to compete.* Often an SER transaction gives the subsidiary more independence, enhancing its ability to compete against other companies, which may include actual customers of the subsidiary's parent company. Alleviating concerns by customers who were also competitors of the parent was a motive behind General Motors' spin-off of its Delphi Components operation.

- *Increasing publicity.* Often there will be increased publicity beyond the initial press release when a subsidiary separates from its parent, which translates into higher visibility with customers, suppliers, and potential alliance partners. The DII Group claimed increased visibility with customers following its spin-off from Dover.

- *Offering employees equity compensation.* Subsidiary competitiveness can be enhanced by offering its employees equity compensation directly tied to the subsidiary's performance, based on a public market value for that equity. Thermo Electron stated that fostering entrepreneurship was a key reason for its SERs.

- *Fostering an independent—and competitive—culture.* Often a formal separation can enhance the performance of the subsidiary—and its employees. Employees gain by being able to operate within their own unique culture that values creativity and competitiveness. This was a primary reason behind the two-step spin-off of Palm from 3Com.

- *Providing needed capabilities.* An SER may bring needed business capabilities to the subsidiary, as did a private equity partnership for Corsair Communications.

- *Facilitating sale of the subsidiary.* Announcing a spin-off or carve-out IPO and filing a detailed disclosure document focuses buyer attention on the subsidiary and sets a deadline by which a potential buyer must act. It also puts a value on the subsidiary.

Creating Tax and Accounting Benefits

SER techniques enable a parent company to create tax and accounting benefits by:

- *Obtaining both tax deferment and cash.* Certain SER alternatives, such as parent securities exchangeable into subsidiary securities, may allow the parent to defer tax on the gain from profitable investments while also providing it with cash. Cox Communications used this technique to cash in on its holdings of Sprint PCS.

- *Obtaining favorable accounting of gain in the parent's income statement.* The increase to the parent's book value from a carve-out may be recorded as nontaxable accounting income by the parent.

- *Reducing the parent's shares outstanding or debt tax efficiently.* Stock in a subsidiary split-off may be transferred tax efficiently to creditors in payment of debt. Lucent used this technique in its spin-off of Agere Systems in 2001. This allows the pretax value of the subsidiary's stock to be used to retire debt. Stock in a subsidiary may also be used in exchange for parent stock, as was done by The Limited in its 1996 split-off of Abercrombie & Fitch.

- *Distributing assets to shareholders in a tax-efficient manner.* One SER transaction, a tax-free spin-off, is a very efficient means to distribute assets to the parent's shareholders without taxation at the parent level and with deferred tax at the shareholder level. An outright sale of the subsidiary may be taxable to the parent and then a dividend to the parent's shareholders of the proceeds of the sale may be taxable again as a dividend. EMC distributed highly appreciated stock in its subsidiary McDATA to its shareholders in this manner.

CHALLENGES INHERENT IN A SUCCESSFUL SER

There are challenges inherent in any SER transaction, including the following:

- *Redeployments are difficult to reverse.* It is expensive and complicated to reverse some SER transactions once they have been completed. This is particularly true of public carve-outs and spin-offs. This is due to the creation of public shareholders who have many rights and protections afforded by the law, the courts, and regulatory agencies.

- *Redeployments are difficult to administer.* Redeployments can be difficult to administer for many reasons, including the fact that the parent may continue to oversee the finances and operations of the subsidiary, the parent may continue to have a commercial arrangement with the subsidiary, and the parent will have to administer the new class of parent stock if a tracking stock is issued.

- *Redeployments may result in a missed opportunity to gain financially.* A reduction in the parent's ownership interest in the subsidiary through an SER reduces the parent's full participation in future appreciation in the value of the subsidiary. This reduction varies from very substantial in the case of a spin-off where the parent has no remaining equity interest, to less significant in the case of a minority carve-out where the parent may continue to own 80 percent or more of the subsidiary after the SER.

- *Redeployments may mean loss of tax consolidation.* An SER for more than 20 percent of the subsidiary (different rules apply to partnerships and limited liability companies) may lead to a loss of tax consolidation with the parent. Consequently, any losses at the subsidiary may no longer be used to offset profits at the parent, dividends from the subsidiary to the parent may incur tax, and a spin-off may be taxable on gain at the parent and as dividend income to the shareholders.

• *Redeployments may monopolize the time and attention of the management team.* A redeployment transaction can monopolize the time and attention of the senior management team of the subsidiary and, often, the parent. This may cost both considerable business momentum. While the long-term impact of an SER may be very positive, preparing for successful equity redeployment can take 6 to 12 months of intense effort.

• *Redeployments may impact the parent's access to credit.* If a subsidiary is making a substantial contribution to the parent's cash flow, lenders may restrict credit or require that cash gained from redeployment be used to reduce parent debt. (However, we have already noted that the reverse may be true if the parent separates from an underperforming subsidiary that is a cash drain.)

• *Redeployments may impact equity incentive plans.* Some SERs, such as a spin-off, may affect the parent's outstanding stock option and stock purchase plan. This happens when parent or subsidiary employees have options that derive some part of their value from the current and future value of the subsidiary. Appropriate adjustments must be made to existing parent option plans to compensate for this loss of value following a spin-off, if the impact is material.

• *Redeployments may impact existing financial instruments.* Some forms of SER, such as a spin-off, may impact existing parent financial instruments, including any restrictions on dividends in loan agreements.

• *Redeployments may create complex corporate structures.* In the post-Enron environment, a complex corporate structure may alienate investors who equate simplicity with transparency and complication with obfuscation.

• *Redeployments may increase the parent's administrative burden.* Most subsidiary equity redeployments create some ongoing administrative burden for the parent's financial and legal staff. Also, if a parent company still has a financial or business interest in a subsidiary, and the subsidiary is not meeting its goals, the parent will spend a great deal of time trying to create—and execute—workable solutions. This is especially time consuming if a turnaround is prolonged.

• *Redeployments generally result in adversarial relationships.* An SER will likely create a relationship dynamic with the subsidiary that is different from the one that existed before. Specifically, subsidiary managers are likely to no longer view themselves as employees of the parent company; instead, they will identify with the subsidiary. This can create a stressful situation when the parent and the subsidiary do not share similar goals during—and after—the SER. For example, a goal of the subsidiary is to act independently of parental oversight, while a goal of the parent is to control—and protect—its interests during the re-deployment process.

However, the dynamic between the management teams at the parent and at the subsidiary will generally vary depending upon the type of redeployment and the degree of independence following the SER. For example, there are fewer areas of contention with a clean spin-off, and they are usually limited to the number, price, and terms of initial option grants to the management team of the subsidiary. In contrast, there may be many fundamental areas of tension with a subsidiary that has many commercial and financial relationships with the parent after the SER. The subsidiary's management will want protocols with the parent that do not jeopardize the success of the subsidiary or limit its ability to run its business in its own best interest, while the parent's objective is often to single-mindedly ensure that its own strategic and operating needs receive complete priority, even at the expense of the success of the subsidiary. If an objective of the parent is to maximize the value of its ownership position through an IPO or merger, attract private equity investors, or attract a top management team, the parent will have to recognize that the subsidiary must be a viable business. Issues of dispute tend to include the capitalization of the subsidiary, the timing of parent liquidity, continuing parent oversight, and the ongoing operating relationship between the subsidiary and the parent after the SER.

- *Stalled redeployments may demoralize the subsidiary management team.* Often, stalled redeployments can result in the resignation of the subsidiary's senior management team. Delays tend to be interpreted by the management team as backpedaling on the part of the parent. Two high-profile examples of this dynamic are Palm and 3Com, which are detailed in a case study later in this book, and General Signal's aborted spin-off of SPX.

- *Aborted redeployments are expensive.* Aborted SERs can be very expensive. Aside from the commitment of management time and the accompanying loss of business momentum, there are often large out-of-pocket expenses incurred in preparing for the SER. This especially applies to public SERs, where the costs of preparing for an SER, including accounting, legal, financial advisory, print-ing, filing fees, and so on, may easily exceed $1 million.

- *Appropriate parental oversight must be maintained.* Until the subsidiary has succeeded as a stand-alone company and fulfilled its obligations to the parent, the parent will need to continue to exercise oversight and ensure accountability. This may be done directly or through an outside board of directors. Parental demands that rigorous performance objectives be set and met are not the same as inordinate and unproductive interference.

It is important to note here that although challenges do exist, they can be reduced by applying the appropriate technique to a particular circumstance and by properly researching, preparing, and executing the most effective SER strategy.

SUMMARY

This chapter reviewed the various types of SER transactions that are available to parent companies and the equity that can be redeployed in those transactions, including the parent's, the subsidiary's, and the combined equity of both entities. It detailed how a business case can be created for undertaking an SER effort, along with the inherent challenges. The next chapter will present an overview of how—and why—to create a public subsidiary to achieve various SER objectives.

CHAPTER **2**

SERs AND PUBLIC SUBSIDIARIES

INTRODUCTION

Many of the SER strategies discussed in the following chapters involve the subsidiary becoming a public company at the time of the SER or later through a spin-off or merger with an already public company or going public through an IPO. Therefore, this chapter will provide an overview of the benefits and challenges of creating a public subsidiary through these means. Subsequent SER-specific chapters will detail the benefits—and challenges—of each strategy in depth.

CREATING A PUBLIC SUBSIDIARY: WEIGHING THE ADVANTAGES

First, to help readers determine whether creating a public subsidiary is the best way to advance an SER strategy, let's consider the reasons that support the creation of a public subsidiary through a carve-out or tracking stock IPO, a spin-off, or a merger with an existing public company.

Increase the Valuation of the Parent

As discussed in later chapters, studies have consistently shown that public market SERs have a positive effect on overall shareholder value of the parent. This is based on recognition by investors of the value of the subsidiary and also, in some cases, that an underperforming parent is now committed to increasing shareholder value.

Obtain Greater Value for the Subsidiary Than in a Traditional Divestiture

There are times when the public markets will value a subsidiary more highly than does a corporate or financial buyer. This is especially the case when a subsidiary is operating in a currently hot industry. The parent's shareholders may benefit from a sale of the subsidiary through a public SER. There are other times when buyers do not recognize the potential of a subsidiary or are not willing or able to pay for full value. The parent's shareholders may benefit from directly receiving the shares of a subsidiary in a spin-off over a traditional divestiture or through other SERs that permit continued participation in the potential of the subsidiary by the parent.

Share the Risks

Many public market SERs allow the parent to share the risk of the subsidiary's future with other investors. If the subsidiary has great prospects but great risk, this may be prudent. This especially applies to large and risky projects.

Increase the Parent's Access to Credit

When a money-losing, capital-intensive, or problematic subsidiary is actually separated from its parent as a result of an SER, creditors take notice and more readily lend cash—or offer a better rate—to a parent based on improved cash flows or lower risks.

Reduce the Parent's Debt

The parent may also repay debt through a tax-efficient exchange of subsidiary stock for parent debt as part of a split-off, and it may, within the bounds of prudence, transfer debt to the subsidiary or receive a cash distribution. The parent may also keep some or all of the proceeds of a carve-out IPO.

Provide Higher Overall Value in a Sale of the Parent

Often shareholders can receive a higher total value for the parent when certain operations that the buyer does not want or does not value are divested via a spin-off. With a spin-off, the unwanted subsidiary becomes a public company owned by the parent's shareholders. (See the example of C-Cube in Chapter 8.)

Allow Continued Participation in the Upside of the Subsidiary

One of the most important benefits of a public market SER is that it allows the parent, or its shareholders in the case of a spin-off, to maintain an interest in the future of the subsidiary and profit from an increase in its value after the SER. This does not apply to a 100 percent majority carve-out IPO.

Attract Different Investors

There are many types of different public stock investors, each valuing a different type of investment more highly. For example, growth-company public stock investors are often willing to pay premium prices for stocks with above-average growth prospects. With a higher growth rate, the subsidiary may command a significantly higher multiple in the public markets than the parent. A number of empirical studies demonstrate that a company's stock-trading multiples (i.e., price-to-earnings ratio and aggregate value-to-revenues multiple) are correlated to the market's perception of its growth prospects. A public subsidiary may attract new and different investors than the parent, increasing the overall level of investor interest and therefore the overall valuation.

Raise Equity Capital on Attractive Terms

An IPO may raise public equity capital for a subsidiary on better terms than those available to the parent. This is especially true when the subsidiary is projected to grow at a more rapid rate than the parent. It then has access to the worldwide universe of growth-oriented stock investors.

Raise Equity Capital Without Diluting the Parent's Ownership Level

Privately held parents can employ a subsidiary carve-out to raise public equity capital without taking the parent public. A closely held, but public, parent may similarly raise public equity capital at the subsidiary level without diluting parent shareholders.

Raise Cash Without Diluting the Parent's Per-Share Price

By taking advantage of the higher multiple often accorded a favored subsidiary, the parent may be able to raise public equity without the per-share dilution to the parent's earnings that usually results from a public offering of its own stock.

Provide Greater Financial Flexibility

Public equity is about the least restrictive and most flexible of any form of capital. It also is the type of capital that does the most to enhance the balance sheet and increase future financial flexibility. In contrast, debt usually has periodic interest payments and eventually has to be repaid. Even convertible debt is still often debt. It will convert into the common stock of the issuer only if the stock of the issuer does well; otherwise, it, too, has to be repaid. Debt—especially bank debt—also often has restrictive covenants that limit the actions of the company. Preferred stock is not usually as restrictive as debt, but it may have numerous rights and privileges. In addition, public equity proceeds retained in the subsidiary increase the creditworthiness and borrowing capacity of the subsidiary and provides a cushion for a cyclical business or a hedge against financial distress in a downturn. Furthermore, a strong balance sheet assures customers that commitments to them in the form of fulfilling orders, service requirements, and future product enhancements will be met.

Provide Growth Capital

An IPO will provide outside capital to grow the business faster than would be possible with only internally generated funds. The operations of the subsidiary may not be generating sufficient cash flow to invest or to use as working capital to take advantage of business opportunities. This may also apply to a mature company that wants to expand or build new facilities, and to growth companies that are often investing to grow but not generating a lot of cash. The parent may have its own restrictions on how much money it is willing or able to put into the subsidiary to finance growth. The capital raised in an IPO, when retained in the subsidiary, may allow greater investment in promising projects, products, and businesses.

Provide Cash to Make Important Cash-Based Acquisitions

A cash acquisition is attractive to a seller because it helps ensure that the deal will actually close regardless of fluctuations in the stock market, and it reduces the need for the seller to make an investment decision on holding the parent's or subsidiary's stock. By going public, the subsidiary, and the parent, can raise needed cash to make critical acquisitions.

Provide the Subsidiary with Its Own Stock for Use in Acquisitions

A subsidiary that wants to grow through acquisition may find that having its own stock is useful for making an acquisition. In many cases, sellers prefer to receive stock rather than cash for their company for reasons including deferment of taxes and the potential return from a continued participation in the combined business if it performs well (see the DII Group example in Chapter 8). Sellers of companies usually prefer to receive a publicly traded stock over a private stock for the following reasons:

• The price is established in the market. Reaching agreement on a price for the subsidiary is generally easier if the market has already established its value.

- There is a greater potential for liquidity, even if there are immediate legal or contractual restrictions on any sale of stock following the merger or a limited market for the stock that makes large sales of stock difficult.

- Public companies listed on a major exchange or quoted on Nasdaq are a safer bet, as they are bound by extensive disclosure and governance requirements and by fiduciary requirements to minority shareholders.

Increase Visibility

When Plumtree Software went public in a difficult IPO market in 2002, it said it was using the offering in part "to provide increased visibility and credibility in the marketplace."[1] As a public company, the subsidiary will issue its own financial statements and reports and be more distinctly identifiable to customers and employees. Credibility is a reason to go public, particularly for companies looking to stand out to potential customers.

CHALLENGES OF TAKING A COMPANY PUBLIC THROUGH AN SER

Subsequent chapters thoroughly discuss the difficulties—and risks—of taking a company public through an IPO. This section provides a brief overview of those challenges.

Considerable Expenses Are Incurred in the Public SER Process

Expenses incurred in connection with a public SER often exceed $1 million. These include fees for accounting, legal counsel, and printing, as well as fees associated with the appropriate agency filings. There are also costs associated with using envestment banks to sell stock to investors in an IPO or as advisors in a spin-off or merger. All these costs are discussed in depth later in this book.

A Public SER Process Is Time Consuming

The entire IPO process is time intensive and prevents senior managers from focusing solely on business matters relating to the subsidiary.

There Is Risk of a Failed Public SER

A good percentage of the companies that embark on a public SER process, particularly an IPO, do not actually close the public SER. Reasons for this include deterioration of the financial markets, poor investor reception to the offering, or adverse changes in the business during the prolonged public SER process. There is substantial trauma connected with an unsuccessful public SER. In addition to the considerable and unrecoverable expenses of preparing and filing for a public SER, there is the extensive time committed by management to the offering process and the impact on morale at the subsidiary.

THE SUBSIDIARY MUST BE VIABLE TO CREATE VALUE

A public market SER has to be a viable business to succeed in creating value in the public markets. This is a theme that will reappear throughout this book. A detailed discussion of the factors that contribute to a successful public company is found in Chapter 18.

Success as a public company is less likely when:

- The subsidiary is not well capitalized (see the example of Agere in Chapter 8).
- The subsidiary is not a good business (see the example of Millennium Chemicals in Chapter 8).
- The subsidiary is a product line, not a business (see the example of CSFB Direct in Chapter 11).
- The parent does not let the subsidiary operate in the subsidiary's best interests (see the discussion of Thermo Electron's SERS in Chapter 6).
- The management team is not up to running a public company (see the example of Endwave in Chapter 15).

CHALLENGES OF BEING A PUBLIC COMPANY

Before an IPO, spin-off, or merger with a public company is undertaken, great thought should be given to whether it is right for the subsidiary. The negative aspects of being a public company include the following.

Living in a Public Fishbowl

Being a public company means living in a fishbowl, where once-proprietary information is now available for public scrutiny, comment, and criticism. Information that may materially affect investors' decisions must be fully disclosed. This opens the company's affairs and every aspect of its business, including senior management compensation, to the general scrutiny of investors, customers, competitors, and employees. This may not always be an agreeable proposition.

Time Demands on Management

At a public company, there are extensive time demands on senior management to deal with investors and financial analysts at investment banks who help create strong investor interest in the stock.

Expense

The ongoing expenses of a public company, including legal, printing, accounting, liability insurance, and possibly an investor relations firm, are considerable. They may exceed $500,000 per year.

Disclosure Requirements

A public company must file extensive disclosure documents on a regular basis with the Securities and Exchange Commission (SEC). These documents include annual financial and business statements (known as SEC Form 10K); quarterly financial and business statements (Form 10Q); prompt reporting of material events (Form 8K); a proxy statement containing the compensation of senior management and directors, and the shareholdings of significant holders and management and directors; and various other reporting requirements. Foreign companies accessing the U.S. public stock markets have similar but slightly less onerous reporting requirements. The primary burden on a foreign company is the annual reconciliation of its financial statements with U.S. generally accepted accounting principles (GAAP).

Public Company Governance Requirements

Being public subjects the subsidiary to public company governance requirements imposed by the stock exchanges, the SEC, and investors. A breach of fiduciary duty to the public investors may well lead to a lawsuit, SEC action, or exchange action. Also, any public company that wishes to have investor interest in its stock needs to conform to requirements initiated by knowledgeable investors, reasonable pay for senior management linked to performance, solid practices regarding transactions between the parent and the subsidiary and other affiliates, and various codes of conduct for directors and officers of a public company. A public company will require a board of directors separate from the parent, with individual directors independent of the parent and with audit and compensation committees. The board assumes fiduciary duties to the public shareholders. Transactions with the parent are subject to special scrutiny.

Risk of Embarrassment

A publicly owned subsidiary that fails to perform in the market will often be a source of negative publicity for itself and the parent. In addition, it has the potential of incurring attention from the securities class action plaintiffs' bar.

Limits on Management's Freedom to Act

The management of a public company has a number of constraints on its actions that do not exist in practice to nearly the same extent as for the management of most private companies. In addition, if a company acts improperly, such as a breach of fiduciary duty to public investors, it often will result in a civil lawsuit by the securities class action plaintiffs' bar or actions by institutional investors, the stock market on which the company is listed, or the SEC. While a private company may also be sued by its shareholders for a breach of fiduciary duty, such lawsuits are rare due to the expense and difficulty of pursuing an individual shareholder action.

Dealing with Public Investors Is Time Consuming

Investors in public companies expect the CEO and senior management to spend time with them. The cultivation of the investor community has to be a top priority of the senior management. This is especially true for newly public companies as they are getting established with investors. A typical CEO of a public company should expect to devote, on average, one day a week to investor issues such as meeting with investors, attending investor conferences, the annual meeting, and quarterly conference calls.

Stock Price Volatility

Even the best-managed public company will be subject to the volatility of the public markets. The consequences of this volatility on employees can be profoundly unsettling and the fluctuating value of employee option and stock holdings can result in serious employee morale issues. Employees may need considerable hand-holding as they watch the stock price fluctuate. There is a natural tendency toward euphoria in a rising market and gloom in a falling market. Employees in both rising and falling markets will need constant reminders that the company and the stock are not the same.

Risk of Hostile Takeover Attempts

Hostile takeovers of public companies are rare, though they do occur from time to time through a tender offer, proxy contest, open market accumulation (known as a *creeping tender*), or other means. The best defense against unwanted interest is to perform and have that performance reflected in the stock price. This is not always possible; almost every public company will stumble at some time and markets do not always accord full value to performing companies. Hostile takeovers are not as much of a concern with a minority carve-out or tracking stock, as the parent retains control. It is more of an issue with a majority carve-out or spin-off, as the parent has ceded control of the subsidiary.

Limited Liquidity for a Large Owner of a Public Subsidiary

Except in a 100 percent majority carve-out IPO or spin-off, the parent will continue to own stock in the subsidiary after it is public. The parent will want a mechanism to eventually ensure liquidity for the remainder of its investment. This is not always easily accomplished (see Chapter 16).

A substantial stake in a smaller-capitalization public subsidiary is often particularly illiquid. There may be no ready exit from many substantial investments in a smaller-capitalization public company, aside from a sale of the subsidiary. Just because the subsidiary is public does not always mean that the parent will be able to sell a substantial amount of stock in the public stock market or in a follow-on public offering.

Also, as a condition of an IPO, the IPO lead manager is likely to require that the parent *lock up* (agree not to sell) its remaining shares for an extended period to enhance marketing the IPO and to ensure a strong aftermarket for the stock of the subsidiary following the IPO. This is usually for a six-month period, but if a parent holds a significant remaining position it may be considerably longer (lockups will be discussed in depth later in this book). The lockup may be released early by the lead manager, in whole or in part, at its sole discretion, if the stock is trading well in the market following the IPO.

Similarly, a condition for many mergers imposed by the merger partner will restrict the parent from selling shares for an extended period following the merger. This will restrict the ability of the parent to sell shares without the approval of the board of directors of the merged company except within defined limits intended to protect the postclosing market value of the parent's stock.

Also, the SEC places restrictions on the sale of stock in the public market by controlling shareholders unless use is made of a follow-on registered public offering or under the limited safe harbors allowed by SEC Rule 144, a safe harbor providing a permitted resale of stock without registration (see Chapter 6 for a fuller description of these provisions).

As a result, if the parent wishes to sell a significant amount of stock following an IPO or merger, it will likely have to sell the share either in the public market over an extended period of time under Rule 144 or in a registered follow-on public offering or a private sale.

Impact of a Large Overhang of Parent-Owned Stock

The existence of a large overhang of stock owned by the parent that may come onto the public market often results in a ceiling on the price of the stock of a public company, as an investor runs the risk of stock sales by the large holder depressing the stock price with resultant losses for the investor. Similarly, market makers and specialists will be unwilling to take positions when there is the danger of a large block coming on the market and lowering the value of the shares that they are holding.

Lack of Sponsorship for Many Public Companies

It is very difficult for many public companies to receive any sponsorship or research coverage from recognized investment banks that creates interest among investors in their stocks. With today's low commissions from brokerage activities and thin margins from the trading of most stocks, commissions alone are not sufficient to support the research effort of most firms in most stocks. Therefore, research may be provided only if the issuer has a broader relationship with the investment bank and engages its services to raise capital or provide other services.

Lack of Investor Interest in Many Smaller and Mid-Capitalization Public Companies

Obtaining interest in a public company from stock investors is never easy. It takes a compelling reason for an investor to own the stock, consistent and excellent company performance, and rapid growth to ensure the stock stands out from the universe of public stocks. This is especially true if the subsidiary is relatively small in size, where the total dollar value of shares publicly traded (this is known as the public *float*) may not be sufficient to attract the interest of institutional investors such as pension and mutual funds, which typically wish to own a significantly large position in any company relative to the size of their fund to justify devoting resources to following the investment. At the same time, however, they also wish to keep their ownership of a public company to less than 10 percent.

Responsibility to Public Shareholders

Responsibility to public shareholders following an IPO or spin-off is an especially relevant concern. Great care must then be taken to ensure that the public shareholders are properly treated. Also, in a merger, the public partner's board will also be very concerned with the provisions regarding the future treatment of the public shareholders by the parent or subsidiary after the merger. If the parent has a large or controlling position following a merger in the combined public company, the board of the partner will often require that extensive protection be given to the public shareholders. This may include an agreed-upon eventual purchase of shares by the parent or subsidiary at a fair price or at a guaranteed value for the shares at a later date (these are known as *contingent value rights*).

Vulnerability to Class Action Lawsuits

Public companies today are increasingly the targets of lawsuits. This activity has now expanded to include officers and directors and is only likely to increase. Even a lawsuit without any merit is costly and time consuming to defend against.

Restricted Dealing with the Newly Public Company

Once the subsidiary has its own public shareholders, the parent is restricted in its interactions with the subsidiary. The parent may not, without potentially alienating public shareholders and incurring litigation or provoking regulators, impose any arrangements on the subsidiary that are highly favorable to the parent at the expense of the subsidiary. Under applicable corporate laws, intercompany transactions must be approved by independent directors and shareholders as fair to the subsidiary. Intercompany transactions and arrangements must also be fully disclosed to public shareholders in SEC filings. As well, the parent and the subsidiary will be subject to the fiduciary duties imposed under state and common law to outside shareholders.

Complying with the Federal Securities Laws

The Federal Securities laws impose significant additional burdens on public companies. The Federal Securities and Exchange Commission is the regulatory agency charged by Congress with administering the Federal Securities laws and protecting public investors against fraud and manipulation.

Once it is public, the subsidiary and parent and their officers and directors will immediately be subject to all the Federal (and state) Securities laws and regulations as well as the regulations and oversight of the stock exchange on which the stock of the subsidiary is listed.

As noted, these laws and the other regulations impose extensive reporting requirements on public companies, their officers and directors, and large shareholders. They also place many restrictions on their actions. If the parent is already a U.S. public company, these requirements will not be a surprise. However, for a foreign or private company they may represent unacceptable intrusions into its activities and limitations on its conduct.

Failure to comply with these laws and regulations is a serious matter subjecting the parent, the subsidiary, and its officers and directors to possible civil actions by the SEC (and sometimes an SEC recommendation that criminal action be brought). On occasion there are actions by individual state securities regulators. There may also be damaging publicity. In addition, as noted, the securities class action bar is active in bringing litigation for damages for actual or perceived violations.

Complying with Stock Exchange Requirements

The stock exchange on which the subsidiary is listed will have its own rules and regulations with which the subsidiary will need to comply. These may include requirements for independent directors and good governance practices as well as financial requirements for continued listing on the exchange.

EMPIRICAL EVIDENCE

In the past 15 years, there have been several hundred SERs involving the issuance of public stocks (carve-outs, spin-offs, and tracking stocks). There is strong empirical evidence to support the value creation of SERs in the form of increased price-to-earnings and sales ratios, and total return to shareholders (stock appreciation and dividend payments). Almost all the studies demonstrate that, on average, each of these forms of public security restructuring creates shareholder value. A review of these studies is contained in the Endnotes for this chapter.[2] See also Exhibit 2–1 for recent public SER activity.

SUMMARY

This chapter examined the reasons to create a public subsidiary through an IPO, spin-off, or merger with a public company in order to achieve key SER objectives. The list of reasons to create a public subsidiary is long and diverse, which can make this action attractive to parent companies. However, as with all of the specific SER transactions detailed later in this book, there are also serious challenges to overcome, which need to be considered during the decision-making process. Chapter 3 will examine the forces that have converged in recent years to make SERs a unique—and timely—option for parent companies looking for a means to increase shareholder value.

EXHIBIT 2–1

Summary of U.S. Public Market Subsidiary Equity Redeployments, 1998–2002

	1998	1999	2000	2001	Q1 2002
Total domestic IPOs					
Total number*	292	483	361	93	14
Total proceeds (billions)	$34.9	$58.8	$60.4	$33.2	$8.9
Minority—50% or less carve-out IPOs					
Number of minority carve-out IPOs	13	33	17	11	4
Amount of proceeds (billions)	$8.0	$9.5	$13.1	$20.6	$6.6
Percent of all IPO proceeds	24%	15%	23%	59%	74%
Majority—greater than 50% carve-out IPOs					
Number of majority carve-outs	2	6	11	8	0
Amount of proceeds (billions)	$6.2	$6.3	$4.8	$3.0	$0.0
Percent of all IPO proceeds	18%	11%	8%	9%	0%
All carve-out IPOs					
Number of all carve-out IPOs	15	39	28	19	4
Amount of proceeds (billions)	$14.2	$15.8	$17.9	$23.6	$6.6
Percent of all IPO proceeds	42%	26%	32%	67%	74%
Tracking stock IPOs					
Number of tracking stock IPOs	0	7	4	2	1
Amount of proceeds (billions)	$0.0	$2.6	$10.4	$2.0	$1.1
Percent of all IPO proceeds	0%	4%	19%	6 %	12%
Total for SER IPOs					
Number of SER IPOs	15	46	32	21	5
Amount of SER proceeds (billions)	$14.2	$18.4	$28.3	$25.6	$7.7
Percent of all IPO proceeds	42%	30%	51%	73%	86%
Spin-offs (including tracking stock spin-offs)					
Number of spin-offs	43	37	38	25	3
Market capitalization of spin-offs at time of spin-off	$42.8	$81.5	$108.7	$81.1	$6.5
Total for SERs					
Total number of public SERS	58	83	70	46	8

*Excludes IPOs with proceeds less than $10 million, investment funds, MLPs, REITs, ADRs, and S&L conversions.

Sources: Securities Data, Dialogic, Needham & Company, SEC filings

CHAPTER **3**

SERs: THE NEW, LEANER BUSINESS MODEL AND GROWTH SUBSIDIARIES

INTRODUCTION

The success of lean companies such as Dell has fueled two business movements which have converged in recent years. One movement entails rethinking the traditional "complete control" business model. In its place, smart companies are following a model similar to Dell's and outsourcing noncore competencies, retaining only those functions that give them a distinct edge in the marketplace and using alliances and partnerships to propel growth. Similarly, smart companies also realize that a traditional cash divestiture of a subsidiary is now only one of a range of available separation alternatives. As well, that greater value for parent shareholders is often obtained somewhere between complete control and complete divestiture. Because this shift in thinking—and action—has been profound, this chapter takes a closer look at the interplay between SER transactions and the new business model.

AVAILABILITY OF A WIDE RANGE OF PROVEN SER OPTIONS

Exhibit 3–1 places growth subsidiary SERs in the context of other subsidiary separation alternatives. Some SERs such as a spin-off may result in total separation of the subsidiary from the parent. However, many SERs provide a middle ground between complete ownership and complete divestiture.

Exhibit 3–1 demonstrates how SERs create a range of options for the parent that fall between complete ownership and control of a subsidiary and complete divestiture.

E X H I B I T   3–1

Subsidiary SERs in the Context of Continuing Parent Control

Degree of parent control of subsidiary	Parent ownership percentage of subsidiary and control	Structure	Representative SER transactions described in this book
Highest degree of parent control	100 Complete parent control	Business unit within the parent	
	100 Complete parent control	Internal disaggregation within the parent	
	100 Complete parent control but some duties to management phantom shareholders	Wholly owned subsidiary possibly with management profit participation or phantom stock (not real stock but cash compensation that simulates stock, usually based on a formula)	
	80–90 Parent control but duties to management shareholders	Majority-owned private subsidiary with actual management ownership/options	
SERs— spanning the range of parent control	100 Parent control but duties to outside shareholders	Tracking stock	AT&T Liberty Media
	50–80 Parent control but duties to outside shareholders	Minority carve-out	Citigroup Travelers Property Casualty
	50–90 Parent control but duties to outside shareholders	Parent-controlled merger with a private or public company	Philips NV FEI
	50–80 Parent control but usually there are contractual agreements that limit the parent's ability to exercise control	Parent-controlled strategic partnership	Roche Genentech
	10–50 Often considerable parent influence through a large ownership position, agreements, or dependence on the parent after the SER	Minority-owned private equity partnership	TRW Corsair
	10–40 Considerable to moderate parent influence	Minority strategic partnership	Schering-Plough Millennium
	20–50 Considerable to moderate parent influence	Minority merger with a private or public company	W.R. Grace National Medical
	20–50 Considerable to moderate influence	Majority carve-out	Du Pont Du Pont Photomasks
	0–20 Moderate to low influence	Full majority carve-out	Verizon Genuity
	0–20 Moderate to low influence	Full majority split-off	The Limited Abercrombie & Fitch
	0–20 Low to no influence	Spin-off	General Mills Kenner Parker
Lowest degree of parent control	0–10 Likely little to no influence	Divestiture to a financial buyer	
	0 Likely no influence	Divestiture to a strategic buyer	

INTERPLAY BETWEEN THE NEW BUSINESS MODEL AND SERs

The greater availability and acceptance of SERs has been instrumental in foster-ing the adoption of this new business model. There are two elements to this new model that relate specifically to SERs.

Focusing Only on Core Competencies and Relying More on Alliances and Partnerships

The new business model stresses that a company should focus only on the core competencies that enable a company to differentiate itself from competitors. It should outsource or partner other activities. Partnerships have turned the traditional vertically integrated business model on its head. Companies that do not form partnerships appear—and often are—dated and lacking vision. The new business model is deeply intertwined with creative use of strategic partnership SERs, which is exemplified in the discussion of LTX Corporation in Chapter 13.

Large corporations are also becoming increasingly comfortable with relinquishing internal ownership and control of all corporate activities and resources, separating out noncritical operations, and forming strategic partnerships. SERs are playing a large role as parent companies rationalize and focus their operations. The 1999 carve-out IPO of Delphi Automotive Systems from General Motors is an example of a vertically integrated parent company that divested itself of noncore operations for the benefit of the parent and the subsidiary through an SER.

Another key difference between the old and the new models is the way in which parents view strategic partnerships. The new model is centered on cooperative, rather than adversarial, arrangements with supplier, customer, and partner companies, for mutual benefit. These arrangements enable a parent to leverage the synergistic capabilities of many other companies to fill its needs. The basis of these relationships is trust.

Fostering Growth Operations

Over the long term the equity markets most highly reward parents that are able to combine a well-run, solid, and well-capitalized business with good growth rates. Growth companies are not a new phenomenon. The Ford Motor Company in the early 1900s, RCA in the 1930s, and Xerox in the 1960s were all highly successful growth companies: however, SERs allow parents greater opportunities to foster growth operations. There have never been more opportunities than there are today for a growth subsidiary to succeed. As alluded to already, SERs can help support the success of a growth subsidiary by these means:

• *Allowing a subsidiary varying degrees of autonomy.* There are now more than a few ways to create—and sustain—the success of a growth subsidiary. A certain degree of autonomy from the parent company is often necessary to take advantage of opportunities unique to that company and the industry in which it operates. SERs can provide this autonomy.

• *Picking and choosing from a wide variety of SER options.* As mentioned earlier, there are a wide variety of SER options now available to help create—and sustain—successful growth operations.

- *Providing support from strategic partners and the equity markets.* Growth operations attract the attention of investors. They also attract the interest of strategic partners looking to enhance their own businesses. As a result, many SER alternatives are available to a growth operation that may not be available to the parent or to a similarly sized mature subsidiary.

GROWTH COMPANY RISKS

While growth is recognized as necessary to create long-term shareholder value, the past few years have brutally highlighted the risks for a parent inherent in growth operations. SERs have become of great interest to parents to help foster growth operations but also to miitgate the risks of growth operations.

These risks are formidable and include:

- The need for a large infusion of capital and resources to get the growth business off the ground—with no guaranteed results.
- The slowed momentum of its other businesses as time and attention are given to the growth business. This may negatively affect overall shareholder value.
- Growth markets do not forgive missteps. Missing a product generation—or market shift—is rarely rectifiable if competitors are awake and well capitalized. This may result in a loss of market position and lead to value loss.
- Growth markets lack reliable historical data on industry and customer behavior. This makes long-term planning very difficult (see the example of Du Pont Photomask in Chapter 7).
- The lack of predictability of a growth company's earnings may cause serious and very unwelcome gyrations in the earnings of a parent.
- The investors in stable, mature, cash-flow-positive, and profitable parents may not appreciate the added risk and uncertainty caused by a capital-consuming, often unprofitable, growth company.
- Credit rating agencies and parent debt providers may take the same view of the growth company. As debt holders, they are not concerned with the long-term equity prospects of the parent shareholders but only with the repayment of their debt.
- Developing the right culture for a growth business may not be easy within the context of the existing compensation plans and operating procedures of a mature parent.
- Recruiting a superior management team also may not be easy, for the same reason. Yet growth businesses desperately need quality, driven, and motivated management talent that can sustain growth against all odds.

In addition, success for a player in a growing market is often defined by market position several years out, rather than by current results. It is also important to measure the performance of a growth company by how quickly it acts to create—and maintain—market position. Time is more critical for growth companies so that opportunities are not lost. And recovery from lost opportunities is not easily, if ever, achieved.

Dell's Use of SER Transactions to Create Shareholder Value and Foster Growth

Let's take a look at how a market leader applied—and benefited from—SERs, in adopting a new, leaner way of doing business and using partnerships and alliances.

Dell is one of the great success stories in American business. Sales ballooned from approximately 10,000 units in 1986 to 17.3 million units in 2001. Similarly, its share of the personal computer (PC) market mushroomed from a negligible percentage in 1986 to over 13 percent in 2001.

At every step, Dell has relied on creative use of SERs, especially those involving partnerships and alliances. And it still depends on partnerships and alliances. It has formed strategic partnerships with a number of suppliers, and it has invested in private equity partnerships with promising customers and suppliers. For example, in March 1999, Dell formed a strategic pact with IBM that involved the purchase of $16 billion in IBM components along with a broad technology-licensing agreement. Later in the year, Dell signed an agreement with IBM Global Services to provide computer-related services to Dell's customers. In 2001, the company entered into a strategic partnership with EMC to resell the Clarion family of midrange storage devices. Dell subsequently announced that it would enter the huge printer business through an alliance with Lexmark.

Dell Computer has used these partnerships and alliances to adhere to the key tenet of the new business model: focus on core competencies and outsource everything else. Dell's core competencies include design, procurement, supply chain management, marketing, sales, and customer relations. Dell was, and still is, so committed to outsourcing that it did not manufacture any of its own components and would not take ownership of components until they hit the final assembly factory floor. It also has now moved to outsourcing part of the design and all of the assembly of some product lines.

SUMMARY

This chapter examined the way in which many smart companies are acting on the belief that they do not need to completely control subsidiary operations to realize the maximum value from them. Instead, subsidiaries—especially growth subsidiaries—are being given varying degrees of independence resulting from SER transactions that create a company structure independent from the parent company. This is in stark contrast to the past, when complete divestiture was one of the most common transactions employed by parent companies. Now parent companies can retain varying degrees of control and investment, which empowers subsidiaries to maximize opportunities and succeed in the marketplace. Ultimately, this creates value for shareholders. Chapter 4 will examine how to successfully prepare for an SER transaction.

CHAPTER 4

PREPARING FOR A SUCCESSFUL SER TRANSACTION

INTRODUCTION

A well-planned and -organized SER process will help ensure that the outcome more closely meets the objectives of the subsidiary and that it is not disappointed in the result. It will also help ensure that disruption to the business of the subsidiary and the parent company is minimized. However, before an SER transaction is initiated the parent must first assess whether an SER is the right strategic choice for the parent and the subsidiary, whether there are better internal alternatives not involving an SER, and which SER is best for the specific needs of the parent and the characteristics of the subsidiary.

To prepare for a subsidiary equity redeployment transaction, the parent, the subsidiary, and their outside advisors should follow a well-planned and well-organized process to ensure the best outcome, with a focus on these goals:

- Meeting the objectives of the parent and the subsidiary concerning the economic terms of the SER transaction, the relationship of the parent and the subsidiary after the SER, certainty of the outcome, continued participation by the parent in the upside of the business of the subsidiary, tax planning, and other needs

- Minimizing disruption to the business of the parent and the subsidiary before, during, and after the transaction

- Ensuring that the transaction actually occurs, and closes within the desired time frame

Therefore, the objective of this chapter is to walk readers through the requisite planning steps to achieve these goals.

It is often valuable early in the SER process to appoint an internal sponsor at a senior management level at the parent, who is charged with shepherding the

SER forward and ensuring that there is continued focus on it. Otherwise, an SER process can easily stall, as the senior management at the parent and subsidiary will usually have other primary responsibilities. The sponsor almost always should come from the parent since the sponsor will understand the internal processes and politics of the parent. Early on, with an SER leading to a separation of the parent and the subsidiary, the parent and the sponsor need to clarify whether the sponsor will go with the subsidiary after the SER or stay at the parent. However, the charter of the sponsor should be to balance the needs of the parent and those of the subsidiary (see the discussion in Chapter 9 of the Palm SER).

INVOLVING SUBSIDIARY MANAGEMENT:
A KEY TO SER SUCCESS

The active involvement of the subsidiary management team is important for SER transactions that rely on the existing management of the subsidiary, such as spin-offs and carve-outs, to prepare for the SER and to manage the subsidiary after the SER. The team does not have to be the original subsidiary leadership, but the ongoing team should be in place before the SER.

With public market SERs, the quality of the ongoing management team is often the most important factor in an investment decision.

Without a capable management team, SER transactions will usually be limited to the following

- A merger with a public or private company that brings along a management team for the combined company

- A private equity partnership in which the investors assemble a management team for the subsidiary

- A traditional sale of the subsidiary to a buyer that is unconcerned about the continuance or existence of a capable senior management team because it intends to fold the subsidiary into an existing operation or already has management available to run the subsidiary after the merger.

CREATING A SUBSIDIARY MANAGEMENT TEAM

Because the subsidiary management team is critical to the success of specific SER transactions, such as carve-out IPOs and spin-offs, it is important to be aware of the three common mistakes parent companies make when putting a team in place.

Putting the Team in Place Late in the Process

Parents often do this to avoid creating two duplicative and expensive management teams before the subsidiary is taken public. However, it is a mistake for several reasons. First, the parent will then make all the material decisions regarding the subsidiary and the relationships and agreements with the parent. This is not healthy for any of the parties involved. For example, the new subsidiary management team members will be frustrated by their lack of input, and decisions may not be in the best interest of the subsidiary. Second, subsidiary management team members do not have the opportunity to work together and coalesce before the public event.

Not Putting a Full Team in Place

In some cases, the parent continues to provide many key services to the subsidiary, and for this reason a full management team is not put in place. This is rarely satisfactory, as conflicts are inevitable and the subsidiary should be able to stand on its own.

Cloning the Parent's Management Structure

This is the most common approach used by parents. However, the subsidiary may require different structures and skill sets and may not need to incur all the costs associated with managing a more mature organization.

The best approach for the subsidiary's future success is to develop a bottom-up organization designed for the subsidiary and put it in place early enough for it to form a cohesive team that can negotiate with the parent on behalf of the subsidiary. However, this is the most difficult alternative to implement. It requires much thought. From the parent's point of view it is also the most divisive, as it creates an independent team at the subsidiary with which the parent must contend. However, the parent should always bear in mind that in most cases, particularly those that involve the public markets, an SER is not just a financial transaction; instead, the goal is to create a successful company after the SER.

Management Compensation

The more different the subsidiary is in size and business from the parent, the more management compensation should differ. This often creates tensions with the parent between the wealth opportunities perceived at the subsidiary and those for managers of similar operations in the parent. Unfortunately this issue cannot usually be ignored. Public stock and private equity investors will require compensation programs appropriate for comparable independent companies. These are likely to include less cash compensation, considerably lower benefits, and a higher portion of total compensation in the form of equity. Not all current employees of the subsidiary will find this new package acceptable.

Now let's turn our attention to the role of advisors in the SER planning and preparation process.

INVOLVING ADVISORS EARLY IN THE PROCESS

The early involvement of accountants, legal counsel, and, as needed, an investment bank should greatly improve the outcome of whatever SER option is pursued.

These professionals will perform the following functions:

- Review the parent's short- and long-term objectives relating to the SER. Advisors need to clearly communicate if objectives conflict or are unobtainable.

- Review the business, finances, and prospects of the subsidiary and their impact on the availability, timing, terms, and value of SER alternatives.

- Review both the proposed and the actual legal structure of the subsidiary and how it may affect various SER alternatives.

- Review how each SER alternative will affect the parent and subsidiary from a tax and accounting perspective.

- Review the proposed and actual commercial, financial, managerial, and administrative relationships between the parent and the subsidiary and understand how they might impact SER alternatives.

- Provide realistic assessments of the potential availability, timing, terms, and value of various SER alternatives, and the current status of the market for each type of SER.

- Highlight issues and deficiencies that are likely to preclude the desired SER or reduce its chances of success or its value, and suggest actions that address these issues and deficiencies.

- Suggest actions that might be taken in advance of an SER that will enhance the likelihood of the SER meeting the parent's objectives.

- Guide the parent and subsidiary through the SER process.

ASSESSING THE OPTIONS

Before assessing SER alternatives, the parent needs to be clear on what it is trying to achieve. Objectives should be developed for the SER. Then the parent should[1]:

- Determine which SER option will best contribute to achieving those business objectives. The reasons that a parent should consider subsidiary equity redeployment were discussed in the previous chapters. These objectives should be listed and the probability of each alternative meeting each of these objectives assessed.

- Determine whether there are better internal alternatives to an SER. Often less disruptive and less costly alternatives not involving an SER are overlooked. Some of these were listed in Exhibit 3–1. However, avoiding an SER may also be costly in terms of lost opportunity.

- Decide if—and when—the parent or the subsidiary will require cash. The parent may require cash immediately for its entire holding in the subsidiary on the best terms available, or it may be willing to delay receiving some or all of the cash because it believes that a deferral will lead to a higher ultimate return. The parent may also require certainty that there will be future liquidity and that the timing of that event will be within its control. Or it may be willing to accept a risk on the timing and certainty of future liquidity. All of these requirements will help determine which option is best for the parent.

- Determine how the SER option will be received in the current market environment. Often, market conditions will dictate which option is the most viable.

- Determine how quickly a deal can be closed. At times, it will be crucially important to close a deal quickly to enable the parent to receive cash in a timely manner. If so, the parent should choose the option that enables it to reach that goal.

- Determine how the deal structure may affect the terms. Often, the way a deal is structured will affect the actual terms. Parent companies need to keep this in mind as they weigh all of the options.

- Determine whether the deal will close—and when. The probability that an SER will close—and when it will close—is a very important criterion when selecting an SER option. In fact, a parent may move forward with an SER that it knows will close quickly, even though the financial or other terms may be less attractive.

- Determine whether the parent needs to remain involved in the business after the SER. Some redeployment options require, or encourage, a continuing active role by the parent, whereas others allow, or require, the parent to sever its involvement in the subsidiary. The parent needs to consider the degree of involvement and responsibility it is willing to maintain following the transaction.

- Assess the capability and commitment of the subsidiary's management team. A number of redeployment alternatives are available to the parent only if the subsidiary has a capable and committed senior management team in place. The parent needs to make a realistic assessment of any management issues.

THE IMPORTANCE OF A BUSINESS PLAN

Almost all SER transactions involve outside parties such as equity investors, strategic partners, and merger partners making an assessment of the subsidiary. The success of certain SER transactions is also contingent upon the support of key intermediaries such as investment bank research analysts and finance professionals who advise on SER transactions and generate interest in IPOs and their aftermarket. In all cases, the involvement of these investors, partners, and advisors often means they commit substantial funds to the endeavor or endorse it to investors. Therefore, they want to make sure that they thoroughly understand the current business and finances of the subsidiary and its future prospects. With this knowledge they can better assess the investment and make a valuation determination.

A business plan is the best vehicle to present the subsidiary to outside parties and to communicate the company's objectives. A realistic business plan can actually help clarify how an SER deal should be structured based on revenue, income, and cash flow forecasts. The importance of realistic forecasts is detailed in the next section.

DEVELOPING REALISTIC FORECASTS
FOR THE SUBSIDIARY

At the core of the business plan, and therefore of the SER alternative review processes, is a realistic revenue, income, and cash flow forecast for the subsidiary. Thus, it is important to remember that the feasibility of specific equity redeployment alternatives and the subsidiary's valuation will be based in part on expectations of future revenues and income.

With a growth subsidiary, expectations will play the largest role in determining alternatives and values. In contrast, with a mature subsidiary, the alternatives available and valuation methods will be based more on current and historical income statements and balance sheets. However, subsidiary forecasts are still important. Decisions by any prospective SER party on the desirability of investing in the SER or merging with the subsidiary, and the valuation it considers reasonable, will be based in large part on the subsidiary's forecasts.

Unrealistic Forecasts Are Common

Unrealistic forecasts do exist, however. In many instances, management may deliberately create optimistic forecasts in order to promote certain business objectives—and incentives. Or their reasons may be more benign. In any case, companies generally create optimistic forecasts because the parent or subsidiary management

- Does not fully understand the dynamics of the industry, including the forces that impact capacity, demand, and pricing, and the impact of economic and industry cycles

- Has a top-down forecasting process that imposes a forecast from above

- Underestimates the time it takes for the development, implementation, and customer acceptance of a new product or service, or has unrealistically high expectations for market size, growth, or timing

- Underestimates competitors

- Believes that senior management at the parent or the subsidiary is committed to a particular SER transaction and does not want to rock the boat

- Does not want to bear bad news

- Has considerable personal career capital invested in the success of the subsidiary and/or the SER that clouds judgment

- Has a personal financial interest in the success of the SER that clouds judgment

- Wants to obtain a higher valuation in an SER transaction from outside investors

- Wants to stretch the organization to achieve higher goals

- Wishes to portray the business in the best light to obtain greater resource allocations from the parent

There are also many reasons for a subsidiary's management team to actually produce forecasts below their real expectations. The primary reason is to ensure that they meet or exceed their forecasts. Often bonuses and favorable reviews are dependent on meeting or exceeding forecasts. In some cases, the subsidiary's management may lowball a subsidiary's forecasts to increase the subsequent value of the equity packages they will receive. For example, the pricing of management options and other equity incentives in the subsidiary following the redeployment is often based directly on a pre-redeployment valuation derived from the forecasts (or on an IPO offering price also derived from those forecasts). For a completely different reason, the subsidiary's management may also lowball the forecast because they do not approve of the transaction and want to kill the deal.

The Consequences of Inaccurate Forecasts

In an equity redeployment process, there are serious consequences to the parent for either overly optimistic or overly conservative forecasts. Both can result in misguided decisions by the parent regarding equity redeployment alternatives and values. For example, unnecessarily low forecasts may economically disadvantage the parent and benefit the new outside investors in the subsidiary by enabling them to invest at a lower-than-fair price. In addition, subsidiary management may benefit due to overly generous management participation in the equity of the subsidiary, as the amount and terms of management equity compensation will most likely be based on a view of the valuation of the subsidiary. As a result, the parent's shareholders will not extract fair economic value from the subsidiary.

Unrealistically high forecasts can harm the subsidiary as well, as they deter well-informed outside parties from investigating the SER.

Unrealistic forecasts, if accepted, will form a basis for an investment in private or public stock of the subsidiary, a decision to underwrite an IPO of the subsidiary, or a merger with another company. If not met later, these forecasts will result in bitter recriminations and even a presumption that the management deliberately misled investors. After many equity redeployment transactions, (e.g., a carve-out IPO, spin-off, merger, private equity investment, or corporate alliance), the management of the subsidiary will have to live with the consequences of its forecasts.

Missing unrealistically high forecasts often results in a private equity partner, corporate alliance partner, public stock investors and equity research analysts, or a merger partner losing faith in the competence of the management team that prepared the forecasts. This loss of confidence may be a serious setback to the subsidiary and to the careers of those involved. It often results in a change of management, the closing of access by the subsidiary to additional capital, embarrassment to the parent, and an eventual sale of the subsidiary at a distress price.

Overly optimistic forecasts may cause the parent to have unrealistically high expectations about the value of the subsidiary and misguided views on the

alternatives available. This may have several consequences. It can create a dispar-
ity in subsidiary valuation expectations between an outside party and the parent,
which may preclude a merger, investment, or an IPO. It may also lead the parent
to pursue an unrealistic alternative, such as an IPO for a subsidiary that will not be
well received by IPO investors and will be an expensive, disruptive, and embarrassing failure.

The Role of a Financial Advisor in Preparing a Forecast

Given the critical importance of forecasts for a successful subsidiary equity
deployment, many parents have benefited from enlisting an advisor to review subsidiary forecasts. Here are some of the key reasons:

• The subsidiary is in an industry with which the parent's staff is not completely
  familiar.
• An outside view is a way to obtain fresh insights or confirmation of the parent's
  view of the subsidiary's prospects.
• The parent's senior management and board of directors feel more comfortable
  with an objective, outside view of the subsidiary.
• The subsidiary's management may feel obligated to produce forecasts supporting a certain course of action, particularly when senior officers of the parent or
  the subsidiary favor a particular redeployment alternative. An objective, outside
  advisor may give balance.
• An outside advisor may ask challenging questions and test the subsidiary's
  assumptions and approaches.
• An outside advisor knowledgeable in the subsidiary's industry will provide a
  reality check for the subsidiary's and the parent's expectations.
• The prospects for the industry over the next 12 months
• The prospects for the industry over the longer term
• Whether the projections properly account for a cyclical business
• Whether the revenue projections are based on customer orders and existing
  backlog, firm expectations, or hope
• How secure the subsidiary's competitive position is in its industry
• How much cash the subsidiary needs to meet its plans

Using Adjustments to Create a More Accurate Forecast

To truly understand the subsidiary's business and prospects, adjustments should
be made to historical and forecast financial statements. The adjustments

• Enable the parent and outside investors, analysts, and partners to understand the
  true operating characteristics of the business.

- Enable the parent, outside investors, and partners to view the subsidiary as a stand-alone entity.

- Enable the parent to understand how certain actions prior to an equity redeployment would affect the valuation of the subsidiary and available options.

Adjusted financial statements may offer a very different picture of the subsidiary's business and valuation. Consequently, equity redeployment alternatives may become available that were not previously considered or thought possible.

The adjustments made will depend on the specifics of the subsidiary and the equity redeployment option under consideration.

Common Adjustments

Adjustments are most commonly made for the following reasons.

Restructuring Before the SER

A large subsidiary often contains many disparate business units, some of which may perform exceedingly well and others that are laggards. These poorer-performing units may be tolerated for historical, strategic, or even political reasons. However, the parent may decide to restructure the subsidiary to exclude these operations, or it may decide to divest itself of them when it understands their adverse effect on the valuation of the subsidiary and its access to certain equity redeployment alternatives.

Discontinued Operations/Extraordinary Items

Adjustments should be made to historical financial statements to reflect any discontinued operations or extraordinary past expenses that are not expected to continue. These adjustments allow the true returns for the business to be brought to the attention of outside investors, analysts, and merger partners.

Putting all these charges behind the subsidiary before the SER is critical. Going forward, outside parties will be skeptical if there are repeated extraordinary items such as an annual write-off of a customer's receivables as part of the costs of the business and also will need to be certain that an extraordinary event does not reflect a fundamental and permanent change in the business.

Eliminating Excessive Parent Charges

Many corporations load subsidiaries with allocations of corporate expenses and charges for services that are excessive, relative to the value of the services provided. Others attempt to extract fees and royalties after an equity redeployment transaction. These transactions will penalize the valuation of the subsidiary by lowering income and deter investors and partners who are wary of being involved in any situation where the parent extracts significant compensation from the operation that puts the parent effectively ahead of any return to an SER party. While these expenses may genuinely be on arms-length terms, this is rarely the case, as it is never easy for a subsidiary's management to negotiate aggressively with its parent for the best terms before the SER.

Showing the True Costs of Parent Services
In contrast, the subsidiary may also be underpaying the parent for services it renders to the subsidiary, such as legal work, human resources management, accounting, management information systems (MIS), or treasury functions. These are costs that the subsidiary will have to bear on its own as a separate company.

With many SER transactions, the parent often continues to provide these services to the subsidiary for a fee, either on a long-term or on a transitional basis. In other cases, the subsidiary will have to find and pay for these services on its own.

It becomes more complex when the parent is providing marketing, field services, or manufacturing for the subsidiary. Agreements need to be made to continue the services either on a long-term basis or for a transition period.

SER parties will be equally concerned that the parent has undercharged for these services, increasing the profit of the subsidiary in the short term. This is of special concern when the multiple of earnings accorded the subsidiary is far higher than that accorded the parent. This provides incentives for the parent to undercharge a highly profitable subsidiary.

Eliminating Intercompany Debt
The capital structure of a subsidiary as part of a parent may reflect a history of loans and dividends. In most cases, intercompany debt should be eliminated along with the corresponding interest charges.

In some cases, the subsidiary will continue to carry debt to the parent after the redeployment. However, for the most part, SER parties will not accept such debt. Sometimes the debt will simply be deducted from the value. But generally, where the use of debt is inappropriate or not in keeping with industry norms, debt to the parent will have a severely negative impact on valuation and will deter many SER parties.

Showing the True Cost of Goods or Services
A large parent may provide a subsidiary with lower costs for the purchase of goods and services from outside vendors through the use of the parent's buying power with vendors. As a separate company, the increased cost of goods and services incurred must be factored into the subsidiary's forecasts. In some cases, increased costs have a material impact on margins.

Adjusting Compensation Levels
Compensation and benefit levels will need to be adjusted to fit with those offered by comparable independent companies. If not, investors and merger partners are likely to be deterred. This may present difficult issues for the subsidiary's managers, who may wish to retain the cash compensation and perks they had at the larger company but also obtain the equity potential of an independent company. These two conflicting desires rarely successfully mesh because

1. Investors and partners expect that management will do well only if the investor or partner does well.

2. The value of the subsidiary to the parent will be materially reduced by such compensation because the subsidiary's value to investors will be reduced.

3. Unless the subsidiary is highly profitable, investors and partners will not have any desire to fund large cash compensation packages and perks.

In other cases, the addition of a strong senior management team with experience to run a stand-alone company will increase costs. For example, an experienced public company chief financial officer (CFO) is usually more expensive than a divisional controller. These additional costs need to be added back in.

Adjusting for Reduced Tax Rates

Generally, an SER party will apply a full tax rate (nominal statutory U.S. tax rate) to any earnings of the subsidiary, regardless of the actual or effective rate. There are several reasons for this:

1. Applying a full tax rate allows an SER party to compare the performance of the subsidiary with that of comparable companies that have different historical circumstances or tax concessions. It also allows SER parties to compare companies in different countries with different tax regimes.

2. While lower rates have a significant cash flow advantage, investors generally do not consider the increased income resulting from low tax rates worth as much as operating income.

3. In many cases, a lower tax rate is due to government concessions. For example, companies domiciled in Israel have significant government tax credits for research and development (R&D). These concessions may extend for only a certain number of years or may be reduced with a change of government.

4. A later change in corporate ownership may eliminate the tax savings.

5. Should the subsidiary have its own net operating loss (NOL) carryforwards (many times these have already been used by the parent in a consolidated tax return), these will not be given great value by SER parties—first, because there are too many circumstances in which their use may be highly restricted, and, second, because the subsidiary has to actually make a profit to use the NOLs. The value attributed to an NOL is likely to be the probability adjusted net present value of the cash savings under various utilization rate cases. Usually this will not be more than 5 to 10 percent of stated value.

Payments that the parent makes to the subsidiary under a tax treaty after the SER (if the subsidiary is making losses and is still consolidated with the parent after the SER for tax purposes) will not be given much value by SER parties beyond the actual cash amount paid in the first year. This is because there is too much risk that the tax consolidation status of the subsidiary may change at any time, as, in some cases, may the tax-paying status of the parent.

Adjusting Accounting Practices to Conform to Comparable Companies
SER parties will adjust the accounting practices of the subsidiary to conform to the predominant practices of comparable public companies. It will be no surprise, following the Enron and Global Crossings cases, that there are significant differences among companies that may materially affect historical statements and forecasts. This is particularly true regarding revenue recognition and how the cost of goods sold is calculated.

In addition, the generally accepted accounting principles (GAAP) of the industry in which the subsidiary operates may be different from those applied by the parent to the subsidiary, especially when that industry is different from that of the parent. Conforming to industry practices may have a material impact on forecasts. Also, the accounting practices of a subsidiary, especially if it is a relatively small part of a large parent, are not always closely scrutinized by the parent's accounting firm and may differ from GAAP.

Adjusting for Public Company Expenses
For an IPO or a spin-off, the increased expenses that result from being a public company need to be factored into forecasts. These expenses include the following:

- *Increased outside legal expenses.* A public company will have increased legal expenses for the preparation and review of SEC and other governmental filings, and from operating in a more legally intensive public environment.

- *Increased outside accounting charges.* A public company will have higher outside audit charges than a subsidiary.

- *Fees for outside members of the board of directors.*

- *Increased internal staffing.* The increased workload of a public company usually requires larger financial and legal staffs and an investor relations staff.

- *Transfer agent fees.* These are not expensive, but they are a cost.

- *Exchange listing fees.* Depending on the exchange, these may be substantial. According to the *Wall Street Journal,* the New York Stock Exchange derives approximately 33 percent of its revenue from its listing fees.

- *Directors and officers insurance.* This is a large expense for a public company post-Enron.

- *Investor communications expenses.* There are expenses associated with attending investor conferences, undertaking investor road shows, and distributing presentations to the wider public as required by SEC Regulation FD, designed to prevent selective disclosure.

- *Outside investor relation firm fees.* It is generally a good practice for a public company to have outside assistance with investor relations.

- *Shareholders communications costs.* These are the costs of preparing, printing, and mailing quarterly and annual reports to shareholders and other shareholder communications.

- *Investor relations website costs.* These are costs of maintaining an investor website or an investor relations portion of the subsidiary's website.

Showing the Impact of Any Cash Raised in an SER
The subsidiary may make reasonable adjustments for changes that will occur after an SER transaction provides additional capital.

Reflecting Postmerger Realities
In transactions involving a merger of the subsidiary, it may be useful to recast the historical financials and forecasts to reflect the postmerger or alliance resources available to the subsidiary.

The subsidiary should make reasonable assumptions of cost savings after a merger, based on the elimination of duplicate functions and sharing of resources, access to lower-cost manufacturing or other resources of the partner, increased combined purchasing power with vendors, and access to lower-cost capital through a stronger combined balance sheet. However, note that merger savings are usually greatly overestimated. Consolidation of operations usually takes much longer than planned, and many expected savings prove ephemeral. Few mergers are as well implemented as they are forecast, and savings usually are less than the amount forecast.

PREPARING FOR THE DUE DILIGENCE PROCESS

The parent and the subsidiary also need to prepare for the due diligence investigations that will be conducted by serious SER parties or their representatives. A well-organized due diligence process greatly minimizes disruption to the business activities of the parent and subsidiary and keeps costs down. If well organized, the due diligence process will not use as much expensive outside legal and accounting time. A well-organized process will also maintain enthusiasm for the transaction from SER parties. A disorganized due diligence process creates concern over the competence of the parent's and subsidiary's organization among potential partners or investors and the managers of a public offering and cast into doubt the reliability of the information provided. In practice, enthusiasm for any SER transaction fades among potential partners or investors if requested or important information is unavailable, slow to arrive, incomplete, or inaccurate.

The scope and time of due diligence investigations can vary greatly, but, in general, they will depend on the following factors:

- The size, complexity, and geographic reach of the subsidiary's business.

- The complexity of the subsidiary's corporate and operating structure.

- The financial health of the subsidiary. A troubled operation or one that was only recently turned around will receive greater scrutiny.

- The number of critical issues that cause concern, such as litigation or questions over the ownership of intellectual property.

- The complexity of the relationship with the parent before and after the SER, and the nature of ongoing protocols.

- The perceived support of the subsidiary by the parent following the SER.

- The willingness of the parent to offer indemnities and retain difficult-to-quantify liabilities.

- The perceived reliability of the subsidiary's financial statements and confidence in the subsidiary's internal control systems.

- The credibility of the subsidiary's management.

- The amount of experience the SER party has with similar transactions and industries.

- Other demands and priorities that distract the SER party.

- How well the parent and the subsidiary control the process.

Advance Preparation of Diligence Materials

The main objective of the parent and the subsidiary in preparing for the due diligence process is to ensure that there are no surprises for an SER party as the transaction progresses. The discovery by a prospective SER party of undisclosed problems, liabilities, potential liabilities, or accounting issues, however innocent, often creates mistrust or leads to concern that there may be other undisclosed issues.

In many cases, the discovery of undisclosed issues or misinformation will result in a loss of confidence by the SER party, which will step back from the transaction—or walk away. Most issues that may complicate an SER transaction do not present major difficulties when known in advance.

Before pursuing equity redeployment and accompanying due diligence, the parent and the subsidiary must ensure that they have carefully and fully documented the following:

- Significant contracts

- Property titles

- Intellectual property rights

- Assets and liabilities that will go with the subsidiary after the SER

- Employment agreements and records

- Stock options and stock ownership records

- Protocols with the parent

- Other relationships with affiliates

- Existing, contingent, and potential liabilities

- Lawsuits and government actions

- The tax basis of the subsidiary's assets

Legal Diligence Issues

Open legal issues, including any outstanding litigation, are usually a major concern to an SER party. Answers should be developed in advance to questions about the potential liability and status of claims, so that the SER party has some sense of the cost of a potential settlement or award after the SER transaction.

An SER party will usually not put much value on potential awards from litigation such as pending patent infringement actions brought by the subsidiary. On the other hand, an SER party will usually assume the worst reasonable case in assessing the potential damages payable in any litigation brought against the subsidiary by others. If the amount of potential damages payable is substantial, some mechanism may be needed to bridge the different expectations, or the parent will need to assume the liability.

Limiting the Distraction of the Due Diligence Process

Even the best-managed due diligence process is very distracting to the parent and subsidiary. There are a number of actions that the parent and subsidiary can take to limit the disruption of the diligence process:

- Limit discussions to the CEO and CFO until the field of prospective SER parties is narrowed down.

- If more than a few SER parties are going to be involved in due diligence investigations, set up a data room on site at the parent or at subsidiary offices that contains copies of all material diligence files.

- Ensure that the prospective SER party can contact important customers and suppliers, but do not disrupt relationships. The parent and subsidiary need to think this through carefully. The approach will depend on the relationship with the customer or supplier and the stage of the SER process. The parent and subsidiary want to avoid customers receiving multiple calls, and should generally allow customer calls only by parties that they feel are serious and about whom they are serious. Customers should be briefed about these calls.

- Channel all information requests through one designated party at the parent and subsidiary. The CFO or general counsel usually fills this role, but the choice of the right person for this role will depend on the organization. This individual is responsible for

- Logging in requests for information

- Obtaining the requested information from within the parent or subsidiary or from outside sources

- Answering questions from prospective SER parties

- Keeping management at the parent and subsidiary, its legal counsel, and its advisors in the loop on information requests and responses

- Ensuring that contacts outside the designated channel are carefully managed to avoid repeated calls to customers and suppliers and to the outside law firm of the parent and subsidiary (which gets expensive)

- Organizing site visits and meetings between the management of the parent and subsidiary and the prospective SER party to minimize disruption

See the comprehensive due diligence checklist at the end of this chapter.

MAKING A SUCCESS OF AN SER: ADVICE FOR TOP MANAGERS OF THE SUBSIDIARY

Management Approach

An SER requires a very different management approach than running either a subsidiary when it is part of the parent or a start-up. A subsidiary often has an existing culture, customer base, and staff—and an existing corporate strategy developed with the parent that must be reassessed quickly and redirected as needed, in light of the new status of the subsidiary. Kevin Ryan, who was CEO from 1995 to 2000 of Jessen VisionCare, an SER from Schering-Plough Corporation, which was sold five years later to Novartis AG, identified the following five actions for the management of the subsidiary to focus on after the SER[2]:

1. Identify a core team of managers who are committed to change, and to the success of the SER. They should not be fence-sitters.

2. Hold people accountable and let them know their future with the company depends on it.

3. Reset objectives. Pre-SER, it is most important to meet the parent's objectives. Post-SER, it is most important to be able to survive as an independent company and to create value.

4. Spend like a start-up. Cash is king for an independent company, since it can't dip into a parent's deep pockets.

5. Reward to the lowest possible level. Establish performance-driven incentives right down to employees on the production floor. This instills a sense of ownership.

Focus on the Right Things After the SER

It is common for participants to be so involved in the mechanics of the SER that they do not pay sufficient attention to the issues that are a key to post-SER success. These issues include:

- *Reach a clear understanding with the parent on post-SER relations.* For a successful SER, the following issues concerning the subsidiary's post-SER status need to be discussed, understood, and decided to the extent possible prior to the separation:

- Financial requirements and the sources of funds
- Capital structure
- Tax structure
- Legal structure
- Governance
- Ownership
- Support from the parent
- Relationship with the parent
- Staffing and compensation plans
- Infrastructure to operate effectively

- *Communicate with all constituencies.* Identify all the internal and external constituencies for the SER and develop a communications strategy targeted at each. These constituencies include employees and their families, customers and suppliers, the parent and investors, and industry analysts. Continual and diversified limited communications are better than occasional massive documents or meetings that overwhelm recipients. Knowledge travels quickly in all corporations; ensure that it is fact, not rumor, that reaches constituents. Communications with key constituencies cannot be delegated; the involvement of the top management of the new entity is important.

  If the SER involves a public equity, it is likely that the dynamics of the public markets for comparable-size companies will need to be explained to employees, the parent, and directors, some of whom may not be familiar with the equity markets at all or only in the context of the large parent. The volatility of many public stocks, the demands of investors and research analysts and their measurement tools, the necessity of meeting expectations going forward, and the consequences of missing them are all often a surprise to those who have not been exposed to the public markets.

- *Put in place the right people and compensation plans to run an independent entity.* In many cases, the sole focus of employee matters prior to the SER is on the extent and terms of equity ownership in the subsidiary post-SER, the treatment of parent options and pension plans, and senior management compensation agreements. These are important; however, there are many equally important issues that are not often addressed. The foremost is who should make up the management team. The talent needed to run a subsidiary post-SER is often very different from that needed as a part of the parent. The post-SER subsidiary generally requires of employees and directors greater tolerance for ambiguity and risk, as well as far fewer resources. The team that runs a division may not be the team, or the complete team, that will succeed on a stand-alone basis. A compensation and measurement plan commensurate with the different requirements after the SER must be put in place. The incentives, assessment and measurement, and compensation plans may be very different from those used at a large parent.

THE ROLE OF EXPERT OPINIONS IN SERs

In May, 2002, the *Wall Street Journal* reported on Georgia Pacific Corp.'s pending IPO of its $12 billion consumer products and packaging business. In the story, the *Wall Street Journal* noted that the boards of the parent and the new subsidiary had hired an independent firm to examine whether a $12.2 billion debt allocation was fair to both sides. This scenario illustrates the benefits of obtaining expert opinions before SER transactions, as a senior bond analyst at a large bank was quoted as saying, "That [opinion] could preclude [the parent] from dumping too much bad stuff on [the new subsidiary]."[3]

After the parent and the subsidiary have agreed on a course of action, it makes sense, in certain situations, to obtain an expert opinion from a qualified and independent financial expert to help ensure that the arrangement is fair to all of the parties involved. These opinions may take a considerable amount of time to prepare and should be started early in the SER process, once the parent decides on a specific SER alternative. Let's look at some of the common questions regarding expert opinions.

Why Should a Parent Obtain an Opinion from a Financial Expert?

An opinion from a financial expert provides a respected opinion that the board of directors may use during financial deliberations and offers significant legal protection for the board of directors if there are creditor or outside shareholder lawsuits at a later date. It may also provide comfort to investors that there has been a review by a reputable party not associated with the SER transaction. However, for many SERs, there is little justification for the expense of an opinion if the risk of a legal or public relations challenge to the parent or the subsidiary is modest.

What Are Common Opinions?

There are a number of types of opinions that are often requested in an SER transaction. These include:

- Fairness opinions from a financial advisor on the fairness of the financial terms of an SER. This is applicable to many types of SERs. These opinions support the goal of creating an SER structure that is fair to all parties.
- Solvency opinions on the subsidiary's financial viability at the time of the SER, should the subsidiary run into financial distress after the SER (most applicable to carve-outs and spin-offs).
- Solvency opinions on the parent's financial viability after the SER (when the parent is financially weakened as a result of the SER transaction—most applicable to carve-outs and spin-offs).

- Valuation opinions for applicable state corporate laws restricting the payment of dividends where a spin-off may be considered a dividend (applicable to spin-offs).
- Valuation opinions on future stock price assumptions for a "poison pill" shareholder rights plan defense measure (most applicable to carve-outs and spin-offs).
- IRS opinions supporting an application requesting a ruling on the tax-free status for a spin-off. These opinions state that the spin-off is being undertaken as a specific non-tax-related financial benefit such as providing easier access to the public capital markets (applicable to tax-free spin-offs).
- Trading price opinion on a spin-off. An opinion as to the expected trading price of the spin-off stock may be required by the stock market on which the stock is to be listed for it to permit "when issued" trading (applicable to tax-free and taxable spin-offs).

When Should an Opinion Be Considered?

An opinion should be considered in any situation in which there is risk of legal challenge to the transaction or there are potential shareholder or public relations pitfalls that make it prudent to have the written support of an outside financial advisor for the SER in hand. The parent often will require that the subsidiary obtain an opinion on a significant SER when there are outside shareholders or creditors. This is especially true when the SER involves a conflict of interest with the parent or where the parent may have ultimate legal liability as indicated in the following scenarios:

- An SER is undertaken in response to a takeover threat of the parent.
- One or more directors or officers of the parent or the subsidiary have a conflict of interest or are interested parties in the SER.
- The subsidiary or the SER is significant to the parent.
- The parent or subsidiary is a public company, and a shareholder vote is required to approve the SER.
- The subsidiary is public, and the transaction is significant.
- The financial condition of the parent after the SER may later be challenged by its creditors or shareholders as impaired by the SER.
- The parent's or subsidiary's banks require a solvency opinion.
- A stock exchange requires an opinion as to expected trading price in a spin-off.

When Is an Opinion Delivered?

In most cases, a draft of the opinion is usually delivered to the management or board of directors of the subsidiary or the parent early in the SER process so that they and their legal counsel may review it for unwanted surprises and make comments. In a spin-off, a draft opinion may be included in the Form 10 Information Statement filed with the SEC, and a signed opinion in the Form 10 when it is sent to shareholders. An updated signed opinion may be delivered when the shares are distributed. In a merger of a public subsidiary, a draft opinion is usually included in the materials filed with the SEC, and a signed opinion is usually included in the materials sent to shareholders seeking approval of the merger. An updated signed opinion is usually delivered at the closing of the merger. In other SERs, the signed opinion is usually delivered only once, at the closing of the transaction.

ACCOUNTING FOR A SUBSIDIARY EQUITY REDEPLOYMENT TRANSACTION

Of course, planning for an SER would not be complete without a brief discussion of the accounting considerations for SER transactions. Although almost every SER transaction has an accounting impact on the parent, a detailed discussion of accounting practices is beyond the scope of this book. The information presented here summarizes some of the major issues. Specifically, this chapter will provide a brief overview of the distinctive accounting rules and regulations that govern subsidiary equity redeployment transactions. We will focus on three common SER transactions that most often involve the public markets: minority carve-outs, majority carve-outs, and tax-free spin-offs. Mergers have many and very complex accounting issues. However, these are a major discussion in themselves, and they are well covered in books on mergers and acquisitions.

Accounting Considerations in a Public Market SER

Consolidation
The parent is usually consolidating the subsidiary for financial reporting before an SER. The balance sheets and income statement of the subsidiary are combined with those of the parent. An SER may change the accounting treatment of the subsidiary. This may be advantageous for the parent if the subsidiary has losses, has a different and more leveraged capital structure, is using cash, or has lower operating margins. Alternatively, the subsidiary may be generating substantial profits or cash flow, and deconsolidating it may make the parent look worse on a stand-alone basis.

The consolidation accounting treatment of three SER scenarios is presented here. The purpose of presenting these scenarios is to show the accounting impact on the parent.

- *The parent retains greater than 50 percent ownership after the SER.* The parent will, in most cases, fully consolidate the subsidiary for accounting purposes. If the parent retained a majority of the voting common stock of the subsidiary (and control), the parent will continue to consolidate all of the income statements and balance sheets of the subsidiary in its consolidated financial statements. The proportion of ownership below 100 percent is treated as a minority interest on the income statement. A minority interest item on the balance sheet is established at an initial amount equaling the book value of the subsidiary times the percentage not owned by the parent.

- *The parent retains 20 to 50 percent ownership after the SER.* The parent will, in most cases, use the equity method of accounting for the subsidiary. If the parent retained a 20 to 50 percent voting interest in the subsidiary, it would generally account for its interest using the equity method. Under the equity method, the parent recognizes the profits and losses of the subsidiary, but not its revenues, proportionate to the parent's ownership interest in the subsidiary in a single line in the parent's income statement, such as "Losses at the subsidiary reduce the parent's profits."

- *The parent retains less than 20 percent ownership after the SER.* The parent will, in most cases, use the cost method. With this method, the parent's ownership in the subsidiary is treated as an investment and is a balance sheet item only. Under the cost method, investments are generally carried at cost and therefore there is no impact on the parent's income statement of profits or losses at the subsidiary. If there is a permanent impairment of value, the investment may be written down but would not be adjusted for temporary fluctuations in fair market value (FMV).

Accounting Gains and Losses

Most SERs involve accounting gains or losses. In a carve-out transaction where the subsidiary sells all or a portion of its stock in an SER, the parent will recognize a book gain or loss calculated as follows: parent's old book basis plus proceeds from share issuance times the percentage retained less old book basis, subject to the applicable income tax rate. The parent takes an accounting gain or loss even though it did not sell any shares itself. Chapter 6, discusses Thermo Electron's use of this technique to increase reported income.[5] The parent will also recognize book gain or loss on any shares of the subsidiary it sells itself.

In a tax-free spin-off, the subsidiary's assets and liabilities are transferred off of the parent's consolidated financial statements at book value (without gain or loss) in the form of a distribution to the shareholders of the parent. Exhibit 4–1 summarizes the accounting impact on the parent of certain SERs (assuming the parent owns 100 percent of the subsidiary prior to the SER).

Accounting Treatment of a Discontinued Operation

The parent may decide to treat the subsidiary as a discontinued operation for accounting if it is intended that all or substantially all (generally greater than 80 percent) of a subsidiary will be sold within a year, except in a spin-off. By treating the subsidiary as a discontinued operation, the assets, liabilities, and financial results of the parent for prior periods may be restated to separately show the results of the operations of the subsidiary separately from the parent's continuing operations. This

E X H I B I T   4–1

Accounting Treatment of Selected SER Alternatives

	Ownership of the Subsidiary by the Parent Post-SER				
	Minority carve-out		Majority carve-out		Spin-off
	80% or greater	50%–80%	20%–50%	Less than 20%	Less than 20%
Parent's accounting treatment	Full consolidation	Full consolidation	Equity method	Cost method	Cost method
Parent's accounting gains and losses on the SER	• Where the subsidiary sells stock the parent will recognize a book gain or loss • Where the parent sells stock the parent will recognize a book gain or loss				No gain, but may be a loss*

*FAS 144, issued in 2001, requires that the parent recognize a loss if the book value of the subsidiary is greater than its FMV at the date of the spin-off.

Source: John C. Michaelson and Robin A. Graham, "Equity Carve-Outs and Spin-Offs of Technology Operations," *The Financier*, vol. 2, no. 4, November, 1995.

may be very attractive in allowing the parent's financial results to be separated from the subsidiary's before the actual subsidiary SER, especially if the subsidiary's operations detract from the real picture of the parent to investors. However, with a spin-off different rules apply. FAS 144 requires that a subsidiary in a spin-off be considered held and used until the actual distribution to shareholders. Only then may it be treated as discontinued.

SUMMARY OF HOW TAXES AFFECT SER ALTERNATIVES

Exhibit 4–2 summarizes the tax impact of the primary SER alternatives. In this exhibit it is assumed that the subsidiary is 100 percent owned by the parent and is consolidated by the parent for tax before the SER.

TAX CONSEQUENCES OF SELECTED SERs: A NUMERICAL EXAMPLE

Exhibit 4–3 examines the U.S. federal income tax consequences of the SERs discussed previously, using a hypothetical transaction for January 1, 2002.

Notes and Assumptions

• *Tax-free spin-off.* The spin-off qualifies as tax free under IRC Section 355.

• *Majority carve-out.* This sale is assumed to be an offering of shares owned by the parent, as opposed to a primary offering of shares by the subsidiary. This chart assumes that a Section 338(h)(10) election has not been made. (See discussion in Chapter 7.)

• *Minority carve-out.* This sale is assumed to be an offering of shares directly by the subsidiary.

E X H I B I T   4–2

Tax Treatment of Selected SER Alternatives

	Type of SER					
	Minority carve-out **Corporate strategic partnership** **Private equity partnership**	**Majority carve-out** **Corporate strategic partnership** **Private equity partnership**			**Spin-off**	**Stock merger with a public or private company**
	Percentage ownership of the subsidiary by the parent post-SER					
	80% or greater	**50%–80%**	**20%–50%**	**Less than 20%**	**0%**	**20%–80%**
Does the transaction result in continued consolidation of the subsidiary by the parent for federal tax?	Yes	No	No	No	No	No
Is the dividend-received deduction on subsidiary dividends to parent __ percent available?	100%	80%	80%	70%	70%	80%
Is a tax-free (Section 355) second-step distribution of remaining shares held by parent available later?	Yes	No	No	No	No	No
Is there tax to the parent on any gain on the initial SER?	No, if the stock is sold directly by the subsidiary*				No	No
Is there tax to the parent's shareholders on a later distribution of remaining subsidiary shares in a second-step spin-off?	No†	Yes, taxable dividend	Yes, taxable dividend	Yes, taxable dividend	Yes, taxable dividend	Yes, taxable dividend

*No, if the stock is sold directly by the subsidiary. Yes, on any gain if subsidiary stock is sold by the parent.

†Taxable gain is deferred until the sale by the shareholder of the subsidiary shares received in the distribution. Tax basis is allocated between the parent and the new subsidiary shares by the shareholder.

- *Parent and subsidiary are U.S. corporations.* Before the proposed transaction, the parent owns 100 percent of the common stock of the subsidiary. The subsidiary has no other classes of equity outstanding.

If the parent and subsidiary can no longer file a consolidated return following the transaction, income or loss from the subsidiary cannot offset income or loss from the parent (or other members of the parent's consolidated group), the parent and/or the subsidiary may be required to recognize gain or income from deferred intercompany transactions, and the parent would be required to adjust its basis in any remaining stock of the subsidiary, if the parent has a built-in loss on the stock of the subsidiary.

In addition, note the following:

- The FMV of the subsidiary is assumed to be $100 million.

- The FMV of the parent, including its investment in the subsidiary, is assumed to be $400 million.

- The subsidiary's tax basis in its assets at December 31, 2001, is assumed to equal $60 million.

EXHIBIT 4-3

Example of U.S. Federal Income Tax Consequences of Selected SERs

	Tax-free spin-off	Majority carve-out	Minority carve-out—less than 20%
Gain or loss recognized by parent.	None. An exception is if debt in excess of $50 million (parent's tax basis in the subsidiary) is transferred to the subsidiary in connection with the spin-off. Section 357(c) would apply if the parent contributes a business (including the related assets and liabilities) to a newly formed subsidiary to facilitate a spin-off.	If parent sells subsidiary stock, a gain of $50 million ($100 million FMV of subsidiary less tax basis in stock of $50 million) times the percentage of shares sold. If subsidiary stock is sold by the subsidiary, none.	None, if subsidiary stock sold by the subsidiary. If parent sells subsidiary stock, a gain of $50 million ($100 million FMV of subsidiary less tax basis in stock of $50 million) times percentage of shares sold.
Gain or loss recognized by subsidiary.	None.	None.	None.
Basis in stock of subsidiary received in the spin-off by a parent shareholder or an investor's basis in stock of the subsidiary purchased in the IPO.	25% ($100 million/$400 million, – FMV of subsidiary/FMV of combined parent and subsidiary) times parent shareholder's original basis in parent's stock.	Price paid for the subsidiary stock.	Price paid for the subsidiary stock.
Holding period in stock of subsidiary received by a parent's shareholders in the spin-off or purchased by an investor in the IPO.	Holding period of the subsidiary stock received in the distribution includes the investor's holding period in parent's stock.	Holding period of the new subsidiary stock purchased in the IPO begins on date of purchase.	Holding period of the new subsidiary stock purchased in the IPO begins on date of purchase.
Parent's basis in remaining stock of subsidiary.	Parent has completely divested its interest in subsidiary.	$50 million times percent of subsidiary stock not sold.	If the subsidiary stock is sold by subsidiary, $50 million. If the subsidiary stock is sold by the parent, $50 million times percent of shares not sold.
Subsidiary's tax basis in its assets.	Same as tax basis at December 31, 2001 ($60 million), FMV of intangibles is not recognized.	Same as tax basis at December 3, 2001 ($60 million), FMV of intangibles is not recognized.	Same as tax basis at December 31, 2001 ($60 million), FMV of intangibles is not recognized.
Filing of consolidated return.	Parent and subsidiary will no longer file a consolidated return.	Parent and subsidiary will no longer file a consolidated return.	Parent and subsidiary will still file a consolidated return.
Effect on net operating losses (NOLs) of the subsidiary.	Subsidiary retains tax attributes, (including NOLs).	Subsidiary retains tax attributes, (including NOLs) but may be subject to limitations.	Subsidiary retains tax attributes, (including NOLs).

Source: John C. Michaelson and Robin A. Graham, "Equity Carve-Outs and Spin-Offs of Technology Operations," *The Financier,* vol. 2, no. 4, November 1995.

- The subsidiary's liabilities do not exceed its basis in its assets. The assets include intangibles with a book and tax basis of $0 and an FMV of $40 million.
- Immediately before the proposed transaction, the parent's tax basis in the stock of the subsidiary is $50 million.
- The parent is assumed to have equal basis in all of its shares.

SUMMARY

This chapter examined the importance of taking the requisite steps to plan appropriately for an SER transaction. Subsequently, we reviewed those steps in depth to help readers understand the planning tasks involved in successful SER transactions. Chapter 5 will examine another important step in the planning process—namely, properly valuing the subsidiary.

Exhibit 4–4 is a list of the typical information requests that will come from SER parties as they investigate a transaction.

Due Diligence Preparation for a Subsidiary SER

Code Key

Parties responsible for providing information/reviewing information before dissemination:

Subsidiary in-house counsel (SIC)	Parent development staff (PDS)	
Subsidiary CEO (SCEO)	Parent operating staff (POS)	
Subsidiary CFO (SCFO)	Parent in-house counsel (PC)	
Subsidiary development staff (SDS)	Parent outside counsel (POC)	
Subsidiary operating staff (SOS)	Parent outside auditors (PA)	
Subsidiary technical staff (STC)	Parent financial advisor (PFA)	
Outside subsidiary counsel (CC)		
Outside subsidiary auditors (SA)		
Subsidiary financial advisor (SFA)		
Consultants (SC)		

Materials requested by:

- SER party CEO/general partner (ICEO)
- SER party CFO (ICFO)
- SER party operating staff (IOS)
- SER party financial analysts (IFA)
- SER party outside counsel (IC)
- SER party outside auditors (IA)
- SER party financial advisor (IFA)
- SER party technical consultants (ITC)
- Outside subsidiary auditors (SA)
- Subsidiary financial advisor (SFA)
- Consultants (SC)
- CEO (SCEO)
- Subsidiary CFO (SCFO)
- Outside subsidiary counsel (CC)
- Outside subsidiary auditors (SA)
- Subsidiary financial advisor (SFA)
- Consultants (SC)

Locations of information / materials:

Subsidiary head office (HQ)	Outside subsidiary counsel (CC)	
Data room (DR)	Outside subsidiary auditors (SA)	
Another subsidiary facility (name)	Parent (P)	

Materials available as:

- Hard copy only (HCO)
- Electronic file (EC)

Checklist

Section	Item	Location of information	Responsibility for review	Reviewed and satisfactory to disseminate	Form of materials	To be copied in advance	Available only on-site	Requested by SER party	Available or date promised available	Responsibility to provide if not available	Provided incomplete — awaiting additional information	Not provided—Incomplete—being assembled	Will not be provided—unavailable	Will not be provided for now—confidential	For discussion with SER party	For senior management decision	Date/Initials/Party
A	**Assets and Facilities**																
A1	List of material assets and equipment including, but not limited to: - computer equipment - manufacturing equipment - vehicles - software (capitalized for resale and internal use) - other If any of the assets listed in this section are leased, summary of lease information.																
A2	Description of real property owned or leased. If the assets listed in this section are leased, summary of lease information.																

A3	For all assets described in A1 and 2, provide the following:
	- cost - location
	- description - depreciated book
	- fair market value
A4	Description of any actual and anticipated environmental compliance issues.
A5	Copies of any environmental studies, the name of consultants and contact person.
A6	Schedule of major capital projects recently completed.
	Schedule of major capital projects in progress.
	Schedule of expected capital requirements over the next 12 months.
B	**Products and Services**
B1	List the products and services being distributed or under development.
B2	For each product and service provide:
	- a brief description of the product or service
	- copies of product documentation, if any
	- the date each product or service was or is expected to be first sold or licensed
	- product brochures and marketing materials
B3	For each product, identify any royalty, ownership, license, or other similar obligations to the parent or other parties. For any third-party inbound license agreements, provide information on the following:
	- cancellation terms
	- identify any volume commitments or special arrangements
	- identify any special discounts, concessions, or accommodations
	- describe any ongoing contract or price negotiations
B4	Description of pricing for each product and service.
B5	Description of any custom projects currently under way for customers and the associated payments or pricing arrangements.
B6	Copies of all material license agreements, development agreements, professional services contracts, and postcontract support agreements relating to the products and services.
B7	Any legal opinions concerning the subsidiary's products or services.
C	**Intellectual Property**
C1	Copies of all copyright registration documents.
C2	A copy of any issued patents, and identify any pending patent applications filed.
	Provide for each:
	- titles, patent numbers, and serial numbers of issued patents; titles and serial numbers of pending patents; and titles of inventions or technology not yet filed
	- names and status of inventors
	- countries filed in (U.S. and foreign)
	If issued, have maintenance fees been paid?
C3	A contact (or name of subsidiary's outside counsel) to review patent files.
C4	List of all products which may be subject to copyright protection.
C5	Copies of nondisclosure agreements with third parties.

Continued

Continued

C6	Description of trade secrets received under nondisclosure agreements.					
C7	List of all products, technologies, patents, copyrights, trademarks, trade secrets (or any other intellectual property) owned by the subsidiary.					
C8	List of all products, technologies, patents, copyrights, trademarks, trade secrets (or any other intellectual property) required or necessary for the subsidiary to carry out its business plan that are not owned by the subsidiary.					
C9	List all trademarks, trade names, service marks and the like, and any domain names issued to or registered by the subsidiary, and the countries in which they are issued/registered.					
C10	Copies of any trademark licenses granted by or to the subsidiary.					
C11	The name(s) of IP counsel and authorization to discuss these matters with them.			†		
C12	A copy of any trademark usage guidelines or quality assurance guidelines used by the subsidiary in connection with its use of trademarks.					
C13	A contact (or name of subsidiary's outside counsel) to review trademark files.					
D	**Legal**					
D1	Description of any litigation (foreign or domestic, federal or state court) in which the subsidiary is currently involved or has been involved in the recent past. This should identify the parties, the court, the case number, the subject of the litigation, and the current status.					
D2	Description of any claims of infringement of a patent, copyright, trademark, or trade secret (or any other intellectual property) made by the subsidiary or the parent against others. Provide the name of any outside counsel on the matter and a copy of any written opinions.					
D3	A copy of any notice regarding any actual or threatened claim and a description of the assertions made or threatened.					
D4	Description of any opposition actions with regard to the trademarks of the subsidiary and a description or copies of any communication, such as phone calls, cease and desist letters, claiming the subsidiary has been infringing or misusing a third party's trademark.					
D5	Description of any pending or threatened environmental actions and any actions brought within the past five years, and contact at environmental counsel.					
D6	List of any of the subsidiary's patents, patent applications, copyrights, trade secrets, or inventions identified subject to any ownership dispute, litigation, reexamination, reissue, or patent interference.					
D7	Description of any pending or threatened product liability actions and any actions brought within the past five years, and contact at product liability counsel.					
D8	Description of any claims of patent, copyright, trademark, or trade secret (or any other intellectual property) infringement raised in writing or otherwise and their status. A copy of any opinion from outside legal counsel. Identify any reserves against these claims.					
D9	Copies of any trademark consent and dispute settlement agreements.					
D10	Summary of pending or threatened state or federal government disputes and investigations, including any claims or inquiries and resolution, if applicable.					
D11	Description of any known or potential personnel litigation issues and any brought within the past five years.					
D12	Description of any pending or potential OSHA actions and any brought within the past five years.					
D13	Description of any outstanding or potential actions by the IRS impacting the subsidiary.					
D14	Copies of letters from internal and external counsel.					

				E	Personnel
				E1	An organization chart for the subsidiary.
				E2	Information for each of the senior executives of the subsidiary - annual salary vested and exercisable - bonus at plan unvested - bonus achievement last fiscal year strike price for each grant - stock options total granted start date - total exercised
				E3	Summary of key management personnel including names, ages (if retirement is expected within the next five years), responsibilities, educational background, and recent business experience.
				E4	Copies of all employment contracts and agreements; summary of verbal agreements, including termination agreements for individuals or classes of employees.
				E5	Copies of all employee benefit plans (health and welfare plans, stock option, stock participation, stock purchase agreements, retirement, bonus, pension plans) in existence or contemplated.
				E6	Summary of management perks.
				E7	Copies of any union contracts and collective bargaining agreements. Description of any pending or threatened union negotiations.
				E8	Headcount summary by function as of most recent two fiscal year-ends, and forecast for current fiscal year separately for full-time employees, part-time employees, consultants, temporary workers, and contractors.
				E9	Proprietary information and inventions agreements with employees.
				E10	Any deferred compensation agreements.
				E11	Any outstanding commitments for relocation or other accommodations.
				E12	A copy of any stock option plan to be created for the benefit of the employees of the subsidiary. A list of the amount of the expected grants and strike price for each recipient.
				E13	A list of all consultants and temporary employees of the subsidiary and the terms of the agreements. Describe independent contractor status classification process and describe any legal action that is pending or anticipated with regard to such classification.
				E14	Description of R&D work contracted out to third parties.
				E15	A list of loans by the subsidiary or parent to subsidiary employees.
				E16	Copy of standard employee confidentiality and noncompete agreements.
				E17	Copy of employee handbook or policies and procedures manual.
				F	Contracts
				F1	Copies of material contracts with third parties. A description of the conditions under which the contracts may be assigned to the subsidiary if held by the parent.
				F2	Copies of government contracts. A description of the conditions under which the contracts may be assigned to the subsidiary if held by the parent.

Continued

E X H I B I T 4-4

Continued

F3 Copies of any standard form contracts. Identify any material agreements containing nonstandard terms relative to the following:
- warranty
- issues with assignment
- right of return
- indemnity exposures
- nonstandard pricing arrangements
- exclusivity
- other special terms or provisions

F4 Copies of all sales, distribution, OEM, manufacturing, and marketing agreements.

F5 Copies of all joint ventures, strategic alliance, and corporate partnership agreements to which the subsidiary is a party.

F6 Description of agreements restricting the abilities of the subsidiary to compete in any lines of business, markets, or geographic areas.

F7 Copies of all other contracts to which the subsidiary is a party, which are material.

F8 Description and copies of all agreements with the parent on the provision of services and support.

F9 Any broad licensing provisions which would give licensee rights to the subsidiary's products.

F10 List of all nondisclosure agreements to which the subsidiary is a party.

G   General Business

G1 Planning documents—copies of:
- management studies, marketing surveys, engineering reports, or other market studies by outside consultants or internally generated
- the subsidiary's business plan for the current year and last fiscal year
- sales projections for the current fiscal year by product and service
- advertising and marketing plan for the last fiscal year and the current fiscal year

G2 List of states in which the subsidiary does business, maintains offices, or has employees.

G3 List of jurisdictions in which the subsidiary is qualified to do business.

G4 List of the subsidiary's principal suppliers:
- Include the suppliers of key supplies as well as the largest dollar volume suppliers.
- Note whether the subsidiary has any special or concentrated sources of supply.
- What is the dollar volume of annual purchases by supplier?
- What are the methods and terms of purchase?
- Are there any ongoing contract or price negotiations with key suppliers? What is the status of these negotiations?
- What suppliers have ceased doing business with the subsidiary in the past year and why?

G5 Description of how the subsidiary sells and distributes its products and services.

G6 Sales and contracting process—description of the subsidiary's:
- sales cycle
- typical terms of sale
- average discount on sales
- credit practices

G7 Summary of major competitors.

G8 What government authorizations, licenses, permits, qualifications, or registrations are necessary for the conduct of the subsidiary's business?

G9	List of revenue from major customer over the last year.	

H Governance

H1	Description of the parent's intention with respect to the board of directors structure and governance of the subsidiary.	
H2	Copies of corporate organization, charter and bylaws, and audit committee reports.	
H3	Capitalization table.	
H4	Shareholder list.	
H5	Copies of any shareholder agreements.	
H6	Copies of any related party contracts, payments, transactions.	
H7	Description of the capital stock of the subsidiary and copies of all documentation of stock securities outstanding and authorized.	
H8	List and chart of all subsidiaries and affiliates of the subsidiary and any predecessor organizations.	
H9	Copies of the subsidiary and any predecessor organizations' board minutes and resolutions and parent board resolutions concerning the subsidiary.	

I Financial

I1	Copies of loan and other financing arrangements with the parent.	
I2	List of bank relationships.	
I3	Copies of loan and bank facility agreements and indentures.	
I4	Copies of material lease agreements.	
I5	Description of tax arrangements with the parent and any tax issues impacting the subsidiary.	
I6	Summary of major accounting practices including revenue recognition policies.	
I7	Contact at the subsidiary's accounting firm and authorization to contact.	
I8	Quarterly internal financial statements for the subsidiary's operation for last four quarters and projection for current fiscal year.	
I9	Copies of audited financial statements for the past five years for the subsidiary and any predecessors (or, if these are not available, consolidating financial information).	
I10	Pro forma combined historical financial statements for the subsidiary, if it is a new entity.	
I11	Copies of any accountant's letters to the board of the subsidiary.	
I12	Description of internal control and accounting systems.	
I13	Copies of monthly financial reports.	
I14	A compilation of the subsidiary's deferred revenue and analysis of when deferred revenue will be recognized.	
I15	List of capital commitments.	
I16	List of all off-balance-sheet obligations and commitments.	
I17	Copies of internal and external accountants letters and observations.	

CHAPTER 5

SOME ISSUES IN VALUING A SUBSIDIARY

INTRODUCTION

The expected value is a key consideration in assessing all SER alternatives. But it can be challenging, as outside equity investors will often value the subsidiary using criteria and methodology that dramatically differ from those used by the parent. Therefore, this chapter will examine some of the techniques used by equity investors to value a subsidiary so that parent companies can understand how both public and private equity investors determine the price they are actually willing to pay for various types of economic interest in different SERs. For the purpose of this discussion, we will look at how outside equity investors approach spin-offs, equity partnerships, IPOs, and mergers.

The purpose of a valuation is usually to approximate what a real third party will actually pay in a specific SER transactions. Bear in mind that a valuation is only a best guess at the price and terms of a future equity redeployment. Nor is valuation a mathematical formula. There is a high degree of judgment in any valuation. Using a formula only supports the application of judgment and experience.

This chapter is not intended to be a general guide for how to value a company. There are many good books published on this topic already. But, as we will see, the parent and private and public equity investors often approach determining value from very different perspectives. Adding to the confusion is the fact that there is no area of business practice where there is a greater divergence between the approaches to determining value now taught in business schools and those used in practice by equity investors. The equivalent would be if American law schools taught only the Napoleonic Code and did not teach common law or statute law.[1]

THE IMPORTANCE OF ACCURATE VALUATION

Valuations rely on many assumptions about the state of the financial markets; the interests, capabilities, and proclivities of SER parties; and the future of the subsidiary and its industry as represented in forecasts. Therefore any valuation is only as good as the assumptions that go into creating it. Valuations based on incomplete data without the full set of facts or inflated sales lead to disappointment, poor choice of SER alternatives, and the potential for a very costly aborted effort. Valuations play a role in all types of SERs and at all stages of the process. For example, many SERs involve an IPO, and valuations occur at many steps in the IPO process. A valuation at the start of the process helps the parent and its advisors determine the feasibility of an IPO. A valuation before the drafting process provides information to managers and directors of the subsidiary and its parent about the expected valuation of shares sold in the IPO. A valuation before printing the IPO prospectuses helps the parent and underwriters of the IPO agree on a target price at which IPO shares will be marketed to potential investors, and guides the parent on whether to continue and incur the expenses of printing and a road show. During the marketing of the IPO, potential IPO investors will perform their own valuations and determine what price they are willing to pay for the shares in the IPO. However, the actual value is only discovered at the end of the IPO process by what real investors are willing to pay. That is when the rubber meets the road. If that price is a surprise to the parent, the professionals preparing the valuation were not doing their job.

KEY POINTS FOR THE PARENT TO CONSIDER DURING THE VALUATION PROCESS

There are many elements of an SER that are within the control of the parent that are interrelated with value and need to be considered together. These include:

- The terms of the ongoing business relationship between the parent and the subsidiary after the SER must be considered. The parent may put in place arrangements that greatly enhance value (e.g., a favorable supply agreement or long-term purchase contract) or completely eviscerate value (e.g., high royalties to the parent).

- The more the subsidiary is structured to look like other successful companies in its industry, the higher the likely valuation under most redeployment alternatives.

- How the parent structures corporate governance at the subsidiary will affect valuation and the interest of SER parties.

- The retention of subsidiary liabilities and assets will have a large effect on attractiveness to SER parties.

- The clear support of a well-respected and financially strong parent will tend to increase valuation as well as increasing the number of SER alternatives available, allowing the parent to select the best SER alternative.

- The quality of the subsidiary's management, sponsors, and board of directors will influence both valuation and the range of available SERs.

- The endorsement of respected private equity and strategic investors and respected customers will enhance value.

- The terms of the securities offered in the SER. If these are different from market expectations or not balanced between the interests of the parent and the other party, it will reduce value.

There are some other issues to consider as well:

- There is not a single value for a subsidiary. Instead, there is a wide range of values for the subsidiary, depending on the specific SER chosen by the parent and its terms. A valuation applicable to one type of SER is not applicable to another. The difference in value between SER alternatives may be a multiple of two or considerably more.

- There is often a trade-off between a priority of speed of execution and obtaining the best terms or values. For example, an organized and competitive process will usually result in obtaining the best terms, but it will usually take longer than negotiating with only one or two parties from the start.

- Most SERs, except a 100 percent single-step majority carve-out, are only one step toward creating parent shareholder value. Even a company that has been spun off is still owned by the parent's shareholders. As a result, the potential success of the subsidiary following the SER is usually more important to creating value for the parent and its shareholders than is the initial value placed on the subsidiary in the SER transaction. For example, unduly maximizing the share price in a minority carve-out IPO produces greater cash proceeds in the IPO but is usually not productive for long-term value. The stock tends to have a weak aftermarket and trade down. Consequently, the IPO does not meet many of the expectations of the parent or create as much value for the parent's shareholders.

- A valuation is valid only at the time it is prepared. As markets change, so will the valuation. Markets may change dramatically between the date of the initial valuation and the actual SER. The closer to the date of the actual SER, the more accurate the valuation is likely to be.

Last, it is important to note that valuations prepared by outside advisors at the start of the SER process and initial indications of interest from SER parties generally are too high and should be taken only as a broad guide, for the following reasons:

- These valuations are often based on accepting the forecasts and business characterization of the subsidiary at face value. Generally for an initial valuation, the forecasts are prepared by the subsidiary. Usually the advisors or SER party have not done the homework at that stage to do more.

- The advisors or SER party may not know any holes in the company's story before due diligence investigations.
- The advisors or SER party do not want to be thrown out of the game early by delivering bad news.

VALUATIONS AND THE TYPE OF SER

Before an SER transaction, it is important that the parent understand that a valuation of the subsidiary may produce many different estimated values at the same time depending on which SER is contemplated, for the purpose of determining the most viable—and profitable—SER transaction. The various SER valuations are categorized and listed as follows from highest to lowest in most circumstances:

Merger Values

- Value in a merger where the partner is in control following the merger
- Value in a merger of equals
- Value in a merger where the parent is in control following the merger

Strategic Partnership Values

- Value where there are close and multifaceted commercial arrangements that are critical and profitable to the partner
- Value where there is a single relationship such as a distribution agreement or where the strategic partner is protecting a valuable, but not critical, relationship

Public Market Values

- Value in an IPO
- Value in a spin-off to the shareholders of the parent without investment bank sponsorship

Private Equity Values

- Value in a private equity partnership where the private equity investors have control
- Value in a private equity partnership where the parent has control

Why are these distinctions so important? Because a valuation of the same operation at the same time, but for a different purpose, will yield a very different result, depending on the proposed SER. Valuations for one SER are not applicable to another. For example, the price a single strategic buyer is likely to pay when purchasing the entire subsidiary will almost always be considerably higher than the value a private equity investor is likely to pay for a minority shareholding in a private company. And the parent's approach to valuation in a sale of the entire subsidiary should also be very different from that with a private equity investment by a value-added investor undertaken to prepare the subsidiary for an IPO. In a sale of the entire subsidiary, the principal objective is usually to maximize immediate value. In a private equity investment, the objective is often to pave the way for a successful IPO and to build a successful public company and increase the total return to the parent's shareholders from its ownership of the subsidiary.

UNDERSTANDING THE VALUATION METHODS

This section will look at some common valuation methods and also examine why they may—or may not—be the best methods to use when valuing a subsidiary before an SER transaction.

Discounted Cash Flow

The valuation methods used by most SER parties are likely to differ from those used internally by the parent. Discounted cash flow (DCF) analysis is the bedrock valuation method used by many parents in assessing investments for budgetary purposes. As the name implies, the future cash flows generated by an investment are discounted at a rate equal to a firm's cost of capital. Building on the seminal research of Franco Modigliani and Merton Miller, as well as other academicians, DCF analysis came into its own in the 1960s.[2] Before this, companies relied on the payback method to decide between investment projects. The payback method measured the time in years that it took for a project to return an amount of cash equal to the investment. Companies typically invested in projects with the shortest payback periods. This approach was unsatisfactory because it assumed that an investment threw off no cash after its initial payback period.

The shift to DCF happened because it is a much more accurate approach in ranking the projects competing for limited funds in a firm's capital budget. Like the payback method, DCF takes into account the timing of cash flows. It favors investments that throw off cash early rather than later. DCF's major advantage, however, is that it takes into account all of the cash flows thrown off by an investment over its life, rather than just in the initial period.

DCF is also more flexible than the payback method. A company usually uses its cost of capital to discount the future cash flows of an investment and then ranks projects according to the net present value of future cash flows. Alternatively, a company can determine the discount rate that equates future cash flows with the size of the investment and rank projects on the basis of their returns.

DCF has proven to be an enormously useful tool in a company's capital budgeting process where cash flows can be estimated with a reasonable degree of precision. However, most SER parties will not rely on DCF analysis to value a subsidiary before an SER transaction for the following reasons:

- In most cases, a DCF analysis generally is predicated on the availability of reliable multiyear cash flow forecasts. A DCF analysis is only as accurate as the projections that underlie the cash flows. DCF results are very sensitive to business assumptions including sales growth, margins, tax rate, required capital investment, success of new products, developments at customers, increases in net working capital, the actions of economic cycles, and the actions of competitors. Although a DCF analysis will almost always be required by investors, it is often used more as a guide to the cash needs of the subsidiary and to help determine the general viability of the subsidiary than for valuation purposes. DCF has proven to be least useful in evaluating investments where the cash flows are much harder to forecast and are necessarily imprecise. This is especially true of SER transactions of many less-mature or cyclical companies.

- A subsidiary with a leading market position in a stable and mature industry that has had sufficient history to understand the impact of economic cycles and of competitive dynamics may be able to forecast cash flows with reasonable accuracy. However, most businesses are less able to reliably project their future cash flows. For example, the ability to project cash flows precisely even a year out is not all that common.

- As well, many subsidiaries considered for an SER are not cash generators. In these cases, the terminal value (value ascribed to the operation at the end of the forecast period) usually represents the most substantial part of the value. Therefore, the assumptions underlying terminal value become the heart of the DCF analysis, negating much of the purpose of the DCF exercise.

- DCF values prepared by the parent or the subsidiary based on the subsidiary's forecasts are often too optimistic and well above the market value SER parties are prepared to pay. SER parties, from good experience, assume that forecasts underestimate difficulties and overestimate opportunities..

Although many SER parties will not rely on DCF analysis as a primary valuation method, some SER parties may still do so. The parties that will place the most reliance on DCF analysis are leveraged buyout private equity investors and corporate partners. LBO investors generally are most interested in stable, mature, cash-generating businesses that are able to support debt. These are also the types of companies most amenable to a reliable DCF forecast. Strategic partners often use DCF analysis. First, their own internal processes may be more comfortable with this approach. Second, a strategic partnership will usually include commercial elements that need to be valued, such as the costs and profits from distribution agreements. This may involve developing complex models with many variables.

Relative Valuation

This is the method most used by SER parties to value a subsidiary, and it looks at the relative value of the subsidiary compared to values in the market for comparable companies and transactions. These values are based on the current market value of public companies, prices paid in recent acquisitions, and the valuation of recent investments in private companies, where information is available. Depending on the stage of development of the subsidiary and its industry, the metrics will vary for comparing companies. Metrics used include the price as a multiple of net income; revenues; operating income; earnings before interest, taxes, depreciation, and amortization (EBITDA); and book value. Many industries also have industry-specific metrics such as price per subscriber for cable systems or per room for hotel chains. Relative valuation has no theoretical basis, is highly flawed, and yet is the method most widely used by SER parties in practice.

With a public market SER such as an IPO, relative valuation completely dominates discussion; public market investors look on stocks as commodities and look at the relative value of one stock against another. Investors in other SERs are usually acutely aware of values in the public stock and merger markets and are highly influenced by them. The extent of this influence will be greater the closer the SER is to a market transaction. But even where the SER is not a market-related transaction, values in the markets will still be a large influence. In a strategic partnership, the partner's board of directors, shareholders, and research analysts, if it is public, will all look at the price paid by the partner for an investment relative to other transactions or market values. Private equity investors will look eventually for liquidity on their investment. Values paid in the stock or merger markets will determine their returns. Private equity investments tend, therefore, to be priced with the current public markets very much in mind.

Relative values are based on external markets, as opposed to the internal market-independent values of a DCF analysis. Therefore, relative valuation says nothing about the fundamental value of a subsidiary. This will be disappointing to the parent where it firmly believes that relative value undervalues the subsidiary. This view was correct in the late 1980s when the public market values accorded companies in many sectors such as cellular communications were depressed well below the value derived from even a DCF analysis using very pessimistic assumptions. In hindsight, the public stock market considerably undervalued these businesses.

Of course, there are other situations, such as in early 2000, where the reverse is the case and the value derived from a DCF analysis under even optimistic assumptions is far lower than the value accorded in the stock market. The very savvy CFO of one Internet software company we know performed many DCF analyses on his company in 1999 and found that the public market value was many times any DCF value, even under the most optimistic assumptions. He convinced his board to sell stock in a large public offering.

As a result of the widespread use of relative values by SER parties, the overall state of the markets will be a major factor in the success, structure, timing, and value of an SER even when the SER itself is not a market transaction such as a strategic partnership. The vicissitudes of the public equity and merger markets will still have a great influence on the overall attitudes, valuation views, and enthusiasm of most SER parties. Even early-stage private equity investors look to the markets for guidance on valuation. Changes in values in the public stock and the merger markets will greatly influence valuations by private equity investors.

Reasons for the Widespread Use of Relative Valuation

Despite its drawbacks, the widespread use of relative valuation among SER parties is due to a number of factors:

- Relative valuation is the most commonly used metric by public stock market investors and is, therefore, a driver of values.

- Relative valuation is convenient. Many SER parties have only a limited amount of time to assess any one potential investment. For example, a research analyst at an investment bank may follow and write research on 15 or more companies and will need to hold views on an equal number of noncovered companies. A portfolio manager at an institution may have a hundred or more stocks actually in the portfolio and be considering many more. Relative analysis permits the conducting of a valuation with available information in a reasonable amount of time.

- Relative valuation is certainly less subjective than DCF valuations. Relative valuation does not depend on long-term forecasts but on recent historical results and near-term forecasts. Debate is narrowed to the correct comparable companies or transactions and the validity of near-term forecasts only.

UNDERSTANDING THE VALUE CYCLE
FOR EMERGING INDUSTRIES

After overall market value levels, the second most important factor in the value of a subsidiary is investor views on its industry sector. Industries rise and fall in investor favor. As a result, values change greatly over time and in many industries access to the public markets is truncated and episodic. On average, access on favorable terms is available for only one or two years at a time. Because this is less true for a very large parent, the parent's management must incorporate into their thinking on timing of subsidiary SERs the state of the private and public equity markets for the particular industry of the subsidiary. This may be a shock for many parents used to unlimited and anytime access to public and private capital. As well, the actual market valuation of the subsidiary may not be closely correlated with its business progress. For example, the subsidiary may make significant business progress over several years and yet the parent will find that its valuation has gone down appreciably because of market factors. Therefore, subsidiaries and parent have to time their transactions accurately to be able to access the markets at the right time. If the timing is off, funding will not be available, or it will be available only on nonadvantageous terms.

This is particularly true for growth companies, where there is an added factor of the investor interest cycle in the industry that tends to exaggerate timing issues. Exhibit 5–1 illustrates a typical investor interest cycle for a growth industry. While this is a chart of the AMEX biotech index over 20 years, it could be any number of other emerging industries dating back to the British railways in the 1840s. It resembles the charts for a number of industries that first came into prominence in the 1980s such as cellular telephony, cable television, personal computers, big-box retailers, and networking. It is likely to resemble the charts for

E X H I B I T   5–1

AMEX Biotech Index

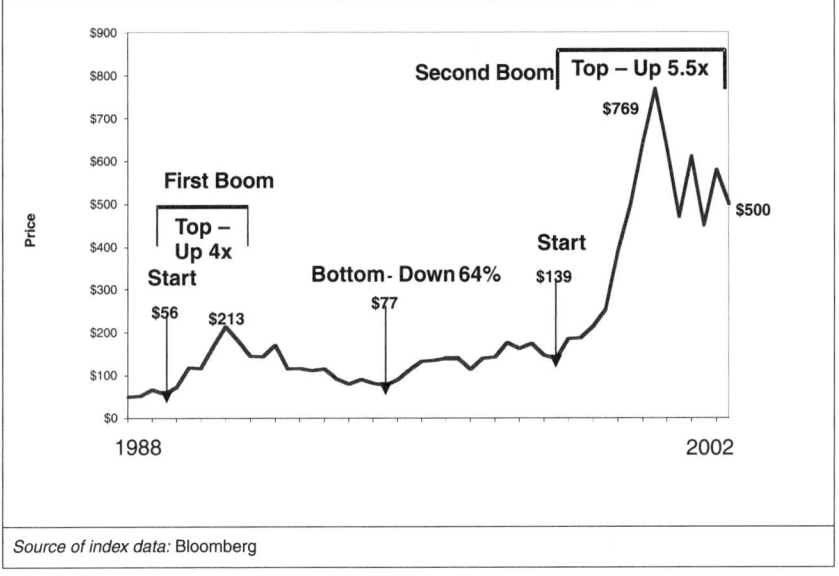

Source of index data: Bloomberg

a number of industries that came into prominence in the late 1990s such as broadband, the Internet, optics, and convergence. These are now coming off their first boom. In most cases the first-boom investors were right and great industries did emerge, but many years later than promised.

The first boom is always short in duration—usually not more than a couple of years. It is always followed by a period of intense investor disappointment. During the down parts of the cycle, few SER alternatives are available, especially those not involving the public and private equity markets. SERs become available again when the industry begins to live up to its promise and there is a resurgence of investor interest in the industry. However, this may be 5 to 10 years later. This cycle is very predictable and occurs in one emerging industry after another. It is the rule, not the exception. Yet it always seems to be a surprise to participants.

CONCLUSION

This chapter detailed the differences in the valuation techniques used by many parents and by many outside equity investors. Understanding the valuation techniques most often employed by outside equity investors will help the parent reach its objectives throughout the entire SER process. In addition, understanding the impact of timing on the valuation process will also help a parent reach its objectives. This chapter has laid the groundwork for a detailed look at the various SER options described in the next section of the book.

SER STRUCTURES AND TRANSACTIONS

CHAPTER **6**

MINORITY CARVE-OUTS

INTRODUCTION

As discussed in the previous section, SER transactions can take many forms and can be utilized to meet specific objectives. Therefore, the purpose of the chapters in this section is to examine each SER transaction in depth, including its structure, purpose, goals, and challenges. We will start this process by first examining minority carve-outs because they are a common SER transaction and often lay the foundation for subsequent SER transactions.

Minority carve-outs are very popular with parent companies because they enable both parents and subsidiaries to achieve important objectives. According to Dealogic, in 2001, 59 percent of all IPO proceeds were from minority carve-outs. During the first quarter of 2002, this trend continued, as the majority of funds raised in U.S. IPOs were based on minority carve-outs. Recent examples of high-profile minority carve-outs include the Citigroup minority carve-out of Travelers Property Casualty, which raised over $3.9 billion, and the Nestlé minority carve-out of Alcon, which raised $2.5 billion. For additional details about the number of minority carve-outs which took place in the United States over the past few years,[1] see Exhibit 6–1.

MINORITY CARVE-OUT DEFINED

A minority carve-out is the sale of a minority equity interest in a subsidiary by its parent to investors. Generally, the subsidiary is majority owned or wholly owned by the parent. The equity interest is usually sold to outside investors in an IPO or to outside private equity investors in a private placement. Exhibit 6–2 provides a graphical representation of a minority carve-out.

E X H I B I T   6–1

Number of U.S. Minority Public Carve-Outs, 1998–2002

Years	1998	1999	2000	2001	Q1 2002
Number of carve-outs	13	33	17	11	4
Amount of proceeds (billions)	$8.0	$9.5	$13.1	$20.6	$6.6
Percent of all IPO proceeds	24%	15%	23%	59%	74%

Does not include closed-end investment funds, rights offerings, or unit trusts.
Excludes underwriters' overallotment.
Source: Dealogic

E X H I B I T   6–2

Minority Carve-Out

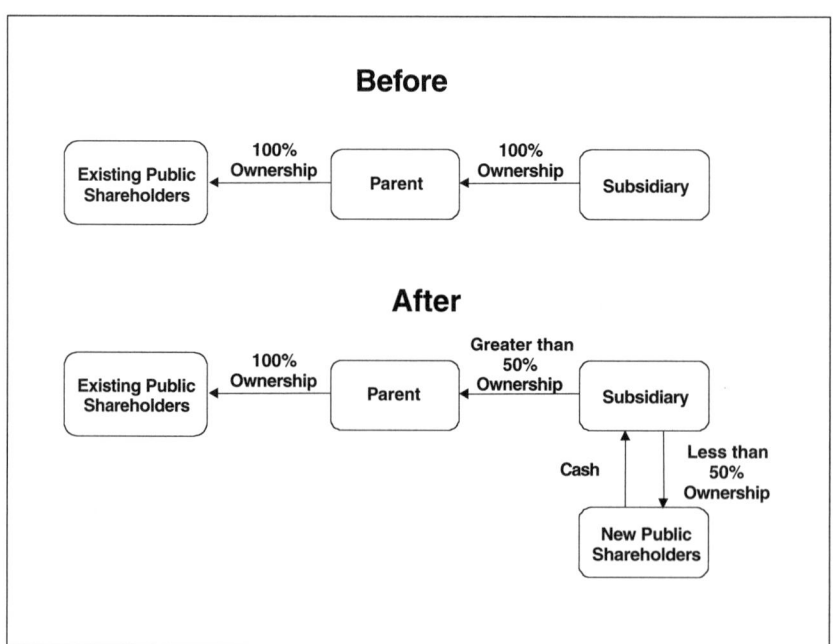

Source: John C. Michaelson and Robin A. Graham, "Equity Carve-Outs and Spin-Offs of
Technology Operations," *The Financier,* vol. 2, no. 4, November 1995.

MINORITY CARVE-OUTS AS AN INTERIM STEP

The parent should anticipate that a minority carve-out will be an interim solution. Minority carve-outs are usually not stable. In most cases a minority carve-out is later followed by another SER alternative. For example, minority carve-outs are often followed by a spin-off to the parent's shareholders, subsequent follow-on public offerings that reduce the parent's ownership interest to a minority, a sale of the subsidiary, or a reabsorption back into the parent.

In fact, studies confirm that minority carve-outs are usually not a long-term situation. For example, a recent study by McKinsey and Company of 204 minority carve-outs before 1998 concludes that after five years only 8 percent of minority carve-outs continue to be parent-controlled public companies.[2] The carve-out of even a small stake in a subsidiary is likely to lead to complete separation over time. The study concludes that 39 percent of minority carve-outs are merged or acquired by another company, 31 percent remain independent of parent control and 11 percent are reacquired by the parent. The parent retains minority ownership of only 8 percent.

The reasons for the likelihood of a complete separation after a minority carve-out include the following:

- Often the minority carve-out is a deliberate first step in a planned series of SERs (see the examples of Du Pont Photomask in Chapter 7 and Palm in Chapter 9). Even a minority IPO gives a subsidiary its own publicly traded stock to issue in acquisitions and options to grant employees. It also enables the subsidiary to raise equity capital to fund growth and stock options. Over time, this leads to the dilution of the parent's ownership position.

- The carved-out subsidiary tends to drift away from the parent due to its new-found independence, including stand-alone compensation programs.

- Carved-out subsidiaries often operate in different industries from that in which the parent operates, resulting in less interaction and value added by the parent over time.

- Carve-out subsidiaries often have higher growth than the parent. A number of studies find that subsidiaries, on average, grow faster than the parent after the carve-out IPO. For example, McKinsey found that revenues for all carved-out subsidiaries in its sample grew at an average annual rate of 13 percent for the first two years after the IPO, compared with 5 percent for the parent. The requirements of growth companies are very different from those of the parent, as discussed. This also leads to less interaction and value added by the parent over time.

- As a public entity, the subsidiary will issue its own comprehensive financial statements and establish a public market value. The presence of these increases the likelihood of a merger offer. Of course, as long as the parent has majority control, it can usually block any undesirable actions by the subsidiary such as an acquisition by a competitor of the parent.

THE BENEFITS OF A MINORITY CARVE-OUT

A minority carve-out may be a better course for the parent and the subsidiary than going straight to a complete public separation through a spin-off or a majority carve-out or a merger with a comparable public company. There are a number of reasons why the interim step may be beneficial to the parent and the subsidiary:

- The parent will maintain control over the subsidiary following the IPO, allowing controlled phaseout of operational interactions.
- The subsidiary will learn to deal with public market investors in a more controlled environment. This is especially valuable if the subsidiary's management has not run a public company before.
- The subsidiary will have time to mature under the supervision of the parent and become a stronger company before a spin-off or sale.
- The subsidiary will need time to develop in-house administrative, financial, or operational capabilities currently supplied by the parent.

ADDITIONAL GOALS OF MINORITY CARVE-OUTS

Companies employ minority carve-outs for a number of reasons:

- *Lowering the cost of raising equity capital.* Many larger companies have high-growth operations in areas that are attractive at any given time to the stock market. A minority carve-out allows the parent to take advantage of the higher price-to-earnings ratios accorded by the market at any given time to favored sectors and provides opportunities to raise capital on advantageous terms for use by either the parent or the subsidiary.

    It also enables the parent to take advantage of the higher valuation that the stock market accords to pure plays over diversified companies. A minority carve-out also provides the parent with an attractive currency for acquisitions in the form of the stock of the subsidiary. This stock may be more attractive to other hot companies rather than either cash or stock in the parent. There are many instances where cash is not attractive because it is fully taxed upon receipt and eliminates participation in the upside of the acquired business and stock in a large, mature parent may have only moderate appeal.

    Studies indicate that parents undertaking minority carve-outs are more highly leveraged overall than their industry peers and have more limited access to capital. These studies indicate that raising equity capital is a leading motivation behind minority carve-outs.

- *Raising equity capital and cash without incurring shareholder dilution at the parent level.* When a family, individual, trust, or another corporation has a significant ownership interest or control of the parent, these shareholders may prefer that the parent not sell stock, as this would dilute their ownership interest in the parent or reduce their control. Or, if the parent's stock price is depressed, its board of directors may not wish to sell parent stock at what they believe is too low a price. When equity capital is needed or prudent, a minority carve-out of a subsidiary permits raising equity capital without the parent selling its own shares. In a carve-out, the subsidiary may (as appropriate) assume parent liabilities, repay debt, or make a dividend to the parent from the IPO proceeds. Repayment of a loan from the parent without tax impact is the usual means to distribute cash to the parent from a minority carve-out. As well, the parent may sell stock directly in the IPO and keep the proceeds (though this may be less tax efficient). For example, Alcon paid parent Nestlé a $1.2 billion dividend at the close of its $2.5 billion minority carve-out IPO. In addition, Nestlé received most of the IPO proceeds through a redemption of preferred stock by Alcon.

- *Creating an acquisition currency.* A carve-out allows the parent to use the subsidiary's stock as a currency in making acquisitions. The parent may not wish to use its own cash or stock in making acquisitions, or the shareholders of the company being acquired may not wish to be paid in cash or parent stock.

- *Uncovering hidden value.* There is strong evidence that the stock market increases the valuation of the parent following the announcement of a carve-out SER.[3]

- *Improving the operating performance of the subsidiary.* Studies show improved performance for the subsidiary after a minority carve-out.[4]

- *Creating business opportunities for the subsidiary.* Competitors of the parent may not be willing to do business with a wholly owned subsidiary. A minority carve-out is a first step to demonstrate that the subsidiary will be an independent business.

- *Maintaining parent control for a time.* After a minority carve-out, the parent continues to remain in control of the subsidiary—subject to its fiduciary duties to minority shareholders—until it intentionally dilutes its position through stock offerings, mergers, or a spin-off. The parent may wish to retain the advantages of control or prevent a competitor from acquiring the subsidiary while bringing in outside equity capital. This is in contrast to straight sale of a subsidiary for cash.

- *Sharing the risk of a promising venture with outside investors.* As with many forms of SER, a minority carve-out allows the parent to bring in outside investors to mitigate its risk in funding a less mature venture. For example, there were a number of Internet efforts by mature companies in the late 1990s financed with public equity and private venture capital.

- *Permitting the subsidiary to offer market-based equity incentives to management, aligned with the subsidiary's operating results.* One advantage of all public SER alternatives is that market value may be placed on equity-related management incentives. This may be preferable to formulas and outside valuations for a private company that often result in contention or are not highly valued by current and prospective employees. Even a clear formula for pricing private options has not prevented acrimonious disputes with employees in the past. These are certainly not desirable with valuable employees, nor are the results always favorable to the employer.

- *Acting as a springboard for a subsequent spin-off.* A carve-out is usually the best way to create an orderly spin-off in a two-step transaction. The initial carve-out allows for an orderly market to be established for the stock of the subsidiary, for research coverage, and for sponsorship to develop before a large number of shares hit the market in the spin-off.

- *Facilitating the sale of the subsidiary.* A minority carve-out places a public value on the subsidiary and creates public documentation (SEC filings, for example), which are extremely helpful if the objective is to ultimately sell the subsidiary. The public documentation greatly speeds the due diligence process for a buyer and increases confidence in the materials. In addition, the existence of a public market price puts boundaries around the price negotiations. The price will have to fall within the market price plus the range of normal premiums in the public markets for comparable acquisitions, or the transaction will not take place.

- *Acting as an enabler for a foreign or private parent.* A minority carve-out enables a public foreign company listed only on a non-U.S. exchange to issue stock options to employees with a clear market value, raise capital in the U.S. public equity and debt markets, and make acquisitions for stock. At the same time, it does not require the parent to comply with the extensive reporting requirements under U.S. securities laws and stock exchange regulations, except regarding the subsidiary, where the parent must comply with all applicable U.S. laws and regulations. With a minority carve-out, only the subsidiary must file U.S. disclosure and reporting. The exception for the parent is the requirement to report actions taken in respect to changes in its stock ownership of the subsidiary. The same advantages apply to a privately owned U.S. parent that has no wish itself to become a public company.

- *Using a tax-efficient way to raise capital.* The proceeds of carve-outs are not taxable to the parent or the subsidiary if the subsidiary issues new shares. There are cases where the parent has preferred to sell shares in the subsidiary itself in the minority carve-out IPO and incur potential tax liability. This happens most often when the parent is foreign or has offsetting losses.

- *Recognizing accounting gains.* When the subsidiary sells stock in a minority carve-out, the parent may elect to recognize a gain (and must recognize a loss). The parent is able to take the accounting gain even though it did not sell any shares itself. In today's environment these would not be considered "quality" earnings. The parent will also recognize accounting (and tax) gain or loss on any shares of the subsidiary it sells itself in the IPO. The pitfall of relying too much on these gains is shown in the Thermo Electron example later in the chapter.

DISADVANTAGES OF A MINORITY CARVE-OUT

Minority carve-outs are far from perfect and do have their fair share of disadvantages:

- *A subsequent tax-free spin-off requires the parent to maintain control after the IPO.* If a later tax-free spin-off is planned following the IPO, the parent must have 80 percent control of the subsidiary at the time of the spin-off. This greatly limits the post-carve-out flexibility of the subsidiary to issue additional shares in a strategic alliance or to raise additional capital, and limits the size of the carve-out SER to 20 percent or less of the equity, as noted in the discussion of the tax issues of spin-offs detailed in Chapter 8.

- *Continued parent responsibility.* When the parent retains majority interest in the new entity after a minority carve-out, it remains bound to the subsidiary in practice as long as it maintains that interest. A number of minority carve-outs over the years were not successful as public companies requiring subsequent parental involvement. In many cases, the parent had vital business interests tied up in the subsidiary's operations and had to step in and finance the operation. In other cases, the parent felt obligated to step in and protect its reputation and relationships. As well, creditors, shareholders, and other aggrieved parties will make strenuous efforts to attach liability to the parent in the event of a minority carve-out subsidiary's failure.

- *Continued responsibility for minority interests.* The responsibilities of the parent's and the subsidiary's board of directors to minority shareholders are particularly acute in a minority carve-out because of what is perceived to be the overwhelming power of the parent. Lawsuits against parents for their actions toward minority shareholders have become more common in recent years.

- *Public markets set a selling price.* A minority carve-out may actually impede a sale strategy by setting a public market price that may be considerably less than real value. In difficult public markets, such as 2002, many public companies were trading below their intrinsic value in the public markets. No matter how strong a case the parent makes for a higher price, a potential buyer will base an offer on the public market price of the stock.

    The market price may work in precisely the opposite way in a bubble market, as it did for Internet stocks in late 1999. The market bid prices up to very high levels, and the only offers for most carved-out subsidiaries that the parent wished to sell were for stock in comparable overpriced companies. Fear of shareholder litigation with a below-market sale price set a floor, however unrealistic, on any sale price.

- *Inevitable tensions with the parent.* After a minority carve-out, the activities of a parent and subsidiary often remain intermixed. For example, if the subsidiary sells products to the parent or the parent provides services to the subsidiary, pricing these activities becomes an issue in the relations between the two companies after the minority carve-out. While intercompany transfer pricing is often an issue of contention between operations in a single corporation, it assumes a new edge when the companies are independent. In general, prices must be set at levels that are fair to each party and their respective shareholders. An independent audit committee of the board of directors, appointed to oversee purchase agreements, is the usual approach to ensuring fairness. If the level of interaction is high because technologies, facilities, or services are shared, these agreements can become complicated. For example, ARCO undertook three equity minority carve-outs between 1987 and 1994, requiring at least 26 separate agreements in all to delimit the boundaries of the various businesses. As a result, it became prohibitively expensive to create all the appropriate tracking mechanisms. ARCO then became exhausted.[5]

• *Funding the needs of the subsidiary can adversely affect the parent.* If the subsidiary requires substantial additional financing following the minority carve-out and sells more stock to outside investors, the parent faces a declining ownership interest in the subsidiary and eventually a loss of control of the subsidiary unless it invests more money in the subsidiary to maintain its ownership percentage.

Often, the parent faces these challenges as its ownership position declines. When this happens, the board of directors and management team of the subsidiary are bound to become more assertive toward the parent. The parent's inability to maintain its initial ownership position also affects its ability to maintain consolidation for tax and financial reporting and control, which is required for a subsequent tax-free spin-off of the subsidiary to the parent's shareholders.

• *Success of the subsidiary may continue to be tied to the success of the parent.* Where a subsidiary is dependent on the parent for a significant part of its business, investors will need assurance that the revenue streams from the parent will continue or the IPO of the carve-out subsidiary will be adversely impacted or not feasible. When General Motors Corporation spun off its EDS subsidiary in 1996, the parent provided about 35 percent of EDS's revenues. This business was conducted on a profitable basis for EDS. As a result, EDS's market valuation was highly dependent on its relationship with General Motors. To facilitate the relationship, GM negotiated a preferred-customer price contract with EDS for a 10-year period to ensure that investors appropriately valued its business with General Motors.

• *Loss of synergies and special relationships.* Most synergies between parent and subsidiary will be lost after a minority carve-out as the two entities operate at the requisite arm's length. Legal protections for public minority shareholders typically demand that all transactions with the parent company take place at fair market terms and conditions as if it were between two independent entities. This greatly reduces the flexibility and ease with which the parent and subsidiary can cooperate to capture any synergies. As well, because of increasing independence of the subsidiary after the minority carve-out IPO, the parent may not always count on the continuation of a special relationship.

This is illustrated by Genzyme Corporation's carve-out of IG Laboratories. Genzyme, a biotechnology company, was dependent on IG Laboratories, its testing division, to test its products. Genzyme carved out IG Laboratories in an IPO in 1990. After the carve-out, Genzyme found that IG Laboratories treated it as just another customer and was increasingly less willing to accommodate its needs. In 1995, Genzyme repurchased the 31 percent public stake in IG Laboratories.

- *Restrictions on sales of stock by the parent after the carve-out IPO.* Following the IPO, the parent will not be able to freely sell shares of the subsidiary in the market. It will be subject to limitations on stock sales except under a safe harbor provided in SEC Rule 144. It will also be subject to the lockup imposed by the investment banks underwriting the IPO. Lockups are restrictions on the sale of stock by significant shareholders following an IPO.

- *Impact of a small initial public float.* The dollar value of the number of shares available for public investors to purchase in the market is called the *public float.* Investors view the public float as an indication of their ability to buy and sell a reasonable position in the stock without a major impact on its price. A large public float is of particular concern to institutional investors that must acquire a reasonably large dollar position in the stock to justify efforts to stay up to date on the company. In an IPO, the float will initially be the same as the proceeds of the IPO. The minimum public float that institutional investors require has increased significantly over the past decade as the average dollar size of institutional funds, while market liquidity in many smaller-capitalization stocks has declined.

   In a minority carve-out, the initial public float often must be small to protect the parent's ability to later spin off the subsidiary tax free. This may be bad news for the success of the IPO, as a small float will deter institutional investors from investing in the IPO. This may also be bad news for the subsidiary, as a small float increases the volatility of the stock. With a small float, even small investor decisions to buy or sell may produce considerable price movement in the stock. This is often upsetting to employees and may get in the way of strategic actions utilizing the stock, such as acquisitions.

STEPS TO ENSURE A SUCCESSFUL MINORITY CARVE-OUT

As mentioned earlier, a parent must recognize that a minority carve-out is not just a short-term financial transaction. Instead, it will very likely lead to complete separation. If the parent does not understand and support the transaction with this in mind, it will probably not help the subsidiary succeed as a separate business. As a result, the subsidiary will fail in the public markets and will not create value for the parent. Value is primarily created in a successful minority carve-out for the parent and the subsidiary after the IPO. Ultimately, the success of the subsidiary should lead to further liquidity for the parent in follow-on public offerings, market sales, a spin-off, or a sale at a premium price.

   Therefore, the subsidiary should look and act like a stand-alone public company because it will need to convince new investors in the IPO, and later in the aftermarket, to buy stock in the subsidiary. In some cases, administrative functions including centralized cash management, legal advice, risk management, benefits administration, tax advice, and financial services continue to be performed by the parent's corporate staff for a fee. A tax allocation agreement is also entered into if tax consolidation is retained.

Also, the subsidiary should adopt director and management stock option and employee stock purchase plans to retain and attract top talent. The parent should implement changes to its own management performance reviews, compensation, and option and restricted stock programs to reflect changes to its operations after the carve-out.

ROLE OF THE PARENT'S OFFICERS ON THE BOARD OF A CARVED-OUT SUBSIDIARY

Officers of the parent serve on the initial board of directors of almost all minority carve-outs following the IPO.[6] Often an officer of the parent is also the subsidiary's initial chairperson. Researchers usually attribute this to the desire by the parent to retain control. While this may be true, there are other reasons. For example, serving on the public board of the subsidiary helps prepare parent managers for senior roles at the parent, it offers additional compensation to managers, and it is often prestigious and interesting to serve on the board of a smaller company.

However, it is important to note that when the parent controls the board of directors of the subsidiary, the subsidiary may be run in a manner that suggests that its primary role is to support the parent. Decisions not made in the best interests of the subsidiary's shareholders, with the usual result of disappointing performance, demoralized management, and investor lack of interest, will tarnish the reputations of all concerned.

In some minority carve-outs, parent executives also serve in executive positions at the subsidiary. For example, in its many carve-outs, Thermo Electron Corporation often named a parent executive as CFO of the subsidiary, as detailed later in this chapter. This was appropriate for the structure of the Thermo carve-outs because the parent functioned as a bank for the subsidiaries.

While such dual executive roles are rife with conflicts, having executives in positions at the parent and the subsidiary may be beneficial for both the parent and the subsidiary. For example, it may improve operational coordination and prevent a carved-out subsidiary from acting in a way that could damage the parent. It may also provide valuable experienced transitional support until the subsidiary's managers become more familiar with operating as a stand-alone public company rather than as a division. In many cases, the parent's senior executives are highly respected by investors and provide an assurance of good management at the subsidiary.

In the wake of corporate abuses such as at Tyco and WorldCom where there were related party transactions between the company and officers and directors, supposedly independent directors were often the beneficiary of the CEO's largesse and acted as lapdogs of the CEO. This is in stark contrast to the role they were hired to perform—namely, that of protecting public shareholders. As a result, there are many initiatives under way to reform public boards. One example is a new rule proposed by the New York Stock Exchange requiring that the majority of the board members for a listed company be truly independent. Under the proposed rule, a director is considered independent only if he or she has not had a material relationship with the company during the previous five years. This, and similar initiatives, as well as the sensitivity of investors to board governance issues, will curtail the practice of having parent representatives sitting on the board of the subsidiary.

SOME TAX ASPECTS OF A MINORITY CARVE-OUT

In many minority carve-outs, the parent sells less than 20 percent of the subsidiary to preserve the option of a later tax-free spin-off under IRS rules. In addition, the shares sold in a minority carve-out are usually sold by the subsidiary directly to the new investors, and the proceeds go to the subsidiary or to repay debt to the parent, with no resulting tax impact. Alternately, the parent may sell shares of the subsidiary that it owns. If a parent sells its own shares of the subsidiary to investors, the parent will recognize a gain on the sale of shares for tax purposes. The gain will be the difference between the proceeds from the offering and the parent's basis in the shares.

If the subsidiary itself sells stock shares to investors, neither the parent nor the subsidiary will recognize a tax gain or a loss on the sale of the shares for tax purposes.

As well, if the parent retains less than 80 percent of the subsidiary's stock following the carve-out, the parent and subsidiary generally will no longer be able to file a consolidated tax return. This is problematic, as tax consolidation may be very useful, for the following reasons:

• If the subsidiary generates tax losses, the losses can be used on the consolidated tax return to offset the taxable income of other members of the consolidated group.

• The parent is eligible for what is the equivalent of a 100 percent dividend-received deduction on any distributions.

Conversely, the loss of tax consolidation can have these effects[7]:

• Trigger taxes from deferred intercompany transactions.

• Trigger taxes if the parent has a negative tax basis in the stock of the subsidiary. This is relevant where the parent pushes debt down to the subsidiary or the subsidiary pays a dividend to the parent.

SECURITIES LAWS AND MINORITY CARVE-OUTS

A minority carve-out that issues shares in an IPO is simply a form of traditional initial public offering. The applicable securities law considerations are the same as those applicable to any quality IPO, including the following:

• The subsidiary, as the issuer of the shares, files a Form S-1 registration statement with the SEC. This is subject to review by the SEC.

• For the purpose of filing a Form S-1 registration statement, the subsidiary must make significant disclosure and supply three-year audited financial statements.

Once public, the company and its affiliates are subject to a number of federal laws and regulations intended to protect investors. Complying with these laws and regulations is expensive and time consuming. The two mechanisms to protect investors are full disclosure and the prevention of fraud and manipulation. These measures give investors confidence in the public equity markets. Following a minority carve-out IPO, the parent (and all other pre-IPO shareholders) is subject to the restrictions on the sale of all unregistered stock still held in the subsidiary unless a sale is made through a registered public offering or under Rule 144. As well, affiliates of the subsidiary are subject to the ongoing stock sale restrictions unless under Rule 144.

Rule 144 is a safe harbor providing a permitted resale of stock without registration. Under this rule, stock not bought by investors in the IPO or held less than one year may not be sold in the public market. As well, such stock held longer than one year may only be sold subject to volume restrictions that limit the number of shares sold in the public market in any three-month period, in reliance on the safe harbor, by any shareholder who has held stock for less than two years and by affiliates no matter how long they have held their shares. Under Rule 144, affiliates are officers, inside and outside directors, and all shareholders that hold 10 percent or more of the stock. It is generally presumed that these persons control the subsidiary, although this presumption may be rebutted in some narrow cases.

SUMMARY

This chapter took an in-depth look at using minority carve-outs as an SER option. Specifically, it examined the benefits, disadvantages, and structures of minority carve-outs and also discussed critical tax implications. Chapter 7 will apply this same framework to another SER option, majority carve-outs.

EXAMPLES OF UNSUCCESSFUL MINORITY CARVE-OUTS

There are many examples of successful minority carve-outs, detailing how the subsidiary prospers and succeeds after the IPO. These range from Kraft Foods (consumer brands) to Maxtor (disk drives) to Delphi (automotive components) to TD Waterhouse (brokerage). They all succeeded because they were viable stand-alone businesses that benefited from the separation from the parent, were properly capitalized, and were allowed by the parent to prosper after the IPO. It is also valuable to focus on some of the less successful minority carve-out experiences and why they failed.

iTurf, Inc., from Delia*s, Inc.: An Opportunistic Carve-Out for Financial Engineering Purposes

In 1999 and 2000, companies that used the Internet as an integral part of their businesses took advantage of high valuations of Internet companies by carving out their Internet operations as a means to raise equity capital very cheaply. This financing allowed companies to attempt to expand their Internet efforts without depleting the capital resources of the parent. Carving out a high-growth Internet subsidiary also enabled the parent to rid itself of the large operating losses generated by the embryonic Internet operation. Of the 11 Internet carve-outs in 1999 and 2000, only two were trading above their IPO price by June of 2001. Delia*s exemplifies this strategy.

Delia*s, a Generation Y clothing retailer, took advantage of bubble Internet valuations by bringing iTurf, its Internet distributor of clothes, public in April 1999. iTurf, which was one of the few Internet companies operating with a profit at the time of the offering, commanded great investor demand and increased the amount of the offering by 75 percent three days prior to the pricing of the IPO.

On its first day of trading, shares of iTurf almost tripled and it achieved a market value of nearly $1.0 billion, with trailing 12-month earnings of $464,000 on revenue of $4.0 million.

Similar to many other Internet stocks, iTurf's stock tumbled from its high of $62.63 during its first week of trading to $0.66 in November 2000. At this point, Delia*s repurchased the outstanding public shares of iTurf it didn't own. Shortly thereafter, Delia*s announced the closing of iTurf due to its high operational costs and lack of separation from the rest of Delia*s business.

In common with a number of other Internet consumer IPOs, iTurf was not a stand-alone retailing business but just another distribution channel for the parent's products, complementing its stores and catalog sales. (See also the examples of the Internet operations of Kmart, CSFB, and Disney later in this book.) Taking advantage of the mania for Internet stocks did raise a large amount of equity capital at a high valuation for iTurf. But costs soared, parent management was distracted, and money was wasted. No value for the parent (or the investors) was created.

When Minority Carve-Outs Went Too Far: Thermo Electron's Minority Carve-Out of 24 Subsidiaries

One of the most intriguing, discussed, profiled, and, in the end, unsuccessful, carve-out stories is that of Thermo Electron Corporation, located in Massachusetts.

Thermo Electron completed 24 minority carve-outs between 1983 and 1998. For a time, many companies closely examined what became known as the "Thermo Model" as a possible standard for their own activities. In the end, the Thermo Model proved unique to Thermo—and ultimately unsuccessful.

Thermo Electron's Vision

Starting in 1956, the founder of Thermo, George Hatsopoulos, built a leading instrument and measurement company. In 1982, Thermo had $200 million in revenue and made energy and environmental equipment. In the early 1980s, Hatsopoulos began to carve out subsidiaries as publicly traded businesses. He envisioned using carve-outs to build a stable of high-tech businesses. He hoped to

(1) increase overall valuation by offering public market investors focused businesses, (2) reduce dilution to the shareholders of the parent of raising equity capital by selling shares directly at the subsidiary level, and (3) push entrepreneurship down the organization by providing subsidiary managers with stock-based incentives based on the subsidiary's performance and exposure directly to the discipline of the public markets.[8]

By 1998, Thermo and its carved-out subsidiaries were a diversified group of industrial companies making different groups of products through 25 different affiliated companies. Thermo's carved-out "children" included such diverse businesses as Thermo Laser (cosmetic hair removal), Thermo Fibertek (recycled fiber and de-inking), Thermo Power (propane gas engines), Thermo Instrument (detection devices for air pollution and toxic substances), Thermedics (explosives detection and biomedical devices), and Thermo Cardiosystems (heart pumps).

As a result, Thermo was a buyer of choice for management teams attracted by the potential for a later carve-out.

Thermo Electron's Model

Thermo's carve-out model involved using the parent firm as a platform from which it developed or acquired new subsidiaries. When an operation looked promising, Thermo would carve out a minority stake through an IPO. Thermo maintained a majority stake in each subsidiary, in part to avoid regulation as an investment company. Thermo supplied its carved-out subsidiaries with human resources, banking, legal, tax, and other services for a fee. In a number of cases, the carved-out subsidiaries, in turn, carved out "grandchildren" of their own. Before a number of its carve-outs, Thermo raised private equity funding for the subsidiary. This brought in outside validation and sponsorship of the subsidiary and imposed outside discipline on its management preparatory to being public.

Note Exhibit 6–3, which illustrates the proliferation of Thermo's minority carve-out activities as it spawned public children and grandchildren. It went from 11 public carved-out subsidiaries in 1993 to 21 in 1997.

Thermomedics, one of Thermo's equity minority carve-outs, is an example of the strategy. In 1983, Thermo sold 14 percent of Thermomedics for $6 million in a carve-out IPO. In 1989, Thermomedics, in turn, sold 40 percent of its heart pump division in a carve-out IPO for $15 million as Thermo Cardiosystems. As the carve-outs continued, the parent Thermo Electron's stock rose from $1.35 a share in 1983 to $44.00 in 1997.

The management of the Thermo subsidiaries received options generally split 40 percent linked to the performance of their own carve-out, 40 percent to that of Thermo itself, and 20 percent to that of the other carve-outs.

The apparent success of Thermo at creating "a firm that is able to move effortlessly from niche to niche [and] is uniquely capable of sustained long-term growth"[9] became an appealing model for other companies. For example, Thermo was cited as a restructuring model by a number of other conglomerates, from W.R. Grace and Westinghouse in the 1980s and The Limited, to Acer, Inc., a Taiwanese computer maker and Idealab!, an incubator of Internet start-ups, in the 1990s.

E X H I B I T   6–3

Year-End 1997: Thermo's Public Company Structures and the Percentage
Owned by Thermo

Parent	Public children		Public grandchildren	
Thermo Electron Corporation	Thermedics	58%	- Thermo Cardiosystems	59%
			- Thermo Voltek	68%
			- Thermo Sentron	78%
			- Thermedics Detection	76%
	Thermo Instrument	82%	- ThermoSpectra	83%
			- ThermoQuest	88%
			- Thermo Optek	92%
			- Thermo BioAnalysis	78%
			- Metrika Systems	60%
	Thermo—Terra-Tech	82%	- Thermo Remediation	70%
			- Thermo Euro-Tech	56%
	Thermo Power	69%		
	Thermo—Trex	55%	- ThermoLase	70%
			- Trex Medical	79%
	Thermo Fibertek	90%	- Thermo Fibergen	71%
	Thermo Ecotek	88%		
	Thermo Information Systems	79%		
Source: Thermo Electron Corporation 10K filings				

The Turning Point

Then the machine stalled. When a subsidiary issued stock in a carve-out IPO,
Thermo elected to take an accounting gain. Thermo became dependent on the
paper profits from its carve-outs to boost its profits and maintain its stock price, as
seen in Exhibit 6–4.

This pushed Thermo into more carve-out transactions. The gains became an
end in themselves. The later carve-outs were not well conceived or successful, and
Thermo lost access to the IPO market for more carve-outs. It became apparent that
the structure was too cumbersome, unmanageable, complex, and without, in many
cases, any real business purpose. Once the public offering engine ran out of steam
in 1996, the share price of Thermo first stalled, and then collapsed. From a high of
$58 per share in March 1996, the share price fell to $12.69 in 1999. Many of the

EXHIBIT 6–4

Breakdown of Thermo Electron's Profitability

Dollars in millions	1992	1993	1994	1995	1996	1997	1998
Pretax realized and unrealized gains from carve-out activity	30.2	39.9	25.3	80.8	126.6	80.1	18.6
Total reported pretax profit	102.6	131.5	206.4	298.8	374.6	488.5	216.5
Carve-out gains as a percent of total reported profits	29.5%	30.3%	12.3%	27.0%	33.8%	16.4%	8.6%
Source: Thermo Electron Corporation 10K filings							

carve-outs also languished after their IPOs. First, they were too small and their public stocks too illiquid to attract investor interest. Investors and investment equity research analysts didn't wish to monitor a conglomeration of 25 thinly traded stocks operating in different industries. Research coverage of Thermo and its subsidiaries fell to two analysts by 1998, only one from a major firm. Providing research coverage of Thermo was, in itself, a full-time job for an investment bank research analyst and not one with great alternative career potential. It did not fit into any one or, even, several research industry groups. Not surprisingly, the only significant research analyst who covered the Thermo companies worked for Thermo's nearly exclusive investment banking firm. Second, the potential for the subsidiaries to independently create value for their shareholders was limited by the desire of the parent to maintain majority ownership and the close operating control actually maintained by the parent over the subsidiaries. The subsidiaries were not able to always make decisions strictly in their own best interest.

Reversal of Course

By 1999, Thermo's founders had retired. A new management team led by Richard Syron completely reversed course and began to reconsolidate Thermo into one publicly traded entity focused on its core instruments business. Thermo's reorganization plan included the divestiture of all businesses that were outside of a focus on instrumentation and the repurchase of all minority interests in core subsidiaries. This program was largely completed by mid-2001. In that year, Thermo combined all 12 of its various repertory care, neurocare, and medical and surgical products operations into one division. These operations had been acquired in 10 transactions dating from 1986 to 1998. In November 2001, 100 percent of the division was distributed to the shareholders of Thermo in a tax-free spin-off under the name Viasys Healthcare, Inc. After the consolidation and divestitures, Thermo's stock went as high as $31.10 in late 2000. Though it subsequently dropped back in 2001 with market corrections, it was still $23.68 per share at the end of 2001.

CHAPTER 7

MAJORITY CARVE-OUTS

INTRODUCTION

Chapter 6 examined minority carve-outs as an SER transaction strategy. This chapter will look at majority carve-outs and detail their structure, goals, and challenges.

DEFINITION OF A MAJORITY CARVE-OUT

In July 2002, Tyco International completed a majority carve-out of all its stock in its wholly owned subsidiary, CIT Group. This IPO raised $4.6 billion for the cash-starved Tyco in the fourth-largest IPO in U.S. history. Tyco earlier had tried to sell CIT in a traditional cash divestiture but received no acceptable offers. A majority carve-out involves the sale of all, or a majority interest in, a wholly owned or majority-owned subsidiary operation in one or more public offerings of stock, using only the traded equity of the subsidiary. A majority interest is defined as 50 percent or more of the economic interest in the subsidiary. Exhibit 7–1 provides a visual representation of the structure of a majority carve-out.

A majority carve-out gives a parent considerable flexibility to decide between a range of outcomes including:

- Selling all the parent's shares in the subsidiary at once in a single-step majority carve-out IPO

- Selling all the parent's shares over time in more than one public offering in a multistep majority carve-out

- Selling a majority of the parent's shares in a single-step or multistep majority carve-out but maintaining a minority long-term shareholding in the subsidiary

101

E X H I B I T   7–1

A Majority Carve-Out IPO

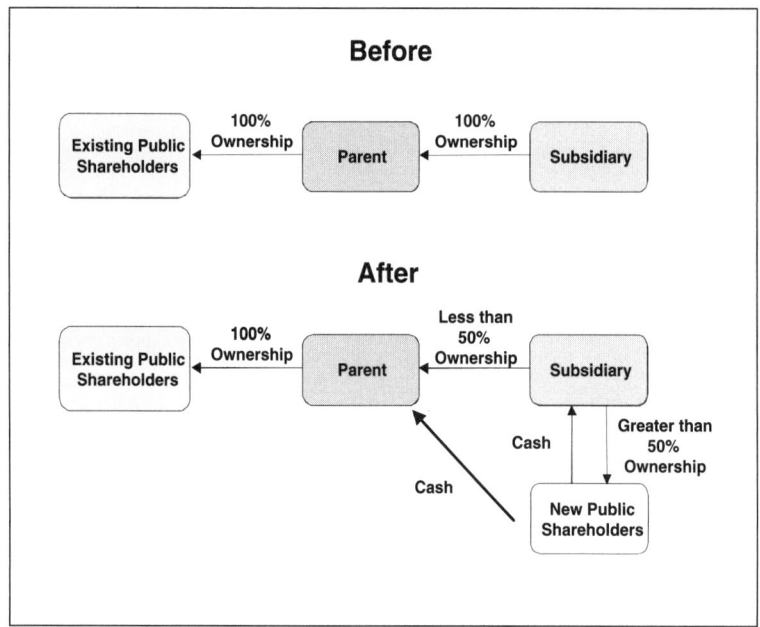

Source: John C. Michaelson and Robin A. Graham, "Equity Carve-Outs and Spin-Offs of Technology Operations," *The Financier*, vol. 2, no. 4, November 1995.

In most majority carve-outs, the parent retains most (or all) of the proceeds from the IPO (and any other public offering). However, if the subsidiary has significant cash needs of its own, sensible IPO investors will require that the subsidiary have sufficient cash to succeed as a public company (see the discussion of Du Pont Photomask later in this chapter). This is also prudent for the parent in avoiding lawsuits, embarrassment, and potential accounting restatements and is certainly in the best interests of the subsidiary and its employees.

As Exhibit 7–2 shows, majority carve-out IPOs are used, but are less common than minority carve-out IPOs. However, in 2001 and 2002 they account for a sizable percentage of the dollars raised by parents in divestitures.

ADVANTAGES OF A MAJORITY CARVE-OUT IPO

Besides its ability to provide a parent with a number of possible outcomes, a majority carve-out IPO is also beneficial in the following ways:

• *It may provide cash for the parent.* Unlike many spin-offs, minority carve-outs, private equity partnerships, or stock mergers, a single-step majority carve-out

E X H I B I T   7–2

Majority (Greater Than 50 Percent) Carve-Out IPOs

Year	1998	1999	2000	2001	Q1 2002
Number of majority carve-out IPO's	2	6	11	8	0
Amount of proceeds (billions)	$6.2	$6.3	$4.8	$3.0	$0
Percent of all IPO proceeds	18%	11%	8%	9%	0%

may generate substantial near-term cash for the parent and/or the subsidiary. In a majority carve-out, the parent and/or the subsidiary will receive the entire current value of the subsidiary.

- *The parent may obtain greater cash proceeds than through a traditional divestiture of the subsidiary.* Public market valuations for subsidiaries at certain times may be considerably higher than the values offered by either strategic or financial buyers. Reasons include (1) a lack of fit between the subsidiary and any single strategic buyer. This is often the case with a diversified subsidiary. (2) The subsidiary is not very profitable or is losing money in the near future and an acquisition would be dilative to the buyer's earnings. (3) The subsidiary does not have the cash flow or balance sheet characteristics to attract a private equity buyer. (4) The subsidiary has significant, or unquantifiable, business or legal risks that deter buyers.

    But, if the subsidiary is in the right industry sector or has good growth rates or a well-known brand, it may be of keen interest to public investors, who will often take in stride, when accompanied by commensurate opportunity, a lack of near-term profitability and significant business risks. All these elements are seen in the majority carve-out of Electroglas, described later in this chapter, where the public markets gave a considerably higher value than any cash buyer had offered.

- *It may allow the parent to terminate its responsibility toward the subsidiary.* Following a majority carve-out where all, or substantially all, of the parent's stock is sold, the parent can distance itself from the subsidiary.

- *It is easier to explain to investors than a minority carve-out.* A majority carve-out is easier for investors to understand. It has far fewer potential conflicts of interest between the parent and the subsidiary than does a minority carve-out, and it avoids the uncertainty over the long-term control of the subsidiary, with resulting uncertainty over its strategy inherent in the instability, discussed earlier, of minority carve-outs.

- *It allows for the option to exercise some continued parental influence.* Alternatively, the parent may maintain (within the limits of good public company governance practices) a more sizable influence on the business and on the direction of the subsidiary than is normally allowed by a buyer following a sale. Should the parent maintain a significant, although minority, position after the carve-out, it will likely be the largest single shareholder in the newly public subsidiary. This may be important to the parent if it continues to have commercial relationships with the subsidiary.

• *It allows continued financial participation by the parent.* The parent may wish to maintain some participation in the financial upside potential of the subsidiary. A majority carve-out allows the parent to maintain a desired ownership position. Cash buyers—particularly strategic buyers—are usually not willing to permit a significant ongoing economic participation by a seller.

• *It allows special provisions.* Using a majority carve-out may allow the parent to have special provisions for its future relationship with the subsidiary that would never be acceptable to a buyer of the subsidiary in a sale. (See the Genuity example later in this chapter.)

• *It may eliminate or reduce the impact of the subsidiary's finances on the parent.* If the subsidiary is unprofitable or has volatile or unpredictable earnings, the losses, or profit swings, of the subsidiary may impact the stock price of the parent. The parent may reduce or eliminate this impact with a majority carve-out. Following a majority carve-out, the parent may not have to consolidate the subsidiary for accounting purposes if the parent owns less than 50 percent (and the subsidiary's earnings or losses will not impact the parent's income statement, absent a write-down of its book value) if it owns less than 20 percent.

• *It can create a significant size for the IPO.* Should the market capitalization of the subsidiary be modest, a majority carve-out may be needed to ensure that there is a sufficient-size IPO to attract a first-tier underwriting team and a large enough public float to interest investors.

• *It may be used to address regulatory issues.* There may be instances when a parent is forced to divest a subsidiary for regulatory reasons. If so, a majority carve-out may be preferable to a straight sale if the parent does not want a competitor to buy the subsidiary and there are no other likely buyers (see the example of Balzers-Pfeiffer later in this chapter).

• *It may be accomplished in several steps.* A majority carve-out does not need to be done all at once. Instead, it can be accomplished over time through several steps. This is advantageous because it allows the parent the flexibility to time its sale. The Du Pont example at the end of this chapter details a multistep majority carve-out process.

• *It offers tax advantages.* An IPO for 80 percent or more of the stock held by the parent in a consolidated subsidiary is considered a sale for tax purposes. Under Internal Revenue Code Section 338(h)(10), a stock sale may be treated as an asset sale by the parent. This allows the tax basis of the subsidiary's assets to be stepped up to the usually much higher fair market value without the parent incurring taxation. This gives the subsidiary the cash flow benefits of a higher tax basis and lower taxes going forward at no additional cost to the parent.

Alternatively, as the IPO market usually does not value tax benefits, the parent may create extra value by having the subsidiary enter into a tax-sharing agreement with the parent in which the subsidiary pays to the parent the cash value of the step-up.[1]

- *It may be used to meet commitments to subsidiary management.* In some cases, the parent will have made commitments to the subsidiary's management to provide independence or not to sell the subsidiary. A majority carve-out allows the parent to meet these commitments yet still divest itself of the operation.

DISADVANTAGES OF A MAJORITY CARVE-OUT

Disadvantages of a majority carve-out include:

- *Limitations on the parent's economic upside.* With a majority carve-out, neither the parent nor (indirectly) its shareholders will participate fully or at all in the upside of the subsidiary. Once the subsidiary is sold, or largely sold, the participation of the parent in the future success of the subsidiary is reduced or ends. However, the parent will receive the proceeds from the sale of the stock, which it can redeploy in other areas.

- *Loss of control.* Once the transaction is completed, the subsidiary will be largely an independent company. While the parent may maintain some contractual links and may be on and appoint the board initially, the two companies will inevitably go their separate ways. Down the road, the former subsidiary may be acquired by a competitor of the parent or compete against the parent in other ways.

- *The subsidiary will need to be a viable public company.* The subsidiary will need to have the elements in place to create a successful IPO and, ultimately, become a successful stand-alone public company such as a full management team. This was discussed in Chapter 4. These attributes may not be required at all for a successful sale. The requirement for the subsidiary to be a viable public company for a successful and value-creating public SER is not unique to majority spin-offs. However, the issue is more pressing with a majority carve-out because continued parental supervision with a minority carve-out or tracking stock IPO gives investors confidence, at least for an interim period, that the wheels will not come off the subsidiary following a majority carve-out. With a spin-off, outside and skeptical investors do not have to be convinced to put up their cash to buy shares. In a spin-off, the shares are distributed to the parent's shareholders rather than sold to IPO investors.

- *Preparation time.* Putting in place the necessary groundwork required by investors for a successful IPO can take time and delay the transaction. As well, time is needed to prepare financial statements, draft the registration statement for the IPO, undergo the SEC review process, and market the IPO. While a majority carve-out IPO may be executed in as little as three months, it usually will take far longer. A one-year process is not uncommon. A sale may also take considerable time, but tends to be faster. With motivated parties, a sale process may take as little as a few months.

- *Gains may be taxed.* The gains received by the parent from the sale of stock in a majority carve-out may result in a substantial taxable gain at the parent level. As well, any distribution of the proceeds to the parent's shareholders will be taxed again as ordinary dividend income at the time of distribution. This is not different than with a sale but does differ from some other SERs such as a spin-off.

- *Greater pressure on the share price during the IPO.* A sale of all or most of the stock of the subsidiary at one time may be more than the public market can absorb easily, resulting in a price discount. This is a heightened risk with a majority carve-out because the size of the IPO will be much greater for the whole company rather than for a portion of the subsidiary, as in a minority carve-out. As well, most investors are less comfortable with IPOs where the parent is a major seller or recipient of the cash, including through dividends, repayment of intercompany debt, and assumption of parent debt or liabilities by the subsidiary, unless the subsidiary clearly will not have any of its own cash needs in the future.

- *Market risk.* During the usually lengthy preparation time for an IPO, the parent is exposed to market risk on the price and availability of an IPO. If the majority carve-out is conducted in several stages, the parent will also be exposed to market risk for the price obtained for the stock of the subsidiary sold in subsequent offerings. Another danger with a multistep majority carve-out is that the later second-step public offerings may not occur at all due to the subsidiary stumbling or because of market conditions. This leaves the parent with an unwanted remaining large position. Note that subsidiary performance largely determines the risk at any given time. In many situations, a cash divestiture may be closed sooner and with greater certainty over price, as the sale price may be formalized early in the process. With any IPO, the price is not known until the completion of the road show and the pricing of the transaction, which may be many months away. Much may change in the markets in the interim to lower (or raise) the actual value received. As well, IPO investors may become uninterested in any company in the subsidiary's industry or at its stage of maturity, preventing an IPO altogether.

- *Business risk.* Because of the greater time usually needed to prepare and execute a majority carve-out than a sale, there is greater risk than with a sale to the parent that the subsidiary's business will deteriorate in the interim, derailing the whole IPO effort.

- *Conflicts between the parent and the subsidiary over the objectives of the carve-out.* The objective of a parent that is divesting most or all of its ownership in a subsidiary through a majority carve-out often focuses on obtaining the greatest proceeds. The objective of the subsidiary is to ensure that it succeeds as a stand-alone company after the transaction. These objectives may be in conflict.

SUMMARY

This chapter examined the structure, benefits, and disadvantages of using majority carve-outs as an SER option. It is best to use this option when a substantial or complete separation is desired from the subsidiary, as it helps to achieve many key objectives, including raising funds for the parent or the subsidiary or providing an alternative to a more traditional divestiture. Conversely, majority carve-outs may not be the optimal choice if the subsidiary is not ready to be a public company or will not appeal to public equity investors at the time. Chapter 8 will examine spin-offs as yet another viable SER option.

SUCCESSFUL MAJORITY CARVE-OUTS

The Divestiture of Electroglas, Inc.: A Successful Majority Carve-Out That Obtained the Highest Proceeds for the Parent in a Sale of the Subsidiary

In 1992, General Signal made a strategic decision to exit the semiconductor fabrication capital equipment industry in which it had a number of operations. The largest of these was Electroglas, Inc., located in California, a maker of automatic wafer probing equipment used to test semiconductor wafers.

General Signal was a conglomerate, comprising primarily mature industrial products divisions such as pumps and valves, with rather predictable market dynamics. A prior CEO of General Signal had made acquisitions of high-technology capital equipment for semiconductor manufacturing a priority, with the belief that this market would grow faster than the existing industrial businesses of the parent and therefore increase overall corporate growth.

However, General Signal struggled with the semiconductor capital equipment businesses, many of which were not profitable. The acquired subsidiaries were a collection of boutique businesses serving market niches that proved difficult to manage from a centralized corporate structure.

General Signal hired a new CEO. Neither he nor the parent's senior staff had experience in high-technology business management, and they were not prepared for the volatility in these highly cyclical markets. Before acquiring the technology businesses, the parent's revenue would fluctuate 5 to 10 percent annually, reflecting the dynamics of its mature, existing industrial businesses. The newly acquired semiconductor capital equipment subsidiaries experienced 40 to 50 percent annual revenue shifts.

Ultimately, the CEO and board of directors succumbed to pressure from institutional investors to divest the company of the semiconductor capital equipment subsidiaries. The CEO was quoted in a business publication as saying his recent experiences were "high tech hell."

Having made the decision to divest the parent of the semiconductor capital equipment subsidiaries, the sole objective of General Signal was then to maximize its cash proceeds from the divestitures.

Looking back, the parent made a mistake in approaching the divestitures of the semiconductor capital equipment subsidiaries by using a financial advisor that focused only on cash divestiture alternatives and did not take a wider look at SER alternatives as well. With a strictly M&A focus, the advisor concluded that the means for General Signal to divest itself of the subsidiaries was to find a single corporate buyer for the entire group of subsidiaries in a cash sale. Unfortunately for General Signal, the financial advisor estimated that such a sale would be at a distress price, with substantial financial write-offs for the parent. In addition, the advisor warned the parent that finding a corporate buyer would not be easy and that the sale process would be long and difficult. The advisor noted that at the time there was little interest by strategic buyers for semiconductor capital equipment makers.

While the advisor, an M&A specialist, was right about the difficulties of a cash sale of the subsidiaries, the advisor was not aware at the time that astute public stock investors and private equity investors correctly believed a great turnaround had begun in the American semiconductor capital equipment industry and they were willing to make large investments in the sector.

A Change in Strategy

Neil Bonke joined General Signal in 1992 to help the company divest itself of its semiconductor capital equipment subsidiaries (he went on to be CEO of one of the subsidiaries, Electroglas). Bonke disagreed with the approach of the parent's financial advisor, believing that divesting General Signal of these businesses in pieces and executing a majority carve-out IPO for the most successful piece, Electroglas, would obtain greater value than the proposed sale.

On a stand-alone basis, Electroglas met the requirements for an equity majority carve-out. It was of sufficient size (nearing $100 million in sales) and had high-quality earnings and at the time had a dominant market position. In other words, it could become a successful public company on its own. It is important to note that Bonke believed that a majority carve-out public offering of Electroglas alone would increase General Signal's net cash return by a factor of two. He based this assumption on comparing the estimate of General Signal's financial advisor for the net cash proceeds of a sale and his own estimate (based on discussions with different financial advisors) for the net cash proceeds of a majority carve-out IPO.

Bonke was right. Electroglas had a successful majority carve-out IPO at the anticipated higher valuation. General Signal was able to achieve its objective of exiting a business area it was uncomfortable with while actually having a modest gain on the divestitures rather than a large write-off.

Electroglas completed its IPO in June 1993. General Signal sold 91.2 percent of its ownership of Electroglas common stock, raising $92.6 million. Electroglas did not receive any of the proceeds from the transaction.

In February 1994, Electroglas completed a follow-on equity offering in which General Signal sold its remaining shares and Electroglas sold off new shares for its own account. In this offering, General Signal raised an additional $15.7 million, and Electroglas $36.6 million.

Electroglas went public at $8.00 (split-adjusted) per share. The price climbed to $39.75 in August 1995. The use of a majority carve-out created substantially more value for the parent than the straight sale alternative.[2]

The Strategy Creates a Conflict of Interest

Neil Bonke shared the following thoughts on the process and the inherent conflict of interest:

> The moment a majority equity carve-out is decided upon, a natural conflict of interest occurs between a parent that is selling most or all of its holdings and the subsidiary. This was true of General Signal's majority carve-out of Electroglas. In this case the sole objective of the parent was to control the transaction and maximize its one time gain. The objective of the subsidiary was to position itself for long-term success.

Conflicts occurred over many issues. All of these areas of contention were major distractions. These issues included:

- *The selection of investment bankers.* Who were they working for? The parent or the subsidiary? The subsidiary needed its own investment bank, which would continue to work with it and provide research and sponsorship after the carve-out. The parent's investment banks had no expertise or interest at the time in the subsidiary's industry.

- *The surviving balance sheet of Electroglas.* The divesting parent wanted to leave no cash behind and preferred to leave some debt on the balance sheet. The subsidiary wanted to have sufficient cash working capital reserves and no debt. The issue was settled in favor of the subsidiary, but only after much contention. The investment bankers and others involved in the IPO argued that a cash-poor, debt-ridden entity would be much less attractive to potential investors and that this would decrease the IPO valuation or might cause the IPO to fail altogether.

- *The assumption of potential liabilities.* These included environmental, product liability, patent infringement, and employment litigation exposures. It was ultimately agreed that the parent would be responsible for liabilities dating back to its ownership and that Electroglas would be responsible for such liabilities going forward—a simple solution, but one that required a great amount of time to negotiate.

- *The establishment of stock option plans, employee bonus plans, executive compensation plans, and overall benefit plans for Electroglas.* The parent wanted to maximize its own proceeds from the sale of Electroglas and therefore wanted to minimize the dilution to its ownership economics of stock option grants. As an older industrial corporation, the parent's own compensation programs leaned more toward structured benefit programs, not equity-based incentives. The subsidiary, as a high-tech company competing for employees in Silicon Valley, required stock options to account for a large percentage of total potential compensation.

After the Transaction: The CEO Communicates the Benefits and the Challenges

After the majority carve-out, Electroglas was able to focus on its business. According to Neil Bonke:

Changing technology and increased global competition make business success challenging even when companies execute well. Being distracted by a corporate parent with somewhat misaligned objectives is a recipe for failure. In Electroglas' case the management group and employee action teams felt like their destiny was really in their own control, a powerful motivator for getting the job done.

The negative of the separation was that Electroglas management team had to learn the responsibilities and costs of being an independent public company fast. The management understood the dynamics of rapidly changing business cycles and of the importance of "time to market" in introducing new products. However, understanding the investment community, SEC reporting and all the associated requirements of being a public company had a certain burden on a new organization. Of tremendous help, however, is the importance of establishing a board of directors who really understand the responsibility of corporate governance. Electroglas was fortunate to have such a guiding board of directors.

Du Pont Photomasks: A Successful Multistep Majority Carve-Out

E. I. Du Pont de Nemours & Company, the nation's largest chemical company, decided for strategic reasons to sell a majority of its ownership of its wholly owned Du Pont Photomasks subsidiary. The subsidiary was only one of two significant domestic participants in its industry, making a strategic sale unlikely for antitrust reasons, as the only likely buyer was its competitor. Also, while the parent determined to divest itself of the subsidiary, the parent believed in its long-term prospects. As a result, the parent was in not in a rush to cash out and wanted to maximize its own long-term proceeds as well as ensure the success of the subsidiary after the divestiture. Therefore, the parent decided to use a multistep majority carve-out. Du Pont's objective was to become a minority shareholder through one or more second-step carve-out public offerings. The first step was a 1996 minority carve-out IPO. The parent then sold additional shares of the subsidiary in two subsequent carve-out public offerings, reducing its ownership to under 35 percent.

Exhibit 7–3 illustrates Du Pont's cash proceeds from each of these equity offerings and the success of the successive public offerings in reducing Du Pont's ownership to the desired level.

Through the initial first-step carve-out IPO and the subsequent second-step carve-out public offerings, Du Pont parent was able to reduce its ownership in Du Pont Photomasks to a minority position, raise a substantial amount of cash for its own use, and allow the subsidiary to fund its growth. The proceeds of the IPO—over $9.1 million—retained by the subsidiary, were used to repay debt to the parent. The parent realized proceeds of over $300 million from the initial first-step carve-out IPO and second-step carve-out public offerings, and retained an equity interest worth over $150 million at the end of 2001. This total of $450 million is a multiple of the author's estimate of what the subsidiary might have been sold for in 1996 in a straight cash sale.

E X H I B I T   7–3

Du Pont's Offering History

Du Pont ownership prior to offering	Date of offering	Security issued	Total proceeds	Proceeds to Du Pont Photomasks*	Proceeds to Du Pont*	Du Pont ownership after the offering[†]
100%	6/13/96	Common stock	$63.2	$9.1	$53.5	72%
69%	3/10/99	Common stock	$75.5	$0.0	$75.5	56%
50%	7/19/00	Common stock	$233.8	$46.4	$187.4	35%

*Debt paid down by Du Pont Photomasks to Du Pont with proceeds from the offerings is included under "Proceeds to Du Pont."

[†]Du Pont's postoffering ownership excludes the effects of the exercise of the underwriters' overallotment options.

Source: Du Pont Photomasks SEC filings

Reasons for a Separation: A Detailed Look

The subsidiary was a service business that manufactured customized photomasks used in the lithography process of making semiconductors. The mask-making business did not fit well with Du Pont's other core chemical and energy businesses because

• The photomask operation had high capital needs for multi-million-dollar mask-making tools. Du Pont would have to make major investments to maintain its competitive position.

• The subsidiary was a highly cyclical business dependent on the ups and downs of the semiconductor market. Du Pont wished to reduce cyclicality in its operations.

• The subsidiary competed against other customers of Du Pont's. Du Pont was a supplier of chemical products to other mask makers.

Also, the subsidiary was not benefiting from the relationship because

• Du Pont was taking cash out of the operation and constraining capital expenditures rather than investing. This weakened the competitive future of the business.

• The photomask business required quick responses to customer needs. The subsidiary was locked into the multiyear planning cycles of the parent more appropriate to mature industrial businesses. It could not respond quickly to customer needs.

And there was still another challenge: the subsidiary participated in the technology sector, which liberally used stock-based incentives. The subsidiary's employees were relatively young, skilled, mobile, and in demand by other technology companies. The parent was not able to offer the subsidiary's employees the stock incentives common in that industry. In contrast to the constrained position of the subsidiary, its main U.S. competitor, Photonics, Inc., was independent, had access to public equity capital, provided equity incentives to retain employees, and was able to quickly respond to customer needs without a lengthy and cumbersome approval process.

Reasons for the Success of the Multistep Majority Carve-Out

The Du Pont Photomasks multistep majority carve-out succeeded because

• The subsidiary was a high-quality company with sound management and a solid, profitable, business.

• Du Pont parent made sure that the attributes of a successful public company were all in place before the carve-out.

• Du Pont parent made sure that the subsidiary was sufficiently well capitalized at the time of the initial first-step carve-out IPO to meet the initial demands of its cyclical and capital-intensive business. After the first-step carve-out IPO, the subsidiary had $18 million in cash, the parent gave it a $30 million revolving credit line, and it had substantial internal cash flow. In addition, the parent assumed the pension liabilities of the subsidiary.

• The parent supported the subsidiary after the first-step carve-out IPO and subsequent second-step public offerings. Du Pont provided transitional administrative services and distribution in offshore markets and assisted with R&D and technical support (all for appropriate, but moderate, fees), licensed trademarks and intellectual property, and expanded its credit support over time.

• The carve-out permitted the subsidiary to grow and attract investor interest. After the carve-out, the subsidiary was able to greatly increase its capital expenditures within a few years, making it a more formidable competitor. Capital expenditure went from $18.9 million in 1995 to $100 million in 1998, and $181 million in 2000. This capital expenditure would probably not have been permitted by the parent had the subsidiary remained fully owned. Had the subsidiary not been structured to be a successful public company after the first-step IPO, there would not have been a receptive public market for its stock and the parent would not have been able to undertake the later second-step follow-on public offerings that allowed it to reduce its ownerships and generate cash.[3]

The Divestiture of Balzers-Pfeiffer GmbH: A Successful Majority Carve-Out for Regulatory Reasons

In February 1995, the U.S. Federal Trade Commission issued a consent order settling alleged violations of U.S. antitrust law by Oerlikon-Buhrle Holding AG, a Swiss-based corporation, resulting from Oerlikon's attempted acquisition of Leybold AG, a German corporation.

The consent order permitted Oerlikon-Buhrle to acquire Leybold, but it required that the company divest itself of both Leybold's compact disc metallizer business and its own Balzers-Pfeiffer turbomolecular pump business within 12 months. However, the likely buyers were all competitors of the parent and it did not want them to obtain the subsidiary, as it would strengthen their competitive position. Oerlikon-Buhrle requested FTC approval to divest itself of its turbomolecular pump business, Balzers-Pfeiffer GmbH, by means of an IPO in the U.S. equity market.

On July 19, 1996, Pfeiffer Vacuum Technology AG completed an IPO in the U.S. market of American Depository Receipts (ADRs) for all the shares of Balzers-Pfeiffer GmbH. In this case, 100 percent of a German company was effectively sold in the U.S. equity markets through an IPO, and the parent was able to use the proceeds from it to settle an antitrust challenge.

A majority carve-out should be considered as an alternative to a traditional sale for regulatory reasons if the parent does not want a competitor to buy the subsidiary and there are no other likely buyers.

The Divestiture of Genuity, Inc.: A Successful Majority Carve-Out for Regulatory Reasons with Special Provisions

This example illustrates the flexibility of a majority carve-out compared with a straight sale to achieve multiple parent objectives to solve regulatory issues. Verizon Communications, a Regional Bell Operating Company providing local telephone service, decided to acquire GTE, a diversified communications services provider. GTE had a subsidiary, Genuity, which offered Internet services that included long-distance telephone services. Genuity had provided the original network for the government-sponsored predecessors to the Internet.

At the time, the Federal Communications Commission precluded Verizon from offering long-distance telephone services. To receive approval for the GTE merger from the FCC, Verizon agreed to sell Genuity. However, Verizon believed that at some point it would be permitted by the FCC to offer long-distance services, and it wanted to keep open an option to later take back control of Genuity. Both objectives of Verizon were achieved with a majority carve-out IPO. This IPO for $1.9 billion closed in June 2000 and the GTE-Verizon merger closed simultaneously. Verizon retained a 5 percent shareholding in Genuity after the IPO, but it was in a special class of stock that was convertible into a control position in Genuity should the FTC later permit Verizon to offer long-distance services.

Lessons
A parent wishing, or required, to divest a subsidiary that may have the potential to be a viable public company should consider a majority carve-out as an alternative to a straight sale. It may offer greater proceeds and more flexible terms.

CHAPTER 8

SPIN-OFFS

INTRODUCTION

The purpose of this chapter is to examine spin-offs as viable SER transactions. As such, we will look at their structure and advantages, as well as the challenges associated with them. Spin-offs became an accepted form of corporate restructuring in the 1990s. Exhibit 8–1 indicates the amount and size of spin-off activity over the past five years.

There has also been considerable spin-off activity in Europe. including the three examples listed here. In July 2001, Sulzer, a Swiss industrial equipment and machinery producer spun off its 74 percent owned subsidiary Sulzer Medica, a maker of orthopedic and cardiovascular products, to its shareholders. Sulzer was in the process of divesting itself of noncore businesses. After the Sulzer Medica spin-off, Sulzer is focusing solely on its industrial products, and Sulzer Medica on health care products. Also in 2001, Kingfisher, a large U.K. retailer, spun off its Woolworth's Group variety store division to the parent's shareholders. Kingfisher was restructuring its business to focus on its more profitable home improvement stores. Previously, Kingfisher had announced that it would sell Woolworth's. However, offers were below Kingfisher's expectations. In 2002, Scottish Power announced that it was spinning off its telecommunications subsidiary. In the 1990s, the newly privatized utility remade itself into a diversified holding company through numerous but only tangentially related acquisitions. These new businesses rarely provided the forecast benefits and are now being unwound.[1]

DEFINITIONS OF TAX-FREE AND TAXABLE SPIN-OFFS

Spin-offs come in two main forms: tax-free and taxable.

A spin-off is a distribution of the subsidiary's stock to the parent company's

EXHIBIT 8–1

U.S. Public Spin-Offs

Years	1998	1999	2000	2001	2002 Q1
Number of spin-offs	43	37	38	25	3
Value of spin-offs at the time of the spin-off (billions)	$42.8	$81.5	$108.7	$81.1	$6.5
Source: Dealogic					

current public shareholders through a dividend. A spin-off uses only the publicly traded equity of the subsidiary. In most spin-offs, shareholder approval is not required unless the transaction can be viewed as a transfer of substantially all of the parent's assets. This requires shareholder approval in most states.

　　Most spin-offs today are tax free. Taxable spin-offs are executed only in special cases. The difference between a tax-free and a taxable spin-off is that a

EXHIBIT 8–2

Tax-Free Spin-Off

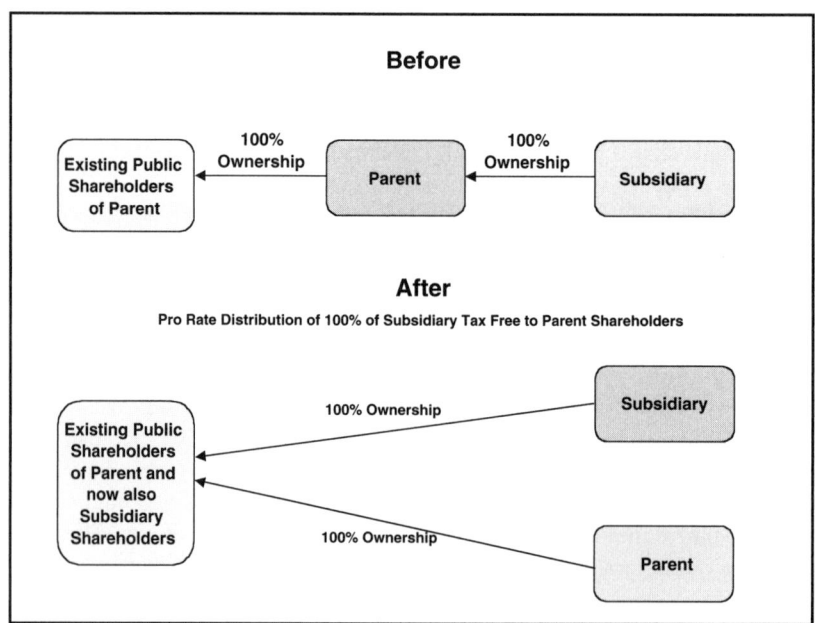

Source: John C. Michaelson and Robin A. Graham, "Equity Carve-Outs and Spin-Offs of Technology Operations," *The Financier*, vol. 2, no. 4, November 1995.

Taxable Spin-Off

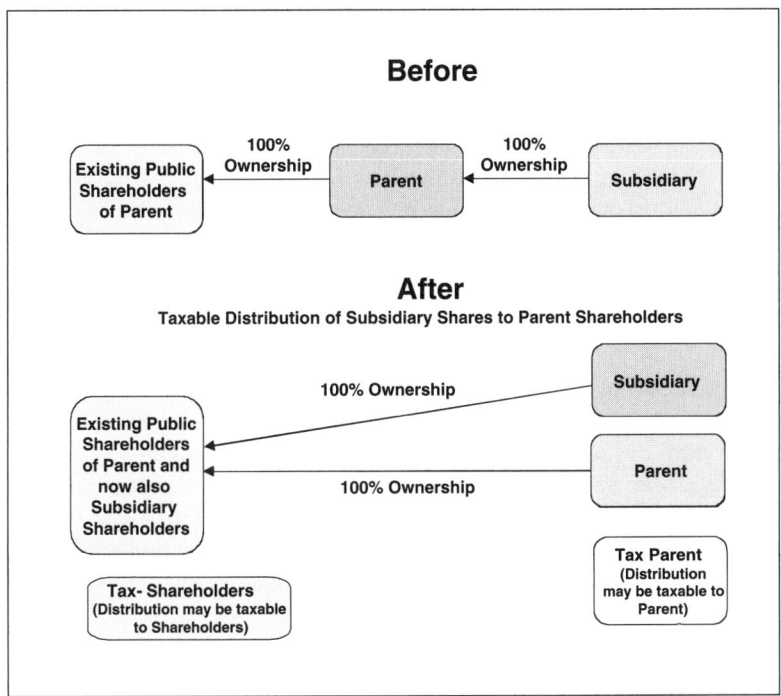

tax-free spin-off incurs no tax at the parent level; tax is deferred until a sale at the shareholder level. In contrast, a taxable spin-off may incur tax at the parent level on any gain upon the distribution. Most taxable spin-offs are taxable only to the parent. In certain circumstances, a taxable spin-off may also be treated as a taxable dividend to shareholders (however, this is rare and the author knows of only one instance where a spin-off was treated as a taxable dividend to the shareholders). Exhibit 8–2 depicts a tax-free spin-off, and Exhibit 8–3 illustrates a taxable spin-off.

SUMMARY OF KEY POINTS ABOUT SPIN-OFFS

Following are some key points common to tax-free and taxable spin-offs, which will be covered later in this chapter:

• Spin-offs are a means to unlock the value of a subsidiary and transfer that value to the parent's shareholders. It is especially useful with a subsidiary that does not completely fit with the core activities of the parent or would benefit from being a stand-alone public company.

• Spin-offs are a means to obtain full value for parent shareholders when divesting an unwanted subsidiary that is a viable business but will not command a reasonable price in a cash divestiture because of market conditions.

• Unlike a carve-out IPO, a spin-off is available to the parent in a depressed public market when there is little demand for IPOs. A spin-off is available when an IPO is foreclosed by market conditions.

• Unlike a carve-out IPO, a subsidiary may be spun off that does not necessarily meet all of the requirements at a given time for a successful IPO (see Chapter 18 to learn more about the criteria that IPO investors use when assessing IPOs).

• Unlike a carve-out IPO, a spin-off does not raise any new capital for the subsidiary. As a result, many spin-offs are preceded by a private equity or strategic corporate investment in the subsidiary, or a follow-on public or private financing after the spin-off to raise capital for the subsidiary.

• Unlike a carve-out IPO, a spin-off does not offer the potential to raise new capital for the parent in a carve-out IPO. However, in some cases the spun-off subsidiary may pay a cash dividend to the parent or assume debt and other liabilities of the parent. As well, a spin-off may be used to reduce outstanding parent debt in an exchange of subsidiary shares for parent debt or to reduce the number of parent shares outstanding in an exchange of subsidiary shares for parent shares (a split-off).

• A spun-off subsidiary does not have the initial send-off into the public markets that comes with a fully marketed IPO. It must take a number of actions after the spin-off to build public market support.

• For a subsidiary management confident in its capabilities, a spin-off is an excellent start to building a successful public company.

A spin-off may be used to reduce parent debt outstanding in an exchange of subsidiary stock for debt or to reduce the number of parent shares outstanding in an exchange for parent shares (split-off).

SPIN-OFFS AND DIVIDENDS

A classic spin-off involves the declaration and payment of a dividend to parent shareholders. The payment of the dividend must satisfy applicable state statutes. The Delaware statute (most states have similar provisions) provides that a company may only pay a dividend out of its "surplus" or its net profits for the fiscal year in which the dividend is declared and/or net profits for the preceding fiscal year. The determination of surplus is usually based on current values rather than historical or book values. In contrast, California's dividend test is based on generally accepted accounting principles.

Directors have a liability to creditors and shareholders for an unlawful dividend and need to assure themselves that there is sufficient surplus to pay spin-off dividends under state statutes, including fraudulent conveyance statutes.

Dividends may also be prohibited under loan agreements, and some equity-related securities, such as convertible debt, might have adjustment provisions for a special dividend, such as a spin-off.

BASIC REQUIREMENTS FOR TAX-FREE STATUS

A spin-off is generally tax free at the parent level and tax deferred to the parent's shareholders, until the distributed shares are sold, if the following conditions are met:

• Prior to the spin-off, the parent has 80 percent control of the subsidiary ("control" is not the same as "consolidation" for accounting or tax).

• The spin-off results in the distribution of at least 80 percent control of the subsidiary to the parent's shareholders.

• There is a corporate business purpose for the spin-off.

• The parent and the subsidiary have both been active businesses for five years.

• The spin-off is not a "device" for the distribution of earnings and profits.

A more detailed discussion of the tax issues in a spin-off is presented later in this chapter.

TAXABLE SPIN-OFFS: AN ALTERNATIVE TO TAX-FREE SPIN-OFFS

If the conditions for a tax-free spin-off are not met, the subsidiary may still be spun off to the shareholders of the parent in a taxable transaction. The transaction is taxable at the parent level on the difference between tax basis and fair market value at the time of the spin-off. It may also be taxable to the shareholders of the parent receiving the shares as a taxable dividend or as a return of capital. While there is a cash tax cost to some taxable spin-offs, a taxable spin-off may, in certain circumstances, still represent increased overall value to the shareholders of the parent either because the overall transaction makes sense or the tax is not large.

ADVANTAGES OF SPIN-OFFS

Regardless of whether the spin-off is tax free or taxable, it contains the following advantages:

• Creates pure-play businesses from within the parent to interest investors.

• Uncovers the value of the subsidiary for investors and analysts and allows the public market to establish the subsidiary's value.

• Permits parent shareholders to retain the entire upside in the subsidiary as they receive all the shares in the spin-off.

- Improves the long-term stock price—and the performance—of the parent and the subsidiary. The empirical evidence strongly supports the value creation potential of spin-offs.[2] Studies find it significant that parents and subsidiaries of spin-offs earn positive returns over three years compared with comparable companies and that long-term gains are significantly positive when comparing spin-offs against comparable companies. Also significant is the fact that there is improved operating performance following the spin-off and increased business focus by the parent.

Additional advantages of spin-offs are discussed in more detail in the following subsections.

Positive Immediate Stock Market Reaction for the Parent

Several studies have found positive returns for the parent's stock price following the announcement of a spin-off. One study finds that there is a positive return for the parent of approximately 3 percent after a spin-off transaction has been announced.[3]

A Valid IPO Alternative in Difficult Markets

In 2001 and 2002, the IPO markets were in disarray and effectively closed to most companies, with the primary exception of a few large carve-out SERs. However, spin-offs still proceeded. ESS spun off Vialta because ESS believed that both companies would benefit from immediate separation, but Vialta was not ready for an IPO. Palm is proceeding with the spin-off of its software subsidiary, Palm-Source, in a very difficult IPO market. Palm's priority is to establish PalmSource as an independent public company. It originally anticipated a first-step carve-out IPO, but market conditions precluded an IPO.

Increases the Competitive Position of the Subsidiary

SABRE Group Holdings, a travel service provider, benefited when it was separated from its parent, AMR Corporation, the parent of American Airlines. It was then better able to position itself to competitors of American Airlines, travel agents, and customers as a neutral and trusted provider of travel services. It was no longer perceived as serving its airline sibling first. Similarly, the spin-off of parts maker Visteon Corporation from the Ford Motor Company was intended, in part, to allow the subsidiary to compete for the business of other automakers.

Enables the Subsidiary to Break Free from Parental Constraints

Host Marriott Services, an operator of airport and toll-road concessions, was constrained from growing as a subsidiary of Host Marriott Corporation because its cash was used to fund the parent. As an independent company created in 1996,

Host Marriott Services had access to internal and external capital and expanded rapidly following the SER, growing its international operations and moving into the shopping-mall food-court management arena.

Mitigates Company Politics

A spin-off may help resolve internal political issues over strategic direction or personalities. In 1989, Cray Research spun off Cray Computer Corporation to resolve conflicts over the costs of developing two immensely expensive competing supercomputer projects.

One project, favored by John Rollwagen, the company's CEO, was a less radical extension to the product line. The other was a revolutionary new machine that was championed by Cray Research's founder Seymour Cray, the Cray-3. The Cray-3 had great promise but required technical breakthroughs.

By 1989, $120 million had been spent on the Cray-3 and it was behind schedule. The Cray-3 project was too risky for Cray Research. In 1989 the Cray-3 and a team led by Seymour Cray were spun off to the shareholders of Cray Research as Cray Computer Corporation. The parent capitalized it with the assets of the Cray-3 project, valued at $55 million and a loan of $100 million. Cray Research kept 10 percent of the new public company. Cray Computer spent over $370 million in its development effort but failed to produce a marketable product. It filed for bankruptcy in 1995 and was liquidated. Silicon Graphics acquired Cray Research in 1996.

Circumvents Tough Regulatory Issues

When the Federal Communications Commission approved AT&T's merger with MediaOne Group, it stipulated that AT&T diminish its market share by either divesting itself of Liberty Media, selling MediaOne's stake in Time Warner Entertainment, or letting go of individual cable systems. AT&T spun off Liberty Media to comply with the conditions set out by the FCC.

And in 2000, Reliant Energy separated into two publicly traded companies, one with unregulated power generation, energy marketing, and telecommunications, and the other with regulated electric and gas distribution utilities. This enabled the unregulated entity to operate with less restriction.

May Separate a Parent from Its Subsidiary's Legal or Financial Problems

A spin-off may enable a parent to insulate itself from the distractions of the subsidiary's financial or legal problems. For example, Goodrich Corporation announced in 2001 that it would spin off its engineered industrial products businesses due to investor concerns over asbestos liability at these operations. Goodrich intended to insulate itself from those liabilities with the belief that the asbestos liabilities would move to a company created through the spin-off.

Goodrich based this belief on the legal opinions it received indicating that it had operated the industrial products businesses separately and was shielded behind a corporate veil. Goodrich also announced that it was assured that the spun-off operation was "viable in terms of its balance sheet and cash flow, which should thwart any potential legal claims of fraudulent conveyance by Goodrich," according to Goodrich chief financial officer Rick Schmidt, as reported in the *Wall Street Journal* at the time of the announcement in 2001.

However, in a counterpoint, in 1998, W.R. Grace & Co. spun off its specialty chemical businesses to its shareholders in a new company named W.R. Grace. The specialty chemical company was given a $1.2 billion capital infusion by the parent. The parent borrowed the capital infusion. The remainder of Grace then merged with Sealed Air Corporation. Grace's shareholders received a 63 percent interest in the combined company that continued the name Sealed Air. The new combined Sealed Air also assumed the $1.2 billion debt taken on by the parent to make the capital infusion into the specialty chemical subsidiary.

Later, the specialty chemical business filed for bankruptcy under the press of asbestos litigation. In 2002, the asbestos litigants won a ruling in the U.S. District Court that the Sealed Air merger was a fraudulent conveyance. Although this ruling will be appealed, it is an interesting development. Very simplistically, there are two tests for proving fraudulent conveyance. The first is that the parent was insolvent at the time of the spin-off. The second is that the consideration received was less than equivalent value. The lawyers for the asbestos litigants contended successfully that the parent was insolvent at the time of the specialty chemical spin-off because of the upcoming wave of asbestos litigation and that the consideration paid by Sealed Air for the remainder of Grace was less than "equivalent value" because the stock portion of the amount paid by Sealed Air went to the shareholders of Grace and not to the company.

May Generate Cash for the Parent—or Lessen Its Debt Load—by Transferring Obligations to the Subsidiary

In a study of 129 one-step spin-offs from 1983 to 1998 by Amy Dittmar of Indiana University, debt was allocated or transferred to the subsidiary or a dividend paid to the parent in 90 cases.[4]

The parent may take cash from a spin-off through several means[5]:

1. The subsidiary borrows funds and then dividends these funds to the parent before the spin-off or uses them to repay loans from the parent before or after the spin-off. When EDS was spun off from General Motors in 1996, it paid GM a special distribution of $500 million before the spin-off, generating cash for the parent.

2. The parent borrows funds from a third party and the sole responsibility for repayment rests with the subsidiary. These loans are repaid from subsidiary cash flows after the spin-off. Kingfisher raised $1.4 billion in the spin-off of Woolworth's. The parent owned the stores occupied by the retailing chain. The parent sold these stores to a third-party real estate company that then

leased the stores back to the now independent Woolworth's, which was responsible for the lease payments.

3. The parent allocates liabilities to the subsidiary. While there is a considerable potential for abuse by the parent in the allocation of the parent's liabilities between the parent and the subsidiary, empirical evidence is that this usually does not occur. In most cases, the allocation is made in line with the ability of each entity to support the liabilities.[5] However, this is not always true, as demonstrated by Lucent's spin-off of Agere, described later in this chapter.

4. The IPO first step in a two-step spin-off may generate funds for the parent in the first-step IPO (see discussion in Chapter 9).

Separates Incompatible Businesses

Some operations are incompatible with the parent. In 1985, General Mills spun off its toy business, Kenner Parker Toys. "The cereal business is a high-margin, predictable business. The toy business is unpredictable, fashion dominated and capital-intensive. The two didn't belong together," said Scott Greiper, managing analyst of "Bits & Pieces" in *Business Week.* Kenner had been a troubled division of General Mills. Once on its own, it prospered. Two years after being spun off at $16 per share, Tonka Corporation acquired Kenner for $51 per share.

In 1998, U S West (subsequently acquired by Qwest Communications International) spun off its cable operation as MediaOne Group. U S West had originally expected convergence to bring the two businesses closer together over time; the opposite occurred. U S West found that its telecommunications and cable operations had diametrically opposed regulatory and business interests that were placing them in conflict.[6]

May Counter a Hostile Bid for the Parent

A spin- off may serve to hinder a hostile offer for the parent by providing the parent's shareholders with immediate value in the form of shares of the subsidiary. The proposal of a spin-off may also provide a bargaining point to obtain a higher price from a hostile bidder. To counter a hostile bid from Northrop Grumman, TRW Corporation proposed spinning off its automotive parts business to its shareholders. In the end, the spin-off did not occur and TRW agreed to be acquired by Grumman at a higher price than the initial offer.

ADVANTAGES OF A TAX-FREE SPIN-OFF

In addition to the advantages for all spin-offs discussed in the preceding section, tax-free spin-offs have these benefits:

• They are a tax-efficient means of distributing subsidiary value to parent shareholders or of divesting the parent of a subsidiary in the most tax-efficient manner for the shareholders of the parent. A tax-free spin-off allows the parent's share-holders to benefit from the value of the subsidiary while eliminating corporate-level taxes on the gain and deferring shareholder-level taxes.

• They are a tax-efficient way to repay parent debt or repurchase parent shares using the appreciated value of the subsidiary shares as consideration in an exchange instead of selling the shares, paying parent-level tax on a sale, and then using the proceeds to repay debt or repurchase the parent shares (see discussion in Chapter 11).

• In addition a tax-free spin-off may provide some defensive value to a parent faced with a hostile bid. A change of control of the subsidiary or the parent shortly after a spin-off may change the status of a tax-free spin-off to taxable. This raises the price paid by the acquirer by the amount of the tax payments.

ADVANTAGES OF TAXABLE SPIN-OFFS

As defined previously, a taxable spin-off is a distribution of a wholly owned or majority-owned subsidiary's common stock to the parent company's current public shareholders, typically through the declaration of a special taxable dividend. There are some solid reasons to employ a taxable spin-off. For example, despite the tax impact, a taxable spin-off may be an attractive way to divest an operation efficiently, quickly, and at the best value for the shareholders. The advantages of the spin-off must be weighed against the tax costs. The parent company may feel the cost is justified when considering a taxable spin-off if:

• The buyer of a major operation of the parent is not interested in all parts of the parent's business and a sale will not maximize value to the shareholders.

• A tax-free spin-off is not available now but is available in the future; however, the parent wishes an immediate separation.

• A tax-free spin-off will likely not be available in the future, and continuing to hold the subsidiary would thwart a business objective.

• The tax cost will not be substantial.

DISADVANTAGES OF ALL SPIN-OFFS

Although a spin-off is appealing under the right circumstances, there are disadvantages and challenges to be aware of, including the following:

• *In many spin-offs neither the parent nor the subsidiary receives any new cash in the SER.* In many spin-offs neither the parent nor the subsidiary receives any cash in the SER transaction itself, which is not the case with a carve-out IPO or a divestiture for cash. While the parent may extract cash from the subsidiary in a variety of ways or may downstream debt on to the subsidiary at the time of the spin-off, the subsidiary must be a viable stand-alone company after the transaction and not be overburdened with debt in order to thrive and fulfill its business promise. As well, tax rules limit the amount of debt that the parent may downstream onto the subsidiary or the amount of cash that the subsidiary may upstream.

In particular, growth and cyclical companies have greater capital requirements than do stable mature companies. These differences need to be recognized and accommodated by the parent at the time of the spin-off by giving the subsidiary a capital structure and sufficient cash as appropriate for its business. An undercapitalized spin-off may flounder. The spin-off of Agere from Lucent illustrates the danger of an undercapitalized spin-off when hit with a severe industry downturn following the spin-off.

One solution is to bring in strategic or private equity investors to provide cash to the subsidiary before the spin-off (see the case study of ESS/Vialta in Chapter 17). Another is a two-step spin-off with a first-stage IPO followed by the spin-off (see Chapter 9).

- *Impact on the parent's stock and creditors.* The parent has to consider the impact of losing the income and cash flow of a valuable asset without receiving any cash in return. This may present difficulties to creditors. It also may seriously reduce the price of the parent's stock. The parent's stock may fall below the $5 needed for margin, and this limits retail interest. The stock price, in a depressed stock market, may even fall below the minimum price requirements for continued listing on its stock exchange. AT&T undertook a 5-for-1 reverse stock split due to the loss of major operations in its restructuring programs. Another alternative is to undertake an exchange spin-off. With this, the subsidiary stock is exchanged for parent stock, mitigating the per-share impact of the spin-off, or for parent debt, mitigating the impact of the loss of cash flow. See Chapter 11 for a discussion of such transactions.

- *SEC requirements.* In order to make a distribution of the subsidiary's stock to public shareholders, the parent must file a Form 10 information statement with the Securities and Exchange Commission and furnish it to the stockholders receiving the shares. Form 10 contains disclosure comparable to that in the Form S-1 registration statement filed with the SEC for an initial public offering.

- *Pension Benefit Guaranty Corporation review.* Based on ERISA legislation, the Pension Benefit Guaranty Corporation can block an SER transaction after it has been submitted to the PBGC for review based on how the parent and the subsidiary plan to treat pension obligations. For example, the PBGC challenged the assumptions for return underlying the proposed allocation of pension liabilities in Anheuser-Busch's spin-off plan for its subsidiary, Earthgrains, and the Minnesota Mining and Manufacturing Corporation (3M) spin-off of Imation. Anheuser and 3M ended up keeping their spin-offs' pension assets and liabilities, lessening the balance-sheet benefit to the parent of the SER.[7]

THE SPUN-OFF BUSINESS MUST BE VIABLE

To create shareholder value, the subsidiary has to have a strong capital structure and a strong business. The problems created by their absence are illustrated by the following two examples.

The Impact of a Weak Capital Structure—Agere

The spin-off of Agere from Lucent closed in 2002. Agere's cash fell from $3.5 billion in March 2001 at the time of its initial carve-out IPO to $1.1 billion in June 2002. By mid-2002, Agere was in a fight for survival, desperately working to raise cash and sell or close businesses. What happened? Partly there was excessive optimism at the time of the SER over the markets for Agere's optical components and semiconductor products. Instead of growing steadily as forecast, revenues collapsed. In the year ended in September 2001, Agere had an operating loss of $967 million. For the nine months ending June 30, 2002, it had an additional operating loss of $1.1 billion. In mid-2002, Agere's headcount was down to 7,200 from 18,500 at the time of the IPO. These industry conditions would have been a challenge under any circumstances.

However, Agere was also burdened by an inappropriate capital structure for a company in a cyclical and capital-intensive business. In addition to exchanging Agere shares for Lucent debt as described in Chapter 11, Lucent also transferred $2.5 billion of short-term debt to Agere prior to the IPO. This added interest expense exceeding $150 million in the first year following the IPO. Agere also had to repay over $2.2 billion of this debt by June 2002 (though it was able to borrow a new $560 million). For Agere, the combination of an improper capital structure for a cyclical business and excessive debt and onerous short-term debt repayment requirements was devastating.[8]

Lucent was so intent on using Agere as a piggy bank that it threatened its viability.

The Impact of a Weak Business Model—Millennium Chemicals

In a 1996–1997 SER, Hanson PLC, the parent, was divided into four focused companies. Three components—Energy Group PLC, Imperial Tobacco PLC, and the new Hanson PLC, a construction-materials company—faired well. The fourth, Millennium Chemicals Inc., a U.S.-based chemicals company, did not fare well in the years following the spin-off. Saddled with old, costly plants and high operating costs, Millennium was a marginal producer. Just as important, the spin-off was weighed down with debt at the spin-off, reducing its flexibility and ability to modernize or make acquisitions. It did not fail, as did many late-1990s Internet SERs; it was a real business. But it did not thrive, either. Sales declined and earnings were sporadic. Millennium closed 2001 with a stock price of $12.60 compared with $24.00 at the time of the spin-off in 1997.

ADDITIONAL CHALLENGE FOR ALL SPIN-OFFS

All spin-offs share a common challenge, namely, the need to build a public interest in the stock on the part of institutional investors after the spin-off. This section will examine why this challenge exists and how it can be mitigated.

A subsidiary that is simply spun off to the parent's shareholders does not begin its public market life backed by a powerful marketing effort from investment banks, which normally accompanies a carve-out IPO. The eventual investor base for a spin-off is likely to be very different from that of the parent, and consequently there is usually considerable initial selling pressure on the newly spun-off stock.

Studies of traded spin-offs highlight the tendency for institutional investors of parents to sell their new dividend holdings in the spun-off subsidiaries.[9] The reasons for this selling by parent shareholders include:

- *Lack of familiarity with the subsidiary.* Investors in the parent may not be familiar with the spun-off business. These investors may sell positions received in the spin-off rather than take on the task of following another company.

- *Index fund selling.* When the parent's stock is owned by index funds, these funds will sell the spun-off stock if it does not fit their index. This is notably the case when the parent is a member of the widely held S&P 500 Index and the subsidiary is not.

- *The subsidiary has too small a market capitalization for the investor.* Many institutional investors have market capitalization minimums that the parent's stock must meet. The large majority of institutional investors are precluded by their charter or internal policies from investing in smaller-capitalization companies. The universe interested in smaller-capitalization stock is primarily limited to retail investors and some specialized value and small-capitalization institutional funds.

- *The subsidiary has a different risk/reward ratio than that of the parent.* The subsidiary's stock may appeal more to investors comfortable with the risks and rewards of high-multiple-growth stocks, while the parent's shareholder base may have investors more oriented toward yield or value investments.

- *The distributed holding in the subsidiary is smaller than the investor's desired minimum holding size.* Institutional investors often have minimum dollar or share number criteria for portfolio holdings. The subsidiary stock distributed in the spin-off may be below this minimum requirement. The investor will then either divest the distributed stock or increase its holdings through purchases of additional stock in the market.

- *Lack of a dividend by the subsidiary.* Certain funds are precluded from holding non-dividend-paying stocks. Should the parent pay a dividend and the subsidiary not pay a dividend, investors will sell. This selling may put considerable pressure on the stock of the subsidiary, as it creates a large supply of stock for sale soon after the distribution. At the time, there may not be an investor base for the subsidiary's stock to buy these shares. While in the end the market may recognize good values, this could take a long time. To accelerate the process, the management of the spin-off must take a number of steps to develop a new shareholder base for the company and obtain research coverage and sponsorship. Investors have thousands of public companies from which to choose. Unless the spun-off company is a complete standout, it is liable to get lost in the clutter, especially if it does not have investment bank sponsorship in research and market making.

The steps required to create a successful public company after an SER are described in Chapter 24. Here are the three additional actions that will help build a new shareholder base specifically after the spin-off:

1. Consider employing an investment bank or banks to advise on the spin-off to start the ball rolling on research coverage and sponsorship. It is money well spent. Don't count on the parent's investment bankers to take an interest in the spin-off; they usually don't. Develop your own relationships among investment banks and analysts attuned to your industry and the size of your company.

2. Hit the road to tell the subsidiary's story in advance of the spin-off of the parent's investors and new investors.

3. Consider a follow-on public offering of stock soon after the spin-off to raise capital, increase visibility, and attract additional research and sponsorship.

DISADVANTAGES OF A TAX-FREE SPIN-OFF

There are also disadvantages specific to tax-free spin-offs, including the following:

• *Strict IRS requirements for a tax-free spin-off.* Strict requirements are imposed by the Internal Revenue Code, and by IRS regulations to qualify for a tax-free spin-off. These also limit corporate actions before and after a tax-free spin-off.

• *Potential for a retroactive shift in tax status.* Any change in control within two years of a spin-off may cause the SER to become retroactively taxable to the parent unless it is established that change in control was not related to the spin-off. However the IRS recently published safe harbor tests that mitigate this risk.

DISADVANTAGES OF TAXABLE SPIN-OFFS

And there are many disadvantages to executing a taxable spin-off, including:

• *Tax at the parent level.* The taxable spin-off creates a corporate-level tax liability that is determined by the difference between the fair market value of the stock distributed at the time of the spin-off and the parent's tax basis in the stock. In cases where the market value of the subsidiary is actually lower than the tax basis, there is no tax consequence. In the past this was rarely the case. It may occur more frequently in the future with spin-offs in depressed stock market conditions. As well, there are many ways to structure the transaction to reduce parent taxable gain.

• *Tax at the shareholder level.* In specific circumstances, a taxable spin-off may also create a taxable dividend liability for the shareholders determined by the fair market value of the stock of the subsidiary at the time of spin-off distribution to the shareholders. Depending on circumstances, this gain may be capital gains and may be offsettable against the individual shareholder's tax basis in the parent stock or dividend income. In most situations, dividend income is more costly to the shareholders. Often there are ways to structure the transaction to reduce fair market value.

- *Limited control by the parent over the tax value.* The fair market value for tax purposes of the stock dividend to the parent's shareholders in a taxable spin-off will likely be determined by the IRS, based on the trading price of the stock of the subsidiary immediately following the spin-off. The parent has little control over this price, which is set by the public stock market. As well, this price is determined after the spin-off is transacted, which will be months after the decision is made to commence the spin-off process. In one case the IRS took a position that the stock market price was not the appropriate measure of fair market value and that the fair market value was the hypothetical price that would have been paid by an arms-length buyer.[10]

- *Added selling pressure from tax selling on the subsidiary's stock.* A spin-off generally results in selling pressure on the stock of the subsidiary immediately following the spin-off, as shareholders adjust their positions. A taxable spin-off has potential to put greater selling pressure on the stock, as shareholders sell in order to satisfy their tax obligation.

- *Added administrative costs and burden of tax filings on the parent and on its shareholders.* Parent shareholders will need to be sent W-8 tax forms by the parent (or the equivalent for overseas shareholders) at the end of the year of the distribution and include the distribution in tax filings and pay taxes on the distribution. There may be an administrative burden in collecting the necessary information and sending the forms, especially if the parent does not itself pay a dividend and therefore has no need for this information.

KEY TAX ASPECTS OF SPIN-OFFS

As alluded to earlier, there can be substantial benefits to structuring a spin-off to be tax free at the parent and shareholder levels. And there are a number of requirements that must be met by the parent and the subsidiary for a tax-free spin-off, as set out by the IRS.

IRC Section 355

Section 355 of the Internal Revenue Code (IRC) determines whether a spin-off will be taxed at the corporate or shareholder level or both or will be considered tax free at the corporate and shareholder levels. Let's take an in-depth look at how Section 355 affects parents, shareholders, and subsidiaries.

Impact of a Tax-Free Spin-Off

- *Parent.* The parent generally does not recognize a gain or loss on the distribution of the stock in a spin-off if the requirements of Section 355 are met for a tax-free spin-off. However, loss of tax consolidation could trigger taxes from

deferred intercompany transactions or to the extent that the parent has a negative tax basis in the stock of the subsidiary. If the requirements of Section 355
have not been met, the parent will recognize a gain (but not a loss) as if the stock
of the subsidiary were sold in a cash divestiture.

- *Parent's shareholders.* If the requirements of Section 355 are met, the parent's
  shareholders generally do not recognize a gain or loss until they sell their shares
  in the subsidiary received in the spin-off and the parent's shareholders basis in
  the stock of the parent before the distribution is allocated between the parent
  and the subsidiary stock. The basis in the stock is determined by the parent and
  subsidiary stocks' respective fair market values on the date of the spin-off. However, if the requirements of Section 355 are not met, the parent's shareholders
  are taxed as if a cash dividend were received equal to the fair market value of the
  subsidiary or, more accurately, as if a property distribution were received. This
  could be a taxable dividend, a return of capital, or a capital gain to the shareholders, depending on the underlying facts.

- *Subsidiary.* The subsidiary carries over the tax basis in its assets after the spin-
  off. It is unaffected.

IRC Section 355 and Tax-Free Spin-Offs
The requirements of Section 355 for a tax-free spin-off include the following:

- Immediately after the distribution of the subsidiary stock, the parent and the
  subsidiary must each be engaged in a trade or business that has been actively
  conducted for at least five years prior to the distribution and was not acquired by
  the parent or the subsidiary during that period except in an entirely tax-free
  transaction. While this may not disqualify the spin-off, such stock would be
  subject to IRS rules concerning "boot."

- The transaction must not be used "principally as a device for distributing the
  earnings and profits of the parent or the subsidiary or both." For example, substantial planned postdistribution sales of subsidiary stock by the parent's stockholders could jeopardize the spin-off's tax-free status.

- The parent generally must distribute all of its subsidiary stock to its shareholders (or an amount of stock that represents control, generally 80 percent or more
  of the stock of the subsidiary) and must establish to the satisfaction of the IRS
  that the retention of the remaining shares was not in pursuance of a plan having
  as one of its principal purposes the avoidance of federal income tax.

Spin-Offs and Internal Revenue Code Section 355(e)

Before 1997, a form of tax-free spin-off of a subsidiary known as a Morris trust was
available to transact a tax-free spin-off of a subsidiary not wanted by an acquirer or
merger partner. This enabled a parent to distribute an unwanted subsidiary to shareholders without a corporate tax being imposed, and sell the rest of the business. In
a Morris trust transaction, the parent spins off the subsidiaries it wishes to keep to

its shareholders and merges the remaining unwanted subsidiary with another company. In a reverse Morris trust transaction, the parent spins off the unwanted subsidiary to the parent's shareholders and then merges it with another company.

The enactment of Section 355(e) in 1997 greatly narrowed the ability of the parent to take advantage of Section 355 by requiring the parent to recognize gain on the distribution of stock of a subsidiary if the distribution is part of a "plan (or series of related transactions)" under which one or more persons acquire, directly or indirectly, 50 percent or more of the stock of either the parent or the subsidiary. An acquisition of the subsidiary or the parent in violation of 355(e) potentially endangered the tax-free status of the spin-off retroactively, with potentially severe tax consequences for the parent (but not for its shareholders). The requirement for more than 50 percent continuing ownership by the parent's shareholders counts only historic shareholders before the spin-off.[11]

A major issue with 355(e) has been defining what constitutes a "plan." Section 355(e) presumes that any change in ownership within two years of a spin-off is pursuant to a plan. It was left to IRS regulations to define the term. Before August 2001, the IRS imposed a two-year period following a spin-off during which a merger of the parent or the subsidiary would retroactively make a tax-free spin-off taxable. Temporary regulations published in 2001 and revised temporary regulations published in April 2002 give considerable relief. Under the temporary regulations, whether a distribution and an acquisition are part of a prohibited plan is determined based on all the facts and circumstances. However, the temporary regulations contain a safe harbor provision that protects a spin-off followed by an acquisition of the parent or the subsidiary from being considered part of a plan if the acquisition occurred more than six months following the spin-off, provided that the spin-off was motivated by a business purpose other than an intent to facilitate an acquisition of the acquired company and there was no agreement, understanding, arrangement, or substantial negotiations concerning the acquisition or a similar acquisition during the year before the spin-off or within six months after it. If the safe harbor test is not met, the two-year period still applies, requiring the parent to rebut the presumption of a plan. The revised temporary regulations also set out a general presumption that an acquisition after a spin-off will not be regarded by the IRS as part of a plan if there was no agreement, understanding, arrangement, or substantial negotiations concerning the acquisition or a similar acquisition during two years before the spin-off.

Tax-free Morris trust and reverse Morris trust SERs may still be accomplished. However, now in either case, the shareholders of the parent have to continue to own more than 50 percent of the combined company following the merger for the spin-off to be tax free.

Tax-Free Spin-Offs and IRC 355(d)

This provision was enacted in 1990 in response to the leveraged buyout activity of the late 1980s. Section 355(d) provides that a parent is not allowed to do a tax-free spin-off of a subsidiary for five years following an acquisition of the parent. The parent not meeting the requirements of 355(d) does not have a tax impact on shareholders receiving the distribution.

Tax-Free Spin-Offs and IRC 357(b) and (c)

Many tax-free spin-offs are preceded by a transfer of the parent's liabilities and assets to a subsidiary in a standard "D" reorganization. The stock is then distributed out to the parent's shareholders. Normally, the conveyance of assets by the parent is undertaken in exchange for stock in the subsidiary and the assumption of an appropriate amount of the parent's liabilities, and is tax free.

However, the parent may be hit with taxable gain where the liabilities assumed by the subsidiary exceed the aggregate basis of the assets transferred to the subsidiary. IRC Section 357(c) states that this excess will be treated as a gain. This section may apply where the parent borrows money in contemplation of the spin-off but has the subsidiary assume responsibility for the repayment of the loan.

In addition, under IRC Section 357(b), liabilities assumed by the subsidiary will be treated as taxable gain if, based on all the surrounding circumstances, the parent's principal purpose was to avoid federal income tax or did not have a bona fide business purpose. Section 357(b) can apply in cases where the proceeds of a loan (particularly a borrowing undertaken in contemplation of the spin-off) are separated from the obligation to repay the loan. One example is if the parent borrows money, retains the proceeds of the loan, and has the subsidiary assume responsibility for the repayment of the loan.

Tax-Free Spin-Offs and IRC Section 368(e)

Under Section 368(e) of the Internal Revenue Code, for a spin-off to be tax free

- The parent must have "control" of the subsidiary to be spun off immediately before the distribution of the subsidiary's stock to the parent's shareholders. Under IRC Section 368(c), "control" means ownership of stock possessing at least 80 percent of the total combined voting power of all classes of stock entitled to vote for the election and removal of directors and at least 80 percent of the total number of shares of each other class of nonvoting stock. One means to mitigate this requirement is to use two classes of stock. See the discussion of this structure in Chapter 9.

- The parent must distribute "control" of the subsidiary as defined in Section 368(c) in the spin-off. This generally means that 80 percent of the stock of the subsidiary must be distributed to the parent's shareholders.

Nonstatutory IRS Requirements for Tax-Free Spin-Off

There are also several nonstatutory requirements imposed by the IRS that must be met for a spin-off to be tax free. These include:

• There must be a corporate business purpose for the separation of the subsidiary from the parent that could not be served without spinning off the subsidiary's stock. The business purpose has to be a corporate business purpose of the parent. As a result, a legitimate business purpose would not include increasing parent shareholder value.

• Both the parent and the subsidiary must satisfy a continuity of business enterprise requirement.

• The historic shareholders of the parent must maintain a continuing interest in both the parent and the subsidiary.

Tax to the Parent's Shareholders

If only IRC 355(e) is violated (as with the C-Cube spin-off discussed later), but all the other requirements of IRC 355 for a tax-free spin-off are satisfied, the parent may recognize taxable gain, but the spin-off is not taxable to the parent's shareholders.

If the requirements of IRC 355 are not satisfied—for example, because the five-year active business test is not met—in addition to the parent recognizing taxable gain, the spin-off is also taxable to the parent's shareholders.

When a spin-off is taxable to the parent's shareholders, it is treated for tax purposes just as if the parent had made any other cash distribution to its shareholders. The value of the distribution is usually the fair market value of the subsidiary's shares at the time of the distribution, and it is usually taxed at the ordinary income tax rate.

However—and this is important in many restructurings—if the parent company's current or accumulated tax "earnings and profits" (calculated after any net gain but not loss on the distribution) are less than the value of the distribution, some or all of the distribution will be a return of capital to the parent's shareholders. The fair market value of the spun-off shares first goes to reduce the basis of the parent shareholder in the parent's stock. Any excess over the shareholder's basis is capital gain and is taxed at the reduced capital gains tax rate if the shareholder is eligible.

When a spin-off is taxable to the parent's shareholders, one approach is to reduce the fair market value of the subsidiary at the time of the spin-off as much as possible. For example, this may be achieved by using a capital structure with preferred stock held by the parent that gives the parent's shareholders participation only in future appreciation of the subsidiary. The parent may also pay a cash dividend along with the spin-off to cover the taxes of the parent shareholders, though this may be expense and some may go to shareholders who are not taxable entities. As well, the dividend itself is taxable.

An alternative when a spin-off will be taxable to the parent's shareholders at the full income tax rate is to use a split-off. This is an exchange of parent shares for subsidiary shares. A split-off is usually treated for tax as if the parent company had simply bought back some if its outstanding shares for cash. Most shareholders are then taxed at the capital gains rate (see the discussion of split-offs in Chapter 11).

IRS Letter Rulings

It is generally the practice for the parent to request a private letter ruling from the IRS that the distribution will be treated as tax free before the distribution of shares in a spin-off. It is a relatively time-consuming endeavor to obtain such a ruling, which typically spans six months from the time of submission to the IRS. If the IRS is not prepared to give a letter ruling, it still may convey to the parent that it will not take "no action" to challenge the tax-free status of the spin-off. While in most cases the parent waits for an IRS determination on the proposed tax status of the spin-off before undertaking a spin-off, the parent may decide to proceed with the transaction for the following reasons:

- It is likely that the spin-off will not qualify for tax-free status (perhaps it does not clearly meet all the tests under Section 355).

- There is a risk that a tax-free spin-off will not be available after a six-to-nine-month ruling delay and the parent suspects that the subsidiary may increase in value during the ruling period, which would increase the potential tax liability.

- The parent may be absolutely committed to a prompt spin-off regardless of the tax impact.

- The parent is highly confident, based on an opinion of tax counsel or its accounting firm, that the spin-off will qualify for tax-free status and wishes to move ahead.

- Section 355(e) may not be met, but otherwise the provisions for a tax-free spin-off are met. The taxable gain would not be large if the eventual ruling is unfavorable, as the expected market value of the subsidiary is similar or less than its tax basis and there will be no tax to shareholders.

EXAMPLE OF SPIN-OFF CREATING SUBSTANTIAL VALUE

In 1996, according to the *Wall Street Journal*,[12] "In an announcement that stunned both the City of London and Wall Street, Hanson PLC said it would split into four parts, dismantling the acquisitive man-of-war built on many a hostile takeover during three decades. Hanson's move caps the end of an era. If the 1980s was the decade of the conglomerate, the 1990s are the decade of the de-merger." Hanson used spin-offs to split into separately traded energy, tobacco, construction, and chemical companies. According to *Business Week*,[13] "Institutional investors would rather diversify their own portfolios than own shares in unwieldy conglomerates. And while Hanson had already shed many smaller pieces, analysts still found the company difficult to follow."

Hanson split into Energy Group PLC (Peabody Coal Co. and Hanson's electricity distribution businesses), Imperial Tobacco PLC (tobacco products), the "new" Hanson PLC (construction equipment and building materials), and Millennium Chemicals Inc. (a U.S.-based chemicals company). Overall, the breakup of

Hanson in 1996–1997 proved highly successful for its investors. The Energy Group was purchased for a 50 percent gain in 1998 by Texas Utilities Company. Imperial Tobacco benefited by the return of investor interest in traditional businesses, and its share price doubled by the end of 2001. The share price of the "new" Hanson increased 54 percent. However, Millennium, as discussed earlier, did not fare as well, and its stock price declined 47 percent through the end of 2001.

The overall lesson to be learned from the Hanson experience is that substantial value may be created for shareholders through spin-offs. Of course, Hanson is a U.K. company and, as with other non-U.S. companies, different tax and securities rules apply.

SUMMARY

This chapter examined how spin-offs are a unique tool to unlock the value of the subsidiary and transfer it to the parent's shareholders. In many cases, this may be done tax free. Chapter 9 will examine two-step spin-offs, including how they compare and contrast to the spin-offs described in this chapter.

EXAMPLES OF OTHER SPIN-OFFS

Example 1, Varian Associates: A Well-Thought-Through and Well-Executed Spin-Off Program That Greatly Increased Shareholder Value

Varian Associates is a classic example of the benefits that can be created through a successful deployment of subsidiary equity values through two tax-free spin-offs, which took place in 1999. Before the restructuring, Varian Associates made health care systems, instruments, and semiconductor production equipment. As a small conglomerate, Wall Street largely ignored it because it was deemed too complicated to follow. Even though Varian had a market capitalization of $1.0 billion, only seven equity research analysts followed it.

To increase shareholder value, Varian Associates spun off Varian, Inc., its instruments business, and Varian Semiconductor Equipment Associates, Inc., its semiconductor equipment business, to its shareholders in April 1999. Immediately after the spin-offs, Varian Associates changed its name to Varian Medical Systems, Inc. This created three independent and focused companies.

Twelve months after the breakup, the three independent business units had a combined market capitalization of $4.6 billion and were covered by 22 equity research analysts. Each of the entities performed well as independent companies following the spin-off. The success of the spin-off can be directly tied to Varian's ability to deliver focused companies in different industries, each able to generate its own investor base and Wall Street research following, and each able to prosper on its own.

Exhibit 8–4 shows the operating performance of the three areas of Varian, Exhibit 8–5 shows the increased shareholder value resulting from the spin-offs,

EXHIBIT 8–4

Varian Summary of Historical Financials

| | Fiscal Year Ending September 30 | | | | | |
| | Revenues | | | Operating Earnings | | |
(dollars in millions)	1998	1999	2000	1998	1999	2000
Varian Semiconductor Equipment Associates, Inc.	$303.5	$206.4	$626.2	$16.3	$(21.3)	$124.1
Varian Medical Systems, Inc.	541.5	590.4	689.7	87.7	24.3	38.4
Varian, Inc.	557.8	598.9	704.4	38.2	15.7	72.6
Total	$1,420.8	$1,395.7	$2,020.3	$142.2	$18.7	$235.1
Source: Varian SEC filings						

and Exhibit 8–6 demonstrates the increased research coverage following the spin-offs.

Example 2, Conexant Systems: A Spin-Off That Was Undercapitalized

In December 1998 Rockwell International spun off its semiconductor business, Conexant Systems, to its shareholders, leaving Rockwell engaged in industrial automation, avionics and communications, and automated call distribution systems. Conexant Systems, a $1.2 billion business based in California, is focused exclusively on semiconductors for communications electronics. Conexant is in a highly cyclical industry, with short design cycles, constant cost pressures, large capital needs, and wide swings in revenues and earnings from year to year. A capital structure appropriate for Rockwell's mature primary businesses was not appropriate for Conexant.

At the time of the spin-off Conexant had only $14 million in cash. This would not have been a problem if it had raised additional equity capital when it had the opportunity when the public market was wide open to it in 2000 and it had a high valuation; instead, it funded its capital needs with $307 million in short-term debt and $765 million in long-term debt. The markets then turned with a deeper-than-normal, but not to be unexpected, cyclical downturn in the semiconductor industry. In 2001, Conexent lost over $400 million. By the end of 2001, Conexant's financial situation had become tenuous. The lesson here is that growth and cyclical companies have very different capital structure requirements than mature companies. These differences need to be recognized and accommodated by the parent at the time of the spin-off.

EXHIBIT 8-5
_____

Varian Market Capitalization Summary

	Market cap as of		
	August 1, 1998	April 2, 1999	April 2, 2000
(dollars in millions)	At announce- ment of spin- offs	At the time of the spin- offs	One-year following the spin-offs
Varian Medical Systems, Inc. (original parent)	$1,037.8	$693.4	$1,409.0
Varian Semiconductor Equipment Associates, Inc.	—	353.7	1,968.9
Varian, Inc.	—	287.1	1,196.9
Total market capitalization	$1,037.8	$1,318.2	$4,574.8
Indexed:			
Varian Composite*	100	99.60	340.51
SP 500	100	115.44	134.38
Nasdaq Composite	100	133.17	225.58

*The Varian Composite index is Varian Associates (parent) until the restructuring spin-offs and the sum of the three units following the restructuring spin-offs.

Source: Bloomberg, Varian SEC filings, Needham & Company

Example 3, DII Group: The Impact of Hard Work on Generating Investor Support for Stock Following a Spin-Off—with Superior Results

The need for a subsidiary to work hard to generate support for the stock following a spin-off is demonstrated by the DII Group spin-off.

Before its spin-off, DII made sure it had the sponsorship of several investment banks and engaged a leading investment bank as an advisor that committed to providing research. Within six months of the spin-off, DII completed a $46 million follow-on public offering of stock that accomplished several goals. The offering increased its sponsorship base on Wall Street by creating a large payday to the investment banks that participated in the offering. They were then obligated to pick up research coverage and provide sponsorship. The offering also raised cash to grow the business, and helped attract institutional investor interest in the company and create a more liquid market for the stock.

E X H I B I T   8–6

Separate Research Analysts at Separate Investment Banks Covering Varian

	Number of different investment banks following company	
	At announcement of spin-offs on August 1, 1998	One-year following spin-offs on April 2, 2000
Varian Associates, Inc. (original parent)	7	—
Varian Medical Systems (successor to the parent)	—	6
Varian Semiconductor Equipment Associates	—	12
Varian, Inc.	—	4
Total number of analysts firms	7	21
Source: Nelson's Research Directory		

DII Background

DII Group, a contract assembler of electronic components, was spun off in May 1993 from Dover Corporation, a diversified industrial holding company. Dover had a substantial business making capital equipment for contract electronic assemblers with well-known capital equipment makers such as Universal. However, it also had built up a small group of contract assembly assets, later named DII Group, that utilized the assembly capital equipment made by Dover to directly serve customers.

Dover decided to spin off the contract assembly operation to the parent's shareholders for five reasons:

1. Dover believed that the growth of its in-house contract assembly group would create conflict with the other contract assembly customers of the capital equipment group, as it was a direct competitor with those customers.

2. There was considerable internal tension when DII purchased capital equipment from outside Dover.

3. The business did not fit with Dover's other businesses. Dover's other companies were mid-to-late-life high-margin cash cows. Conversely, DII was the only company to have strong potential to grow from within. As a result, it needed cash to grow.

4. While it did not fit inside Dover, DII offered strong appreciation potential for Dover's shareholders.

5. The business had an aggressive and talented management team that could run a public company.

For these reasons, DII was spun off from parent Dover. The stock price chart (Exhibit 8–7) of DII shows the temporary price pressure that occurred at the time of the spin-off. The subsidiary had to build a new investor base, as the Dover shareholders sold their positions. This is to be expected in any spin-off.

However, the initial pressure was quickly followed by recovery. DII sought out its own investor base and quickly launched a public stock offering to build sponsorship on Wall Street. This support was cemented by a follow-on public stock offering in November 1993 that raised $46 million and created a war chest for acquisitions. DII then went on to build the company. At the same time, its management never missed an opportunity to present their vision of industry consolidation and DII's role in it to investors and equity research analysts. DII quickly had sufficient size, growth, and management talent to attract institutional investor sponsorship and rapidly built a strong base of institutional investor support. In April 2000, DII was acquired for $3.2 billion by Flextronics International. At the time of the sale, the stock price of DII had increased over 15 times from the price at the spin-off in 1993, as compared to 3 times for the S&P 500 index for the comparable period.

The management of DII did a superb job of taking what was at the time of the spin-off a not-very-promising miscellaneous collection of contract assembly

E X H I B I T   8–7

Stock Performance of the DII Group Right After Its Spin-Off (1993)

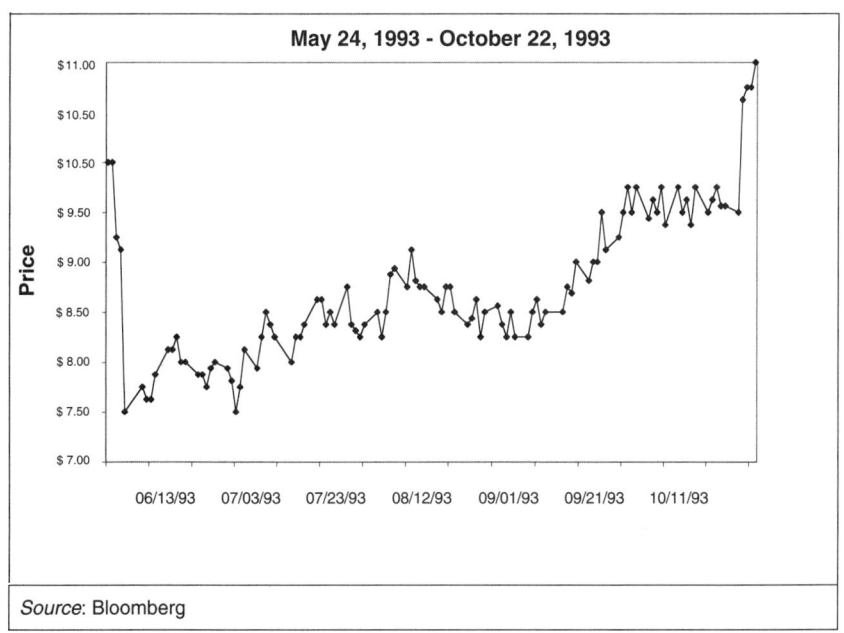

Source: Bloomberg

assets and building a major integrated outsourcing company in the following seven years. This was achieved through the superior operation of the business, a high degree of energy by the management team, efforts to recruit Wall Street support, constant communication with investors, raising cash through public offerings, and growing the business through acquisitions.

From the time of the spin-off to its acquisition by Flextronics International, DII made over 12 acquisitions in the United States and abroad and undertook two stock offerings and a convertible debt offering. Through these transactions it transformed itself from a smaller player into a worldwide leader in its industry.

By 1999, DII had coverage from research analysts at 13 investment banks. It had a vibrant liquid trading market in its stock, access to the capital markets for funds, and a stock that it could use instead of cash for acquisitions.

One key lesson from the story of DII is that hard work by the management of the subsidiary after the spin-off to cultivate investors and research analysts will speed up the recognition of its company's value by the investor community.

How aggressive the management of the subsidiary is with Wall Street depends partly on the strategy of the subsidiary. DII played in a capital-intensive, rapidly consolidating industry. Initially it was not a leader, nor did it have the best manufacturing equipment. It had to have a stock valuable enough and attractive enough to be used to make acquisitions and to raise substantial amounts of equity capital in the public markets for expansion and acquisitions. If it did not move quickly, it would fall by the wayside. A vibrant stock was not a luxury but a necessity.

After the sale to Flextronics, Carl Vertuca, the COO of DII, offered the following suggestions for a subsidiary contemplating a spin-off:

> Get at least [one] person from the outside that has been in the public company environment. I think it is critical.
>
> We were not happy with the option plan for executives and employees. However, we figured we could change it later, and we did. Two Dover executives sat on the initial board of directors; my suspicion is that it was to control our remuneration—since Dover continued to hold 60 other subsidiary companies with executives who could see our remuneration in our public filings and might get upset. However, reasonably soon after the spin-off executive compensation was heavily geared towards stock and stock options. We were highly paid at the top—partly because we had such a flat organization.
>
> Try to spin debt-free—this gives you huge leverage for future growth. We wanted to be debt free in order to grow. We argued that our shares were going to their shareholders, so why not give us a good chance to fund growth.
>
> Try not to take any contingent liabilities—or cap your exposure. We wanted a cap on any historical environmental issues. We argued that they wouldn't want it to look like Dover was spinning us out to shed their environmental issues. Our exposure was capped at $5 million.

Vertuca also had this advice for the CEO of a parent: "If you spin off a subsidiary debt free, keep 19% of the stock. This is not for control, but because they will probably reward you with better returns than your own company."[14]

Exhibit 8–8 shows the value created by the DII Group for its stockholders.

EXHIBIT 8–8

Stock Performance of the DII Group, 1993–2000

DII Group, Inc.
Daily Indexed Price Performance
May 24, 1993 - April 28, 2000

Source: Bloomberg

Example 4, Tripos: A Successful Spin-Off, but Without Early Traction in the Stock Market

In contrast to the stellar performance of the DII Group is the more conventional performance of Tripos, a developer of software for life sciences. In May 1994, Tripos was spun off from Evans & Sutherland Computer Corporation, a maker of hardware and software primarily for flight simulation. For five years, Tripos stagnated as a stock, though the business was performing well (see Exhibit 8–9). In contrast to DII, Tripos was a non-capital-intensive software company, did not need outside capital to grow, and was not interested in large acquisitions. A vibrant stock soon after the spin-off was a luxury, but not a necessity.

In 2001 the stock of Tripos performed much better. The reason, according to Jim Kloppenburg, portfolio manager of the Needham Aggressive Growth Fund and a Tripos supporter, was the addition of a new CFO, who brought financial and business discipline to what had been a classic "engineering playpen" that was run more for the intellectual stimulation of its engineers than to make money for investors. The new CFO also focused the company on commercial success. Good products were finally shipped to customers on a timely basis. The stock responded to the increased upside potential in Tripos's earnings resulting from these changes. However, in the first quarter of 2002 the stock suffered from its associa-

EXHIBIT 8–9

Stock Price Chart of Tripos Following the Spin-Off in 1994

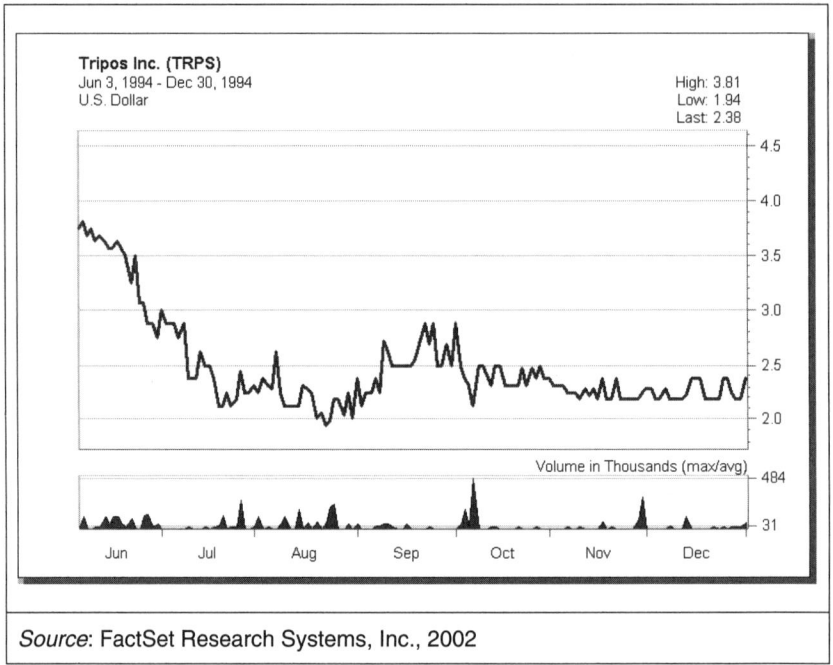

Tripos Inc. (TRPS)
Jun 3, 1994 - Dec 30, 1994   High: 3.81
U.S. Dollar   Low: 1.94
                                     Last: 2.38

Source: FactSet Research Systems, Inc., 2002

tion with the poor performance of other biotech tools companies and an overall decline in the stock prices of the biotech group.

Tripos still has only moderate sponsorship on Wall Street; only three research analysts covered it at year-end 2001.

The spin-off of Tripos was a success in the end, but not the stunning success experienced by the DII Group, as shown in Exhibit 8–10. This demonstrates that real value will win out in the end and that efforts by the subsidiary after the spin-off will accelerate the recognition of those values. This will permit the subsidiary to access the public equity markets and make acquisitions with newly raised cash or by using its fully valued stock to grow faster.

Example 5, C-Cube Semiconductor: A Successful Taxable Spin-Off

In October 1999, C-Cube Microsystems, a California-based industry leader in the development of digital video and systems solutions, agreed to sell its DiviCom business to Harmonic, a manufacturer of fiber-optic solutions for cable television companies. The selling price was approximately $1.9 billion in an all-stock transaction.

EXHIBIT 8–10

Tripos Stock Price, 1999–2002

Source: FactSet Research Systems, Inc., 2002

C-Cube Microsystems had two distinct businesses: DiviCom, the leading developer of digital video solutions, and C-Cube Semiconductor, a leading designer of semiconductors for CD and DVD players in the consumer electronics markets.

Harmonic did not want to own the C-Cube Semiconductor operation. C-Cube determined that the most tax-efficient structure for selling just the DiviCom operation to Harmonic was to sell the entire company to Harmonics in a tax-free stock transaction and simultaneously spin off the C-Cube Semiconductor operation to the shareholders of C-Cube in a spin-off that was taxable to C-Cube but not to its shareholders. The tax liability arose because there was a change of control under 355(e).

In May 2000, C-Cube Semiconductor simultaneously spun off from C-Cube Microsystems, and Harmonic completed its acquisition of DiviCom. After the close, C-Cube Semiconductor took the original company name of C-Cube Microsystems.

C-Cube incurred a substantial tax penalty for the spin-off.. The tax liability was calculated as the difference between the fair market value of the shares of C-Cube Semiconductor stock distributed to the shareholders and the tax basis of its assets. It came to approximately $203 million, based on an assumed valuation of its semiconductor business of $975 million.

The board of C-Cube correctly believed that the overall benefit to the parent's shareholders was higher using this approach than through a taxable sale of the DiviCom operation and a fire sale of the C-Cube operation to a cash buyer. C-Cube had $303 million in cash and short-term investments as of March 31, 2000, that it used to settle this tax liability.

In May 2001, the spun-off company, C-Cube Microsystems, was purchased by LSI Logic Corporation for $850 million, justifying the approach taken by the board, as demonstrated by its stock price appreciation, shown in Exhibit 8–11.

E X H I B I T   8–11

C-Cube's Stock Price

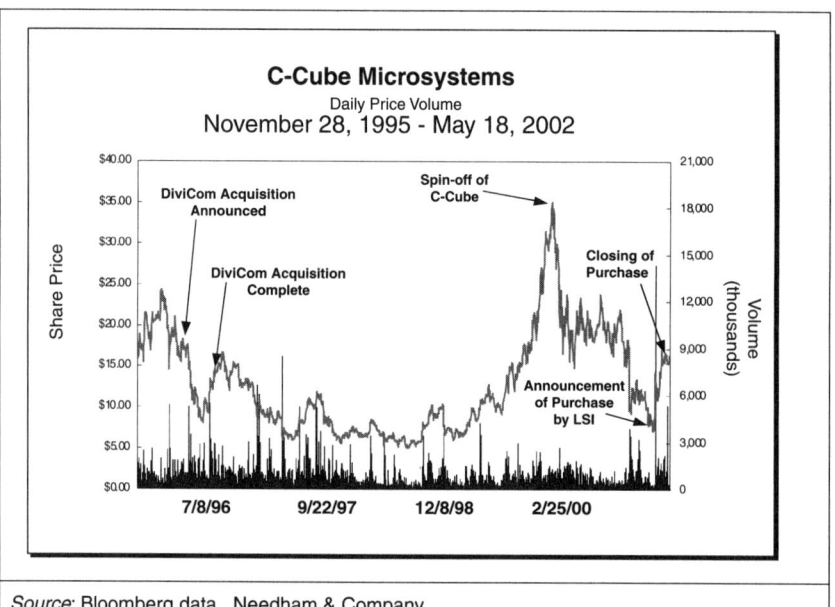

Source: Bloomberg data, Needham & Company

CHAPTER **9**

TWO-STEP SPIN-OFFS

INTRODUCTION

The previous chapter discussed tax-free and taxable spin-offs. This chapter examines two-step spin-offs, which have become a common means of transacting a spin-off. Two-step spin-offs can be very successful if handled properly.

DEFINITION OF A TWO-STEP SPIN-OFF

The first step in a two-step spin-off is a conventional minority carve-out initial public offering of shares in the subsidiary. These shares are sold either by the subsidiary or by the parent to public investors. The second step is a conventional spin-off of the remaining shares of the subsidiary held by the parent to the parent's shareholders.

A two-step spin-off uses only the publicly traded equity of the subsidiary. After the first-step IPO, the subsidiary becomes a public company. After the second step of the spin-off, the parent and subsidiary become stand-alone entities. In most cases, the parent tries to construct the second step as a tax-free spin-off.

Exhibit 9–1 presents a graphical representation of the two steps in a two-step spin-off.

TWO-STEP SPIN-OFFS AND TAX CONSOLIDATION

As mentioned previously, the parent usually tries to construct the second-step as a tax-free transaction. This requires that the parent control the subsidiary at the time of the spin-off. The provisions governing tax-free spin-offs were described in Chapter 6. As discussed, control generally requires that the parent own 80 percent

E X H I B I T   9–1

Two-Step Spin-Off

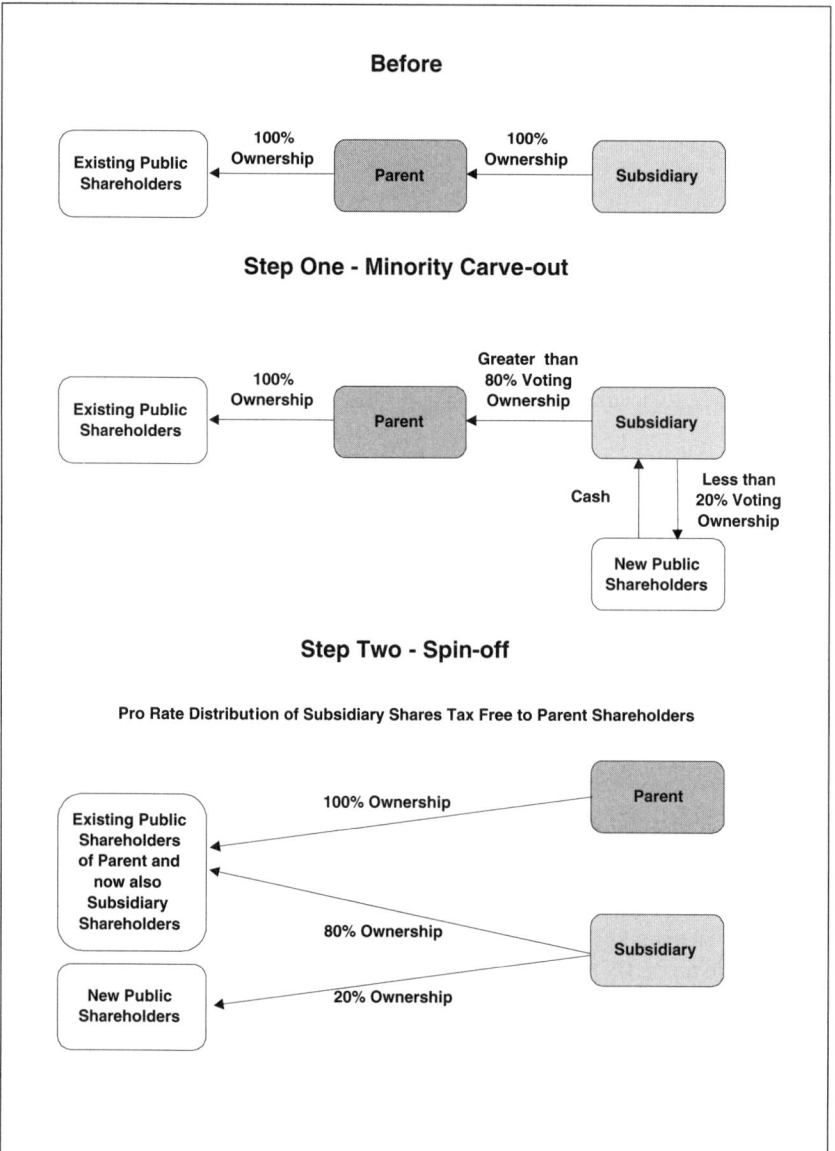

of the subsidiary's voting stock after the first-step IPO. The parent then may dispose of its remaining interest in the subsidiary in a second-step tax-free distribution to its shareholders.

On occasion, complex structures are employed to allow the parent to sell more than 20 percent of the subsidiary after the first-step IPO but still retain control. However, all of these structures create a number of issues and are rarely used in practice. Parents do often consider issuing two classes of stock, which will be discussed later in the chapter.

SELECTION OF A ONE-STEP OR TWO-STEP SPIN-OFF

When planning for a spin-off, the question often arises about the relative merits of a two-step spin-off with a first-step IPO versus a simple one-step spin-off without bothering about the first-step IPO. Each approach has merits and disadvantages.

The choice of approach—one-step or two-step—depends partly on the parent's objectives and the characteristics of the subsidiary. The questions the parent should initially ask include the following:

• *Does the parent or the subsidiary need cash?* A two-step spin-off raises cash in the IPO phase. A spin-off by itself does not raise cash.

• *How important is it to establish a formal separation quickly and with assurance?* A one-step spin-off is faster, and the outcome is more certain.

• *How important is the publicity and "bang" of a marketed IPO?* Only a two-step spin-off offers the marketing and promotion of an IPO.

• *Are the restrictions (discussed later) needed to maintain eligibility for a second-step tax-free spin-off acceptable to the parent?* If not, the choice of a one-step spin-off is easy.

• *Does the subsidiary fit the profile for a quality IPO? Is the current IPO market receptive to its industry and characteristics?* If not, a first-step IPO is not an available option.

• *Does the parent or subsidiary not want to go through the expensive and time-draining IPO process?* If so, a one-step spin-off may be best.

The depressed IPO and public market valuation environment of 2002 has led to increased interest in one-step spin-offs. For the past few years, a first-step carve-out IPO was often not an available option for many subsidiaries and even when an IPO is available, valuations in the public markets are such that an IPO large enough to attract institutional investors may exceed the 20 percent limitation for a second-step tax-free spin-off and also may give too much of the subsidiary away to suit the parent. A one-step spin-off still allows a tax-free SER to be successfully executed even in a depressed IPO and valuation environment.

As an example, in 2000 Adaptec, Inc., had a subsidiary, Roxio, that developed consumer software. Roxio filed for a conventional carve-out IPO in September 2000 with the announced intent to follow the IPO with a tax-free spin-off.

However, the valuation of Roxio came down after the IPO filing, and Adaptec found that it could no longer execute a quality first-step carve-out IPO large enough to appeal to institutional investors and still have a later tax-free spin-off. As a consequence, Adaptec withdrew the IPO filing and instead distributed its holdings in Roxio in a one-step tax-free spin-off in May 2001.[1]

ADVANTAGES OF TWO-STEP SPIN-OFFS

A two-step spin-off is often used as an alternative to the standard spin-off described in the Chapter 8. The first-step IPO adds expense, risk, delay, and complication over just going directly to a spin-off. However, there are a number of reasons why the parent often prefers a two-step IPO followed by a spin-off, as opposed to a simple one-step spin-off. These reasons are as follows:

• *An IPO establishes a public market.* The principal reason for the first-step IPO of a two-step spin-off is that it establishes a public market for the subsidiary's stock in advance of the larger spin-off. The public market sets the price, the security is traded, and investors have the opportunity to become familiar with the subsidiary. Subsidiary management also has the opportunity to tell its story to public stock investors and build demand for the stock that will be sold by the parent shareholders after a spin-off.

• *An IPO ensures investment bank research coverage and aftermarket support.* The investment banks underwriting the first-step IPO market the stock of the subsidiary. Through the IPO, they develop an independent investor base for the subsidiary. After the IPO, they will support the stock of the subsidiary in the aftermarket with research and trading. In contrast, as discussed before, there is often little research coverage or support by investment banks with a simple one-step spin-off, because a one-step spin-off does not generate the large investment banking fees of an IPO.

• *An IPO subjects the subsidiary to critical scrutiny.* With an IPO, the subsidiary will be subject to the intense scrutiny of investment bankers, lawyers, and investors. This usually will make it a stronger public company. There is no such outside scrutiny or quality control with a one-step spin-off.

• *An IPO raises cash.* Spin-offs do not generate additional cash. If the parent or subsidiary needs cash, the first-step IPO is one way to raise these funds.

• *An IPO creates an event.* The parent and subsidiary may want a first-step IPO to create a well-publicized event that will get considerable attention within the industry and in the press. It also is a single event on which employees may focus. A spin-off on its own will provide much less bang.

DISADVANTAGES OF TWO-STEP SPIN-OFFS

The primary disadvantages of the two-step approach include the following:

• *An IPO creates risk.* An IPO is dependent on a good IPO market and will be held up by poor market conditions. A protracted delay in executing the first-step

IPO may create morale, financial and strategic problems for the parent and the subsidiary.

- *An IPO is time consuming.* The IPO process is lengthy and involved. It takes management time and attention away from the subsidiary's business and often takes the parent's management away from the parent's business. This distraction may even put the subsidiary at risk of stumbling, with the senior management team not engaged day to day in the business during the IPO process. A single-step spin-off may be much less time consuming, depending on how extensive a stock-marketing effort the parent and subsidiary undertake.

- *The company must put the pieces in place.* In order to create a successful two-step spin-off, a company must first meet the profile for a quality IPO. This is discussed in detail in Chapter 18. This may take quite a bit of time, or it may not be feasible.

- *The parent must have control of the subsidiary.* For a spin-off to be tax free, the parent must have control of the subsidiary immediately before the distribution of the subsidiary's stock to the parent's shareholders. In addition, change of ownership tests will limit extensive stock sales and mergers after the spin-off for a limited period; see the discussion of IRC 355(e) and 368(c) in Chapter 8.

- *The float may be too small for a quality IPO.* The number of shares available for public investors to purchase is called the float. Stocks with small floats are generally less attractive to institutional investors because they are not as liquid, meaning it is hard to buy or sell a significant position.

  As such, there is an important factor inherent to a two-step spin-off that contributes to a smaller float. Specifically, in order to maintain control by the parent of the subsidiary following the carve-out IPO, the parent must continue to own 80 percent of the subsidiary. Control is required if the subsequent spin-off is to be treated as tax free by the IRS. This leaves only 20 percent of the stock available for public and other pre-spin-off investors.

  The number of shares available for the IPO will be reduced further if the subsidiary raises private capital before the carve-out from private equity investors, or intends to bring in private equity investors after the carve-out IPO but before the spin-off. The reason for this is that these shares will count against the 20 percent total. While there are techniques used to avoid this limit, such as issuing parent debt that is exchangeable into the equity of the subsidiary only after the spin-off to strategic or equity investors or two classes of stock, these are complex and often are not acceptable to the parent or to the partner.

- *The market may prevent the subsequent second-step spin-off.* Much may go wrong after the carve-out IPO that prevents the second-step spin-off of the remaining shares. The market may deteriorate, the industry sector may go out of fashion, or the subsidiary may crash and burn. A depressed stock price at the time of the spin-off may prevent the parent from undertaking the spin-off. This occurred in several cases with subsidiaries that completed first-stage carve-outs in the buoyant stock market of 1999–2000, but were unable to complete the second-stage spin-off. The impact on the subsidiary in these cases was disruptive and depressing, with a broken stock price, a low market capitalization, and low-liquidity public stock that was unable to attract sponsorship or investor interest. The parents ended up with an unwanted public subsidiary. In several instances, the parent had to buy back the first-stage public stock. For example, UtiliCorp United Inc. spun out a 20 percent equity stake of its subsidiary Aquila Inc. in 2001. At the time, UtiliCorp intended to spin off the remainder of Aquila. However, the stock declined, and the spin-off never occurred. In late 2001, UtiliCorp bought back the public shareholding in Aquila. In another example, Phoenix Technologies carved out 20 percent of inSilicon in 1999. The stock of the subsidiary did not perform well after the market decline of 2000, and a second-step spin-off was not viable. inSilicon became an orphan stock with little liquidity or investor interest.

- *The first-step IPO is expensive.* The costs and fees involved in an IPO are discussed in Chapter 18. These are substantial.

- *A two-step spin-off doesn't guarantee Wall Street support after the IPO.* The investment banking industry is in turmoil, and many quality companies are not receiving the post-IPO attention they were promised from their investment banks. (See the following example of Palm.) This will be compounded if the subsidiary's industry goes out of favor or the subsidiary stumbles in its performance.

TWO CLASSES OF STOCK

One solution to the 80 percent control requirement that is often studied by parents in evaluating a two-step spin-off is to use two classes of common stock, one with a large number of votes per share that is retained by the parent and one with fewer votes per share that is sold to the public in an IPO, or before or after the IPO to corporate or private equity investors. Although this may seem like a viable option, it is usually not employed due to a number of inherent challenges, including the following:

- It will usually reduce investor interest in the private investment and in the IPO, and, in some cases, it will create outright distaste, as many investors prefer a simple capital structure and do not like to have an inferior class of stock. With the emphasis investors place today on transparency and responsible governance, the use of two classes of stock will be subject to special scrutiny.

- The lower-vote stock may trade at some discount to the higher-vote stock, resulting in some economic loss to the parent. Studies consistently indicate a discount of up to 10 percent imposed on the value of lower-vote stock.

- Such arrangements are hard to reverse at a future date due to an IRS requirement that prohibits the implementation of a two-class structure with the intent of reversing it later. The parent will need to file a statement that it has no intention of changing the structure at a later time. In order to later exchange the high-vote shares for ordinary shares, there would have to be a material event sufficient to cause the parent to determine that two classes would no longer be appropriate. Such events may include an unforeseen merger of the subsidiary or a requirement for raising capital in which new investors would not participate with two classes of stock outstanding.

• Investor attitudes toward two classes of stock are not enhanced by the questionable governance practices of many companies that have issued two classes of stock in the past. That control has too often been used for the benefit of the control shareholder or to protect poor management performance over an extended period. Adelphia Communications is only one of numerous recent examples.

CONCLUSIONS

Overall, the advantages of a two-step spin-off outweigh the negatives if the subsidiary fits (or can be strengthened to fit) a quality IPO profile, and there is a good IPO market overall and for its industry. In most cases, a subsidiary that is spun off when there has been no prior carve-out IPO will, at least initially, struggle to obtain research coverage and sponsorship.

The reasons for a two-step spin-off are less compelling if the spin-off will attract attention anyway because of its size or interest, or if the parent allows the subsidiary to build its value over time.

SUMMARY

As this chapter describes, two-step spin-offs can be used to meet key parent criteria to ensure SER success such as creating a public market for the subsidiary's stock—and ensuring aftermarket support for the stock and raising capital for the parent or the subsidiary. The next chapter examines tracking stocks as a viable SER option.

Example of a Two-Step Minority Carve-Out IPO Followed by a Spin-Off: Palm, Inc.

The purpose of this example is to illustrate a well-conceived two-step spin-off in which the parent, 3Com, made the right decision to spin off a subsidiary, Palm. The SER of Palm was well conceived and well timed under the guidance of the chairman of 3Com, Eric Benhamou. This SER generated great value for the parent, which received a substantial amount of cash from the first-stage carve-out IPO of the subsidiary in March 2000, and for the parent's shareholders who received substantial value in the distribution of Palm shares in July 2000. However, while 3Com and Palm did a fine job in creating shareholder value, its IPO managers did a questionable job of executing the IPO for the benefit of 3Com's shareholders. And they certainly did a worse job of providing aftermarket support following the IPO, despite being paid huge fees.

Background on the Transaction
Santa Clara–based Palm, a networking equipment company, dominated the market for handheld computing devices. Palm was a subsidiary of 3Com. The parent

EXHIBIT 9–2

Operating Performance of Palm, Inc.

Fiscal year ended June	1997	1998	1999	2000
(dollars in millions)				
Revenues	$114	$272	$563	$1,057
Operating income	(13)	6	50	63
Net income	(7)	4	31	48

acquired Palm in 1997, when it merged with U.S. Robotics. Palm was founded in 1992 by Donna Dubinsky and Jeff Hawkins. Palm was bought by U.S. Robotics in 1995 when it was unable to raise capital from private equity investors. The sales of Palm's simple and inexpensive computing devices took off in the late 1990s.[2]

In 1999, Palm's sales totaled $570 million and accounted for about 68 percent of the worldwide handheld computer market at the time. Exhibit 9–2 shows Palm's explosive revenue growth.

Step 1: The Palm IPO
In March 2000, 3Com sold 23 million shares of Palm's common stock in an IPO, representing 4.1 percent of the Palm's total outstanding stock. Ninety-four percent of shares remained in the hands of 3Com. The IPO raised $874 million, with all the proceeds going to 3Com.

Step 2: The Spin-Off of Palm to 3Com's Shareholders
In July 2000, after a ruling by the IRS confirming the tax-free status of the spin-off, 3Com distributed its remaining holding of 532 million shares of Palm to the 3Com shareholders. Exhibit 9–3 details the two transactions.

Eric Benhamou, chairman of both Palm and the parent, 3Com, has these comments on the spin-off:

EXHIBIT 9–3

The Two-Step Palm Spin-Off

Transaction	3Com ownership prior to offering	Date of transaction	Security issued	Proceeds to 3Com	3Com ownership after the transaction
Palm's IPO	100%	3/2/00	Common stock	$874 mm	94%
Remainder of 3Com's holding in Palm spun off to 3Com's shareholders	94%	7/27/00	Common stock	None	0%

From the time we acquired U.S. Robotics (and its subsidiary, Palm), we knew that Palm was a distinct business from the networking business of 3Com. Also, in terms of synergies, there were very few, and they were less technology related and more centered around consumer branding and retail selling. While we recognized that at some point in the future all Palm devices would have access to networks, creating opportunities for 3Com, there was nothing we could not do as separate companies from the perspective of connecting Palm devices to a network. As a result, from the very start, we regarded a spin-off of Palm as a very serious possibility. To keep this option open, unlike all the other U.S. Robotics divisions that came with the merger and were quickly tightly integrated into 3Com, Palm was actually managed as an autonomous stand-alone business unit. Also, Palm was allowed to operate on a basically break-even model, and was not required to conform to the 3Com financial model that demanded operating margins of 15 percent from all major business units.

Even before the U.S. Robotics merger with 3Com had closed, the founders of Palm were demanding to be spun off. So, I knew that from the start I was dealing with entrepreneurs who relished their independence. However, for a while we felt that it was desirable to keep Palm inside 3Com for these reasons:

First, we wanted the 3Com organization to learn about the consumer markets, about the retail channels, about what it takes to create a consumer oriented organization and a consumer marketing organization. I looked to Palm to teach 3Com about the consumer markets for networks. At the time, I was also hoping that there would be a rapid broadband deployment that would open up a market for 3Com for home networking devices. Of course, the broadband build-outs never really happened—certainly nowhere close to the scale that at the time I was hoping. Therefore, the market for home networks never really became a big market in the '90s. It will eventually, but it will be a much slower process than I imagined then. I thought that by the end of 2000, there would be a need for 3Com to have its own home-networking consumer units.

Second, there was a feeling that there was a new industry segment in the making, and Palm could emerge as a leader within that segment. So this was viewed as a shareholder value creation opportunity. I first wanted Palm to build up its brand, build up its reseller organization and the Palm industry segment to get more recognition so as to maximize 3Com shareholder return. Palm benefited in the following period from significant investments by 3Com that allowed it to grow its product line, build up momentum, build up visibility, and build up its brand. You just have to show that the subsidiary you're spinning off has strong business fundamentals.

Third, I didn't think that Palm was ready to run on its own. The founders were creative entrepreneurs, but I didn't think they had the management team nor the maturity needed to run a potentially large business.

Fourth, I had a difference with the founders over the direction of Palm. They wanted to build a device company, and I felt that a device company could never amount to a significant business by itself. I believed (and still do) the core value of Palm was the operating system. From the start, I asked the management of Palm to consider licensing the operating system and to treat it as a separate business within Palm. The founders opposed licensing the Palm software to others, believing that it was much better to keep the operating system inside Palm and optimize it for the Palm device only. The example of Apple clearly indicated to me that this device would fail. Microsoft was now challenging Palm with its own PDA software. Apple developed the superior Macintosh operating system in the late 1980s but resisted licensing it to others. In the meantime, rival Microsoft licensed its Windows operating system widely and became the industry standard.

Fifth, for a successful spin-off, the parent needs to make a clear-cut case to investors that the sum of the parts is greater than the whole and that the parent is creating shareholder value and better focus. We were not yet ready to do this as the PDA market had not yet emerged for investors.

After one year (following the 3Com–U.S. Robotics merger), the founders decided to leave the company. They asked for a license for the operating system—I had no problem granting the license. I felt they would be a great test case. So, they built Handspring on a Palm OS license. We gave Handspring a very favorable license as they were the first licensee.

We took another look at a spin-off in the late spring of 1999, and at the time Palm was already a $200-million-plus revenue operation, had the critical mass required to go public, and had successfully licensed the operating system software to other hardware makers. This reality combined with the fact that the potential of the PDA market was now recognized by investors and therefore the pure-play aspect of Palm would be highly valued by the investment community. 3Com did an exhaustive survey of all the possible ways of doing the spin-off. We looked hard at a one-step spin-off. However, a two-step spin-off involved an IPO, which we viewed as a branding event. Because Palm sells to consumers, brand matters. We did sell equity before taking the IPO to a few strategic investors like Nokia, Motorola, and AOL. This proved to be the right thing to do. The choice of a two-step spin-off was clearly the right thing to do at the time. Securing strategic investors prior to the IPO was also the right thing to do. We went through a relatively fast process. One of the problems we faced was that we had to figure how much cash we should raise. We didn't want to raise too much, because there was a limit to what we could raise on a tax-free basis, Besides, neither Palm nor 3Com needed a whole lot of cash. As a result, we raised only as much cash on the IPO as we could bring back into the parent company on a tax-free basis plus a comfortable level for Palm to run itself. This led to a relatively small percent of Palm being offered in the IPO.

During the IPO process, momentum for Palm built up among investors. Our investment bankers had advised us to start with a low price, then progressively move up and create a momentum effect. We had a very intense road show—the order books filled up to an incredible level—we were oversubscribed. A problem was that we could then only increase the price by 20 percent without having to refile an amended prospectus, and this would have delayed the pricing. This is how we ended up pricing the IPO at $38. Of course, the first day, it ran up over two and half times.

Today's environment is totally different from the time of the Palm spin-off. Today there would no froth, no hype—it would be very sober. Today is probably a better environment for a spin-off. Palm went public at the peak of a bubble. As a result, its early culture was spoilt and its values somewhat distorted. Later on, the bubble burst. Palm had to go through a sobering-up process. Today, Palm is a far better company than it was at the time of the IPO, even though it was worth 20 times more than today.

Benhamou has the following comments on the frictions between the parent and the subsidiary during the spin-off preparation process:

> There were minor frictions having to do with the fact that Palm was perceived at the time as a hot business within 3Com. Back when we were building the management team and preparing it to make Palm an independent company, there were key positions that opened up. A race opened to compete for these positions. Some of the people who didn't get them became resentful and thought that the selection was unfair and perhaps politicized.

As well, all of a sudden two people who had been close colleagues found themselves split between the two different companies. They would start arguing over issues related to the spin-off, and you realized then that circumstances create conflicts. This is where the CEO of the parent retains the best objectivity on maximizing the total shareholder value of the parent and the subsidiary. The CEO must serve as the tiebreaker and arbitrate these situations. So, I was called upon to do this several times.

Benhamou has the following advice for a CEO contemplating an SER:

There were a few things that worked out well for us more because of the circumstances than because we were particularly brilliant. However, we learned many things that could turn into useful advice for others. First, appoint an internal sponsor. Take a senior employee who has been with the parent a while and understands a lot of the innards of the company's organization, personalities, and processes, and have this person run the spin-off program full time and oversee all of the steps of the separation process. If you try to do a spin-off with part-time executives who also have day jobs, it does not work; many things will fall through the cracks. What we did at the time was leverage Judy Bruner [3Com's corporate controller and later Palm's CFO] to work on the spin-off on a full-time basis along with program management staff. And we did not hesitate to use outside help and consultants. Having a senior person oversee the program was very helpful.

Second, have a strong management team in place at the subsidiary prior to the spin-off. The primary thing that we did not do as well as we could have with Palm was to have a strong and complete enough management team at Palm at the time of the IPO. It wasn't a conscious choice; it was tough to recruit at that time—it was the height of the Internet bubble—so searches took longer and offers were easily turned down. But, in retrospect, we probably should have moved a few more senior 3Com people over to Palm, as these transfers would have created a more mature management team from the start.

Third, unless there are substantial reasons to deviate, clone the parent's basic administrative structure and replicate it at the subsidiary. There is no need to reinvent the wheel for things that are clearly not strategic, like the way the books are closed or the way performance reviews are administered. The subsidiary management may try to make a case for a completely different structure to be independent. The parent has to say, "You shouldn't change this to be different from the parent; you should only change this if it helps you to be the best in the market."

Fourth, do not forget to highlight the parent along the way, as it gets recast across a narrower scope. It turned out that Palm was such a visible company—a visible brand—that it cast a shadow on 3Com during the IPO and spin-off process. We should have pushed 3Com harder, even though it was more fun to talk about Palm.

Philippe Morali, vice president of corporate development at Palm, adds this comment: "An SER is not about a transaction but creating a new solid and successful public company with long-term prospects."

A Wild-Ride Transaction

Exhibit 9–4 shows Palm's price performance after the IPO and through the spin-off.

Palm was not well served by its IPO managers in the execution of the IPO and afterward. On the first day, Palm's stock went from its IPO price of $38 to

E X H I B I T   9–4

Palm's Stock Price

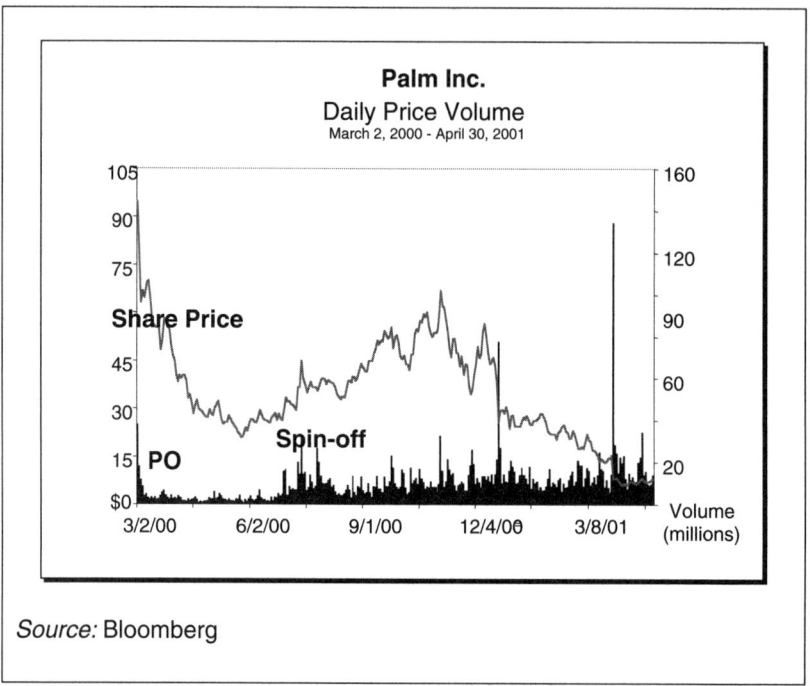

Palm Inc.
Daily Price Volume
March 2, 2000 - April 30, 2001

Source: Bloomberg

close at $95 per share. Palm's stock price then dropped in the three months following the IPO to $20.81 per share—and eventually went as low as $1.22 in June 2001. Obviously, hindsight is always perfect, and the conditions of the bubble market in early 2000 were astonishing.[3] However, to better manage the price swings, the IPO managers might have started the IPO process at a fair price. It was well known in advance that Palm would be a hot stock. Perhaps nothing would have worked in that environment, but it does appear that this approach would probably have dampened demand. Also, 3Com's shareholders and not the favored IPO investors would have reaped more of the value.

The principal beneficiaries (at least in total dollars) of the Palm IPO were not 3Com or Palm but the favored investors chosen to receive shares by the primary managers of the IPO, many of whom then sold their shares for huge gains right after the offering. These included fast-turning hedge funds that paid large commissions and corporate executives and venture capitalists being courted for their next investment banking deals. Over 58 million shares changed hands in the market in the two days following the IPO, compared with the total of 23 million shares sold in the IPO itself.

Palm paid $45,885,000 in underwriting fees alone to the investment banks for this butchered IPO. The IPO had two primary managers, Goldman Sachs and

Morgan Stanley, who received the majority of that fee. By the end of 2001, one of these had dropped research coverage of Palm completely, and the other was on the third research analyst assigned to cover Palm in two years, the first two having left the firm in the interim. For the amount of fees Palm paid, it should have expected better.

Subsequent Events

In 2002, Palm decided to split itself in two, separating its hardware and operating system software operations, by spinning off the software operation, PalmSource. This was intended to facilitate the licensing of the software. Eric Benhamou and the head of PalmSource, David Nagel, believed that Palm had to propagate its operating software as widely and quickly as possible to obtain support from third-party software vendors. This supoort was needed to compete with Microsoft. Hardware and software are very different businesses. Palm wants to propagate its operating software as widely as possible to ensure support by third-party software vendors and to compete with Microsoft. It felt that PalmSource, on its own, would be more focused and more able to attract other customers to use its software. While Palm at first considered an initial carve-out IPO for PalmSource, it reconsidered this approach in light of the weak IPO market in mid-2002 and instead decided to raise the capital that would be needed by PalmSource after the spin-off through a private placement of stock to corporate investors, including licensee Sony.[4]

CHAPTER 10

TRACKING STOCKS

INTRODUCTION

Tracking stock is a unique SER option that can create many benefits for both the parent and the subsidiary. Perhaps its appeal is best measured by its ability to create value for both the parent and its shareholders without the corresponding need to change complex organizational structures relating to tax, legal, and governance issues. This chapter will examine the unique features of this SER alternative while also examining its inherent disadvantages. Tracking stocks are certainly the most controversial SER, and the reasons for this will be discussed in this chapter as well. Exhibit 10–1 summarizes recent tracking stock IPO activity.

DEFINITION OF A TRACKING STOCK

Tracking stock, also known as *letter stock* or *alphabet stock,* is a class of parent common stock that provides a return to investors linked to the performance of a particular business unit, or groups of units, within the parent.

E X H I B I T   10–1

Domestic Tracking Stock IPOs

	1998	1999	2000	2001	Q1 2002
Number of domestic tracking stock IPOs	0	7	4	2	1
Amount of proceeds (billions)	$0.0	$2.6	$10.4	$2.0	$1.1
Percent of all domestic IPO Proceeds	0%	4%	19%	6%	12%
Source: Dealogic					

E X H I B I T   10–2

Tracking Stock IPO

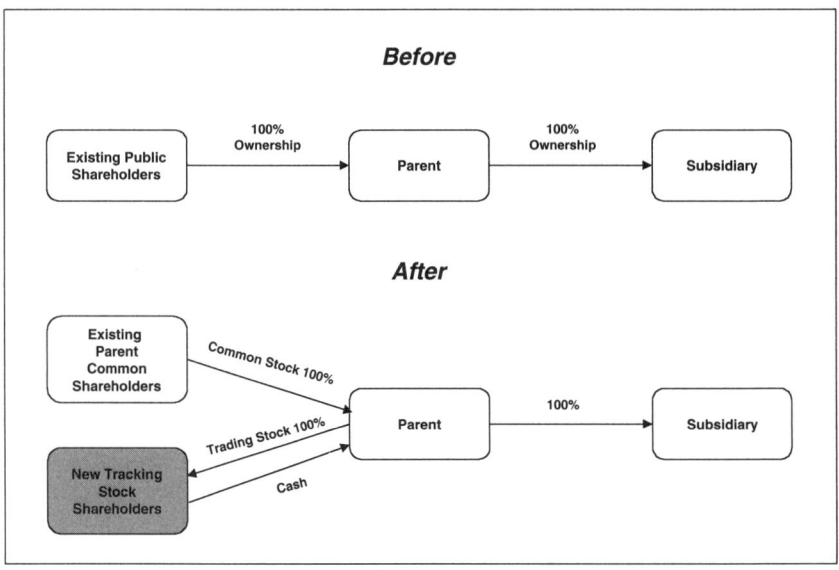

Tracking stock may be sold to investors in an IPO, as was the case with the Loews Corporation in 2002. In that transaction, Loews, a diversified holding company, sold in an IPO $960 million of Loews CG stock that tracked The Carolina Group, its tobacco business. When a tracking stock IPO is successful it can raise capital to further create shareholder value through acquisitions and follow-on public offerings. Exhibit 10–2 illustrates a tracking stock IPO.

A tracking stock may also be distributed to parent shareholders in a tax-free dividend or exchange, similar to a spin-off, as was the case of Quantum HDD discussed later in this chapter. Exhibit 10–3 illustrates a spin-off issue of a tracking stock.

THE APPEAL OF TRACKING STOCKS TO PARENTS

Parents will more than likely consider tracking stocks while they assess other options such as a carve-out and a spin-off. The principal appeal to the parent of a tracking stock over these other SERs is that a tracking stock is another class of parent common stock. Therefore, it does not require that the parent make the tax, legal, governance, and organizational changes required for a carve-out or a spin-off, in which the subsidiary becomes a separate public company with its own board of directors and issues its own stock. A tracking stock also does not affect parent loan agreements, leases, licenses, and contacts.

We will take an in-depth look at the specific advantages of tracking stocks later in this chapter.

E X H I B I T   10–3

Tracking Stock Spin-Off

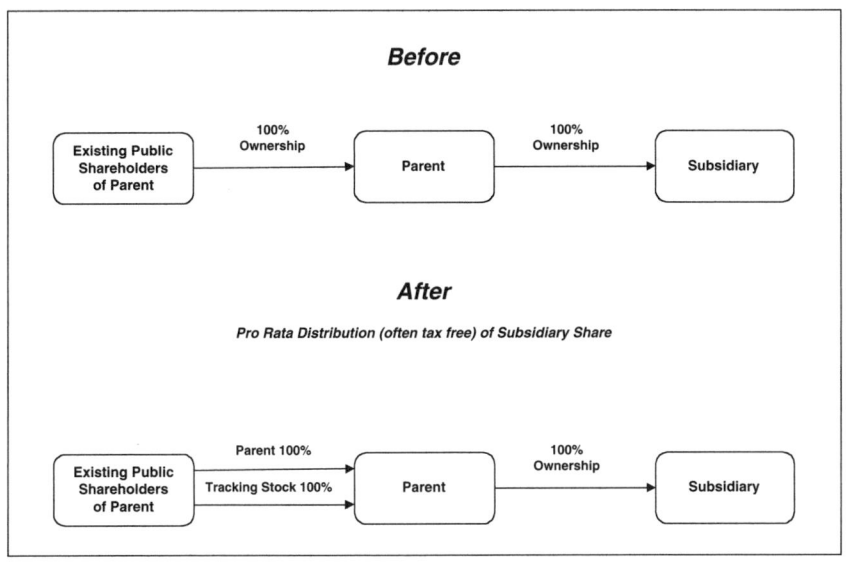

HISTORICAL BACKGROUND

Tracking stocks were first introduced in 1984 by General Motors Corporation to track the performance of its Electronic Data Systems (EDS) division. This tracking stock was known as "E" common stock. The GM "E" stock met the specific needs of the largest shareholder of EDS, its founder Ross Perot. GM offered each EDS shareholder two payment alternatives. The first alternative was cash only. The second alternative was a combination of cash, GM class "E" shares, and a note. The ownership of GM class "E" stock allowed Mr. Perot, and other stockholders of EDS if they wished, to continue to participate in the upside potential of EDS after its sale to GM. It also permitted EDS's management team to receive equity incentives after the acquisition that were tied to EDS's performance rather than to that of GM overall. Concurrently, it also enabled GM to obtain complete control and consolidation of EDS.

GM used tracking stock again in 1985 to facilitate its acquisition of Hughes Aircraft Company (later named Hughes Electronics) from the Howard Hughes Medical Institute. The Institute wanted to divest its ownership of Hughes and put Hughes up for auction. GM was competing with other bidders to buy Hughes. A stumbling block for the bidders was that the institute believed in the future potential value of Hughes and wanted to continue to participate in the value growth of Hughes after the sale. To meet this need and secure the transaction, GM created a new class of GM common stock, GM class "H" common stock that tracked the performance of Hughes Aircraft after the acquisition. GM issued this tracking

EXHIBIT 10–4

Stock Price Comparison 1985–1995, GM and GM-H

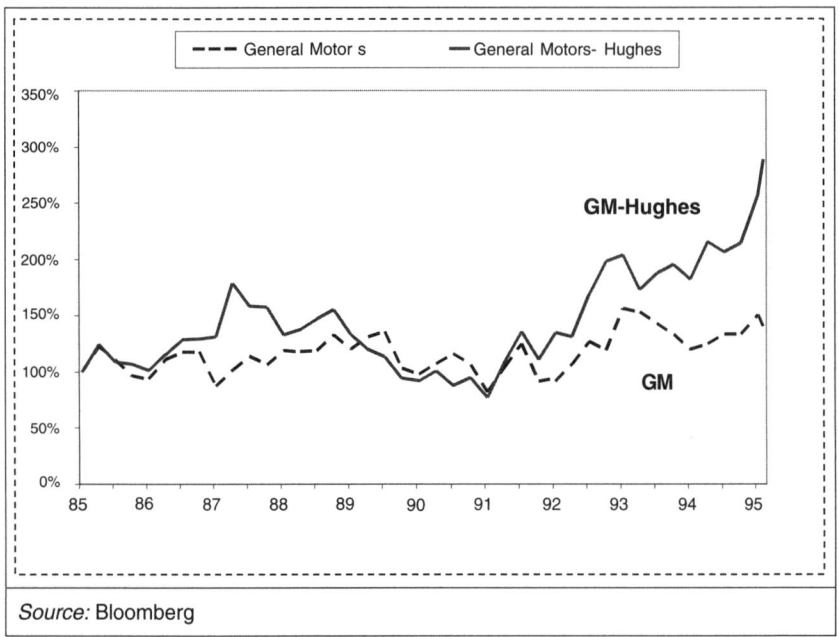

Source: Bloomberg

stock to the institute as part of the purchase price for Hughes. The tracking stock enabled the institute to continue to participate in increases in the value of Hughes. This decision by the institute proved prescient, as the value of Hughes surpassed that of GM over the following years.

Exhibit 10–4 is a comparison of GM and GM-H stock price from 1985 to 1995, indexed to 100.

The next company to adopt a tracking stock did not do so until 1991, when USX Corporation separated its energy operations from its steel business. Tracking stocks remained relatively rare until the late 1990s, when tracking stocks were used as a means of redeployment in a wide range of industries, from retailing to biotechnology. Subsequently, tracking stock has been used by a number of established U.S. companies in a variety of different roles. Some were exceptionally successful over a reasonable period, such as Celera Genomics and Sprint Corp. PCS Group, and others less so, such as Continental Baking.

The first technology company to use a tracking stock was Genzyme Corporation in 1994. The tracking stock was issued to facilitate Genzyme's acquisition of BioSurface Technology, Inc. Genzyme combined BioSurface with its own related internal programs to form a new Tissue Repair Division and issued a tracking stock for that operation. Genzyme issued shares of the Tissue Repair Division tracking stock representing a 50 percent equity interest in the combined operation to BioSurface's former stockholders and distributed shares representing 33 percent of the equity interest to Genzyme's then existing stockholders.

Genzyme went on to issue three more tracking stocks for each of its divisions—for a total of four. The other three were Genzyme General (a profitable developer of drugs for rare genetic diseases), Genzyme Biosurgery (a loss-making producer of products for use in surgery), and Genzyme Molecular Oncology (a loss-making developer of cancer therapies). Genzyme believed that this structure encouraged each division to operate independently and ensure that stock value of each division reflected its own success. At the same time, the tracking stock structure permitted the combined company a large cash savings by allowing it to offset the losses in the unprofitable Genzyme Biosurgery and Genzyme Molecular divisions for tax purposes against the profits of the Genzyme General division.

Tracking stocks have been issued in recent years for subsidiaries in businesses as diverse as cigarettes, cable TV, car dealerships, analytical instruments, oil and gas production, building materials, paper products, Investment banking, education, freight transportation, wireless telecommunications and equipment rental. Tracking stock IPOs have ranged in size from $40 million to $8 billion. When used under the right circumstances, tracking stocks are a very useful financial tool for creating value for the parent, the subsidiary, and public investors.

However, investor support for tracking stocks, more than spin-offs or carve-outs, requires investor faith in the parent's probity, good governance, and willingness to protect shareholders. Investors in a tracking stock have fewer rights than do spin-off or carve-out shareholders, as a separate public company is not created. Investor faith in good corporate governance is being sorely tested with the recent behavior of some American companies. Investors going forward are likely to only make this assumption on a selective basis.

TRACKING STOCKS OUTSIDE THE UNITED STATES

Unlike spin-offs and carve-outs, which have been widely utilized in Europe and even in Japan, the predominant tracking stock activity has been in the United States. There have been some tracking stocks issued in Europe and Japan. In 2001, Sony Corporation issued the first tracking stock in Japan. This was a tracking stock for Sony Communication Network Corporation, the third-largest Internet service provider in Japan.

The first tracking stock in Europe was Alcatel SA's 2000 IPO of Class O stock. This tracked its subsidiary, Alcatel Optronics, a maker of components used to amplify optical signals to ensure good data transmission along fiber-optic networks. The Class O shares were listed on the Paris Bourse and in Berlin and an ADR traded on Nasdaq. It performed well relative to its sector peers. Fletcher Challenge Ltd., in New Zealand, has issued four classes of tracking stock. However, the level of activity is small. One reason for this lack of activity is that standards of corporate governance are even more suspect in many other countries. As the *International Herald Tribune* reported,[1] on Sony's offering: "In a country

([Japan]) where corporate governance is not clearly established, management accountability toward investors has a spotty record, and accounting rules are lax, tracking stock owners could find themselves disregarded even more than regular shareholders."

BUSINESS PRESS VIEW OF TRACKING STOCKS

The business press has not been favorable to tracking stocks. It generally views tracking stocks as an inferior alternative to carve-outs or spin-offs for investors. "Tracking stocks can be better deals for the corporation issuing them than for investors," *Business Week* wrote in March.[2] "Collectively, the trackers' showing has been pretty unimpressive," wrote *Forbes* in December 1999.[3] "The advantages to shareholders are less clear. The performance of most tracking stocks ranges from lackluster to downright dismal," wrote *U.S. News and World Report* in December 1999.[4]

This view is not warranted. There were certainly disastrous tracking stock IPOs in the excesses of the late 1990s and 2000. But, there were many disastrous IPOs of all types in that period. There is substantial empirical evidence that tracking stocks perform well in relation to their peers and are beneficial to the parent's valuation, which we will see subsequently.

TRACKING STOCK EMPIRICAL EVIDENCE

Because of the controversy over tracking stocks, a close look at the empirical evidence is in order. Empirical studies[5] have largely supported the use of tracking stocks. Most studies indicate that the announcements of tracking stocks have an initial positive impact on the market value of the parent. Studies have found a mean positive impact of 3 percent surrounding the announcement of a tracking stock issue. In 30 of 35 issues in one study, there was a positive impact. This is comparable to the announcement returns for spin-offs and carve-outs.[6]

In relation to longer-term effect, a 1995 J.P. Morgan study[7] analyzed the trading multiples of eight tracking stocks. The study finds that tracking stocks trade at a small discount (some 10 percent) to their independent peers, as might be expected, with reduced shareholder rights and less potential for a sale of the subsidiary at a premium. A comprehensive study by two professors at Boston College[8] finds that the long-term performance of tracking stocks is positive and similar to that of equity carve-outs. They also find a significant positive impact on the valuation of the parents issuing tracking stocks. The price-to-sales ratios of parents issuing tracking stocks "was significantly lower than those of industry counterparts (prior to the issuance) but the difference becomes insignificant after restructuring." Exhibit 10–5 details this effect.

McKinsey & Company also found positive value creation effects for tracking stocks and concluded that "tracking stocks can create shareholder value."[9]

In contrast, an unpublished study by two professors at the University of Iowa[10] came to a much less positive conclusion concerning tracking stocks. They

EXHIBIT   10–5
───────────────────────────
Impact of Tracking Stocks on Valuation

	Tracking stock issuers	Matched firms
Median price-to-earnings ratios		
Parents before	13.65 x	16.47 x
Parents after	16.12 x	17.80 x
Median price-to-sales ratio		
Parents before	0.60 x	1.14 x
Parents after	0.81 x	1.06 x
Source: Thomas J. Chemmaneur and Imants Paeglis		

examined the postissue returns and the market performance of tracking stocks issued in the U.S. market during the period from 1984 to 1998 and their long-term returns through December 2000. They found that tracking stocks earn negative buy-and-hold excess returns during a three-year period following the issue date. They conclude: "The evidence suggests that tracking stock stocks do not outperform their benchmarks over a three-year period. In fact, they under perform." This study also found no evidence of a positive impact on the parent following the announcement of a tracking stock issuance.

While the research here does conflict, overall the author believes that tracking stocks are a very useful tool for parents. However, as is most often the case, there are examples of tracking stock that created value for parents and shareholders, and those that did not. This chapter will examine examples of both. Of course, the key is to use tracking stocks in the right situation and to make sure that the preconditions for their use have been met.

ADVANTAGES OF TRACKING STOCKS

There are many advantages to using tracking stocks, including the following.

Creates Greater Overall Value

A tracking stock may enhance the parent company and shareholder value if the combined value of the parent's stock and the tracking stock is greater than just that of the parent's stock. Subsequent value can be created if the tracking stock is used appropriately in acquisitions, IPOs, or follow-on offerings.

No Formal Separation of Operation

With a tracking stock, a parent can realize some, or all, of the economic value of a business segment without formally separating the operation. Parent company management continues to control the business segment and maintain ownership of its assets.

Raises Capital on Attractive Terms

A tracking stock is created for a subsidiary with a higher price-to-earnings ratio than that of the parent company. This may result from the subsidiary having a higher growth rate or a more attractive business-to-investors ratio than the parent. The tracking stock can be used for acquisitions, raising public capital for the subsidiary, or, for the parent's nontracked business, creating a lower cost of capital.

Allows Attractive Unwinding Provisions

At most companies today, change is almost certain. A subsidiary on which the tracking stock is based may later be completely spun off to the parent's shareholders or sold by the parent. A tracking stock enables the parent great flexibility to make any of these changes with a minimum of disruption. This is discussed later in the section called "Planning for Next Steps."

Lower Vulnerability Than a Stand-Alone Subsidiary to Hostile Takeovers

Issuing a tracking stock makes sense if the parent is concerned that the subsidiary might be the target of a hostile takeover on a stand-alone basis due to its smaller size and lack of structural complexity. In order to use a tracking stock as a subsidiary takeover vehicle, the parent must be taken over as well.

Creates Subsidiary Compensation That Can Be Tied to the Public Market

A publicly traded tracking stock establishes a public market value for the business of the subsidiary to which management compensation programs can be tied. The equity component of compensation can then be linked to company performance as recognized by the public market.

Parent Retains Strategic and Operating Synergies

A tracking stock preserves the operating benefits of a single, integrated corporation. For example, the company can retain strategic synergies such as brand name and marketing, a single finance group, one purchasing function, and a single management team. A tracking stock may be the only viable SER transaction when there are significant shared operations such as R&D, manufacturing, and customer service that make a clean separation of assets and capabilities too complex and difficult. This is in contrast to a spin-off, carve-out, or joint venture, which creates two separate and independent legal entities. USX used a tracking stock for its Delhi energy operation in part because Delhi shared gas-processing plants with USX's other energy operations.

Encourages Cooperation Among Business Units

A single, integrated company with synergistic divisions is more likely to foster cooperation among its business units to maximize long-term opportunities than would separate companies created from a spin-off or carve-out. Following a spin-off, for example, the former parent and subsidiary may even go into direct competition with each other. For example, this happened with Pacific Telesis Group after it spun off AirTouch Communications in 1993.

Maintains Parent Control and Operational Integrity

With a tracking stock, the parent maintains control of the subsidiary. It may raise additional equity for the subsidiary and achieve many of the other benefits of a carve-out or spin-off without altering control or cooperation among its various business units.

Facilitates Acquisitions and Creates a Higher-Value Acquisition Currency

A tracking stock may be a useful tool in facilitating an acquisition in the following situations:

• The acquired company CEO or management team of a public or independent company does not want to completely lose independence within a large parent. At the same time, the parent wants the benefits of consolidating the acquired business operation. A tracking stock allows both these wishes to be met. In the AT&T and TCI case detailed subsequently, AT&T was able to use tracking stock to structure a deal with TCI, enabling it to acquire TCI on terms acceptable to its chairman, John Malone. Without this flexibility, it is doubtful that AT&T would have been able to complete this crucial transaction.

• The shareholders of the potential subsidiary believe that the offer price does not reflect its true potential value. They want continued participation in the upside of the subsidiary after the acquisition. The parent could accommodate this objective by leaving a minority in the subsidiary in the hands of the old shareholders or having an earn-out arrangement; however, the parent wishes to avoid the considerable complications of a minority equity interest or earn-out in the subsidiary. With a tracking stock, the former shareholders of the subsidiary may participate more directly in the success of the subsidiary after the acquisition, as did the Hughes Institute in Hughes Aircraft.

• The parent may use the tracking stock as acquisition currency to develop a promising business area without diluting the overall shareholders' interest in the earnings of the other units. U S West had a forward multiple of 17, while the tracking stock of its Media Group was accorded a multiple of 76. The tracking shares of the Media Group were then used to acquire Continental Cablevision on far more favorable terms than if the parent had used its primary stock.

• A parent with a low price-to-earnings ratio creates acquisition currency by developing a tracking stock for the acquisition of a subsidiary with a high price-to-earnings ratio. When General Motors issued tracking stock to acquire EDS, GM had a forward price-to-earnings ratio of just 5, while EDS was accorded a multiple of 38.

A Tracking Stock Tax-Free Spin-Off Can Meet IRS Criteria at a Later Date

Complex IRS criteria must be met before a subsidiary can be spun off to the parent's shareholders on a tax-free basis. When a subsidiary does not meet these tests, a tracking stock for the subsidiary may still be distributed tax-free to the parent's shareholders. This lays the groundwork for a tax-free spin-off to tracking stock shareholders should the subsidiary later meet the requirements for a tax-free spin-off. Later this chapter will examine how USX first used a tracking stock for its U.S. Steel operation and then spun off U.S. Steel as an independent public company.

Continues Tax Consolidation

Unlike a carve-out, with a tracking stock, ownership may be reduced below 80 percent while still maintaining tax consolidation for federal corporate income taxes. The parent may maintain tax consolidation without any restriction on the percentage of the subsidiary that is sold or distributed as a tracking stock.[11] The advantages of maintaining tax consolidation with tracking stocks include the following:

• The parent may offset losses at one operation against profits at another. The tax attributes of the parent and the subsidiary are unaffected by a tracking stock, and the benefits of tax consolidation remain. Tracking stocks are useful where the parent or the subsidiary has net operating losses that may be used to offset taxable profits. Genzyme benefited from using the losses arising from the research and development spending of its Tissue Repair operation to offset profits from other operations at the corporate level. Similarly, USX offset the profits of its oil and gas operations with the losses at its steel operation.

• The parent may receive cash distributions from the subsidiary without an additional layer of tax, regardless of the parent's percentage interest. With a carve-out IPO, the parent has to maintain tax consolidation to receive tax-free distributions, though there is a smaller-dividend-received deduction equal to 70 to 80 percent of the distribution.

- If the parent decides to sell its interest in the subsidiary to a single buyer, the hybrid structure inherent in a tracking stock will allow the parent to offer the buyer a tax basis step-up without incremental tax liability, even if the parent's "ownership" of the tracked operation falls below 80 percent. With a carve-out, the parent would have to maintain tax consolidation to offer this benefit to a buyer.

Preserves Existing Legal Structure

With a tracking stock, there is no change to the underlying legal structure of the businesses. This prevents any interference with existing credit and debt agreements or borrowing capacity. Since there is no change to the parent's legal structure, the rights of the parent's lenders, suppliers, and bond and note holders are unaffected by the issuance of tracking stock. With other forms of equity redeployments, creditors may have their rights or asset bases reduced.

Does Not Require a Separate Board of Directors for the Tracked Operation

Unlike a carve-out or spin-off, there is no need for a separate board of directors for a tracked operation. The parent's board retains full control and discretion.

Attractive to Large Foreign Corporations with U.S. Operations

Foreign companies are not always comfortable with the U.S. equities market and are less inclined to create separate public companies. Creating a tracking stock on the U.S. operations alone, primarily for use in pricing management equity incentives, may make the U.S. subsidiary more attractive to prospective employees.

Use to Reduce Parent Debt

A tracking stock may be exchanged for parent debt or equity on tax-advantageous terms, reducing parent debt or shares outstanding. (See the example of ATT in Chapter 14.)

Track an Investment Operation

One interesting use of a tracking stock is to offer public investors a way to participate directly in the returns from an internal investment operation within the parent, such as one that invests in real estate or venture capital, without creating an entity that has to be registered under the Investment Company Act of 1940, with all its onerous restrictions. According to the 1940 Act, an "investment company" is "any issuer" that "(a) is or holds itself out as being engaged primarily, or pro-poses to engage primarily, in the business of investing, reinvesting, or trading in securities . . . or (b) is engaged or proposes to engage in the business of investing, reinvesting, owning, holding, or trading in securities, and owns or proposes to acquire investment securities having a value exceeding 40 per centum of the value of such issuer's total assets."

In 2000, the Division of Investment Management at the SEC issued a no-action letter to Comdisco which would have permitted Comdisco to issue two series of stock to track the economic performance of two business groups of Comdisco, one of which is engaged in venture financing activities (Comdisco Ventures). The effect of such a letter is to permit an operating company to issue stock that tracks the performance of a business unit engaged in investment activi-ties without registering the business group as an investment company, as the sub-sidiary would have to do were it a separate public company.

While this stock was never issued, it is an interesting use of a tracking stock that may find application at a later date.[12]

CHALLENGES OF TRACKING STOCKS

Tracking stocks pose challenges for both investors and the parent company.

For the Parent

Vehicle for Large Parent Companies Only

Tracking stocks are best suited for large parents because an investor in a tracking stock is actually purchasing common stock of the parent and therefore is depend-ent on the parent's financial and business stability as well as the success of the tracked operation. If the parent goes under, the tracked stock will be worthless, even if the tracked business is still great. With spin-offs and carve-outs, the investor has a direct equity interest in the subsidiary and is not dependent on the solvency of the parent (except where the success or failure of the parent impacts the sub-sidiary's business such as when the parent is a large customer of the subsidiary).

This is not true with tracking stock. A large, established, and well-known parent will much more easily give assurance to investors in the tracking stock of its own stability, solvency, and longevity. This is because there is often an existing familiarity with the parent on the part of investors, there is more likely to be research coverage and information on a large parent, and large parents are more likely to have higher credit ratings and are considered to have less business risk. Also, buying a tracking stock requires considerable trust by the investor in the quality of the governance and the board of directors of the parent. These do tend to be stronger with large, established companies.

Intergroup Transactions Must Be Conducted with Care

The parent issuing a subsidiary tracking stock must create firewalls between the subsidiary and the rest of its operations to preserve the economic claims of the subsidiary shareholders on the value of the subsidiary.

These firewalls can one of two forms:

• Legal restrictions in the parent's charter

• Procedures guiding the management and board of directors on how the parent may conduct business with the subsidiary

Issuers of tracking stocks must create programs that prevent the movement of assets and cash among different businesses of the parent and the subsidiary without fair compensation to the subsidiary. A portion of the economic benefit of the assets of the subsidiary must also flow to the tracking stockholders. This includes the benefit of any sale of assets, net of taxes and expenses. The combined company's fixed costs must be allocated among each business segment.

There are currently no rules for these allocations. The board of directors and management are only required by law to use proper "business judgment." For maximum flexibility, such policies can be changed by vote of the board of directors without stockholder approval.

Increased Complexity and Administrative Burden on the Parent

Because a tracking stock is another series of parent common stock, the subsidiary will usually not have its own stand-alone financial and legal staff. Therefore, the burden of administering the additional public security will most likely fall on the parent's existing staff. They will be tasked with preparing for the transaction and continue to administer the structure after the transaction. This administrative burden includes:

• Increased reporting and accounting arising from issuing an additional equity security outstanding for the parent. These tasks include preparing separate financial reports and SEC filings.

• Increased complexity of internal operations from having to allocate various shared facilities, capabilities, and services and adjudicate conflicts between internal operations

• Increased burden on senior parent management arising from the need to cultivate and communicate with an additional investor base for the tracking stock

Conflicts of Interest at the Parent Level

A company that issues a tracking stock creates the potential for a conflict at the board level between the interests of the two sets of shareholders. New York Law School professor Jeffrey Haas has written a detailed review of the issues facing directors of parents issuing tracking stocks.[13] Among the potential conflicts that he lists between divisions with different outside investors are these:

• The allocation of scarce corporate resources, corporate opportunities, corporate expenses, or merger or acquisition consideration

• Whether to promote or discourage particular public policies or laws beneficial to one division but harmful to another

• Dividend policies relating to the various classes of stock

- Intergroup transactions and dealings
- Decisions relating to capital-raising activities and the use of the proceeds

Professor Haas also offers a number of points of advice to parent directors to avoid potential litigation. These include ensuring the following:

- "Disinterested directors" should make all board decisions regarding conflicts between divisions.
- Each outside director should own all series of the parent's common stock and in the ratio of shares outstanding,
- Any officer who is a member of the board should have duties running the entire parent, not just one division.
- Decisions are fair and reasonable for all involved.

In some cases, the parent's actions in respect to the subsidiary have led to litigation. General Motors was unsuccessfully sued by the EDS tracking stock shareholders regarding a $500 million distribution that it took from the subsidiary before its spin-off as an independent company. However, so far, such litigation is not common.

Limits on the Economic Upside to the Parent's Shareholders if the Tracking Stock Is Sold Through an IPO
When a tracking stock is sold through an IPO, the business is partially sold or completely sold following an IPO. As a result, neither the parent nor its shareholders will fully share in the economic upside of the subsidiary. With a spin-off of a tracking stock, the shareholders of the parent have the opportunity, should they hold the tracking stock, to participate fully in the success of the business.

Increased Complexity for Investors
At a time when transparency is one of the uppermost of investor concerns, a tracking stock adds a level of complexity to the parent's story for investors and analysts and makes it more difficult to understand.

The Tracked Operation Must Be a Separate and Viable Business
Unlike a carve-out or spin-off, a tracked subsidiary does not have to be a stand-alone, independent business. However, it does need to be a separate operation that investors are able to value separately from other operations of the parent. It also needs to be an attractive business that investors will initially want to own and then continue to want to own. This was not the case with a number of Internet portals for which some large parents issued tracking stocks during the Internet bubble. The parents later found that these were neither separate businesses nor viable stand-alone public investments.

Structure Should Accommodate Future Eventualities
Chapter 6 outlined the inherent instability of minority carve-outs. In contrast, tracking stocks are not fundamentally unstable, and they were very stable for a

long time. Of the 23 domestic tracking stocks issued from 1984 till 1998, fully 19 were still trading as tracking stocks at the end of 1998. Two had been sold and two spun off.[10] However, that picture changed radically in the late 1990s. Of the 12 tracking stocks issued in 1999 and 2000, 9 were gone by the end of 2001. This largely reflected the unviable Internet businesses of a number of tracking stocks issued in that period—50 percent of the tracking stocks issued in 1999 and 2000 were for Internet operations and only one of those remained outstanding at the end of 2002. However, as business strategies and operations do change and few business structures are permanent, the parent needs to ensure that it has planned for these eventualities in structuring the tracking stock. This challenge is discussed in detail later in the chapter.

Embarrassment to the Parent
A tracking stock that has failed as a business and is trading well below its IPO price is often an embarrassment to the parent out of all proportion to its relative size. As well, the parent must continue to make public disclosures for the subsidiary, highlighting the failure of a small operation that otherwise would not be noted. Parents of some dot-com tracking stocks later redeemed or exchanged the shares more to eliminate embarrassment and disclosure than out of any business purpose or wish to buy the shares back at a discounted price.

For the Investor

The disadvantages of a tracking stock for the investor include the following.

Less Tax Efficient for Shareholders if the Subsidiary Is Sold
The sale of the assets behind a tracking stock may result in taxation of gains at the corporate level (though the gain to shareholders from a redemption of tracking stock is generally a capital gain). This is not the case with a sale of a spun-off subsidiary, as there is usually no tax at the corporate level. Unfortunately, the option of a last-minute tax-free spin-off just before a sale to avoid parent taxation is not available. Within a limited time before or after a sale, IRC Section 355(e) prevents a tax-free spin-off. In a carve-out, the public investors in the subsidiary receive capital gains treatment should the subsidiary be sold, while there is usually no tax at the subsidiary level.

Sharing Parental Risk
For a tracking stock and its holders to receive the desired tax and accounting treatment, investors must share the economic benefits and risks of the parent. The interests of all holders of common shares are subject to the claims of creditors of the parent. Holders of tracking stock have no claims on specific corporate assets, but share in any distributions of assets available to all holders of common stock.

Tracking Stock May Be Impacted by Problems in Other Parent Company Operations
A tracking stock is vulnerable to problems anywhere in the parent company. In the mid-1990s, Pittston issued tracking stocks for its coal, Brinks armored trucks, and

air cargo units. Investor concerns over pension and health care liabilities at the coal company, from which investors in the tracking stocks of the other operations (holding parent securities) were not insulated, severely affected the value of the other two tracking stocks. Pittston later undid the tracking stock structure.

Limited Market Experience with Tracking Stocks
While tracking stocks have been around since 1984 until recently not many were issued. Therefore, the performance—and investor history—is limited and colored by the fact that many of these recent issues were undertaken only to take advantage of the stock market bubble of the late 1990s.

Optional Redemption Rights May Cause Contention
Any optional redemption rights are typically stipulated at the time of the issuance of the tracking stock and are usually at a small premium to the market price at the time of redemption. The parent may choose to redeem the tracking stock from its investors at a time when it is highly undervalued for extraneous market reasons and the holders of the tracking stock are thereby deprived of fair value. This is obviously an attraction to the parent and a potential deterrent to investors.

The IRS May Rule That Dividends of Tracking Stock Are Taxable
There is always the risk that the IRS will, at some point, attempt to close down the tax-free distribution of tracking stock to parent shareholders or otherwise challenge the tax status of tracking stocks. However, while there have been proposals in the past, there are no announced plans at this time to do so.

For a Tracking Stock Spin-Off to Be Nontaxable, Parent Itself Must Issue the Tracking Stock
A separate issuer will be determined to exist within the parent if interests are issued in a pool of assets legally segregated from the parent's other assets, those assets are held primarily for the benefit of the tracked stockholders as the sole measure of their investment participation, and those interests do not confer significant rights in other assets of the parent. The SEC also has guidelines for determining whether a tracking stock is a parent stock or the stock of the tracked entity with major repercussions on registration. These are discussed later.

Tracking Stocks Are Issues of the Parent's Stock
If the parent is public, the same requirements apply to tracking stock issue as would apply to any issue of the parent stock. If the parent is not public in the United States, the tracking stock is an IPO of the parent and subject to all the requirements of a traditional IPO.

The SEC Might Deem the Tracking Stock a Separate IPO by the Subsidiary—Not a Variety of Parent Stock
The SEC has enumerated a number of factors that it looks at for securities law purposes in determining whether a public tracking stock is a parent stock issue. If

the stock is not a parent issue, the tracked subsidiary is a separate issuer subject to the securities laws. This is not a desirable determination and these should be looked at in detail.

Tracking Stocks Are Complex to Understand
Critics of tracking stocks assert that the intricacies of tracking stocks are too complex for most investors to understand.

PLANNING FOR NEXT STEPS

As mentioned earlier in this chapter, tracking stocks are often terminated when the situation of the subsidiary and/or parent changes. As tracking stock termination may be expected at some point, the parent should structure the tracking stock to allow flexibility for this event. Unlike a carve-out, a tracking stock may include specific provisions that enable the parent to redeem the tracking stock or exchange it for another stock relatively easily should such a move be advantageous for business, valuation, or strategic reasons. Let's look at the likely later events that cause the termination of a tracking stock, and how termination may be made less painful for the parent.

Sale of the Tracked Operation

The parent sells the tracked operation. It then redeems the tracking stock with the sale proceeds. For example, in 2001 Quantum sold the disk drive operation that its Quantum-HDD stock tracked to Maxtor Corporation for Maxtor stock, as described in the example later in this chapter. Quantum then redeemed the HDD tracking stock, distributing to the Maxtor common stock to HDD shareholders.

Spin-Off of the Tracked Operation

The parent decides to spin off completely the tracked operation. It then exchanges the tracking stock for shares of a new public company in a tax-free spin-off to the tracking stock shareholders. For example, in 2002, USX Corporation exchanged shares of a new public company, U.S. Steel, for shares of its USX-U.S. Steel tracking stock. Each share of the tracking stock was exchanged for a share of the new public company. Similarly, the transaction that originated tracking stocks— General Motors's acquisition of EDS—was unwound in 1996 when GM spun off EDS as an independent company.

Buy-In of the Tracking Stock for Cash

The parent decides it no longer wants the tracked operation to have its own public stock. It then repurchases the shares of tracking stock held by the public for cash. For example, in 2001, Credit Suisse Group tendered with cash for the 18 percent of CSFB Direct, its Internet discount brokerage operation tracking stock held by the public.

Buy-In of the Tracking Stock for Stock of the Parent

The parent decides it no longer wants the tracked operation to have its own public stock. It then exchanges parent stock for the shares of tracking stock held by the public. For example, in 2001 Disney exchanged shares of Disney common stock for the publicly held shares of the tracking stock of its Internet operations, the Walt Disney Internet Group.

CREATING STRUCTURAL FLEXIBILITY WITH A REDEMPTION PROVISION

Tracking stocks typically contain both mandatory and optional redemption provisions that strike a balance between giving the parent great flexibility to react to changed circumstances and protecting the tracking stock shareholders. A redemption provision is defined as a right by the parent to redeem the tracking stock for cash or another security, usually parent common stock. There are two primary types of redemption provisions.

Optional Redemption Provision

Optional exchange redemption provisions enable the parent to redeem or exchange the tracking stock on a preset basis should it no longer be a desirable element of the parent's capital structure. This allows the parent to use a tracking stock to obtain certain objectives, knowing that there is a simple means to terminate it at a future date. These provisions usually enable the parent to exchange parent stock for the tracking stock or redeem it for cash, at a preset premium, to the market price of the tracking stock at the time of the redemption. This limits the price the parent will have to pay to unwind a tracking stock but also provides some protection to investors. The alternative is redemption at fair market value that, in practice, will almost always be a magnet for dispute and litigation, or at a preset fixed price, which is certain to result in a price at the time of the redemption that will be either too low and unfair to the investors or too high and unfair to the parent.

Mandatory Redemption Provision

There is a usually a mandatory redemption requirement to protect the investors in the event of a sale of the tracked business. There is a wide range of terms for mandatory redemptions. Some provisions may allow the parent to use the proceeds from the sale of the tracked operation to redeem the tracking stock at the current market value. Others provide for the parent to declare a dividend of the aftertax disposition proceeds, and still others provide for an exchange of the tracking stock for parent common stock at a pre-agreed premium, typically between 10 and 20 percent, to the average market price of the tracking stock for a period of time before the announcement of the redemption.

See Exhibit N–6 in the Notes section for representative unwinding terms for tracking stocks in the event of a sale of the subsidiary and at the option of the parent.[14]

SUMMARY

This chapter examined the unique features of a tracking stock, which provides an opportunity for a parent company to create value for the organization—and for its shareholders—with the need to make complex organizational changes.

Chapter 11 examines exchange spin-offs, which are a tax-efficient way to create value for the parent's shareholders.

TRACKING STOCKS IN ACTION
Example 1, AT&T Wireless Group: Use of a Tracking Stock to Raise Cash on Advantageous Terms

AT&T issued two tracking stocks for two business lines to the public over the last few years. One stock tracked its Wireless Group. At the time, the high growth rates shown by the wireless business and exuberant forecast for its future growth were exceptionally appealing to some public stock investors who were less concerned with profitability. In contrast, the traditional investors in AT&T were more concerned with dividends and earnings. Separating out the wireless operation allowed AT&T to appeal to certain growth stock investors who would be otherwise uninterested in its other operations. However, AT&T did not want to carve out the wireless operation at that time. The wireless operations benefited from consolidation with AT&T for support of its massive capital needs, and AT&T benefited from the tax losses generated by the depreciation on the wireless infrastructure to offset against other income. As well, AT&T believed that there would be close operating synergies among its different businesses.

Exhibit 10–6 illustrates the higher growth rate of the wireless business, but its lack of profitability.

In April 2000, AT&T completed the largest IPO in U.S. history by issuing a tracking stock for 15.6 percent of the AT&T Wireless Group, raising approximately $10.6 billion. The majority of the proceeds were allocated to fund the wireless operations. Each share of tracking stock was structured to contain one-half of a vote, redeemable at the option of AT&T's board of directors at any time following May 2002, subject to certain tax-related events or other significant transactions, using AT&T common stock at a 10 percent premium, and not likely to receive cash dividends. In addition, AT&T Wireless tracking stock could be exchanged later by AT&T, should it so desire, for shares of a subsidiary holding substantially all of the assets of the wireless group.

Exhibit 10–7 demonstrates the performance of the AT&T Wireless tracking stock against that of AT&T itself. As can be seen, it outperformed the parent. Separating out the wireless operation created value for AT&T's shareholders by

E X H I B I T   10–6

Summary of Historical AT&T Financial Data

	1997	1998	1999	2000
AT&T Corporation	*($ in millions)*			
Revenues	$51,577	$53,223	$62,600	$65,981
Operating income	6,836	7,487	12,365	11,306
Net income	4,415	6,398	*3,428*	4,669
AT&T Wireless				
Revenues	$4,668	$5,406	$7,627	$10,448
Operating income	(70)	(343)	(666)	(38)
Net income	69	164	(405)	658
Source: SEC filings				

allowing it to raise equity at a lower cost by appealing to growth investors who were enthusiastic about the growth prospects of the wireless business but were uninterested in AT&T's other, lower-growth businesses. Exhibit 10–7 shows the relative performance of the two stocks.

AT&T's grand vision of offering home and business customers broadband, wireless, long-distance, and local telephone service by bringing together cable, cellular, and telephone services ultimately failed because of poor execution, resulting in not achieving the hoped-for integration and synergies. At the same time, AT&T's long-distance business began to flounder under intense competition. AT&T came under intense pressure from shareholders to completely separate the successful cable and wireless operations from the failing long-distance operations. It eventually proceeded with a break-up plan, and AT&T spun off AT&T Wireless Services as an independent company on July 9, 2001.

Example 2, AT&T and Liberty Media Group: Use of a Tracking Stock to Facilitate an Acquisition

The second AT&T tracking stock was issued in connection with AT&T's acquisition of Tele-Communications, Inc. (TCI). As noted, AT&T had a strategy of offering combined cable, wireless, and telephone services. It believed that it needed to buy large cable systems to provide it with direct access to customers. One of the largest cable operators was TCI, controlled by its chairman, John Malone. TCI would make a plum acquisition for AT&T. Along with its cable operations, TCI had an extensive entertainment business, Liberty Media, which owned cable program channels and entertainment content production operations. Entertainment

EXHIBIT 10-7

AT&T Wireless Group Stock Performance

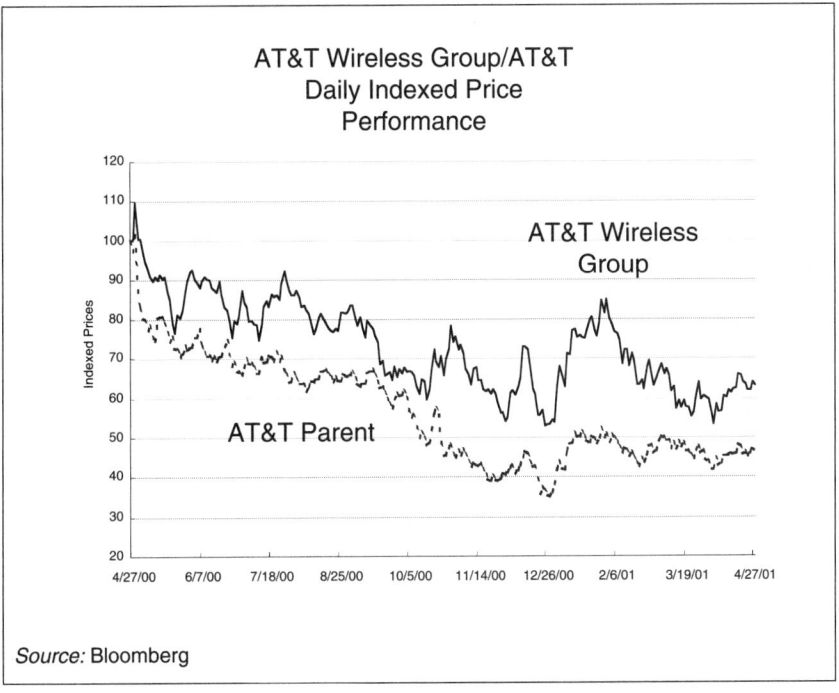

AT&T Wireless Group/AT&T
Daily Indexed Price
Performance

AT&T Wireless Group

AT&T Parent

Source: Bloomberg

programming is a very different business from operating cable systems and appeals to different investors. In 1995, TCI issued a tracking stock for just Liberty Media to its shareholders in a tax-free distribution.

Malone wished to sell the cable operations of TCI in a tax-efficient manner but also wished to continue to control and benefit economically directly from Liberty Media. An acquisition of TCI by AT&T hinged on meeting these two needs of Malone. In March 1999, in a deal valued at $43.5 billion, AT&T acquired TCI. AT&T paid for TCI by exchanging AT&T common stock for the stock of TCI. AT&T also exchanged a new AT&T-Liberty Media tracking stock for the outstanding TCI-Liberty Media tracking stock. The plan was for Malone to head Liberty Media.

AT&T had two objectives in issuing the tracking stock for Liberty Media:

1. The new AT&T Liberty Media tracking stock was critical to winning the support of Malone for the acquisition of TCI by AT&T. The tracking stock provided Malone with a way to divest TCI but retain control of Liberty Media and participate economically directly in Liberty Media's growth.

2. By issuing a tracking stock for Liberty Media, AT&T would widen its overall investor group to include investors who were interested in an

entertainment business. Liberty Media appealed to a very different set of public investors than did the other operations of AT&T. The tracking stock investors in Liberty Media were unlikely to be interested in owning AT&T parent stock and would likely sell any AT&T shares that they received. Instead, they were offered a means to continue their interest in Liberty Media.

This flexibility to facilitate structuring an acquisition that meets the needs of both the parent and the seller is an inherent advantage of a tracking stock.

The lesson to be learned from this example, as with EDS, is that a tracking stock is useful to the parent in making an acquisition where there are particular needs of a large shareholder of the other company. However, both cases also illustrate the difficulty of keeping a strong entrepreneur corralled, once he or she sells the business. In this instance, relations between the parent and John Malone deteriorated after the acquisition with well-publicized and acrimonious disagreements between Malone and the senior management of AT&T. In the end, after debilitating infighting, AT&T agreed that Malone would leave AT&T and that AT&T would spin off Liberty Media to its tracking shareholders as an independent public company headed by Malone. This was done in August 2001.

Example 3, USX Corporation: Successful Use of Tracking Stocks to Increase Shareholder Value

At the beginning of 1991, USX Corporation consisted of two entities: U.S. Steel, then the nation's largest integrated steel producer, and Marathon Oil Group, an integrated oil and gas producer. The stock of the parent, USX, traded at a discount relative to other comparable public companies in the market. It was clear that the stock of USX was heavily penalized in the public stock market, as it was not understood by either steel or oil analysts.

Exhibit 10–8 shows the low valuation of USX compared with comparable public companies.

E X H I B I T   10–8

USX Valuation Summary

Valuation as of January 1, 1991	USX Corporation	Median of public U.S. integrated oil companies	Median of public U.S. integrated steel companies
Market price to projected 1991 EPS	8.8x	11.3x	15.0x
Enterprise value to last 12 months EBIT	10.1x	12.5x	13.8x

Source: SEC filings, Needham & Company

EXHIBIT 10–9

USX Business Unit Operating Income Losses

Operating income/losses		
Steel Group		
	1991	$(617)
	1992	(241)
Marathon Group		
	1991	358
	1992	304
Source: SEC filings		

In 1991, USX issued tracking stocks on U.S. Steel Group and Marathon Group. The impact on shareholder value was considerable relative to the peer groups. USX cited the tax savings at the corporate level from offsetting Marathon's profits with the losses generated by the U.S. Steel business as the reason to issue a tracking stock rather then spinning off Marathon. Exhibit 10–9 shows the tax advantages of offsetting the losses at U.S. Steel with the profits at Marathon.

USX distributed one-fifth share of USX-U.S. Steel Group tracking stock for each share of USX Corporation stock and exchanged one share of USX-Marathon Group tracking stock for each share of USX Corporation stock, retiring the USX shares.

As a consequence, within two years, the value of each of the components of USX traded at a premium relative to that of their respective public peer groups of companies.

Exhibit 10–10 shows this increase in valuation relative to comparable companies within a few years. The combined value of the two components of USX went from a significant discount relative to comparable companies to a premium after the tracking stock issues. This created significant value for the parent's shareholders.

Between January 1992 and July 1993, USX Corporation raised $1.5 billion in four tracking stock public offerings. One was a follow-on offering for Marathon, two were follow-on offerings for U.S. Steel, and one was a convertible offering for U.S. Steel.

As with many SERs, the separation of the steel and energy operations of USX was preceded by a catalyzing event—in this case a struggle with a large shareholder, corporate raider Carl Icahn, who owned 13 percent of the company. Since 1982, USX had spent $10 billion on energy acquisitions in a strategy to balance steel's cyclical earnings. But USX's stock has only slightly

E X H I B I T   10–10

USX Valuation Summary as of January 1, 1994

	U.S. Steel Group	Comparable public U.S. integrated steel companies	
		Mean	*Median*
Market price to 1993 EPS	37.6x	17.6x	17.6x
Market price to projected 1994 EPS	12.2x	11.5x	11.3x
Enterprise value to net capital	2.2x	1.8x	1.7x
Enterprise value to steel production capacity in dollars per ton	$365.4	$236.2	$252.5
	Marathon Oil Group	Comparable public U.S. integrated oil companies	
		Mean	*Median*
Market price to 1993 EPS	22.2x	20.0x	18.3x
Market price to projected 1994 EPS	20.0x	18.1x	15.1x
Enterprise value to latest 12 months EBITDA	7.5x	6.1x	5.6x
Market value to latest 12 months cash flow from operations	8.3x	5.9x	6.0x
Implied market value of oil and gas reserves per barrel of oil equivalent	$5.44	$4.85	$4.20
After-tax SEC discounted value of oil and gas reserves	$1.88	$1.66	$1.81

Source: SEC filings, Needham & Company

outpaced peer steel stocks, while greatly underperforming the energy sector. At USX's 1990 annual meeting, Icahn had proposed a nonbinding vote on a proposal to split USX in two by spinning off 80 percent of its $5.7 billion steel unit to shareholders. USX was under great pressure to improve the performance of its stock price.[15]

The tracking stock served the purpose of increasing shareholder value while maintaining tax efficiency.

As a postscript, at the end of 2001, USX split into two independent public companies: the former parent, USX, was renamed Marathon and contained the energy operations. The tracking stock of the U.S. Steel Group subsidiary was exchanged for common stock of a spun-off independent U.S. Steel.

Example 4, Quantum Corporation: Use of a Tracking Stock When a Carve-Out or Spin-Off May Have Made More Sense

In 1999, Quantum Corporation was a maker of hard disk drives (HDDs) used primarily for relatively inexpensive data storage in personal computers and also in higher-end storage systems. It also made digital linear tape (DLT) and accompanying storage systems. The disk drive business was (and remains) a highly competitive and low-margin business with periodic excess capacity and little differentiation among vendors other than price.

By contrast, the tape business enjoyed higher margins and Quantum had proprietary DLT products. Quantum's stock had not performed well in the late 1990s.

Quantum believed that this mediocre performance of Quantum's common stock was related to the low multiples accorded by public investors to participants in the disk drive industry. It also believed that the public markets did not give Quantum credit in its valuation for the higher multiples that were accorded stand-alone tape and storage systems companies comparable to the DLT & Storage Systems (DSS) group. In August 1999, Quantum Corporation converted each of its common shares outstanding into one tracking share of its DSS group stock and 0.5 of a tracking share of its Hard Disk Drive (HDD) group stock.

Issuing tracking stocks was viewed by Quantum as a way to bring out DSS's market value and thereby increase overall value. Quantum was correct in viewing the disk drive operation as a lower-multiple business. It was also correct in seeing the storage operation as a stand-alone entity with higher value potential After the tracking stock issues, the DSS operation did trade at a significant multiple premium relative to that of Quantum alone before the issues. However, the disk drive operation traded at a considerably lower multiple, leaving the combined value of the two stocks unchanged, despite a small increase in revenue. The assumption that investors did not appreciate the real value of the DSS operation was not correct; investors actually had already recognized the full value of the two separate operations. And while the tracking stocks did not increase in value, maintaining two tracking stocks instead of one combined common stock considerably increased costs, administrative burden, and operating complexity. This was compounded by the need to manage two separately tracked operations.

Instead, it should simply have been carved out or spun off. In the end, the hard disk drive business was sold to another disk drive maker, Maxtor Corporation, the DLT stock was exchanged for new parent stock, and the DSS group continued as an independent public company.

Two Tracking Stocks for Dot-Com Operations

Before a business is separated from the other operations of the parent with a tracking stock, the parent must think through whether it is actually a distinct business. This was not done before issuing tracking stocks for the Internet operations of some large companies, as the following three examples illustrate.

CSFB Direct

In May 1999, Donaldson Lufkin & Jeanrette (DLJ) carved out 18 percent of its online brokerage operation, DLJdirect, in an IPO of a tracking stock, raising $346 million. The IPO price was $20 per share. The stock subsequently traded down in the public market to $2.50 per share as the market lost its enthusiasm for Internet stocks. DLJ, including DLJdirect, was subsequently purchased by the large Swiss bank Credit Suisse Group and merged with its Credit Suisse First Boston investment banking and brokerage operation. DLJdirect was renamed CSFBdirect.

After the purchase of DLJ, Credit Suisse First Boston realized that the online brokerage business was not a separate business. Instead, it was simply another channel for its existing brokerage activities. Credit Suisse First Boston decided to reintegrate the online brokerage operation into its mainstream product lines. The public holding of the tracking stock was repurchased for $6 per share at a cost of $110 million in August 2001. While the public shareholders did not make money on this transaction, they fared well compared with most shareholders of stand-alone Internet stocks.

At the end of 2001, new management at CSFB decided that the retail discount brokerage business did not fit its strategic plan, and it sold the operation to the Bank of Montreal, which had other discount retail operations.

Infoseek Corporation

The Walt Disney Company reached a similar conclusion: its Internet operations were not a stand-alone business, but part of its other entertainment operations.

In November 1998, Disney acquired 43 percent of Infoseek Corporation, a publicly traded Internet search company. During January 1999, Disney and Infoseek together launched go.com, an Internet portal. In July 1999, Disney agreed to acquire the remaining 58 percent of Infoseek that it did not then own. Both Disney and Infoseek stockholders approved the deal in November 1999, and Disney combined its Internet and direct marketing operations with Infoseek to create a single Internet business. Disney issued in exchange 29 percent of a new class of its common stock, Walt Disney Internet Group, to track the performance of the Internet business. The share of Disney Internet Group tracking stock issued to the public shareholders of Infoseek was valued at the time at $1.535 billion. In March 2001, Disney recognized that the Internet operations were not a stand-alone business and repurchased the public tracking stock for Disney common stock valued at $241 million.

A Comment on the Dot-Com Tracking Stocks

While the shareholders in each of these tracking stocks suffered mightily, overall they have suffered less than the shareholders in the equivalent independent Internet public companies—many of which have gone out of business. In many cases, the parent was willing to step in and reacquire the tracking stock to reintegrate the operation, to reduce the complexity of its capital structure, to support the tracked operation, sustain its reputation, and eliminate the requirement to make embarrassing public disclosures about the subsidiary. Because tracking stocks are a parent security, it is much more difficult for the parent to walk away from it than from a spin-off or carve-out. In a 1999 *Business Week* article, James Andrew, vice president at Renaissance World, a consulting firm, said, "Stand-alone Internet companies will have a hard time financing negative cash flow and growth in tough times, so a mother-ship company provides a more stable platform." This largely proved to be correct.

CONCLUSION

Tracking stocks have a very mixed reputation in the press. This has not stopped their continued use by parents or continued interest by investors, as demonstrated by the success of the tracking stock IPO of Loews Carolina Group in the first quarter of 2002, referred to in the introduction to this book. There have been inappropriate tracking stock IPOs, but there were many inappropriate IPOs of stand-alone companies in the late 1990s as well. There certainly are governance issues relating to tracking stocks that must be considered, and trust is important in these issues. However, they are very much worth considering. There is no more flexible tool for achieving complex parent objectives than a tracking stock.

CHAPTER **11**

SPLIT-OFFS

INTRODUCTION

A split-off is an exchange by a parent of shares it owns in a subsidiary for shares of the parent or for parent debt. Split-offs for parent shares may be voluntary, where each parent shareholder decides individually whether or not to participate in a tender offer by the parent or mandatory when authorized by the terms of a class of parent shareholders or by shareholder vote. Mandatory split-offs are usually pro rata to all the parent shareholders or all the holders of a particular class of parent stock. Debt split-offs are usually voluntary unless already provided for in the debt agreements. Split-offs for parent debt are also receiving attention as a part of debt restructuring.

DEFINITION OF A SPLIT-OFF

A split-off is a way to create value for the parent's shareholders by reducing the parent's outstanding shares or debt. A tax-free split-off offers the advantage of using appreciated subsidiary shares in exchange for parent shares or debt without incurring tax at the parent level. A split-off is tax-free to the parent if the subsidiary is eligible for a tax-free spin-off and other tests are met. A taxable split-off still may create value for the parent's shareholders, particularly where there is not substantial tax incurred. This chapter examines split-off transactions in detail, including their advantages and disadvantages and the conditions that must be met in order to attain tax-free status.

In a split-off the subsidiary's shares are exchanged for the parent's shares or debt. The purpose of reducing the parent's shares outstanding is to increase the earnings and cash flow per share and, thereby, the value of the remaining shares or to meet the needs of particular shareholders. The purpose of reducing the parent's debt is to reduce interest expense, principal repayment obligations, and financial risk. In contrast, a typical spin-off distributes the subsidiary's shares to the parent's shareholders.

Of course, if the parent wants to retire its debt or reduce its shares outstanding and has a valuable asset in the subsidiary, it can always sell the subsidiary cash or shares of the subsidiary in an IPO and then use the posttax cash proceeds to retire parent debt or repurchase parent shares through market purchases or through a tender offer. However, with this approach, the parent will have to pay tax on the gain if the subsidiary's shares are worth more than their tax basis and shareholders will be taxed on any capital gain. A tax-free split-off is an alternative for the parent that may save tax. With a tax-free split-off, no tax is incurred on the appreciated value of the subsidiary shares exchanged for parent shares at the parent or the shareholder level. For this reason, this transaction may be more beneficial to the parent than an outright sale of the subsidiary or its shares.

To obtain this benefit, the split-off must be tax free. This requires that the exchange meet the requirements of Internal Revenue Code (IRC) Sections 355 and 368(c). As discussed in Chapter 8, these stipulate, among other tests, that the parent controls, before the split-off, more than 80 percent of the subsidiary and that more than 80 percent of the subsidiary is distributed in the split-off, and that more than 50 percent of the shares are held after the exchange by historic shareholders of the parent. For reasons set out below, the last requirement means in practice that a split-off for parent debt must be combined with a simultaneous traditional spin-off to the parent's shareholders of shares in the subsidiary. Last, to minimize confusion, it is worth mentioning that the use of the term *exchange* in this chapter should not be confused with exchangeable (convertible) securities, covered in Chapter 14.

Exhibit 11–1 depicts a typical tax-free stock split-off for parent stock. A tax-free split-off for parent debt is illustrated in Exhibit 11–2, after the discussion of the Lucent debt exchange at the end of this chapter.

ADVANTAGES OF A SPLIT-OFF

Besides helping to retire parent debt and shares, a split-off also mitigates concerns of parent shareholders over the earnings impact on the parent of spinning off a significant subsidiary. For example, the spin-off of a profitable subsidiary reduces the parent's earnings per share, as the subsidiary's future earnings will no longer contribute to the parent's future earnings. This can alarm shareholders. Employee option holders may also worry about a reduced appreciation potential of their options. Through a split-off for parent shares, the number of parent shares outstanding is reduced, which mitigates the decline in earnings per share.

The spin-off of a profitable subsidiary will also concern the parent's lenders and credit agencies, because the subsidiary's cash flow and asset base will no longer be available to service and support the parent's debt. It will also worry the management of the parent's remaining operations, which will then have to support

Split-Off for Parent Stock

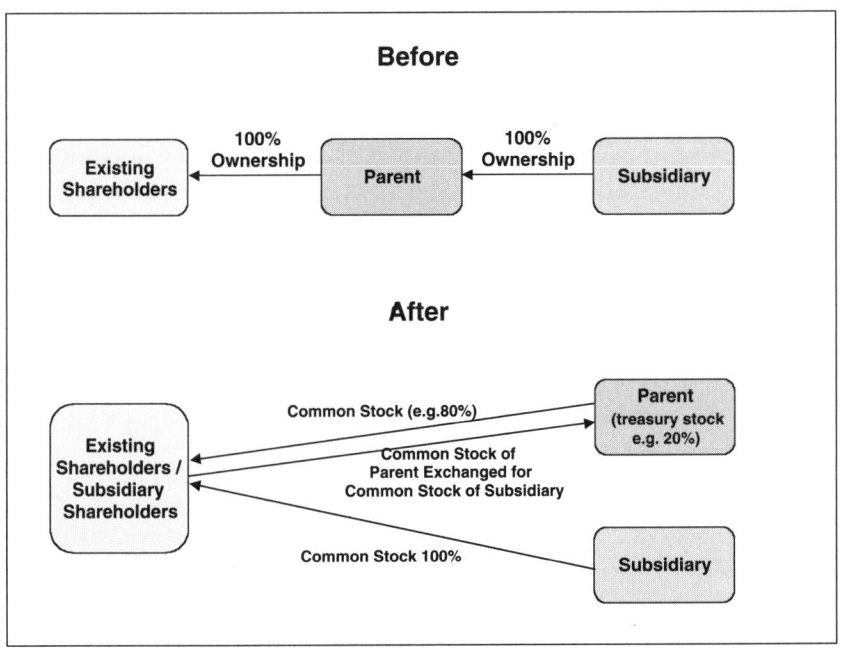

the parents's debt load entirely from their own cash flow. With a split-off for parent debt, the parent debt is reduced to compensate for the loss of the subsidiary's cash flow. A split-off for debt is also an alternative to transferring parent debt to the subsidiary as part of a traditional spin-off when the subsidiary's business would be adversely impacted by the cash demands of servicing the debt.

PRECONDITIONS FOR A SUCCESSFUL SPLIT-OFF

There are three main conditions that must be met before holders of parent stock and debt holders will support the split-off.

First, it is critical to correctly price the exchange ratio used in the split-off so that holders of the parent's stock or debt will tender their holdings. It is important to note that an initial carve-out IPO prior to the split-off establishes a market price and helps to create a liquid market in the subsidiary's stock following the split-off, similar to a two-step spin-off. But, it is possible to consummate a split-off directly as part of a subsidiary spin-off rather than in a two-step approach involving a carve-out IPO followed by a split-off if a parent or debt shareholder is willing to take a risk on the eventual actual market price of the subsidiary's stock following the split-off. This is likely to require a substantial discount to fair market value as an inducement.

Second, it is useful to have a liquid market for the subsidiary's stock before the split-off to guide correct ratio for the exchange, and to allow arbitrageurs to buy the parent's shares or debt in the market and tender them in the split-off, facilitating the transaction. The arbitrageurs play a valuable role in ensuring the success of the split-off.

Third, it is important to ensure that there is a liquid market in the subsidiary's stock after the split-off so that the parent's shareholders or debt holders who receive the subsidiary's stock in the split-off are able to easily sell the shares that they receive. Otherwise, they will also not be enthusiastic about offering their parent debt or shares for illiquid subsidiary shares.

The need for a liquid market in the stock of the subsidiary before and after the exchange makes this SER more suitable for a larger-capitalization subsidiary with a very liquid public market in its stock.

CHOOSING THE EXCHANGE RATIO

The exchange ratio, defined as the number of subsidiary shares offered in exchange for each share of parent stock or each debt security, has to be set at just the right level to ensure that the split-off appeals to investors but is not too appealing. If the parent sets the initial fixed ratio too low, investors will not be interested, and the parent will have to go back to investors with a higher amended offer. This will cause delay and expense. If the parent sets the initial ratio higher than necessary, investors will line up to accept the offer, and the split-off will be very successful, but the parent will receive less benefit by retiring less debt or by receiving fewer shares. The exchange ratio is generally set in relation to the market prices of the subsidiary stock and the parent stock or debt, with some added premium to induce investors to go along with the split-off. If any of the securities are not traded on a market, an informed view of the fair market price is used.

However, there is a twist in setting the exchange ratio. When setting the exchange ratio, there are two elements that also need to be considered in addition to the current market prices of the securities. The first element is the impact on the price of the parent's stock or debt and the subsidiary's stock of the split-off itself. This requires determining what the parent's stock or debt, and the subsidiary's stock, will trade for in the market *after* the split-off—*not* before it. The second element is that the activity of arbitrageurs will influence the price of all the securities involved in the split-off before the close. This also has to be factored into the ratio. As a result of arbitrage activity, the price of the parent's stock or debt will rise, and the price of the subsidiary's stock will fall, as arbitrageurs purchase parent shares or debt to exchange for subsidiary stock and then lock in a profit by selling short the subsidiary's shares.

A Dutch auction tender may also be used to let the market set the exchange ratio within bounds set by the parent. In a Dutch auction, each investor sets a minimum exchange ratio that it is willing to accept. The exchange ratio is then set at the lowest single ratio at which all the desired stocks or bonds are offered by investors. All investors who would have accepted a lower ratio receive the benefit of the higher ratio. All those who desired a higher ratio do not get to participate at all. The advantage of a Dutch auction is that (if the bounds are correctly set) it should eliminate the risk that the parent might set the initial fixed ratio too low or too high. The disadvantage of a Dutch auction is that it adds a whole additional level of complication to an already complex transaction.

TYPES OF SPLIT-OFFS

As with most SER transactions, split-offs can be modified to reach specific objectives. With this in mind, the most widely used split-offs are detailed here.

Voluntary Split-Off for Parent Stock

Instead of a straight spin-off through a distribution of the subsidiary's stock to the parent's shareholders, the parent offers to exchange the subsidiary shares it holds for its own parent stock, at a ratio representing a sufficient premium to the current market price for the parent's shares needed to encourage parent shareholders to agree to the exchange. This premium, depending on the liquidity of the subsidiary's stock, may range from 5 to 30 percent. The parent's shareholders then have the option of exchanging their parent shares for subsidiary shares on attractive terms or not doing anything. This is a tax-efficient way for the parent to use an appreciated asset (the subsidiary's stock) to reduce its shares outstanding. Tracking stock may also be used in this transaction. Split-offs for parent stock have also been used to satisfy an individual or group of parent shareholders who no longer wish to own the parent's stock but are not able or are unwilling to sell their holdings in the market.

Mandatory Split-Off for Parent Stock

When it is provided for in the provisions governing the parent's stock or, more usually, a class of the parent's stock or authorized by a shareholder vote, the parent is able to make a mandatory exchange of subsidiary stock for parent shares. The terms of the exchange are usually already defined in the governing documents for the stock. Many tracking stocks (a class of parent shares) have provisions for the mandatory exchange of the tracking stock for the regular parent stock. Some mandatory split-offs may be authorized by shareholder vote of the parent, such as split-ups, which are described below.

Split-Up

A split-up is a form of split-off where there is a mandatory exchange by the parent of the shares of two or more subsidiaries for all the parent's outstanding stock. This is usually followed by liquidation of the parent. In a split-up, the parent's shareholders become shareholders only of each of the subsidiaries. A split-up is another way to break up a parent into two or more independent companies.

Direct Split-Off for Parent Debt

An alternative to an exchange of parent stock for subsidiary stock is an exchange of parent debt for subsidiary stock. With a direct exchange, public debt investors or commercial banks exchange parent debt for shares in the subsidiary. The former debt holders then hold or sell the shares. One advantage of this approach is that it is a very tax-efficient means of retiring debt through the use of an appreciated asset (the subsidiary's stock) without the parent first having to sell the subsidiary stock for cash to investors, incurring tax on any gain on that stock sale, and then using the posttax cash proceeds to repay parent debt. One challenge with this transaction is that most debt holders have no interest in owning shares of any description, because it is not their charter. Therefore these holders often sell the shares they receive immediately. This results in pressure on the subsidiary's stock through uncoordinated sales of subsidiary shares following the split-off. With a direct split-off for parent debt there is no placement effort by an investment bank to market the subsidiary's shares to stock investors. The parent will need to factor in the impact of these subsidiary's shares coming on the market on the price of the subsidiary's stock in calculating the exchange ratio. Another reason to use a split-off is when parent debt holders prefer receiving an ownership interest in the subsidiary such as when the subsidiary has fewer financial or business issues than the parent or when control of a smaller asset than the entire parent is desired. As well, the parent may prefer to use the subsidiary's stock rather than its own to avoid dilution of the ownership of shareholders of the parent.

Many companies today are considering approaches to restructuring their debt. Split-offs for parent debt are a tool that should be looked at with any parent that has or anticipates difficulties meeting its debt service or has a capital structure that is impeding its business. In many cases, the debt is now held by distressed debt investors that may take a more flexible approach to equity ownership than will traditional debt funds.

Indirect Split-Off for Parent Debt

A variation of the preceding transaction is one in which an investment bank purchases the parent's debt from public debt investors or banks for cash, and then exchanges this debt, which it now owns, with the parent in return for shares in the subsidiary. The investment bank then places the subsidiary's shares it owns with institutional investors. This approach ensures a coordinated and marketed placement of the stock. However, the requirements of Section 355 discussed in the following section still have to be met. Generally speaking, the risk involved in such a transaction means that an investment bank will enter into it only if market conditions are buoyant and if it is confident that there is a sufficient demand for the subsidiary's stock for it to place the stock it receives. In the case of Lucent's split-off of Agere for parent debt described below, the parent is reported to have leaned heavily on the investment bank to buy its debt and exchange it for Agere shares. Using an intermediary circumvents the reluctance of many debt holders to own shares, and it allows a coordinated marketing effort to place the subsidiary stock. A variation is where a large equity-oriented investor acquires the parent debt from its holders and privately exchanges the debt for a desired ownership of the subsidiary's shares.

A challenge to any tax-free split-off for parent debt comes from the provisions of IRC Section 355, described in the following section.

TAX CONSIDERATIONS IN A SPLIT-OFF
Split-Off for Parent Debt

When a parent transfers appreciated property to a creditor to repay debt, the transfer is usually treated as a sale of property, on which gain or loss must be recognized for tax purposes. However, this rule does not operate when a parent transfers subsidiary stock taking advantage of IRC Section 355. This rule also does not operate when a parent transfers subsidiary stock to a creditor and when the transfer occurs as part of an otherwise qualifying tax-free spin-off under IRC Section 355. This may be very advantageous to the parent when it uses appreciated subsidiary stock to repay debt without paying tax on any gain. Lucent Technologies, in its SER of Agere Systems, first used subsidiary stock to repay debt on a tax-advantaged basis. However, the requirement of Section 355(e) for more than 50 percent continuing historical ownership will still apply in this situation. Creditors who receive subsidiary shares in exchange for their parent debt will not count toward the 50 percent test historical ownership requirement, as they are not historic parent shareholders. The parent must take care that the split-off still meets the 50 percent historic ownership test after all the shares exchanged with creditors for parent debt are taken into account, including shares issued in a first-step carve-out IPO. Also, IRC Section 368(c) requires that more than 80 percent of the subsidiary be spun off for the exchange to be tax free. As noted previously, the 50 percent test, when combined with the 80 percent test for a tax-free spin-off, usually requires that a split-off for debt be combined with a traditional spin-off of the remaining shares in the subsidiary.

Split-Off for Parent Shares

If all of its requirements of IRC Section 355 are met, it provides for tax-free treatment to the parent and its shareholders on any distribution of subsidiary stock, regardless of whether the distribution is a pro rata spin-off or a non–pro rata split-off. A split-off will be tax-free to shareholders if all of the requirements of Section 355 are met. If a split-off meets all of the requirements of Section 355 except that it fails to meet Section 355(d) or 355(e), it will be taxable to the parent but tax free to the shareholders. If the split-off fails to meet one of the basic requirements of Section 355 (such as the five-year active business requirement) the split-off will be taxable to parent's shareholders. Unlike a spin-off, which is taxable to shareholders as a dividend, a split-off is usually taxable to the parent's shareholders as a capital gain.

However, control and large shareholders in split-offs are subject to the same rules as for stock buybacks. Gain for them will be taxed as a dividend unless there is a "substantial disproportionate reduction" in that shareholder's proportionate interest.

SUMMARY

This chapter examined a unique SER alternative that provides a tax-efficient means of creating value for the parent's shareholders. Yet caution must be exercised with this transaction to ensure that a tax-free basis is attainable and that the proper exchange ratio is achieved. Chapter 12 discusses how private equity partnerships can create successful stand-alone subsidiaries that create value for parents and shareholders.

EXAMPLES OF SPLIT-OFFS
Example 1, Agere Systems/Lucent: Split-Off for Parent Debt

Lucent Technologies first used this structure in its carve-out IPO of its subsidiary, Agere Systems, in March 2001. Simultaneously with the carve-out IPO, an investment bank exchanged Lucent debt, which it had purchased in the market from debt holders, for shares in Agere, which it then resold to institutional investors. The IRS ruling on the Agere transaction also permitted the investment bank to purchase additional debt directly from Lucent and exchange this debt for Agere shares, effectively allowing Lucent to sell Agere shares for cash without incurring any gain.

Exhibit 11–2 illustrates split-off for parent debt in an indirect transaction.

Example 2, AT&T Wireless Services/AT&T: Split-Off for Parent Debt

In July 2001, AT&T, as a selling shareholder, issued 94.5 million shares of AT&T Wireless common stock. AT&T Wireless Services, formerly a wholly owned subsidiary of AT&T, was split off by AT&T and became a separate public company before the offering. This split-off occurred through a redemption of all outstanding AT&T Wireless Group tracking stock and a dividend distribution of the remaining shares of AT&T Wireless common stock to holders of AT&T common stock, less 185.3 million shares retained by AT&T. A distinction between the AT&T and Agere split-offs for parent debt is that Agere was a newly formed entity that had previously been a division of Lucent. The Agere assets were dropped down in a "D" reorganization that permitted the exchange of subsidiary shares to the holders of any parent debt. Without a "D" reorganization, only the holders of the parent's long-term debt would be eligible to participate.

AT&T shareholders received 0.3218 AT&T Wireless shares for each AT&T parent share held in a standard tax-free spin-off. In addition, investment banks agreed to purchase approximately $1.0 billion of the parent's debt from debt holders; they then exchanged that debt to the parent for subsidiary shares. The investment banks then placed those subsidiary shares with institutional stock investors.

EXHIBIT 11–2

Split-Off for Parent Debt

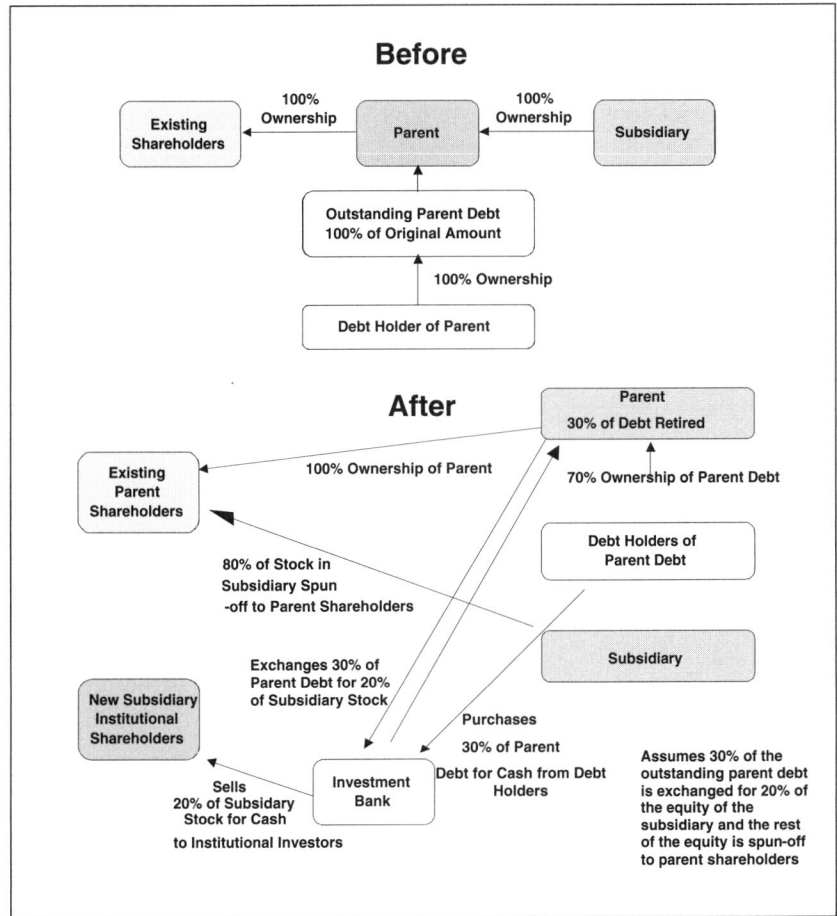

The exchange served the parent as a means of tax-free debt reduction as well as a means of divesting a subsidiary to create value for the parent's shareholders. This structure allowed the parent to use an appreciated asset, its interest in the subsidiary, to pay off debt without incurring intermediate corporate-level taxes.

Example 3, Abercrombie & Fitch/The Limited, Inc.: Split-Off for Parent Stock

In September 1996, The Limited, Inc., sold 8.3 million shares, or 16 percent, of its wholly owned subsidiary Abercrombie & Fitch in a carve-out IPO. In April 1998, it offered to exchange parent shares for the 43.6 million shares, or 84 percent, of

Abercrombie & Fitch that it still held. The exchange was a Dutch auction in which the parent's shareholders could tender the parent's shares for 0.73 to 0.86 a share of A&F for each parent share they held. This was equivalent to a minimum premium of 8.9 percent and a maximum premium of 28.3 percent over the market price of parent shares. The exchange was tax free. In May 1998, the tender closed successfully. Four times as many parent shares were offered for exchange as were specified, and the premium was at the bottom of the range—8.9 percent. As a result, 47.1 million shares of the parent's stock were retired. The Limited was able to spin off Abercrombie & Fitch as an independent company to its shareholders and mitigate the impact on the share value of its own stock by no longer owning this valuable asset. The split-off required a first-step carve-out IPO of the subsidiary to set a value on the Abercrombie & Fitch shares for the exchange.

CHAPTER 12

PRIVATE EQUITY PARTNERSHIPS

INTRODUCTION

Increasingly, partnerships with private equity investors are being used as an SER technique to create shareholder value. This chapter will focus on how private equity partnerships can be used for a range of objectives from providing collaborations to develop emerging technologies into powerful stand-alone businesses that create value for the parent and its shareholders to divestures of large and mature operations. Some private equity partnerships are highly successful, as evidenced by TRW's Corsair, discussed later in this chapter. However, this technique is not always successful, as evidenced by Kmart's Bluelight.com, also discussed later in this chapter. This chapter will examine the structure of private equity partnerships, their advantages and disadvantages, and the goals of private equity investors. The chapter will also provide criteria to help select the best private equity partner.

In today's difficult business environment, private equity partnerships are receiving considerable attention by parents as a means of financing emerging operations with great prospects that the parent can no longer support and for creative ways of divesting noncore activities when a cash divestiture is unavailable or undesired. Overall private equity investing activity has fallen from 1998–2001 levels. However, while activity is down considerably in 2002 from 2000 levels, by historic standards it is still very high, and quality companies continue to receive funding (see Exhibit N–7 in the Endnotes[1]). Private equity funds still have large cash and callable capital available to invest in the right situations. Three years ago, the focus of many private equity investors was on "concepts" that could quickly get public in an overheated IPO market with incredible valuations. In contrast, most established businesses were of no interest. Today most earlier-stage and unproven companies attract less interest from these investors and the focus is more on established businesses with meaningful revenues and customers. Also, investments are now being made with a much longer time horizon and more reasonable return expectations. The advantage of this shift is that a wider range of parent operations may now be of interest to private equity investors. The disadvantage is that promising early-stage operations are receiving less attention. For private equity investors in 2002, divestitures and spin-offs provide an important source of potential investment flow.

Private equity investors today are particularly interested in investing in a subsidiary in conjunction with a spin-off. A pre-spin-off investment by a private equity firm in a spin-off allows the private equity firm to invest a large amount of cash, at a reasonable price with low risk.

Private equity partnerships can also be created for use as financial or accounting vehicles, such as special-purpose off-balance-sheet borrowing and trading partnerships. However, this chapter will not examine these special-purpose partnerships. It likewise will not discuss straight cash divestures of operations to financial buyers where the parent has no further involvement.

DEFINITION OF PRIVATE EQUITY PARTNERSHIP

For the purpose of this chapter, a private equity partnership transaction is defined as an investment by a private equity firm (or firms) in a subsidiary of a parent company. The investment is generally substantial and takes two forms: capital and expertise. The goal of the private equity investors is to transform the subsidiary into a successful company so that they receive a return on their investment after the company is sold, recapitalized, or taken public.

Exhibit 12–1 is a graphical depiction of a private equity partnership.

OUTLINE OF A TYPICAL PRIVATE EQUITY PARTNERSHIP STRUCTURE

Private equity partnerships may take many forms and may be structured in various ways. However, the components of the structure detailed as follows is common to most equity partnerships:

- A new subsidiary is formed and the parent contributes operations, facilities, employees, customers, revenues, expertise, intellectual property, products, and other resources to it.

- Outside equity funding is obtained from private equity investors.

- The outside investors actively participate in building the new company. They may hire management, recruit directors, provide strategic direction, foster alliances, and take the lead in obtaining additional capital. They may also sponsor strategic mergers and acquisitions to grow and strengthen the business.

- The parent may perform ongoing services for the new company for which it receives payment.

EXHIBIT   12-1

Private Equity Partnership

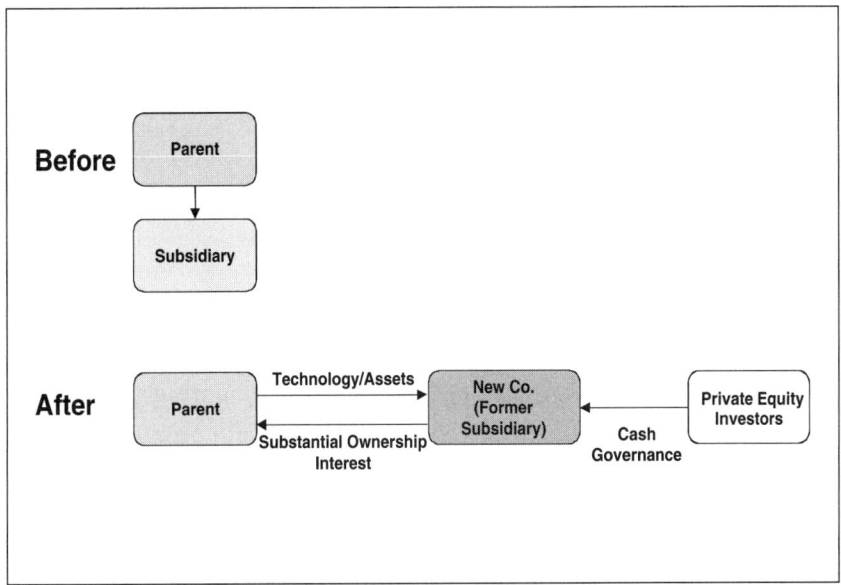

For its initial and ongoing contribution, the parent receives some combination of equity ownership, royalties, cash, notes, and commercial contracts negotiated with the private equity investors. Generally, with an earlier-stage business, the bulk of new cash from the private equity investors goes into the new company. With a more mature operation that is generating cash, all or a considerable portion of the new cash may go to the parent.

• The private equity investors will usually require that the parent relinquish strategic control of the operation. The objective is to create a stand-alone successful company that goes public, is sold, or otherwise generates returns for its shareholders.

ADVANTAGES OF A PRIVATE EQUITY PARTNERSHIP FOR PARENT AND SUBSIDIARY

The contribution made by private equity investors to the partnership depends on the stage of development of the operation. The roles will differ considerably between an emerging and a mature operation. These include:

• *Provides experienced support to build an emerging business.* Experienced private equity investors can greatly assist in building the subsidiary, recruiting a management team, forming relationships with customers, and setting business strategy. Certain private equity investors may have more experience than the parent in building a specific business. Private equity investors are also often more plugged in than many parents to an alliance framework where collaboration is common and can greatly accelerate the success of the subsidiary.

- *Provides needed cash for building the business.* Private equity investors invest cash into the subsidiary and assist in funding key business initiatives. They will also raise additional capital for the subsidiary from other private equity investors. Where the parent does not wish or is unable to fund the subsidiary and its divestiture potential is limited at the time, the alternative to a private equity partnership is an entirely lost opportunity.

- *Provides a higher overall return route to a complete divestiture.* A private equity partnership may provide immediate cash to the parent and a means to obtain additional value later. Where the parent wishes to divest itself of an operation but believes that its value will be significantly greater in the future, a private equity partnership allows the parent to participate in that upside. This is especially relevant for well-positioned businesses that have been hit by cyclical downturns in markets.

- *Sponsors the subsidiary to go public.* The involvement of experienced and respected private equity investors is a significant asset to the subsidiary in an IPO. Private equity firms are in touch with the IPO market and provide an assessment of the readiness of the subsidiary and its management team to go public. As the IPO market has evolved in recent years, even after the setbacks of 2000 and 2001, the involvement of certain experienced and respected private equity firms is still an asset to assure IPO investors.

  Respected private equity investors demonstrate to IPO investors that there are quality corporate governance practices in place, the relationship with the parent is fair, there is a strong management team, there is a focus on creating shareholder value, and timely action will be taken on issues of importance.

  IPO investors are well aware that studies have consistently shown that IPOs with respected private equity investors generate higher returns in the aftermarket following the IPO, compared to non–private equity IPOs. Several studies have found significantly higher returns for venture capital (VC)–backed IPOs.[2] For example, one study finds that the five-year returns on IPOs are significantly higher for a sample of venture-backed firms than for non-venture-backed firms (though this is partly correlated to the larger size of venture-backed IPOs).[3]

  The leading private equity firms know how to generate favorable buzz about a company and introduce it to investment banks, industry analysts, and the press. This often results in more interest from investors, who have already heard about the company during the IPO process.

- *Assists in a spin-off.* In conjunction with a single-step spin-off, a private equity investor may help place a value on the subsidiary and provide some of the support and visibility for the subsidiary with Wall Street that would otherwise come from a first-step carve-out IPO.

- *Increases the ability of the subsidiary to respond to market demands.* Today's markets require that the subsidiary move quickly to exploit market opportunities. The equity and governance provided by private equity investors can create a culture of quick decision making so that it can respond to market demands quickly. For example, a study by two Stanford Business School professors[4] demonstrates that companies with private equity backers were three times more likely to get a product or service to market in any given time period.

- *Allows entry into new areas.* The parent may have opportunities to enter into new markets based on available technology, facilities, or the strength of its brand. However, it may be unfamiliar with the requirements to succeed in these markets. A private equity partnership can help the parent create a successful subsidiary that will maximize these new opportunities.

- *Allows radical initiatives to succeed.* Radical new initiatives are often lost inside large companies because their charter is not in line with the existing business focus, or they face intense competition for budget and staffing and lack the support of operating management. Even with the support of senior management they often flounder. Separating these units out with venture funding may be the only means for them to provide returns to the parent's shareholders.

- *Provides a reality check.* Private equity investors will also provide a reality check on projects. While far from infallible, a lack of interest by private equity investors in a project may be an indication that there are greater problems or less potential than is believed by the internal team. In particular, private equity partners know from experience that successful commercialization of a product creates success—not the underlying technology of the product in and of itself. Private equity investors will not be impressed by great technology unless there is clear commercial appeal.

- *Sets unwavering focus on the bottom line.* Private equity investors are good at increasing focus at the operation on meeting budgets. They also are good at identifying immediate commercial opportunities, and curtailing investment in projects that are less commercially viable. They are also less encumbered by long-standing relationships and take a fresh look at all aspects of the business. The parent can be confident that the private equity investors will do everything possible to create shareholder value by a sole focus on maximizing its investment. As long as the parent and the private equity firm have this interest aligned, the private equity firm will work to build value for the parent.

CHALLENGES OF PRIVATE EQUITY PARTNERSHIP FOR THE PARENT

The challenges of a private equity partnership for the parent include the following.

The Subsidiary Must Meet Specific Requirements

Most subsidiaries will not meet the criteria for a private equity investment. These criteria range from those of:

- Traditional venture private equity investors who look for large markets, growth, and a proprietary position and are willing to take reasonable risk. Although venture funds have been getting much larger in recent years, projects requiring hundreds of millions of dollars are usually not available from this group. Venture funds are used to providing company building assistance.

- Buyout investors who look for large, stable, cash-generating businesses and are very willing to make multi-hundred-million-dollar investments. They are masters at financial engineering and building companies through mergers.

DISADVANTAGES OF PRIVATE EQUITY PARTNERSHIPS
Culture Shock at the Subsidiary

The employees of the subsidiary may be in for a shock. For example, there is the shock of working within a very profit-orientated culture, reduced cash compensation and benefits compared to that offered by the parent, and intense pressure to demonstrate continuous progress. Some will thrive; others will be out of place. Furthermore, subsidiary employees may not be able to return to the parent if the venture fails.

Viable Stand-Alone Business

For the type of partnership discussed in this chapter, the subsidiary should be a viable stand-alone business. This usually requires the parent to turn over to the partnership all critical assets and employees.

Control

As a general rule, a private equity firm will not invest in an entity when the parent controls its strategic direction. This requirement comes from a well-founded belief that the parent may have other agendas than the sole pursuit of equity return for the shareholders of the subsidiary, even though the parent is also one of those shareholders.

Private equity investors also want control because they know that parents tend to change objectives and agendas. Also, staff turnover is common, and corporate decision making is often slow, impeding the parent's ability to react quickly to changing market demands.

The Timing of Exit Strategies May Not Mesh

Private equity investors are not long-term investors and are interested in an exit strategy within a reasonable time frame that depends on their stage of investment (and the market for IPOs and mergers). In the late 1990s, time frames went down dramatically as high-value IPOs and sales were so very available. In normal times, private equity investors will have a five- to eight-year time horizon to realize an investment. Late-stage investors typically have a shorter time horizon. The need for a liquidity event may not fit the parent's timetable.

Because private equity investors need a route to liquidity, the company must be working toward this objective from early on. Friction will occur if the parent does not recognize and support the time/return needs of private equity investors.

Buyback Options Are Limited

If the parent later decides that separation was not a good idea, buyback options for the parent may be limited. The parent will probably not have an option to buy back the holdings of the private equity investors at an up-front agreed price or at a fixed rate of return to the private equity investors—even a generous one. This is often requested by the parent but is usually unacceptable to the private equity investors who see it as a means for them to share the higher early-on risk of a project but not share the full potential return. Even an option for the parent to have the right to buy out the private equity investors based on an agreed formula or a right of first refusal will be very contentious, as it could limit the profit alternatives for the private equity investors. Should the parent later decide that it prefers to have ownership of the subsidiary, this may be very expensive to achieve.

High Return Expectations

Private equity fund return-on-investment requirements, reflected in the percentage of the subsidiary they will insist on owning for economic gain, often appall corporate managers and can be a roadblock to investment. The best private equity investors sell much more than money; they are also selling the value of their time, connections, and experience. They recognize that their involvement may contribute to the subsidiary's success—and want to be duly compensated for it. Private equity investors can be involved in only a limited number of portfolio companies at one time and need to make a high return to justify their involvement in these investments.

The return expectations do vary by type of private equity fund. Venture capital funds usually have the highest return expectations, reflecting investments in smaller, riskier, and earlier-stage operations. Buyout funds tend to have considerably lower return expectations, reflecting investments in larger, safer, and more mature operations.

The issue for the parent is not what it is giving up to the private equity investors, but the value that it is receiving from them. Parents need to ask themselves if the end value of the subsidiary will be higher with the involvement of the private equity investors to justify the percentage of the subsidiary they will need to give to the private equity investors. It is also important to figure in their ability to later promote lower-cost capital in subsequent private financing rounds and earlier access to the public markets.

Complex Corporate Structures May Limit Interest

Structurally complex companies usually do not interest venture capital (VC) investors because the VC model is based on a very simple corporate structure. In contrast, buyout funds are happy to consider complex structures. The restructuring of Seagate is a good example of a complex structure that created value for Seagate's shareholders.

Private Equity Transactions Are Involved and Time Consuming

Private equity partnerships are complex transactions incorporating business, investment, and technical agreements; intellectual property transfers; and many issues regarding assumption of liabilities and obligations. The partnership negotiations may take up to a year to close.

Bureaucratic Delays Frustrate Private Equity Investors

Private equity investors generally have a high frustration level when working with larger companies. Private equity investors make decisions fairly fast with little bureaucracy. They have small staffs that need to keep moving forward to close transactions and cannot devote inordinate time to one investment possibility. The parent, in contrast, will have its own timetables and procedures. In many cases, private equity investors abandon a partnership prospect if it is taking too long. The parent must recognize the limited resources of a private equity firm if it is interested in a successful close.

Additional Funding Requirements from the Parent

Private equity funds have grown considerably larger in recent years, and the size of possible fund commitments to a single investment project has grown considerably as well. Still, the willingness of a fund to commit additional capital to any individual portfolio company following the initial investment is limited by a continually updated view on the expected returns. This is particularly a concern where the subsidiary is of strategic importance to the parent. Should the subsidiary not meet its forecasts or offer a good prospect of a return on the new investment, the private equity investors may decide not to provide further funding. If the parent then does not wish to see the operation constrained or terminated for lack of funding, the burden of future funding will be placed back onto the parent.

SELECTING THE RIGHT PRIVATE EQUITY FIRM

Choosing the right equity firm is critical. In the late 1990s, many private equity funds, particularly venture capital funds, enjoyed high returns. In hindsight, this had a great deal more to do with the extraordinary market conditions at the time than the genius of the investors. The parent should not be overawed by the reputation of a private equity firm. First, the partners who were responsible for building the firm reputation may now be less active. These partners almost always had operational backgrounds before turning to investing and as a result brought great value to their portfolio companies. Today, many of the professionals at private equity firms do not have this operational experience. Some of the most idolized private equity investors of the late 1990s who received great media attention and applause and made large fortunes were actually just carnival promoters, not builders of companies. These promotional skills are useless today, when it is necessary to build real companies to build value.

Unless a particular private equity fund and the professional within that fund have deep experience in the industry and the subsidiary's stage of development, the private equity investor's contribution to the subsidiary will be disappointing to the parent.

Private equity partnerships usually involve a close and continuing relationship with the private equity partners. There need to be trust and respect on both sides. There also needs to be sufficient commitment of time by the private equity professionals actually working on the project for the success of the partnership. A "drive-by" investor (the industry term for an overstretched private equity professional who sits on many boards of directors and does not have the time to learn about or make a meaningful contribution to any portfolio company), however talented, will not be an asset.

PROFIT REQUIREMENTS DRIVE PRIVATE EQUITY FUNDS

Before examining the various types of equity funds, it is important to note that there are some elements common to most funds—namely, demanding rates of return and fund compensation arrangements. Let's look at each more closely.

Rate of Return Demands

Private equity investors are driven by the internal rate of return. In their world, the clock is always ticking. They need to demonstrate high returns to their own investors to continue to receive funding.

Fund Compensation Arrangements

Private equity funds are generally compensated in two ways. They are paid an annual management fee and an incentive fee based on the success of investments. Some firms also charge portfolio companies various fees and expenses, though additional fees are more typical in the leveraged buyout world than in the venture world.

In most cases, the incentive fee is paid to the private equity fund only when an investment is actually realized. Realization may be a sale in which cash proceeds or stock of the acquirer are distributed to the investors in the private equity fund or it may be the distribution of nonrestricted stock to the investors following an IPO. The motivation to be a private equity investor is the incentive fee. The management fee is nice and covers expenses, but the incentive fee is the pot of gold.

The Structure of Private Equity Funds

Private equity firms typically organize and manage a series of limited partnerships to make investments. The limited partners, who put up the majority of the capital for the partnership, are typically institutions such as state pension funds, insurance companies, charitable foundations, and university endowments, as well as wealthy individuals. Some family, corporate, and bank funds get all their funds from one investor—the sponsoring family, company, or bank. The private equity firm usually has sole responsibility for managing the fund, making investments, and monitoring investments. Some private equity funds are small business investment corporation (SBIC) affiliates licensed and partially funded by the U.S. Small Business Administration (SBA). There are many restrictions on eligible investments imposed by the SBA.

A typical private equity partnership starts with a fixed commitment of capital from the limited partners. The limited partners agree, in advance, to fund up to a certain amount, known as *committed capital,* when called upon by the private equity firm. The partnership then draws down the committed capital from its limited partners by calling in capital as it makes investments over an investment period that ranges from one to five years. At the end of the investment period, or earlier if the available capital has been fully committed to investments, the private equity firm stops making new investments in that particular partnership, except for follow-on investments in existing portfolio companies. In most cases, private equity firms do not make initial investments with the entire committed capital of a partnership. They will leave a significant portion of the committed capital available for anticipated follow-on investments in existing portfolio companies in that partnership.

Liquidating Nature of Most Private Equity Funds

After making its initial investments, most private equity partnerships liquidate as the companies in the portfolio go public or are sold. Generally, funds distribute to their investors or limited partners cash and public stock received in the sale of a portfolio company and stock in a portfolio company that goes public when the shares become unrestricted. The investors or limited partners make their own decision on whether to hold or sell the shares received in the distribution. Institutions tend to sell shares received in a distribution. This may put pressure on the stock in the immediate period following the distribution. If a private equity firm has a sizable stock position in a portfolio company, it may delay or stagger distributions of stock in that company to limit pressure on the market. They invest once and then liquidate. After the investment period on a given partnership, the firm will raise another partnership to make new investments. The raising of new partnerships every few years is an ongoing activity for these firms. Some of the older firms have raised 10 or more successive partnerships. Some family, corporate, and bank funds are *evergreen* funds that retain proceeds to fund new investments.

As a result, every few years, most private equity firms must generally go back to the well of existing and new investors and raise a new fund. In order to receive new funds, they need to show high rates of return on investments made in prior funds and actual liquidity events that return real cash or cash-equivalent public unrestricted securities to investors.

In addition, most private equity funds have a limited time horizon, which is compounded by the fact that the partnerships themselves are usually of only limited life—usually 10 or 12 years from closing.

TYPES OF PRIVATE EQUITY FIRMS MAKING INVESTMENTS IN SUBSIDIARIES

Previously this chapter defined equity partnerships and examined their advantages and disadvantages. This has laid the groundwork for an in-depth look at the various types of equity funds operating today that invest in partnerships with parents. They fall into six main groups:

- Traditional capital venture firms
- Later-stage venture funds
- Corporate investors
- Commercial and investment bank private equity affiliates
- Nonleveraged buyout and restructuring funds
- Leveraged buyout funds

Let's look at each in more detail.

Traditional Capital Venture Firms

The cash resources of traditional venture firms range from tens of millions of dollars to several billion dollars.

Many of the original private equity investors after World War II were family funds such as J. H. Whitney & Company (Whitney family) and Venrock Associates (Rockefeller family) that invested in a range of transactions from early-stage seed capital to management buyouts. These funds defined the institutional venture capital industry and built fabled reputations. However, the relative influence of the family funds has, in recent years, been eclipsed by funds with broader funding from large managers of money such as state pension funds and college endowments, and by generational changes at the sponsoring families leading to reduced support for the venture operations.

Traditional venture capitalists tend to be active investors. They are usually involved in day-to-day decision making and all significant strategic and financial decisions. Depending on the experience and capabilities of the individual venture capitalist, the value of this participation may be stellar. Traditional venture capitalists are also actively involved in recruiting and changing senior management of portfolio companies. Some of the most active American venture firms in 2002 are Accel Partners, Alta Partners, Menlo Ventures, New Enterprise Associates, Polaris Venture Partners, Sequoia Capital, and U.S. Venture Partners. Some of the most active European venture firms in 2002 are 3i Group (United Kingdom), Advent Venture Partners (United Kingdom), Apax Partners (United Kingdom), GIMV (Belgium), Sofinnova Partners (France), and STAR Ventures (Germany).

Today, many traditional venture firms are less interested in start-up and early-stage ventures. This is understandable given the large amount of cash these funds have available to invest, the lowered experience levels at many of the firms, the poor recent returns from early-stage investing, the drying up of the IPO and merger market, and the disappearance of sources of follow-on capital. While most traditional venture firms today are primarily focused on making larger investments in more mature operations, there are still some smaller funds that remain committed to making early-stage investments. These include Still River Ventures in Boston, Selby Venture Partners in Silicon Valley, Alta Partners in San Francisco, and Sequel Ventures in Boulder, Colorado. The choice of venture firm to approach for a given project should take into account the size of the project relative to the fund.

Later-Stage Venture Funds

Later-stage funds are private equity funds that generally invest in the last, or near last, private round of an already venture-backed company before its IPO or sale. Later-stage investments are often called *mezzanine* investments. This use of the term reflects that these equity investments fit between traditional venture capital and the public markets. This use of the term is unconnected with the use of the term *mezzanine* in leveraged buyouts, where it refers to the subordinated debt above the equity but below the senior debt in the capital structure.

Until the mid-1990s, this sector of investing was made up of a small number of established later-stage investors and reasonable valuations. Later-stage funds focused exclusively on lower-risk investments in companies with a reasonable expectation of a near-term IPO or sale. With a shorter time horizon and lower expected risk, later-stage funds were comfortable with somewhat higher valuations than traditional venture firms. Leading late-stage firms included crossover investors such as Integral Capital Partners and Technology Crossover Ventures (*crossover* investors invest in both the public stock market and also the later stage venture market).

In the late 1990s and 2000, the nature of the later-stage market private equity completely changed. A large range of financial institutions delved into late-stage financing as a way to participate in the expected profits of the Internet and telecom bubbles. These investors included insurance companies, pension funds, public mutual funds, and hedge funds that invest primarily in public equities. The later-stage market became characterized by valuations unconnected with reality. Many disastrous investments were made. Most of these new entrants withdrew from the market after 2000 with large losses, finding that private equity investing was not as easy as it looked.

Corporate Investors

Corporations make long-term strategic venture capital investments to grow markets and gain access to promising new small companies. However, corporate venture investors have a justified reputation (with notable stalwart exceptions such as Intel and Cadence) for entering and existing the venture area in response to short-term financial market and business conditions and not supporting portfolio companies in more difficult times.

Corporate venture capital goes in and out of favor with large corporations. Corporate venture capital was very popular in the early 1980s when companies such as Exxon established venture operations. This period of activity was followed by large losses, and most corporations decided that they should not be venture capitalists after all. Corporate venture capital was fairly dormant until the late 1990s, when large corporations as diverse as Starbucks, News Corporation, Amazon.com, and Dell Computer launched corporate venture capital operations. Corporate venture investing grew from some $800 million in 1997 to $17 billion in 2000—more than twice the overall growth rate of venture investing, according to PricewaterhouseCoopers.

After some early successes, there was again a drumroll of setbacks. In the second quarter of 2001 alone, write-offs by corporate venture funds totaled over $9.5 billion, according to *Corporate Venturing Report.* Corporate venture investing has fallen faster than overall venture activity to less than $1.2 billion in the first half of 2002. Many corporations such as Lucent, E. W. Scripps, and Accenture closed their venture operations entirely. Others have scaled venture activities way down. For example, Dell Ventures invested in 55 financings in 2000 but only 3 during the first six months of 2002.

Corporate investors tend to invest in areas of strategic importance to the parent's businesses. In common with later-stage investment funds, many corporate investors also prefer to invest in companies that already have the involvement of traditional VC fund corporations. They make venture investments through a number of different vehicles, including internally managed venture funds (Intel Ventures), dedicated outside venture funds with management from the parent (Cadence's Telos Ventures), and outside funds with their own independent management (KLA-Tencor's KT Ventures), dedicated funds run for the parent by established venture firms (Adobe's Adobe Ventures, administered for many years by Hambrecht & Quist), consortium funds of a number of corporations with a common investment interest (Allegis Capital), and as limited partner investors in traditional venture funds.

A strategy for corporate venture investing after the bubble is stated by Mike Volpi, senior vice president at Cisco:

> Cisco invested approximately $500 million in 100 venture investments in 1999. We expect to invest approximately $100 million in 10 to 15 investments in 2002. Cisco generally does not lead investments; we do not play the role of venture capitalist. We provide start-ups with credibility and access to key customers. Our expertise is not in helping small companies grow. We tend to be mid- to later-stage investors where we can add value. We do look for financial returns, but we invest for the strategic relationship. For Cisco, a model investment was TIBCO (an Internet software provider). It was financially successful, but more importantly the companies were jointly successful in developing and driving a new market segment.

Commercial and Investment Bank Private Equity Affiliates

A number of the large commercial and investment banks are active private equity investors. Their activity spans the spectrum from traditional venture capital to leveraged buyouts. These include J.P. Morgan Ventures, Sprout Group (CS First Boston), Morgan Stanley Ventures, Goldman Sachs Partners, and Needham & Company. Their activities range from traditional venture capital to leveraged buyouts.

Nonleveraged Buyout and Recapitalization Funds

There are now several large funds that make majority or significant minority investments in larger, established growth companies or subsidiaries. Like traditional venture funds, these investors are interested primarily in companies or subsidiaries with growth potential and do not use much, if any, debt. Like leveraged buyout funds, they favor control or very significant ownership positions in substantial and established businesses with large revenues and earnings, and they are comfortable, when appropriate, with the parent receiving all or part of their investment. These funds have the financial means, interest, and expertise to structure large and complex transactions. Silverlake Partners is an example of such a fund. Some traditional venture capital funds also focus on making major investments in established growth subsidiaries. These funds include Advent International, Summit Partners, Francisco Partners, General Atlantic, and TA Associates.

Leveraged Buyout Funds

These funds also focus on majority investments in established subsidiaries. These funds employ debt and look primarily to pay off this debt from cash flow to generate returns. The best candidates to support high debt levels are generally mature businesses that have predictable, steady, and current cash flow available for debt service after meeting all the needs of the business. These funds are very active buyers of subsidiaries in sale divestitures. They have been less active in partnerships, as these are not their traditional model of buying entire mature businesses. A business generating substantial cash flow with large noncash charges will often be more attractive to an LBO investor than it might be to an investor more focused on public market potential.

Most buyout funds may accept a need to strengthen the management team but rarely will go into a situation requiring a completely new management team.

SUMMARY

This chapter examined the role that private equity partnerships can play in creating successful subsidiaries that create value for both the parent and its shareholders. Of course, partnerships come with inherent risks, as equity partnerships have strict performance criteria that must be met, which may be unsettling to employees. Nevertheless, when executed properly, these partnerships can transform company culture and performance to create companies that survive and thrive in today's competitive marketplace. (See Exhibit 12–2.) Chapter 13 will examine the use of corporate strategic partnerships as a viable SER alternative.

EXAMPLES OF PRIVATE EQUITY PARTNERSHIPS

Example 1, Corsair Communications, Inc.: A Successful Venture Capital Partnership Followed by an IPO

TRW is a large automotive and defense supplier headquartered in Cleveland, Ohio, with a substantial space and military electronics operation based in Redondo Beach, California, in what is known as Space Park.

The Space Park operation has implemented a series of partnerships with venture capitalists and corporate partners to commercially exploit its outstanding military technology. Because of its utilization of partnerships and alliances, Space Park has been among the most successful large military contractors commercially exploiting its military technology, including a corporate alliance with venture-backed RF Micro Devices.

Space Park's first experience with a partnership to commercialize a military technology was with an advanced technology developed for better friend-or-foe identification in the military. With this TRW technology, each individual U.S. military radio transmitter in the field was uniquely fingerprinted, preventing an enemy from impersonating a friendly asset with stolen codes. In 1994, TRW believed that this technology could prevent analog cellular telephone cloning fraud, then a prevalent and unsolvable multi-billion-dollar problem in large urban areas. TRW believed that its radio-frequency fingerprinting technology was the solution to the cloning problem.

TRW had unsuccessfully attempted to market this technology on its own to the cellular industry. After considerable expense and wasted effort, TRW came to recognize that it did not have either the skills to adapt the "fingerprinting technol-

Summary Characteristics of the Types of Private Equity Investors

Type of fund	Capital structure preference	Areas of investing comfort	Typical exit strategy	Advantages	Disadvantages
Traditional venture capital (VC) funds	Traditional venture funds finance their investment entirely through equity capital. Convertible preferred is the standard venture security. Terms used to be very simple. Recently there has been a greater focus on trying to ensure returns in uncertain times through complex terms.	Most focused on smaller and earlier-stage technologies, and subsidiaries. Prefer all funds to go into the business.	VC buyers look to build value by growing the business rapidly. IPOs have been the traditional preferred liquidity alternative of VC buyers. In recent years, a sale to a strategic buyer is becoming the dominant exit.	The best bring a wide range of relationships in the business and financial communities, operating experience, and deep knowledge of company building. Are very active to ensure the success of the business. The only institutional investors interested in earlier-stage operations.	Time sensitive once invested. Younger generation of VCs often do not have operating experience and have not been through difficult times. Valuation sensitive with high return expectations.
Later-stage venture capital funds and crossover/mezzanine funds	Convertible preferred is the standard security. However, often add "bells and whistles" to reduce risk and lock in a level of return.	These funds are comfortable with growth companies. Taking control positions and complex structures are not of interest. These funds tend not to lead transactions but participate with later-stage VC funds. These funds do not like turnarounds or investments without a near-term IPO or sale.	IPOs have traditionally been the preferred liquidity alternative of VC buyers. Increasingly, a sale to a strategic buyer is also considered.	Higher valuations. Connections with investment banks for a later IPO. Do not interfere. Few of the many new entrants in the late 1990s are left.	Will generally only invest following top-tier VCs. Terms often are complex and limit future financial flexibility. Very time sensitive once invested. Looking to maximize its realized internal rate of return. Not great value-added. Often will not invest in follow-on later rounds.
Corporate investors	Similar to later-stage VC funds.	These funds are comfortable with risk within their industry. These funds tend not to lead transactions but participate with later-stage VC funds.	The primary investment motive in normal markets is not return but furthering corporate strategic goals.	May pay the highest valuation due to lower return hurdles than other private equity investors. Synergies may be available to a strategic investor.	Often will not invest in follow-on later rounds. Despite rhetoric about "long-term strategic" commitment, most corporate investors exit the private equity area in difficult times.

Type of fund	Capital structure preference	Areas of investing comfort	Typical exit strategy	Advantages	Disadvantages
		These funds tend to look to situations where the corporate relationship has value-added.		Longer time frame. Some corporate investors are solid support through all seasons.	
Nonleveraged buyout funds	Comfortable participating in complex structures with multiple layers of equity and redeemable preferred and subordinated debt. The nonleveraged buyout funds use little or no bank and high-yield market debt.	These funds combine the control and structuring emphasis of the LBO funds with the comfort of high-growth companies of later-stage VC funds.	These buyers look to build value through growth, asset sales, and the restructuring of operations. These buyers look for liquidity through distributions of the proceeds of asset sales, an IPO, or a sale to a strategic buyer.	Not dependent on the availability of debt to finance the large part of the investment. An equity-oriented capital structure is generally more appropriate for growth or turnaround subsidiaries where cash is needed to grow the business and not debt service.	A relatively small source of capital.
Traditional LBO funds	LBO funds finance their investment primarily by borrowing against the assets and future cash flows of the company in which they are investing.	These funds are comfortable with complex financial engineering structures. Investing in high-growth companies is not the primary activity of LBO funds, though they will, from time to time, make such investments.	LBO fund buyers look to build value through paying down the acquisition debt through operating cash flows, asset sales, and the restructuring of operations. LBO buyers look for liquidity through distributions of cash flow, distributions of the proceeds of asset sales, releveraging the company, an IPO, or a sale to a financial buyer or a strategic buyer.	Large funds for large deals. Often able to take the entire transaction up front and later syndicate it (a "bought deal").	Usually require control. Often large fees. Financial orientation. Lack of experience with growth companies. Dependent on the availability of senior and subordinate debt capital to finance most of the investment. Focus is back on current cash flow after disastrous forays into speculative areas in the late 1990s.

ogy to the demands of the cellular industry nor the expertise to exploit commercial markets.

The primary objectives of TRW in considering the SER of its fingerprinting technology were as follows:

• *Bringing in commercial expertise.* TRW needed to obtain outside expertise and experience in commercial wireless services from outside the company to make a commercial success of the fingerprinting technology.

• *Eliminating losses from TRW's income statement.* TRW's attempts to develop and market the fingerprinting technology for commercial uses had already resulted in large losses at TRW. Also it anticipated additional large losses before the technology succeeded in the commercial market and became profitable. These would hit TRW's reported earnings and therefore its stock value.

• *Generating revenues.* TRW wished to manufacture the electronic hardware that went with the fingerprinting technology to produce revenues and profit for the parent.

• *Retaining a continued equity interest to reward TRW shareholders for its investment in the technology.* TRW maintained a reasonable equity interest in Corsair, and its shareholders profited from the value of this holding.

Before deciding on a private equity partnership, TRW also considered a sale of the technology to a strategic buyer and an alliance joint venture with a large industry partner. No other alternative allowed TRW to meet all the aforementioned objectives. Therefore, TRW decided to seek a partnership with experienced venture investors to commercialize the technology.

The negotiations between the parent and the private equity investors took nine months. The first hurdle was valuation. TRW had locked onto unrealistic revenue forecasts for the fingerprinting technology's success in the commercial market before the negotiations. This set unachievable valuation expectations, which took time to recalibrate. Most of the other issues hinged on the requirement by the private equity investors that the fingerprinting technology be handed over to a new stand-alone company not controlled by TRW after the SER. This was a new concept for TRW and therefore created conflicts within TRW and between TRW and the investors. These conflicts had to be negotiated as follows:

• *Equity for the TRW employees transferring to the new company.* The private equity investors required that employees of the new company receive substantial equity positions. This created a perception at the parent that the employees of TRW transferring to the new company were receiving disproportionate rewards compared to parent employees.

• *Intellectual property rights.* TRW required protection for the identification technology that it viewed as strategic to its defense and satellite businesses. The private equity investors required that the new company have freedom to use the technology in commercial applications. There were prolonged negotiations over what technology would be leaving TRW and the ability of the new company to use it.

• *Engineering team.* TRW wished to retain at TRW the key engineers on the identification technology. The private equity investors required that a reasonably strong engineering team go with the new company.

However, over the course of the discussions, TRW Space Park came to understand the needs of the private equity investors and agreement was reached.

In December 1994, the new company was launched to exploit the fingerprinting technology with the name Corsair Communications. TRW and the private equity investors owned it. The new company raised $13.2 million in cash and $3 million in notes from four venture capital firms: Kleiner Perkins Caufield & Byers, Norwest Venture Partners, Sevin Rosen Funds, and Needham Capital Partners. After the financing, the venture capital firms owned approximately 68 percent of Corsair, TRW owned 22 percent, and management owned approximately 10 percent.

At the same time, Corsair paid TRW $9.2 million ($6.2 million in cash and $3 million in notes) for a perpetual license for the "fingerprinting technology for use in commercial wireless telecommunications markets, as well as in process R&D and the assignment of contracts. Corsair assumed the lease of the TRW facility in California, where the fingerprinting capability was based. The majority of the TRW engineering team working on the fingerprinting product transferred to Corsair and successfully transitioned to a commercial environment.

What the venture capitalists obtained in the partnership was a raw technology that was promising but far from ready for the commercial market. It took several years of intense effort to bring the cost and size of the military product down to a level where it would be attractive to cellular operators. Selling the cellular industry on a new product that took scarce real estate at a cellular base station (often atop a pole) also took several years of intense effort to qualify the product and then successfully sell it. The venture capital investors brought in an entire new senior management team with a CEO from the cellular industry, Mary Ann Byrnes.

While TRW gave up control and a substantial part of the ownership, it obtained expertise, considerable funding, and a fine return.

After the formation of Corsair, TRW continued to play an active role in the technological development of Corsair. With its strong VC sponsorship, Corsair later raised two additional rounds of private financings.

Corsair performed well, as seen in Exhibit 12–3.

Corsair completed an IPO on attractive terms in July 1997. TRW had 10.2 percent of Corsair following the IPO, valued at $21 million at the end of 1997.

The financing history of Corsair is set out in Exhibit 12–4. This illustrates a progression of private financing at higher valuations followed by an IPO. This is exactly what should happen in a successful venture capital partnership.

E X H I B I T   12–3

Corsair Communications Summary of Operations

	1994	1995	1996	1997	1998
($ in millions)					
Revenues	$0	$8	$20	$47	$65
Operating income	(6)	(9)	(13)	(1)	(5)
Net income	(6)	(8)	(13)	(1)	(7)

TRW Applies the Lessons Learned

The lessons that Space Park took away from the Corsair process served it well in its next SER, the tremendously successful strategic partnership with RF Micro Devices, described in Chapter 13.[5]

Example 2, Kmart: An Unsuccessful Venture Capital Partnership

In December 1999, Kmart Corporation, the nation's second-largest discount retailer and the third-largest general merchandise retailer, announced the formation of the BlueLight.com subsidiary. BlueLight.com was responsible for the online sales of Kmart's products as well as offering free Internet access. K-mart became the majority shareholder of BlueLight.com with an approximately 60 percent ownership. Softbank Venture Capital led the initial financing round, investing $62.5 million, and Martha Stewart Living Omnimedia, a retail partner of Kmart, made a strategic investment as well.

E X H I B I T   12–4

Corsair Communications Financing History

Private venture capital financings			IPO
$12,200,000	$9,050,000	$18,000,000	$37,500,000
6,100,000 shares	2,011,111 shares	3,272,728 shares	2,500,000 shares
Series A	Series B	Series C	Public offering
Preferred stock	Preferred stock	Preferred stock	Common stock
December 1994	October 1995	October 1996	July 1997
Valuation: $20 million	Valuation: $55 million	Valuation: $84 million	Valuation: $199 million

BlueLight.com was created to give away free Internet access, with the hope of boosting sales of Kmart's products online and generating independent revenue through advertising. Kmart's goal was to take BlueLight.com public within two years of its formation, but due to the bursting of the Internet bubble, that did not occur.

As a business, BlueLight's free Internet service, supported by advertising and e-retailing, was not a viable model. In July 2001, Kmart announced it was abandoning the free service. The revenue to support a free Internet service provider business model was not there. As well, with the speculative bubble over in Internet retailing, Kmart had to make the site work as a business, not just a concept for investors. It also recognized that its customers needed to be served by one unified company across a range of sales channels from physical stores to an online shopping site.

In July 2001, Kmart announced its plan to buy back the 40 percent of BlueLight.com that it didn't already own for $84 million in cash and stock. Due to the purchase, Kmart had to take a charge of $120 million to write down the value of BlueLight.com on its balance sheet. In addition, Kmart agreed to pay $15 million in cash and $6 million to its partners, Martha Stewart Living Omnimedia and Softbank Venture Capital. The buyout caused Kmart's partners to lose less than $3 million in their investment in BlueLight.com, while Kmart lost considerably more from its participation in the third and fourth financing rounds, the last at a $400 million valuation. Based on the repurchase, BlueLight.com still carried a valuation of $210 million. This was far above its market value after the Internet bubble burst.

It is important to note here that the VCs were perhaps too enthusiastic about profiting from the application of their e-retailing expertise to an old-line brick-and-mortar retail operation. As a result, they overlooked the fact that the business model itself was flawed. This venture unquestionably hurt an already ailing Kmart. Even top-tier VCs cannot make a success out of a business with a flawed model.

Kmart also probably made a mistake worth noting in bringing in as an investor its premiere supplier, Martha Stewart Living Omnimedia. The continued support of Martha Stewart was crucial during a troubled time for the company (it later filed Chapter 11 bankruptcy). Retaining that goodwill, it may be speculated, led Kmart to buy back the venture from the outside investors including Martha Stewart, at nonmarket valuation. Having an important supplier as an investor is usually not a good idea.

Example 3, Conexant Systems: A Partnership with a Buyout Group

The purpose of this example is to illustrate how a buyout partnership can provide needed funding and alliance connections to create a successful subsidiary. This is a model for a parent on divesting an operation that it cannot sell in a distressed market. While the partnership contributed to the parent's short-term goal of receiving additional funding, it is too soon to tell whether it will create shareholder value, as the deal had just been completed at the time of this writing.

The growing interest in partnerships by more traditional buyout funds is demonstrated by the 2002 partnership of Conexant Systems and the Carlyle Group, a large private equity firm that made its name by acquiring mature defense businesses. Conexant and Carlyle formed a new specialty foundry subsidiary to fabricate high-performance integrated circuit chips using silicon germanium. The technology comes from Conexant. Carlyle brings deep experience and connections in the military and aerospace worlds, where much of the demand originates for high-performance silicon geranium chips. Carlyle believes it can reduce costs and send business from its other military holdings through to the facility. Carlyle paid Conexant $20 million in cash and contributed $30 million to the new venture. In return, it received 55 percent ownership of the entity. This partnership raised needed cash for a financially hard-pressed Conexant and brought in a partner with deep pockets and expertise to exploit the Conexant technology in defense markets.

Example 4, SRI International: A Successful Partnership Program

SRI is an independent R&D institute in Menlo Park, California that primarily works for government clients. SRI has engaged in more than 25 strategic and private equity partnerships, primarily to commercialize promising technology that it developed for the government. Typically, SRI retains an ownership position in a newly created subsidiary and receives a royalty. A member of SRI's senior management team often will sit on the subsidiary's board of directors. However, the SRI staff that created the technology usually stays with SRI.

One of SRI's earliest partnerships was with Nuance Communications. Nuance was started by SRI in 1994 to commercialize speech recognition and voice authentication software technology that SRI had developed for the government. In this case, SRI brought in venture capital firms to finance and build the commercial company. By 2000, Nuance's customers included American Airlines, UPS, OnStar, and Sprint PCS. Nuance went public at $17 per share in April 2000. SRI owned 10.7 percent after the IPO—fairly typical for a corporate private equity partnership where the parent primarily contributes technology. The stock climbed after the IPO, hitting $175 and valuing the company at $5.5 billion in mid-2000. In September 2000, SRI sold 10 percent of its holdings in a follow-on public offering for $36 million. Unfortunately, Nuance stumbled and at the end of 2001 was valued at $300 million with $40 million of revenues in 2001. Still, it is a good example of a successful commercialization by SRI of a government technology.

Lessons Learned by SRI

After spinning off more than 25 strategic and private equity partnerships, Dr. Norman Winarsky, vice president for ventures and strategic business development at SRI, believes that the following lessons apply:

• Work only with premier partners at the highest level, and engage them very early in the process. They should be involved in choosing the management team, identifying potential customers, and building corporate strategy.

- Get external validation of the commercial potential of the technology from leading analysts, market consultants, and current clients as much and as early as possible.

- Cool technology isn't enough. There has to be an important market need, a compelling approach to meeting that need, and superior value relative to the cost of the competition's solution.

- Be flexible in approach and in plans.

- Provide internal rewards. All SRI staff participate in a royalty and equity sharing program from the partnerships.

According to Dr. Winarsky, the major mistakes made by SRI in its partnership program occurred when it committed too much internal funding and built a management team and staff for a project without first validating the attractiveness of the project by seeing whether private equity investors were willing to commit capital. It then found that outside funding was not available. The other problem SRI found when it did not bring in outside private equity investors early into the project was that it could not recruit top-quality management, as these people were not attracted to joining a company without sufficient financial runway and outside validation.

CHAPTER 13

CORPORATE STRATEGIC PARTNERSHIPS

INTRODUCTION

This chapter will examine corporate strategic partnerships. As this chapter will demonstrate, this SER alternative has the opportunity to create value for shareholders and for all parties involved, if it is planned and executed properly. If so, the parent can often gain some of the same benefits of a merger without the associated cost—and risk—inherent in a merger.

DEFINITION OF A CORPORATE STRATEGIC PARTNERSHIP

A corporate strategic partnership is a relationship between a parent or subsidiary and a public or private outside company. The parent's objective is to increase the value of the subsidiary by obtaining added resources. The partnership may be between the parent or subsidiary and another large company or with a smaller company. The term *strategic partnership* is used loosely to describe interactions ranging from simple commercial agreements such as a distribution arrangement to close long-term alliances. This chapter will focus on the latter type of partnership, which can create true shareholder value when executed properly. Close long-term relationships may take the form of a new joint venture company that is independent of the parents, such as Dow Corning. However, few go this far. For this reason, true stand-alone joint ventures are not discussed in this chapter. The type of strategic partnerships discussed here generally also involves the parent taking an equity interest in the strategic partner.

When well crafted, strategic partnerships can achieve many of the same objectives for the parent as an acquisition of the other company, including access to the resources of the strategic partner at a lower cost and without the risk associated with an acquisition. It is also important to note that many strategic partnerships do not lead to acquisitions, and may be disbanded over time once strategic objectives have been met. Successful strategic partnerships are often followed by other SERs such as IPOs.

Exhibit 13–1 illustrates a typical strategic partnership.

ADVANTAGES OF A CORPORATE STRATEGIC PARTNERSHIP FOR THE PARENT

A strategic partnership with the right partner can help the subsidiary increase in value while meeting the parent's objectives. For example, it can:

• Respond more quickly to changing market demands and reduced time to market

• Obtain access to promising new technologies

• Access new markets

• Exploit synergies in complementary areas by combining product offerings

• Get to know a smaller independent partner better as a prelude to a possible acquisition

• Retain the services of key founders or senior management at an independent partner who might cash out or lose interest following an acquisition

• Work with a smaller independent partner that does not wish to be acquired

• Enable the parent to own a substantial equity position in a smaller independent outside partner or other partnership structure while keeping incentives and company cultures separate

• Increase the credibility of the parent as an industry leader by associating it with a respected partner

ADVANTAGES FOR THE STRATEGIC PARTNER

By entering into a strategic partnership, the partner can benefit by:

• Accessing the technical, distribution, financial, manufacturing, or other resources of the parent

• Sharing the risk and cost of a promising new project

• Accessing the technology or other strengths of the subsidiary or parent to enhance its growth and success

• Increasing credibility with customers, suppliers, and investors

• Accessing capital on better terms than are normally obtainable from financial investors

• Holding on to a substantial ownership position

Strategic Partnerships

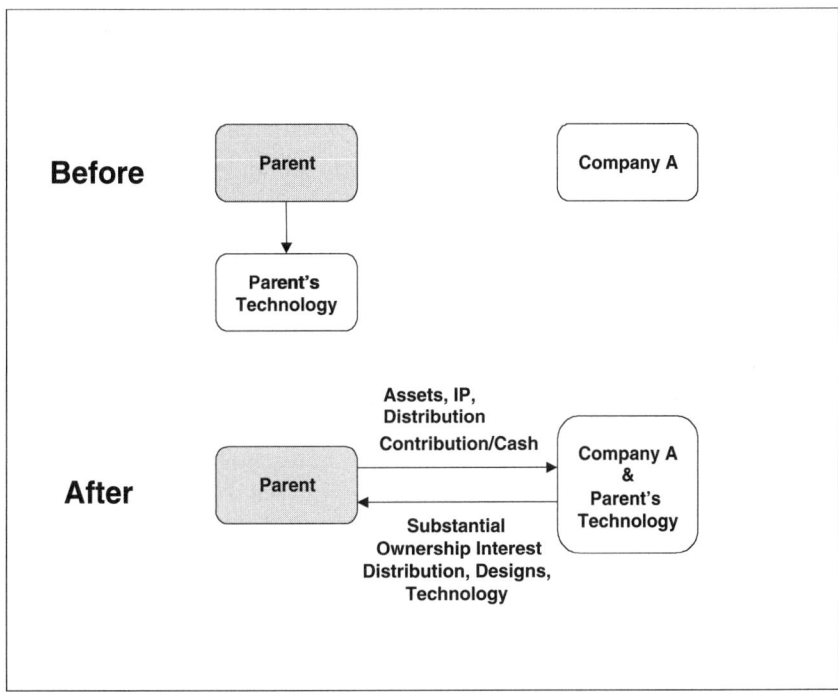

- Retaining its corporate culture and not being stifled as part of a large parent
- Keeping compensation incentives in place

NEGOTIATING THE TERMS OF THE STRATEGIC PARTNERSHIP

Although partnerships can be advantageous to both parties, there are numerous conflicts that can hinder a strategic partnership. They include:

- *Unrealistic expectations of the parent.* The parent often really wants the benefits of ownership and will try in every way possible to back into them. It will want the partner's resources dedicated solely to its projects and will try to limit the partner's ability to work with other companies. It will also want to impose its own procedures on the partner, create its own time schedule, and do an inordinate amount of negotiating, reviewing, and researching to ensure that no mistakes are made.

- *Unrealistic expectations of the partner.* The partner will want all the benefits that come with access to the resources and funds of the parent with no strings attached and no delay, and will resist even the most reasonable protections for the parent. It will also, almost always, have a highly inflated view of its own value.

How to Reach Agreement

Following is a list of suggestions to help a parent, a subsidiary, and a partner reach agreement:

- *The parent has to recognize that it is not buying the partner.* If it wants complete control, it must make an acquisition. It must realize that stifling the partner will not help it perform and that the partner does not have the resources to support an extended negotiating and diligence process. It has limited management time to spare and is on a tight time schedule.

- *The partner needs to understand the internal processes of the parent.* The partner has to recognize that the parent will have to work through its procedures, will not put its strategy or cash at risk without reasonable protections, and cannot present a wish list of demands but must be realistic in its expectations.

- *Prioritize what is most important.* There are only ever a few really key points. Focus on those. Ask on each point: "Do we really need this or is it nice but not essential?"

- *Don't take extreme negotiating positions.* Taking extreme positions does not usually enhance long-term relationships. Unreasonable demands build up hostility and mistrust. They incite unreasonable responses and a breakdown of discussion.

- *Don't overreact to an overreaction.* Even when the other party makes what appears to be an unreasonable demand, don't overreact. Stay reasonable and in the middle.

- *Don't negotiate by tossing hand grenades.* Throwing term sheets back and forth, especially by e-mail or fax, usually leads to each side growing suspicious of the other. The tendency is to assume the worst intentions, even if the terms are innocuous.

- *Recognize that the other side almost always has alternatives.* Don't negotiate on the presumption that the other side has no alternatives. This is rarely the case. There is almost always some alternative. If pushed hard enough, emotional reactions alone may cause a choice of another alternative, even if it is less advantageous.

- *Assume good faith.* Assume the other side is acting in good faith until there is evidence to the contrary. Never attribute to bad faith what can be explained by lack of thought or simply incompetence.

- *Recognize that you will have to live with the partner after the negotiations.* The deal has to make sense for both sides. The parent is often in a position to impose a very one-sided deal on a smaller partner. Negotiating too hard on terms may mean winning the battle and losing the war. Both sides have to feel committed for a strategic partnership to succeed. A deal that leaves little on the table for the other side is unlikely to last or meet the partner's objectives. The object is not to extract the last point but to have a reasonable deal that both sides are happy about and will continue to be happy about as circumstances change.

- *If negotiations get off track, sit down together.* Get together and explain the reason for each and every term and any changes to terms. This often clears away misunderstandings.

GROUND RULES FOR A SUCCESSFUL CORPORATE STRATEGIC PARTNERSHIP

After the deal has been finalized, it is important to follow these ground rules to pave the way for a successful strategic partnership.

- *Set clear rules for the strategic partnership.* The certainty of change in any business requires that the partners have clearly established goals for the strategic partnership and clearly understood respective responsibilities that transcend the original terms of the contract. This will allow the strategic partnership to respond flexibly to changing conditions. The partners must consider whether they have the same objectives at the outset and thereafter an ongoing basis.

- *Work hard at maintaining trust.* It is also important that both companies deal with each other in a fair and reasonable manner. It is equally important that there be a perception of fair dealing. Without any intent to alienate, large companies may easily treat the smaller partner with arrogance and indifference. As in any marriage, maintaining trust takes work.

- *Maintain ongoing communication.* Constant communication at a senior level is needed to ensure that the strategic partnership develops and that the partners respond with trust to the inevitable unexpected events.

- *Appoint an internal sponsor.* Appoint as the sponsor for the partnership a senior person who has the authority to make things happen and clear roadblocks, but also put a more junior manager in day-to-day charge to ensure ongoing activity.

- *Provide unwinding capability should the objectives of each party change.* It is very important to pay attention to the "unwind" provisions in the contract and other arrangements in case one or both parties wish to separate at some point in the relationship.

- *The parent should provide incentives to support the strategic partnership.* Often the employees at the parent assigned to the strategic partnership will be operating outside of their usual reporting structure and standard career-enhancement system. An evaluation and promotion system is needed that defines and rewards success based on the activities of the strategic partnership. Otherwise, the parent may create the perception that working with the strategic partnership is not career enhancing.

• *Expand organizational buy-in.* Support for the strategic partnership has to spread beyond a few sponsors within both organizations. It is necessary to involve personnel at multiple levels in each organization and expand the circle of committed parties. Strategic partnerships often wither when the key sponsors at the parent move on to new assignments. A prevalent cause of failure of strategic partnerships is that the larger partner loses interest.

• *Provide for contingencies.* While it is difficult to provide for every potential contingency, it is necessary to provide a framework from which to deal with the inevitable issues during the life of the strategic partnership. Contingencies should include mechanisms for dispute resolution and for terminating the strategic partnership.

• *Do not interfere excessively.* The parent has to resist the desire to interfere in the activities of the partner and thereby lose many of the benefits that the smaller company brings to the strategic partnership. The perceived need to interfere is often great, especially should all not go according to plan.

• *Do not overstress the resources of the smaller company.* The parent has to resist overstressing what are usually very limited resources of the smaller partner.

• *Require firm resource commitments.* Specifying in detail the specific resources that each side will commit to the partnership, their respective responsibilities, and the detailed timetable will help ensure that action results. Financial and performance metrics should also be set to judge results. Undoubtedly these will change over time, but accountability requires benchmarks.

• *Require good governance practices at the partner.* There is no substitute for a strong, experienced, independent outside board with a significant financial interest in the smaller company to help create a mature and reasonable process for dealing with issues at the smaller company. A board that includes experienced current or former CEOs of larger companies will be invaluable in building the relationship with the parent. The management of the smaller company and many venture investors and other directors of smaller companies have had limited experience working with a larger company. The right directors fill this gap. The limited perspective of the initial team at the smaller company may result in behavior that may even seem bizarre from the viewpoint of a larger corporation.[1]

CHALLENGES OF A CORPORATE STRATEGIC PARTNERSHIP FOR THE PARENT

Now that we have detailed the ground rules for making a strategic partnership work, let's look at some of the inherent challenges not covered in the preceding list.

- *An option to purchase the partner or extensive restrictions on its later sale is usually denied.* In certain situations, a parent may want to purchase or affect whom the partner can be sold to. However, even a right of first refusal is unlikely to be acceptable if such a right, in practice, prevents the partner from eventually selling itself to another party to obtain the best price. The partner will respond that the parent has not bought the partner and therefore cannot control its destiny.

- *Partnerships are almost never permanent.* There is a certainty of change in any business relationship as strategic objectives and agendas alter over time and people move on. This even applies to successful partnerships that have met all their objectives. It is important to pay attention to the unwind provisions in the contract and other arrangements in case one or both parties wish to separate at some point in the relationship.

- *The parent shares in only a portion of the upside.* The other dilemma for the parent is that its contribution may create most of the value in the partner over time but it will share in only a portion of the upside. This is legitimate and does occur. However, the contributions of the management team and investors at the partner are easy to underestimate.

- *The parent may not be willing to intervene when problems arise.* From time to time, the partner may encounter financial difficulties, business setbacks, and management problems that will impair its ability to fulfill its obligations in the strategic partnership. The parent may not have the power to step in with the financial and managerial resources to deal with the problem.

- *The parent must view the arrangement from a broad perspective.* One reason partner companies are attracted to these relationships is the attractive terms of the arrangement. While these terms may not always seem advantageous to the parent, it must remember to value the total package, not just the financial arrangement.

THE CHALLENGES OF A CORPORATE STRATEGIC PARTNERSHIP FOR THE PARTNER

The parent needs to be cognizant that a failed strategic partnership may be an embarrassment for the parent, but it may be fatal for a smaller independent partner. The smaller partner's approach to issues will be colored by this view.

Smaller companies face significant risks in entering into corporate strategic partnership discussions. The parent should be aware of the likely causes of the ambivalence of the potential strategic partner and recognize the need to ameliorate some of these concerns so that the strategic partnership can proceed. For example, the partner will have these specific concerns:

- The partner will be very concerned that the demands of the parent may defocus it from its own objectives. This is a justifiable concern. The parent cannot expect to have all the advantages of ownership, including directing resources, without acquiring the partner.

- Once the larger partner obtains its objectives it may not step up for future financing rounds. The parent may believe it obtained what it desired from the relationship with the initial investment. However, the partner may want additional financing rounds.

- A strategic partnership with the parent may preclude other strategic alternatives for the partner.

- Dealing with a large company may completely consume the limited senior management resources of the partner.

- Corporate priorities and personnel are constantly changing at many parents. This complicates communications between a parent and the partner. With a strategic partnership, there is usually an exchange of information directly between the partners and there is less control over its subsequent use.

TWO-STEP STRATEGIC PARTNERSHIP TRANSACTIONS

A version of a strategic partnership is one that is structured to allow a later acquisition of the partner.

A two-step transaction involves a purchase by the parent of a substantial position in a public or private strategic partner for cash. Subsequently, the parent may have control of, or a substantial minority interest in, the strategic partner while leaving the remaining shares outstanding. At the same time, commercial arrangements are put in place that benefit the business of the parent and provide support to the strategic partner. This often leads to the later purchase of the rest of the strategic partner by the parent in a second step.

There are a number of events that may trigger the decision to move from a strategic partnership to a second-step acquisition. These include the following:

- The partner's technology proves out and the parent now wants to own it and control it.

- The partner is now profitable. As a result, the parent is willing to consolidate the partner's results on its own income statement, which it has to do if it owns the partner.

- There are differing agendas between the partner and the parent, and ownership is the best way for the parent to see that its objectives are reached.

- The partner has developed to a point where it is now a mature company, and the parent is no longer worried about the partner losing its entrepreneurial edge as part of a big company.

- The partner is not succeeding at a task vital to the parent and the parent needs to take control.

The express purpose of a two-step partnership is to provide the parent with these benefits:

- A means to get to know the strategic partner before a subsequent acquisition. This allows both parties to get comfortable with one another.

- A means to assist the strategic partner with any immediate cash needs. This may ultimately induce it to agree to a strategic partnership, while also giving it the financial means to meet the strategic objectives of the parent.

- Encourages the shareholders of a strategic partner to support the strategic partnership by allowing shareholders to take some money off the table in the form of a cash dividend or share repurchases.

However, the parent needs to make sure that there is an acceptable mechanism to extract itself from the investment in the strategic partner if the relationship does not progress.

Exhibit 13–2 provides a graphical representation of a purchase of a substantial position in a public strategic partner followed by an acquisition.

SUMMARY

This chapter detailed the advantages and disadvantages of using corporate strategic partnerships as an SER alternative to create shareholder value. One of the key advantages is combining the complementary resources and capabilities of the alliance partner and the subsidiary. This chapter also studied the risks of the partnership to the strategic partner and provided a framework for the parent company to consider—and negotiate—the actual deal. When the arrangement is negotiated for the benefit of all parties involved, it will truly support the critical SER objectives of importance to all of the entities. Chapter 14 will examine exchangeable securities as an SER alternative that enables parents to realize the current value of an investment in a public company without actually selling the shares at that time.

EXAMPLES OF CORPORATE STRATEGIC PARTNERSHIPS

Example 1, TRW: A Highly Successful Corporate Strategic Partnership Followed by an IPO

TRW's satellite and military operation at Space Park in Redondo Beach had developed a highly advanced Gallium Arsenide (GaAs) semiconductor with heterojunction bipolar transistors (HBTs) for satellite and military uses that created exceptionally high-speed communications. HBTs also helped produce semiconductor devices and were superior to any product commercially available in the late 1990s for cell phone handsets. TRW had built an advanced GaAs semiconductor manufacturing facility (known as a fabrication plant or *fab*) at Space Park primarily to provide chips for its internal use using HBT technology that gave it a competitive edge in winning large satellite and military systems contracts over other defense and satellite contractors with less advanced technology.

E X H I B I T   13–2

Two-Step Strategic Partnership Followed by Acquisition

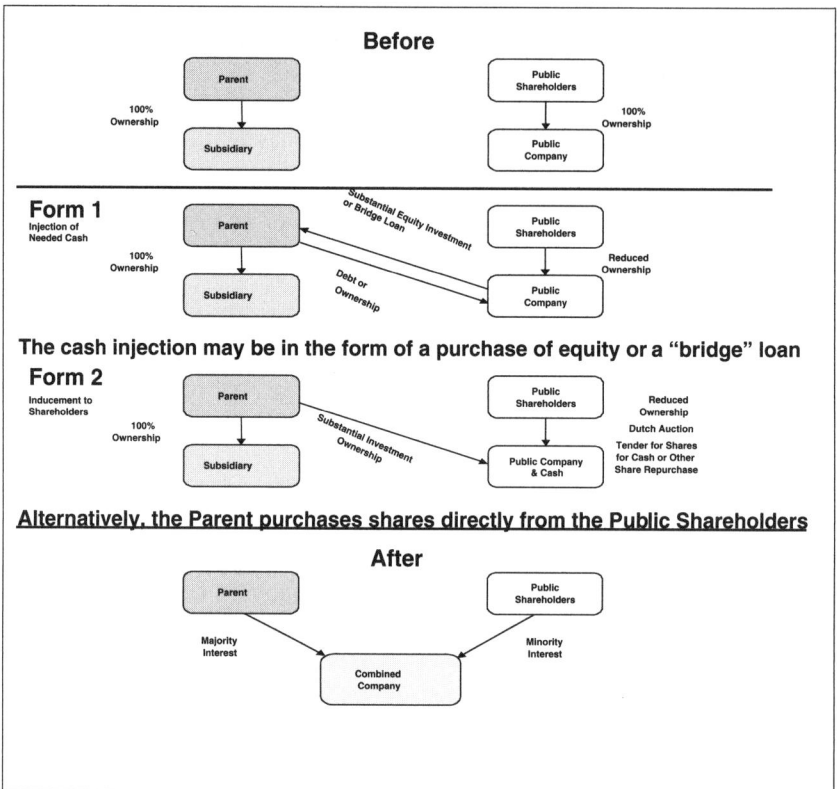

However, the internal demand for semiconductors by TRW did not initially fill the production capacity of TRW's fab for making GaAs HBT semiconductors. In 1995, TRW had considerable excess capacity at its GaAs HBT fab at Space Park. As semiconductor fabs are very expensive to build and have high fixed costs, TRW filled the excess capacity by providing a limited quantity of advanced GaAs HBT semiconductors on a merchant basis to outside customers who did not compete in the defense and satellite business with TRW.

In 1995, RF Micro Devices (RFMD) was a small, venture capital-backed semiconductor designer in North Carolina, founded four years previously. RFMD's strategy was not to invest in its own very capital-intensive manufacturing fab; instead, it was to rely on outside semiconductor fabs to make semiconductors to RFMD's design for the emerging cellular handset market on a contract basis. This strategy promised a high return on a limited amount of capital investment, as the capital cost of plants would be borne by its vendors. This is known as a *fabless* model. RFMD copied this model from that used by many successful silicon-based fabless semiconductor companies. These relied on a number of vendors (primarily in Taiwan) that owned fabs and produced silicon semiconductors solely on a contract basis (known as *foundries*). By the mid-1990s there was a competitive silicon foundry industry offering fabless silicon companies ample capacity with advanced technologies.

The success of a fabless approach by RFMD depended on the availability of competitive GaAs foundries. However, the GaAs industry was less developed than that for silicon and there were no comparable contract GaAs fabs with the advanced technology offered by TRW. In reality, RFMD was completely dependent on TRW. RFMD became the largest customer for the excess TRW fab capacity. With the help of the superior performance of the TRW product, RFMD's business took off.

RFMD's growing need for wafers began to fill the excess capacity at the TRW fab and TRW would run out of capacity to supply RFMD's growing needs by 1998 unless it built additional fab capacity. This prospective lack of capacity resulted in the loss of a major RFMD customer. In 1996 QUALCOMM represented 32 percent of RFMD's sales. The upcoming restraints on production at TRW resulted in QUALCOMM changing to another supplier with its own fab.

Initial Position of the Future Partners

RFMD's position was that it was a fabless company and that TRW should spend the money to build additional fab capacity to meet RFMD's needs. In this way, RFMD would not incur capital expenditures and would maintain complete flexibility to later change vendors. However, at the time, there were no other vendors, and RFMD needed TRW to build the additional fab capacity.

TRW had no desire to build this additional fab capacity for the use of RFMD. While TRW was willing to sell fab capacity excess to its own needs when it was available, it did not wish to be a contract foundry as a primary business. As well, TRW's corporate office in Cleveland was not receptive to committing more than the minimum necessary cash to the Space Park fab, as TRW at the time was contending with pressing capital needs for other TRW operations.

The division general manager of Space Park, Tim Hannemann, astutely recognized the great commercial potential in TRW's HBT technology and it did not wish to waste the opportunity. However, Hannemann also believed that with its space and defense orientation, TRW did not have the internal skills to successfully sell into the commercial markets, and it needed a partner. Hannemann set out to see whether there was a way to allow TRW to benefit from its technology through a closer partnership with RFMD. Hannemann and his team at Space Park had a very clear vision for the project from the beginning.

Hannemann's objectives for structuring a strategic partnership with RFMD included:

- Taking TRW's HBT technology successfully into commercial markets
- Obtaining as much equity in RFMD as possible for TRW
- Ensuring that RFMD would succeed so that TRW's equity would have considerable value and its HBT technology would win in the commercial area
- Accommodating the reluctance of TRW corporate to spend cash; the less short-term cash outlay, the better

Hannemann and his staff at Space Park fully understood that to succeed in the fast-changing commercial markets, RFMD needed independence and could not be dominated by TRW. RFMD needed flexibility to:

- React quickly to a changing marketplace.
- Build its business rapidly without the constraints of a large organization.
- Obtain the needed outside capital to build its business rapidly.

However, Hannemann also recognized that to succeed, RFMD was going to need extensive technical support and strong backing from TRW.

RFMD's management, under the leadership of its CEO, David Norbury, also recognized the critical need for a closer partnership with TRW. Norbury's objectives for a strategic partnership with TRW included:

- Securing an adequate and expanding supply of HBT semiconductors for its rapidly growing cellular handset business
- Using the backing of TRW to convince large customers that RFMD was a reliable supplier
- Obtaining in-depth technical and business support from TRW
- Succeeding in a fast-moving commercial marketplace with as few restraints as possible
- Giving up as little equity to TRW for all this as possible
- Ensuring that TRW interfered in RFMD's business as little as possible

In 1996, RFMD and TRW entered into a broad strategic relationship. The key goals of the strategic partnership agreed to by both parties were that:

- RFMD would construct a fab of its own to manufacture GaAs products using TRW's GaAs HBT technologies licensed to RFMD. TRW would provide technical assistance to RFMD in connection with the design, construction, and operation of the fab and would invest in RFMD to help pay for its cost.
- While the fab was being built, TRW would provide RFMD with an assured supply of semiconductors.
- TRW would support RFMD's sales efforts, including large customers concerned about depending on a small supplier.

In support of these goals, TRW committed the following to RFMD.

Commercial Agreements

- A royalty-free license for existing and future GaAs HBT products and the MBE process for commercial wireless communication applications on signals having a frequency of less than 10 GHz. The license with respect to the GaAs HBT patent rights was effective immediately, and the MBE process license would become effective when RFMD's GaAs HBT wafer fabrication facility became operational. Both licenses were exclusive. However, TRW had the right to make the licenses nonexclusive if RFMD failed to meet set revenue goals following the opening of RFMD's GaAs HBT wafer fabrication facility.

- A supply arrangement for TRW to continue to provide RFMD with minimum quantities of GaAs HBT wafers and GaAs epitaxial wafers for five years from the Space Park facility.

Financial Resources

To support the goals, TRW invested $15 million of equity and debt financing in RFMD in exchange for a complex package of securities, effectively giving TRW a 40 percent equity position in RFMD should all business targets be met, all convertible debt and preferred stock converted, and all warrants exercised. The components of the investment were as follows:

- 826,446 shares of RFMD Class C preferred stock in exchange for $5 million in cash from TRW.

- 2,683,930 shares of RFMD common stock in exchange for TRW's execution and performance of the license agreement.

- A 6 percent subordinated convertible note in exchange for $10 million in cash. This note was convertible at $9 per share into 1,111,111 shares of RFMD common stock at any time before December 31, 1998. Subject to the prior conversion, the note would be due in full in 2003. There was mandatory conversion of the note upon a quality IPO.

- A warrant for the purchase of up to 1,111,111 shares of RFMD common stock at a price of $9 per share. This warrant was only exercisable should the note not be converted into common stock. If the note were converted into common stock in full, the warrant would terminate at such time without being exercised. If the note were not converted in full, the warrant would remain outstanding and would terminate at the earlier of the full conversion of the note or December 31, 1998.

- A warrant for the purchase of 1 million shares of RFMD common stock at $10 per share. The warrant became exercisable only when the RFMD wafer fabrication facility became operational. The warrant would be cancelled if not exercised by TRW for cash on the earlier of the second anniversary of the RFMD fab becoming operational or 90 days after market price of RFMD's common stock traded for at least 20 consecutive trading days at greater than $12 per share. The warrant would also terminate if the fab did not become operational by December 31, 1998.

Overcoming Objections

Once the partnership structure was agreed on, both TRW and RFMD had to overcome internal objections to the partnership structure.

Internal Objections at TRW

A partnership without control was a new structure for TRW, and the corporate office was not comfortable with many aspects of the structure; it wanted a much greater degree of control over RFMD than was stipulated—such as desiring to approve all management hires at RFMD. Hannemann worked hard to convince the corporate office that RFMD would not thrive on such a tight a rein. The corporate office was first wary, but then embraced the structure.

Internal Objections at RFMD

While RFMD's CEO understood the value of a close partnership with TRW, surprisingly some of the venture capital investors who controlled RFMD did not initially support the strategic partnership with TRW, though in the end it created great wealth for them. With a fabless model in mind, these venture capitalists did not wish to vary from a strategy that used TRW simply as an arms-length merchant wafer foundry. As well, some of the venture capital investors in RFMD were determined not to give up any equity to TRW. In the end, David Norbury—and lack of alternatives—pushed through the strategic partnership with TRW over the objections of these venture capital investors.

As a consequence of TRW's superior technology, RFMD's design capabilities, and TRW's financial and business backing, RFMD became a dominant vendor of GaAs semiconductors to the cellular industry.

The Transaction Creates Value

Nokia in Finland was well on its way to being the largest maker of handsets in the world. Orders from Nokia were critical to the success of RFMD. However, Nokia was apprehensive about relying on RFMD as a first-source vendor. From Nokia's perspective, RFMD was a small company with untried ability to meet high-volume demands. Nokia required that TRW ensure it that TRW would provide needed semiconductors from its own facility should RFMD falter as a vendor. Tim Hannemann stepped up and put the full weight of TRW's resources behind RFMD's commitments to Nokia. This support from TRW was instrumental in RFMD obtaining major design wins at Nokia.

The Outcome

TRW's objectives were achieved:

- Outstanding success for TRW's technology in a commercial arena—the wireless handset market

- Considerable financial upside, as RFMD achieved a peak market valuation of $8 billion following an IPO

- A limit on TRW cash outlay for the project to $15 million ($25 million with the later exercise of the warrant)

TRW also benefited from the strategic partnership in the following ways:

- Volume from RFMD for TRW's GaAs fab for a period until TRW's own needs filled the production facility
- A close customer relationship with Nokia that later benefited other TRW operations
- Gaining know-how for creating and executing a successful strategic partnership in the commercial arena that it could apply to later partnerships

In addition, RFMD's objectives were achieved:

- The new foundry opened successfully in 1998. Capacity expansion for growth was achieved. Its business exploded.
- RFMD had the autonomy necessary to succeed.
- RFMD had the management incentives to recruit a top-quality team.
- RFMD was able to go public and went on to create considerable wealth for its shareholders and employees. Its value in the stock market exceeded that of TRW for a time.[2]

Exhibit 13–3 demonstrates the rapidly expanding sales of RFMD after the TRW partnership.

Subsequent Transactions
In June 1997, RFMD went public through an IPO raising $37 million. In January 1999 it followed with an offering raising $133 million. In August 2000 it issued $300 million of 3.75 percent convertible notes. RFMD had ample funds to build its business and create value for its shareholders including TRW. The IPO and subsequent success of RFMD as a public company provided TRW with a liquid stock

E X H I B I T   13–3

RF Micro Devices Statement of Operations Data

(dollars in millions)	Year ended March 31,						
	1995	**1996**	**1997**	**1998**	**1999**	**2000**	**2001**
Revenues	$2.7	$9.5	$28.8	$45.3	$152.8	$289.0	$335.4
(Loss) income from operations	(4.2)	(5.2)	1.6	1.4	23.8	73.9	46.7
Net (loss) income	(4.1)	(5.1)	1.7	(0.5)	19.6	50.6	35.0

Source for Exhibits 13-3 to 13-8: RFMD and TRW SEC filings

E X H I B I T   13–4

Investment and Returns by TRW in RFMD—1

Return on Shares Purchased by TRW in RF Micro Devices as of December 31, 2000				
Initial investment by TRW				
	Number of RFMD shares			
Shares	**Original number**	**Split adjusted**	**Investment cost**	**Notes**
Common	826,446	6,611,568	$5,000,000	Series C preferred automatically converted into common stock 1 for 1 at the close of the IPO
Common	2,683,930	21,471,440		
Warrants	1,000,000	8,000,000	$10,000,000	Exercised at $10/share
Convertible note	1,111,111	8,888,888	$10,000,000	Automatically converted into 1,111,111 shares of common stock at $9 per share at the close of the IPO
Initial cash exchange			$15,000,000	
Total shares acquired		44,971,896	$25,000,000	
Weighted price/share		$0.56		

market into which to sell the shares of RFMD stock it obtained in the partnership. By the end of 2000, TRW had received over $500 million for RFMD shares that it sold in the market and still held RFMD shares valued at another $600 million.

Exhibits 13–4 through 13–8 trace the TRW investment and its returns to TRW.

Subsequent Transactions Create Shareholder Value for TRW

In late 1999, TRW and RFMD expanded their strategic relationship through several agreements that licensed RFMD to use TRW's technology to manufacture products

E X H I B I T   13–5

Investment and Returns by TRW in RFMD—2

Sales of RFMD Stock by TRW			
	Number of shares		
Dates of sales	**Original number**	**Split adjusted***	**Realized value**
12/99– 5/2000	8,350,000	22,720,000	$554,387,160

*Shares still held by TRW are valued at the closing price of $27.43 on 12/29/2000.

E X H I B I T 13–6

Investment and Returns by TRW in RFMD—3

Remaining Holdings of RFMD Stock by TRW at December 31, 2000			
	Number of shares		
Type	Original number	Split adjusted*	Market value*
Common	11,500,948	23,001,896	$630,572,117

*Shares still held by TRW are valued at the closing price of $27.43 on 12/29/2000.

E X H I B I T 13–7

Investment and Returns by TRW in RFMD—4

Summary of TRW Realized and Unrealized Values on its RFMD Investment			
	Number of shares (split adjusted)		
Transaction	Number	Price per share	Total pretax value
Shares purchased	44,971,896	$0.56	$ (25,000,000)
Shares sold	22,720,000	$24.40	$ 554,387,160
Shares still held*	23,001,896	$27.43	$ 630,942,007

*Shares still held by TRW are valued at the closing price of $27.43 on 12/29/2000.

E X H I B I T 13–8

Investment and Returns by TRW in RFMD—5

Summary of TRW Pretax Realized and Unrealized Gains on its RFMD Investment	
Realized pretax return after cost*	$ 541,757,050
Unrealized pretax return after cost[†]	$ 618,572,117
Total return to TRW	$ 1,160,329,167

*Average split adjusted average share price of shares sold by TRW was $24.40

[†]Shares still held by TRW are valued at the closing price of $27.43 on 12/29/2000.

for commercial coaxial and other nonfiber wire applications. Products include cable television distribution amplifiers, cable modems, digital television converters, and television tuners. TRW received additional warrants in this agreement.

A Successful Relationship Winds Down

Once RFMD's first and then second large fabs were operational, RFMD no longer needed TRW's fab capacity. This reduced the frequency and intensity of interchanges between RFMD and TRW. In 2001, RFMD finally discontinued its purchases of GaAs products for handsets from TRW's fab. However, RFMD and TRW continue to maintain a good working relationship.

Lessons to Be Learned

There are many important lessons to be learned from this example, including the following:

- Each company was able to overcome internal roadblocks to the transaction by strong sponsorship from the CEO of RFMD and the head of Space Park at TRW. These roadblocks are common to such deals because of differing internal agendas, lack of focus on moving the deal forward, and the time and expense involved.

- The management team at each company worked together closely to create shared objectives and an execution plan that supported these key objectives.

- The management team at each company built on a shared learning experience to create a successful strategic partnership.

- The management team at each company acted with maturity and professionalism when dealing with difficult partnership issues. For example, they had the skills to listen well and find common ground, respond flexibly to each situation, calm damaged interpersonal relations as they occurred, and operate in ambiguous and unstructured situations.

- There was trust between the organizations and good personal chemistry among the senior management.

- The senior management at the partners was visible and clearly committed to the strategic partnership.

In fact, according to Tim Hannemann, its sponsor and architect, the TRW-RFMD strategic partnership succeeded because of the following factors:

- High-level commitment from TRW management
- Effective relationship management, especially among technologists
- Collaboration, rather than competition, among partners
- Confluence of market need, technology advantage, customers willing to gamble on new technology, and missteps by RFMD's competitors

Hannemann also laid out the elements that will usually cause a strategic partnership to fail, even if there is a good fit and real purpose:

- Hidden agendas
- Partner weakness/indecision
- Unclear business objectives
- Failure to plan for strategic partnership evolution

Example 2, Barnes & Noble: A Corporate Strategic Partnership to Share Risk and Increase Resources

Barnes & Noble launched its online retail business, barnesandnoble.com, in March 1997. By March 1999, barnesandnoble.com was the fourth-most-trafficked shopping site and was among the top 30 largest Web properties on the Internet, according to an Internet and digital media measurement company. However, it was a distant follower to the clear leader in the book space, Amazon.com, and it was experiencing very large losses. This created a tough dilemma for Barnes & Noble. The store chain was being heavily criticized in the press, by investors, and by Wall Street stock analysts for being too slow to react while Amazon.com appeared to steal its market share. However, the massive investment needed to fund the Internet operation to compete with Amazon.com was generating considerable losses that reduced the earnings of the parent and hurt its stock price. Furthermore, these losses were forecast to increase.

Compounding these problems was the fact that, as a traditional bricks-and-mortar retailer, Barnes and Noble was held to traditional standards of profitability by investors and research analysts. In contrast, the stock market did not appear to require any semblance of profitability from Amazon.com. Worse, the public markets were willing to provide Amazon.com with virtually unlimited amounts of capital at a very low cost, while Barnes & Nobel had a depressed stock price and a high cost of raising capital.

Barnes & Noble felt that it needed a means to respond to Amazon that did not destroy its earnings and that enabled it to access outside capital. However, the parent also wished to continue to consolidate the substantial operating losses of barnesandnoble.com against profits at the parent for tax purposes, as this provided a major cash savings. In addition, tax consolidation allowed the parent to receive tax-free dividends from the subsidiary in the future, maintain the ability to offer tax step-up to a later buyer of the subsidiary, and maintain the availability of a later tax-free spin-off of the subsidiary to the parent's shareholders.

Exhibit 13–9 demonstrates the impact of the losses at barnesandnoble.com on the parent's earnings.

The Partnership

In October 1998, Barnes & Noble sold Bertelsmann AG a 50 percent equity interest in barnesandnoble.com in a strategic partnership. This enabled barnesandnoble.com to benefit from Bertelsmann's international direct marketing channels and increased barnesandnoble.com's access to global markets. It also provided needed capital to fund the business. The strategic partnership was structured to allow Barnes & Noble the advantage of no longer consolidating the subsidiary's losses for accounting purposes against its other earnings, while still continuing to consolidate the subsidiary's losses for tax purposes, reducing its taxes.

E X H I B I T   13–9

Barnes & Noble Summary Historical Financial Data

	1997	1998	1999	2000
Barnesandnoble.com				
Revenues	$11,949	$61,834	$193,730	$320,120
Operating income	(13,552)	(83,856)	(122,640)	(181,940)
Net income	(13,552)	(83,148)	(48,150)	(65,400)
Barnes & Noble				
Revenues	$2,796,850	$3,005,610	$3,486,040	$4,375,800
Operating income	147,269	188,560	232,110	240,660
Net income	53,170	92,380	124,500	(51,970)

Source: Barnes & Noble SEC filings

The IPO

In May 1999, barnesandnoble.com completed a majority carve-out IPO of 25 million shares of Class A common stock at $18 per share, raising $450 million. It sold all of its Class A common stock in the offering. The stock of barnesandnoble.com closed as high as $25.63 after its second day of trading, but then traded down 90 percent off that high by the end of 2001. The fall in the stock price reflected the bursting of the Internet bubble and affected many online retail public companies. The structure of the IPO has not been particularly noted upon as a negative.

After the IPO, the public holders of barnesandnoble.com owned over 54.5 percent of the economic interest in the public company, but under 7.0 percent of the combined voting power of the stock due to the creation of Class B and Class C common stock with 10 votes per common equivalent share. The holders of these classes of stock, Barnes & Noble (Class B) and Bertelsmann (Class C), were able to effectively control all matters requiring stockholders' approval, including election of directors, approval of significant corporate transactions, and dividend policy. Classes B and C, each with one share outstanding, also had the right to convert these shares into a total of approximately 40 percent of outstanding Class A shares.

Analyzing the Unusual Structure Used by barnesandnoble.com

The barnesandnoble.com IPO involved an unusual structure that enabled Barnes & Noble to continue to enjoy the tax benefits of consolidating the subsidiary's losses after the IPO.

With this structure, Barnes & Noble and Bertelsmann each contributed their ownership in the subsidiary to a limited liability company (LLC) in exchange for a passive membership in the LLC (similar to the interest of a limited partner in a limited partnership). The LLC's other member was a newly formed corporation that raised capital in the IPO and used the proceeds to pay for an interest in the

LLC. In the barnesandnoble.com IPO, public investors bought shares of barnesandnoble.com (a newly formed public holding company) that gave them a 99.9 percent economic interest and 2.2 percent voting interest in that company, with the balance held by Barnes & Noble and Bertelsmann. Barnesandnoble.com, in turn, used the proceeds of the IPO to purchase an 18 percent equity interest in the LLC—the actual operating entity—and became the LLC's sole manager (similar to the role of the general partner in a limited partnership), thereby controlling all of its affairs. Barnes & Noble and Bertelsmann each owned a 41 percent passive equity interest in the LLC, although they had actual control over the LLC through their joint control of its sole manager, barnesandnoble.com (the public company).

When the IPO was completed, the public held an indirect 18 percent equity interest in the actual operating entity, and Barnes & Noble and Bertelsmann shared the remaining 82 percent of the equity and also voting control.

The primary advantage of the structure used for barnesandnoble.com was that it enabled Barnes & Noble to consolidate the subsidiary for tax purposes to offset its own profits with the losses of the subsidiary. The structure also allowed the parent all the flexibility of a tracking stock or carve-out in respect to any future acquisitions for stock by the subsidiary. Barnesandnoble.com later bought a public competitor, Fatbrain.com, for stock.

In addition, the structure had the added advantage that it allowed a subsequent tax-free spin-off. The ownership test with this LLC structure is 50 percent (the IRS requirement with a partnership type structure) rather than the 80 percent required with a traditional carve-out, allowing greater flexibility to use equity for acquisitions, funding, and alliances while still maintaining the later option of a tax-free spin-off to the parent's shareholders.

And because the IPO vehicle, barnesandnoble.com, did not house the operating business and had few assets other than its equity interest in the LLC, the structure required that care be taken so that barnesandnoble.com would not be inadvertently deemed an investment company by the SEC and subject to the Investment Company Act of 1940 that governs mutual and other investment funds sold to the public. This required barnesandnoble.com to have voting control of the operating LLC that actually owned the business.

However, it is important to note that the structure involved great complexity, which increased the difficulty and cost of legal, tax, and accounting compliance and made it more difficult for public investors to understand. This is in contrast to a more traditional SER, which is relatively simple and well understood by investors. It is not clear, in the post-Enron environment, if public investors would again look favorably on this high degree of complexity.

Exhibit 13–10 lays out the barnesandnoble.com structure.[3]

Example 3, Roche and Genentech: A Two-Step Partnership and Investment Followed by an Acquisition, and Then a Carve-out IPO

In the late 1980s, Roche Holding AG, a large Swiss-based manufacturer of pharmaceuticals and other fine chemicals, believed that many new and exciting drugs

EXHIBIT 13–10

Structure of the barnesandnoble.com Transaction

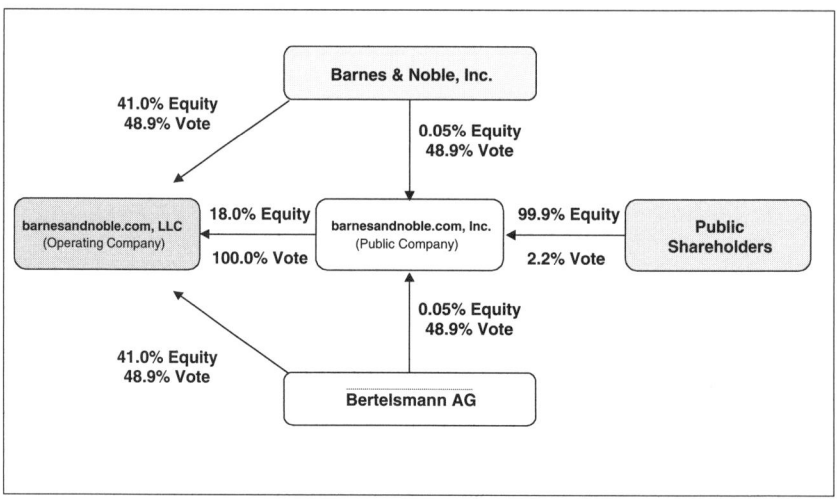

would come from the emerging biotechnology industry. It wanted to participate in the new area and obtain access to new drugs to develop and sell through its sales and distribution system. However, it also recognized that the entrepreneurial culture that made the early biotech companies successful would be stifled if these companies were acquired and became part of a giant company.

Genentech was a leading biotechnology company that discovered, developed, manufactured, and marketed drugs produced by recombinant DNA technology. Genentech was founded in 1976 and its launch marked the start of the commercial biotech industry. While Genentech was well capitalized for a young, independent company, the process of discovering, developing, testing, gaining government regulatory approval, and marketing a new drug is fraught with risk. It takes many years, often a decade or more, and costs many hundreds of millions of dollars to gain approval of a single new drug. Worse, most promising drug discoveries fail to ever come to market as approved drugs, often after great expenditure.

Genentech and Roche had much to offer each other. Roche had huge financial and technical resources and a worldwide sales and distribution system. Genentech had potential blockbuster drugs in its pipeline to offer Roche and also provided Roche with a way to be close to the emerging biotech area.

The Partnership

In 1990, Roche entered into a strategic partnership with Genentech. One part of the partnership was an investment by Roche. The shareholders of Genentech received a large amount of cash, and Genentech received funds to develop and market new drugs.

Roche benefited from the licensing, marketing, and collaborative development arrangements for a number of Genentech's promising drugs. For Roche, it was access to Genentech's drug pipeline that made the deal worthwhile from a business standpoint.

The Partnership Transaction

In the transaction with Roche, the Genentech's stockholders received, for each share of common stock that they owned, $4.50 in cash, for $1.5 billion in total from Roche and one half share of a newly issued redeemable common stock of Genentech. As well, Genentech issued additional shares of common stock to Roche for $487.3 million in cash. The shares of common stock that Roche acquired represented approximately 57 percent of the total. Roche received an option to purchase the remainder of the company by June 30, 1995. Roche had the right to require Genentech to exercise its redemption right, providing it did so for all shares of outstanding redeemable common stock at a price increasing to $15 per share on April 1, 1995. Roche first had to deposit sufficient funds in trust to pay the aggregate redemption price of all outstanding shares of redeemable common stock. This allowed Roche to purchase the remaining shares of Genentech it did not own at a pre-agreed price.

In addition, Roche was permitted to acquire additional shares of Genentech's stock through open market or privately negotiated purchases, provided that Roche's aggregate holdings did not exceed 75 percent of the company's stock outstanding on a fully diluted basis.

However, Roche did not have control. Genentech acted independently with an independent outside board in control. This served Genentech well, as it had both independence and the relationship with Roche.

With the 1990 transaction, Roche entered into a governance agreement defining and limiting its role in the affairs of Genentech. The board of directors grew from 11 to 13 members, and Roche could not designate more than two representatives to the board unless it acquired 100 percent ownership of Genentech. A board nominations committee was established to nominate new individuals to serve on the board. The nominations committee had one director designated by Roche, and all nominations for members of the board had to be unanimous, except for the two representatives designated by Roche.

This marked the beginning of a long relationship and subsequent investments made by Roche in Genentech.

Subsequent Transactions

Over time, Roche bought additional shares of Genentech in the market, bringing its stake to over 63 percent. In 1995, Genentech extended for an additional four years Roche's option to purchase the remainder of the company at an option price of $15.63 during the quarter ending December 31, 1995, to $20.63 during the quarter ending June 30, 1999. In conjunction with the extension, Roche was granted a 10-year license option to use and sell specific Genentech products in non-U.S. markets. Roche granted to the public shareholders a right to require the purchase by Genentech (backed by Roche) of all or a portion of their shares at the option of the holder at a price of $15 per share, exercisable during the 30-business-day period following June 30, 1999.

Roche continued to buy shares before exercising its option on the final third of Genentech it didn't own for $3.7 billion in June 1999. The shares were purchased at an exercise price of $20.75 per share. Roche also announced at the time of the purchase of the final public shares of Genentech its intention to take Genentech public again in a minority carve-out IPO later in the year.

Lessons to Be Learned

Though a seemingly very complicated and contradictory transaction, the steps Roche took along the way were beneficial for a number of reasons. Circumstances had changed, and its relationship with Genentech needed to change also. The initial partnership provided Roche with access to Genentech's drug pipeline and a window on the emerging biotech world. The structure permitted Genentech significant independence and allowed it to offer equity-related compensation. These were of great value in attracting scarce top talent. Retaining the talented research team and the entrepreneurial culture of Genentech was a major priority of Roche. At the time, Genentech was young and fragile. However, the structure was not completely satisfying to Roche. Despite Roche owning a majority of the stock, Genentech was free to form partnerships with other large pharmaceutical companies—and did so. Also, the commercial arrangements with Genentech were favorable to Genentech. Circumstances changed in the intervening decade. Genentech was no longer a fledgling; it had grown up into a multi-billion-dollar company.

The purchase of the remainder of the public stock of Genentech allowed Roche to take complete control of Genentech. Once it fully owned Genentech, Roche was able to enter into new commercial arrangements on terms it preferred.

One other difficulty with the original partnership structure was that Genentech's stock price before the 1999 final acquisition by Roche was always capped by Roche's option price. This presented a problem by capping the potential return to shareholders and to employees granted options. The carve-out IPO enabled Genentech to issue equity-related compensation packages to employees to attract and retain talented researchers that did not have a cap that limited the potential upside of these options.

Postscript

In July 2000, Roche completed a minority carve-out IPO of 88 million shares of Genentech common stock (all share amounts are adjusted for splits). The shares were priced at $24.25 per share. Thus, Roche's ownership in Genentech was reduced from 100 percent to about 83 percent. On October 26, 1999, Roche completed the sale of an additional 80 million shares of common stock at $35.88 per share. On March 23, 2000, Roche completed the sale of an additional 34.6 million shares at $81.50 per share. At the end of 2001, Roche owned 58 percent of Genentech's common stock. The proceeds to Roche from the three public offerings exceeded $8.5 billion.

Roche obtained access to the drug pipeline of Genentech without acquiring the actual company, knowing that it might destroy Genentech's culture and lose the technical team. When Roche felt the time had come for the relationship to be altered, it had a purchase option in place to acquire Genentech on acceptable terms and restructure the relationship to its advantage.

Two Other Partnerships in the Pharmaceutical Industry

Two other examples of strategic partnerships between large pharmaceutical companies and smaller companies with promising drugs are discussed here. These partnerships are becoming common as the large drug companies search for new products to sell through their distribution systems.

Schering-Plough Ltd. and Millennium Pharmaceuticals formed a partnership in June 1998 to launch Millennium's antianginal drug, Integrilin. In this partnership, Schering provided manufacturing and manufacturing support services, designed and conducted advanced clinical trials, and comarketed Integrilin in the United States. Under the agreement, the partners share any profit or loss. The profit sharing ratio between the two companies depends on the amount of promotional effort contributed by each company. Since the launch of Integrilin, these efforts have been equal. Schering and Millennium collectively target health care providers. In addition to this effort, Schering has the sole responsibility for marketing Integrilin to wholesalers in the United States. Outside of the United States, Schering has exclusive marketing rights to Integrilin, and Millennium collects royalty payments based on sales volume. The partnership is working well, and annual sales of the drug approached $300 million in 2001.

Quintiles formed a partnership with Scios Inc. in January 2001 to commercialize Scios's congestive heart failure drug, Natrecor, in the United States. Quintiles provided complete sales and marketing effort for Natrecor. This included hiring, training, and deploying a dedicated sales force. However, in June 2003, Scios assumes complete control of this Natrecor sales force. Quintiles provided $30 million in sales and marketing costs to launch Natrecor. In return, it received a royalty on certain sales of Natrecor through early 2008. Also as part of the agreement, Quintiles received a warrant to purchase a substantial number of Scios shares.

Example 4, LTX Corporation: Becoming a Leader by Maximizing Strategic Alliances and Challenging the Industry Business Model

LTX Corporation employed strategic partnerships to transform its business into a growth powerhouse. In 1997, LTX was a struggling, third-tier, vertically integrated manufacturer of test equipment in a highly cyclical industry with high fixed and operating costs and bleak prospects for long-term survival. It barely made money in boom years, and lost money in other years. Investors had no interest in LTX, and its market capitalization at the end of 1997 was under $120 million, with 1997 revenues in excess of $200 million. But in 1997 a brilliant new management team led by Roger Blethen and David Tacelli made a series of "bet the company" moves that transformed LTX into the rising star of the semiconductor equipment industry. By the end of 2001, despite a vicious industry downturn, LTX's market capitalization had grown to $1.1 billion and its stock price had increased five times from the beginning of 1998 and 22 times from its low in late 1998. In contrast, LTX's main competitor's stock went up less than 50 percent from the beginning of 1998 through the end of 2001. In addition, its market share increased in 2001 to 20 percent—up from a low of 6 percent three years earlier. How did this amazing transformation happen?

LTX narrowed its product line to a single innovative and advanced new product platform that offered customers a migration path for their entire test needs—something never offered in the industry before. Prior to that, semiconductor manufacturers required several narrowly focused testers, each capable of testing only digital, memory, or mixed signal devices, but not all three (this was not trivial, as testers cost up to $4 million each).

The new LTX platform handled all three, eliminating the need for mutually exclusive expensive testers. Having one product that tests any type of circuit not only simplified the customer's decision, it also benefited manufacturing, hardware and software development, marketing, and service functions. It also allowed the other two pieces of LTX's strategy: outsourcing of all noncore operations and relying on strategic partnerships to add unique functions to the LTX tester.

LTX reduced operating costs by outsourcing all noncore functions including manufacturing and customer service. The impact on LTX of the adoption of a lean, focused business model, a single platform, and outsourcing of manufacturing and service as part of product development is seen in the change in its headcount from 1998 to 2002, shown in Exhibit 13–11.

An example of LTX's willingness to break with the traditional approaches of its industry was its strategic partnership with StepTech, a small, complementary maker of test equipment that allowed LTX to supplement its internal development capabilities for its single platform.

In 2000, StepTech was a small, private company based in Massachusetts. StepTech specialized in the design and manufacture of low-cost testers for wireless and mixed-signal semiconductor testing. In October 2000, LTX made an equity investment of $10 million and entered into an agreement with StepTech, resulting in the development of a low-cost test technology for the new LTX standard test platform. This enabled LTX to broaden its reach into the high-volume, low-cost commodity semiconductor market.

The traditional approach in LTX's industry was to develop products inhouse or acquire, and thereby control, a smaller company with promising technology. Before the alliance deal with StepTech was pursued, LTX had weighed the benefits of developing the product on its own. LTX believed that it could obtain the low-cost tester for its platform faster and cheaper by outsourcing the development to StepTech. LTX also weighed the merits of acquiring StepTech.

EXHIBIT 13–11

LTX Corporation—Composition of Headcount

Function	1998	2002	Change percent
Manufacturing	348	45	–87
Service, sales, general and administrative	411	266	–35
Internal engineering and customer applications software internal	332	524	+58
Engineering dedicated to LTX projects at outside partners	0	140	
Total engineering and customer applications software dedicated to LTX projects including at outside partners	332	664	+100
Total LTX internal headcount	1091	835	–23

Source: LTX Corporation

LTX management believed that the control advantages that come with an acquisition were outweighed by the likely negative impact on StepTech's entrepreneurial, low-cost culture. These decisions proved correct. LTX sold its first platform with the StepTech technology within a year of the alliance. Internal development may have taken up to an additional two years and diverted scarce R&D resources from other projects. LTX's management strongly believes that StepTech performed as it did only because it remained an independent company.

And StepTech benefited from the partnership with LTX in a number of ways as well. First, it received a needed cash infusion. Second, StepTech was a small company with limited sales, service, and support infrastructure of its own. LTX provided all of these. Third, it obtained a reliable customer for its low-cost technology.

Example 5, Coca-Cola and Procter & Gamble:
The Adverse Impact of an Aborted Strategic Partnership

An example of the pitfalls in creating a successful strategic partnership is shown in the aborted and much publicized strategic partnership between Coca Cola and Procter & Gamble to market existing and develop new juices and snack foods.

The two companies began work on a strategic partnership in 2000. The impetus for Coke to enter the discussions with P&G was the rejection by its own board of a proposed acquisition of Quaker Oats that would have provided Coke with a snack food and other complementary product lines to compete with Pepsi, which offered snacks and dominated this product area. Pepsi also dominated the juice business, where Coke had not been successful at product innovation. P&G had a vaunted new product development capability that Coke wanted to use to develop new juice products that would improve its competitive position against Pepsi in that area as well.

The impetus for P&G was the limited access to distribution, both domestically and overseas, that impeded sales of its food products. P&G was under pressure from shareholders to improve its stock performance and made a commitment to investors to exit these lagging businesses or find a way to make them successful quickly.

A strategic partnership was publicly announced in early 2001 to great fanfare. In September 2001, the strategic partnership was cancelled. As reported in the *Wall Street Journal* at the time, Coke had found that after trials, the distribution of snack foods through its bottling system was not a success. Coke had also been criticized by investors for the impact of the structure on its earnings. In the end, P&G wasted a year, and its problems with its food brands were still unresolved. Similarly, Coke still did not have snack foods to compete with Pepsi. It was a major—and embarrassing—setback for both.

CHAPTER 14

EXCHANGEABLE SECURITIES

INTRODUCTION

This chapter will examine various types of exchangeable securities that enable a parent to realize the current value of a substantial investment in an independent company or a subsidiary without selling the investment at that time. Exchangeable securities may also be used in an exchange offer of new parent securities for outstanding securities to restructure the parent's obligation to creditors.

EXCHANGEABLE SECURITIES DEFINED

Exchangeable securities are similar to the familiar convertible securities. Securities are termed *convertible* when they can be converted into the stock of the issuer of the security. Securities are termed *exchangeable* when they can be exchanged for shares of a company that is not the issuer of the security. An exchangeable security is generally debt issued by the parent that gives the investor who purchases the debt the right, or the obligation, to exchange the debt for the parent's investment in an independent company or subsidiary other than the parent. At times, an exchangeable security may also be in the form of preferred stock or trust certificates. However, for the purposes of this chapter we will assume that the exchangeable security is debt.

Exchangeable debt is generally sold to the public in a registered underwritten public offering, sold privately to large institutions under the registration exemption provided for in SEC Rule 144A, or exchanged for existing parent debt obligations. The investment may be in:

- A subsidiary of the parent
- A company in which the parent made a successful venture-type investment
- A company in which the parent acquired an investment through a corporate partner alliance
- A company in which the parent acquired an investment as part of a sale of an operation

Exhibit 14–1 shows a representative sampling of exchangeable debt, which illustrates its diversity and the market's ability to absorb a large offering of this type.

Exhibit 14–2 represents a typical exchangeable offering.

CORPORATE OBJECTIVES OF THE PARENT IN ISSUING EXCHANGEABLE DEBT

Commonly, the parent has a large holding in a subsidiary or an unrelated company that it does not desire to sell at the time or is precluded from selling, but it wishes to realize the cash value of its holdings today. The parent may defer the sale because:

E X H I B I T 14–1

Representative Exchangeable Securities Offerings

Issuer	Security	Date	Size of Offering
Cox Communications Inc.	Debt exchangeable into shares of Sprint Corporation's PCS Group	April 2000	$700 mil.
Korea Deposit Insurance Corp.	Debt exchangeable into shares of Korea Electric Power Corp.	October 2000	
Comcast Corp.	Debt exchangeable into cash based on the value of shares of AT&T Corp. stock.	March1999	$718 mil.
Tribune Co.	Debt exchangeable into cash based on the value of shares of shares of AOL stock.	April 1999	$1.1 bil.
Bell Atlantic Financial Services, Inc.	Debt exchangeable into its shares of New Zealand Telecom Limited.	February 1999	$2.4 bil.
Bell Atlantic Financial Services, Inc.	Debt exchangeable into shares of Cable & Wireless Corporation Plc.	August 1998	$3.2 bil.
MediaOne Group, Inc	Debt mandatory exchangeable into shares of AirTouch Communications, Inc.	July 1998	$1.5 bil.
Source: Kaye Scholer LLP			

EXHIBIT   14–2

Exchangeable Offering for a Subsidiary Stock

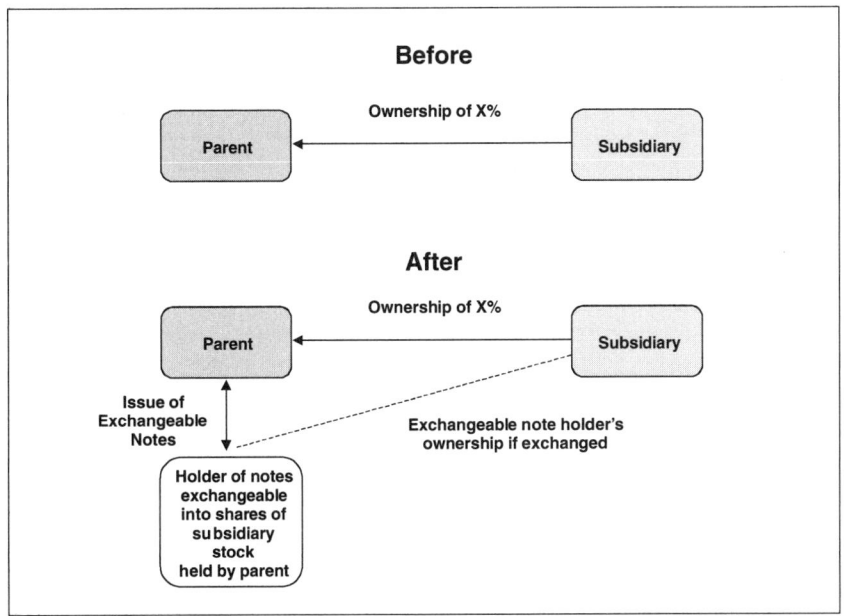

- The parent has considerable appreciated value in the holding with an attendant significant tax liability were it sold today. An exchangeable security realizes the value today but defers tax on the gain.

- The parent is restricted from selling its holdings for a period of time due to the terms of the purchase of the securities or to restrictions on sale under the securities acts.

- The parent wishes to obtain cash now but also wishes to participate (albeit in a more limited way) in the upside from the holding through either a premium to the current stock price or a reduced interest.

- The market is not able to absorb directly the size of the holding that the parent wishes to dispose of without depressing the stock price and the resultant value received by the parent.

- The parent wishes to maintain its voting rights and influence over the public company or subsidiary for a period of time.

- The parent wishes to issue debt with a lower coupon than straight debt. The exchangeable feature on a debt offering results in a lower interest rate than the equivalent straight (nonexchangeable) debt.

- The parent wishes to receive a price for its holding that is higher than the current market price. With most exchangeable debt for already publicly traded shares of the independent company or subsidiary there is an exchange premium over the current market price of the public stock. The exchange premium is the amount by which the exchange price exceeds the then market price for the underlying stock.[1]

- The parent wishes to issue debt with less impact on its credit rating. Most exchangeable debt is subordinated to senior debt. Subordinated debt is generally viewed more favorably by rating agencies and by senior creditors than senior or straight debt. Mandatory exchangeable debt, a form of exchangeable debt discussed later that does not have to be repaid in cash, is even more favorably viewed by rating agencies and senior lenders.

FORMATS OF EXCHANGEABLE DEBT

There are many exchangeable debt formats. The two broad classes are those where the exchange rate into the underlying public company shares is fixed at the time of issuance and those where the exchange rate is set at the time of the exchange ("reset"). These structures are found in all the most common types of exchangeable debt, including:

- Fixed exchange rate, optional exchangeable debt
- Fixed exchange rate, mandatory exchangeable debt
- Reset exchange rate, mandatory exchangeable debt
- Fixed exchange rate, zero coupon optional exchangeable debt

Let's look at each form of debt more closely.

Fixed Exchange Rate, Optional Exchangeable Debt

With this debt the investor has the option, but not the obligation, to exchange the debt for the underlying stock. This is equivalent to traditional convertible debt. Should the investor, at his or her discretion, decide not to exchange the debt for the public stock, the debt must be repaid in cash by the parent at call or maturity. In practice, exchange will occur only if the value of the public stock is greater than the redemption price of the debt at the time of call or maturity. However, if the underlying stock has decreased in price so that the exchange value is below the redemption price, holders will opt for cash. With optional exchange debt, exchange into the public stock can occur at any time at the option of the holder. The exchange rate is fixed at the time of the offering, subject to adjustments for stock dividends, splits, and so forth. As with most traditional convertible debt, the holder will not exchange the securities for the public shares and thereby forgo the coupon, the protection of a debt instrument, and the alternative of a return of capital in full at the fixed maturity, until the debt is called before maturity by the parent or at the final maturity of the debt.

There are often either provisions that prohibit a call for a period of years (usually two or three) or a requirement that the public stock must trade at a significant premium to the exchange price during that period for a number of days before a call, or both.

With optional exchangeable debt, the parent generally receives a premium over the price of the public stock at the time of the issue of the exchangeable debt. However, the parent is obligated to make periodic interest payments on the exchangeable debt and repay the debt at maturity (or at an earlier call) in cash should the investor decide not to exchange the debt for the public stock.

Should the investor decide not to exchange the debt for the public stock, the debt has to be repaid by the parent at maturity in cash. As a consequence of the very real potential that the parent will have to issue cash at maturity or call, rating agencies and banks look upon optional exchange debt as debt, albeit benign debt that is generally subordinate and long term and with few restrictive covenants.

Fixed Exchange Rate, Mandatory Exchangeable Debt

With this debt, the investor is required to exchange the debt for the underlying stock at call or maturity. Unlike the case with optional exchangeable debt, there is forced exchange into the public stock at maturity or at call—the parent is not required to repay the debt in cash. However, in some cases, the parent reserves the right to pay the cash value equivalent to the public shares rather than the shares themselves.

Exchange into the public stock automatically occurs at maturity or call. The exchange rate is fixed at the time of the offering, subject to adjustments for stock dividends, splits, and so forth. The investors do not get to choose whether to take stock or cash.

Mandatory exchangeable debt, similar to traditional optional exchangeable debt, requires periodic interest payments during the life of the debt. These payments must be made as due. The important distinction with mandatory exchange is that the principal does not have to be repaid.

Mandatory exchangeable debt is viewed much more favorably than optional exchangeable debt by credit rating agencies and banks. In fact, they treat it as equity. Because fixed-rate mandatory exchangeable debt most closely resembles straight equity, a fixed-rate mandatory exchangeable debt appeals to equity investors as well as traditional convertible debt investors.

However, there is a cost to the parent for obtaining the mandatory exchange feature. With fixed-rate mandatory exchangeable debt, the coupon tends to be higher, the exchange premium lower, and the term shorter than with optional exchangeable debt. In 2001, an average coupon for mandatory exchangeable and convertible debt was about 7.5 percent, compared with an average coupon payment of about 4.5 percent for optional exchangeable debt. The average exchange or conversion premium was about 20 percent for fixed-rate mandatory exchangeable debt, compared with an average of about 29 percent for optional exchangeable debt. The term of mandatory exchangeable debt ranged from 3 to 5 years, compared to up to 10 years for optional exchangeable debt.

Reset Exchange Rate, Mandatory Exchangeable Debt

Similar to a fixed-rate mandatory exchange, this exchangeable debt is never repaid in cash.

As in a fixed-rate mandatory exchange debt, exchange into the underlying stock automatically occurs at maturity or call. However, with reset exchangeable debt, the nominal exchange rate is a cap but not a floor. The exchange rate is not fixed at the time of the offering, but floats with the price of the underlying stock until the time of the exchange.

Fixed Exchange Rate, Zero Coupon Optional Exchangeable Debt

This is discount debt that does not pay interest in cash periodically, unlike more traditional exchangeable debt. Rather, the debt is sold at a discount to the price at maturity and the interest accumulates. This is called *zero coupon exchangeable debt*. A feature of zero coupon exchangeable debt is a very high exchange premium. Zero coupon exchangeable debt was exceptionally popular with parents in the late 1990s and 2000 for two reasons: (1) the high exchange premium, which meant that fewer shares of the public stock would be issued at maturity or call; and (2) the lack of cash interest payments. However, an unfortunate aspect of these securities for the parent was that, to induce investors to accept the high exchange premiums, most zero coupon exchangeable debt provided investors with the ability to put the debt back to the parent for cash after one or two years.

DISADVANTAGES OF EXCHANGEABLE DEBT OFFERINGS
Exchangeable Debt Is Still Debt

Exchangeable debt is a debt obligation of the parent. This is particularly true of optional exchangeable debt that may have to be repaid in cash on maturity or call. With optional exchangeable debt, the exchange premium is not a guaranteed sale price for the public stock; it is only an option granted to the investor that will only be exercised if the price of the public stock exceeds the exercise price. This is an important distinction that is often not stressed by investment bankers when marketing optional exchangeable debt. (This is also true with traditional convertible debt.)

The lower coupon and the premium over the market price on the public stock on exchangeable debt are the compensation that the parent receives for giving to the investors an option, but not a requirement, to take the public stock.

There Are Interest Obligations

Additionally, except with zero coupon exchangeable debt and some reset exchange rate debt that does not carry a coupon, there is a requirement to make interest payments on the debt. While these payments are usually lower than for straight debt, they still are a cash requirement so long as the debt is outstanding.

Put Features in Zero Coupon Exchangeable Debt May Be Disastrous

Most zero coupon fixed-exchange rate exchangeable debt issuers give the investor the right to put the debt to the parent for cash after a fairly short period. The high exchange premium should not distract the parent from the considerable likelihood that the public stock will not appreciate sufficiently in the short term to deter investors from exercising the put right. Because of the put provision, in many cases zero coupon exchangeable debt in practice becomes short-term debt. At the time of issue of this debt, it was not perceived to be a risk by the parent, as there was great optimism over the continued rise into the future of stock prices. The parent fully expected that the price of the public stock would appreciate considerably so that the investors would ultimately exchange the debt for shares. It often did not work out that way. With the weak stock markets of 2001 and 2002, the high exchange prices were not obtainable and many of these issues of debt in 2002 are being put back to the parents for cash by investors. The considerable risks in these securities were not adequately understood by parents—or they were ignored. A number of issuers of these securities face financial distress. These securities are poorly conceived and inappropriate for many issuers.

Resettable Debt May Create a Trap

Reset exchangeable debt offers many problems for the parent. Reset mandatory debt is also known as *toxic* or *death spiral* securities. Quality issuers do not use this type of security, and quality investors do not purchase such securities. However, a number of investment banks push this product, as it is easy to sell and has large fees attached. The buyers are often hedge funds and offshore funds. In general, only a distressed or an ill-advised parent will issue securities with reset exchange provisions. With these securities, the interests of the parent and the investors are diametrically opposed: the lower the stock price of the subsidiary at the time of the exchange, the more shares the investors are issued. Any manipulation with the purpose of bringing down the stock price of the underlying shares before the exchange and hedging activities is generally precluded by contractual agreements with the purchaser of these securities. However, frequently there is manipulation of the underlying stock to drive the price down prior to conversion. The incidence of this manipulation can almost never be proved, as offshore investors operate in secret and without any regulatory scrutiny.

A major disadvantage of toxic debt is that the parent has no idea how many shares it will have to issue in the exchange. Therefore, it has to ensure that there are sufficient shares to meet any eventuality. In the case of a majority-owned subsidiary, an affiliated or a nonaffiliated company has only so many shares to issue. The parent will either have to reserve a reasonable number of shares and put a floor on the price adjustment or be prepared to pay cash for the difference between the number of shares it owns and the number it is obligated to issue.

Issuing such debt will usually have an immediately adverse effect on the parent's stock also, because any intelligent shareholder will run for the hills when such a debt issue is announced.

The Ultimate Tax Bill May Be Higher

The parent will have to pay taxes on the appreciated value of the subsidiary or unrelated company stock underlying the exchangeable debt at the time of exchange, rather than at the time of issuance of the exchangeable security. This is important. Although there will be an offsetting interest deduction, the value of the public equity at the time of exchange may be considerably higher than at the time of the issuance of the debt. This results in a much larger taxable gain than at the time of issue. The deferral of taxes using exchangeable debt has to be balanced (or hedged) against the potential for an unknown tax liability later.

Investors Will Require Confidence in Two Entities

An investor in an exchangeable debt issue is buying into two securities. One is a debt issue by the parent. Investors will need assurance that the parent will be able to meet its obligations on the debt security to pay interest and, in an optional exchange, on the principal on call or maturity or upon a put. The second security is the public equity into which the debt is exchangeable. Investors will need reason to believe that this will appreciate in value to compensate for the lower coupon and the premium over the market price at the time of issue.

Cooperation Is Needed from the Other Company

The cooperation of the company (or subsidiary) that issued the holding is usually required for two reasons. First, if a publicly registered offering is made, a registration statement will need to be filed by the public company covering the shares to be owned by the parent that will be exchanged for the debt so that these shares are freely marketable upon exchange. Second, to induce investors to buy the exchangeable debt, it is often useful to have the management of the underlying company assist in the marketing effort in selling to investors the second part of the story—the appreciation potential of the underlying stock.

Exchangeable Debt Is Generally Marketable Only in Larger Sizes

The market for an underwritten public or 144A offering of exchangeable debt is generally limited to an issue amount above $100 million. Under that size, buyers have concerns over the liquidity of the debt should they wish to sell their holdings.

While smaller issues may be done, there is usually a substantial cost to the parent in higher interest expense and/or lower conversion premium. An illiquid private placement may be smaller, but will be considerably more costly and have a more limited investor group to approach.

Complex SEC Registration Is Required

A public offering of exchangeable debt involves the registration of the securities of two different issuers: the parent and the issuer of the public stock. This may complicate the registration/disclosure process beyond that of a simple sale of the holding by the parent. This also contrasts with traditional convertible debt, where the issuer of the debt and the stock are the same, or a traditional exchange offer. It is certainly more complex than an exchange using a 3(a)9 offering circular.

SUMMARY

Exchangeable securities are a unique SER alternative that enables the parent to realize the current value of the subsidiary without selling shares in the subsidiary or another public company at that time. Chapter 15 will look at how mergers can create shareholder value by exchanging the subsidiary's stock or assets to create a successful company that can be sold or taken public at a later date.

EXAMPLES
Example 1, Tribune Company: Optional Exchangeable Debt

In 1999, Tribune Company issued $1.25 billion of 30-year exchangeable subordinated debentures. The debt carried an interest rate of 2 percent and could be exchanged for cash based on the value of America Online, Inc., common stock. In this optional exchange transaction, the market value of AOL serves as the public security, or reference share, that determines the value of the exchangeable debt and the cash value for which it will be exchanged at any time until its maturity in May 2029.

Each of the 7 million exchangeable debentures was issued based on a principal amount of $157, which was the price per share of AOL's common stock at the time of the debt issuance on April 7, 1999. (After a 2-for-1 split, the equivalent price was $78.50.) This principal amount represents the minimum amount payable to the investors in the debt upon maturity or call.

Upon maturity, holders of the debt are entitled to receive either the principal amount of the debt or the current market value of AOL shares on the maturity date plus any deferred quarterly payments of interest, whichever is higher.

Tribune owned 11 million shares of AOL. This debt allowed it to realize the value of its holding in AOL without creating a taxable event at that time. Tribune was able to set up hedging strategies based on its AOL position that deferred any gain.

Tribune was able to raise $1.25 billion on very favorable terms by using its AOL shares. At the time, the value of nonexchangeable debt with equivalent terms would have been around 60 percent of the value of the exchangeable debt—$500 million less in proceeds to Tribune.

Example 2, Cox Communications, Inc.:
A Partially Mandatory Exchangeable Security

In August 1999, Cox Communications issued $1.6 billion of exchangeable subordinated discount debentures due in 2020. The debt was sold at a price of $429 per bond. At maturity in 2020, the investor would receive $1000 per bond in cash. The debt had a 1 percent cash interest rate and a yield to maturity of 5 percent. It was exchangeable into 7.59 shares of Sprint PCS stock (equivalent to a price of $56.52 per PCS share). The market price of the PCS shares at the time was $47.75 per share (a 20 percent premium). At that time, Cox owned 127.1 million shares of Sprint PCS Series 2, including shares issuable upon the exercise or conversion of warrants and preferred stock.

The debt has two significant terms. If the holder exercised the exchange right before April 19, 2002, the holder received cash equal to the value of the Sprint PCS shares. If the holder exercised this right on or after April 19, 2002, the holder received only shares in Sprint PCS, or, at Cox's discretion, cash equal to the shares in Sprint PCS or a combination of both. The right was exercisable only every five years beginning in 2005.

This debt allowed Cox to realize the value of its holding in Sprint PCS immediately without creating a taxable event at that time or violating restrictions on the sale of the shares. Cox was able to set up covered hedging strategies to protect itself until April 19, 2002, against any optional conversions by debt holders that would have required it to pay cash rather than shares.

Sprint PCS stock closed on March 31, 2002, at $10.29 per share. The debt created value for Cox's shareholders by locking in 20-year funds on attractive terms with a very low cash coupon and a low yield to maturity. Additionally, Cox was able to deduct for tax purposes the full 5 percent yield to maturity.

Example 3, AT&T Corporation:
A Mandatory Exchangeable Security

In October 2001, AT&T Corporation realized the value of most of its stake in Cablevision Systems Corporation through two concurrent public offerings. One offering was of AT&T's Cablevision stock. The other was of interests in a trust that had as its principal asset a contract with AT&T to deliver Cablevision stock to the trust in November 2004 for mandatory exchange of interests in the trust into Cablevision stock.

At the end of 2000, Cablevision Systems Corporation owned cable television systems and had approximately 3 million subscribers. In addition, Cablevision's majority-owned subsidiary, Rainbow Media Holdings, Inc., owned a number of programming networks, the Madison Square Garden sports and entertainment business, movie theaters, and other operations. Cablevision's revenues for 2000 were $4.4 billion.

On April 1, 2001, 133 million shares of Cablevision Class A common stock and 42.1 million shares of Cablevision Class B common stock were outstanding, for a total of 175.1 million shares of common stock outstanding. Only the Cablevision Class A common stock ("Cablevision stock") was available to the public.

Each share of Cablevision stock had one vote per share. Each share of Cablevision Class B common stock had 10 votes per share. The holders of the Class B common stock voted as a separate class to elect 75 percent of the board of directors. The chairman, Charles F. Dolan, controlled a majority of the Class B common stock and therefore controlled Cablevision.

AT&T Corporation owned 48.9 million shares of Cablevision stock, equivalent to 28 percent of the total common stock outstanding of the combined Class A and B. AT&T had obtained the Cablevision stock position when it bought Tele-Communications Inc. in 1999.

During 2000, AT&T's debt had increased 81 percent to $65 billion because of its $100 billion purchase of Tele-Communications and other cable companies. In 2001, AT&T was under pressure from its lenders and the rating agencies to reduce its debt level, and so began selling assets to raise cash.

As part of its debt reduction, AT&T decided to divest its entire holdings in Cablevision through public offerings of those shares. On October 17, 2001, AT&T undertook two concurrent public offerings of its shares in Cablevision, raising $1.5 billion to repay debt.

One concurrent public offering consisted of a sale through a traditional secondary offering of 20.5 million of the 48.9 million shares of Cablevision held by AT&T. These were sold at $36.05 per share, with gross proceeds of $737 million, realized through the sale of 19.3 million shares in the initial offering and 1.3 million shares in the overallotment.

The other concurrent public offering was more unusual in its structure. A trust was set up ("the trust") to sell Equity Trust Securities ("the trust securities") in a public offering. The trust securities represented all of the beneficial interest in the trust. They were listed on the New York Stock Exchange and were freely tradable. A total of 26.9 million trust securities were sold at the offering price of $36.05 per trust security, representing the closing price of Cablevision stock on the date of the offerings. The gross proceeds of $970 million were realized through the sale of 23.9 million trust securities in the initial offering and 3 million trust securities in the overallotment.

AT&T entered into a contract with the trust requiring it to deliver to the trust between 22.1 and 26.9 million shares of its remaining Cablevision stock or its cash equivalent in November 2004. The exact number of shares depended on the Cablevision stock price before the November 2004 date. After this, the trust would distribute the Cablevision stock or its cash equivalent, and any other assets, to the investors in the trust, and then terminate. The trust used the proceeds of the public offering to prepay expenses and then to purchase two new assets:

1. Zero coupon U.S. Treasury securities that matured every quarter during the term of the trust. This provided the cash to pay the quarterly distributions on the trust stock due over the term of the trust, at $0.5858 per trust security, equivalent to a rate of 6.50 percent per annum. The U.S. Treasury securities initially represented approximately 19 percent of the assets of the trust.

2. A prepaid forward contract between the trust and AT&T under which AT&T was required to deliver to the trust on the exchange date in November 2004 (subject to certain adjustments) either Cablevision stock or its cash equivalent.

Under the terms of this contract, the number of shares or their cash equivalent which AT&T was to deliver to the trust would vary between 0.82 shares and 1 share, but would not exceed 1 share. The provisions were that AT&T would deliver to the trust:

• For each trust security, 0.82 shares of Cablevision stock, or the cash equivalent if the average price of Cablevision stock for the 20 trading days prior to the exchange date was more than $43.98 per share; or

• Shares of Cablevision stock worth exactly $36.05 for each trust security (i.e., the issue price of the trust securities), or the cash equivalent if the average price of Cablevision stock for the 20 trading days prior to the exchange date was more than $36.05 per share but less than or equal to $43.981 per share; or

• Shares of Cablevision stock for each trust security, or the cash equivalent if the average price of Cablevision stock for the 20 trading days prior to the exchange date was $36.05 or less per share.

In some limited circumstances, AT&T would deliver the Cablevision stock, or its value in cash, to the trust before November 2004. In other limited circumstances, AT&T had the right to extend the exchange date to February 2005 if it were delivering cash instead of Cablevision stock. The forward contract with AT&T initially represented approximately 81 percent of the assets of the trust.

After AT&T completed delivering the shares or their cash equivalent to the trust, the trust would distribute its assets to the trust security holders and terminate.

Cablevision had no affiliation with the trust, did not receive any of the proceeds from the sale of the securities by the trust, and did not have any obligation to the trust.

Attractiveness of the Trust to Investors

The trust was attractive to investors because its trust securities provided them with a quarterly distribution equivalent to 6.5 percent per annum, in contrast to the

Cablevision stock, which paid no dividends, as well as participation in the upside of Cablevision stock.

However, this dividend came with a cost for investors. Although this arrangement allowed them to receive a 6.5 percent per annum quarterly distribution and participate in the appreciation of the California stock, they had a lesser opportunity for gain from its appreciation after the offering than if they had purchased the equivalent Cablevision stock, and yet they would incur full participation in any decline in its value. Investors would realize a gain only if the value of Cablevision stock increased by more than approximately 22 percent between the offering and the exchange date, and then they would receive only 82 percent of the increase beyond that level.

Risk of Default

This transaction did present some risk in the event that AT&T defaulted on its forward purchase contact to deliver the Cablevision shares to the trust due to bankruptcy. The trust did not actually own the underlying Cablevision stock. It had a forward purchase contract with AT&T obligating AT&T to deliver the shares or their cash equivalent on the exchange date. There was a small potential risk of delay or loss of principal in the event that AT&T were to go bankrupt before its delivery of the shares.

AT&T stated that the prepaid forward contracts in this arrangement constituted securities contracts for purposes of the U.S. Bankruptcy Code. In the case of a securities contract, the obligation of AT&T to the trust would generally not be subject to the automatic stay provisions of the U.S. Bankruptcy Code in the event that AT&T filed for bankruptcy.

However, the forward contract was a sizable asset and it might be presumed that the other creditors in a bankruptcy would challenge its validity. As a result, there was a small risk that the forward contract would be determined not to qualify as a securities contract and then the trust would simply be a claimant on the bankrupt estate. AT&T believed that this determination was unlikely. However, AT&T noted that were it to be made, it would delay payment at best and jeopardize the recovery of the principal amount at worst.

Because there is some risk of a delay in the event of a bankruptcy of the parent, a trust arrangement with forward delivery such as this one will generally be available only if investors have confidence in the long-term creditworthiness of the parent.

Benefits to AT&T

The trust was attractive to AT&T because it provided the company with $970 million in immediate cash while still permitting it to share in part of any increase in the value of Cablevision stock before the exchange date. Even in the worst case, this arrangement would result in AT&T having to deliver the full 26.9 million shares to the trust with no further obligation. In the best case, it would cause AT&T to deliver only 22.1 million shares, allowing the company to retain 4.8 million shares of Cablevision stock, or 18 percent of the maximum, still with no further obligation. In exchange, the forward contract allowed the trust to pay AT&T at the closing of the offering the equivalent of $28.12 per share of Cablevision stock, compared to the then market price of $36.05—equivalent to a discount of 22 percent.

Another benefit to AT&T was that this offering attracted a different investor group, which included dividend-oriented retail investors, than did the straightforward concurrent stock offering.

Because it used two concurrent offerings, AT&T expanded the available size of the total offering that could be placed without increasing the price pressure on the Cablevision stock.[2]

The offering was also attractive to AT&T's banks and the credit rating agencies because it contained no further cash obligation to AT&T other than delivering the shares to the trust.

CHAPTER **15**

MERGERS WITH PUBLIC AND PRIVATE COMPANIES

INTRODUCTION

Mergers can take many forms. For the purpose of this discussion we will examine merger structures that use subsidiary equity redeployment transactions to create shareholder value. Based on these criteria, we will examine only those transactions that exchange subsidiary ownership positions—usually stock or assets—between a parent and its public or private merger partner, creating a combined entity. In the end, the primary goal is to structure a merger deal that enables the parent—and its shareholders—to benefit from the success of the newly merged entity by taking it public, or selling it, at a later date. At times when there is a limited conventional IPO and private equity market, there is increased interest in mergers as a means to grow a promising emerging business. Similarly with a noncore subsidiary that the parent wishes to divest, when the cash divestiture market is not offering premium values, a merger may provide an avenue to greater shareholder value in the long-term for the parent rather than an immediate sale for cash at a low price. However, most mergers are not successes. Choosing the right partner is critical to creating value.

ADVANTAGES OF A MERGER WITH A PUBLIC OR PRIVATE COMPANY

For the purpose of this chapter, a merger makes sense if it generates some of these benefits:

- Creates a stronger company that is better able to meet the parent's objectives than the subsidiary on its own.
- Allows the parent to divest the subsidiary but also retain a significant equity interest in its potential upside.

263

- Through a merger with an already public company, enables the subsidiary to become a public company.

- Through a merger with a strong private company, increases the probability that at a later date the combined company will go public and become a successful public company or be sold at a premium price.

- Enables the subsidiary to become a public company when a traditional IPO is unavailable for market reasons and the parent does not want to wait for the market to come back, or when the parent or subsidiary does not want to labor through the time-consuming and expensive IPO process.

- Creates a springboard for full ownership of the combined company at a later date. In many cases, it may make sense for the parent to eventually buy the merged entity if it creates value for parent shareholders. However, in the short term, it may make more sense to keep the merged entity independent to maintain an exceptional internal culture or equity incentives for managers, or to avoid consolidating the company losses on the parent's income statement.

- Lessens concerns by the parent that a stand-alone public subsidiary will be a takeover target, depriving the parent's shareholders of the benefit of its long-term potential.

DISADVANTAGES OF A MERGER WITH A PUBLIC COMPANY

However, there are disadvantages to merging a subsidiary with a public company, including:

- *Limited liquidity for a large owner.* Owning shares in a smaller-capitalized public company does not mean that there is a liquid market or that the shares can be easily sold. As well, the parent may be subject to the stock sale restrictions of SEC Rule 144.

- *Limited control.* Even if the parent has a majority ownership, any actions that might be perceived as disadvantaging the public shareholders will be scrutinized. An example is the transfer of assets or personnel to other divisions.

- *Increased public disclosure.* The subsidiary will be subject to increased scrutiny and stringent public disclosure rules.

- *Risk of damaged reputation.* There is always the chance that a merger may not succeed. If this is the case, the failure takes place in a public forum.

- *Increased cost.* There are many costs that come with being a public company. These costs have been thoroughly covered in previous chapters.

It is also worth noting that a merger rarely results in an infusion of cash for the newly created entity unless the merger partner has cash that it can contribute to the combined company. In many cases the parent must supply cash to the subsidiary to make it an attractive merger partner. After a merger, the parent may also have to supply cash to ensure that the newly combined company succeeds on its own.

CHALLENGES OF MAKING A MERGER WITH A PUBLIC COMPANY WORK

There have been many books written about the challenges of making a merger work. For our purposes, we will take a brief look at the key challenges parents face as they undertake the process of merging a subsidiary with a public company.

Finding the Best Merger Partner May Be Difficult

The most difficult part of using a merger to go public is finding the right merger partner. Once the partner is found, agreeing on terms acceptable to both sides is equally difficult.

Also, the list of potential candidates can be truncated by conditions that are preset by the parent. Often, for example, a parent may look for a merger partner with a stellar track record. There is a short list of companies that meet this criterion.

If the parent wants control or a substantial influence after the merger, it will often reduce the potential field still further. Attractive public companies are often not willing to give up control or are only willing to do so as part of a complete acquisition of the entire public company at a premium price. Usually there will be no merger candidate that meets all the parent's criteria. The parent will then have to compromise on its requirements.

When an acceptable partner is found that is willing to consider a merger, agreeing on valuation is equally difficult.

Valuation issues also complicate the selection process, as parents will look for merger partners that have a relative value consistent with the goals of the parent. For example, if the parent wants a substantial interest or a majority of the combined company after the merger, either it will need to find a merger partner of appropriate value relative to the value of the subsidiary or it will have to contribute additional cash or other assets.

The Merger May Go Public with a Whimper

As with a spin-off, a merger with a public company usually has none of the splash of a traditional IPO. For a star subsidiary, a merger may not be the best way to be introduced to the public market. If the subsidiary is eligible for a quality IPO and the market is receptive, it is usually a better alternative. A desirable merger is often best delayed until the subsidiary is public, when the subsidiary has cash in the bank, is a well-sponsored public company, has a glow, and has its own public market value established for valuation discussions.

Mergers with Public Companies are Complex and Take Time

Most merger deals take up to five months to close due to numerous approvals that need to be requested and received. For example, federal and state agencies, and the listing exchange need to approve the timing, structure, and financial arrangements relating to the merger deal.

Other obligations that hold up mergers include the need to put the merger to a shareholder vote. A merger with a public company where the parent has control of the combined entity after the merger will almost always require a vote of the public company's shareholders. This is a lengthy process involving drafting and filing a proxy, receiving comments from the SEC, responding to comments, circulating the proxy, and calling and holding a shareholder vote.

Compounding the time challenge is the fact that the details surrounding a public merger must be disclosed, including the terms, price, and structure of the transaction. Any special arrangements with management and shareholders must also be disclosed.

Mergers with Public Companies Are Expensive

During the merger process, many documents need to be filed with appropriate oversight agencies along with the necessary fees. In addition, mergers often involve investment bankers who charge large fees.

The Merger Process with Public Companies Contains Inherent Risks

During the merger process there is always the chance that another bidder may step in with a better offer. The board of a public company may be obligated to consider a better offer if one is made.

Loss of Momentum

There is the risk that the subsidiary and the partner will lose their momentum due to distractions caused by the merger.

There Are Obstacles in Making Mergers Work

The low success rate of mergers is widely known. Most mergers do not create long-term value. Making a merger work is hard and takes skill, experience, and luck. Customers, suppliers, and above all employees will be unsettled and apprehensive. In addition, there is always the risk that the subsidiary and the merger partner may lose their momentum due to distractions caused by the merger. Mergers with well-run and pristine partners are difficult enough. The problems are compounded if the partner or the subsidiary is a turnaround or is troubled.

There Are Few Structure Options with Public Company Mergers

In a merger with a public company intended to take the subsidiary public, subsidiary stock or assets are exchanged for an ownership position in the already public company, whatever the actual form of merger used. The public company survives and maintains its public trading. This generally means that the parent has to take the public company in its entirety, including its liabilities. It also means that few public companies, or their shareholders, will be interested in anything but a plain vanilla deal of a fixed number of the partner's common shares for the subsidiary or its assets. While it may be possible to devise more complex transactions, doing so will limit later interest by analysts and investors in the stock of the combined company, defeating much of the purpose of merging with a public company—obtaining a vibrant public stock.

Share Transaction Limits May Be Placed on the Parent

Often, the board of the merger partner will create an agreement that restricts the parent's ability to buy and sell the combined company's stock. This is usually the case when the parent gains a controlling interest in the company. For example, the board may require a "stand still" agreement prohibiting the purchase of future shares without board approval.

The Parent May Inherit Public Relations Problems

In a merger, the combined company inherits the history and reputation of the public company. This is problematic if the public company has not performed well in the past or has engaged in questionable business practices.

BENEFITS OF A PRIVATE COMPANY MERGER

Having spent a great deal of time detailing the disadvantages of merging with a public company, we now turn our attention to the benefits of merging a subsidiary with a private company. As stated previously, the primary benefit of such a merger is to create a company strong enough to successfully make its way through the IPO process or be a better candidate for a sale or an eventual acquisition by the parent. Other ancillary benefits include:

- *Increased flexibility in how the merger deal is structured.* Because the subsidiary is merging with a private entity, the parent can pick and choose the assets it wants to buy and the liabilities it wants to leave behind. In this way it can create a merger transaction that truly benefits the subsidiary, the parent, and its shareholders.

- *Increased governance flexibility.* Governance arrangements are much more flexible with a private company than with a public company. For example, the parent may receive many rights via separate classes of stocks and shareholder agreements. This is true even if the parent is a minority shareholder.

DISADVANTAGES OF A PRIVATE COMPANY MERGER

At the risk of stating the obvious, many of the disadvantages of a public merger also apply to a merger with a private company. For example, it can be as difficult to find a private company merger candidate as it is to find a public company merger candidate. Having said that, there are risks inherent to merging with a private company. These are detailed in the following paragraphs.

An IPO Event Is Not Guaranteed

The parent has usually entered into the merger to take the newly combined company public. This may not occur because of market conditions, the performance of the combined company, or reluctance by its other shareholders. If the parent only owns a minority position in the company, it will be difficult for it to force the combined company to go public or take another liquidity action such as sale, assuming there is a market. Therefore, it will have to consider creating an exit strategy such as a put after a reasonable period to ensure that it is not permanently locked into a minority private investment. None of these exit strategies are usually of much use in practice if the combined company is significantly underperforming, with the exception of the ability to force a sale at a distress price.

Minority Shareholders Will Want Protection

When the parent is in control of the private combined company after the merger, the shoe is on the other foot and the other shareholders of the private company will be reluctant to accept a minority position in the combined company without substantial protections for both its independence and a path for liquidity. The parent will need to expect that the shareholders will demand fairly onerous protections such as a cash put of their shares to the parent if a liquidity event does not occur in a certain time.

THE PRIMARY MERGER OPTIONS

Having covered the advantages and disadvantages of mergers as an SER tool, we will now review the three basic types of merger transactions that can create value for parents and their shareholders. The balance of the chapter will touch on all of these but will focus primarily on the merger of a subsidiary with a public company in which the parent retains a significant or majority interest in the combined company after the transaction. The three basic merger types are:

1. A majority merger of the subsidiary with a merger partner in which the parent has majority ownership of the combined company after the merger

2. A merger of equals in which the parent has a very large economic position in the combined company without outright control

3. A minority merger in which the parent has a minority interest in the combined company

All of these merger types can be transacted between the subsidiary and a public company or between the subsidiary and a private company with a view to a subsequent IPO.

Let's look at each alternative in more depth.

A Majority Merger

A majority interest transaction can take the following forms:

• A merger of the subsidiary with a private company (or the purchase of specific assets or operations from another company) in which the parent has control of the combined private company with an intent to later take the combined company public or effect some other form of equity redeployment at a later date. This is, in reality, an acquisition of the private company. To effect the transaction, the private merger partner may issue its shares, or the parent may purchase the private merger partner for cash or notes, or both. The advantage to the parent is that the subsidiary has an opportunity to become a public company at a later date while the parent retains control.

• A merger of the subsidiary with a public company in which the parent has control of the combined public company. This is, in actuality, an acquisition of the public company. To effect the transaction, the public company issues additional stock to the parent in exchange for the stock or assets of the subsidiary, thereby continuing as a public company. The advantage is that the subsidiary becomes a public company without going through the IPO process, while the parent retains control.

Exhibit 15–1 provides a graphical representation of the merger of a subsidiary with a public company for a majority interest.

Later, this chapter will take an in-depth look at this transaction by examining the merger of Lockheed Martin's subsidiary Calcomp with a public company, Summagraphics Corporation.

A Merger of Equals

In a merger of equals, the parent has a very large economic position in the combined public or private company, but not outright control of the company. The "equals" nature of the merger is reflected in the composition of the board of directors, which is controlled by neither the parent nor the owners of the merger partner.

The advantage of a merger of equals is that it permits a merger when a merger partner is not willing to cede control to the parent but the parent wants substantial influence. As well, in practice, a 50-50 split is often the easiest merger to

EXHIBIT 15–1

Merger of a Subsidiary with a Public Company for a Majority Interest

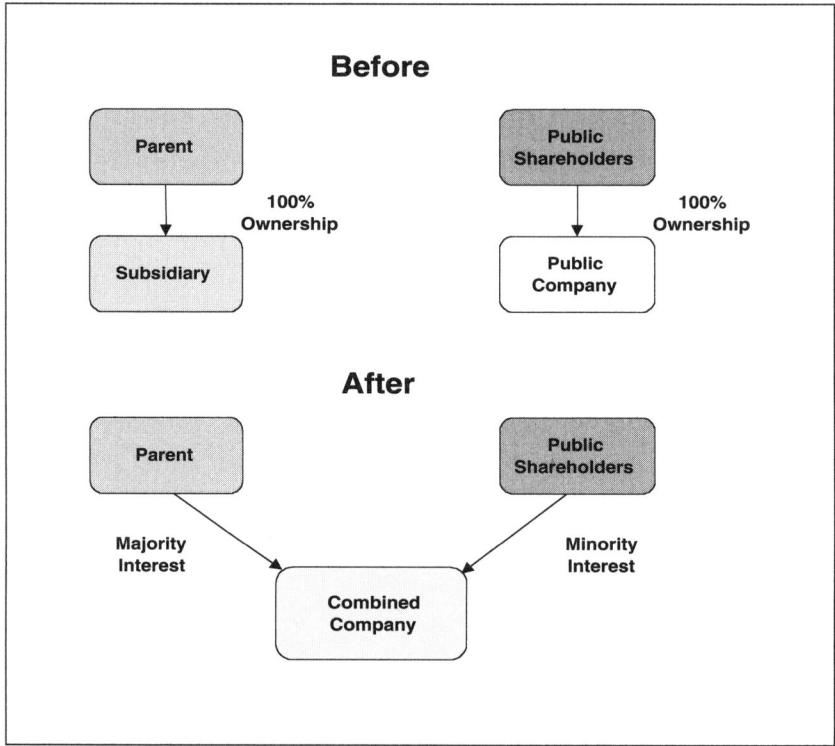

negotiate. It is a simple concept that takes away all the valuation issues that are often the major impediment to an otherwise attractive merger. These valuation issues are especially daunting with private companies, where there is no market price on either side to provide some valuation anchor. Valuation issues in particular complicate most attempts to merge private entities and turn them into an exercise in futility as merger discussions get bogged down in the credibility of comparative forecasts, weighting given to various balance sheet and income statement items, and valuation metrics to be employed. Later, this chapter will take an in-depth look at a merger of equals transaction by examining the merger of a subsidiary of parent TRW Miliwave with an independent venture capital–backed merger partner, Endgate Corporation.

A Minority Merger

A minority interest transaction entails a merger of the subsidiary with a private or public merger partner in which the parent has a minority ownership position and

EXHIBIT   15–2

Merger of a Subsidiary with a Public Company for a Minority Interest

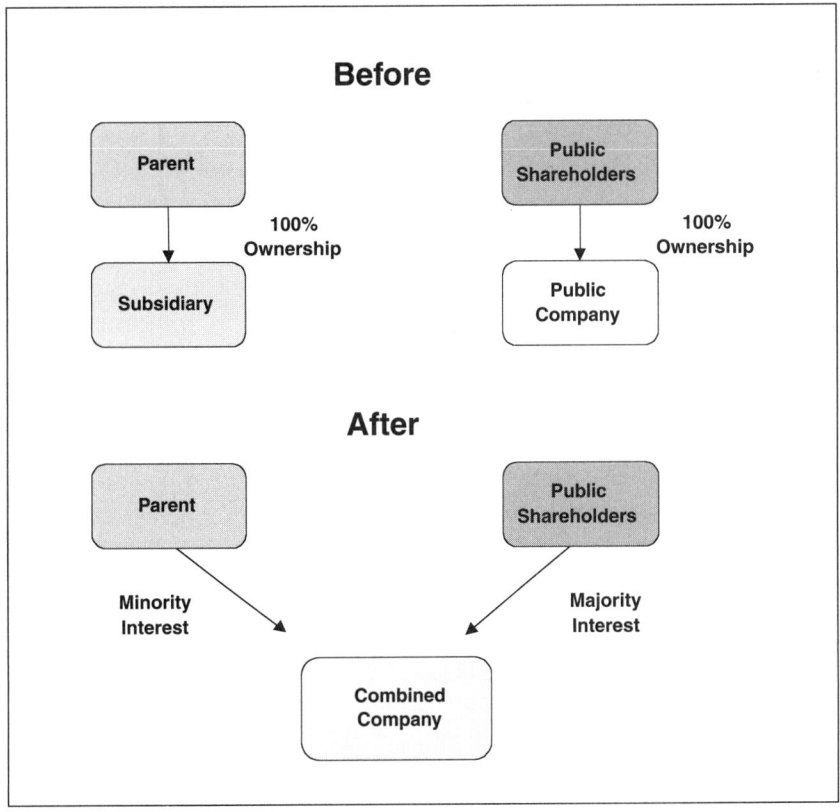

does not have control of the combined company. The advantages are that this structure permits the subsidiary to become a public company through a merger with a strong public (or about to be public) merger partner and it removes the parent from primary responsibility for the postmerger company. Exhibit 15–2 provides a graphical representation of a minority merger with a public company, and Exhibit 15–3 shows a merger with a private company for a minority or majority position followed by an IPO.

Later, this chapter will take an in-depth look at this transaction by examining the merger of a subsidiary of Philips with FEI Corporation.

AN ALTERNATIVE MERGER STRUCTURE: MERGING WITH A SHELL COMPANY

Another way for a subsidiary to go public is to merge with a public "shell" company. A shell company is listed on a stock exchange but has no meaningful operations. In some cases, promoters create shell companies as merger candidates,

EXHIBIT 15–3

Merger of a Subsidiary with a Private Company for a Minority or Majority
Position Followed by an IPO

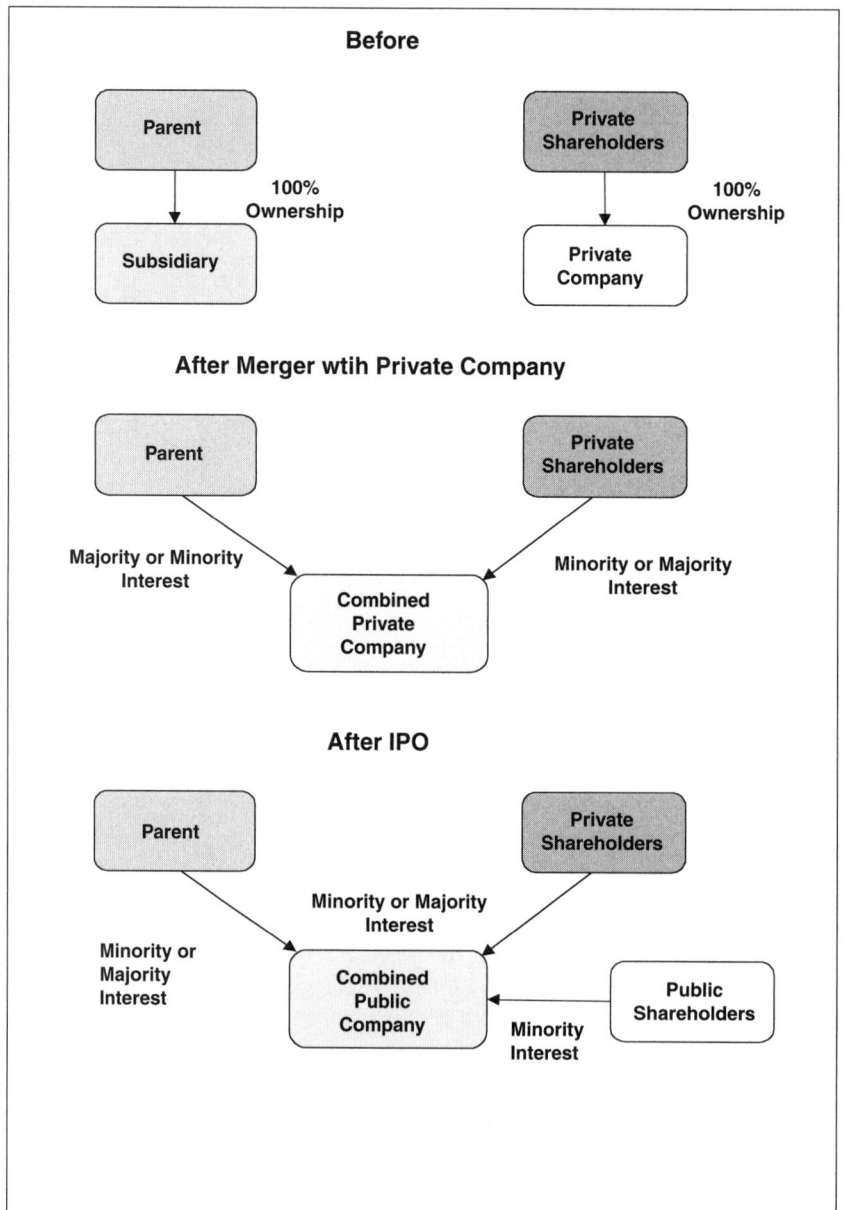

although most shells are the public remains of sold or failed businesses. Often the only assets of a shell are some cash and a public stock listing. Some advantages of merging with a shell without its own operations are that there are no merger issues of combining with another business and valuations of shells tend to be low. As a result, control is ensured for the parent, which may end up owning 80 or 90 percent of the combined public company. In most cases, a subsidiary going public through this process will attract even less investor interest than other mergers. For these reasons, a merger with a shell is generally not recommended, unless executed properly, as detailed in the Micro General example later in this chapter.

SUMMARY

This chapter has examined the role of mergers as an SER option to create shareholder value. As with any SER option, mergers must be planned and executed carefully to ensure that key objectives are met. Unfortunately, this challenge is compounded by the fact that mergers come with inherent risks in the form of selecting the best merger partners—which are often hard to find—and coming to agreement about the true value of the subsidiary.

EXAMPLES OF SUCCESSFUL SER MERGERS
Example 1, Philips NV/FEI Company: A Successful Minority Merger

In February 1997, Koninklijke Philips Electronics NV ("Philips"), the international electronics company headquartered in the Netherlands, merged its wholly owned European-based operation, Philips Electron Optics, with FEI Company, an Oregon-based public company traded on the Nasdaq in a stock transaction worth approximately $100 million. The FEI businesses had 1997 revenues of approximately $78 million and the Philips operation had revenues of $90 million for a combined $168 million. In this transaction, Philips Electronics International NV acquired 9.7 million shares of newly issued stock from FEI, representing a 55 percent ownership of FEI in exchange for the assets of Philips Electron Optics. Existing FEI shareholders retained the remaining 45 percent of the outstanding shares of the company. The combined company retained its Nasdaq listing with a market capitalization of approximately $200 million. Its stock price was $10.50 at the time the merger was announced, a bit above its 1995 IPO price of $9 per share. The stock reached $12.50 at the time of the merger.

FEI made workstations used to design, manufacture, and test integrated circuits. Philips Electron Optics produced electron microscopes and was a supplier to FEI before the transaction.

After that transaction, FEI became a majority-owned subsidiary of Philips. FEI entered into agreements with Philips that defined the operational arrangements between the companies. The FEI board of directors mandated a policy that any transaction or arrangement with Philips be on terms no less favorable than could be obtained in independent negotiations with outside third parties and had to be approved by a majority of disinterested directors. The arrangements with Philips included access to Philips's patent cross-license agreements, technology portfolio, and research laboratories; Philips's name and trademark; a $75 million line of credit provided by Philips; and a range of worldwide services through Philips and its affiliates.

The combination agreement gave Philips the right to purchase additional shares in FEI after the close of the transaction to keep Philips's ownership percentage in the combined entity at 55 percent. Philips increased its share ownership to 14.2 million shares by the beginning of 2001, maintaining slightly under 50 percent ownership of FEI.

In August 1999, FEI bought its leading competitor, Micrion Corporation of Peabody, Massachusetts, for $63 million in cash and stock. Revenues in 2000 were $320 million. In April 2001, FEI sold in a public offering 9.2 million shares of stock at $30.50 per share. Philips sold 6.1 million of these shares for $186 million. The share price of FEI at the end of 2001 was $33.75, valuing the remaining original shares Philips received in the merger at $121 million at a total of $308 million. In 2002, FEI merged for stock with another equipment company, Veeco Instruments. Veeco's offer valued FEI at $1.0 billion.

Philips achieved significant value for its shareholders by assembling a world-class single company from three underscale competitors and by taking advantage of the U.S. public markets to finance the combined company and to sell some of its own position at a premium price.[1]

Example 2, Lockheed Martin's CalComp Subsidiary/ Summagraphics: An Unsuccessful Majority Merger

In 1996, Lockheed Martin Corporation merged its private subsidiary, CalComp, into a Nasdaq-listed public company, Summagraphics Corporation. CalComp, based in California, produced high-end computer peripherals such as plotters, printers, digitizers, and scanners for complex business applications. It was a leader in the sector. Summagraphics, based in Texas, manufactured digitizing tablets, cutters, and large-format color printers that were complementary with CalComp's products in some cases and competitive in others.

In an all-stock transaction, Summagraphics issued (following a shareholder vote) approximately 40.7 million shares to Lockheed Martin in a tax-free exchange for all outstanding common shares of CalComp. Upon closing in July 1996, Lockheed Martin owned approximately 90 percent of the combined entity, whose name was changed to CalComp Technology, Inc. Summagraphics shareholders held the remaining 10 percent of the shares. The combined entity remained a Nasdaq-listed public company.

Summagraphics merged with CalComp to gain financing going forward. It was running out of money and had no reasonable prospects for raising cash to fund its operations or for a sale for cash of the entire company at any reasonable price. The most likely alternative to the merger was bankruptcy. Prior to the transaction, Summagraphics had been posting continuing operating losses and was in violation of some of its debt covenants. By joining forces with CalComp, a much larger company that produced many of the same products and complementary products, Summagraphics was able to ease these liquidity problems as well as increase its product offerings and distribution channels. The transaction also enabled the two companies to discontinue some of their unprofitable operations and close duplicative manufacturing facilities.

Given the bleak alternatives available to Summagraphics, the merger represented a very favorable outcome for its shareholders. The stock of Summagraphics did well for a time following the merger. However, the business of CalComp and Summagraphics received hammer blows from advances in technology that dramatically brought down the price of printers and input devices. Plus they had to contend with vigorous competition from makers of printers and input devices that could offer goods at a lower cost.

The revenues of the combined entity declined from $235 million in 1996 to $153 million in 1998 and the business had an operating loss of $49 million in 1998. The stock, which reached $6 after the merger, fell to under $1. In early 1999 the stock was delisted from Nasdaq and in late 1999 CalComp formally liquidated with no proceeds to the shareholders (primarily Lockheed).

Once the merger was completed, the parent did not make any use of the public currency it now had in CalComp to make sensible acquisitions or raise additional capital. The merger did enable the parent to take control of Summagraphics and combine the businesses without any outlay of cash to the Summagraphics shareholders.

Example 3, TRW Milliwave/Endgate: Merger with a Private Company as a Prelude to an IPO

Background on Endgate

In early 2000, Endgate Corporation, based in California, was a designer and maker of radio frequency subsystems that enabled the transmission and reception of data signals in high-data rate, or broadband, wireless systems. The products were used in high-speed cellular backhaul, point-to-point access, and point-to-multipoint access applications. The products were sold to wireless systems integrators that provided the broadband wireless equipment used by communications service providers to offer data services.

Endgate had highly regarded venture backers including Crescendo Ventures, Goldman Sachs, Company Greylock Equity Partners, Morgenthaler Partners, Oak Investment Partners, and Sigma Partners. It also had respected venture capital partners on its board of directors. It had a management team with the right resumes. It had the quality pieces in place for a high-visibility IPO; it just lacked a meaningful business. After seven years, the company still had not achieved traction in the market and had missed its projections repeatedly. Endgate faced the additional challenge of a continuing need for substantial capital to fund growing operating losses. While there was some improvement in revenues, it was not substantial. The company was incurring large losses and, while it had prospects for

E X H I B I T   15–4

Endgate Corporation Statement of Operations

(dollars in thousands)	Years ended June 30,			Nine months ended March 31,
	1997	1998	1999	2000
Revenues:				
Product revenues	$ 1,133	$ 1,560	$ 1,084	$ 2,384
Development fees	239	373	519	2,689
Total revenues	1,372	1,933	1,603	5,073
Total costs and expenses	11,970	12,375	18,254	20,787
Loss from operations	(10,598)	(10,442)	(16,651)	(15,714)
Source: Endwave S-1				

major contracts, the reality was thin. In late 1999 Endgate was running out of money and faced the need to raise yet another major financing round with little actual business improvement to support a premium valuation. As well, Endgate has missed its projections year after year.

Prior to 2000, Endgate had received over $60 million in venture capital financing beginning in 1994. Endgate was a problem for its venture capital backers: Exhibit 15–4 demonstrates the lack of revenue traction and the large losses at Endgate.

Background on TRW Milliwave

In early 2000, TRW Milliwave was a wholly owned subsidiary of TRW. It was based within TRW's Space and Electronics Group. Milliwave manufactured transceiver modules employing gallium arsenide millimeter-wave monolithic integrated circuits for broadband systems for commercial customers. It was gaining good traction in the markets. The support of the parent gave it considerable credibility with large customers already familiar with the parent. Its revenues were rising and its losses very moderate. The stock market at the time was accordingly very high values to companies similar to Milliwave. This, combined with the view that its commercial business would do better outside of TRW, led TRW to decide that Milliwave should be public. However, TRW also believed that Milliwave lacked the management team and other features needed for a quality IPO. What it did have was excellent customers and the support of the TRW parent. TRW had the choice of building a quality public company by recruiting management outside board and putting in place the other attributes for a quality IPO or finding the right merger partner to immediately enhance its ability to go public. TRW decided that a merger with Endgate would provide the needed components for a quality IPO.

Exhibit 15–5 demonstrates the burgeoning success of Miliwave.

E X H I B I T   15–5

TRW Milliwave Statement of Operations

(dollars in thousands)	Years ended December 31,		
	1997	**1998**	**1999**
Revenues:	$5,520	$7,030	$12,419
Total costs and expenses*	6,096	9,242	13,917
Loss from operations	(576)	(2,212)	(1,498)

*Excludes amortization of goodwill and deferred stock compensation.
Source: Endwave S-1

Given the limitations of each company, neither Endgate nor Milliwave on its own had the opportunity to exploit this market through a high-quality IPO. However, the IPO market would be available to the combined company, as each participant appeared to bring to the combined company the components the other needed for a quality IPO.

The Merger
In March 2000, Endgate merged with Milliwave in a stock transaction. The combined company was renamed Endwave Corporation. Concurrent with the merger, and predicated on the merger closing, Endgate raised $25 million in additional later-stage capital funding at a postmoney valuation of over $130 million ($10.12 per share). In the merger, TRW ended up owning 53 percent of the combined company and the former Endgate shareholders, including the new private later-stage investors, ended up owning 47 percent. Based on the last private financing, the combined valuation was $293.2 million, valuing TRW's ownership at $154.2 million.

Along with Milliwave's business and its manufacturing and product development facilities, the combined company obtained a valuable working relationship with TRW that included a long-term supply agreement for gallium arsenide devices and two agreements to license TRW circuit technologies and provide Endwave access to technical support and design expertise as detailed in the following list:

- *The supply agreement.* The supply agreement enabled Endwave to purchase specified quantities of particular gallium arsenide devices from TRW through March 2003. This was significant because TRW was one of the world's leaders in making these devices.

- *The license agreement.* TRW granted Endwave a royalty-free, fully paid, worldwide license to TRW intellectual property existing as of February 2000

EXHIBIT   15–6

Endwave Corporation Statement of Combined Pro Forma Operations

	Year ended December 31, 1999		
	Endgate	TRW– Milliwave	Combined
(dollars in thousands)			
Revenues:			
Product revenues	$ 1,326	$ 12,419	$13,745
Development fees	1,302		1,302
Total revenues	2,628	11,221	15,047
Total costs and expenses	20,693	13,917	33,612
Loss from operations*	(18.065)	(1,498)	(19,563)

*Excludes amortization of goodwill and deferred stock compensation.
Source: Endwave S-1

that was incorporated into specified products made by Milliwave. In addition, Endwave was granted a license to changes or improvements in this intellectual property that was developed by TRW on or before February 28, 2001. Although there were restrictions on the license, TRW granted a nonexclusive, royalty-free, perpetual, irrevocable, and worldwide license to TRW-owned intellectual property related to products incorporating TRW-produced devices.

• *The service agreement.* TRW agreed to provide Endwave with access to technical support related to the production of products incorporating TRW-produced devices, as well as access to TRW's radio frequency design and process expertise for certain other products. TRW also agreed to provide general design assistance. The agreement, which expired in March 2002, was significant because TRW's assistance was vital to the success of the combined company.

Exhibit 15–6 demonstrates the combined operations of the two companies for the year ending December 31, 1999.

The IPO
Following the merger, Endwave immediately began the IPO process. On July 12, 2000, Endwave filed a Registration Statement for an IPO. On October 16, 2000, it priced the IPO, with leading investment banks managing the offering, including Deutsche Bank Alex. Brown (lead manager) and J.P. Morgan & Co., U.S. Bancorp Piper Jaffray, and Epoch Partners (comanagers). The offering raised $84 million at $14 per share in a buoyant IPO market for wireless telecommunications suppliers. However, the public experience of Endwave was not successful. On October 24, 2000, Endwave reported record quarterly revenues for the September quarter

and issued bright prospects. The stock initially surged to $19.25, which valued the company at over $600 million. However, shortly thereafter, on December 5, 2000, Endwave issued a press release that stated it would miss its forecasts for the December 2000 quarter. The stock collapsed, dropping from $12.56 to $2.56 within a week.

The market for the products of Endwave quickly evaporated with the bursting of the wireless equipment purchasing bubble in 2001. Many customers withdrew from the industry, such as Hughes, or fell into financial distress, such as P-Com. The stock of Endwave fell to $1 by the end of 2001. The total market capitalization at that time was $36 million. The company had over $60 million in cash at the time. Revenues had fallen from $12.2 million in the September quarter of 2000 to $6.4 million in the September quarter of 2001.

Lessons to Be Learned

Endwave had some of the pieces in place to become a successful public company. It had first-tier venture backers, a strategic relationship with TRW, and a fine board of directors. However, Endwave missed its forecasts the very first quarter following its IPO. The public markets are unforgiving of such disappointments, especially right after an IPO. It is very difficult to recover from a stumble this early out of the gate. Part of the reason Endwave missed its forecasts was that the market for wireless telecommunications devices underwent a breathtaking decline between 1999 and 2001, as the end customer service providers were unable to obtain financing and also found their business models wanting. Many of these service providers went under. Missing a forecast has little impact on a private company with a tolerant board of directors and continued access to equity capital; however, the effect of missing projections on a public company is considerable, especially before its credibility is established in the market with investors.

The bigger problem was that Endwave was not a good choice of merger partner. As in any large company, there were multiple agendas at TRW. The manager at TRW responsible for directly supervising the SER was determined on Endwave and no other. The rest of the team believed that the prospect of associating with the prestigious venture investors in Endwave might have been seductive.

Example 4, Sabre/Preview Travel: A Merger with a Public Company Structured to Maintain Tax Benefits

In March 2000 SABRE Group Holdings, Inc. merged its wholly owned Travelocity Division, an Internet-based seller of airline, hotel, and cruise reservations, with a public competitor company, Preview Travel, Inc. The combined company was renamed Travelocity.com, Inc. The merger and its structure served several purposes:

- It created the leading Internet-based seller of travel services. For several years, Travelocity and Microsoft's Expedia had been fighting for leadership in the online travel arena. The merger gave Travelocity a clear advantage.

- The merger provided Sabre with a means of turning Travelocity into a publicly traded entity. It gave Travelocity access to the public equity markets. At the time, online ticket seller Priceline.com Inc. had a multi-billion-dollar public market. Sabre was looking to capitalize on the values investors accorded to Internet businesses.

- It clarified for Sabre investors the financial performance of the parent by separating out the operations of Travelocity. The management of Sabre believed that losses at the subsidiary had been adversely affecting the valuation of Sabre.

Sabre contracted to manage the operations of the merged company and also was given a contract for the merged company to use the Sabre reservations system. As a result, Sabre recognized considerable revenue from the combined operation.

The Wall Street Journal wrote at the time: "[T]he move not only gives Travelocity access to capital markets, but also clarifies its financial performance to analysts. Travelocity, which has yet to make a profit, has been a drag on Sabre earnings, and the company has wrestled with the question of how much to invest in functions such as marketing for Travelocity."[2]

The structure was interesting. Sabre contributed its Travelocity Division and gave $50 million in cash to a new partnership, Travelocity.com LP, a Delaware limited partnership. Publicly traded Preview Travel then merged into a subsidiary of Sabre, Travelocity.com Inc. Preview Travel stockholders received Travelocity.com Inc. common stock in the merger. Travelocity.com Inc. then contributed the Preview Travel business to the new partnership, Travelocity.com LP, in exchange for a minority interest in the partnership, with the remainder held directly by Sabre. The public Travelocity.com Inc.'s sole asset was its interest in Travelocity.com LP. The partnership became the owner and operator of the combined assets and liabilities of the former Travelocity division of Sabre and Preview Travel. Sabre acquired a 70 percent economic interest in Travelocity.com, Inc.

This structure had the following effect:

- It enabled Sabre to offset its share of Travelocity.com LP's losses against its taxable income without owning 80 percent or using a tracking stock. However, Sabre did not retain the ability to undertake a later tax-free spin-off of its interest in Travelocity.com, as it did not control 80 percent or more in Travelocity.com LP; a partnership is not eligible for a tax-free spin-off under IRC Section 355.

- Unlike many dot-coms, the stock of Travelocity.com performed reasonably well following the merger. While the stock price did decline from a peak of $46.75 per share in March of 2000, it ended 2001 at $28.71. In 2000 the company had operating losses of $113 million on revenues of $196 million and in 2001 it had operating losses $92 million on revenues of $301 million. However, excluding amortization of goodwill resulting from the merger, the operation was profitable by the end of 2001. Exhibits 15–7 and 15–8 provide a graphical representation of the Travelocity.com transaction.

EXHIBIT   15–7

Travelocity/Preview Travel Merger: Premerger

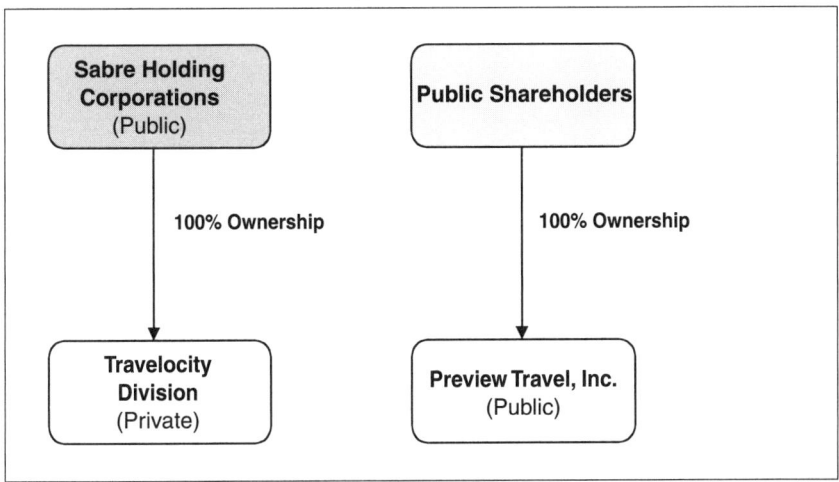

Travelocity became one of the most successful consumer Internet sites. By March 2002, it was the number two travel site, close behind the number one, Microsoft's Expedia. As a side note, Expedia was also an SER. Microsoft developed the site internally and then entered in a private equity partnership with Technology Crossover Ventures to bring in venture capital investors' business-building skills to foster the success of a business unrelated to Microsoft's primary activities.

In April 2002, Sabre paid $420 million to acquire in a cash tender offer the 30 percent of Travelocity it did not own. Interestingly, Sabre used a tender offer rather than the more traditional merger for this going private transaction. Tenders are increasingly being used by parents to reacquire public minority ownership positions. In a conventional merger, a parent and special committee for the subsidiary negotiate a price for the acquisition of the minority interest from the public shareholders, opine on its fairness to shareholders, and enter into a merger agreement. However, if the special committee does not agree with the proposed share price, the parent has few options other than to increase the price or withdraw the offer. A tender allowed Sabre to bypass the Travelocity board. Two recent Delaware cases have increased interest in tenders as they bar the public minority shareholders of a Delaware company from suing to block a tender on fairness reasons unless the parent company engaged in fraud or other illegal activity.

However, post-Enron, the boards of directors of public subsidiaries controlled by a parent are asserting the right to review the parent's offer regardless of its form and the Delaware court's views that the board of the subsidiary is not required to opine on the fairness of the parent's offer to the minority shareholders.

E X H I B I T 15–8

Travelocity/Preview Travel Merger: Postmerger

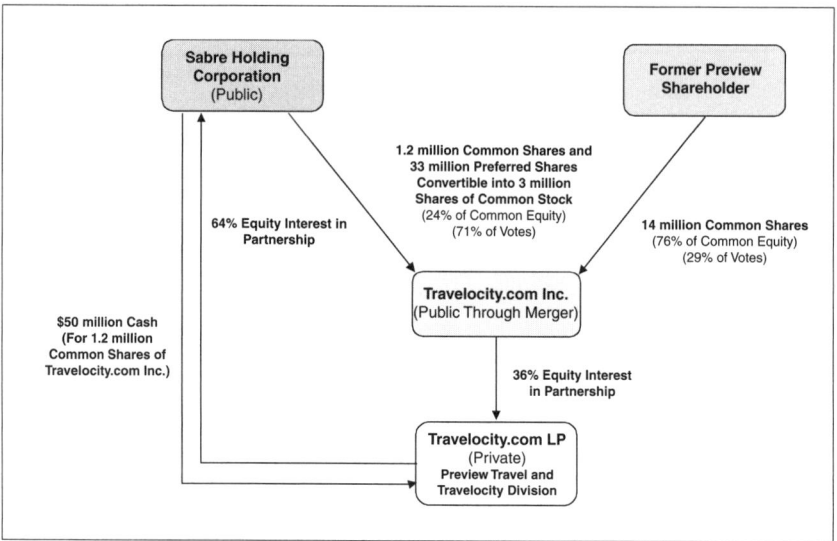

The initial offer from Sabre was $345 million. The board of Travelocity did not remain neutral on the Sabre offer. It treated the tender as it would a merger proposal, set up an independent committee of the board to assess the offer, determined it was inadequate, and recommended that shareholders reject the Sabre offer. One month later the committee recommended acceptance of a new Sabre offer that was raised to $420 million.

Example 5, National Medical/Fresenius: A Defensive Merger with a Public Company

In 1994 W.R. Grace & Co. proposed spinning off its National Medical Care Inc. division to shareholders after rejecting a $3.5 billion offer to buy National Medical by National Medical's chairman, who had earlier sold National Medical to Grace. The spin-off included a $1.4 billion special dividend to the parent, which would come from debt incurred by the subsidiary without liability to the parent. National Medical was the largest dialysis treatment business in the United States.

However, the spin-off was delayed by an investigation by the U.S. Department of Health and Human Services over federal payments received for treatment of older patients on Medicare. The actual liability that would arise from this investigation was not clear.

In February 1996 Baxter International Inc. made an unsolicited offer to purchase National Medical. Baxter was a leader in producing products used in kidney dialysis. Baxter's offer limited its potential liability for any claims from the federal investigation to $100 Million.

Three days later, Grace agreed to combine National Medical with the worldwide dialysis business of Germany's Fresenius AG. Fresenius merged its Fresenius USA, Inc., public subsidiary into the combined company. Fresenius USA traded on the American Stock Exchange. Grace's shareholders received 44.8 percent of the new company, called Fresenius Medical Care. Fresenius and the U.S. public shareholders received 55.2 percent. Grace's shareholders also received a preferred stock with a nominal value of $200 million linked to the value of the new company. No cash was involved. All liabilities were assumed by the new entity. While the transaction was tax free under rules at the time, this was a pre-IRC Section 355(e) transaction. Today it would have to be constructed so that the Grace shareholders owned more than 50 percent of the combined company[3]—not a difficult change.

Example 6, Fidelity National/Micro General: A Merger with a Public Shell

In 1997 Fidelity National Financial, a title insurance company, merged a subsidiary that developed title insurance software into Micro General Corp. in exchange for 74 percent ownership of the combined company. The subsidiary was valued in the transaction at a nominal $6.9 million. Years earlier Fidelity National had made a small cash venture investment of $860,000 in Micro General. Micro General was a small public company that had unsuccessfully attempted to develop a new postage meter. When this development did not succeed, Micro General wound up these operations and became a public shell.

The software business proved a considerable success and Micro General's stock went from $1.84 per share at the end of in 1997 to $14.15 per share at the end of 2001, creating considerable value for the parent and for the outside public shareholders. In 2002, Fidelity National arranged for the merger of Micro General with another majority-owned public subsidiary, Fidelity National Information Services, Inc., that sold real estate–related data. The merger valued Micro General at $17.50 per share or a total value of $310 million, up from approximately $10 million at the end of 1997. The parent, Fidelity National, held 72 percent of the combined entity after the merger. The objective of the merger was to integrate the two real estate information subsidiaries.

In 2002, Fidelity National arranged for the stock acquisition of Micro General by another majority-owned public subsidiary that sold real estate–related data. The merger valued Micro General at $16.65 per share. The parent, Fidelity National, held 72 percent of the combined entity after the merger. The objective of the merger was to integrate the two real estate information subsidiaries. This is a good example of a successful merger of a subsidiary with a shell company that created considerable value for the parent's shareholders.[4]

Exhibit 15–9 shows a summary timetable for a merger with a public company.

E X H I B I T   15–9

Summary Timetable for a Merger with a Public Company

Timing	12–9 months prior to closing	9–6 months prior to closing	6 months prior to closing	6–4 months prior to closing	4–2 months prior to closing	2–1 month prior to closing*	1 month prior to closing	Closing
Responsible party†	Define objectives and issues	Preparation	Solicitation of public partners	Evaluate public partners	Negotiation	Draft proxy	Solicit shareholder vote	Close
Parent†	Define the parent's and subsidiary's objectives: • Maximum value • Commercial factors • Outside funding availability • Quick closure • Minimum hassle • No continuing role for the parent following the merger • Control of the combined company by the parent following the merger Prioritize these objectives. Engage professionals. Come to a preliminary conclusion on which objectives for the merger are obtainable. Review with advisors the best structure for the merger for the parent: • A sale of assets? • A stock merger? • A stock merger with a step-up in basis? Define any postmerger interactions between the parent and the combined company and review with advisors.	Review with advisors the structure of initial proposals for potential merger partners. Review with advisors any likely "show-stopper" issues that would delay or prevent a merger or a merger on acceptable terms. Discuss premerger actions that would make the subsidiary a more attractive merger partner. Decide to proceed with a merger process. Implement measures to mitigate any tax and accounting impact of the merger. Take steps to eliminate or mitigate these "show-stopper" issues. As appropriate and practical, implement premerger actions to make the subsidiary a more attractive merger partner. Review with advisors the structure of any postmerger operating agreements between the parent and the future combined company. Host an organization meeting of the key internal players and outside advisors to kick off the process and discuss: • Objectives • Issues • Likely success • Timetable • Responsibilities • Next steps	Review general criteria and priorities for qualifying potential merger partners: • Business logic • Needed complementary capabilities • Probability of it accepting satisfactory governance conditions • Financial capability • Valuation • Likelihood of closing Review list of potential merger partners. Define any requirements to be included in the definitive agreement and specify any mandatory requirements and any "nice to have" requirements. Ensure that complete and accurate due diligence materials are prepared by the subsidiary: • Financial data • Product data • Strategic data Review the draft confidentiality agreement for potential merger partners. Prepare any postmerger operating protocols between the parent and the combined company. Contact assigned potential merger partners. Meet with potential partners and exchange presentations.	Conduct diligence investigations into the potential partner. Invite the selected merger partners to participate in detailed mutual due diligence. Review the results of the due diligence process. Reflect on what is learned in due diligence. Work with the subsidiary and advisors to address as far as possible issues raised in the diligence process by potential partners. Discuss (as appropriate) with potential partners: • Outstanding issues • Relative values • Board of director composition • Management roles • Postmerger operating protocols for the parent with the combined company Review draft merger agreement. Develop with the subsidiary a communication plan for press, subsidiary and parent employees, and customers and suppliers (include the partner in these discussions for shareholders and communicating to its employees as events evolve).	Discuss with advisors the status of the negotiations with potential partners. Review the recommendations of advisors on: • The partner(s) for the final round of negotiations • Reasonable terms with the selected potential partner(s) Determine partner for final negotiations. Negotiate (together with advisors) the final merger agreement with the selected partner. Submit proposal to the board of directors (if appropriate) of the parent to approve the terms of the merger agreement. Sign merger agreement. Implement with the subsidiary and the partner the communication plan for press, subsidiary and parent employees, partner employees and shareholders, and customers and suppliers and divide responsibilities between the parties. Review press release with subsidiary and the partner. Decide whether to hold a joint press conference. Issue joint press release with the partner on the merger.	Review with the merger partner and subsidiary the proxy filing with SEC (and, as negotiated, the S-4 registration statement).	Make any requested presentations to public investors of the partner. Review closing documents.	Final board of directors approval (if required). Issue joint press release on the closing of the merger. Make closing audit or other adjustments (if required in the merger agreement). Fulfill closing condition requirements. Sign postmerger operating and other protocols with the combined company.

Financial advisor to the parent or the subsidiary

- Review the subsidiary's forecasts and business plan and test the assumptions.
- Make requested presentations on the alternatives for equity redeployment to the management and (as requested) the board of directors of the parent.
- Review the business and financials of the subsidiary.
- Advise on the feasibility of the proposed merger.
- Give a preliminary view on expected:
  - Certainty of closing
  - Feasibility
  - Values
  - Timing
- Specify what are the needed enhancements to increase the:
  - Probability of a successful merger
  - Number and type of potential partners
  - Valuation
  - Probability of meeting the parent's and the subsidiary's objectives
- Offer objective advice.

- Learn the business of the subsidiary.
- Review and comment on the parent's priorities in context of the practicality of meeting each of the objectives and the trade-offs between objectives.
- Advise on the suitability of the subsidiary to merge with a public company.
- Advise on necessary enhancements to make the subsidiary a more attractive merger.
- Advise on any "show-stopper" issues that will:
  - Deter a merger
  - Greatly affect valuation
  - Result in substantial delay
- Discuss the impact of these issues and recommend how these issues might be immediately addressed.
- Prepare a preliminary valuation range looking at:
  - How does the subsidiary compare to its peer group?
  - What are comparable public companies trading at?
  - What do cash flows indicate?
  - What special factors will increase or decrease value?
  - What is the supply of and demand for similar operations?

- Work with the parent and the subsidiary and other advisors to clean up outstanding major issues that might impair a merger.
- Advise the parent on separation issues for the subsidiary.
- Update the valuation.
- Work with the parent and the subsidiary on putting in place enhancements that will increase the probability of a satisfactory merger or the valuation of the subsidiary.
- Make presentations on positioning and on valuation.
- Identify potential public and (as appropriate) private merger partners.
- Qualify potential merger partners based on the parent's criteria and present list to the parent and the subsidiary.
- Determine the best means of approaching each potential merger partner.
- For each potential partner, recommend who should be assigned to contact the potential partner:
  - Parent?
  - Subsidiary?
  - Financial advisor?
  - Others?
- Set up the master list and keep records of all parties with potential merger partners.
- Contact assigned potential merger partners.

- Screen potential merger partners:
  - Nature of interest
  - Business logic
  - Fit
  - Management capabilities
  - Financial capability
  - Likelihood of the merger receiving partner shareholder approval and closing
  - Realism of the partner's valuation expectations relative to actual performance and likely prospects
  - How the combined company would be received in the public markets
- Compile written summary of visits and diligence conclusions for the parent and subsidiary consisting of:
  - Comparative analysis
  - Supporting analysis
- Ascertain preliminary interest of potential partners.
- Make recommendations on next steps.
- Review draft merger agreement.
- Review pro forma combined financial statements for the subsidiary and merger partner.
- Assist in negotiations with potential merger partners.

- Discuss status of interest by potential partners.
- Make recommendations on next steps with each potential partner.
- Assist in negotiating with selected potential partner(s).
- Assess next steps to conclude the merger agreement with leading partners.
- Review:
  - Key parameters of proposals
  - Conditions, if any, to proposal
  - Requirements to conclude merger agreement
  - Expected value
  - People
  - Time to close
  - Requirements to eliminate contingencies
  - Certainty of closing
- Assist the parent and subsidiary to understand each element of the proposals.
- Assist in determining the partner for final negotiations.
- Assist in final negotiations.

- Assist in drafting proxy.
- Review closing documents.

- If the partner is public, work with legal counsel to:
  - Assist the partner and its advisors to secure shareholder approval including helping organize shareholder information meetings
  - Assist the subsidiary and parent in preparing any requested presentations to the partner seeking approval for the merger
- Assist the parent in preparing any advisable communications to the parent's shareholders, for informational purposes, on the merits of the merger.

Continued

285

Continued

Subsidiary	Prepare credible forecasts and a business plan on a stand-alone basis.	Prepare management presentation to potential merger partners. Set up due diligence files. Contact assigned potential partners. Meet with potential partners and exchange presentations. Assist in preparing assessments of each potential partner for business fit. Assist in organizing diligence on potential partners.	Hold management presentations and meetings with potential partners. Host site visits by potential partners to the subsidiary. Respond to additional due diligence requests. Assist in preparing pro formia combined financial statements. Assist in site visits to the potential partners. Assist in due diligence investigations of potential partners. Address as far as possible issues raised in the due diligence process by potential partners. Assist in developing and implement the communication plan.	Assist in determining the partner for final negotiations. Assist in final negotiations. Hold meetings with employees and customers (as appropriate, include partner).	Assist in drafting proxy. With the guidance of legal counsel, make any requested presentations to public investors of the partner.	Fulfill preclosing conditions. Make any requested presentations to public investors of the partner. Review closing documents. Assist in closing audit (if required in the merger agreement).	Fulfill closing condition requirements. Sign closing documents. Issue joint press release on the merger closing.
Legal counsel to the parent and/or the subsidiary	Advise on the alternative structures for separating the subsidiary and effecting a merger. Advise on any "show-stopper" legal issues and propose a resolution to these "show-stopper" issues.	Set up the subsidiary's legal structure, if not now separate. Clean up outstanding legal issues such as documentation of contracts, employment agreements, intellectual property, etc. Review any potential antitrust and other regulatory issues that might delay a merger.	Assist in setting up of due diligence files. Prepare draft merger agreement. Prepare draft postmerger operating protocols between the parent and the combined company. Advise the management of the parent and the subsidiary of disclosure and insider trading rules. Highlight any potential antitrust and regulatory issues with specific merger partners.	Take the primary responsibility for negotiating the merger agreement. Respond to additional legal due diligence requests. Review communications plan and prepare draft press releases. Assist in negotiations with potential merger partners. Assist in preparing and negotiating postmerger operating protocols between the parent and the future combined company. Prepare defense measures review of the future combined company and recommend any actions. Provide an in-depth appraisal of antitrust and other regulatory issues with the specific partner.	Draft final documents. With the merger partner, review antitrust and other issues with regulatory authorities. With the merger partner, prepare filing packages for regulatory approvals: • Federal industry regulators • Federal antitrust regulators (e.g., Hart-Scott-Rodino) • Securities regulators • State regulators • State industry regulators • SEC and stock exchange filing Draft and coordinate with the partner the final press releases.	Assist the partner in drafting the proxy. Review any presentations by the parent or the subsidiary to public investors of the partner.	Follow up on regulatory approvals. Assist in response to SEC comments on the proxy. Prepare closing documents.

Subsidiary's accounting firm	Assist with preparing pro forma stand-alone financial statements for the subsidiary. Assist in preparing an assessment of the accounting and tax effect on the parent and on the subsidiary of a merger under various scenarios. Discuss any likely SEC issues with the subsidiary's financial statements.	Ensure all required audited financial statements are available for later public filings. Review financial controls and recommend changes for a public operation. Point out tax and accounting potholes and recommend alternatives to mitigate their impact.	Assist with any premerger restructuring of the balance sheet and capital structure. Prepare and review audited financial statements.	Review the accounting practices and statements of the proposed merger partner. Highlight accounting issues. Highlight potential issues with the combined company. Respond to additional accounting due diligence requests from potential merger partners. Assist in preparing pro forma combined financial statements for the subsidiary and merger partner.	Prepare financial statements for inclusion in the merger agreement.	Prepare financial statements for inclusion in the proxy filed with the SEC. Assist in response to SEC comments on the financial statements in the proxy.	Conduct closing audit (if required in the merger agreement).	Present closing audit.
Merger partner and its legal counsel and financial advisor	Determine interest in the proposal. Determine views on relative values. Meet with subsidiary and parent and exchange presentations. Prepare for site visits by subsidiary and parent.	Respond to additional due diligence requests. Respond to proposed operating and other protocols between the parent and the future combined company. Reach agreement on relative values and management roles. Respond to draft definitive merger agreement.	Communication with employees and customers. Review draft fairness opinion (if appropriate). Board of directors of the public company approve terms of the merger. Prepare filing packages for regulatory approvals. Issue joint press release on the merger. Issue press release on the filing of the proxy.	Draft proxy. File proxy with SEC for shareholder vote. Respond to SEC comments.	Mail proxy to shareholders. Organize shareholder information meetings to inform shareholders on the merger. Fulfill preclosing conditions. Solicit shareholder vote. Conduct closing audit (if required in the merger agreement). Prepare closing documents.	Hold shareholder vote. Sign closing documents. Issue joint press release on the merger. Receive final fairness opinion (if requested). Make closing audit or other adjustments (if required in the merger agreement). Fulfill closing condition requirements.		
SEC			If requested, hold discussions with the partner, the subsidiary, the parent, the accountants for the subsidiary and the partner, and legal counsel regarding likely problems.	Review proxy statement. Issue comment letter. Review responses to comment letter. Resolve comments.		Declare proxy effective.		

*This assumes that the merger partner will need a shareholder vote. State law, charter provisions, and the requirements of any stock exchange on which the partner is listed will govern this. The time for shareholder approval of a private company is the statutory notification period. There would be no additional period of 1 to 2 months for SEC review of the proxy filings (and S-4 if used) and responses to comments before the proxy is mailed to shareholders. This substantially reduces the time needed to close a merger with a private company over a merger with a public company.

†The distinct roles of the financial advisors and legal counsel to the parent as against such advisors to the subsidiary vary case by case. In some equity redeployments the parent and its advisors are in complete charge, in others the responsibilities are split with the subsidiary, and in others the subsidiary takes the main role and keeps the parent appraised of its actions. Similarly, the roles of the parent as against the subsidiary in the choice of merger partner and the control of the process will vary on a case-by-case basis. Generally, the parent takes an active role at least in the initial stages of the process including the selection of the merger partner. For this reason the roles divided between the parent and the subsidiary and their respective legal counsel and financial advisors are different with each transaction.

287

CHAPTER 16

EXIT ALTERNATIVES: USING SER TRANSACTIONS TO CREATE CASH FOR THE PARENT[1]

INTRODUCTION

At some point following an SER, the parent will almost always want cash for its ownership interest in the subsidiary. This may be shortly after the SER or many years later. *Cash,* as used in this discussion, refers to cash and to securities readily turned into cash such as highly liquid stock of a large buyer.

This chapter sets out the exit alternatives for the parent to obtain cash for its ownership interest in the subsidiary following an SER. Exit alternatives are also known as liquidity alternatives. The advantages and disadvantages of each of the exit alternatives are discussed in this chapter.[1]

COMMON EXIT ALTERNATIVES

Before we examine some of the more common exit alternatives, it is important to mention that parents should prepare for eventual exit alternatives at the start of the SER process. It is also important for parents to understand that undertaking an exit strategy after an SER can be complex, as the parent can no longer make unilateral decisions. Instead, numerous parties are involved, including outside shareholders in the subsidiary, strategic partners, and the subsidiary's management team and board of directors.

Most SERs are only intermediate steps for the parent to an eventual sale or distribution of the parent's ownership position in the subsidiary. The exceptions are a majority carve-out of all the shares owned by the parent, a spin-off of all the shares owned by the parent, or the issue of an exchangeable security for all the shares owned by the parent. After these SERs, the parent no longer holds a significant position in the subsidiary. With almost all the other SERs, the parent continues to hold shares in the subsidiary after the SER. Of course, often the exit is another SER that disposes of the parent's remaining shares, most typically a spin-off.

Some exit alternatives are available to a private as well as an already public subsidiary. Others are available only if the subsidiary is already public.

Depending on the attributes of the subsidiary and market conditions at any given time, none, or only a few, of these exit alternatives may actually be available in practice or at least on acceptable terms. For example, public market liquidity alternatives and most sales to nonstrategic buyers such as LBO funds and follow-on public offerings are available to the parent only when the subsidiary has a capable and committed management team in place and is performing well. If the subsidiary has a weak management team or is underperforming, the parent is more likely to be successful with a sale as an exit strategy. Therefore, exit alternatives and terms vary greatly. Differences include the following:

- The timing and certainty of receiving cash

- The certainty that the transaction will actually close

- The impact of liquidity alternatives on tax planning

- The impact of the liquidity alternative on subsidiary and its management and employees

  Following are explanations of the more common exit alternatives.

ALTERNATIVES AVAILABLE TO A PARENT WITH A PUBLIC OR PRIVATE SUBSIDIARY
Sale of the Subsidiary for Cash or for a Very Liquid Public Stock

A sale of the entire subsidiary for cash or for the stock of a large public company that has a readily traded liquid stock is among the most common exit strategies by a parent. It is the exit alternative most often used for getting cash for a large holding in the subsidiary. A sale is available to the parent with a public or a private subsidiary. The reasons for its popularity include that such a sale:

- Is the only alternative that may be available when there is not a strong senior management team or the subsidiary is underperforming.

- Is the most available liquidity alternative in a wide range of circumstances.

- May offer the only liquidity alternative in cases where the subsidiary is not attractive to public or private investors.

- Offers the best means of obtaining complete or substantial liquidity in the short term.

- Usually provides the highest current value, as a control premium is obtained from the buyer. A control premium is the additional price that a buyer will pay for control of the subsidiary. With a public company it is usually a premium to the public price for the stock at the time of the offer.

- Is often the best exit alternative for a parent when a subsidiary faces strategic or business issues that are best solved by a combination with a strategic buyer that has greater resources.

- Is often the best strategic exit alternative for a parent if the subsidiary has management issues but a strong business.

- Is the preferred liquidity alternative when a private subsidiary may have access to the IPO market, but the parent or subsidiary prefers not to deal with the demands and uncertainties of being a public company.

- Is often the best strategic exit alternative if the parent wants immediate and full cash for all its shares.

- May be the only available exit alternative for a subsidiary that is underperforming and/or does not have business characteristics such as type of industry, size, growth rates, and margins that are demanded at any given time for an IPO.

Buyback of the Parent's Stock by the Subsidiary

A buyback offers the potential for immediate substantial liquidity for the parent by selling its shares back to the subsidiary for cash. A buyback may be accomplished by the subsidiary using its own cash resources, obtaining bank debt, or bringing in another investor. A buyback may be the only exit alternative for the parent if it is a minority owner in a private subsidiary and the other shareholders do not want the subsidiary to go public or be sold.

Buybacks have these challenges:

- The valuation paid for by the shares purchased from the parent is almost always less than that obtained through a sale of the subsidiary.

- If the subsidiary is private, it is usually difficult to reach agreement on the valuation unless it is clearly spelled out in the investment agreements.

- Only cash-positive businesses are likely to be suitable for a buyback that involves substantial payments to the parent.

- Many subsidiaries do not have access to the cash for a buyback.

- For a larger subsidiary with a long-established business and excess cash flow that enables it to safely pay out its current working capital resources or support extensive debt, a buyback may be a good way to provide cash to the parent.

EXIT ALTERNATIVES AVAILABLE ONLY WITH AN ALREADY PUBLIC SUBSIDIARY
Open Market Sales of Stock by the Parent

With a strong public market in the subsidiary's stock, the parent may achieve considerable liquidity by selling, over a period of time, a reasonable number of shares relative to the float in the open market. Open market sales may occur following the expirations of the lockup period imposed by the lead manager of the IPO (discussed later in the book) and if the parent has held the shares at least one year. These sales will also be subject to any restrictions under SEC Rule 144 on the amount that may be sold in any one quarter.

The advantages of selling shares in the open market include the following:

- The timing and amount of sales are controlled by the parent.
- The acceptable price is set by the parent and no sales need take place below that price.
- The expenses are limited to brokerage commissions.

The disadvantages of selling shares in the open market include the following:

- The market may not be able to absorb a meaningful quantity of stock in a short period except at a severe discount. Most smaller-capitalization stocks have a relatively illiquid market for sales of stock in any large size. In many cases, attempting to sell a large block of stock in a short period of time for smaller-capitalization stock will force the price down severely, if it can be done at all. It is not uncommon for an illiquid stock to drop 50 percent in price when a parent sells a large number of shares in the open market.
- The sale in the open market of a substantial block may need to be staged over a considerable period of time to meet the requirements of SEC Rule 144, as discussed in Chapter 6.
- Unlike a follow-on offering marketed through investment banks with a road show, there is no mechanism with open market sales to create new demand for the stock of the subsidiary. Open market sales may be accomplished through normal brokerage sales or through a block trade in which an investment bank's trading desk buys a large block at a small discount to the market price and then places it with one or a number of investors.

For a detailed look at parent open market sales, see the case study of TRW in Chapter 13.

Follow-on Public Stock Offering by the Parent

An efficient method for a parent to sell a large block of stock following an IPO is through an underwritten public follow-on offering of stock. For a more detailed look at a follow-on offering, see the Du Pont Photomask case in Chapter 7.

The use of a follow-on offering by the parent to sell a large stock position in the subsidiary may have considerable benefits for the parent, including the following:

- A follow-on offering usually impacts the subsidiary's stock price (i.e., the best average price) the least when a significant amount of stock relative to the float of the subsidiary is being sold.

- A follow-on offering usually is the best means to quickly move a significant block of stock. A follow-on offering may be the only means to move a significant amount of an illiquid stock in a reasonable period of time.

- A follow-on offering is organized by the lead manager, removing the responsibility of the sales process from the parent.

The disadvantages of using a follow-on offering include the following:

- A follow on offering requires that there be a market for the shares being sold by the parent. This in turn generally requires that the subsidiary be performing well and have a vibrant stock.

- A follow-on offering involves considerable expenses that may have to be borne by the parent. There will also be an underwriting discount. The parent may prefer not to pay these expenses.

- The lead manager of the follow-on offering generally will require that the parent enter into another lockup agreement on any remaining shares. The parent may not wish to incur this limitation on its flexibility to sell its remaining shares at a time of its own choosing.

- The lead manager of the follow-on offering will usually require an indemnity for any liability under the securities laws concerning the registration statement. The subsidiary is often not willing to give such an indemnity for shares sold by parent, as it does not receive the proceeds from the sale of those shares. And the parent may be unwilling to incur liability for the contents of a registration statement over which it has no knowledge.

- A follow-on offering is likely to be priced at some discount to the public market price for the subsidiary's stock at the time of the offering.

- With a traditional follow-on offering, the time involved in the process of preparing registration and road show materials and then conducting the road show exposes the parent to considerable market risk on the price actually obtained for its shares. While the time for a follow-on may be considerably shorter than for an IPO, there is still time risk.

- If the subsidiary is listed on the Nasdaq, under SEC rules, any market makers who are lead-managing or comanaging the public offering or are in the underwriting syndicate will have to withdraw from market making right before the pricing of the public offering. This may include all the firms supporting the stock of the subsidiary. Because of this rule, there always seems to be a last-minute drop in the subsidiary's stock price at the most critical time—the pricing of the offering.

- The parent may be a statutory underwriter exposed to securities law liability for three years following the offering.

Obtaining the Cooperation of the Subsidiary
One of the major hurdles with a follow-on offering is that the cooperation of the subsidiary is required. This is not always forthcoming, especially if the parent is

no longer in a control position. It is very difficult to execute a follow-on public offering without the cooperation of the subsidiary in marketing the offering. However, often the subsidiary will not view a follow-on public offering as beneficial for it and will not cooperate enthusiastically—or at all. From the subsidiary's viewpoint, especially if it is not raising any cash itself in the offering, a follow-on offering has many negatives. A follow-on offering imposes costs and burdens on the subsidiary by:

- Requiring a major time commitment by the management of the subsidiary in preparing the registration materials and road show presentation and in marketing the offering to investors.

- Involving considerable legal, filing, printing, and possibly accounting expenses in connection with preparing and filing a registration statement, printing prospectuses, and traveling on a road show. The parent is not always required to reimburse these expenses.

- Creating a temporarily depressive effect on the subsidiary's stock price as the market brings the price down to accommodate the offering.

- Requiring that the subsidiary be in a quiet period, which limits its communications under the SEC regulations regarding registered offerings.

Because a follow-on offering requires the cooperation of the subsidiary, it is worth discussing why the subsidiary might support a follow-on offering rather than having the parent sell stock in the open market. A follow-on offering benefits the subsidiary by:

- Giving the subsidiary an opportunity on the road show to visit its existing shareholders and acquaint them with its progress. It also allows the subsidiary an opportunity to get in front of new investors and diversify its shareholder base. If the subsidiary has stumbled in the past and needs to rebuild its shareholder base, a follow-on offering is a very good means to reintroduce the subsidiary to the investor community.

- Marketing the subsidiary's stock to investors around the forum of an offering focuses the attention of the investment bank's sales forces and of investors. An offering provides a catalyst with a definite time frame for a salesperson at an investment bank to make a call to an institution and for that institution to take an action step of investing.

- Encouraging a new institution to consider investing in a subsidiary with an illiquid market for its shares by allowing an investor to buy a large number of shares without disrupting the market.

- Creating another large payday for investment banks. This may be used by the subsidiary to reward the investment banks that have supported the subsidiary up to that date with research coverage and to provide an incentive for new research analysts to take up coverage and increase the research base.

- Increasing quickly the public float in the subsidiary's stock, which improves liquidity in the stock and increases institutional interest.

- Reducing the continuing depressing effect on the stock price of the subsidiary from a large overhang of stock that might come on the market from the parent.

- Putting less pressure on the subsidiary's stock price than sales in the open market.

- Enabling the subsidiary to also raise additional capital in the follow-on offering.

- Ensuring the parent does not put the subsidiary in play for a takeover by offering its block of stock to a single buyer with hostile intentions.

- Ensuring that the parent does not transfer a large position to a single investor that might be proactive in interfering in the subsidiary's affairs.

Executing a Follow-on Offering
With an IPO there is a fairly standard execution formula: a lead manager and several comanagers, a syndicate, a substantial road show, and then the IPO is priced. However, follow-on offerings provide various alternatives to the traditional IPO process because there is already a public market.

Following is a list of some of the ways that a follow-on offering can be executed:

- *A traditional offering with a full road show.* In this method, the subsidiary approaches the follow-on offering in a similar fashion to an IPO. A registration statement and prospectus are drafted. A one- or two-week road show is conducted to generate demand. A number of firms are chosen as managers of the offering to cement and increase research support. A syndicate may also be employed. This is the best approach in a difficult market or where the subsidiary needs to retell its story to investors.

- *A traditional offering with no road show.* With this approach, the offering is sold by the lead manager without a marketing program or with only a very limited road show to a few cities. This reduces wear and tear on management. Such an offering may be done in one week or less. A well-known and followed subsidiary with an established investor base may place a follow-on offering quickly and without a marketing effort, relying simply on a small discount to the then market price to generate demand.

- *A "bought deal" offering.* In very robust markets, investment banks will take the risk on these offerings. A bought deal is one where the investment bank first purchases the shares for its own account before lining up investors. Having purchased the offering, the investment bank then markets the offering to investors.

A Private Investment in Public Equity (PIPE) Offering

A first cousin to a follow-on public offering is a private placement of stock by the parent with institutional investors in a private investment in public equity (PIPE) offering. PIPEs are not public offerings and there is no filing with the SEC until the offer closes. As a result, PIPEs are usually done without publicity until they close. With a PIPE, a placement agent generally places the stock of the subsidiary with institutional investors without going through a public offering or the open market. To facilitate a PIPE offering, the subsidiary will need to commit to registering the shares sold by the parent following the PIPE offering. PIPEs are generally sold at a small discount to the then market price. The parent may also place a PIPE without an agent when it knows the potential investors or has been approached by investors looking to buy stock in the subsidiary. PIPEs may be done for smaller size than a public offering and need less cooperation from the subsidiary, as they may be placed with one or a few investors who are often already knowledgeable about the subsidiary.

SUMMARY

This chapter details the most common exit alternatives used by parent companies to obtain cash after an SER transaction. Obtaining cash, also known as exit strategies, can be accomplished immediately after the transaction or years later. In most cases the determining factor is the performance of the market at a given point in time, and timing the transaction to take maximum advantage of market conditions. Chapter 17 contains a study of an SER transaction by ESS. This case will show how one company successfully worked through a myriad of SER-related issues to truly create value for shareholders.

PUTTING IT ALL TOGETHER: CASE STUDY OF ESS

INTRODUCTION

This chapter examines the 2001 spin-off of Vialta, Inc., from ESS Technologies. We will study this transaction for two reasons. First, ESS management did an excellent job of identifying and exploiting an SER opportunity to create shareholder value. Second, this transaction illustrates many of the SER concepts presented in earlier chapters, including how to:

- Determine which SER transaction is most appropriate.
- Create the SER transaction that has the greatest chance of receiving Wall Street support.
- Structure an SER transaction to meet multiple objectives.
- Comply with IRS requirements.
- Comply with SEC rules and regulations.
- Treat pre-spin-off stock options.
- Issue new stock options.
- Prepare to trade the subsidiary's stock before and after the transaction.

This case study will walk readers through each step of a lengthy and complicated SER process.

Before studying the reasons for the spin-off effort, along with its deployment, it is important to understand the interplay among the product line of ESS, its changing competitive position, its challenges in dealing with Wall Street, and its goals and objectives for the spin-off.

THE INTERPLAY

In March 2001, the senior management team at ESS considered various ways to get the stock market to recognize the underlying values in ESS. At the time, ESS was a leading maker of semiconductor devices for use in the rapidly growing digital consumer home electronics industry. The senior management team included Dr. Fred Chan, founder and chairman; Bob Blair, president and chief executive officer; and Jim Boyd, chief financial officer. At the time, the company's stock was trading near a two-year low at $6.50 and was valued at a severe discount on revenue and earnings multiples compared to ESS's main comparable public competitor, C-Cube Microsystems. In addition, ESS received no value in the stock market for its investment in its well-capitalized and promising majority-owned subsidiary, Vialta, a development stage company focused on producing an advanced DVD player/digital home entertainment system and the first usable home videophone.

At the time, ESS had a market capitalization under $275 million and cash on its balance sheet in excess of $50 million. Vialta had cash of over $90 million. ESS was enjoying accelerating revenues and increasing market share in its major product lines, but a stubbornly low valuation, as previously mentioned.

As of March 31, 2001, the undervaluation of ESS compared to its most comparable public pure-play semiconductor competitor, C-Cube Microsystems, was substantial, as illustrated by Exhibit 17–1. This shows that ESS had significantly lower multiples of its stock market value to earnings and revenues than did its competitor on a historic basis and in forecasts for 2001.

The senior managers of ESS believed that they understood the reason for this undervaluation, namely, Vialta. Where the ESS team saw opportunity in Vialta to build an exciting new business, investors and analysts saw complication, risk, and distraction. And ESS's undervaluation had adverse strategic consequences for ESS: it restricted the company's ability to make acquisitions for stock, raise capital in the public equity markets, attract much-needed engineering talent, and reward current employees through valuable equity incentives. Because the undervaluation caused significant problems for ESS, we will examine the cases in the following paragraphs.

Lack of Investor Interest in ESS

Compared to its most immediate public competitor, C-Cube Microsystems, ESS was not receiving the same attention from Wall Street. This was a significant deterrent to investors for several reasons.

Research Analysts Are an Important Resource to Many Investors

Investors rely (to varying degrees) on investment bank research analysts to keep them apprised of interesting stock investments, develop models for the future of those companies, and communicate news about the companies they follow to

EXHIBIT 17–1

C-Cube and ESS Valuation Comparison

Comparable Valuation at March 30, 2001									
		Stock price	Market value	Stock price as a multiple of calendar earnings			Enterprise value/revenue*		
Company	Ticker symbol on Nasdaq	Closing price on 3/30/01	(Mil.)	LTM[†]	2000	2001E[‡]	LTM[†]	2000	2001E[‡]
C-Cube Microsystems	CUBE	$12.31	$554.5	23.3x	22.8x	25.1x	2.2x	2.1x	2.0x
ESS Technology	ESST	$5.56	$176.3	6.9x	8.7x	16.4x	0.7x	0.6x	0.7x

*Enterprise value is the stock market value at March 30, 2000, plus any debt and minus all cash. This adjustment helps compensate for differing capital structures and cash positions.

[†]Latest 12 months ending March 31, 2001.

[‡]Earning and revenue estimates for 2001.

Source: Bloomberg and Multex as of March 31, 2001

investors. C-Cube had research coverage from powerhouse large investment banks. In contrast, the only investment bank providing research coverage of ESS was a midsize retail firm. While a fine firm, it did not have the same clout with investors. The result of the lack of research coverage of ESS was less investor familiarity and comfort with ESS.

Without research coverage and market making support from major firms, there was a less liquid market in ESS's stock, which precluded investors from easily buying and selling holdings. It did not help ESS that the lead manager of ESS's 1995 IPO and the comanagers had all effectively dropped research coverage due to either analyst turnover or a loss of interest in ESS when it did not look like it would generate large trading or advisory revenues.

Exhibit 17–2 highlights ESS's lack of research sponsorship as of March 31, 2001.

C-Cube undoubtedly benefited from recent transactions that paid large fees to investment banks—a good way to get support at the time. It also did not hurt that C-Cube had a management team comfortable with marketing stock.

The management of ESS held discussions with investors and investment bank research analysts and came away convinced that the causes of the lack of interest in the stock of ESS by investors, particularly institutional investors, were several:

- *Unwillingness of investment bank analysts and institutional portfolio managers to learn about two separate businesses.* Institutional portfolio managers told the management of ESS that they were deterred from investing in ESS because of the confusion surrounding Vialta. Similarly, the investment bank analysts also told the management that they were not comfortable analyzing or valuing ESS as long as its semiconductor business was combined with a consumer electronics division. ESS was a pure-play semiconductor company, selling to major

E X H I B I T   17–2

Research Coverage of ESS as of March 31, 2001

C-Cube Microsystems	ESS Technology
Firm name	Firm name
Credit Suisse First Boston	A.G. Edwards
Lehman Brothers	
Robertson Stephens	
Thomas Weisel Partners	
Source: ESS management	

original equipment manufacturers (OEMs) and it possessed considerable ability to scale itself up and down with cyclical revenue flows associated with macroeconomic cycles. On the other hand, Vialta was a consumer products company with the dynamics of a vendor to the retail trade. Many investors who were knowledgeable and comfortable with the semiconductor business of ESS did not understand, and were not comfortable with, the consumer electronics focus of Vialta and had no interest in learning that business. These investors assigned little or no value to Vialta as part of ESS. In fact, many discounted ESS for the uncertainty of Vialta or simply avoided the stock altogether.

• *Concerns over the financial impact of a large cash drain on ESS.* Vialta was a research and development company that was accumulating large losses and was at a much earlier stage of its business cycle than ESS. Because Vialta's losses affected ESS's financial statements, it was difficult for investors to value the core business of ESS and to recognize the distinct growth prospects currently inherent in ESS. Moreover, the cash burn at Vialta represented a significantly different risk profile than that for ESS.

• *Concerns that ESS's management was spread too thin.* Investors and analysts also expressed concern about the amount of time management was allocating between the two companies. Because Vialta was still in its development stage, investors and analysts worried that ESS's management was devoting a large amount of time to Vialta at the expense of ESS's other operations.

The management of ESS believed that the stock price of ESS would remain depressed until ESS removed these issues and concerns for investors and their supporting investment bank research analysts.

THE PARENT: ESS TECHNOLOGY

In early 2001, ESS designed, marketed, and provided customer support for highly integrated and mixed signal semiconductors. The company operated without semiconductor manufacturing plants of its own (a "fabless" business model) and relied on third-party contract semiconductor manufacturers to test and assemble its devices. This enabled ESS to focus all its resources on what it did best—the design and marketing of innovative semiconductors. ESS had a genius for producing highly integrated chipsets that had greater functionality than those of its competitors. While not the cheapest chipsets on the market, ESS's highly integrated chipsets enabled manufacturers of electronic products to produce lower-cost products and offer more features for consumers. ESS's chipsets often replaced solutions using many components at much higher cost.

The strategy of ESS was to compete on product innovation, unique features, and high integration of many functions into one or a few chips, not on the low-cost manufacturing of commodity semiconductors. However, ESS did have a number of competitors that would soon copy any innovations from ESS. The market lead of any new ESS product (the period when margins were highest) was measured in quarters rather than years. Therefore, ESS had to continually develop new and exciting products to prosper. Fortunately, ESS was very good at conceiving and developing innovative products.

In March 2001, ESS focused on producing comprehensive chipsets for Digital Video Disc (DVD), Video Compact Disc (VCD)/Super Video Compact Disc (SVCD), MP3 player, Internet-related communications, and PC audio applications. VCD and SVCD players were primarily sold in Asia as a low-cost alternative to VCRs using CDs instead of tape (SVCD players offered higher quality in the same format). A VCD player might sell for $39 and movie discs might rent for $0.10 per use. With these products, ESS strategically positioned itself to benefit from the convergence of television, telephone, and Internet devices and had developed both the hardware and software that enabled the convergence of appliances that combined data, entertainment, and communications.

Dr. Chan, a brilliant creator of innovative semiconductor devices, founded ESS in 1984. He repeatedly identified future industry developments and repositioned ESS to be a leader in each new generation of products. For example, ESS started out designing consumer speech/sound chips used in toys, games, and other consumer products. But, in late 1992, ESS changed its focus to the much larger PC audio market. In 1993, ESS began shipping large volumes of PC audio chips. Sales of ESS's PC chips grew rapidly. ESS came to dominate this market. By the mid-1990s, Dr. Chan foresaw declining demand in the PC market for separate PC audio chips as the capabilities offered by ESS's separate chips were taken over in the PC by the rapidly increasing power of the PC's central microprocessor. As microprocessors packed in more and more power, PC makers no longer needed to buy stand-alone chipsets for these functions, except at the high-performance end of the market.

ESS then developed a range of advanced chips for VCD and SVCD players. By 2001, ESS dominated the VCD market with a 75 percent unit share and the SVCD market with a 50 percent-plus market share. However, ESS believed that the growth of this market would slow as superior-quality DVD players came down in cost.

E X H I B I T   17–3

ESS Revenues by Sector and Outlook in Early 2001

	1998	1999	2000	2001 estimated	2002 estimated
PC audio	$130,951	$149,112	$109,237	$48,997	$36,132
VCD/SVCD	87,301	161,539	148,683	132,672	128,510
DVD	—	—	45,515	89,862	161,213
Total revenues	$218,252	$310,651	$303,436	$271,531	$325,854
PC audio	60.0%	48.0%	36.0%	18.0%	11.1%
VCD	40.0%	52.0%	49.0%	48.9%	39.4%
DVD	0.0%	0.0%	15.0%	33.1%	49.5%

Source: ESS public filings with the SEC and Needham & Company research estimates for 2001 and 2002 from March 2001

Dr. Chan recognized that the next market opportunity for ESS was in the emergence of lower-cost DVD players offering superior quality and features. In the late 1990s, DVDs were a high-end product costing up to $1000. The integration of the electronics on a few chips, Dr. Chan believed, would result in a rapid and dramatic reduction in the cost of DVD players and the market for DVD players would then explode. This happened. By the end of 2001, DVD players were selling for under $100. By March 2001, ESS commanded a growing world market share in DVD chipsets (by mid-2002, ESS had a 50 percent world market share in these chips).

Looking past the stand-alone DVD player, Dr. Chan formed a view in 1998 that traditional analog-based televisions and stereos were migrating to digital-based content and technology with the advent of digital TVs, DVDs, audio CDs, MP3s, home DVD recorders, Internet access, and large-capacity disk drives to store video content taken from cable, satellite, or broadcast sources. The increasing digitalization of these functions and the increasing processing capabilities of these digital controller chips would allow the development of simple-to-use appliances that integrated and combined data, entertainment, and advanced communication technology into one easy-to-use unit. Dr. Chan believed that these would begin to supplant stand-alone DVD players starting in 2002. He wanted ESS to be the leader in this new and potentially much larger emerging market of digital home systems.

The growth in the new DVD products at ESS and the decline in the older PC-related businesses are illustrated by the following breakdown of revenues prepared in March 2001. The breakdown illustrates that while the ESS legacy PC audio and modem market was declining and the VCD/SVCD market was stagnant, ESS experienced great growth in the DVD market. In March 2001, ESS's management felt that ESS was also well placed to be a leader in chips for the next generation of integrated home consumer electronics appliances.

Exhibit 17–3 illustrates the changing revenue base of ESS.

THE SUBSIDIARY: VIALTA

In early 1999, ESS began development of a digital home system in the form of an enhanced DVD player and other consumer electronic devices including the first practical and inexpensive videophone for home use, the "Beamer". This development was an offshoot of work ESS had been performing to assist its customers in the development of consumer electronics products that used ESS chips. In order to focus efforts on the development of the new consumer electronics product lines, ESS set up Vialta in April 1999 as a potentially stand-alone operation. ESS invested $10 million in Vialta at the time of its formation, and then invested an additional $52 million in November 1999. At the time of its formation, Vialta also acquired certain technologies from ESS and entered into joint research and development agreements that permitted Vialta to complete development of its initial products. Dr. Chan decided to devote his full-time efforts to Vialta. He made Bob Blair, then the president of ESS, the CEO of that company and removed himself from the management of ESS.

Between November 1999 and March 2000, Vialta raised an additional $80.6 million from strategic and private investors including Dr. Chan. In total, Vialta raised $144.2 million. ESS owned approximately 58 percent of Vialta and the rest was owned by outside investors, the largest being United Microelectronics of Taiwan. By the spring of 2001, Vialta had developed an advanced DVD player, the ViDVD, which combined many features at a reasonable cost and was well along with the development of the videophone for introduction in the summer of 2002.

The first generation of ViDVD players used chips from ESS. Vialta was under no obligation to continue to use chips from ESS, but would do so as long as ESS had the most cost-effective and functional chipset for the ViDVD and its other products.

As Vialta developed its product, it had no revenues and sustained operating losses of $29.1 million for the year ending December 2000 and operating losses of $7.8 million for the quarter ending March 31, 2001. As of March 31, 2001, Vialta was well capitalized with cash, cash equivalents, and short-term investments of $98 million. While it expected only small revenues in the second half of 2001, Vialta forecast significant annual growth thereafter. However, Vialta estimated that it would spend over an additional $100 million for product development and working capital to support increasing revenues, marketing and promotion expenses, and general expenses. While Vialta still had a substantial amount of cash, this would not be sufficient to support its success. Vialta would need to raise additional capital to reach its potential in a very competitive marketplace.

ESS, the principal shareholder in Vialta, did not then have the cash to finance the large future capital requirements of Vialta. On March 31, 2001, ESS had a total of $58.6 million in cash to fund its own capital needs and for promising potential acquisitions of technology to enhance its own capabilities. This was the minimum cash reserve that the management of ESS believed was prudent for ESS. ESS's depressed stock price made raising additional equity in the markets for ESS an unattractive alternative.

ESS Wanted Vialta to Succeed

Although ESS did not wish to invest further in Vialta, it did want Vialta to succeed for the following reasons:

- ESS looked to Vialta to prove the market for advanced consumer electronics products using ESS's latest technology. This would open up large new markets for ESS's chips.

- ESS also looked to Vialta for a close working relationship to assist ESS in developing its next generation of multimedia chips.

- ESS, of course, had a strong financial interest in the success of Vialta and wished to obtain a return from the ESS technology contributed to Vialta and its cash investment in Vialta. Vialta's success as an independent would increase the value of ESS's equity investment in Vialta.

- ESS had a strong preference that Vialta remain independent for some time so that it would continue to provide close cooperation on new products.

HELPING VIALTA SUCCEED CONTRIBUTES TO THE SEPARATION DECISION

According to Jim Boyd, chief financial officer of ESS, the primary motives for the ESS/Vialta separation included supporting Vialta while supporting ESS at the same time, as detailed here:

- "Separate the management teams to allow both to focus on their respective businesses. This also applied to the development efforts of the two companies. It was hoped that an independent Vialta would be able to hire its own management team and operate on a more arm's-length basis with the parent. As well, ESS and Vialta would each be able to reward its employees through incentive compensation and option plans tied directly to the performance of their respective businesses. We believed that there would never be true separate management teams and true independent strategies for addressing the future development of both companies without a truly independent company in every way. ESS' R&D resources were being significantly distracted by Vialta related activities. It often happened that ESS' R&D resources were pulled away from ESS goals and focused on Vialta goals. This situation was frequent and often of indeterminate duration."

- "Allow ESS and Vialta to separately finance their businesses going forward and separate their risks. We believed that as long as the two companies were financially and legally connected there was true financial risk to ESS. There was the potential for ESS to be pulled into commercial or financial transactions with Vialta."

- "Alleviate customer concerns. The first product to be introduced by Vialta was the ViDVD player. This multi-function DVD player would compete directly with ESS' own customers in the consumer electronics business that also made DVD players."

• "Alleviate investor concerns. The investor community of research analysts and current and potential shareholders were confused and concerned by ESS' getting into a business that was foreign to its traditional chip business. They were concerned about our ability to be successful and by the amount of cash it would take to make it successful. In addition they were concerned about ESS' chip customers' reaction to ESS entering their markets as competitors. As well, the improved performance of ESS was not visible to investors because the operating results (losses) of Vialta were consolidating for accounting statements with those of ESS."

THE SPIN-OFF DECISION

After ESS determined that a separation made sense, it hired Needham & Company (Needham) as financial advisor to address the alternatives available to ESS in respect to Vialta.[1]

The alternatives considered were a sale of ESS's interest in Vialta to a third party; external strategic or additional private equity financing that would dilute ESS's ownership to less than 20 percent, as this would allow ESS to completely deconsolidate Vialta's losses from ESS's income statement and treat it as an investment; and a merger with a smaller or larger public entity. However, the option considered most seriously was a true carve-out IPO for Vialta once Vialta had revenues and income prospects.

However, Needham concluded that a carve-out IPO to raise capital for Vialta and establish a strong public market was not practical at the time because of the then dormant state of the IPO market, especially for companies without revenues. While a carve-out IPO would have been the preferred alternative, as Vialta still needed to raise capital, a public offering in the IPO market of 2001 would have to wait until Vialta had made considerable business progress in establishing consumer demand, building revenues, and showing a route to profitability. By Vialta's forecasts, these requirements would not be met for almost two years.

Needham also concluded that additional private financing of Vialta would not be advisable for the following reasons:

• It did not address the issue of investor confusion and concern generated by Vialta, reflected in the stock price of ESS.

• It would probably preclude any possibility of ESS spinning off Vialta's shares tax free because its ownership interest would continue to drop (see discussion in later sections).

• A private placement of Vialta stock was likely to be exceedingly expensive in the then hostile state of the private equity market for nonrevenue, loss-making, venture-type capital.

Needham also concluded that there was no obvious merger partner. Meanwhile, both management teams wanted to proceed with an SER separation as soon as possible.

Based on these challenges, Needham concluded that a spin-off of Vialta was the quickest and most feasible means of achieving ESS's objectives. Fortunately, for the time being, Vialta did not need funds and could wait to access the capital markets. (A significant disadvantage of spin-offs is that they do not raise additional funds, unlike carve-out IPOs.)

STRUCTURING THE SPIN-OFF

ESS wanted the spin-off structure to meet a number of goals and objectives as outlined in the following sections.

The Spin-off Should Be Tax Free to ESS and Its Shareholders

There were a number of requirements that had to be met to transact a tax-free spin-off. First, Vialta had to meet the active trade or business requirements as an expansion of ESS's historic business. Second, ESS had to transfer enough of its shares of Vialta stock to Vialta to satisfy obligations under the new Vialta option plan because any retention of shares by ESS could jeopardize the tax status of the spin-off. Third, Vialta had to undergo a recapitalization to create high/low-vote common stock to satisfy the requirement of the Internal Revenue Code that ESS possess control of Vialta immediately prior to the distribution of Vialta's stock.

In order to comply with the requirements for a tax-free spin-off, Vialta went through a recapitalization before the spin-off. The recapitalization effort involved the following steps:

1. The holders of all shares of Vialta's preferred stock converted their shares into common stock.

2. Vialta separated its outstanding capital stock into Class A common stock with 3.8 votes per share and Class B common stock with one vote per share.

3. ESS received one share of Class A common stock for each share of Vialta common stock held, and all other Vialta stockholders received 1.1 shares of the lower-voting Class B common stock for each share of Vialta common stock held. The objective of the extra 0.1 shares to Vialta shareholders was to compensate them for an increase in ESS voting power.

4. Vialta established a nonstatutory stock option plan under which it granted ESS option holders, immediately before the distribution, options for Vialta Class A common stock on terms that mirrored the terms of those option holders' existing ESS options.[2]

Following the recapitalization, ESS transferred shares of Class A common stock to Vialta to be issued upon exercise of options that were granted by Vialta to

ESS option holders (or returned to treasury stock if the options were canceled or not exercised).

Vialta Would Have Proper Governance, Management, and Agreements with ESS in Place

One of the requirements of the Internal Revenue Service was that after the distribution Vialta would continue to actively conduct its business independent from ESS and with separate employees. However, Vialta was using engineering resources, the human resources department, and leased office space from ESS. It also shared certain technology. Vialta could continue to rely on ESS for certain services and related matters as long as they were properly documented in agreements that were negotiated at arm's length. These agreements had to fairly allocate resources and properly compensate the provider in order to qualify. In order to comply with this requirement, Vialta and ESS entered into a series of separation agreements with the understanding that the two organizations would be completely separate 12 months after the distribution.

The intercompany agreements included:

- *Master Technology Ownership and License Agreement.* Allocated ownership rights generally along ESS and Vialta product lines.

- *Employee Matters Agreement.* Allocated responsibilities relating to current and former employees of Vialta and their participation in any benefits plans that ESS sponsored and maintained.

- *Tax Sharing and Indemnity Agreement.* Allocated responsibilities for tax matters between ESS and Vialta. Under the agreement, Vialta indemnified ESS in the event the distribution initially qualified for tax-free treatment and later became disqualified as a result of actions taken by Vialta.

- *Real Estate Matters Agreement.* Addressed real estate matters relating to property owned by ESS that ESS leased to Vialta, as well as other properties currently leased by Vialta.

- *Master Confidentiality Disclosure Agreement.* Provided that Vialta and ESS agree not to disclose confidential information except in specific circumstances as might be permitted in an ancillary agreement.

- *Master Transitional Services Agreement.* Governed corporate support services that ESS agreed to provide to Vialta, including information technology systems, human resources administration, customer service, buildings and facilities, and finance and accounting services.

The Spin-off Would Be Fair to ESS and to Vialta

Another objective in the preparation of the spin-off was to ensure that it would be fair to both companies and their respective shareholders.

E X H I B I T   17–4

Spin-off Time Schedule for Vialta

Dates	Event
March 1	Organizational meeting and management due diligence.
March 7–May 25	Drafting sessions with ESS and company counsel.
May 25	Form 10 information statement filed with SEC.
June 13	Filed amendment #1 to Form 10 with SEC.
June 27	Received SEC comments.
July 17	Responded to SEC comments. Filed amended Form 10. Filed ruling request letter with Internal Revenue Service.
July 30–August 3	ESS road show to sell the "new" post-SER ESS to institutional investors.
August 6	Filed posteffective amendment #1 to the Form 10 with SEC.
August 7	Limited Vialta road show to gain market support upon spin-off.
August 8	Filed posteffective amendment #2 to the Form 10 with SEC.
August 16	SEC notifies ESS's counsel that they have no further comments on the Form 10, enabling the spin-off to proceed.
August 16	When-issued trading in Vialta's shares begins. This is the trading of a security in advance of its issue. (See text discussion.)
August 21	Distribution to ESS shareholders of shares in Vialta.
	Regular trading begins in Vialta's shares

THE SPIN-OFF PROCESS BEGINS

ESS began the spin-off process by drafting the Form 10 information statement to be filed with the SEC. This process took about two months. The actual spin-off timetable is detailed in Exhibit 17–4.

Unlike a Form S-1 IPO registration statement, a Form 10 automatically becomes effective after 45 days. However, a parent is unlikely to actually commence a share distribution until the SEC has resolved any comments, since the stock will not be accepted for listing on a stock market until the SEC issues a no further comment.

DISTRIBUTION TO ESS SHAREHOLDERS

In preparation for the spin-off, Vialta created two classes of common stock: Class A common stock and Class B common stock. Vialta's common stock was divided into two classes of common stock with disparate voting rights in order to facilitate

EXHIBIT 17–5

Principal Stockholders of Vialta

Beneficial owner	Class of common stock	No. of shares prior to spin-off distribution	% of shares outstanding prior to spin-off distribution	No. of shares after spin-off distribution	% of shares outstanding after spin-off distribution
ESS Technology	Class A	60,400,100	56.7%	0	0.0%
United Microelectronics	Class B	20,900,000	19.6%	20,900,000	19.6%
Other private investors	Class B	25,200,000	23.6%	25,200,000	23.6%
	Total	106,500,100	100.0%	46,100,000	43.2%
ESS shareholders		0	0.0%	60,400,100	56.7%
Total		106,500,100	100.0%	106,500,100	100.0%

Source: Vialta's Form 10 filing with the SEC

ESS's request with the IRS for a tax-free distribution. Holders of the Class A common stock were entitled to 3.8 votes per share on all matters to be voted upon by the stockholders. Holders of Class B common stock were entitled to one vote per share on all matters to be voted upon by the stockholders. ESS's shareholders received only shares of Class A common stock in the distribution. All Vialta shareholders before the distribution, other than ESS, continued to hold Class B common stock after the distribution.

Exhibit 17–5 sets forth the principal stockholders of Vialta's common stock as of June 30, 2001, and is adjusted to reflect the distribution of common stock as described.

NEW VIALTA MANAGEMENT TEAM

In keeping with separating the two businesses, Vialta needed a complete management team of its own. The first priority for Vialta after deciding on the spin-off was finding a CEO who could build the rest of the management team and the internal infrastructure. Didier Pietri joined Vialta as CEO in April 2001. Prior to joining Vialta, Pietri had served as president and chief executive officer of TVA/Motion International, a global entertainment production and distribution company, and was a senior vice president of the ABC Television Network Group, as well as president of ABC Pictures, a division of The Walt Disney Company. This was an excellent background for running Vialta's business going forward and completely different from the semiconductor and software engineering backgrounds of the management of ESS. Pietri was granted options for 1 million shares (1 percent of the outstanding stock).

Vialta also recruited its own board with members able to assist it in its business. There was no other overlap of directors between ESS and Vialta other than Dr. Chan, who served as chairman of the board for both Vialta and ESS.

CHALLENGES WITH THE VIALTA SPIN-OFF

There were many challenges with the Vialta spin-off, and patience and creative thinking was required to get past them. Note the following examples.

Unknown Tax Consequences at the Time of the Distribution

The U.S. federal income tax treatment of the receipt of Vialta Class A common stock was not certain at the time of the distribution. It depended on whether the distribution qualified as tax free under the Internal Revenue Code. ESS applied for a private letter ruling from the IRS on the spin-off's tax-free status. However, this normally takes six months or more months (in the case of ESS it took nine months). If the distribution was deemed taxable, ESS believed that the tax liability could greatly increase during the period before receiving a letter as the business prospered. Consequently, ESS distributed its shares in Vialta before receiving a letter ruling from the IRS.

Because ESS did not know if the distribution would be tax free, the company was forced to collect information from its shareholders to properly fill out IRS Form W-9 for issue to ESS's domestic shareholders and Forms W-8 BEN or W-8 IMY for issue to international shareholders. If shareholders did not provide the appropriate tax information to the transfer agent, shares would be withheld by the transfer agent and sold on the open market in the first three days of trading to satisfy the tax withholding requirements of the IRS for taxable distributions.

While there was certainly a risk in distributing shares before receiving a ruling from the IRS, ESS determined that the benefits to its shareholders of not delaying the spin-off for an extended period outweighed any potential tax liability to ESS and its shareholders.

Automatic Recapitalization If ESS Did Not Receive a Favorable Ruling from the IRS

Vialta's common stock was divided into two classes to comply with the IRS requirement that ESS distribute control of Vialta in the spin-off. However, only the Class A shares were registered with the SEC, leaving the holders of the Class B shares in a less liquid position by comparison. In order to respond to the demands of the Class B holders, Vialta agreed that each share of Class A common stock and each share of Class B common stock would automatically be converted into one share of nonclassified Vialta common stock when the first of these events took place:

• A ruling by the IRS that the distribution was a taxable event

• The abandonment by ESS of its request for a ruling from the IRS that the distribution was a nontaxable event

- ESS not receiving a ruling from the IRS by June 30, 2002, that the distribution was a nontaxable event

    After such conversion, the holder of each share of Vialta common stock would be entitled to one vote per share.

Nasdaq OTC Bulletin Board Trading Status for the Vialta Shares

ESS and Needham did not believe that Vialta would qualify for listing on the Nasdaq National Market or another national exchange. Vialta met all the tests for listing on the Nasdaq National Market except one: that the minimum bid price be above $5 per share. Reaching this price point was unlikely based on a valuation of Vialta prepared by Needham. Vialta might have transacted a reverse stock split to reduce the number of shares outstanding and thereby raise the likely trading price above $5. However, Vialta decided not to do this, given particular issues in its case relating to its overseas private investors. Therefore Vialta was listed on the Nasdaq's secondary market, the OTC Bulletin Board. Needham filed an SEC Form 211 on behalf of Vialta for its stock to be listed on the OTC Bulletin Board, and also allowing Needham to be a market maker in the stock. The Nasdaq OTC Bulletin Board is a quotation service that displays quotes, last sale prices, and volume information regarding over-the-counter (OTC) equity securities. An OTC equity security is generally not listed or traded on the Nasdaq or a national securities exchange. The OTC Bulletin Board is only a quotation medium and not an issuer listing service. Market makers for Nasdaq OTC Bulletin Board securities are usually required only to match up willing buyers and sellers. Generally, market makers are not required to purchase securities directly from willing sellers or sell securities directly to willing buyers. While inferior to the national markets, the Bulletin Board was the best alternative available at the time. When Vialta had succeeded as a business, and its stock price reflected that success, it could later apply to have its stock listed on a national exchange.

Vialta's Form 10 was declared effective by the SEC on August 16, 2001, enabling Vialta to trade when issued until the distribution date of August 20, 2001. Vialta's stock began trading on the OTC Board when issued on August 16, 2001, under the ticker symbol VLTAV. According to the OTC Bulletin Board there is no specific rule promulgated by either the OTC Bulletin Board or the NASD that addresses when-issued trading. Such trading is normally allowed on the record date for the distribution, but that is premised on the availability of a Form 10 that includes a pricing range listed on the cover and a valuation established by the investment banks, either in the Form 10 itself or in a valuation opinion issued by an investment bank. In this case, Vialta had neither, and so Nasdaq did not allow trading until the SEC specifically approved the registration statement (normally a Form 10 registration becomes effective 30 days after filing). With Vialta, when-issued trading was not allowed by the OTC Bulletin Board on the record date for the distribution to the parent's shareholders but on the effective date of the Form 10 Information Statement filed with the SEC. On the distribution date of August 20, 2001, Vialta's stock began trading the regular way under the ticker symbol VLTA.

Determining the Amount by Which ESS Traded Ex-Dividend

In order to determine the value by which ESS would trade ex-dividend, defined as the value of ESS excluding the value of Vialta, it was necessary to know the value of Vialta. Nasdaq normally required a when-issued price quote on the spun-off stock to determine the amount by which ESS's stock price would be reduced when it traded ex-dividend, although Nasdaq was willing to use a third-party valuation of Vialta if (1) ESS established when-issued trading but no trades actually occurred or (2) ESS told Nasdaq it didn't want to trade when issued.

Regardless of the valuation methodology, ESS could not begin trading ex-dividend until the first business day after the distribution date. In this case, there were no meaningful Vialta when-issued trades before the distribution, in order to determine the value of Vialta. While there were several market makers willing to trade Vialta when issued, it was extremely difficult to execute a trade.

Almost all brokerage firms refused to accept buy or sell orders for Vialta's stock on a when-issued basis prior to the distribution. The reasons for this were that executing these trades would have been time consuming and the sizes small. As a result, any seller or buyer needed an account at the market maker's firm to transact a trade. Few had such accounts.

As a result of the lack of when-issued trading in Vialta, Nasdaq was forced to rely on ESS's valuation opinion of Vialta in order to determine the opening price of ESS on the day the stock began trading ex-dividend.

Determining the Cost Basis for ESS Shareholders

Shareholders needed to know the value of Vialta near the spin-off date regardless of whether the transaction was tax free. If taxable, the value of Vialta determined the amount of the dividend received by ESS shareholders. If tax free, the shareholders' basis would be allocated between the ESS shares and Vialta shares.[3] While there are specific IRS rules on the cost basis allocation of a tax-free spin-off, this is not the case with a taxable spin-off, where the criterion is fair market value. ESS and Needham did not believe that the initial when-issued trading price was a meaningful indicator of the market value of the Vialta shares, as almost no shares traded during that period. ESS and Needham believed that the weighted average of Vialta's volume and average opening and closing price on the first day of active trading following the distribution was a reasonable guide to valuation of the shares where the distribution was held to be taxable. However, shareholders of ESS were advised to consult their own tax advisors to determine the most appropriate allocation methodology in the event of a taxable spin-off.

Determining the Potential Tax Liability for ESS

The same valuation issue also concerned ESS's potential corporate tax liability if the spin-off was held by the IRS to be taxable.

On the first day of trading in Vialta following the distribution, it was clear that, as expected, the market price of Vialta was below ESS's tax basis in its Vialta stock holdings of approximately $1.10 per share and thus no corporate tax consequence would arise whether the distribution was deemed taxable or tax free. From the parent's point of view, an unfavorable tax determination by the IRS on the tax status of the spin-off would actually have been favorable to the company due to the fact that it would alleviate any potential lawsuits that could arise if control of Vialta or ESS changed hands due to a sale by either company that would then cause a tax-free distribution to become taxable retroactively at a later date. However, it still would have penalized the ESS shareholders. Additional tax-related issues and challenges are detailed in the following text.

TAX ISSUES SURROUNDING THE SPIN-OFF

The Vialta spin-off presented some unusual tax issues for ESS and its shareholders. Because these issues are complex, they are worth examining in more depth.

Section 355 of the Internal Revenue Code deals with the requirements a corporation needs to satisfy in order for a spin-off/distribution to be tax free to the corporation and its shareholders. It is generally standard practice for a corporation to request a private letter ruling from the Internal Revenue Service before the distribution of shares from a spin-off to its shareholders. It is a relatively time-consuming endeavor for the corporation to obtain such a ruling, which typically spans six months from the time of submission to the IRS. By doing so, assurance is obtained that the distribution will be treated as a tax-free distribution. If the IRS is not prepared to give a letter ruling, it still may convey to the parent that it will not take action to challenge the tax-free status of the spin-off.

However, for the reasons just stated, ESS distributed its shares of Vialta to shareholders on August 21, 2001, before receiving a tax ruling from the Internal Revenue Service. ESS anticipated receiving the ruling from the IRS sometime in December 2001. When it applied for the tax-free ruling, ESS believed that it had satisfied the following issues necessary for ESS to qualify for a tax-free distribution to its shareholders.

ESS strategically accelerated the spin-off/distribution date of Vialta in anticipation of the initial shipping date for Vialta's product. It felt that the best interests of both companies were better served by a quick Vialta separation. The risk associated with separating the two companies before receiving an IRS ruling was perceived to be worthwhile even if ESS's shareholders had to pay a reasonable amount of taxes on the distribution. As well, if ESS waited for a tax ruling from the IRS prior to the distribution of Vialta and did not receive a favorable ruling for any reason, it was possible that favorable developments at Vialta in the intervening period would increase the value of Vialta to a point where the potential tax liability with a taxable distribution would have been much more significant for the parent and the shareholders.

Moreover, if the distribution was determined to be a taxable transaction, the tax liability for ESS might have increased greatly due to an increased value of Vialta at the time of the IRS ruling. Were the tax liability large enough, ESS might have then determined that it was not feasible any longer to distribute the stock in a taxable spin-off and the separation might have been set back several years until an attractive alternative such as an IPO was available. Therefore, the delay incurred in waiting for an IRS ruling might have delayed the separation plan several years. Thus a quick distribution was worth the risk. ESS declared Vialta a discontinued operation on April 25, 2001, and simultaneously filed a ruling request letter with the IRS.

ESS and its advisors believed that ESS had a strong case for a determination by the IRS that the spin-off was tax-free. However, there were several issues on which the IRS would need to be satisfied. These are summarized in the following sections.

Did Vialta meet the active trade or business requirement as an expansion of ESS's historic business even though Vialta was recently incorporated, its customers would not be the same as ESS's historic customers, and its products would be complete electronic systems rather than electronic components?

Treasury Regulation $\S 1.355\text{-}3(b)(3)(ii)$ provides that if a corporation engaged in the active conduct of one trade or business during the five-year period preceding the distribution "purchased, created, or otherwise acquired another trade or business in the same line of business, then the acquisition of that other business is ordinarily treated as an expansion of the original business, all of which is treated as having been actively conducted during that five-year period, unless that purchase, creation, or other acquisition effects a change of such a character as to constitute the acquisition of a new or different business." Numerous Internal Revenue Service private letter rulings supported the belief that Vialta would meet the active business requirement of section 355(b) after the proposed spin-off. Vialta was an expansion of an existing five-year historic business. Vialta's business was based upon technology that ESS acquired more than five years earlier and was directly related to the product development work undertaken by ESS to assist its customers. As a result, ESS believed that Vialta's business was an expansion of a historic business of ESS and satisfied the five-year active trade or business requirement of IRS Section 355(b) by reason of regulation Section 355-3(b)(3)(ii).

Did the recapitalization of Vialta with two classes of stock before the distribution ensure that the control requirement was satisfied?

In Revenue Ruling 86-25, a recapitalization transaction was found to be a reorganization within the meaning of Section 368(a)(1)(E) where the transaction had a valid business purpose, was an isolated transaction, and was not part of a plan to increase periodically the proportionate interest of any shareholder in the assets or earnings and profits of the corporation. To relate this back to Vialta:

- At the date of the distribution of Vialta shares, there was no plan or intention to alter the capital structure of Vialta resulting from the recapitalization by which ESS acquired control of Vialta as defined in Section 368(c).

- The purpose for the recapitalization was to permit the tax-free distribution of the Vialta shares.

- The recapitalization transaction was an isolated occurrence that would not result in an increase in the proportional interest of any shareholder.

- Further, the recapitalization was not a step in a series of transactions, the goal of which was to distribute the earnings and profits of ESS. Quite the contrary, the recapitalization was necessitated by that fact that other investors provided a significant portion of Vialta's invested capital. ESS provided only a portion of Vialta's capital requirement.

Therefore, ESS believed that the IRS would conclude that the recapitalization allowed ESS to satisfy the control requirements of Section 355(a)(1)(D)(ii) by reference to Section 368(c).

DISPOSITION OF THE TAX ISSUES

The IRS declined to issue a letter ruling on the tax-free status of the Vialta spin-off. However, ESS ensured that it complied with all the requirements of a tax-free spin-off, such as maintaining the high-/low-vote stock, and the IRS took no action.

ESS also changed the automatic conversion feature on the two classes of stock in Vialta's articles from one where the A and B classes converted to a new class of single vote common if a favorable letter ruling was not received from the IRS by June 30, 2002, to one where the A and B converted only if the distribution was treated as a taxable distribution by the IRS.

TELLING THE ESS STORY TO INVESTORS

Now that we have explored the spin-off in depth, we need to examine whether it met a key objective, namely, mitigating investor concerns. In the past, investor concern had resulted in the undervaluation of ESS stock.

Immediately following the spin-off of Vialta, ESS's senior management team went on a road show to visit institutional investors to tell them how ESS was attacking the high-growth digital home consumer electronics market and had spun off Vialta. ESS met with some 70 institutions in 11 cities. The "new" ESS was extremely well received by institutional investors. During the road show, investors recognized the growth opportunities inherent in ESS. As a result of the spin-off, ESS's stock increased substantially and continued to perform well for a time in a difficult market, as illustrated in Exhibit 17–6.

The stock appreciation of ESS following the Vialta spin-off illustrates how companies such as ESS (after the spin-off of Vialta) engaged in a single business

E X H I B I T   17–6

ESS Technology Stock Price Chart

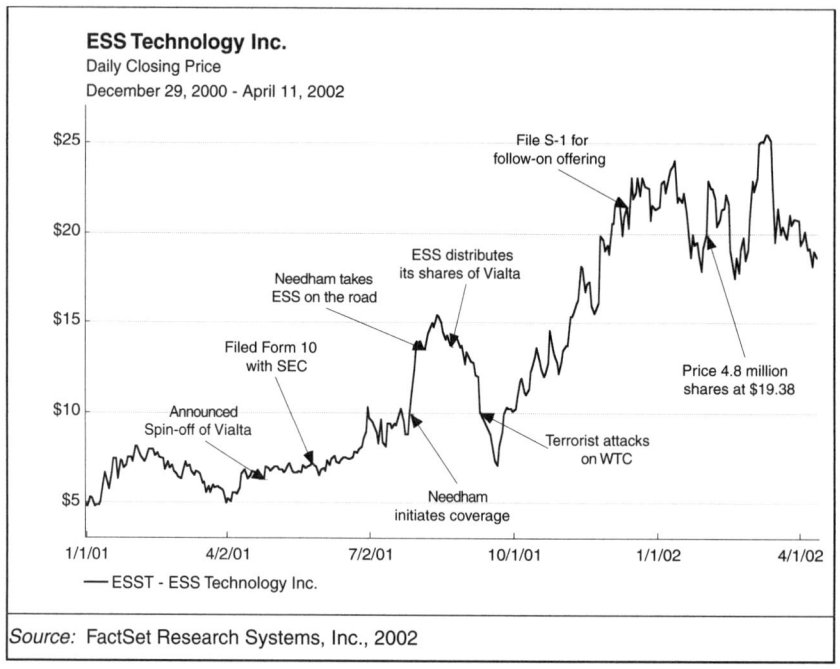

ESS Technology Inc.
Daily Closing Price
December 29, 2000 - April 11, 2002

File S-1 for
follow-on offering

ESS distributes
its shares of Vialta

Needham takes
ESS on the road

Filed Form 10
with SEC

Price 4.8 million
shares at $19.38

Announced
Spin-off of Vialta

Terrorist attacks
on WTC

Needham
initiates coverage

— ESST - ESS Technology Inc.

Source: FactSet Research Systems, Inc., 2002

with high growth and performance characteristics are rewarded by investors. This is in contrast to companies involved in several unrelated businesses and where the growth potential is partially masked, as demonstrated by ESS before the spin-off of Vialta.

Exhibit 17–6 tracks the progress of ESS's stock before and after the spin-off.

ESS'S FOLLOW-ON PUBLIC OFFERING

Given the successful spin-off of Vialta and positive investor response to ESS's nondeal road show, ESS decided on a share follow-on stock offering for ESS. ESS believed the offering would enable the company to achieve several important objectives:

• Substantially increase institutional ownership

• Reduce the Chan family's ownership holding from approximately 35 percent to 17 percent and thereby alleviate investor concerns over stock overhang, given that Dr. Chan was no longer the CEO of ESS as he had been earlier

• Build a support base for the stock

EXHIBIT 17–7

Vialta Stock Price Chart

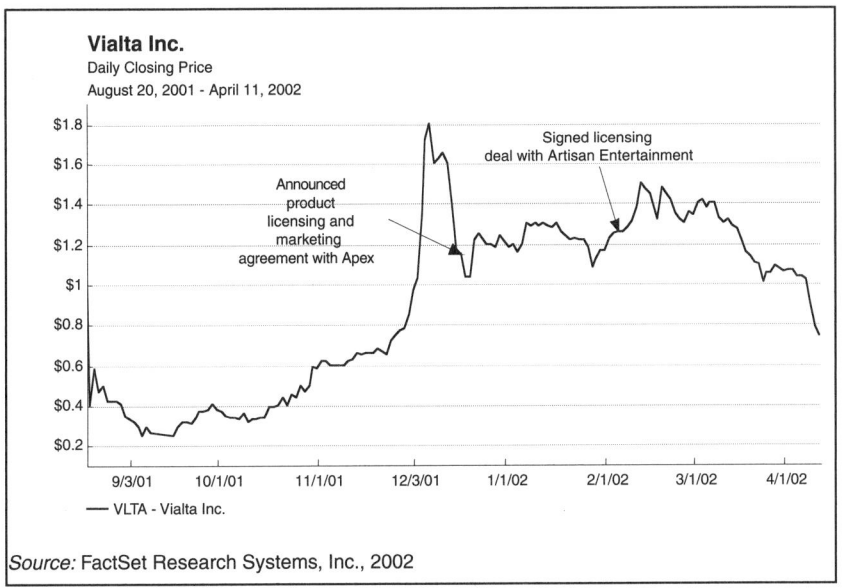

Source: FactSet Research Systems, Inc., 2002

• Provide a war chest of capital to pursue acquisitions of complementary and advanced technologies

In December 2001 ESS filed an SEC Form S-3 registration statement for a follow-on offering of 4 million shares. ESS met with some 76 institutions in 28 cities in the United States and Europe over two weeks. The offering was well received by investors and the size of the offering was increased from 4 million to 4.8 million shares. Including the Green Shoe (see Chapter 23), ESS sold 5.52 million shares at an offering price of $19.38 with gross proceeds of $107 million in February 2002.

TELLING THE VIALTA STORY TO INVESTORS

Before the distribution of ESS's stock in the spin-off, Vialta also went on a road show to generate market support for its stock. Vialta met with value-oriented investors appropriate for the company and its long-term business vision.

Vialta's stock did not fare as well in the market following the spin-off. Exhibit 17–7 displays the price and volume of Vialta, beginning with its inception as a publicly traded entity. Investors declined to take any interest in unproven companies in 2001. At the time of the spin-off, Vialta had no revenues, had substantial ongoing losses, and presented considerable risk to investors.

In the year following the spin-off, Vialta did have some positive announcements:

• In December 2001, Vialta announced a product licensing and marketing agreement with Apex Digital, the leading U.S. manufacturer of DVD players, to market Vialta's products through Apex's extensive U.S. retail distribution channel.

• In the summer of 2002, the Beamer home videophone was launched to favorable reviews.

REFLECTIONS ON THE PROCESS BY ESS'S MANAGEMENT

The following thoughts from Jim Boyd are helpful for readers contemplating an SER transaction.

Key Decisions That Supported the Success of the Spin-Off

• "Declaring Vialta a discontinued operation early on separated its finances and committed both companies to the spin-off."

• "Proceeding with effecting a distribution simultaneously with submitting the revenue-ruling request. Had this not been done ESS would have lost a year in the distribution effort with great cost to both companies."

• "Recognizing the need for continual management and coordination of the various constituents, i.e. the lawyers, accountants, government entities, and business managers of: Vialta, ESS, the financial advisor, Nasdaq, State of California and Delaware, various government entities including SEC and IRS."

Suggestions for the CEO of a Parent Contemplating a Spin-Off

• "Get someone else to champion it within the organization. A spin-off will take a senior person 100 percent of his or her time for an extended period."

• "Do the spin-off in as little time as possible because it is hugely disruptive to both the parent and the subsidiary."

• "Get input from every department in both organizations."

Suggestions for a Division Manager Who Is Going to Run a Spin-Off

"The spun-off subsidiary is going to operate totally on its own and it therefore needs to develop its own independent culture, infrastructure, and strategy. It needs all the traditional functions of a truly public company including accounting, legal, investor relations, budget discipline, strategic plan, and strong managers of all necessary departments including operations, marketing, sales, finance, HR, and last but not least a president and CEO."

Additional Thoughts

"The management teams and R&D departments are now truly separate. This has been tremendously beneficial for both companies. As well, ESS's strategy has solidified and clarified tremendously since the distribution, as ESS's management is no longer distracted by trying to also run and develop a large-scale start-up company in another sector."

SUMMARY

This chapter examined how ESS used SER transactions to successfully create shareholder value and meet other key objectives including simplifying its business. In addition, the chapter explained how the company was able to meet these objectives while also balancing the various requirements for a successful transaction, including meeting IRS requirements, following SEC rules and regulations, and communicating the story to investors. Chapter 18 will look at laying the groundwork for a successful IPO, because understanding how to properly execute an IPO can affect current or future SER transactions.

SECTION **III**

A SUCCESSFUL PUBLIC SER

LAYING THE GROUNDWORK FOR A SUCCESSFUL IPO OR SPIN-OFF AND PUBLIC COMPANY

INTRODUCTION

The previous chapters explained and demonstrated that enabling a subsidiary to become a public company through a spin-off, IPO, or merger can create value for parent company shareholders. It was also explained that one of the goals of many SER transactions is to create a company that is strong enough to be a successful public company at the time of the SER or at a future date. Therefore, many SER transactions involve a transition from a private entity to a public entity.

As mentioned, the primary means to transition a company from a private entity to a public entity are mergers, spin-offs, or IPOs. The next section of the book will focus on how to successfully plan, structure, and execute an IPO or spin-off. The reason for this focus on the IPO and spin-off process is that, although there are many books available on IPOs, the environment has recently dramatically changed for the public stock markets, IPOs, and Wall Street.

We will begin our study by examining the key validation criteria that are used by investors to evaluate IPOs and the stock distributed in spin-offs. While the focus of the first two chapters of this section is on IPOs and spin-offs, keep in mind that much of the information also applies equally to other forms of public SERs. For example, investors often use the same criteria when assessing an investment in the stock of a merged company. It also applies to preparing any company for a successful experience in the public markets.

Public stock investors have had a hard time in the past few years and have become very selective. The results of U.S. IPOs have been especially dismal. Most IPOs executed between 1995 and 2001 are trading below the initial offering price, as demonstrated in Exhibit 18–1. In fact, 82 percent of the IPOs in 2000 were trading well below their IPO offer price at the end of the first half of 2002.

E X H I B I T   18–1

Results of U.S. Domestic IPOs

Year of IPO	Total no. of IPOs in study	No. of IPOs from that year trading below the IPO price	Percent below IPO price
1998	315	205	65
1999	548	355	65
2000	345	285	83
2001	78	35	45
Totals	1,313	887	68

As of March 28, 2002.

Source: Dealogic, Needham & Company

Forget the late 1990s and 2000! In the bubble, all investment disciplines were ignored. In the post-bubble and -Enron world, investors are back to looking at the basics in assessing any public company and demanding a high degree of quality. The subsidiary will need to conform to high investor expectations if it is to have a successful IPO or interest in the stock after a spin-off or other public market SER and a successful performance as a public company after the SER. These criteria will also be of great interest to private equity investors, as these investors will often be looking to a future IPO to ensure the success of their investment.

WHAT INVESTORS WISH TO SEE IN SUBSIDIARIES UNDERTAKING IPOS AND SPIN-OFFS

In normal times, IPOs are not readily available for most subsidiaries. While there was a massive and unprecedented IPO boom in the late 1990s through 2000, this has ended. However, there has been a reasonable IPO market each year since 1976 for quality companies. Even in the depressed markets of the first half of 2002 there were still 54 U.S. IPOs. The key elements that institutional investors—the primary buyers of IPOs and spin-offs—look for in assessing an investment are called *quality validators.* These criteria are the same regardless of the subsidiary's industry or development stage. Experience repeatedly has taught (and recently retaught) investors that the probabilities of a company succeeding as a public company and thereby creating wealth for its investors are much higher when these quality validators are in place. They not only increase the probability of success, but, as or more important, they significantly decrease the potential for failure.

These quality validators are also what outside investors will look for before investing in the stock of a spin-off. It is obvious why interest among new investors is needed for a successful IPO—in an IPO investors have to put up hard cash and buy shares for it to succeed. In a spin-off, the shares are distributed to the parent's shareholders and no new cash is required for the SER to succeed. The spin-off will technically succeed regardless of investor interest in the shares. However, creating interest among new investors is equally as important with a spin-off as it is with an IPO if the spin-off is to create value for the parent's shareholders. The parent shareholders receiving shares who are eligible to hold the shares distributed in the spin-off by their charter or investment guidelines will then make an investment decision whether to hold or sell those shares. They will usually apply the same criteria they would use to assess any new investment. Some will want to sell and will want cash for their shares; those that continue to hold will want to see the value of their shares increase. Unless there is interest among new investors in putting up cash to buy shares after the spin-off, the spun-off stock will be illiquid and not easily sold and its price will languish. As well, the subsidiary may want or need its own access to public equity capital after the spin-off. This is available only if there is significant investor interest in the stock.

However, unlike an IPO, a spin-off may still be undertaken even when there is an understanding by the parent that there will not be much investor interest in the stock after the spin-off. There may be a belief that the benefits of separation outweigh the disadvantages of a likely lack of investor interest, or there may be significant shareholders who intend to hold the stock and do not care, or the parent may believe that with time the subsidiary will grow into a strong public company and decide not to wait.

It should also be noted that certain of the quality validators are also what private equity investors will either want to see in place before they invest or at least be confident that they can be put in place after the investment so as to allow a successful future IPO.

The parent will want to ensure that most, if not all, of the quality validations are in place before the subsidiary's IPO or spin-off. With an IPO especially, the tremendous costs involved in actual expense and time commitment to prepare for and execute an IPO make it imperative that the subsidiary not undertake an IPO unless it has reasonable certainty that it will actually close.

The number of aborted IPOs each year is eye-opening, as seen in Exhibit 18–2.

E X H I B I T   18–2

U.S. Market IPOs Withdrawn After Filing

Years	1998	1999	2000	2001
Withdrawn IPOs	200	132	263	165
Completed IPOs	393	601	581	135
Source: Dealogic				

Compare the 167 IPOs withdrawn in 2001 with the 135 that actually closed! An aborted IPO is always hugely expensive in its out-of-pocket cash costs and in the commitment of management time and attention to preparing for the IPO (these will be discussed in later chapters) and may be devastating for the subsidiary and the parent in its impact on employee morale, retention and recruitment, forgone capital, loss of business momentum, competitors trumpeting the failure to customers, missed strategic opportunities, and public failure. However, equally devastating to the parent and the subsidiary is a broken IPO where the stock trades to a fraction of the issue price and further strategic steps and SER transactions are closed off. The subsidiary will not have a second chance for a successful entry into the public markets. As well, all problems and retooling will be exposed to the full light of the public eye. Finally, class action lawsuits often follow, regardless of merit. These lawsuits can tie subsidiary management—often for years—casting a cloud over the subsidiary and generating great expense in legal costs and eventual settlement costs.

KEY QUALITY VALIDATORS

Knowing now that quality validators are crucial to the success of an IPO or a spin-off, here are the actual quality validators most looked for by investors today:

1. Simple capital and corporate structure
2. Simple common stock offering
4. Simple business model
5. Relationship with the parent that allow the subsidiary to thrive as a stand-alone company
6. Strong balance sheet after the IPO or spin-off
7. Strong corporate governance practices
8. Validating relationships with respected outside parties
9. Experienced, capable management team
10. Reasonably liquid and solid market for the stock
11. Reasonable restrictions on additional stock coming on the market
12. A good business with predictable revenue and earnings

Let's look at each of these in more depth.

Simple Capital and Corporate Structure

Investors in public companies prefer simple capital structures. In a bubble market there is tolerance of all types of ingenious and complex financial structures and securities. In normal markets, investors will only tolerate a capital simple structure that has only one type of equity—common stock—and only one class of common stock—with equal rights. It also must have debt appropriate to the cash flow of the company and comparable companies in its industry. Complex capital structures with twists and turns take too much time to understand, and investors believe that complexity benefits the subsidiary or the parent, not the investor. They are generally right in this assumption.

In addition, institutional investors will be particularly wary if there are equities outstanding after the IPO or spin-off that are senior to the common stock that they are purchasing in the IPO or receiving in the spin-off. In the end, the parent has to put its wish list aside and recognize that investors want all equity holders to have the same rights and run the same risks.

Investors also want to invest in a single, unified corporate structure. Holding companies with multiple subsidiaries, complex partnerships, and joint ventures are a source of concern. Post-Enron, there is even deeper suspicion of complexity. Although some degree of complexity may be tolerated with a large company, it is generally not acceptable with a smaller company or a growth company, where investors want all equity investors to have the same economic interest.

Simple Common Stock Offering

Investors in IPOs today prefer simple common stock offerings. Unit deals of stock and warrants, or debt and other complex packages, are rarely seen in quality IPOs. They are usually indications of penny stock offerings and distract investors from the subsidiary's story. From time to time there are IPOs of stock with concurrent debt offerings. The different components of these offerings are usually sold to different investors. These most often occur where the success of either of the offerings is dependent on the success of both, such as where a recapitalization is needed. The terms of both offerings are generally penalized somewhat for the added complexity.

Simple Business Model

As already noted, investors prefer pure plays, simple (and easily understandable) businesses, and simple and understandable operating relationships. Complex, multisector companies are penalized in the public markets, and investors are well aware of this. There are various ways to simplify a business before an IPO or spin-off, including the divestiture of nonrelated operations back to the parent or to an outside buyer in a sale. The parent should consider keeping only related businesses in the subsidiary, regardless of the current organizational structure of the subsidiary. It should also consider adding other, similar operations to the subsidiary even if the subsidiary is now in a different business unit. The parent should also retain nonoperating or nonstrategic investments held by the subsidiary before an IPO or spin-off, as the public markets will not value these and will find them distracting.

Value-enhancing acquisitions before the IPO or spin-off may also add to the appeal of the subsidiary's business model to investors in the IPO or after the spin-off. Value-adding acquisitions include those that:

- Achieve critical mass in the industry
- Add new products that offer growth potential
- Add a critical distribution channel

Relationships with the Parent That Allow the Subsidiary to Thrive as a Stand-Alone Company

Complex and one-sided relationships between the subsidiary and the parent can muddy an otherwise attractive story. Examples of such transactions include excessive royalty payments, loans, consulting agreements, partnerships, and continued ownership of key assets or parts of the business by the parent. This also applies to relationships with other investors, management, and directors. Investors view these transactions as good reasons not to invest. Therefore, it is best to get them cleaned up before the IPO or spin-off.

However, practical and reasonable transactions between the parent and the subsidiary often are necessary, at least for a transition period. These include normal service contracts for continued parent support of the subsidiary's operations, distribution and supply agreements, and agreements covering the use of intellectual property. These are acceptable and usually not an issue if the terms are reasonable and the relative costs are not too large. Where substantial economic benefit goes to the parent, investors will look very carefully at the arrangements and at what they, as new shareholders, get out of the deal.

However, if the subsidiary is dependent on the parent for a large part of its business or operations, investors will require that adequate agreements to protect the business from the parent be put in place before the IPO or spin-off. For example, when General Motors spun off EDS, GM accounted for a substantial part of EDS's business. GM entered into a long-term agreement with EDS to continue as a customer.

Also, unless the subsidiary is a fully established stand-alone operation, as was the situation with Allstate Insurance and Sears, investors will want to see that the parent will continue to be supportive of the subsidiary. Chapter 7 details how Du Pont provided crucial support to its Photomask subsidiary.

Strong Balance Sheet After the IPO or Spin-Off

Investors will look carefully at the cash needs of the subsidiary after the IPO or spin-off and will want complete assurance that the subsidiary will have adequate cash to meet its business objectives for at least several years following the IPO or spin-off. Investors will also want to know that the subsidiary is financially sound after the IPO or spin-off. In an IPO or spin-off, investors will not want to see the parent or other shareholders take out any cash unless the subsidiary is well capitalized and will not need cash in the future. With an IPO, the offering will need to raise enough cash for the subsidiary to make any required debt repayments with the proceeds and to provide sufficient proceeds to fund the subsidiary's growth.

Investors in an IPO or after a spin-off will also require that any remaining debt not be due for an extended period. They will not be willing to invest in an IPO or spin-off subsidiary with financial distress just around the corner.

Investors will also be wary of an IPO or spin-off for a subsidiary that has too much debt, or of any growth subsidiary that has any debt at all after the IPO or spin-off. Investors are hesitant to take on both balance sheet risk and business risk. Investors in an IPO or after the spin-off will look for a strong balance sheet as a necessary competitive weapon to attract good employees, and a strong balance sheet is a must in order to be perceived as a credible vendor to customers. Investors also prefer that growth and cyclical companies be overcapitalized to reduce the risk of financial distress in the event of setbacks. The pitfalls of an inappropriate capital structure were discussed in relation to Agere earlier.

Strong Corporate Governance Practices

IPO and post-spin-off investors want to see an independent board of directors at the subsidiary with strong outside directors, and a commitment to shareholder value for all the shareholders. A board dominated by the parent or management will deter IPO and post-spin-off investors. In the wake of Tyco and WorldCom, there is intense scrutiny of board composition today. New rules requiring genuinely independent boards are likely from the major stock exchanges.

Validating Relationships with Respected Outside Parties

The following relationships can help validate a quality IPO.

Strategic Alliances

Strategic alliances are a source of comfort to investors in an IPO and after a spin-off. These alliances include strategic partnerships with other corporations, often industry leaders, and are integral to the business success strategy of many companies. Strategic partnerships often include an investment by the strategic partner in the subsidiary. These alliances can expand the subsidiary's business and financial resources and increase its stature in the industry.

Strategic investments by industry leaders are also of value in the marketing of the subsidiary's stock in an IPO and after a spin-off, by providing important validation to investors and, with an IPO, the investment banks involved in the IPO. These parties will assume the strategic partners have done their homework on the capabilities of the subsidiary. This is particularly important for a subsidiary lacking a sizable revenue and customer base or with forecasts predicated on the success of a new product or service.

Recognized Customers

Investors look for familiar names—especially large customers within specific industries. These are an indication that the subsidiary itself is a leader or is on its way to becoming one. A customer list consisting of second- and third-tier names

is not in itself an insurmountable barrier, but it is certainly better to have Target
and not Kmart or Dell and not eMachines as the largest customer.

Quality Pre-IPO or Spin-off Private Equity Investors
Depending on the stage of development of the subsidiary, the involvement of
respected private equity investors may be beneficial to the success of an IPO or
spin-off. With a more mature subsidiary, the numbers and business will speak for
themselves. With an earlier-stage subsidiary that is selling its future prospects
rather than its current or past performance, outside validation of the subsidiary by
respected private equity firms may provide comfort to the IPO or post-spin-off
investors. The types of these firms are discussed at length in Chapter 12.

Experienced, Capable Management Team

Before the IPO or spin-off, investors will require that the subsidiary have a strong
team in place, consisting of experienced managers. In particular, it is difficult, if
not impossible, to have a successful IPO without a designated and well-respected
CEO. The CEO may be the current division head or an outsider. If the CEO does
not have direct experience of running a public company, it is strongly recommended that a COO or CFO be brought in with public company experience (see
discussion in Chapter 4).

Reasonably Liquid and Solid Market for the Stock

Investors in an IPO or in stock distributed in a spin-off will assess whether there
will be a liquid market for the subsidiary's stock before investing. Investors holding a significant position in an illiquid stock will face severe losses if they want to
sell their position. These investors will look at the following factors to assess
whether there will be a liquid market.

Sufficient Public Float
The number of shares available for public investors to purchase is called the *float*.
Institutional investors view the public float as an approximation of liquidity.
    In an IPO, the float will initially be the same as the proceeds of the IPO. In
a spin-off, it will be the value of the shares distributed to nonaffiliated shareholders. The minimum public float that institutional investors require has increased
over the past decade along with the average size of institutional funds as the fund
management industry has grown in assets.
    While the baseline will fluctuate depending on markets, in mid-2002, the
size of IPOs provides a good guide. $30 million is the base minimum public float
required by institutions to even consider investing in an IPO. However, the market
at this size is very limited. Many institutions have much larger requirements and
will not participate in an IPO that results in such a small public float. A minimum
float approaching $100 million is often needed for an IPO that will attract reason-
able institutional interest. In general, the larger the float, assuming the overall valuation of the subsidiary is there to support it, the easier it actually is to sell an IPO

E X H I B I T   18–3

Average Size of Offering of Domestic Issuer IPOs, 1990–2001

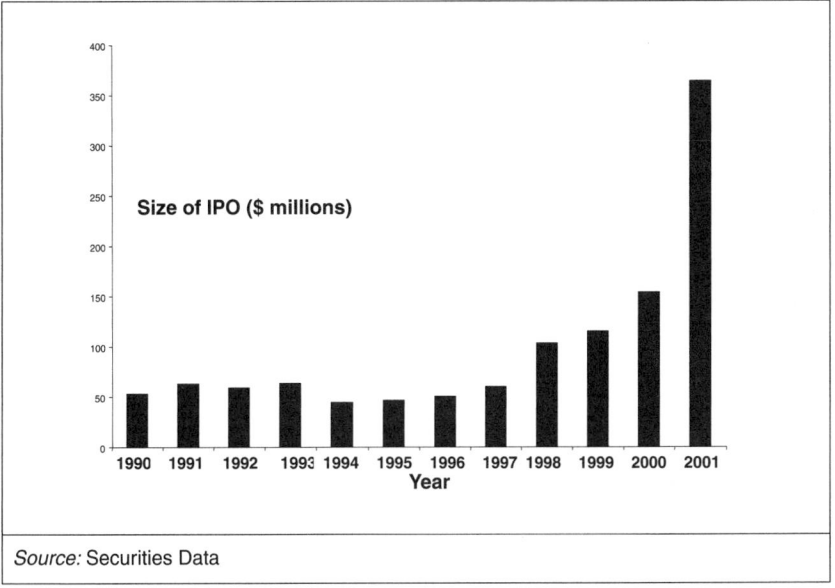

Source: Securities Data

or find new investors for a spin-off and the wider the range of potential institutional investors.

Exhibit 18–3 indicates the increasing interest by IPO investors in larger IPOs over the past five years.

An indicator of the increased minimum float requirements by institutions is the average size of venture-backed IPOs. The average size of these IPOs went from $30 million in 1994 to around $120 million in 2001. While some of this increase is explained by overall higher valuations, much of it arises from a desire to meet the requirements for a quality IPO in an environment where average fund size has increased dramatically.

Investors generally view small IPOs and small-float spin-offs in the same way that they view investments in a private placement of stock that is not readily marketable. Accordingly, they will expect a discounted price for investing in a small-float IPO or spin-off that compensates them for the lack of a deep and liquid market following the IPO.

Sufficient Overall Market Capitalization

While there is no fixed minimum total market capitalization, investors are increasingly requiring a large market capitalization before they take an interest in a stock. For this discussion, market capitalization is the total aggregate dollar value of all shares outstanding, including those held by the parent and management. It is calculated by multiplying the total number of shares outstanding by the market price per share.

A sufficient market capitalization is required because many institutional funds are precluded by policy from owning more than 5 percent of any company, and few funds have a desire to own more than 10 percent of the outstanding shares, as this would subject them to onerous SEC restrictions regarding affiliates. For example, it would require them to return so-called short-swing profits to the company.

In addition, larger funds do not want to have numerous small positions that they have to monitor and track. They will pass on a very promising investment if they are precluded from acquiring enough stock in value to be meaningful to the particular fund. Many institutions require a $500 million minimum market capitalization to even consider investing in a public company.

There are a relatively limited number of institutions that are willing to invest in micro-cap companies—those with under $100 million in market capitalization. As a result, the demand for IPOs for these companies or interest in the stock after a spin-off is limiting.

Reasonable Restrictions on Additional
Stock Coming on the Market

In addition, investors in an IPO will want to ensure that additional stock does not come onto the public market before the subsidiary establishes itself solidly there. For this reason, the parent and other large shareholders are restrained from selling shares for a period of time after the IPO. In a spin-off all, or almost all, the shares are available for sale into the market following the distribution unless there is a large shareholder. While the provisions covering sales of stock by an affiliate may restrict sales by that shareholder, it may also need to consider other restraints on its sales for a vibrant market to develop in the stock.

A Good Business with Predictable Revenue and Earnings

A company that is an industry leader and that shows consistent high return on capital over an extended period and has visibility on its revenue and income in the future is the best candidate for continued success as a public company. Demonstrating higher growth than the industry is also well received and leads to a higher valuation.

If the subsidiary has some operations that have erratic earnings, these may reduce the overall value of the subsidiary because of the premium placed by investors on earnings predictability. Therefore, it is often advisable to separate or divest those operations before considering an IPO. Similarly, acquisitions that increase the momentum of the subsidiary's earnings and revenue demonstrate to IPO and post-spin-off investors the subsidiary's commitment to growth.

A subsidiary with a mediocre market position, low return on assets, and little ability to accurately forecast revenues and earnings will usually disappoint investors and have an unhappy experience as a public company. Therefore, other alternatives not involving the public markets should be considered by the parent.

If a subsidiary does not have the required quality validation or market capitalization for an IPO, it may become a stronger IPO candidate by merging with another private company in the same industry or by acquiring a smaller public company in the same industry to create a combined entity with sufficient size and other attractions for an IPO.

DISCUSSION OF PROFITABILITY

The reader will notice that profitability was not listed as a basic criterion for a successful IPO or spin-off. The reasons for this are detailed in the following text.

In some markets, investors are willing to ascribe great value to the promise and potential of a business and ignore historical and current financial performance. In other markets, investors require a considerable history of revenue growth and a profitability trend for several quarters to ascribe value to a business. In general, high forecasted growth and an exuberant market mean that lower revenues are required to attract investment.

There is no set guideline for the level of revenues or the expectation of profitability in a subsidiary that is undertaking the IPO process. As Exhibit 18–4 indicates, profitability is important but not always necessary for a successful IPO or spin-off if other attractive attributes are in place. For example, a subsidiary that shows consistent significant revenue growth over an extended period with the expectation of solid growth in the future will obtain investor support in virtually any market if it has quality validation.

However, there is certainly a renewed focus on profits by IPO investors. For example, the percentage of profitable issuers and the age of the company at the time of the IPO have greatly increased in 2002.

Exhibit 18–4 illustrates the changing profitability and maturity of successful IPOs. After a period in the late 1990s and 2000 when unprofitable young companies were able to go public with an IPO, investors are returning to the earlier standard that a company undertaking an IPO be seasoned and profitable.[1]

PREPARING FOR THE FISHBOWL LIFE OF A PUBLIC COMPANY

Part of laying the groundwork for a successful IPO or spin-off is mentally preparing for life as a public company. Often the transition can be quite difficult, especially relating to the disclosure of information that was at one point proprietary. For example, the subsidiary will be required to make extensive and timely disclosures of:

• All aspects of its business and financial affairs

• Senior executive salaries, stock options, benefits and transactions with the parent, officers and directors, and overall stock option programs

In addition, the management of the parent and the subsidiary and their boards of directors should be thoroughly familiar with SEC rules for public companies, including those relating to other disclosure requirements such as:

• *Insider trading.* A public company must put in place measures to ensure that access to sensitive information that may be of value in the market is protected

E X H I B I T   18–4

Maturity at the Time of the IPO

Year	% of IPOs by profitable issuers*	Median age of companies going public[†]
1990	86%	9
1992	72%	10
1994	75%	7
1996	62%	7
1998	48%	7
1999	22%	4
2000	16%	6
2001	28%	12
2002 Q1	58%	16

Source: Dealogic

[†]*Source:* Professor Jay R. Ritter, University of Florida

and that all employees and directors are aware of the restrictions on using or distributing inside information.

- *Timely disclosure.* A public company must periodically disclose known trends and uncertainties if they are reasonably likely to have a significant effect on the company's financial performance. While the SEC does not require the disclosure of projections, investors expect the disclosure of projections.

- *Disclosure of all material developments.* The SEC requires the public disclosure of significant events. However, the timing of that disclosure is often open to considerable discretion.

- *Selective disclosure.* Regulation Fair Disclosure (FD) requires the simultaneous widespread public disclosure of material nonpublic information.

- *Forward-looking disclosures.* A public company must disclose known trends and uncertainties if they are reasonably likely to have a material effect on the company's financial performance.

- *Restrictions on stock sales.* SEC Rule 144, in effect, imposes restrictions on the sale of shares by the parent, management, directors, and large shareholders, as well as any shareholder who has held shares for less than two years by only providing limited specific safe harbors for such sales.

In addition, the parent and the subsidiary and their boards of directors must be familiar with the following:

- The fiduciary duties to outside shareholders under state and common law of the parent and the board of the subsidiary
- The various codes of conduct for directors and officers of a public company
- The standards for blackout periods imposed by companies on purchases and sales of stock by officers and directors to safeguard against the reality or perception of insider trading
- Corporate governance requirements imposed by the NYSE, ASE, or Nasdaq or as a result of SEC disclosure requirements

IPO ALTERNATIVES

If a subsidiary does not have all the required quality validation or market capitalization for an IPO in the current market environment or for a successful market to develop for its stock after a spin-off but the parent believes that is will succeed as a public company, it still has public market alternatives already discussed, such as a merger with an already public company. In addition, as noted, a spin-off may still be undertaken even when there is an understanding that there will not be a liquid market for the stock after the spin-off.

SUMMARY

This chapter examined the criteria that investors use to evaluate investing in IPOs and shares distributed in a spin-off. The challenges of life as a public company were also discussed. It is important to remember that many of the concepts in this chapter can also be applied to alternate ways to create a public company, such as mergers.

CHAPTER **19**

DEFENSE MEASURES TO PUT IN PLACE PRIOR TO BECOMING A PUBLIC COMPANY

INTRODUCTION

Although rare, hostile takeover bids do happen. In a stock market where many companies are trading at or below cash, hostile attacks are likely to become more common. In essence, these are attempts by an outside firm to purchase a company without approval from the board of directors at the company that is the takeover target. Instead, the hostile bidder tries to go around the board and deal directly with the shareholders who may not understand the long-term potential of the business or the alternatives available to achieve higher value. The hostile bidder's objective may be to actually win the bid. More usually it is to put such pressure on the company that it accedes to a merger on favorable terms to the bidder. For instance, many institutional investors have begun to insist that all takeover bids be considered—even if they are hostile—as long as the offer raises the company's short-term share price.

Unlike the 1980s, when hostile bidders were buccaneering Wall Street predators looking for quick financial gains by breaking up conglomerates, most hostile attackers today are respected corporations making long-term strategic moves, not looking for quick financial profits. In most cases, the hostile bidder has already been rebuffed in a friendlier overture.

For an independent subsidiary, a hostile takeover can be disastrous as it may seriously jeopardize the company's ability to reach its goals and is a major distraction. As such, the purpose of this chapter is to help parent companies understand the defensive measures that should be put in place before a subsidiary becomes public through an IPO, spin-off, or merger, to help ensure that an unfriendly offer is not made in the first place.

WHY COMPANIES BECOME TAKEOVER TARGETS

Although the purpose of this chapter is to detail how to put measures in place before an IPO to discourage the takeover of a newly public company, it is worth reviewing, in a general sense, the reasons why public companies become takeover targets. They include:

• *Strategic necessity.* The hostile bidder must own the target company for strategic reasons (AMC/Read Rite).

• *Underperformance.* The hostile bidder believes it can do a better job of managing the attractive strategic assets of a target company that is underperforming or unfocused (AlliedSignal/AMP).

• *Turnaround.* The target is on the cusp of a turnaround or an exciting new growth period. However, its stock price does not yet reflect the improvement (Philips NV/VLSI).

• *Undervaluation.* The target is undervalued because it is in a depressed industry sector or a depressed stock market, or the bidder's stock is overvalued because it is in a hot stock market sector at the time (Qwest/U S West).

• *Aftereffect of an announced merger.* The target has entered into a friendly merger with another party and the hostile bidder sees this as an opportunity to strike because the target is now in play (GE/Honeywell) or it does not want to see the merger succeed, which would create a more formidable competitor (Mentor/IKOS).

• *Multibusiness operation.* The target is unfocused and in several businesses, one of which is a gem. The bidder wants the gem and is willing to buy the entire target and break it up to get the gem (Northrop Grumman/TRW).

Because even the best companies can have their stock price battered, it is best to put the appropriate defensive measures in place to guard a newly public company against a hostile takeover bid. Having said that, it easiest to do this while the company is still private, as getting the necessary approvals for these measures is more difficult as a public company.

CORPORATE ATTACK AND DEFENSE OVERVIEW

Hostile attacks take three main forms including (1) a creeping acquisition of a controlling interest through open stock market purchases; (2) a tender offer or the threat of a tender offer at a price that does not reflect the subsidiary's value or is coercive; or (3) taking control of the subsidiary's board without giving shareholders time to consider the consequences.

Unless the target company has a control owner unwilling to sell, all defensive measures will do is buy time for the board. However, it is important to note that the board cannot shield the target company from a hostile takeover if the majority of the shareholders support the offer and if the acquirer is determined, patient, well capitalized relative to the amount of the offer, willing to spend a great deal of money on legal bills and other expenses and, above all, willing to pay a premium price. Such a bidder will eventually obtain control of the board of the target company and repeal the defensive measures including a poison pill. Or it will put such pressure on the board from litigation, a proxy contest, and creating shareholder agitation that the target company negotiates with the bidder or pursues another, higher-value alternative. A 1995 study by two professors at the University of Rochester found that anti-takeover measures "increase the bargaining position of target firms but do not prevent many transactions."[1] An update in 2002 reached similar conclusions for mergers in the intervening period.[2] Once a credible hostile bid is launched at a premium price by a credible bidder, the target company usually does not stay independent. Such a bid will almost always result in a sale of the target company to the bidder or to another buyer. In 2000, half of target companies remained independent after a hostile offer. In most years the percentage is lower; in 1999, less than 20 percent remained independent.[3] However, hostile bids by strategic buyers are expensive and time consuming for the bidder and therefore are not usually launched unless the bidder believes it has a good probability of success. Therefore, the key to deterring a hostile bid is making the subsidiary appear to be a tough nut to crack.

THE DEFENSE PROGRAM

The first objective of any defense program is deterrence. If a target has strong defenses in place, it may cause a hostile bidder to look elsewhere. The second objective is to force a hostile bidder to negotiate directly with the subsidiary's board of directors so that the board may ensure that the best interest of the shareholders is served by exploring available alternatives such as a restructuring, searching for an alternative buyer, or continuing on a stand-alone basis. By doing this, defensive measures protect the ability of the board to act in the long-term best interests of the shareholders.

For many public companies, a shareholder rights plan (poison pill) is the first line of defense in averting a hostile bid. When Motorola recently put in a new poison pill, the board of directors stated that the poison pill would "ensure that all shareholders receive fair treatment in the event of an unsolicited attempt to gain control of the company."

Empirical evidence on the impact of poison pills supports their use. The 1995 study by the University of Rochester professors finds: "Poison pills and control-share laws are reliably associated with higher takeover premiums for selling shareholders." However, some large shareholder groups such as the Council of Institutional Investors oppose any defense measures. including poison pills. as against the interests of shareholders. Using dual classes of voting stock as a defensive measure enables a shareholder controlling the high-voting class to deny an unwanted suitor control indefinitely. However, as discussed, dual classes of stock are not popular with investors.

Also, recognize that some protection measures described in the next section, such as supermajority voting and removing voting by consent, may restrict the parent's own freedom to act when it is the one that holds a control position.

RECOMMENDED DEFENSE MEASURES

The three most common and successful defenses intended to discourage a hostile bidder from even considering hostile action that are also palatable to investors include:

1. Shareholder rights plan (also known as a poison pill)
2. Blank check preferred stock
3. Classified board of directors[4]

A majority of larger public companies now utilize these measures, as do an increasing number of smaller public companies. These and other defensive measures are examined in Exhibit 19–1.

SUMMARY

A smart defense program put in place before a private/public company transition will protect a public subsidiary from becoming a takeover target. As discussed in this chapter, at some point any public subsidiary may be vulnerable to attack because its true market value may not yet be apparent to investors for a variety of reasons. This undervaluation attracts hostile bidders who want to snap up a deal that makes strategic or financial sense. This chapter also examined the various defense measures that are available that can also be applied to companies going public through IPOs, spin-offs, or mergers. These are easier to put in place while the subsidiary is still private. Chapter 20 will examine the next step in the process, which is to create the external team to take the company public.

Summary of Defensive Actions

Measure	Threat	Defense description	Deterrent effect
1. Establishing board of directors control			
Shareholder Rights Plan ("poison pill") Board decision/may need shareholder approval if an insufficient number of shares are authorized.	A raider takes control of the subsidiary through a: "Creeping tender" (i.e., buying up stock in the open market until it has a control position) and leaving the minority shareholders exposed; or A tender offer for a majority of the shares (that may be closed in 20 business days) at an inadequate price, limiting the time the board of directors has to consider alternatives.	A plan that gives all the shareholders other than the hostile raider rights for additional stock at a reduced price when a raider has crossed a preset ownership threshold.	Lethal to a hostile raider. An SRP enables shareholders to confiscate a substantial portion of the raider's investment and redistribute that value to the company's other shareholders. However, a tenacious raider willing to pay a high and firm price may eventually obtain control of the board and redeem the poison pill.
Blank Check Preferred Charter amendment	A raider takes advantage of a limited flexibility of the subsidiary to respond to a variety of threats based on a lack of flexibility in the types of securities it may issue.	A class of authorized but unissued preferred stock that has terms set by the board at the time of issuance. A blank check preferred may be used in a wide variety of defenses such as a poison pill, alliances, and acquisitions.	Gives the board great flexibility in structuring a shareholder rights plan and advantageous alliances with strategic partners.

Continued

2. Business Combination Restrictions

Super Majority Provisions	A control shareholder forces a merger that disadvantages the other shareholders.	Requires some percentage greater than 50 (typically 80%) of all outstanding voting stock or a "majority of the minority" to authorize a business combination or a bylaw amendment.	Gives minority shareholders the right to independently assess the proposed combination.
Charter amendment			
"Fair Price" Provisions	A raider pressures shareholders into selling their shares in a tender by offering a better price to those who tender first.	Mandates that shareholders receive equivalent consideration at both ends of a two-tier bid.	Prevents coercive offers.
Charter amendment			
Changing state of incorporation to Delaware	A raider takes advantage of weak state laws or untested defense protections.	Places shareholder issues in the jurisdiction of the Delaware Chancery Court under the provisions of Delaware law including 2203 that limits second-stage mergers with a company controlled by an investor acquiring shares in a creeping tender.	Delaware has the best developed, most predictable, and most expeditious corporate legal systems of any state. Delaware also has strong statutory takeover protections and well-settled precedent supporting the use of shareholder rights plans.[5]
Reincorporation			

3. Protecting board powers

(a) Board Provisions

Classified Board	A raider wages a proxy contest to take complete control of the board without giving the shareholders time to carefully consider the consequences and alternatives.	Staggers directors' terms and provides for terms of service longer than one year. Allows the board time to consider all alternatives.	Forces a raider attempting to take majority control of the board to wait more than one year.
Charter amendment			

Power to Fill Vacancies Charter amendment	A raider forces a vote to expand the board and inserts its own nominees in the newly created openings.	Restricts power to fill vacancies to a majority, or supermajority, of remaining directors.	Allows the board to ensure that long-term shareholder interests are not threatened.
Size of Board Charter amendment	A raider forces a vote to expand the board and inserts its own nominees in the newly created openings.	Caps the number of directors on the board.	Allows the board to ensure that long-term shareholder interests are not threatened.

(b) Shareholder Action Provisions

Special Meetings Charter or bylaw amendment	A raider calls a special meeting of the shareholders to enact proposals favorable to the raider or elect directors favorable to the raider.	Provides that only certain parties (e.g., board, chairperson, president) can call special meetings.	Ensures that management and the board have sufficient opportunity to react to shareholder proposals.
Advance Notice of Action Bylaw amendment	A raider makes surprise proposals favorable to the raider at the shareholder meeting.	Requires advance notice of any business planned for a shareholder meeting.	Ensures that management and the board have sufficient opportunity to react to shareholder proposals.
Action by Consent Bylaw amendment/charter amendment	A raider bypasses the shareholders meeting as the forum for shareholder action to make favorable changes, including changing the composition of the board without giving shareholders time (and a process) to carefully consider the merits.	Restricts the use of written consent.	Prevents bypassing a shareholder meeting.

Continued

343

Continued

4. Ensuring continuity of control

Dual classes of voting stock	A control shareholder desires to ensure that the subsidiary stays independent but does not wish to inhibit the subsidiary from issuing stock for acquisitions, raising capital, and options.	With dual classes of stock, one class has a higher number of votes (Class A stock) and the other has a normal number of votes (Class B stock).	Completely effective long-term protection. Gives the Class A stockholders the ability to prevent an undesired change of control.
Charter amendment			

CHAPTER 20

CREATING THE EXTERNAL TEAM TO TAKE THE SUBSIDIARY PUBLIC

INTRODUCTION

In order for the subsidiary to achieve a successful IPO, the parent must have a strong internal and external team and understand the roles of this team and also those of the regulatory agencies and stock exchanges. Therefore, the focus of this chapter is on identifying the key players in taking a subsidiary public through an IPO and detailing their roles. There are key differences in the processes of an IPO and a spin-off. The primary difference is that most IPOs are sold to new investors through investment banks in an underwritten and marketed public offering, while spin-offs are not. However, the roles of the members of the team not involved in the underwriting process will be similar in most respects.

A comprehensive overview is provided in the following sections.[1]

THE ISSUERS OF IPO STOCK

The Parent

If the parent is selling shares it owns in the subsidiary in the IPO, the parent must execute a selling agreement with the lead manager of the IPO. The parent will usually also be required to indemnify the underwriters for liability under the federal securities acts in addition to the indemnity provided by the subsidiary.

The Subsidiary

The subsidiary, parent, and lead manager will determine the number of shares the subsidiary will sell (or "issue"), the number of shares that any other shareholders may sell in the IPO alongside the subsidiary, and the price range at which the IPO will be marketed. The subsidiary will need to enter into the underwriting agreement with the underwriters, represented by the lead manager, upon the pricing of the IPO. The subsidiary and any selling shareholders will need to deliver the title to the shares sold in the IPO at the closing.

Other Selling Shareholders

Other shareholders include any private equity firms, corporate partners, and past and current employees who own shares in the subsidiary. These parties may be permitted to sell some or all of their shareholdings in the subsidiary in the IPO. The lead manager of the IPO will determine the amount of shares (if any) that it believes the market will accept from each type of selling shareholder.

THE PARENT

In its capacity as an exclusive or substantial owner of the subsidiary, the parent determines the equity redeployment strategy for the subsidiary. The parent often selects the lawyers, accountants, and all or some of the investment bank underwriters for the IPO. The parent must separate operations and systems from those of the subsidiary. It must recapitalize and restructure the balance sheet and capital structure of the subsidiary as appropriate to provide a public company structure that is acceptable to the IPO market (and that will enable the subsidiary to thrive after the IPO). The parent generally will decide or have substantial influence in determining the IPO offering structure and filling in the board of directors of the subsidiary. In many cases, the parent must negotiate with the subsidiary about post-IPO operating and tax protocols.

Board of Directors of the Parent

Depending on the size of the subsidiary relative to the parent, and on governance practices at the parent, the board of directors of the parent may play a significant role in the IPO process or simply be apprised of developments. The board of the parent usually must approve the decision to go forward with the subsidiary IPO before the process begins. In some cases the board of the parent delegates to the parent's management full authority over the execution of the IPO. In other cases the board desires to review the preliminary and/or final terms of the IPO before the parent commits to the transaction. In still other cases, one or several members of the board are delegated by the board to work with the parent's management on the IPO.

Senior and Divisional Management of the Parent

The management of the parent may play a dominant or supporting role in a subsidiary IPO. The division of responsibilities between the parent and the subsidiary is different in each situation. In some cases, the parent makes all the decisions about the IPO and works on a daily basis with the professionals executing the transaction. In other cases, the parent orchestrates the overall strategy of the IPO but leaves the details to the subsidiary. In other IPOs, the subsidiary's management functions essentially as an independent company and merely keeps the parent advised. Regardless, it will be up to the subsidiary's management to market the IPO to investors.

Internal Counsel at the Parent

The in-house counsel at the parent will often be charged with giving preliminary guidance regarding the legal issues of the IPO. Internal counsel will ensure that the parent's interests are looked after in the preparation of the IPO, including issues that might result in legal liability for the parent in the representations made in the IPO documents. Internal counsel will be responsible for working with outside legal counsel and with the management of the parent and the subsidiary to prepare any agreements between the parent and the subsidiary that will come into effect after the IPO. These include licensing, production, and distribution agreements between the subsidiary and the parent; arrangements for any ongoing services to be provided by the parent to the subsidiary; and any arrangements for ongoing financial support of the subsidiary by the parent after the IPO.

Once the decision to go forward with the IPO is finalized, the internal counsel of the parent may be responsible for engaging the various outside legal counsels to effect the transaction. The parent's internal counsel may play a leading role or an observer role in interacting with legal counsel for the subsidiary; any patent, management compensation, or regulatory advisors and lawyers; and other experts to ensure the success of the separation of the subsidiary and the IPO. It may also share with the management of the subsidiary the responsibility for drafting the registration statement and preparing exhibits. Internal counsel will brief the parent and subsidiary management on restrictions relating to discussion of inside information before and after the IPO, and restrictions on sales and purchases of parent shares before and after the IPO. The parent's internal counsel will generally take the lead in negotiating the underwriting agreements with the lead manager of the IPO. It will also negotiate with the subsidiary, its counsel, and the IPO managers on any intercompany agreements after the IPO.

Outside Legal Counsel to the Parent

Outside legal counsel to the parent reviews the legal structure of equity redeployment alternatives for the parent and gives legal advice on steps needed for the subsidiary to become a public company. It also gives legal advice regarding the parent's separation from the subsidiary. It will generally review the underwriting agreement and the subsidiary's SEC filings and provide advice to the parent throughout the IPO process on issues relating to its liabilities. The counsel will brief the parent on any anti-takeover defenses appropriate for the subsidiary as a public company, which should be implemented before the IPO. It will explain to the parent how these measures will affect its control over the subsidiary.

The legal counsel to the parent (as may other advisors) will make suggestions on the appropriate law firms and investment banks for the IPO and offer to make introductions. The parent and subsidiary should recognize that there is a well-established exchange of lucrative referrals back and forth between law firms, accountants, and investment banks.

Outside Financial Advisor to the Parent

The parent may employ a financial advisor to review SER alternatives and advise on the feasibility and potential valuation of the IPO. The advisor often assists in the selection of the IPO team, recommends a structure for the offering, reviews the proposed capital structure, and advises on composition of the board and the strengthening of the senior management of the subsidiary and any needed enhancements to ensure a successful IPO. The financial advisor may also be a manager of the IPO. If this is the case, compensation for the advisory role may come in full or in part from its role as a manager of the IPO.

In many spin-offs the parent employs one or more investment banks to advise on the structure of the spin-off, assist with valuation, help the parent inform the parent's shareholders and new investors about the merits of the shares of the subsidiary, and provide market making and sponsorship for the subsidiary. The investment bank may also be called upon to provide opinions to the IRS supporting the spin-off and to provide information to the exchanges.

Outside Employee Compensation Advisors

The parent's legal advisor or an outside compensation expert will assist the parent in understanding management compensation plans for the subsidiary based on other comparable public companies and the specific nuances of the parent. The parent will need to understand the differences between the programs it has and those appropriate to the subsidiary as a newly public company if it is to attract and retain needed employees. These terms will also be of interest to IPO investors, who will expect the subsidiary's compensation programs to be similar to those of other successful comparable public companies. The most important distinction is usually the increased role of options and equity-related incentives versus traditional pension and benefits.

Outside Tax Advisor (Often the Parent's Accounting or Legal Firm)

This person or team advises about the tax implications of the proposed IPO structure and also gives tax advice to the parent regarding separation issues. Tax advice will often play a large role in structuring the IPO.

Outside Accounting Firm of the Parent

The parent's accounting firm assists with balance sheet restructuring and the capital structure of the subsidiary. It may assist in preparing pro forma financial statements for the parent and the subsidiary before and after the IPO as a decision support tool for the parent. It will also advise on the accounting and tax implications of the IPO.

THE SUBSIDIARY
CEO of the Subsidiary

At the beginning, the parent may play the dominant role in the IPO, choosing the team and setting strategy for the offering. However, as the process progresses, the burden will often shift to subsidiary management. The first role of the CEO is to help the external team understand the business and affairs of the subsidiary and its strategy, and to describe these in the prospectus. Weaknesses as well as strengths must be fully communicated. During the marketing of the IPO, the CEO of the subsidiary has the primary responsibility of marketing the IPO to investors in conjunction with the investment bankers. With an operating business, it is very difficult to accomplish an IPO without a strong and capable CEO as investors look closely at the CEO in making an investment decision. During the road show, the CEO must present the company in a favorable light, telling a story sufficiently compelling to encourage investor purchase of the offering. The CEO may also play a critical role in preparing the IPO by incorporating company vision into the strategy components of the offering materials, keeping the process moving forward, and ensuring that problems are overcome.

CFO of the Subsidiary

The CFO and internal counsel of the subsidiary will share primary responsibility for the drafting of the prospectus and registration statement and assembling the many exhibits and schedules that are attached to it. The CFO will also be responsible for the preparation of financial statements and exhibits and for supervising the accountants. The CFO generally coordinates the due diligence process of the lead manager and comanagers and their legal counsel as well as the subsidiary's own outside legal counsel. The CFO prepares, with the subsidiary's outside accounting firm, the financial disclosures included in the prospectus and the forecasts prepared for the managers of the IPO and investors to value the IPO. The CFO is also responsible for the financial part of the presentation to prospective IPO investors, and for ensuring that there is a financial forecasting system for the subsidiary that will give confidence to the managers and investors involved in the IPO that representations about the financial condition of the subsidiary are accurate and that the subsidiary will perform according to its forecasts after the IPO.

Board of Directors of the Subsidiary

The board of the subsidiary will need to approve any charter or bylaw changes attendant to the offering and will need to approve and sign the registration statements and other SEC and regulatory filings. It will also need to pass resolutions

authorizing the filings of the registration agreement and give management authority to sign the underwriting agreement within a specific range of terms.

Outside Legal Counsel for the Subsidiary (Company Counsel)

To avoid conflict, it is normal for the subsidiary to have a separate legal firm from
that of the parent. The division of labor between the parent's legal counsel and the
subsidiary's legal counsel will vary case by case. For this purpose, it is assumed
that subsidiary's counsel (company counsel) will be the primary legal counsel on
the IPO. Detailed laws and regulations govern the disclosures of information in
the prospectus for the IPO and the registration statement and the conduct of officers and directors. The company counsel coordinates works with the parent's
internal and outside counsel to prepare the registration statement and is the primary interface with the SEC. The company counsel may assist in negotiating the
underwriting agreements with the lead manager of the IPO.

The company counsel generally takes the lead in conducting a review and
cleanup of the subsidiary's files to prepare it to be a stand-alone public company.
It helps to ensure that there is good documentation of all material contracts and
agreements including employment agreements, leases, intellectual property,
trademarks, and titles to real estate and other assets. It generally prepares the documentation for any changes to state of incorporation, charter, and bylaws in anticipation of the IPO. The company counsel also cleans up, or at least clarifies, any
outstanding legal issues and litigation. It seeks out and reviews any potential problems that will impede or delay the IPO, helps draft and then files the preliminary
registration statement with the SEC, files a listing application with the applicable
stock exchange, and drafts press releases.

Following the filing of the registration statement, it works with the subsidiary and other members of the team to respond to SEC comments and eventually clears the registration statement with the SEC, files the final registration
statement after the pricing of the IPO, and ensures that the closing of the IPO
goes smoothly. Company counsel should also review all press releases relating to
the IPO, and all press releases, presentations, and speeches by the management
of the subsidiary in the time leading up to the IPO, to ensure that the subsidiary
(or the parent) does not violate the SEC guidelines on preoffering publicity. The
company counsel will assist the subsidiary in its negotiations with the parent
regarding intercompany agreements after the IPO, and with the implementation
of new employee compensation plans at the subsidiary.

In addition to its other duties, company counsel will usually be required to
provide an opinion letter to the lead manager stating that, to the best of its knowledge, there is no pending or threatened legal action or proceeding not disclosed in
the registration statement. This letter also states that the terms of the underwriting
agreement are not in conflict with the charter or bylaws of the subsidiary, the
terms of any loan or debt agreements, any regulation, or any court or regulatory
agency order and that nothing has come to the attention of the counsel that would
lead it to believe that the prospectus has any material misstatements or omissions
(known as a *10b-5 opinion*).

If the shares will be listed on the NYSE, ASE, or Nasdaq National Market, company counsel will file a Form 8A registration statement with the SEC to register the shares as a class of securities to be listed on an exchange. Company counsel will also apply to the CUSIP Service Bureau, operated by Standard & Poor's for the American Bankers Association, for a unique number to identify the shares for electronic trading, known as a "CUSIP" (named for the ABA's Committee on Uniform Security Identification Procedures).

Inexperienced or understaffed company counsel often causes considerable and avoidable delay and missteps in the IPO process. Delays can culminate in missing a market opportunity to go public. Therefore, it is important to use this criteria checklist when screening prospective counsel:

- Experience with IPOs
- Industry knowledge
- Name recognition among IPO investors
- Availability of specialist capabilities within the firm
- Appropriate size focus for the subsidiary
- Industry contacts
- Capabilities of the partner working on the transaction
- Sufficient staffing at the firm to ensure that the process is not impeded
- Cost

Let's look at the most crucial criteria in more detail.

Experience with IPOs
The selected law firm should be familiar with the underwriting process, including the rules, regulations, and protocols that govern it. The actual attorneys working on the IPO should be accustomed to dealing with federal and state securities regulators including the SEC, the National Association of Securities Dealers Regulation (NASDR), and any state securities commissions regarding prospectus approval. Company counsel should know how to coordinate communications with the regulatory agencies and handle SEC filings, and should be familiar with the registration process. Such familiarity not only ensures that proper procedures are followed, it also helps to avoid delays to the extent that potential issues can be anticipated and addressed before filing. For non-U.S. companies, it is important that the company counsel be familiar with the rules and regulations relating to foreign issuer IPOs in the U.S.

Industry Knowledge
Knowing the subsidiary's industry will help company counsel draft the prospectus, especially the sections relating to the description of the subsidiary's business and risk factors and the managements' discussion and analysis. In addition, knowing the industry enables company counsel to determine what disclosures the SEC has required in comparable situations and whether the SEC disclosure information is adequate.

Name Recognition Among IPO Investors

The involvement of a well-known IPO law firm matters to IPO investors. These investors take comfort in the involvement of these firms because the firms are perceived as providing some base level of scrutiny and quality control. But the names that count most to IPO investors are not necessarily those of the traditional large metropolitan law firms; rather, they are the law firms most associated with the premier IPOs. Investors in IPOs know this and look for the names of these firms on IPO registration prospectuses.

There is a relatively small universe of law firms that handle the majority of IPOs each year as either company counsel or underwriters' counsel.[2] These firms are the attorneys of choice on most IPOs by all but the largest companies, and all of them have deep and substantial IPO expertise. A final sad note: these firms also have considerable experience defending against class action securities lawsuits, which are now an all too common occurrence among even successful public companies.[3]

As with any large purchase, it is definitely best to interview several law firms and to get a detailed price estimate in advance. For a guide to the out-of-pocket expenses for the subsidiary in an IPO, see Exhibit 22–2 in Chapter 22. Fees of company counsel may range from $200,000 to $2 million depending on the complexity of the IPO and how much preparatory work is needed.

Spin-offs are sufficiently different in detail from IPOs that legal counsel needs specific experience in spin-offs. For example, ensuring tax-free status is a major part of planning many spin-offs. While many attorneys are familiar with IPOs, the number experienced in spin-offs is considerably fewer. As well, legal counsel may be called upon by the parent to present to it an opinion on the tax-free status of the spin-off and to negotiate with the IRS.

Outside Experts

In some industries, investors and regulators will look in the registration statement for an opinion from a recognized expert on certain areas to provide a level of comfort before approving or investing in the transaction. Examples include an opinion from a patent counsel on the validity of patents; from an oil and gas reserve appraiser on the size and value of oil and gas reserves; from a mining reserve appraiser on the value of mineral deposits; from a real estate appraiser on the value of large real estate holdings; and from Federal Food and Drug Administration counsel on the status of applications and approvals for a drug or medical device. These experts will also advise the working group drafting the prospectus on areas of their expertise and review drafts of relevant sections of the documents.

Outside Accounting Firm for the Subsidiary

The primary role of the outside accounting firm for the subsidiary is to prepare all required audited financial statements and schedules for the registration statement. The accounting firm should start by laying out a program to develop financial statements that conform to the requirements of the SEC and to identify any issues—for instance, SEC financial disclosure requirements that are broader than generally accepted accounting principles (GAAP). It prepares financial statements and schedules for the registration statement and helps draft the "Management's Discussion and Analysis of Financial Conditions and Results of Operations" section of the prospectus. The accounting firm responds to comments from the SEC on the accounting parts of the filing. It also prepares updated financial statements, if necessary, for inclusion in amended filings. The accounting firm also may review the subsidiary's financial controls and recommend changes suited for a public stand-alone operation.

The accounting firm also works with the managers on their financial due diligence. Under the Securities Act of 1933 and clarifying court decisions, the underwriters of an IPO are responsible for carrying out a "reasonable investigation" of all the information included in the registration statement other than "expertized" information. However, they may rely for certain matters on representations by experts, such as the subsidiary's accountants, as defense from liability. The lead manager will require a comfort letter from the subsidiary's accountant attesting to the accuracy of the financial statements of the subsidiary to provide this defense.

Before the filing of the registration statement, the accounting firm prepares a draft comfort letter for discussion with the lead manager and underwriters' counsel. The content of the comfort letter is an area of negotiation. The accounting firm will attempt to limit the scope of the comfort letter; the lead manager will want it to be as expansive as possible to provide the greatest protection. The subsidiary's accountant will be expected to provide comfort on financial data not contained in the audited financial statements, such as unaudited and interim financial statements, pro forma financial information, and per-share net income.

Generally, for any unaudited number, the accountant will only provide comfort that nothing adverse has come to its attention. As well, the accounting firm will usually only provide comfort on matters to which its professional expertise is relevant beyond the audited financial statements. For example, it will usually not provide comfort on the number of employees or order backlog.

A signed comfort letter is delivered to the lead manager when the registration statement is declared effective and the shares are sold. A "bring-down" comfort letter is given at the closing attesting that there has been no material change in the financial condition of the subsidiary. A second bring-down comfort letter is given should the underwriters' overallotment option (Green Shoe) be exercised. The Green Shoe permits the managers to purchase up to a specified number of additional shares from the subsidiary at the offering price for up to 30 days following the IPO. The Green Shoe is usually for 15 percent of the offering. For a more detailed explanation of the Green Shoe, see Chapter 23.

Except in a few industries that have respected specialized accounting firms, the use by the subsidiary of one of the four remaining large national accounting firms is a requirement by investors and IPO managers. IPO investors view the involvement of one of these firms as a validation of the accounting and also see the firm as a deep pocket to sue if there are problems. The investment bankers will also want a Big Four accounting firm, as they are relying on the auditor's comfort letter as a statement from financial statement experts to protect their own liability. The accountants working on the IPO should have industry experience and be knowledgeable about how revenue and expenses are recognized in the subsidiary's particular industry.

Each industry has different nuances in its accounting practices, and the accountants should be aware of acceptable reporting alternatives, the alternatives used by comparable public companies (so that nonnormal accounting practices are not an inadvertent red flag issue with investors), and the limits allowed by the regulators so that delays are not incurred by regulator requirements to clarify or restate financial statements.

For non-U.S. companies, the accountants selected for the IPO should have an understanding of the accounting policies of the home country and also of translating or reconciling foreign financial statements to U.S. GAAP.

The accounting firm will often play a key role on the tax aspects of a spin-off. Tax issues usually play a more prominent part in preparing for a spin-off than an IPO. Understanding the tax consequences of each proposed structure, developing the materials to present to the IRS for a letter ruling, and responding to IRS issues are often roles performed by the accounting firm. The accounting firm may also be called upon to provide an opinion to the parent on the tax status of the spin-off.

Outside Depositary Bank

A non-U.S. company undertaking an IPO in the United States may issue either American Depository Receipts (ADRs) or the company's regular common shares to U.S. investors. With ADRs, the foreign company appoints an authorized depositary that is usually part of a large U.S. bank or trust company. If a parent already has a relationship with a banking institution, it is likely to use that bank's depositary services. However, the parent should also talk to depositaries that represent other issuers from the same home country. Most foreign companies use ADRs. With ADRs, a depositary takes ownership of the non-U.S. underlying shares and then offers certificates, each representing one or more of these shares, to U.S. investors. ADRs have advantages for the investor and the issuer. The advantage for U.S. investors is that they are able to trade ADRs in the United States without the expense and difficulty of having to transfer the underlying shares back in the company's country of origin. ADRs are traded in the same manner as U.S. securities for clearance, settlement, transfer, and ownership purposes. Another advantage is that in many countries, shares are traded in small denominations by U.S. market standards, which call for a $10 to $20 initial offering price on an IPO. With ADRs, a number of underlying shares may be offered together to meet typical U.S. dollar initial offering prices. ADRs are also much more convenient for the issuer. The depositary bank distributes investor communications to U.S. investors, pays dividends, and administers changes of ownership.

Outside Transfer Agent and Registrar of Shares

The transfer agent and registrar is an independent third party responsible for administering issuances and sales of stock and for keeping accurate records of stock ownership. The New York Stock Exchange (NYSE) and the American Stock Exchange (ASE), but not the Nasdaq, require the use of a transfer agent and registrar. However, with Nasdaq-listed IPOs, use of these resources is often required by the lead manager of the IPO, as keeping these records in-house is often a source of friction with shareholders and regulators.

Outside Investor Relations Counsel

It is advisable to retain an investor relations firm early in the IPO process. The primary responsibility of the investor relations firm in the IPO process is to disseminate press releases about the IPO. Some companies prepare press releases in-house; others have company counsel or the investor relations firm draft press releases. After the press release is approved by management and reviewed by company counsel, the investor relations firm is used to distribute the press release. Charges for financial investor relations counsel range from $2,500 to $20,000 or more per month, depending on the type of firm and the workload. Small firms often do a perfectly adequate job at a lower cost. An experienced investor relations firm is especially valuable in the pre-IPO period and immediately following the IPO, and until the subsidiary's management is completely comfortable with the demands of public investors and meeting the disclosure requirements of the SEC.

Road Show Preparation Advisors

There are professionals who specialize in helping the subsidiary prepare for the IPO marketing road show. They help prepare the presentation and coach management in presentation techniques. Some management teams are natural presenters, while others benefit from a little coaching. A subsidiary management that has not been exposed to public investor meetings and presentations will often benefit from this help. A road show advisor may cost anywhere from $5,000 to $50,000. In many cases, outside graphics and visual arts companies are also engaged to assist in preparing the road show and prospectus.

Printer

In most cases, the printer prints the preliminary and final registration statements and prospectuses and files the registration statement electronically with the SEC on EDGAR (the SEC's electronic document system) and with the NASDR. There are only a few specialized financial printers experienced in SEC filings and related documentation. These companies add value by ensuring that mistakes do not happen in assembling the registration statement and exhibits. The costs of printing vary greatly depending on the size of the registration statement and exhibits, the number of copies to be printed, and the number of changes made after the initial draft has been submitted to the printer. For convenience, final drafting sessions are often held at the printer. Choose a printer that has an office close to the location of the main drafting work. The next criterion is price, which is negotiable and will depend on the individual workload of each printer at a given time. The parent or subsidiary should get quotes from several different printers, as there is often a wide difference in price.

THE INVESTMENT BANKING GROUP SELLING THE IPO (UNDERWRITERS)

Lead Manager

The lead manager is the investment bank that is in charge of organizing and selling the offering. It has the most important job among the investment banks involved in the IPO. Choosing the right lead manager is a key decision by the parent. A lead manager that is not familiar with the subsidiary's business and industry or is ambivalent about the company, inexperienced in IPOs, disorganized internally, or overloaded and distracted by other assignments will butcher an IPO. The right lead manager will at least make an IPO go smoothly, if not be a joy.

The lead manager has responsibility for a successful IPO. The lead manager is typically the investment bank whose name appears first on the left side of the prospectus cover. Here is a list of some of the more important responsibilities of the lead manager:

• Early in the IPO process, provides an assessment of the marketability of the IPO and advises on any actions that will help ensure a successful IPO

• Provides an initial assessment of the IPO structure, size, valuation, and timing and also recommends an allocation of shares in the IPO between institutional and retail investors

• Assists in drafting the prospectus and registration materials and preparing road show presentations

• Assists in conducting due diligence investigations

• Negotiates the documentation between the investment banks in the selling syndicate and the subsidiary, parent, and selling shareholders

• Organizes the syndicate and selling group

• Organizes the marketing program including the road show to sell the IPO to investors

• Keeps the "book" (the master record of orders for the shares in the IPO)

• At the end of the marketing program, advises on the appropriate price for the IPO

• Recommends the allocation of the shares in the IPO among institutional investors and retail interest from its own retail sales force, the comanagers and the syndicate, and the selling group as the retail distribution channels

- Collects and finalizes indications directly from institutional investors and from the retail distribution channels

- Gets agreement on the price, the size of the IPO, the allocation of shares sold in the IPO between the subsidiary and any other selling shareholders, and the underwriting discount

- Executes the underwriting agreement with the subsidiary and any selling agreements with shareholders

- Confirms allocations of shares with institutional investors and with the retail distribution channels

- Provides net proceeds to the subsidiary and other selling shareholders at the closing

- Places "tombstone" advertisements announcing the offering in appropriate publications

- Stabilizes the aftermarket for the stock of the subsidiary immediately following the IPO and determines whether to exercise the Green Shoe

The lead manager has the plum position with an IPO and will usually get a larger percentage of the fees than any other firm. However, this is only one of many benefits of being the lead manager on an IPO. Other benefits include:

- *Ability to allocate shares.* As explained in Chapter 21, the lead manager controls the allocation among potential investors of most of the shares in an IPO. This control is of great economic value to the lead manager, especially with a hot IPO where allocating shares is the equivalent of handing out dollar bills to the initial IPO buyers. During the late 1990s and 2000, the underpricing of IPOs was a prevailing practice by many investment banks. In 1999 and 2000 alone, companies raised $121 billion in proceeds from IPOs. But an additional $60 billion of first-day gain went to the initial IPO investors, not the issuer.[3] The IPO share allocation process for this bonanza was often abused for the benefit of the investment banks not the issuer. These abuses took a number of forms, including:

  - *Allocating shares in hot IPOs to induce investment banking business.* CS First Boston orchestrated many of the most overpromoted Internet IPOs and Citigroup's Salomon unit orchestrated those in the telecom area. These firms are reported to have given allocations of shares in hot IPOs to CEOs and venture capitalists. In many cases, these allocations were perfectly legitimate. However, there appear to have also been instances where these allocations were used to induce future investment banking business. There is no benefit to the issuer from these allocations. One example reported in the *Wall Street Journal*,[4] Bernard Ebbers, then CEO of WorldCom made over $11 million from allocations of shares in hot IPOs managed by WorldCom's investment banker Salomon Smith Barney. In many cases Ebbers sold the stock within hours or days.

  - *Allocating shares in IPOs in exchange for future stock commissions.* This practice led to a greatly disproportionate number of IPO shares being allocated to momentum hedge funds because of their high trading volumes from rapid turnover. These were often exactly the wrong investors for the long-term interest of the issuer. CS First Boston was also a stand-out participant in this practice, reportedly directly tying IPO allocations to commission payments. CS First Boston was certainly not alone in this practice.

- *Command of the aftermarket order flow.* Buy and sell orders from investors in an IPO usually go to the lead manager for the four to six months immediately following the IPO. Investors correctly assume that the lead manager has the best handle on who are the natural buyers and sellers of the stock following the IPO. Many IPOs turn over several times in the days following the offering and then sustain high volumes for months thereafter. The lead manager will capture a high percentage of this order flow. The lead manager may make a multiple of the revenues that it earned on the IPO itself trading stock in the aftermarket.

- *Prestige.* The large investment banks are much attuned to their standing in the "league tables," which rank the IPOs completed by each investment bank during a year. The league table for lead manager is an important marketing tool for firms as they compete for lead manager positions on IPOs. A decline in ranking from year to year causes consternation within these firms and is also often picked up in the press.

- *Selecting the underwriters' legal counsel.* The lead manager of an IPO usually selects the law firm that represents the underwriters in the IPO. Acting as underwriters' legal counsel is attractive business for law firms. A firm that lead-manages a large number of IPOs, and is thereby responsible for allocating considerable legal fees, will likely receive referrals of business from law firms.

Comanagers

In recent years the role of the lead manager has increased from that of first among equals to commanding general. This has occurred for a number of reasons. It is convenient for the issuer; and, because there are now many more comanagers on an IPO, the role of each is reduced. In addition, lead managers have become less willing in recent years to share as the culture of Wall Street has changed from one of cooperation in the interest of the issuer to one of pure greed. As a result, the role of comanagers has been somewhat reduced to providing research support, market making, and sponsorship after the IPO.

The comanagers appear on the prospectus cover to the right of the lead manager. There may be one or more comanagers. In recent years the number of managers has increased considerably on an IPO of a given size (see Exhibit 21–3 in Chapter 21), reflecting the recognition by issuers of the need for research and sponsorship in the aftermarket. Comanager positions are also used by the parent or the subsidiary to reward investment banks that have provided advice and services in the past.

Syndicate and Selling Group

The role of a syndicate often causes confusion for issuers. It is arcane and a remnant of history. In an underwritten IPO, the subsidiary and selling shareholders do not sell shares directly to investors; the shares are sold to a syndicate of investment banks that have agreed to underwrite the IPO at an agreed discount to the price at which the shares will be then resold to investors. The investment banks then own the shares and sell them to investors and dealers at not more than the offering price.

Most IPOs and almost all quality IPOs are sold through a group of investment banks that act as firm commitment underwriters of the subsidiary's stock in the IPO. As such, they are known as a syndicate. The syndicate structure originated in the days when Wall Street firms were small and had little capital. The syndicate was divided into firms that had relationships with the issuers of public offering stock, and different firms focused on the sale of stock to investors who would distribute the offering. To effectively sell an IPO, a group of firms would need to band together to put up the capital, share the risk, and market a public offering. Each assumed pro rata liability for any losses incurred in relation to the offering, stabilized the shares in the aftermarket, and shared in any profits.

Today, most investment banks are fully integrated, combining corporate finance deal origination and sales and trading capabilities, and are very well capitalized. As a result, the role of syndicates is minimal, except for very large IPOs aimed at retail investors. While syndicates are no longer important, the structure and nomenclature remain. A good syndicate for an IPO may still serve a function for the issuer. For example, it helps get the issuer's name in front of firms that may at some point take an interest in the issuer, involve firms other than the managers in the IPO, and obtain any needed specialized distribution capabilities that complement that of the managers (such as regional retail or overseas distribution), and may lead to additional research coverage and market making. An illustrious syndicate also adds validation to the IPO. Too much should not be expected of a syndicate today, as there is rarely much time or attention invested in the IPO by syndicate members, except for the managers and a few firms with a special relationship with the issuer.

Depending on the size of the offering, the number of geographic markets in which the issuer may wish to offer its securities, and the mix of retail and institutional investors the issuer hopes to reach, the syndicate could range from as few as 3 to as many as 50 underwriters. In addition, there may be a selling group. This is another group of firms that assist in the distribution of the IPO but are not underwriters. Instead, they are paid on the shares they sell.

Legal Counsel for the Investment Banks (Underwriters' Counsel)

Underwriters' counsel has two specific roles in the IPO. The first, and most important, is to protect the underwriters from legal liability under the securities laws by ensuring that all material facts are fully and fairly presented in the registration statement, and that the offering complies with all federal and state securities laws and SEC and NASDR regulations. Underwriters' counsel prepares NASDR filings, responds to NASDR questions and comments, and makes any required state "blue sky" filings. Underwriters' counsel supports business due diligence by the managers, and takes primary responsibility for legal due diligence such as reviewing material contacts, employment agreements, option plans, loan agreements, corporate documents, board minutes, and intellectual property rights. Underwriters' counsel also assists in drafting the prospectus and registration materials and in highlighting legal and business issues.

The other role of underwriters' counsel is to negotiate the underwriting agreement with the parent, subsidiary, and any other selling shareholders and their respective legal counsels. Terms that are often negotiated include restrictions on the sale of stock following the IPO by significant shareholders (lockups) and any agreements with other shareholders for selling shares in the IPO.

Underwriters' counsel will also have primary responsibility to organize the closing of the IPO and make payment to the subsidiary and selling shareholders of the proceeds of the IPO. An underwriters' counsel will typically earn from $100,000 to $750,000 on an IPO depending on its size and complexity. The underwriters pay for underwriters' counsel.

THE REGULATORY BODIES THAT REVIEW THE IPO
The Securities and Exchange Commission (SEC)

The SEC is a federal agency that is charged by Congress with administering the federal securities laws and protecting public investors against fraud and manipulation. The focus of the federal securities laws is on ensuring full and fair disclosure. Offers of securities (the solicitation of a sale) and sales must be registered with the SEC unless a specific exemption applies. The SEC does not take a position on the investment merits of an IPO. Instead, the SEC reviews the registration statement to see that all appropriate information has been disclosed, and issues a comment letter detailing its questions, issues, and desired changes. After the SEC receives responses to its comment letter, it will often create one or more additional rounds of comments. Once the SEC is satisfied with the disclosures, and also that all required regulatory filings have been submitted, and the NASDR has issued a "no objections" letter on the underwriters' compensation, the SEC will accede to the issuer's request to declare the registration statement effective, permitting the sale of shares to investors in the IPO.

The National Association of Securities Dealers Regulation (NASDR)

The NASDR reviews the fairness and the terms of underwriters' compensation on all IPOs, not just those listed on the Nasdaq. The SEC will not declare an IPO effective until the NASD has concluded its review and issued a letter expressing "no objections" to the proposed compensation and arrangements. Excessive underwriting compensation is most often an issue when a manager of the IPO has also participated in a recent private placement of subsidiary stock. Any profit on the investment, defined as the difference between the price paid and the proposed

IPO price, may be included by the NASD in underwriters' compensation. If any of the underwriters of the IPO have participated in a recent financing by the subsidiary, this issue should be flagged.

Various State Securities Administrators

There are provisions for review by individual states of securities sold within a state when the shares will not trade on an exempt market. These are known as blue sky laws. Exempt markets include the major national stock exchanges and Nasdaq. State review is not an issue with most quality IPOs, as these are almost always listed on an exempt exchange. In a few states, the state securities regulator still examines IPO filings. Compliance with blue sky laws is the responsibility of underwriters' counsel, but the cost is paid by the subsidiary.

Various Industry-Specific Regulatory Agencies at the State and Federal Level

Many industries are regulated by state and federal agencies that may review IPO offerings of a subsidiary operating in that industry. Such regulatory bodies include state public utilities, banking and insurance commissions, the Federal Communications Commission, federal banking regulators, and the Department of Defense.

THE STOCK MARKETS ON WHICH THE SUBSIDIARY WILL LIST ITS STOCK
Exchanges and Markets

There are two primary markets on which to list SER shares: the Nasdaq national market and the NYSE. The American Stock Exchange is no longer widely used for SER listings. Each exchange has its own listing, reporting, and governance requirements for listed companies. Each has merits and disadvantages as a choice for the listing.

Nasdaq Market Makers

The Nasdaq national market is an electronic market of competing market makers that use their own capital to buy and sell the stocks they trade. Each market maker trading a stock competes for customer orders by displaying buy and sell quotations. In theory, there is a liquid and competitive market for all Nasdaq listed stocks, but in practice this only applies to larger-capitalization, actively traded companies. Nasdaq market makers will usually not commit capital to buy or sell significant positions in most stocks without knowing they have a matching order from a buyer or seller. As a result, the market in many Nasdaq stocks is fairly illiquid for a large buyer or seller.

NYSE and ASE Specialists

The NYSE and ASE use an agency auction market system. A specialist is a firm assigned by the stock exchange to make a market in each listed stock. The responsibility of the specialist is to ensure that there is a fair and orderly market in its assigned stocks. The specialist is required to use its capital to bridge temporary imbalances of supply and demand. The quality of the markets made by different specialist firms varies greatly among the firms. Some specialists are very good; others are a nightmare. On the NYSE, it is now possible to pick a specialist from among several names presented by the exchange. On the ASE, it is possible to nominate a desired specialist firm. There has been considerable consolidation among the specialist firms and only a few significant ones are left.

The Right Exchange for the Subsidiary

Selecting the right exchange depends on the subsidiary's expected capitalization, the market of its peers, and its industry. While the parent may be listed on the NYSE, this may not be the right choice for the subsidiary. The parent should look at where companies comparable to the subsidiary are listed. Today the Nasdaq is the exchange chosen by most new SER IPO companies. However, the author believes that there will be increased interest in the NYSE in the future.

Although Nasdaq IPO listings consistently outpaced NYSE IPO listings for more than a decade, this has changed, as illustrated by Exhibit 20–1.

This is due partly to the falloff in the number of growth company IPOs. A *Wall Street Journal* article in April 2002 noted that "The New York Stock Exchange—not the Nasdaq Stock Market—has had 16 of the 24 major underwritten initial public offerings this year. It is a rare time that the Big Board can cite dominance in new stock issues by sheer numbers. But the kinds of companies that are listing nowadays play into some of the NYSE's strengths. They are more-mature companies, either at or near profitability, in fairly stable businesses."[5]

However, this change may also reflect a reassessment of the relative merits of the two exchanges. The reasons for this include the fact that the Nasdaq is still something of a "Wild West," meaning there is increased volatility and inexplicable moves by shares traded on the Nasdaq. As well, when a Nasdaq-listed company undertakes a follow-on public offering of stock, under SEC rules, the managers and members of a syndicate must stop making a market in advance of the offering for a limited period (known as "stepping out of the box"). This usually results in a fall in the stock price just as the offering is being priced. Also, the NYSE, under Richard Grasso's leadership, is finally serious about marketing to emerging companies.

As well, in the past, the managers of an IPO made more money on a Nasdaq-listed stock because they would be market makers and make trading profits following the IPO. On an NYSE stock, the specialist did the trading and made the profit. This imbalance resulted in some bias toward Nasdaq listings of IPOs, but this is no longer true, as institutional investors have squeezed margins in many

E X H I B I T   20–1

IPO Listings by Exchange and Market

Year	1999	2000	2001	2002*
NYSE				
NYSE-listed IPOs	38	22	29	17
Dollar amount of IPOs in billions	$27.1	$23.5	$31.2	$12.2
Percent of number of IPOs	8.0%	6.4%	39.7%	51.5%
Percent of dollar amount of IPOs	40.8%	42.5%	80.6%	89.7%
Nasdaq				
Nasdaq-listed IPOs	438	323	54	16
Dollar amount of IPOs in billions	$39.1	$37.2	$7.5	$1.4
Percent of number of IPOs	72.0%	93.6%	60.3%	48.5%
Percent of dollar amount of IPOs	59.2%	57.5%	19.4%	10.3%

*Through May 31.

Source: Dealogic

stocks. IPO managers now have less incentive to promote a Nasdaq listing than in the past.

SUMMARY

This section has taken a very comprehensive look at the role of each issuer of IPO stock including the parent, the subsidiary, and current shareholders. It also detailed the parties that support each of the issuers during the IPO process and provided some general guidance about what to look for when selecting those parties. Chapter 21 will take an in-depth look at the investment bank selection process.

SELECTING THE INVESTMENT BANKERS

Today, there is considerable and justified mistrust of investment bankers. Some of the most prestigious investment banks in the past five years squandered reputations for trustworthiness carefully built over generations of good service in the pursuit of short-term profits. The purpose of this chapter is not to chronicle abuses; the objective is to give constructive guidance on how parents and subsidiaries should approach Wall Street.

INTRODUCTION

Collectively, the subsidiary and the parent select the investment bank to manage the IPO. As we will see later in the chapter, not only is this an extremely important decision, it is also very challenging, as the parent and the subsidiary may have different selection criteria. In the end, however, the most important criterion is the investment bank's ability—and willingness—to support the newly public company and its stock in the aftermarket. The purpose of this chapter, therefore, is to thoroughly walk readers through the selection process and explain how the investment bank is compensated so that issuers can use this knowledge to keep the bank motivated and focused throughout the process and in the aftermarket.

This chapter and those that follow it will look at ways to ensure that a transaction is conducted for the best interests of the parent and the subsidiary rather than those of Wall Street.

In recent years, the pressure at many investment banks to produce business has been so intense that it is very hard for investment bankers not to focus solely on maximizing short-term revenues. This is even more true in 2002 when Wall Street is cutting so many jobs. In this environment, the parent has to work very hard to ensure that its objectives come first in any dealings with Wall Street. An

IPO creates a multi-million-dollar payday for Wall Street. It is up to the parent to ensure that this money is used to encourage wide support and sponsorship for the subsidiary after the IPO and that right types of investors for the subsidiary are favored in the allocation of shares in the IPO. It simply will not happen if left to the discretion of today's Wall Street deal makers.

BENEFITS OF USING AN INVESTMENT BANK

That said, almost all quality IPOs are underwritten by investment banks, which are also known as underwriters. While theoretically an issuer could raise funds on its own from the public, investment banks have the distribution channels to reach a broader group of investors and the expertise to make the process more efficient. Investment banks also add credibility and risk capital to the IPO. Along with the importance of this sponsorship, research coverage helps develop a liquid after-market for trading shares.

THE INVESTMENT BANKING UNIVERSE

Because investment banks are integral to a successful IPO, it is important to understand some basic facts about the industry today. The investment banking world is in disarray and is consolidating. The industry is under assault from all sides. In 2002, many firms faced hundreds of class action lawsuits arising from the failed Internet and telecommunications deals of the late 1990s, IPO allocation abuses and research conflicts, investigations by state attorneys general and the SEC into a host of questionable practices, scrutiny by Congress and the press, and the lost confidence of investors. This traumatic process is not ending but will continue for several more years as more scandals are unearthed and then publicized. At the same time, the industry is suffering a dramatic decline in revenues resulting from the end of the great merger wave and frantic IPO activity of the late 1990s, declining trading volumes, and lower commissions.

As if this was not enough, the industry is also suffering the disruptive after-effects of a number of mergers and acquisitions that took place within the last five years. Many investment banks were purchased, with unsatisfactory outcomes in most cases. As a result, there are today only a limited number of investment banks available as serious choices to manage an IPO, and soon there may well be fewer still.

There is a strong possibility that these pressures will produce further consolidation. There is also a strong likelihood that the current organizational structure of investment banks will change significantly under regulator pressure.

THE INTERNAL STRUCTURE OF AN INVESTMENT BANK CREATES CONFLICT

The professionals at a full-service investment bank serve three distinct constituencies with very different agendas: the corporations that are selling shares in the IPO, called *clients;* the investors in equity securities (individuals and institutions), who are called *customers;* and the firm itself, which requires revenues to pay salaries. There are inevitable and irreconcilable conflicts and tensions in serving all these constituencies at once.

This situation is compounded by the fact that investment banks are structured in such a way that different departments within a bank support these three different constituencies. Let's look at each of these divisions in more detail.

Corporate Finance Bankers

Within the investment bank, the corporate finance professionals (known as *bankers*) represent the corporate client in the IPO and are the primary interface for the parent and subsidiary with the investment banking firm. When the author first started in the industry at the old First Boston Corporation, the senior investment bankers there viewed themselves as trusted intermediaries and advisors providing capital for well-screened companies and offering quality securities to investors. The large fees in the M&A boom of the mid-1980s permanently changed the culture in the corporate finance area at this and other large firms from one where the only question was "What is the right thing to do for the client" to one where the only question is "What transaction has the biggest fee for us?" In the late 1980s, the transaction culture spread to the capital markets area of the investment banks as the growth of complex derivative securities, the relaxation of the SEC Rule 144, and the increasing use of high-yield securities all brought the capital markets area into a daily sales relationship with corporate clients. Finally in the 1990s, the research area was brought into the transaction culture with the boom in equities. This mentality is exacerbated by the lack of training of younger bankers in general finance. The way to maximize personal income at most firms in recent years was to become a narrow specialist. Many specialists are most comfortable promoting solutions employing their specialty. Others simply do not know about alternatives. For example, it often seems that the solution to all issues proposed by an M&A banker is some M&A transaction—divest, acquire, merge.

While only a few bankers are to be relied on for good advice on whether to undertake a transaction, what transaction to undertake, or how to ensure the parent's objectives are met, most bankers are skilled at executing transactions. That is the role for which they should be used.

Capital Markets Professionals

The capital markets professionals, consisting of the sales, syndication, and trading areas, represent the buyers of securities.

To capital markets professionals, each transaction is a *trade* to be executed for the benefit of the revenues of the capital markets group. Increasing that revenue comes from pleasing the buyers, who, in turn, reward the capital markets group with greater business. In a normal environment, there is a natural and usually healthy tension between the bankers and capital market professionals. For example, in an IPO, the corporate client generally wants a fair price for the shares it sells, while the buyers always want the lowest price. The corporate client wants the stock in the IPO placed only with quality long-term investors, while the capital markets professionals want to disproportionately reward their best customers, the active traders, who are not good long-term holders but generate massive commissions. In a well-executed IPO, the bankers representing the corporate client and the capital markets professionals representing the buyers negotiate a reasonable balance that gives the corporate client a fair price and predominantly good holders while allowing the buyers a reasonable profit and placing some of the shares with traders. However, this mechanism clearly broke down in the 1990s as other agendas intervened.

Research Analysts

The third group within the investment bank involved in IPOs is equity research professionals, known as *analysts*. The primary job of research professionals is to provide stock investors with advice on which stocks to buy and sell. Because of their industry expertise, they may also provide corporate managers with advice on mergers and financing options. As of this writing, these are tormented individuals. The job of a research analyst was already among the most difficult in the investment bank. It has become significantly harder in the past few years. Research is a cost center within an investment bank. It earns no direct revenues. The pay of most research analysts at a typical investment bank has come, in the past decade, primarily from two sources. These are analysts' contribution to the revenues earned by the corporate finance area from deals such as IPOs, mergers, and advisory assignments and only to a lesser degree from revenues earned by the capital markets area from brokerage commissions and trading profits in the analyst's stocks. In some firms, the asset management area also contributes to research revenues from the fees it earns managing money.

The equities research area of investment banks did not play a large role in the lucrative merger boom of the 1980s. Cash deals financed with high-yield and bank debt drove that boom. As a result, the principal beneficiaries within the investment banks were the merger kings and bond traders. In that period, American corporations did not issue much equity, and stock options, while used, were not issued excessively. As well, with the exception of some brief moments of activity, such as in 1983, growth stocks had not been a hot area since the "Nifty Fifty" collapsed in the early 1970s. An aging and declining number of well-trained and highly principled equity research analysts toiled in relative obscurity for relatively low pay through the 1980s. These analysts saw their role as providing quality research to investors. While research analysts did help out corporate finance from time to time, research at many firms for investment banking clients was even published with a different header color prominently worded "Corporate Finance Research" as a notice to investors. When the stock market took off in the 1990s and the focus of investment banks turned with a vengeance to the lucrative business of issuing and trading stocks, analysts moved from the wings to center stage. Certain research analysts had the ability to promote stocks. From the perspective of the venture capitalists looking to cash out of portfolio companies at high prices and of senior corporate managers compensated primarily with stock options, the ability of an analyst to move stocks to higher prices was the key differentiator among competing investment banks. Research analysts became the most important players in the investment banking business; they were the star athletes.

The more promotional private equity investors coveted the sponsorship of the less principled analysts and investment banks and made a willingness to promote the stock their only selection criterion in choosing IPO managers. The only concern of these private equity investors was that the stock stayed up long enough for them to get out with a huge profit from what they were fully aware was actually a worthless investment. Some corporate managers with large option positions were also believers in this new system. Smaller investors, of course, still had faith in the objectivity of analysts and the integrity of the brand-name investment banks.

Since 2000, the wheels have come off the two primary revenue sources that supported the research area. Deals are running at a fraction of their pace in the boom years; revenues from sales and trading are also well below their boom levels. The days of star analysts are over for these reasons alone, at least for a time.

But at the same time, investment banks are coming under great outside pressure to reform their research practices. What this will mean is still not clear at the time of this writing. In the author's view, proposals to completely separate research from investment banking—while in theory the solution to many of the abuses—may, depending on the implementation, actually be counter to the interests of investors and many companies. Commissions and trading revenues alone are so squeezed today that they cannot support the level of research expense at most firms. If completely separated from investment banking revenues, the research areas must shrink considerably. They will do this by focusing solely on the higher-volume stocks that generate the bulk of commission and trading revenue. In that case, smaller companies and companies with lower turnover in their stocks will lose research coverage. Investors will then have fewer resources to find out about these companies. It is not at all clear that stand-alone research boutiques would survive in any case. Sanford Bernstein, held up as a model, has a large asset management business to defray the costs of its research effort.

INVESTMENT BANK PLAYERS IN THE IPO WORLD

A number of investment banks are capable of managing an IPO. These range from the major international investment banks to smaller firms. However, within this universe, a very limited number of firms are consistently the lead managers and comanagers of most quality IPOs.

The investment banking universe that is specifically relevant to IPOs consists of the following firms, as detailed in Exhibit 21–1. This is a subjective categorization and some firms would argue with their noninclusion or their placement.

In addition to these firms, there are smaller firms focused on various industries that are well-regarded within that industry such as Keefe, Bruyette, & Woods for banks; Sandler, O'Neill & Partners for financial services; Fox-Pitt, Kelton for insurance; Simmons & Company for oil service; and Gerard Klauer for communications.

Investment Banking Players

Large firms also known as the "special bracket"
CS First Boston (owned by Crédit Suisse Group)
Goldman Sachs
Lehman Brothers
Merrill Lynch
Morgan Stanley Dean Witter
Salomon Smith Barney (owned by Citigroup)

Commercial banks and financial conglomerates that purchased equity-oriented investment banks in the late 1990s and 2000
BankAmerica—*Montgomery*
Canadian Imperial Bank of Commerce—*Oppenheimer*
Deutsche Bank—*Alex. Brown*
J.P. Morgan Chase— *Hambrecht & Quist*
Royal Bank of Canada—*Wessels, Arnold & Henderson*
Société Générale—*Cowen*
US Bancorp—*Piper Jaffray*

Some of the more active independent specialty firms
Adams, Harkness & Hill
Allen
Friedman Billings
Jefferies
Lazard Freres
Needham
SoundView
Thomas Weisel Partners

Significant national firms
Bear Stearns
Prudential Securities
UBS Securities

Some of the more active regional retail firms
A.G. Edwards (St. Louis)
Legg Mason (Baltimore)
Morgan Keegan (Memphis)
Raymond James (St. Petersburg)
Stephens (Little Rock)
Wachovia (Richmond)
William Blair (Chicago)

The criteria used in the selection of the investment banks for the IPO of the subsidiary may differ among the parent, the subsidiary's management, and any outside private equity investors. The parent may have its own long-standing investment bank relationships with firms that it trusts. It may also be under pressure from its commercial banks to use their investment banking affiliates. The subsidiary's management will be looking for firms that will provide them with advice and counsel during and after the IPO process and will stay involved in the long term. The private equity investors often want more promotionally oriented firms that will allow them to sell or distribute their shares at a good profit. An understanding of these different perspectives is important, particularly when private equity investors are involved, because there is a tendency to defer to them as experts on Wall Street.

TYPE OF INVESTMENT FIRMS MOST OFTEN INVOLVED IN IPOs

There are several types of investment banks that are most active in IPOs. They are the very large special-bracket firms, which dominate the IPO business as they do almost all other areas of investment banking today, and a limited number of full-service smaller firms. Increasingly active are a few of the larger regional retail firms. The remaining smaller national firms manage IPOs from time to time. Let's look at each of these in more detail.

Special-Bracket Firms

The special-bracket firms (also known as the *bulge bracket*) are the very large investment banks that focus on serving large national and multinational corporations. These firms have been gaining market share throughout the past 20 years and now dominate almost all sectors of the investment banking industry. They offer a full range of services worldwide.

Increasingly, the large corporations that these firms serve are demanding that investment banks provide relatively low-margin loans and bridge financing as a condition for obtaining the more attractive investment banking business. The corollary is also true. While tying investment banking to commercial lending is illegal, the commercial banks that own investment banks have been more than assertive in letting existing and new borrowers know that they are expected to use the banks' higher-margin investment banking services as well. The demand by clients for loans and the pressure by banks for borrowers to use their investment banking services, if it continues, is likely to cause other special-bracket firms to consider mergers with giant commercial banks.

Two of the special-bracket firms, Morgan Stanley and Goldman Sachs, have had a long-standing commitment to equities in general and have stayed the course in this area through up and down IPO markets. Most of the top-quality IPOs are lead-managed by one of these two firms. Credit Suisse First Boston was traditionally not that active in equities but made a push into the IPO area in the late

1990s. It became the darling of the more promotional venture capitalists. It developed very close relationships with the less reputable momentum hedge funds that took stocks to nosebleed prices. Salomon, a firm traditionally focused on debt and trading, became a leader in the telecom IPO area, but at great cost to stock investors in the ensuing collapse of this sector. Of the special-bracket firms, the reputations of CS First Boston and Salomon were, perhaps, the most damaged in the aftermath of the bubble. Merrill Lynch has shown a repeated pattern of cutting back when the revenues disappear. Lehman was a leading player in the IPO area in the 1980s and early 1990s. It went quiet (perhaps with great sense) in the mid-1990s but appears now to be reemerging as a stronger player.

Advantages of Using a Special-Bracket Firm

There are many advantages to using a special-bracket firm. These include the following:

- *The parent is often comfortable with the investment bank.* In many cases, the parent has a special-bracket investment bank that performs splendidly in meeting its needs. The use of the parent's traditional investment bank for a subsidiary SER IPO allows the parent to maintain existing relationships and provides considerable comfort to the parent that the IPO will receive high-level attention and that it will get straight information about the IPO.

- *Prestige.* There is no question that the right special-bracket firm adds prestige to the subsidiary's IPO. This is often particularly helpful if the subsidiary has business overseas and wishes to impress European and Asian customers. In the author's view, the two firms that most add prestige to an IPO are Morgan Stanley and Goldman Sachs.

- *Broad product range.* Special-bracket firms have many capable specialist resources that may be valuable to the subsidiary. These include assistance with project finance, foreign exchange, debt issuance, and execution of various derivative transactions. Special-bracket firms may also have greater merger deal flow because of their relationships with large companies. This will help the subsidiary if it has a growth-through-acquisition strategy.

- *Geographical reach.* The special-bracket firms have operations worldwide. Should the subsidiary need introductions, or if it is undertaking a transaction in an area other than the United States, a special-bracket firm is able to staff the project and give advice on local laws and regulations.

- *Relationships.* Special-bracket firms have relationships and contacts with large corporations that may prove useful as introductions to strategic partnerships.

Disadvantages of Using a Special-Bracket Firm

The special-bracket firms usually serve the needs of a large parent exceptionally well. However, they are often not the right choice to work with a subsidiary. The parent's special-bracket investment bank may not be right for the subsidiary, or, as is often the case, the parent and subsidiary will do better in the IPO if the special-bracket firm is teamed in the IPO with a smaller firm. Much depends on the size of the subsidiary and its industry. The special-bracket firms are structured to give the most attention to large clients who use many services. If the subsidiary is large, it will clearly benefit from a relationship with a special-bracket investment bank. However, if it is smaller, the right choice may be different.

- When business is slow, the special-bracket firms will chase small transactions. These firms have a history of losing interest in smaller companies when there were no imminent transactions or the subsidiary stumbles (see the case study of Palm in Chapter 9).
- Smaller clients suffer disproportionately from the high staff turnover at the special-bracket firms, as they are not priority clients.
- Smaller transactions tend to be assigned to junior staff who are inexperienced and, on not a few occasions, are surprisingly arrogant.
- The special-bracket firms are structured to serve the needs of large and sophisticated corporations. The professionals at these firms are often narrow product specialists. Their job is to pitch transaction ideas and to execute these with great skill. This means that they are often not good at giving objective advice on whether a transaction is appropriate, whether a different transaction might be better, or, as is often the case, whether no transaction at all is the best option. The parent often has a large and experienced staff of its own to sift through the "ideas of the week" presented by investment bankers. The subsidiary may not have the expertise or the time.

Many parents are competently served at the parent level by one or more special-bracket firms but disappointed with the work done by these firms with smaller subsidiaries.

Full-Service Smaller Firms

A group of smaller full-service investment banks first emerged in the 1960s that focused solely on equity securities, primarily those of growth companies. These firms are also known as *specialty* investment banks. While small, these firms are not boutiques. The smaller full-service firms have banking, capital markets, and research capabilities. In contrast, the boutiques specialize in a single service such as M&A or stock trading. At that time, the large investment banks were focused on large companies and turned up their noses at company upstarts such as Intel. It was not until the early 1990s that most of the large firms became serious about equities. A particular group of smaller full-service firms made their names in providing services to emerging growth industries such as technology, biotechnology, health care, and specialty retailing. A major factor in the emergence of the smaller full-service firms was the concurrent emergence of a limited number of large institutional investors as the dominant players in the equity markets. This concentration allows the relatively small but focused sales forces of the smaller full-service firms to be every bit as effective as those of the giant but general-purpose distribution systems of the large firms in selling growth equities.

Until the mid-1990s, the relationship between the smaller full-service firms and the special-bracket firms was symbiotic. The large firms were not focused on equities, were busy elsewhere, and did not have major outreach efforts in this area. The smaller firms had the outreach and relationships to private companies and their investors. The smaller firms would lead-manage most IPOs but would feed the most important IPOs to the special-bracket firms to lead-manage. The special-bracket firms welcomed these referrals and supported the involvement of the smaller firms' offer of a generous participation in the economics of the IPO to the smaller firm. In the mid-1990s, the special-bracket firms greatly expanded their own outreach efforts to private companies and their investors, eliminating the origination role of the smaller firms. However, the special-bracket firms still tended to be very selective, and there were plenty of opportunities for the smaller firms. By 2000, the special-bracket firms had the marketing infrastructure in place to directly chase most IPOs. Also, they were willing to undertake IPOs for companies of less than top quality. Therefore, not very much was left for the smaller firms. These were reduced to secondary comanager roles on most IPOs with ever thinner economics.

There is no question that the competitive position of the smaller full-service firms as a group continued to decline in 2001 and the first half of 2002. Partly, this reflects the changed characteristics of IPOs in 2002. IPOs in this period were dominated by large carve-outs of mature companies, a special-bracket competence. It also reflects the turmoil and disruption in the smaller firms after mergers with large banks. However, mostly it reflects a changed competitive dynamic in the industry. Some of this dynamic is a temporary consequence of overcapacity in the large firms as they lag in adjusting headcount to lower revenues. However, there may no longer be the supportable market for smaller full-service firms below and alongside the special-bracket investment banks that existed even five years ago. What factors could change this dynamic? One is that a prolonged downturn in the equity markets causes some or the entire special bracket to lose interest in the equities area. Another is that a reorganization required by regulators makes it unprofitable for the special-bracket firms to do business with any but the largest corporations.

Most of the smaller full-service firms were bought within the past five years by international and regional commercial banks and other large financial institutions. These firms have not fared well and have all but disappeared within their parents or been closed. Only a few smaller full-service firms still remain independent. Most of these are losing money and will need to rethink their business.

The smaller full-service firms divide broadly into three orientations: trading, research, and advisory. These distinctions did get somewhat blurred in the late 1990s, as many firms expanded their strategy, but they still define the underlying character of the firms. Thomas Weisel and Jefferies are leading firms with a trading focus; SoundView and Adams Harkness, a research focus; and Lazard and Needham, an advisory focus.

The stock promotion system practiced at some investment banks in the second half of the 1990s and 2000 to support distributions and sales of public stocks by private equity firms and corporate executives was described by a senior executive at one of the leading trading firms as follows: "First, the firm and its partners would buy a position in the stock. Then the 'A' list of favored hedge funds and 'friends of the firm' would get the whisper and buy positions in the stock. Then the trading firm's formidable stock promotion machine would go into high gear. At the same time the company would put out favorable press releases. Momentum would quickly build in the stock attracting less sophisticated investors. The stock would run from $20 per share to $80 per share. Along the way, the firm and its partners, the favored 'A' list investors, and the private equity firms or management would sell their positions. The stock would then collapse, leaving the employees of the company to pick up the prices. The author notes that the trading-oriented firms will object to this characterization and claim to be very relationship oriented.

In contrast, the primary focus of the research firms is on providing institutional investors with quality research and quality executions of trades. Among these are SoundView and Adams Harkness. These firms do fine research and focus on institutions that are longer-term holders. Other smaller full-service firms are most focused on quality financial advice. These include Lazard Freres, Needham, and Allen. These firms may not admit it, but they do not excel at promoting stocks and therefore are not the usual choices of promotionally minded private equity investors. They do offer the subsidiary and parent superior advisory capabilities and adequate capital markets capabilities.

For a look at the changing competitive position of the top smaller full-service firms and the special-bracket firms over a 10-year period, see Exhibit 21–2.

The increasing concentration of IPO activity into fewer hands is clearly apparent, as is the implosion of the smaller full-service firms in 2002. The market share of a few special-bracket firms has gone from 17.4 percent of lead-managed IPOs in 1990 to 60 percent in the first quarter of 2002. In the 1990s the special-bracket firms squeezed out the national and regional firms. In the 2000s they squeezed out the smaller full-service firms as well.

However, a few smaller full-service firms are still thriving because they did not become overly dependent on IPOs and kept their expenses under control.

Advantages of a Working with a Smaller Full-Service Firm

There are some key advantages in working with a smaller full-service firm:

- *Senior-level attention.* Having access to the senior management team is a key benefit companies gain when working with a smaller full-service firm. Access to the top level is often invaluable, especially with a difficult transaction.

- *Attention between transactions.* The smaller full-service firms tend to be more committed to servicing smaller clients between transactions.

- *Industry focus.* The smaller full-service firms often have the most expertise in specific industry segments. They also tend to be the first to develop expertise in emerging sectors.

- *Objective advice.* The better-trained and more senior bankers at the better of the smaller full-service firms are often good generalist advisors. They provide good objective advice on transactions.

E X H I B I T   21–2

Special-Bracket Firms Come to Dominate the Industry

Selected Specialty Firm Lead-Managed IPOs					
Name of the firm in 1990	Alex. Brown & Sons	Hambrecht & Quist	Montgomery Securities	Robertson, Coleman & Stephens	Total
Name of the firm in 2002	Deutsche Bank	J.P. Morgan Chase H&Q	BankAmerica Securities	FleetBoston Robertson Stephens Closed in 2002	
Lead-managed IPOs in 1990	15	3	0	6	24
As a percentage of total IPOs	9.7%	1.9%	0.0%	3.9%	15.5%
Lead-managed IPOs in 2000	30	29	9	33	101
As a percentage of total IPOs	7.7%	7.4%	2.3%	8.4%	25.8%
Lead-managed IPOs in Q1 2002	0	0	0	0	0
As a percentage of total IPOs	0.0%	0.0%	0.0%	0.0%	0.0%
Selected Special-Bracket Firm Lead-Managed IPOs					
	Morgan Stanley	Goldman Sachs	CS First Boston	Merrill Lynch	Total
Lead-managed IPOs in 1990	7	9	5	6	27
As a percentage of total IPOs	4.5%	5.8%	3.2%	3.9%	17.4%
Lead-managed IPOs in 2000	38	48	56	30	172
As a percentage of total IPOs	9.7%	12.3%	14.3%	8.4%	44.7%
Lead-managed IPOs in Q1 2002	3	2	3	4	12
As a percentage of total IPOs	15.0%	10.0%	15.0%	20.0%	60.0%
Does not include IPOs of closed-end funds and investment trusts.					
Source: CommScan Equidesk Data & Software					

Disadvantages of a Smaller Full-Service Firm

There are also some disadvantages in working with a smaller full-service firm:

• *Limited product range.* The smaller full-service firms have only a few arrows in their product quivers. They are focused primarily on equity and equity-related (e.g., convertible debt) securities. There are a range of products such as commercial paper, derivatives, and foreign exchange that a company may wish access to from time to time. Most smaller full-service firms either do not offer these products or are only marginal players. The specialty firms that are now part of large financial conglomerates have many product offerings and capabilities available within the parent. However, the actual delivery of products from sister divisions has often been spotty, and they are not necessarily the best vendors available for these products.

- *Limited geographical reach.* The smaller full-service firms are essentially domestic organizations, although some of the specialty firms are now part of financial organizations with international capabilities. However, the delivery of international services by the smaller firms has usually not been competitive. There is no question that the special-bracket firms have considerably greater international capabilities than do the smaller firms.

Regional Retail Firms

In contrast to most of the industry, a few of the quality regional retail firms are thriving. These firms have always been good in a supporting role to place IPOs with long-term retail investors. Note that even though some of these firms are growing and becoming national in scope, they do not come close to matching the size or resources of the special-bracket firms. For this reason, they are being treated together with the specialty firms, which they resemble in the size and scope of their corporate finance capabilities and research capabilities. Recently a few of the regional retail firms are making a concerted effort to emerge as the heirs to the imploding specialty banks with focused equity efforts targeted at specific industries. They may well succeed in this effort. These firms are increasingly looking like the specialty firms in their capabilities.

Smaller National Firms

The smaller national firms have all but faded away under the onslaught of the special-bracket firms. There used to be a large number of these firms such as Paine Webber; Donaldson, Lufkin & Jenrette; Dean Witter; Kidder Peabody; and Smith Barney. These all merged. The few remaining smaller national firms, other than Bear Stearns, appear to be searching for a role. Only Bear Stearns is still active in IPOs.

Foreign Banks

From time to time, the large foreign commercial banks have made a push to be major factors in the U.S. investment banking business, as they are in their home countries, and compete head to head with the U.S. special-bracket firms. These efforts have been unsuccessful so far. Recently, several foreign banks seem to be making inroads by focusing on smaller growth companies in specific industries. These banks include Société General, Royal Bank of Canada, and UBS.

The foreign banks also make a push from time to time to comanage U.S. IPOs by claiming massive placement power offshore. However, today the principal overseas buyers of U.S. IPOs are very well covered by even the smaller U.S. investment banks because there are actually not that many of them and they are easy to identify. As well, outside of IPOs by large and established household names, there is not widespread interest in U.S. IPOs in Europe, and less still in Asia. If the IPO is very large and the subsidiary's name well known overseas, there is a good case for involving foreign banks to help place the IPO. If the parent is an overseas entity, it may have important relationships of its own that it does not wish to slight and will find a place for these firms in the IPO. With moderation, this is fine.

Now that we have gained an understanding of the various types of investment banks from which an issuer can choose to manage an IPO, we will now review the actual manager selection process and the importance of optimizing the working relationship with the manager—or managers, if more than one are selected.

OPTIMIZING THE RELATIONSHIP WITH THE MANAGERS

At its best, a relationship with a manager of an IPO is long term, trusting, and close. The parent and the subsidiary will need to work closely with the managers in the preparatory stages of the IPO, through the completion of the offering, on subsequent public offerings, and on future mergers and acquisitions. A good working relationship is therefore important, and the management of the subsidiary should be involved in the selection process for two reasons: first, to ensure that there is chemistry between the managers and the management of the subsidiary; second, to ensure that the managers understand that they are also working for the subsidiary and not just the parent.

APPROACHING POTENTIAL MANAGERS

The process of selecting managers is a two-way street. A potential lead or comanager may not be interested in the subsidiary's IPO, most commonly because of lack of industry expertise or research coverage within the firm of the subsidiary's market sector. Other reasons include a negative or less-than-enthusiastic assessment of the subsidiary's business, prospects, state of development or management, or unresolved due diligence issues. The potential manager may also have conflicts with existing clients in the same industry or disagreement over structure and evaluation. And, of course, an unfavorable IPO market or other offerings in the firm's pipeline might impair its ability to successfully distribute the IPO or to develop investor interest in it. Because the managers are generally compensated only if the IPO is completed, potential managers will not want to commit time and resources unless they are reasonably confident that the offering will be completed. Other issues include the size of the IPO and disagreement over the role or the economics offered the specific firm in the IPO.

Conducting a Manager Interview Process

Once the parent and the subsidiary have prepared a reasonably short list of potential lead and comanagers, they should interview the parties and ask them to make presentations. There are two ways to interview investment bankers. The first is to interface with one firm at a time. The other approach is to have a "beauty contest" by interviewing a number of investment banks concurrently.

If the offering is small in dollar size, or the subsidiary is early in its development, or the market for IPOs is not buoyant, securing the support of one manager at a time is the best process to ensure that the IPO is well structured and proceeds. In contrast, if the IPO is large in dollar size, the subsidiary attractive, and the IPO market strong, an openly competitive process will work very well to create greater interest, more responsiveness, and firmer commitments by potential managers.

As parent and subsidiaries work through the selection process, they should not use valuation as a selection criterion. The initial valuations of an IPO early in the process by investment banks tend almost always to be on the high side and should be viewed with a large degree of skepticism.

For example, for an initial valuation, the investment bankers will usually simply take the forecasts prepared by the subsidiary and apply to them a valuation model. The bankers usually have not done the homework at that stage to do more. These forecasts are usually toned down during the IPO process after critical review. Unfortunately, prospective clients often take a high initial valuation from an investment banker as indicating that the banker is enthusiastic about the IPO.

AFTERMARKET SUPPORT: A CRUCIAL SELECTION CRITERION

The most important distinguishing factor among investment banks is not the actual execution of the IPO, which is now of similar quality across many firms, but how the subsidiary is supported by the investment bank after an IPO. Let's take a closer look at aftermarket support.

Components of Aftermarket Support

Aftermarket support has two important components: creating a liquid trading market for the stock in the aftermarket and disseminating information about the stock—and the issuer—after the IPO. In addition, it is the responsibility of the lead manager to create a selling strategy for the stock after the IPO, which may include the assumption of a market maker role by managing underwriters and syndicate members if the stock is listed on the Nasdaq market.

Another important component of aftermarket service is the ability of the firm to provide financial advisory services. The managers of the IPO should have the resources to continue to provide the subsidiary with investment banking services once it is independent. This includes obtaining additional capital as the need arises and advising on proposed mergers or acquisitions.

Factors That Contribute to Aftermarket Support

When choosing the investment banks to lead and comanage the company's IPO, the following factors should be considered.

Industry Focus

Today a primary consideration in picking an investment bank to lead-manage or comanage an IPO is the commitment, reputation, and involvement of the firm in the industry of the subsidiary. A firm that is committed and experienced with the industry is more likely to:

• Be seen as a respected information resource by investors in the industry.

• Understand the subsidiary's business.

• Add value with industry intelligence and knowledge of potential acquisitions.

• Have a sales force knowledgeable and comfortable with the industry and conversant with the investors who follow it.

• Be more committed to seeing the IPO through to completion and staying with the subsidiary through its ups and downs after the IPO.

Although the overall commitment and experience of the firm in the subsidiary's specific industry should be the primary consideration in picking an investment bank to lead-manage or comanage an IPO, the reputation of the firm's industry equity research analyst is also important. Once the IPO is distributed, the analyst is a primary interface between the subsidiary, the sales force at the investment bank, and investors. Recent events have shown the importance to institutional investors of a knowledgeable analyst who, though enthusiastic about the company, is also respected for independence.

Research Capability

At the time of writing, the role of the research areas at investment banks is in turmoil. The following discussion is relevant only should the research area continue to work with corporate finance. Certainly, this involvement will be greatly curtailed. Though the issuer has the primary responsibility for disseminating information to the public on a current basis once the IPO is distributed, an important component of developing and maintaining market interest is research analysis of the subsidiary and its industry by investment bank research analysts. Thus the manager's research department should have the resources necessary to produce that information, and it should have a reputation that commands the respect of investors—particularly institutional investors—and the financial community in general.

It is helpful to ask analysts of prospective managers for copies of their past IPO reports regarding representative companies that their firms have taken public. Consider how professionally written the reports are, whether their ratings are logical based on the information they provide, and how the reports treat any problems which arose at the company.

In many cases, the subsidiary is in too small an industry sector or is in an industry area with insufficient comparable-quality public issuers to attract dedicated research analysts. The parent and the subsidiary will then have to look at adjoining sectors for an appropriate analyst. Analysts are usually fairly versatile and they readily go into adjoining sectors. However, if the subsidiary is the only one in the area that the analyst will cover, the economics involved raise a natural concern about how committed the firm will be to providing research about the subsidiary on a continuing basis. Firms and analysts may find it inefficient to learn an entire new industry just to follow one company. Therefore, be alert as to whether the analyst really understands and covers the subsidiary's industry or is being dressed up to get the business.

It is also useful to look at whether the analyst covers companies with a market capitalization similar to the subsidiary's. An analyst who covers only very large capitalization names is probably not interested in smaller companies, while an analyst who specializes in small or mid-caps may not have a focus on larger companies. There are also some analysts whose interests are in special situations, rather than following specific companies over a long period.

The analyst will have to explain the subsidiary to investors. Is the analyst genuinely interested in the subsidiary? Is the analyst knowledgeable about the subsidiary or willing to devote the time to getting up to speed? Note that wild-eyed enthusiasm, while no doubt flattering, should raise caution flags. Such enthusiasm may only be a tool to bring in new business.

Make sure that the track record of a firm reflects the current staff at the firm; whole industry groups have left some firms and there have been many recent layoffs.

Other Selection Criteria

Stability

Look for a stable firm. Firms with high turnover are unlikely to either prosper or keep commitments to the subsidiary. Also, look for a firm that is succeeding as a business—that ensures it will be around to fulfill its promises. Historically, Wall Street has never been very good at taking a long-term perspective and subsidizing loss-making operations. These are closed or cut back. Most Wall Street firms undertook cutbacks in 2001 and 2002 to adjust to the depressed markets for equity offerings, debt, and mergers. Entire groups have been closed. These cutbacks look to be far from over. Some firms are serial exiters. They enter hot areas in good times, claim they are in for the long term, and exit yet again in a downturn.

Professionals Working on the Offering

Who is actually working on the offering? In the end, investment banking is a people business. As with law firms, much comes down to the talents, experience, and skills of the actual people working on the IPO. Bait and switch by investment banks is not unheard of as a tactic for soliciting business. The senior banker or analyst may appear for the sales pitch, but then not be seen again once the selection is made. Make sure that the people who pitch the business are the same people who will work on the offering and afterward.

Reference Checks

The parent and subsidiary management can best evaluate the investment bank's long-term commitment to clients by talking to the senior management of a representative sampling of IPOs managed by the firm. The issuer, not the investment bank, should select deals of different sizes over a number of years. In most cases senior management will be pleased to share their experiences with reference checkers, especially if these experiences have been less than satisfactory. Ask when the last comprehensive research report on the company was issued by the investment bank, when the last visit by a banker or an analyst from the firm occurred, or when firm personnel met with institutional investors not related to a live transaction. Surprisingly, a number of issuers do not extensively check prospective managers.

The references should include checking with companies that stumbled after the IPO. The true test of an investment bank is whether it stays in touch with companies that stumble, particularly those with no short-term additional revenue prospects.

Here are some questions to ask during the reference check:

• Did the manager provide you with all the services it promised?

• Did the manager make a contribution appropriate to or exceeding its relative position in the IPO?

• Did the manager provide support in the aftermarket for the stock?

• Did the manager provide other services to you after the IPO, such as financial advice? Did the bankers continue to call?

• Did the manager take you on a post-IPO road show to investors?

• If a lead manager, did it significantly reduce the proposed selling price during the registration process without adequate market changes to justify the reduction? Did it employ bait-and-switch tactics?

• If a lead manager, were you satisfied with the placement of your shares? Were they placed in good long-term hands?

• Would you use the same manager again on your IPO?

Also do reference checks with institutional investors. They are the primary consumers for the IPO. What do they think and why? Do reference checks as well with other comparably sized companies that the investment bank has worked for in the recent past.

CHOOSING COMANAGERS

As this chapter will demonstrate, there is a trend toward using multiple comanagers in the IPO process. When selecting comanagers for an IPO, parents should use the following criteria.

Research Coverage

As noted already, research coverage is important because it is a primary communications channel between the issuer and institutional investors during and following the IPO. And more managers increase the likelihood of adequate research coverage of the subsidiary following the IPO. The reasons for this are as follows:

- The economics of a research effort are such that an issuer should assume that the only investment bank research coverage that it will receive will be from the managers of the IPO. Therefore, managers of the IPO should be picked to ensure the widest possible research coverage by the appropriate analysts.

- Analysts continually change firms and industry areas; some leave the industry altogether. This creates a risk that research coverage will not continue. Therefore, it is best to hedge this risk by spreading coverage among firms as widely as possible.

Support in the Aftermarket

The primary support for most IPOs in the aftermarket comes from the IPO's managers. For this reason, more managers also increase the likelihood of adequate support following the IPO.

Banking Advice

A firm that provides good ongoing advice on financial matters but is not chosen to be lead manager may be valuable as a comanager to ensure its advice throughout the IPO process and to reward it financially for those services.

THE INVESTMENT BANK AND THE SUBSIDIARY'S COMPETITORS

A question often arises over the advisability of using an investment bank that also manages public offerings or performs advisory work for direct competitors of the subsidiary. The dilemma is that there is a declining number of investment bank alternatives, so most investment banks may be working with a competitor. As a general rule, work for a competitor is not an issue with a firm in a comanager role. However, it is an issue with a firm in a lead-manager role. It is not grounds for automatic disqualification, but it is reason for concern because the lead manager is the firm most associated with the subsidiary and it will be asked by investors which of the competitive companies it prefers more. It may also have conflicts such as which client is shown an attractive acquisition opportunity first.

ISSUER EXPECTATIONS OF INVESTMENT BANKS

After the selection process is complete, issuers need to have realistic expectations of their investment bank. Thus, let's take a look at what is reasonable and unreasonable to expect from an investment bank. Realistic expectations are that after the IPO the managers will:

• Provide research coverage promptly after the 40-day research quiet period following the IPO. After the IPO, the investment bank should issue research reports to inform the market about the company's affairs and prospects. These reports should both be periodic and appear whenever there is a significant business transaction such as an acquisition. Under new regulations, the draft report may be shown to the issuer, but without ratings, conclusions, or price targets. Of course, the relationship of investment banks to research may change greatly in the future.

• Invite the issuer to its conferences and to meet institutional investors.

• Organize investor road shows from time to time to introduce new investors to the issuer and allow one-on-one time with existing ones. As with the IPO road show, the issuer pays its own out-of-pocket expenses while on these road shows, whereas the investment bank pays for the costs of lunches and meetings.

Unrealistic expectations are that the managers will

• Proceed with the IPO if there is not investor demand for the shares.

• Guarantee a valuation in the IPO. The price per share quoted by investment bankers when soliciting IPO business or put on the cover of the preliminary prospectus is only an estimate. The actual price will be determined by what the leading institutional investors are actually willing to pay for the shares. The only exception is a *bought deal,* whereby an investment bank commits to purchase shares in a public offering at a fixed price regardless of having final buyers. However, virtually no IPOs are ever bought deals. These are largely confined to follow-on offerings for established large-capitalization stocks in great demand and where the commitment is only made immediately before the actual offering.

• Promote the stock with a "strong buy" research rating. While the research area, at least for now, should provide information for investors on a company for which the investment bank undertakes an IPO, the research analysts will come to their own determination of what rating and expectations investors should have of the stock.

• Commit serious capital to support the stock after the IPO if there are more sellers than buyers. Trading desks today will not expose themselves to the prospect of serious losses to support a stock.

DETERMINING THE FINANCIAL ARRANGEMENT WITH THE INVESTMENT BANK

As with all important financial transactions, it is critical to understand how the other party is compensated. This is particularly true of IPO compensation to investment banks, as it is generally the single largest expense in a public offering, and it tends to be fixed for any given size of IPO. The objective of the issuer should be to pay no more than the average compensation for comparably sized recent Ipos. For the investment banks, IPOs are unquestionably very profitable, but they do involve a large number of well-paid players, including professionals in corporate finance, capital markets, and equity research. There is also an implied ongoing commitment to support the stock following the IPO with expensive equity research and trading.

The NASD limits overall underwriter compensation to 10 percent of the proceeds of an IPO. (There are additional charges allowed by the NASD for expenses, and some firms charge as much as an additional 3 percent of proceeds for expenses. The underwriters are also allowed to receive warrants to purchase shares in the subsidiary after the IPO, and some firms take warrants for as much as 10 percent of the shares offered in the IPO.) There are no regulatory guidelines on underwriters' compensation below this limit. However, compensation for each size of IPO is fairly standard. Third-party data services produce exhaustive tables tabulating and recounting all the details of prior offerings including the compensation to the underwriters. The parent or subsidiary should ask each of the managers of the IPO for an analysis of the investment banking compensation on comparably sized Ipos. This should be a complete, not select, list of recent IPOs of similar size. The limited range of investment banking compensation for each type of IPO will be apparent from reviewing the list. Factors influencing underwriting compensation on a specific IPO are the difficulty of marketing the IPO and whether the IPO will appeal mainly to retail or to institutional investors. IPOs sold mainly to retail investors may have slightly higher compensation, reflecting the higher costs of this distribution channel.

HOW INVESTMENT BANKS MAKE MONEY FROM AN IPO

With a "firm commitment" (the usual for a quality IPO) type of underwriting, the underwriters do not receive a fee for placing the shares but rather are compensated by reselling discounted shares to investors that they had purchased from the issuer. This is known as a spread or *underwriting discount.* The gross spread is the numerical difference between the offering price public investors pay and the net price set by the issuer. As discussed earlier, almost all quality IPOs between $30 million and $175 million in proceeds have spreads of 7 percent.

While there is almost no price competition to date on IPO spreads, the number of managers (as comanagers) for each IPO has increased considerably in recent years, effectively reducing the compensation to any firm participating in an IPO by dividing the pie among more firms. In the 1970s, the typical IPO had only one manager; in the 1980s, two; in the 1990s, three; and today, four or more. As long as the spread is reasonable and supported by comparable data, it should not be debated. There are more important issues, including:

• The amount, identity, compensation, and role of the comanagers

• Participation of the syndicate

- Extent of the marketing program for the IPO including qualifying proposed institutional investors
- Analyst coverage of the subsidiary at each firm

How the Spread Is Divided

The agreement between the investment banks underwriting the IPO divides the gross spread in three ways.

Management Fee

The management fee, paid only to the lead and comanager(s), is typically 20 percent of the gross spread. In many investment banks, this is the amount that is credited to the corporate finance area of the firm. Some firms credit both corporate finance and capital markets with the entire gross spread received by the firm or split it evenly between the two.

Selling Concession

The selling concession is generally 60 percent of the gross spread. This goes to the capital markets area for the majority of firms, and it includes the payment to the sales professionals who sell the IPO. Institutional salespeople are typically on a base pay plus a bonus. The bonus is generally related at least in part to revenues. Retail salespeople are almost always on direct commission with a payout of up to 40 percent of the sales concession.

Underwriting Fee

The remaining 20 percent of the spread is first used to pay the expenses of the IPO incurred by the managers and for any losses on stabilizing the offering in the open market following the IPO. If there is anything left over, this is paid to all the underwriters as a fee for making a capital commitment and for incurring underwriters' liability. The lead manager remits this fee, net of the expenses of the offering, at syndicate settlement, with all underwriters on a pro rata basis of securities underwritten. Usually, there is little underwriting fee left after all the expenses, except on very large IPOs. The parties in an IPO tend to look upon IPOs as an opportunity to recapture any expenses even remotely associated with the solicitation or execution of the IPO. Therefore, participation in the underwriting syndicate, by itself, does not mean that the syndicate member will be paid much or anything. In the event that expenses exceed the underwriting fee (possible on a small IPO) or there is a later lawsuit against the underwriters for which legal and settlement costs or damages are incurred, they are billed to the syndicate members pro rata. The only way a syndicate member will make any meaningful amount from an IPO is either by receiving a sizable retention of shares to sell itself or for the lead manager to write it a check in lieu of retention shares. The number of shares that appears in the final prospectus by the name of a syndicate member in most cases is only an indication of the pro rata liability assumed by that firm, not its compensation.

Although syndicates played a much larger role in selling IPOs to investors than they do today, they can still be useful. Syndicates may be used by the parent or subsidiary to reward an investment bank for past services, add to potential research coverage, or draw on expertise in a particular area.

Forming the Syndicate

After the registration statement is filed with the SEC, the lead manager will issue invitations to other investment banking firms to participate in the underwriting syndicate. Depending on the size of the offering, the style of the lead manager, and the wishes of the issuer, the syndicate may include 2 to 20 underwriters. However, the average size of syndicates is shrinking rapidly. According to Dealogic, in 1997 the average IPO had 13.3 nonmanager syndicate members, while in 2001 it had 6.7. The concept of a syndicate is transitioning from being a large group of firms included because of a historic relationship with the lead manager to a small, focused group of firms that will assist the subsidiary after the IPO with support in the aftermarket. Syndicates have a diminishing role each year. Their future use is not certain, given the much greater number of comanagers on recent IPOs.

Each of the investment banks in the syndicate commits to underwrite a certain number of shares. However, the underwriting commitment is simply an assumption of liability and a share in any funds left, after all expenses, in the underwriting account. It has no relation to the number of shares that the syndicate member is given in the IPO to sell and on which it is then paid a selling concession. A syndicate member may ultimately be given no shares at all or far fewer shares to sell than the number it underwrites. Allocation of shares to syndicate members is at the discretion of the lead manager. In most cases very few shares are allocated to syndicate members. Ensuring that a syndicate member receives a large number of shares to sell is never an easy process. It requires the lead manager to give up substantial dollars out of its (and its comanagers') own pocket. In most cases, this is done very reluctantly.

One thing to make sure of is that senior management of the lead manager, not just the account officer, knows that a syndicate member should receive a large allocation of shares to sell in the IPO. This ensures that the capital markets group that does the actual allocations is made very aware of the preference. Often it is best to put specific instructions relating to the syndicate in writing to the lead manager.

Using the Spread as a Motivational Tool

It is in the best interest of the subsidiary to structure the financial arrangement with the investment banks so that it motivates all of the parties involved. This will help ensure that all of the investment banks support the shares of the company in the aftermarket following the IPO.

The first step in the process is determining how many managers will appear on the cover of the IPO, their respective roles as lead or comanagers, and the split of the management fee and selling concession between the various managers. The

E X H I B I T   21–3

Average Number of Firms as Managers on IPOs by Size of Offering

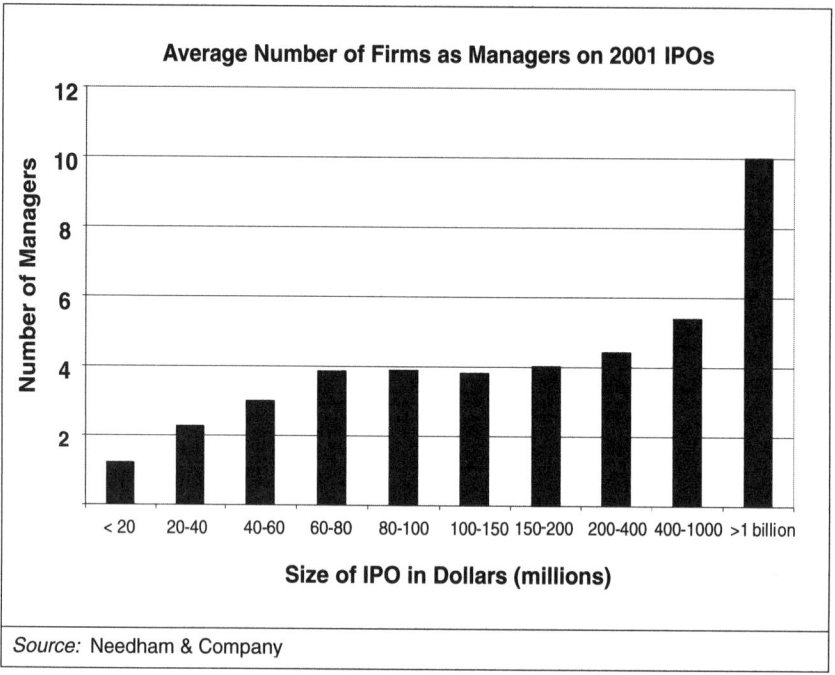

Average Number of Firms as Managers on 2001 IPOs

Source: Needham & Company

number of managers on an IPO is related to the size of the IPO. To get some sense of the ratio of managers to dollars, see Exhibit 21–3.

In March 2002, the $4.2 billion (including the Green Shoe) IPO of Travelers Property Casualty Corporation had no less than 15 comanagers.

Once the number of managers has been determined, it will be necessary for the issuer to decide how the discount will be allocated among the lead and comanagers. Years ago, investment banking was a more genteel profession and issues of economics and order were settled fairly among the managers. This is no longer true, and the parent and subsidiary must ensure that they have the final and definitive say in determining who gets what percentage of the discount. This decision should definitely not be left to the lead manager. It is not fun to get in the middle of a split discussion, but it is necessary for a successful IPO. However, the IPO outcome will be better if you tell the investment bank what the economic split will be before you commit to it. Before they are chosen, all investment banks are fairly reasonable. Once they are in the deal, they get tougher to negotiate with.

A reasonable division of the fee splits for a $100 million IPO is as follows:

- Special-bracket firm as lead manager, two smaller firms as comanagers: 50-25-25
- Special-bracket firm as lead manager, three smaller firms as comanagers: 50-20-20-10
- One smaller firm as lead and one as comanager 50-50 or 60-40
- Smaller firm as lead manager; two smaller firms as comanagers: 40-30-30
- Smaller firm as lead manager, three smaller firms as comanagers: 40-25-20-15

Prospectus Listing Can Be as Important as Spread Allocation—Almost

Larger firms are often unwilling to be listed on the prospectus in a secondary position after firms they do not consider their equal. Generally, this is a matter of prestige, and investment banks have walked away from IPOs for this reason. Sometimes an issuer wants two firms, but neither is willing to go behind the other and one drops out after an order selection has been made. All of this is bizarre, arcane, and frustrating for issuers. However, be aware that while most of the intramurals among investment banks over economics are mere negotiation posturing, maneuvers on positioning tend to be more real. Positioning is very visible (it is printed on the cover) while economics are not disclosed, and precedents on position are important. As a comanager, a special-bracket firm may appear ahead of the other comanagers in order on the prospectus cover. The rest should be alphabetical, except that it is acceptable for small firms to appear last. There has been a trend in recent years to appoint several firms as joint lead managers. According to Dealogic, the percentage of IPOs with joint lead managers went from 3 percent in 1997 to 55 percent in 2001. This allows various bragging rights to all the joint leads and does no harm.

INSTITUTIONAL INVESTORS ORDER IPO SHARES

Now that we know how investment bankers are compensated, we will detail how orders from institutional investors are placed and tracked. Institutional investors typically purchase their shares directly from an "institutional pot," usually managed by the lead manager, rather than from individual underwriters. This is done for the convenience of institutional investors who want to place one order and not assemble shares from among various underwriters. Additionally, this procedure gives the managers a truer picture of total institutional demand, as there could be double counting and double ordering without it. The pot can also serve a marketing purpose, as the lead manager can adjust its size and allocations so that institutions do not get all their needs filled. This keeps the overall interest in the deal high to generate aftermarket orders that are essential to a successful offering. It is also a way for the lead manager to substantially reduce the shares allocated to institutions it does not believe capable of properly digesting a large order. Ideally the lead manager should ensure that shares are only allocated to investors with a reputation for holding stock for the long term. Unfortunately, in the late 1990s this appears to not always have been the case, and some firms favored buyers beneficial to the firm's own revenues but not the long-term interests of the issuer.

HOW LEAD AND COMANAGERS ARE COMPENSATED FOR INSTITUTIONAL ORDERS

The compensation among the lead and comanagers for purchases made by institutions from the pot is either fixed (a percentage agreed in advance among the managers) or jump ball (effectively, the lead manager allocates the percentage among the managers). Let's look at each more closely.

Fixed Pot

A fixed pot is defined as a system in which the split of the selling concession is predetermined as a fixed percentage of the institutional pot. Usually this allocation will mirror the split of the management fee. The principal benefit of a fixed pot is that it encourages teamwork among the managers because the compensation is already set. Such teamwork may reduce infighting between the lead manager and comanagers. A fixed pot will also encourage the comanagers' institutional sales forces to make calls because they know that they will be paid for their effort.

Jump Ball

A jump-ball pot enables institutional investors to indicate which firm actually sold them on the IPO so that the proper firm receives sales credit. Once the actual order is placed, it is known as a *designated* or *directed* order. On the surface, this system should provide incentive for the lead and comanagers to compete to sell the IPO and encourage salespeople at all the managers to make calls. However, in practice the impact is the opposite. With a jump-ball pot the lead manager is solely responsible for allocating shares to institutional investors and deciding on designations. Not surprisingly, if unrestrained, the lead manager will, sometimes, decide that 90 percent or even 100 percent of the designations go to it. Issuers have figured this system out and the arrangement that is now standard is to have the lead manager capped at 50 to 70 percent of the jump-ball shares, with the remainder up for grabs among only the comanagers. Not too much should be expected of the comanagers with any system. This is especially true in busy times, when each firm's first priority will be pushing to a close its own lead-managed IPOs. The lead manager's securities analyst and sales personnel actually do much of the heavy lifting in terms of convincing institutions to purchase the IPO.

OTHER COMPENSATION TO INVESTMENT BANKS

As mentioned earlier, the largest cost of any IPO is the underwriting discount. However, underwriters may ask for other forms of compensation from an issuer of a small IPO, or if the offering will be difficult to sell and requires an overabundance of preparatory work. Other compensation could include the following items.

Underwriters' Warrants

In addition to the discount, some managers on smaller IPOs will negotiate for stock warrants to buy shares of stock of the issuer. From the managers' perspective, warrants will increase the economics without increasing the spread. Generally, warrants are divided among the managers pro rata according to the split of the management fee. A distribution among all the managers is in the best interests of the issuer and should be insisted upon if warrants are granted. Post-IPO, the warrants may serve to ensure that the managers have an economic interest in continuing to support the issuer. Warrants are typically given for between 5 and 10 percent of the shares issued in the IPO. They typically have a term of five years and are exercisable at a price that is a 20 percent premium relative to the IPO price. Often there is a cashless exercise privilege that allows the holder to use some of the warrants to exercise the others. This is attractive for the holder, as it does not have to put up cash and the safe harbor for sale according to Rule 144 starts at the date of the warrant issuance rather than the exercise date as with a cash exercise.

Reimbursement of the Managers' Expenses

In quality IPOs, the managers assume the risk for their own expenses should the offering not close. These expenses include prep time, the costs incurred by the managers in the road show, and the fee of underwriters' legal counsel. For quality firms, broken-deal expenses are a cost of doing business.

Advisory Fee

Paying an investment bank an advisory fee for helping to structure an SER is proper, should the parent or the subsidiary wish to ensure that it receives sufficient attention and impartial advice. This would be in addition to the compensation received by the firm as a manager of the IPO. Note that the fee will be subject to scrutiny by the NASDR for excess underwriters compensation issues.

Right of First Refusal

Some lead managers will request a right of first refusal on any future public offerings or advisory services for the issuer. Such a request may not first appear onerous, but it can be very expensive and can adversely affect future public and private offerings and advisory support. Other investment banks will be reluctant to invest time in supporting the issuer or offering advice on acquisitions and capital raising if there is already another firm with a right of first refusal. If a right of first refusal is unavoidable, it should be limited in duration to one year.

Letters of Intent

Some investment banks may require the parent or the subsidiary to sign a formal letter of intent before starting work on an IPO. Letters of intent are rarely used by quality investment banks and rarely accepted by quality issuers. Usually the only binding parts of a letter of intent lock the issuer into using the services of the investment bank, sometimes for a prolonged period, and to require the issuer to pay expenses and fees regardless of whether the IPO actually closes. There almost always is no binding reciprocal obligation on the part of the investment bank to do anything at all. The issuer's position should be that if the investment bank does an acceptable job before and after the IPO, the firm will be rewarded with additional work. But if the investment bank performs poorly during or after the IPO, the issuer is under no further obligation to use the services of the investment bank.

While most quality lead managers do not require a letter of intent, they may legitimately ask that the parent bind itself to compensate them if an offer is made and accepted to purchase the subsidiary during the IPO process. Depending on circumstances, the parent may decide that this compensation arrangement should be solely with the lead manager or with all the managers. It is not uncommon for the filing of an IPO to generate an attractive offer to purchase the subsidiary. Indeed, one strategy for selling a subsidiary is to draft an IPO registration statement and use this as a selective sale document. This approach is effective because it provides documentation and creates a time deadline for prospective buyers without appearing to put the subsidiary up for sale. Some compensation is justified in these circumstances.

SUMMARY

This chapter detailed the recommended process by which investment banks should be selected. It also examined how investment banks are compensated, which is key to understanding how to keep them motivated and focused throughout the process and in the aftermarket. Now that we know how to select the investment bankers and the rest of the external team, we will describe how to organize the IPO effort for maximum result.

CHAPTER 22

ORGANIZING THE IPO EFFORT

INTRODUCTION

This chapter will examine how to best organize all of the activities relating to an IPO including preparing for due diligence, structuring the IPO, and drafting and filing the registration statement. The proper organization, synchronization, and execution of these activities is challenging, complex, and critical to the success of the IPO. One misstep can seriously jeopardize the success of the offering. One crucially important step in organizing and executing a successful IPO is marketing, which will be touched on in this chapter and covered in depth in Chapter 23.

Although IPOs vary in size and structure, the time frame—and process—to bring them to market is fairly consistent. Thus, a comprehensive schedule has been provided in Exhibit 22–1. This schedule is applicable for any traditional underwritten IPO, but is directed at a carve-out IPO.

Before reviewing the schedule, it is important to note that the time needed to obtain the necessary regulatory approvals and consents is largely outside the control of the parent company.

The main activities contained in the schedule are as follows:

- Performing corporate housekeeping tasks to establish the subsidiary as a stand-alone company and prepare the subsidiary for a quality IPO and success as a public company

- Engaging an IPO team including investment bankers, legal counsel, accountants, investor relations advisor, financial printer, transfer agent, and stock certificate printer

- Working with the investment bank lead and comanagers of the IPO on the marketing strategy of the IPO, the positioning of the subsidiary to investors, the creation of operational forecasts used in marketing the IPO, and performance of

Typical Timetable for a Carve-out IPO

	1 year before the IPO	1 year–6 months before the IPO	6–3 months before the IPO	3–1 months before the IPO	4–1 weeks before the IPO	10–1 days before the IPO	1 day before the IPO	Day of the IPO	3 days after the IPO	Up to 30 days after the IPO
The parent	Determine strategy for SER. Select going-forward accountants (if new) for the subsidiary. Identify missing and useful enhancements for an IPO as outlined in Chapter 18. Identify "show-stopper" issues that might impede the IPO to be immediately addressed.	Begin separation of operations and systems of the parent and the subsidiary. Determine what services will be provided by the parent to the subsidiary on a transitional basis and longer term following the IPO. Work with the subsidiary to fill out the subsidiary's management team. Select the core IPO team of investment banks, accountants, and subsidiary legal counsel. Review and approve any changes to subsidiary structure, state of incorporation, charter, and bylaws. Put in place any defensive measures at the subsidiary. Review revised charter and bylaws, defense measures and draft option plan, and management compensation plan for the subsidiary. Elect officers for the subsidiary.	Host the organization meeting to kick off the IPO. Decide on offering structure (number of shares, any parent shares). Fill out board of directors at the subsidiary. Negotiate post-IPO operating agreements and tax protocols with the subsidiary. Negotiate the lockup agreement on the parent's remaining shares with the lead manager and underwriters' counsel. Negotiate the selling shareholder agreement (if the parent is selling shares directly in the IPO) with the lead manager and underwriters' counsel. Reply to directors' and officers' questionnaire. Elect new board for the subsidiary.	Select the financial printer and transfer agent. Select a financial PR firm to work with the subsidiary on the IPO. Issue a press release on the filing of the preliminary registration statement. If the subsidiary will be listed on the NYSE or ASE (together with the subsidiary) interview and agree on the specialist on the exchange who will make a market in the subsidiary's stock.	Monitor progress. Review the subsidiary's road show presentation. Keep the board of directors of the parent informed of progress (as appropriate) on the IPO. Execute any credit agreements with the subsidiary effective on the closing of the IPO. Execute post-IPO operating agreements and tax protocols with the subsidiary effective on the closing of the IPO.		Agree on the terms of the IPO with the lead and comanagers. Execute the selling shareholder agreement (if the parent is selling shares in the IPO). Issue a press release on the IPO.		Provide share certificates and receive proceeds of the sale (if the parent is selling shares in the offering).	Provide additional share certificates; receive additional proceeds (if the parent is selling shares in the underwriters' overallotment option (Green Shoe) and it is exercised by the lead manager.
The parent's Financial advisor (this firm may also be the lead or a comanager on the subsidiary's IPO)	Review for the parent the available alternatives for an SER. Advise on the suitability of the subsidiary to be a public company and the steps needed to get the subsidiary ready for a quality IPO.	Assist the parent in selecting the IPO team. Working with the parent on cleaning up parent-subsidiary issues such as the appropriate capital structure for the IPO and inter-company agreements following the IPO.	Review the structure and terms of the IPO proposed by the prospective lead and comanagers. Assist the parent in determining the structure for the IPO.	Together with the lead and comanagers for the subsidiary's IPO, hold a prefiling structure and price review with the parent. Monitor progress. Provide advice to parent, as requested, on overall market conditions and specific deal issues.			Together with the lead and comanagers for the subsidiary's IPO, hold a prepricing structure and price review with the parent.			Together with the investment banks for the subsidiary, hold a postpricing review with the parent.

	1 year before the IPO	1 year–6 months before the IPO	6–3 months before the IPO	3–1 months before the IPO	4–1 weeks before the IPO	10–1 days before the IPO	1 day before the IPO	Day of the IPO	3 days after the IPO	Up to 30 days after the IPO
	Provide a timetable and list of actions and responsibilities to prepare the subsidiary for an IPO. Provide an assessment of the IPO markets and likely size and valuation for a subsidiary IPO.	Develop an IPO timetable. Work with the parent and the subsidiary on putting in place IPO enhancements. Assist the parent and subsidiary in choosing the investment banking team for the IPO, determining the economic split between the lead, comanagers, and syndicate. Assess nonmanagers for special allocations of shares in exchange for research support. Assist in introducing potential additions to strengthen the board of the subsidiary.	Together with the lead and comanagers of the IPO, recommend to the parent and exchange for listing the subsidiary's shares. Advise on appropriate option and compensation plans for the subsidiary in line with industry norms. Advise on appropriate defensive measures for the subsidiary.							Provide additional share certificates; receive additional proceeds from Green Shoe (if it is exercised). Issue press release. Ensure compliance with FD disclosure rules going forward.
The subsidiary	Develop business plan and forecasts on a stand-alone basis. Begin to put in place missing "success factors" for a quality IPO. Address "show-stopper" issues. Put in place public company forecasting capability, financial controls, and option programs. Fill out the subsidiary's management team. Ensure that audited financial statements are prepared.	Prepare restructuring of the balance sheet and capital structure (if any) coincident with the closing of the IPO. Develop stand-alone financial statements on a post-IPO basis. Make presentations to prospective lead and comanagers of the IPO. Prepare due diligence files for the lead and comanagers of the IPO and underwriters' counsel. Prepare files for the subsidiary's legal counsel.	Review for the attendees the business and forecasts for the subsidiary. Assist in drafting the prospectus and preparing the registration statement. Respond to due diligence inquiries from the lead and comanagers of the IPO and underwriters' counsel. Meet with the research analysts for the managers and present on the business of the subsidiary. Review research analyst financial model and draft research reports. Reply to directors' and officers' questionnaire.	Prepare road show presentation. Hold board of directors meeting or conference call to approve filing final prospectus. Issue press release on filing of preliminary registration statement. Negotiate post-IPO operating and tax protocols with the parent. Apply for ticker symbol. If listing is on NYSE or ASE, interview and agree on specialist. Ensure that the lead and comanagers have obtained all their internal approvals to proceed.	Kick of road show with subsidiary management presentations to the lead manager's and comanagers' internal sales forces. Launch road show for investors with subsidiary management team making presentations.	Make additional road show presentations as requested by the managers of the IPO.	Execute the underwriting agreement. Implement any restructuring of the balance sheet and capital structure coincident with the closing of the IPO. Hold board of directors' conference call to approve filing final prospectus.	Issue press release on IPO.	Provide share certificates; receive proceeds from the offering.	

Continued

Continued

	1 year before the IPO	1 year–6 months before the IPO	6–3 months before the IPO	3–1 months before the IPO	4–1 weeks before the IPO	10–1 days before the IPO	1 day before the IPO	Day of the IPO	3 days after the IPO	Up to 30 days after the IPO
The subsidiary's legal counsel (also known as "company counsel")		Conduct review and clean up company records. Prepare defense measures review. Prepare any changes to state of incorporation, charter, and bylaws. Assist in cleaning up outstanding legal issues and litigation. Assist in cleaning up documentation of contracts, employment agreements, intellectual property, etc. Assist in preparing due diligence files for the lead and comanagers of the IPO and underwriters' counsel. Provide advice on changes to charter, bylaws, and state of incorporation of the subsidiary to go into effect with the IPO. Work with the parent and its counsel to structure intercompany agreements between the parent and the subsidiary to go into effect following the IPO. Prepare draft option plan for the subsidiary. Prepare draft subsidiary employment and other management compensation plans.	Prepare first draft of the S-1 registration statement. Prepare registration materials. Hold discussions with the SEC regarding potential problems. Circulate draft registration statements to all participants for comment. Prepare applications to list on an exchange. Negotiate the underwriting agreement with the underwriters' counsel. Brief the subsidiary's board of directors on their responsibilities and duties of a public company. Brief the subsidiary's board on the proposed management compensation and option plans, changes in charter and bylaws and defensive measures, and obtain appropriate resolutions.	Issue a press release on the filing of the registration statement, giving size in shares and naming the lead and comanagers. Provide preliminary registration statement to the board of directors of the subsidiary for approval and signing. File preliminary registration statement with the SEC. File listing application with exchange. Draft press release. Apply for a CUSIP number to identify the subsidiary's shares for electronic trading.	Respond to SEC comments on the registration statement. File Form 8A with the SEC to register the class of securities to be listed on an exchange under the Exchange Act.	Clear the registration statement with the SEC.	Provide final registration statement to the board of directors of the subsidiary for approval and signing. Request acceleration; file final registration statement. Draft press release.		Deliver documents/opinions.	Update closing documents.

	1 year before the IPO	1 year–6 months before the IPO	6–3 months before the IPO	3–1 months before the IPO	4–1 weeks before the IPO	10–1 days before the IPO	1 day before the IPO	Day of the IPO	3 days after the IPO	Up to 30 days after the IPO
The subsidiary's accounting firm	Prepare audited stand-alone financial statements for the subsidiary. Ensure all required audited financial statements are available for IPO filings. Review financial controls and recommend changes for a public stand-alone operation.	Assist with IPO restructuring of the balance sheet and capital structure. Prepare and review audited financial statements.	Circulate directors' and officers' questionnaire to assemble information for the registration statement. If necessary, hold discussions with the SEC regarding potential problems.	Prepare draft comfort letter and give to the lead and comanagers and to underwriters' counsel for comment.	Prepare updated interim financial statements, if necessary. Respond to SEC comments on the financial statements.	Deliver final draft comfort letter to lead and comanagers and to underwriters' counsel.	Deliver final comfort letter to lead manager.		Deliver bring-down comfort letter to lead manager.	Deliver second bring-down comfort letter to lead manager.
The IPO lead manager's corporate finance department and the comanagers' corporate finance departments	Call on the parent and discuss ideas for an SEP for the subsidiary.	Visit with the parent and the subsidiary and learn about the business of the subsidiary. Begin an IPO dialogue with the parent and the subsidiary. Make presentations on market conditions and potential structures for the IPO. Present proposed timetable. Make presentations on qualifications. Provide advice (as requested) on syndicate participation. Advise the impact of proposed management option and compensation plans, bylaws, and charter proposals and defensive measures on the marketability of the IPO.	Prepare agenda and materials for the organization meeting. Highlight all issues that will need to be addressed relating to the IPO. Ensure all issues are discussed and responsibilities for resolution are assigned. Make presentations on positioning. Make recommendations on structure, size of the offering and values, pricing, road show, syndicate strategy, and marketing strategy. Assist in drafting the prospectus and registration statement. Conduct due diligence. Negotiate lockup agreement with parent and other shareholders of the subsidiary.	Hold profiling structure and price review and lay out road show and syndicate plan and objectives with the parent and the subsidiary. Assist subsidiary to prepare road show presentation. Hold discussion with subsidiary and parent. Prepare marketing materials. Prepare kickoff of road show discussion.	Organize and make arrangements for the roads show. Accompany management on the road show. Host group meetings as appropriate.		Update due diligence. Participate in the discussion among the lead and comanagers to prepare a recommendation to the parent and the subsidiary. Participate in the pricing meeting.		Update due diligence.	Hold a postclosing review with the parent. Later, the lead manager hosts a closing event for the parent and the subsidiary's senior management and the comanagers and other professionals engaged in the offering.

Continued

Continued

	1 year before the IPO	1 year–6 months before the IPO	6–3 months before the IPO	3–1 months before the IPO	4–1 weeks before the IPO	10–1 days before the IPO	1 day before the IPO	Day of the IPO	3 days after the IPO	Up to 30 days after the IPO
the IPO lead manager's and comanagers' research departments		Meet with the subsidiary to learn the business. Prepare positioning strategy for marketing the IPO.	Prepare financial model for use in research report and IPO marketing. Prepare draft research report and marketing materials. Assist in due diligence calls and research. Help prepare internal commitment committee materials for the individual firm to approve, moving forward with the IPO.	Update business review with the subsidiary. Update financial models and materials. Assist subsidiary to prepare road show presentation. Prepare internal sales force marketing materials to assist in selling the IPO. Hold a touch-in with the internal sales force.	Talk to investors about the financial model, industry conditions, and the subsidiary's business. Provide forward estimates to investors.					Update review of the business with the subsidiary. Issue initiating coverage research report.
The IPO lead manager's capital markets department		Participate in presentations on market conditions.		Hold a prefiling market and price review with the parent and the subsidiary. Participate in marketing discussion with the parent and the subsidiary.	Organize the road show. Kick off road show of institutional management presentation to internal sales force. Take the lead in setting up sales presentations with investors and any visits to retail offices. Accompany management on the road show and attend meetings with investors. Solicit expressions of interest from potential investors. Issue invitations to the syndicate. Apply to be a market maker (if listing is on Nasdaq).	Form syndicate. Form "order book" of institutional indications of interest. Keep the parent and subsidiary appraised of the status of the order book.	Host a discussion with the comanagers to prepare a recommendation made jointly by the lead and comanagers to the parent and the subsidiary on price, number of shares, and spread. Hold a pricing meeting with the subsidiary and the parent; discuss the order book; agree on price, number of shares, and spread. Execute underwriting agreement.	Confirm orders with buyers. Allocate shares.	Provide net proceeds to the subsidiary and/or parent and selling shareholders. Place tombstone ad in Wall Street Journal and, as applicable, in other national newspapers and in the newspapers local to the parent and subsidiary.	Exercise Green Shoe (overallocation) option (if warranted) and provide net proceeds to the subsidiary and/or parent and selling shareholders. Place tombstone advertisements, as applicable, in trade and other periodicals.

	1 year before the IPO	1 year–6 months before the IPO	6–3 months before the IPO	3–1 months before the IPO	4–1 weeks before the IPO	10–1 days before the IPO	1 day before the IPO	Day of the IPO	3 days after the IPO	Up to 30 days after the IPO
The IPO comanagers' capital markets departments		Participate in presentations on market conditions.		Participate in the prefiling market and price review with the parent and the subsidiary. Participate in the marketing discussion with the parent and the subsidiary.	Kick off road show with subsidiary management presentations to internal sales forces. Assist the lead manager in setting up investor presentations. When applicable, attend meetings with investors. Solicit expressions of interest from potential investors. Apply to be a market maker (if listing is on Nasdaq).	Give to lead manager institutional indications of interest.	Assist the lead manager in forming a recommendation on price, number of shares, and spread to be given the parent and the subsidiary. Participate in the pricing meeting.		Provide stabilization for the IPO in the immediate aftermarket. Provide long-term sponsorship and support for the subsidiary's shares following the IPO.	Advise the subsidiary if the Green Shoe option will be exercised.
The IPO managers' legal counsel (also known as "underwriter counsel")			Begin due diligence. Assist in drafting the prospectus and registration materials. Conduct blue sky review of the applicability of various state securities laws. Negotiate the underwriting agreements with the subsidiary's legal counsel. Negotiate selling shareholder agreements (if any) with the parent's counsel and any other selling shareholders.	Prepare NASDR filing. Make applicable blue sky filings with state securities regulators. Review post-IPO operating and tax protocols between the parent and the subsidiary.	Clear NASDR comments. Clear with applicable state securities regulators.	Continue due diligence. Assist in responding to SEC comments.			Assist in closing.	Assist in second closing. Make applicable filings with state securities regulators.

Continued

EXHIBIT 22-1

Continued

	1 year before the IPO	1 year–6 months before the IPO	6–3 months before the IPO	3–1 months before the IPO	4–1 weeks before the IPO	10–1 days before the IPO	1 day before the IPO	Day of the IPO	3 days after the IPO	Up to 30 days after the IPO
The financial printer				Print preliminary registration statement. Prepare filing packages for SEC and NASD.	Print preliminary prospectuses (red herrings). Deliver preliminary prospectuses.		Print final registration statement. Prepare filing packages for SEC and NASD. Print final prospectuses. Deliver final prospectuses.			
Securities and Exchange Commission (SEC)			If requested, hold discussions with the subsidiary, the parent, their accountants, and counsel regarding potential problems.	Review preliminary registration statement. Issue comment letter.	Review subsidiary's responses to comment letter. Resolve comments.		Declare offering effective.			
NASD Regulatory (NASDR)			Request prefiling advice, if necessary.	Review preliminary registration statement. Issue comment letter.	Resolve comments.		Declare no objections.			
Stock market on which the subsidiary's stock will be listed				Review preliminary registration statement. Issue ticker symbol. If listing is on NYSE or ASE, appoint specialist after consultation with the subsidiary and/or parent. Preliminary approval of listing.	If listing is on Nasdaq, approve applications of broker-dealers to be market makers. Final approval of listing.			Begin trading.		

the due diligence on the subsidiary to ensure the completeness and accuracy of the disclosures in the prospectus

• Drafting the prospectus and registration statement, preparing exhibits, and responding to SEC and NASDR comments

• Marketing the IPO to potential investors through the distribution of the prospectus and investor meetings

What follows is a step-by-step list of the most important tasks to execute during the organization phase of the IPO process.

ORGANIZATIONAL MEETING

The organizational meeting is the kickoff to the IPO process and is usually hosted by the parent or the subsidiary and the lead manager once all the parties who will work on the IPO have been selected.

The primary purpose of the organizational meeting is to define the structure of the IPO, allocate responsibilities, discuss marketing strategy, agree on a timetable, review open issues that might delay or impact the IPO, and bring all those involved up to speed on the business of the subsidiary so that they may contribute to drafting the offering documents and valuation discussions. Those present at the organizational meeting should include the management team of the subsidiary, any representatives of the parent who desire to be present, the lead and comanagers of the IPO, the subsidiary's accountant, legal counsel to the subsidiary (company counsel), and the investment banks' legal counsel (underwriters' counsel). The parent's legal counsel and accountants may also be present if issues pertaining to the parent will be discussed.

The first part of the meeting should be devoted to housekeeping matters including a discussion of the following:

• The actual or proposed corporate structure of the subsidiary, management team, and board of directors

• Open issues that will need resolution before the IPO, and the timing of their resolution.

• The structure of the IPO (e.g., the number of shares to be offered by the subsidiary and any selling shareholders such as the parent), and the lead manager's proposed timetable for all of the steps in the process

• The use of proceeds generated by the IPO

• The Green Shoe and who will provide the shares for it—the subsidiary, the parent, or other selling shareholders

• The proposed marketing strategy and draft road show itinerary

• The due diligence process

• The projected valuation of the subsidiary in the IPO and the proposed spread (the fee paid to the underwriters) based on comparable IPOs (see Chapter 23)

- The proposed split of the spread between the lead and comanagers and any special syndicate allocations

- The timing of the availability of historical financial statements, the date of the last audit, and subsequent interim or quarterly information to be included in the prospectus

- The adequacy of financial statements for all the businesses included in the subsidiary

- The authorizations from the parent and the subsidiary that will need to be obtained to proceed

At the organization meeting the lead manager will also circulate the following items for corrections and additions:

- A contact list for all the individuals involved in the IPO
- A schedule of the division of responsibilities between the parties
- A timetable for the entire process

The second part of the meeting includes an in-depth explanation of the subsidiary's business to the group and the start of the due diligence process. If appropriate, this may be followed by a tour of the subsidiary's major facilities.

STRUCTURING THE IPO

The structure of the IPO includes the transaction size, defined as the amount of money to be raised in the IPO. Among the factors that determine transaction size are the capital needs of the subsidiary, the liquidity interests of the parent and other selling shareholders, minimum IPO investor size requirements, and market conditions. The structure of the IPO also includes a discussion of the filing price range per share to be put on the cover of the prospectus.

To obtain a price per share of $10 to $20, the number of shares outstanding at the subsidiary is adjusted through a stock split or reverse split. There is nothing magical about this range, but it is customary. A price below $10 per share runs the risk of going below $5 per share in the aftermarket, eliminating many intuitional investors who have a minimum-price-per-share threshold of $5. This is also a floor for eligibility for margin, a concern of retail investors (though some brokerages may have an internal requirement for a higher floor before extending margin loans). If the price continues to decline, the stock will be subject to delisting on the stock exchange. A price above $20 per share limits retail interest, as a round lot (100 shares) becomes pricey.

The structure of the IPO also includes determining the mix of primary and secondary shares, which is defined as shares offered by the subsidiary and the parent or other selling shareholders. The mix is determined by balancing the subsidiary's capital requirements, the liquidity desires of the parent and other selling shareholders, and the market's likely reaction. Let's take a look at some of the issues surrounding selling shareholders.

SELLING SHAREHOLDERS

The tolerance of the market for sales by the parent and other shareholders of the subsidiary in the IPO will vary by the type of shareholder and the buoyancy of the IPO market. Generally, investors are least receptive to more than nominal sales by current management of the subsidiary, while sales by former employees with no current involvement are much more acceptable. The percentage of shares offered in the IPO from selling shareholders that the underwriters believe will be acceptable to investors in the IPO may be substantial, if the subsidiary does not need additional capital to fund its operations and does not have excessive business risk. In other IPOs, selling shareholders are only permitted to offer shares in the underwriters' overallotment option or Green Shoe, should this be exercised following the IPO by the underwriters. If the subsidiary has substantial capital requirements or still has considerable business risk, sales by selling shareholders are likely to be a negative for IPO investors. The various selling shareholders, within the constraints set by the lead manager and any contractual agreements between the shareholders, affect whether to sell shares in the offering.

In addition, the lead manager may restrict the sales of shares from these shareholders to support the success of the subsidiary. For example, funds raised in the IPO should be used to finance the needs of the subsidiary—not to buy outstanding shares from shareholders.

The subsidiary may have contractual agreements with private equity or corporate strategic partners who are investors in the subsidiary to register their shares upon an IPO. However, the lead manager usually may exclude such shares from the IPO entirely or in part if it believes that the market requires this. It is always best to get this exclusion provision in the original investment documents; otherwise, the investors will need to agree to an amendment before the IPO may proceed.

Lockups

The parent and other selling shareholders will, in most cases, be required by the lead manager of the IPO to commit to a lockup of shares still held following an IPO for an extended period—a minimum of six months and sometimes several years. If the parent is a disproportionately large shareholder, its lockup may be longer than that of other investors.

DEVELOPING THE MARKETING PLAN

During this discussion, the managers will give advice on the most likely investors in the IPO. They will also give advice about when to best offer the IPO based on the company's performance within a specific period and the availability of audited financial statements.

PREPARING FOR DUE DILIGENCE

Due diligence is the term used to describe the process undertaken by the lead and comanagers and their legal counsel to verify the accuracy of information contained in the IPO prospectus. The due diligence process helps the company counsel and the underwriters' counsel decide what additional information should be disclosed. It also involves conducting a *legal audit* of the company's corporate records. All of the participants in the offering should be aware of the importance of being completely open and honest with the managers and their legal counsel during the due diligence process.

The due diligence process is time consuming for the subsidiary and its counsel. The parent may also be extensively involved. The more advance preparation, the less time consuming and easier the process. If there is a lack of detailed records of contracts and agreements or where financial statements have not been audited, the subsidiary, its professional advisors, and the managers will spend considerable time in sorting out the documentation.

At the organizational meeting, a due diligence schedule is usually agreed on. This may include site visits by one or all of the managers to the subsidiary's operations and customer and supplier interviews. The lead manager or underwriters' counsel will provide a document request. If actual or forthcoming patents, licenses, or government approvals are a meaningful part of value, a process for the review of these, possibly by outside experts, will also be agreed on. If there are large asset values such as real estate holdings or oil and gas or mineral reserves, a process for appraising these will also be needed. If material, such appraisals are often a required part of the registration statement.

The due diligence part of the organization meeting usually will include management presentations on various aspects of the business. The managers and their counsel (and often the subsidiary's counsel if it is new to the situation) will typically ask numerous questions to understand the company's business, its products, and markets or potential markets. It is during these sessions that the company's story begins to take shape for the purpose of drafting the prospectus and the road show presentation.

Typically, the underwriters' counsel and the lead manager will each provide the subsidiary with due diligence request lists. The underwriters' counsel's list will focus on legal due diligence, such as reviewing the subsidiary's corporate documents, material contracts, loan agreements, employment agreements, litigation files, shareholder lists, terms of equity securities, protocols with the parent, insurance, ownership and licenses off intangible assets and intellectual property, ownership of tangible property, tax and other required government filings, environmental compliance, information on foreign operations, and any affiliations between shareholders and NASD member firms (especially relevant where there are private equity firms as shareholders in the subsidiary), and many other documents.

The lead manager's due diligence list will include business plans, industry information and studies, and historical and projected financial statements. In addition, the lead and comanagers will expect to have conversations with significant customers and vendors, and visit the most significant facilities of the subsidiary.

As well as reviews of documents, due diligence will include extensive interviews with the management of the subsidiary and, as relevant, the parent.

In some cases, the lead manager will engage experts to review specific areas of concern such as the patent portfolio, the status of government approvals of new drug or device applications, and the status of specific litigation such as asbestos lawsuits.

Due diligence doesn't end with the initial investigations; it is conducted throughout the entire IPO process. In drafting sessions, the participants critically review the disclosures and will recommend disclosure of any risks particular to the company and general to its industry, confirming the accuracy of the information presented.

While the due diligence process is time consuming for the management of the subsidiary and the parent, the more informed the managers and their counsel are on the business of the subsidiary, and the more confident they are that there will be no surprises, the more effectively they will market the IPO.

DRAFTING THE REGISTRATION STATEMENT AND PROSPECTUS

Federal securities law requires the filing of a registration statement before making any offer to sell shares in the IPO. The registration statement is a public document filed with the SEC. It consists primarily of a prospectus that includes descriptions of:

- The history of the subsidiary, its business operations, facilities, employees, significant tangible and intangible assets, actual and contingent liabilities, significant contracts, customers and vendors, and any other material information
- The details of the offering and the underwriting arrangements with the investment banks
- The use of proceeds
- Risks for investors who purchase shares in the IPO
- The backgrounds and compensation of officers and directors of the subsidiary and any transactions between them and the subsidiary
- The relationship of the subsidiary with the parent before and after the IPO
- The capital structure of the subsidiary before and after the IPO

The prospectus also includes audited financial statements, recent interim financial statements and a management discussion of operations, financial results, and changes from prior periods. In addition to the prospectus, the registration statement will include documents such as the underwriting agreement, corporate organization documents, and material contracts. The preliminary prospectus is the only written information that may be supplied to potential investors during the marketing of the IPO.

A prospectus is prepared with two completely conflicting objectives. First, it is the primary document for marketing the IPO to investors. Second, it discloses all material information and risks. These conflicting objectives are not easy to reconcile. The art in drafting a prospectus is to have a document that is effective in selling investors that the shares are a good investment while fully disclosing all material facts and risks. Full disclosure is a good idea for the reputations of all involved. In addition, the securities laws provide that the subsidiary, certain members of its management, directors, underwriters, accountants, and the parent may all be liable to investors in the IPO for any material misrepresentation or omission of facts in the registration statement.

The subsidiary and company counsel usually prepare the initial draft of the registration statement. This is logical, as they are the most familiar with the business. Confidential treatment may be requested where documents include confidential information. The company counsel will have to submit a justification for each portion of documents for which confidential treatment is requested. These documents should be identified early to ensure that the confidential treatment process does not cause delay.

Before the first filing of the registration statement, the parent, the subsidiary, and the managers of the IPO should have a formal valuation discussion to ensure that they are all on the same page. For this discussion, the managers should prepare a *valuation book* for the parent and subsidiary that lays out the analysis behind the expected valuation of the IPO and provides an estimate of the valuation. This formal valuation discussion gives the parent and the subsidiary a basis for setting their valuation expectations and also for terminating the IPO before incurring the expense of filing and then printing prospectuses if the expected price is too low to be acceptable.

FILING THE REGISTRATION STATEMENT

When the drafting process is complete, which can take from one month to several months, the finished registration statement is filed with the SEC in Washington, D.C. This is done electronically via the EDGAR electronic filing system that makes all public filings available online to the public. Once information has been submitted on the EDGAR system it cannot be altered or removed. After the registration statement is filed with the SEC, it is sent to the Corporation Finance Division of the SEC and assigned to two examiners. One examiner reviews the business and legal aspects of the document, and the other reviews the financial aspects. These examiners do a preliminary review, which is then presented to their supervisor at the SEC.

A few days after filing, the SEC will call company counsel to let it know whether it intends to review the registration statement. Almost every IPO is reviewed. Approximately 30 days after the registration statement is filed with the SEC, a letter of comment on the registration statement is sent by the SEC to the subsidiary. The letter will contain a number of comments and questions that need to be addressed either in the prospectus or in a supplement to the prospectus.

The SEC does not comment on the merits of the offering. Rather, its focus is on whether there has been adequate disclosure. For example, the SEC may ask the subsidiary to provide more detail about the impact of a proposed business expansion or to provide information to support qualitative factual assertions regarding the company's expertise or innovative developments. Another area of frequent comment is the basis for accounting treatments and substantiation of restructuring charges. At any given time, the SEC will also have some hot buttons on which it particularly focuses. At the time of this writing, off-balance-sheet liabilities and revenue recognition are receiving close scrutiny in the wake of the meltdowns of Enron and Global Crossing.

When it is apparent in advance that there will be significant SEC issues with the subsidiary, the subsidiary and its counsel or accountant may request a conference with SEC staff to discuss the issues and receive guidance from the SEC on how to treat them before filing and drafting the registration statement.

RESPONDING TO SEC COMMENTS

The subsidiary, through its counsel, will respond to SEC comments by letter and, if appropriate, with changes in the prospectus, which will be filed as part of an amendment to the registration statement. There may be a number of amendments filed. Most often when compliance with an SEC comment is not burdensome or it adds effective disclosure, the company will comply with the request, even though, in many cases, the new disclosure may seem unnecessary. However, in some instances the company will be unable to provide the requested disclosure or will otherwise take issue with the comment. This comment-and-response process often continues through an exchange of letters, telephone calls, and amendments over a period of several weeks. However, remember that the SEC has the final word since it has to approve the issuer's request to declare the registration statement effective.

Several months may now have passed since first filing the registration statement, and it may need to be amended to reflect any material changes in the subsidiary's business or finances in the interim.

Exhibit 22–2 provides some guidance on the average time between filing the preliminary registration statement and pricing the IPO. Not all this delay is

E X H I B I T   22–2

U.S.—Time from Filing to Pricing: Marketed IPOs (1995–2001)

Years	1995	1997	1999	2001
Average number of days from filing the preliminary registration statement to pricing the IPO.	74	88	93	143
Source: Dealogic				

due to the SEC. Market conditions also play a role. In the first half of 2002, the average delay was 147 days.

All agreements with the managers should be made before the filing of the registration statement. Before filing the registration statement, the parent and the subsidiary are in complete control. For example, they may replace a lead or comanager, add new comanagers, or postpone or restructure the IPO without public exposure. After the filing, the replacement of a manager, especially a lead manager, while not unheard of, will raise questions among investors—perhaps the manager found out something bad and voluntarily withdrew.

Generally, the preliminary prospectus ("red herring") is not printed or circulated until the SEC is satisfied or nearly satisfied with the disclosure. If the preliminary prospectus is printed and circulated before sign-off by the SEC, there is always a risk that the SEC may require the issuer to recirculate an amended version of the preliminary prospectus. This is expensive and embarrassing. The preliminary prospectus will have language in red print on the cover that cautions investors that the prospectus is not yet final. The preliminary prospectus will include the estimated price range, the number of shares being offered by the subsidiary in the IPO, and the number of shares being sold by any selling shareholder. It usually has blanks for the actual price of the shares, total proceeds, the underwriters' discount, the composition and commitments of the syndicate, and the estimated expenses of the offering. After all outstanding issues have been resolved with the SEC there is technically a 20-day waiting period before the IPO may be sold to investors (under the delaying amendment filed as part of the original registration statement). However, company counsel and the lead manager usually file a request that the SEC waive the 20-day waiting period and declare the registration statement effective immediately. This is an acceleration request. The SEC usually approves these requests, provided that it has already signed off on the registration statement and it has been notified already by the NASDR that it has no objections to the compensation terms and by the chosen stock exchange that it has no objection to the listing. The SEC then declares the registration statement effective, and the shares may be sold in the IPO.

HONORING THE QUIET PERIOD

The SEC places severe restrictions on the public activities of companies during the registration process. These restrictions apply during the *quiet period,* which starts when there is an agreement with the managers to begin the IPO process and continues to 40 days after the IPO has been priced. During the quiet period, certain restricted activities could be interpreted as part of the marketing effort and are therefore prohibited.

During the period before initial filing of the registration statement, the federal securities acts prohibit the subsidiary from offering the security. There is a broad interpretation by the SEC of the meaning of *offering* to include, in the words of the SEC, "the publication of information and statements, and publicity efforts, made in advance of a proposed financing that have the effect of conditioning the public mind or arousing public interest in the issuer or in its securities." However, the restrictions do not prevent the subsidiary from advertising its products and services in the usual course of business, including press announcements about important accomplishments relating to current activities. The restrictions do prevent the subsidiary from starting a new publicity program or issuing financial forecasts.

There are serious consequences for violating these SEC restrictions. These include the SEC imposing a cooling-off period. This is always an embarrassment. It may have worse consequences, including the disruption of the IPO process, particularly if a cooling-off period is imposed during the IPO marketing or just prior to pricing. By significantly delaying the IPO, a cooling-off period may lead to postponement or even termination of the IPO should market conditions change. To prevent any possibility of even inadvertently triggering SEC action, once an IPO is considered a reasonable possibility, the subsidiary should involve its legal counsel in reviewing its conference appearances, press releases, and press interviews. For example, on occasion, magazine interviews granted months before an IPO didn't appear in print until the middle of the IPO and led to the imposition of a cooling-off period by the SEC.

There are also specific guidelines with respect to sales materials given to prospective investors after the registration statement is filed with the SEC. Except for the preliminary prospectus, no other written sales literature may be given to investors between the filing of the registration statement and the completion of the IPO except for a limited notice of the offering. Any sales materials given to investors are required by the SEC to be accompanied by the prospectus. During this period, oral offers may be made, but any oral statements that are inconsistent with the registration materials and that are materially misleading may give rise to liability.

A FIRM COMMITMENT UNDERWRITING

Quality IPOs are always done with what is called a *firm commitment* underwriting. In this type of IPO, the lead manager, on behalf of the underwriters, purchases the entire agreed number of shares from the subsidiary or other selling shareholders and then resells the shares to investors. While it is called a firm commitment, no binding commitment is made until after the marketing efforts are completed, the lead manager knows the order book for the IPO, and the pricing of the IPO is agreed on. With a firm commitment underwriting, there is no obligation on the part of the subsidiary (or the parent) to proceed with the IPO until the underwriting agreement is agreed on and signed. However, the same is true for the lead manager. In some cases, the lead manager will purchase shares in an IPO without having buyers for the shares. But this will occur only in unusual circumstances. In general in an IPO, shares will be purchased by the lead manager only if it already has solid indications of interest from investors. When there is insufficient demand, the lead manager will not proceed with the IPO.

Early in the IPO process, the lead manager will send company counsel its standard underwriting agreement for review. The contents of the underwriting agreements used by quality investment banks are very similar in form. Any change to the standard underwriting agreement is unlikely, and company counsel should not waste too much billable time on an extensive markup of this document. In contrast, the underwriting agreements of the investment banks that undertake speculative IPOs often contain very negotiable provisions regarding the reimbursement of expenses, warrants and other compensation, and ongoing commitments by the issuer.

The primary alternative to a firm commitment underwriting is a best efforts underwriting, in which the investment banks only act as an agent of the issuer and never purchase any shares for their own. A best-efforts underwriting is not used with quality IPOs except in limited applications such as the conversion of financial institutions from mutual to stock ownership.

MOVING INITIATION OF COVERAGE FORWARD

As of this writing, there is a newly enacted 40-day quiet period following an IPO distribution which restricts the managing and comanaging underwriters from publishing research reports on the subsidiary. After this period, the managers should release the first of many in-depth research reports on the issuer as a reference for new and existing investors.

CLOSING THE DEAL

The closing of a firm commitment IPO takes place three business days after the registration statement is declared effective. At that time the lead manager wire-transfers the proceeds of the IPO, net of the underwriting discount, to the subsidiary and any other selling shareholders.

A *tombstone* advertisement is usually placed by the lead manager, at the expense of the underwriters and paid for from the underwriting portion of the offering spread, in the *Wall Street Journal* and other publications. Tombstones are positive for the subsidiary, as they highlight the IPO. Placement in the subsidiary's local paper is often requested. The tombstone includes the size and price of the IPO, lists the lead and comanagers, and lists the names of the members of the syndicate alphabetically, grouping each size of underwriting commitment separately.

RESTRICTIONS ON MARKETING THE IPO

The stock of the subsidiary may not be sold to investors until the SEC declares the registration statement effective. However, marketing is permitted within limits set by the SEC. The first action is to send a press release concurrent with the first filing of the registration statement. The SEC limits the information in this press release to a description of the offering, a summary description of the subsidiary, the names of the managers, and where prospectuses may be obtained. Note that the subsidiary is not required on an IPO to issue a press release on the filing. This is known as a *silent filing*. However, filings are public documents and today are instantly picked up by data services and available over the Internet.

The subsidiary should take care when marketing the IPO to avoid making any statements or projections that may be misleading. Also, copies of road show slides, presentations, or any other written materials other than the preliminary prospectus and press release announcing the filing should not be distributed to prospective investors while marketing the IPO.

COSTS AND EXPENSES OF AN IPO

The transition from a private company to a public company is a tremendously expensive undertaking. The costs of going public are extraordinarily high and must be taken into consideration before the IPO begins. The total cost of the IPO process will easily exceed 10 percent of the proceeds (including the investment banking costs). Let's look at which party is responsible for specific expenses.

The subsidiary is responsible for the following expenses:

• Preparation and filing of the registration statements, the preliminary and final prospectus, and any amendments or supplements

• SEC filing fees

• Preparation, issuance, and delivery of the subsidiary's shares sold in the IPO to the transfer agent and register and their fees

• Costs of the subsidiary's accountant and legal counsel and any experts and appraisers

• Printing and delivery of the registration statement, the preliminary and final prospectus, and any amendments or supplements

• Printing and delivery of copies of any state securities law (blue sky) survey and legal investment survey prepared by the underwriters' counsel relating to applicable states and types of investors

• Legal fees of the underwriters' legal counsel specifically incurred to ensure compliance with blue sky laws, which are ordinarily reimbursed by the subsidiary, as it is in its interest to have the IPO available in as many states as possible, provided that the expense is not onerous

• Fees for the depository for a foreign issuer using ADRs

• Fees and expenses of listing the subsidiary's shares on a stock market

• Fees and expenses for filing with the NASD

• The hotel and travel costs of the subsidiary's management during the road show

The underwriters are responsible for the following expenses:

• Underwriter's legal counsel fees

- Hotel and travel expenses for the investment bankers for drafting and due diligence, and on the road show

- Road show expenses for group and individual investor breakfasts, lunches, dinners, meeting rooms, audiovisual equipment, and limousines

- Office and miscellaneous expenses

Smaller investment banks that undertake more speculative IPOs may require that the issuer also reimburse the investment banks' out-of-pocket expenses including legal, travel, and road show expenses. Many times, the investment banks will require that they receive this reimbursement even if the IPO does not close and no funds are raised. Neither practice is customary with quality investment banks that assume responsibility for their traditional costs and also bear the risk of the IPO not closing and absorbing the associated expenses. Broken-deal expenses are a part of the cost of doing IPO business, and the major cost of a broken deal is usually the charge of underwriters' legal counsel. However, in practice, the amount actually paid by the investment banks in legal broken-deal expenses is usually less than if the IPO closed.

Exhibit 22–3 shows typical IPO expenses paid by an issuer IPOs of various sizes. The source for the information in this exhibit is SEC filings made by the issuers, which are a good indication of the direct costs of an IPO. Not included, of course, is management time.

There are also many direct costs associated with being a public company following the IPO. These include:

- Considerably higher legal and accounting fees after the IPO, with the added costs of producing periodic and special SEC filings, ensuring compliance with disclosure requirements, and the greater liability for professional firms working with a public company. This cost has increased significantly with consolidation of the accounting industry and the massive damages, litigation costs, and settlements borne by accountants in recent large fraud cases.

- Annual stock market listing fees and expenses

- Preparing, printing, and filing required periodic and special reports with the SEC

- Preparing, printing, and mailing annual and quarterly reports to shareholders

- Maintaining an investor access website

- Directors' and officers' (D&O) liability insurance (usually necessary to attract outside directors and prudent for officers, especially in today's litigious environment) for a public company. Since the Enron scandal, the cost of D&O insurance has skyrocketed.

- Investor relations professionals in-house and on retainer

- Increased financial staff to meet the requirements of SEC filings and to ensure that no mistakes are made with these important filings

- Fees for outside directors

Representative IPO Underwriting Discounts and Out-of-Pocket Expenses of the Issuer

Issuer	REMEC, Inc.		CoSine Communications Inc.		KPMG Consulting Inc.	
Size of offering	$72,000,000		$230,000,000		$2,024,676,000	
Underwriting discount in percent	7.0%		7.0%		4.0%	
Underwriting discount in dollars	$5,040,000		$16,100,000		$80,987,040	
Out-of-pocket expenses	In dollars	In percent of total out-of-pocket expenses	In dollars	In percent of total out-of-pocket expenses	In dollars	In percent of total out-of-pocket expenses
SEC registration fee	$ 10,707	1.4	$ 51,612	1.7%	$ 975,241	9.4%
NASD filing and listing fee	39,844	5.1	120,800	4.0	125,500	1.2
Printing	75,000	9.7	600,000	20.0	4,000,000	38.6
Company's legal fees and expenses	250,000	32.3	1,000,000	33.3	2,000,000	19.3
Accounting fees and expenses	200,000	25.8	800,000	26.7	3,000,000	28.9
Blue sky fees and expenses	15,000	1.9	15,000	0.5	2,500	0.0
Transfer agent and registrar fee and expenses	6,000	0.8	77,210	2.6	10,000	0.0
Miscellaneous expenses	53,449	6.9%	335,378	11.2%	251,759	2.4
Total out-of-pocket expenses (excluding underwriting discount)	$650,000	100.0%	$3,000,000	100.0%	$10,365,000	100.0%
Total out-of-pocket costs and discount	$5,890,000		$19,190,000		$91,352,000	

Source: SEC Filings

- Any additional state filings and expenses

- Expenses of attending investor conferences and going on investor road shows

- Costs for complying with Regulation FD such as the costs of webcasting conference presentations and teleconferencing investor calls

The additional costs of being a public company will easily total $500,000 to $1 million without expensive extras such as full-color annual reports.

SUMMARY

Organizing all of the activities relating to executing an IPO can be complex and challenging. This chapter provided an understanding of the breadth of the activities that need to be organized to help ensure the success of the IPO. It also offered advice about the best way to organize various activities once they are identified. Chapter 23 will take a look at marketing and pricing the IPO, a subject that is treated separately because of its importance.

MARKETING PRICING THE IPO FOR MAXIMUM RESULTS

INTRODUCTION

There are many important steps involved in successfully marketing an IPO to the investor community, and then pricing it appropriately. This chapter identifies each step, details its purpose, and explains how each can be successfully executed. At the time of writing, there is an exceptionally difficult IPO market. This may well last for some years. A reader might ask, why then this attention on IPOs? The reasons are several. First, even in the worst markets, IPOs are almost always available for quality companies; the difference is the price at which the IPO is transacted. Second, a stronger IPO market will come back at some point—it may take years, but it will come back. It always does. Third, although this discussion is focused on IPOs, most of it is also relevant to marketing spin-offs, public mergers, and any already public subsidiary to investors. This marketing work continues regardless of the depressed state of the public equity markets or the availability of IPOs.

The following sections discuss the steps involved in marketing an IPO.

UNDERSTANDING THE TARGET MARKET

At the heart of any successful marketing campaign is knowing who the target market is and crafting a message that will resonate with that market. The following sections discuss the organizations that constitute the target market.

Institutional Investors

Today, strong institutional interest is needed for an IPO to succeed. All sophisticated investors and brokers understand that institutional interest makes the aftermarket. Usually there is less liquidity in a stock without institutional interest.

The largest group of investors in IPOs is major institutions. These are private and state pension funds, endowments, and mutual funds. These are the primary targets for marketing an IPO. While there are thousands of institutional buyers, there are relatively few important ones. The growth of concentrated buying power for IPOs in the hands of only a few hundred large institutions has changed the marketing of IPOs.

In general, these institutions must be catered to when marketing most IPOs. For example, the senior portfolio managers at the significant institutions expect to be visited on their own premises by the CEO of the subsidiary that is going public.

Retail Investors

In general, retail investors, defined as individual investors, do not make IPOs a success, though they do bolster institutional interest by adding another group of buyers for an IPO. Despite protestations by the retail brokerage firms, there is no evidence that most retail investors are longer-term holders than institutional investors in IPOs. But some retail firms do appear to deal with more long-term investors than do other retail firms. These tend to be the quality regional retail firms.

Although retail is not the primary distribution route for an IPO, retail interest will be substantial for large IPOs of stocks offering high dividend payments or for those issued by household names. A large retail system will be effective in marketing such an offering and may be an essential channel for the stock. However, in most cases, retail brokers will sell an IPO only if there is already strong institutional buying interest. A good retail broker will be well aware of the level of institutional interest in the IPO—there are even websites that offer this information.

Retail is not usually a reliable marketing channel except for specific large IPOs that will appeal to retail investors. For example, the large retail firms will not always make shares received in an IPO available to their retail brokers. The large retail firms have their own institutional businesses and very often the majority, or even the entire, allocation of shares received in an IPO by a retail firm will actually be placed with a few significant institutions rather than with individuals, as these institutions generate the bulk of the day-to-day trading revenues for most investment banks. As well, retail customers tend not to come into the aftermarket and buy more shares, which can be critical to the success of an IPO.

Smaller retail firms generally do a better job of placing shares in the typical IPO in true retail hands than do large retail firms. The amount of stock is more meaningful to their smaller organizations, and their institutional commitment to supporting their retail efforts tends to be higher. For this reason, the smaller retail firms such as A.G. Edwards and Raymond James are often the best choice if the parent desires retail distribution. Their role may be that of an extra comanager or as a syndicate member.

Foreign Investors

Foreign interest in U.S. IPOs waxes and wanes with the strength of the overall U.S. stock market, the quality of IPOs offered, and the vicissitudes of the dollar against other currencies. At times, up to a third of an IPO may be placed with

EXHIBIT 23–1

Typical Allocation of an IPO Among Investors

Type of investor	Typical portion of the total stock offered
Major U.S. institutions	65–75%
International institutions	10–15%
Retail	10–20%

European investors. At other times, there is less interest. The center of interest in U.S. stocks overseas is in London. There are also some buyers in Milan, Paris, Stockholm, and Edinburgh. In general, most European institutions buy only large-capitalization, recognizable names among U.S. IPOs. Also, companies with significant operations or business activity in Europe are likely to have more appeal to European investors.

Depending on the size of the IPO and the advice of the managers, a trip to Europe is often justified to market the IPO. Marketing may be confined to London or spread more broadly. Even if the meetings do not result in sales in the IPO, they may be good exposure for the subsidiary to another group of future investors. On some IPOs, European investors will buy 30 percent of the shares; on most, the number is much lower. There is loss of confidence in the U.S. stock markets by overseas investors in 2002. If this continues, little should be expected from Europe until confidence is restored.

Except for subsidiaries that are very large and are household names, there is rarely any interest in U.S. IPOs in Asia, and almost never any in Japan. For that reason, a marketing trip to Asia for a typical IPO is exceptionally tiring for the subsidiary's management team and of no sales value. It is usually undertaken for the sole benefit of a lead manager that is trying to increase its own visibility with Asian investors. Exhibit 23–1 sets out a typical allocation among investor groups of an IPO. Exhibits 23–2 and 23–3 show representative lists of leading buyers of recent IPOs.

CRAFTING THE MESSAGE—CREATING THE STORY

The first part of preparing to market the IPO is crafting the story. This tells the target market why they should buy the stock of the subsidiary over all the other thousands of choices of stocks to buy.

A road show is the most effective way to market the IPO by getting the story out in front of key buyers. But the road show process is very challenging because of the diverse audience and the large and concentrated time requirement.

Generally speaking, the audience for the road show will consist of institutional investors, larger retail investors, members of the underwriting syndicate,

E X H I B I T   23–2

Representative List of the Leading Buyers of Large-Capitalization IPOs in 2002

Company	City	State
Capital Research & Management	Los Angeles	CA
Dresdner RCM Global Investors	San Francisco	CA
Essex Investment Management	Boston	MA
Fidelity Management	Boston	MA
Harbor Capital Management	Boston	MA
John Hancock Advisors	Boston	MA
Putnam Investments	Boston	MA
Wellington Management	Boston	MA
T. Rowe Price	Baltimore	MD
Alliance Capital Management	New York	NY
Citigroup Asset Management	New York	NY
J&W Seligman	New York	NY
Mutual of America	New York	NY
Neuberger Berman	New York	NY
Oppenheimer Capital	New York	NY
Columbia Management	Portland	OR
US BANCORP Trust	Johnstown	PA
Strong Capital Management	Menomonee Falls	WI

Source: Needham & Company

and salespeople for the underwriters who, in turn, market the IPO to their customers. But there is also another audience that needs to be addressed: employees and customers, who will often see the road show presentation.

The institutional audience at a road show presentation tends to be sophisticated and skeptical. They have heard many presentations before and may view 5 to 10 IPO presentations a week in a buoyant IPO market. The challenge for the issuer is to capture investor interest and appear in charge of the facts and numbers. Even though the road show is challenging mentally and physically, the management must retain its enthusiasm, freshness, and even passion about the issuer.

COMMUNICATING WITH THE TARGET MARKET

The road show presentation has to be basic enough for a relatively uninformed generalist investor to make sense of the subsidiary and its industry but also deep

E X H I B I T   23–3

Representative List of the Leading Buyers of Smaller- and
Mid-Capitalization IPOs in 2002

Investment company	City	State
Capital Research & Management	Los Angeles	CA
Barclays Global Investors	San Francisco	CA
Berger	Denver	CO
Invesco Funds	Denver	CO
Janus Funds	Denver	CO
Hartford Investment Management	Hartford	CT
Northern Trust Global Advisors	Stamford	CT
State Street Research & Management	Boston	MA
Wellington Management	Boston	MA
Legg Mason Capital Management	Baltimore	MD
Arbor Capital Management	Minneapolis	MN
Winslow Capital Management	Minneapolis	MN
Beekman Capital Management	New York	NY
Credit Suisse Asset Management	New York	NY
J.P.Morgan Fleming Asset Management	New York	NY
MacKay Shields	New York	NY
Morgan Stanley Dean Witter Investment Management	New York	NY
Oppenheimer Funds	New York	NY
The Vanguard Group	Valley Forge	PA
Pilgram Baxter	Wayne	PA
State of Wisconsin Investment Board	Madison	WI

Source: Needham & Company

enough to keep the attention of the knowledgeable specialist investor in the industry of the subsidiary.

Preparedness varies greatly among investors. Some investors are obviously looking at the prospectus for the first time in the meeting with the management of the issuer; others have done considerable homework and have pages of notes and questions. Some meetings will be with investors that already own stocks of competitors. Some of these investors may be genuinely interested in the IPO; others may only be looking for information.

In addition, different buyers of IPOs have different holding period expectations and therefore are looking for different things in the road show presentation. Some buyers of IPOs are genuine long-term investors who only buy stock in IPOs with multiyear holding periods and accumulate additional positions in the aftermarket. These investors are looking at a road show presentation to answer questions on fundamental attributes of the business. They are focused on long-term prospects, strategy, and management capabilities. Other buyers of IPOs (such as many hedge funds) are short-term investors who only buy IPOs with the intent of selling the stock within a few days. These buyers are looking solely for signs that an IPO will be hot and trade to a premium. Some investors who like the story will buy in the IPO. Other investors who like the story will monitor the issuer for a period and then take a position later in the aftermarket. These investors may turn up as stockholders a year or more after the road show. So, even though there may not be an immediate purchase order for shares in the IPO, it may still turn out to have been a worthwhile meeting.

Keep track of the names and addresses of all investors and research analysts who listen to the road show presentation and stay in touch with them following the IPO. Send a thank-you note to each investor and research analyst who attended the road show.

TIPS FOR A SUCCESSFUL ROAD SHOW

Following are recommendations for a successful road show.

Rehearse

Run through the presentation first internally, then with the managers of the IPO. Listen to their comments, as the rough presentation is likely to be too long, contain too many generalities, and focus too much on points of interest to the management of the subsidiary but not to investors. Avoid banalities—does every company doing an IPO road show have to include a slide reading "superior management"?

Insist on a Good Briefing

Before each road show presentation to individual institutional investors, the lead manager's or comanager's salesperson who is accompanying the subsidiary's management to the meeting should give the management a briefing on the prospective buyer being visited. Information in this briefing should include:

- *The investment focus of the fund.* Each fund tends to have a sweet spot by market capitalization and by style of investor (e.g., whether the manager is a growth at a reasonable price, or GARP, investor or a momentum investor interested primarily in high-velocity, high-value stocks). Know the focus of the fund. In addition, have the salesperson provide a list of the other holdings in the fund's portfolio.

- *Whether the manager has many smaller holdings or concentrates on larger positions in fewer stocks.* Some managers hold a relatively small number of large positions. Other funds have many small positions. The manager with fewer large holdings is less likely to buy the IPO but is worth cultivating for a long-term relationship.

- *Whether the portfolio manager is a generalist or a specialist in the industry.* Some portfolio managers are very focused on a few industries. These managers go to industry events and conferences and read the trade press. They are informed about all the public companies in the industry and have visited with many of the private companies. The presentation to these managers should focus on the subsidiary's position in the industry. These managers will want a thorough explanation of the differentiation of the subsidiary's products or services. Other portfolio managers are generalists who have investments in a range of industries. For these managers, an industry overview is often helpful and is a necessary underpinning for the rest of the presentation. These managers may be more focused on financial criteria.

The subsidiary will probably have the characteristics at any given time to appeal to only one or the other of these types of investors. A sizzling-hot early-stage subsidiary with very high growth prospects, name backers and alliances, and a lofty multiple may be very interesting to a momentum investor, but may hold no interest for a GARP investor. In contrast, a solidly profitable, prosaic company with steady 15 percent growth may appeal greatly to a GARP investor but completely bore a momentum investor.

Follow Up on Unanswered Questions

The IPO managers' sales forces will usually take note of any unanswered questions at road show meetings and try to get back with answers. But it is a good idea for a member of the management team to be delegated to likewise note unanswered questions and ensure that they are answered.

Regroup Each Day

Despite the long hours on the road show, at the end of each day, the management and the lead manager should review what transpired that day. They should critique each meeting, including the issues that arose in the meetings, open issues, and any changes that need to be made to the presentation.

View Every Meeting as an Opportunity

One objective during the road show should be to lay the groundwork for future investors. Many portfolio managers do not buy stock in IPOs but are still interested in the subsidiary. They will follow the subsidiary's progress and may invest at a later date. Approach each meeting as an opportunity to win over a new investor either now or in the future. Stay in touch. Follow up later with additional meetings, mailings, and e-mails.

Keep the Road Show Story Simple and Address Key Concerns Up Front

A typical mistake in a road show presentation is to say too much. Much of what is of great interest to the management of the subsidiary is of little interest to an investor in making an investment decision. An investor needs to come away from a road show presentation with only a few key points as to why an investor should own the stock. The most effective presentations last no more than about 20 minutes and are supported by a PowerPoint presentation.

It is also important to directly address issues that might cause an investor concern or lead to a rejection. If the issuer has lost money for the past three years and has declining revenues, there needs to be good explanations. Understandably, issuers avoid unpleasant subjects—but this is always a mistake. Have good answers to all likely tough questions beforehand. If a question recurs, incorporate the question and the response into the road show. Don't assume that investors will ask about issues that are of concern; often, instead, they simply do not buy into the IPO at all.

Present Obtainable Forecasts

It is important to present to investors forecasts that are not only obtainable but will be beaten in the quarters following the IPO. As discussed, any short-term gain in excitement for the stock from aggressive forecasts will be lost if those forecasts are missed. If this happens, investors will quickly lose confidence in the stock. After an early stumble based on missing forecasts, it is extremely difficult to rebuild credibility with investors. One missed quarter may be forgiven by investors, after the company spends a period in the penalty box. However, two missed quarters are generally fatal to the stock. It may take years to restore credibility and interest in the issuer within the financial community. In the meantime, the issuer's stock will be an orphan stock, with many resultant problems. Also, overly optimistic forecasts that are not met may have negative career effects for the management team, particularly the CFO. Blame will, inevitably, fall on management alone. Very often a new CFO or an entire management team will need to be brought in to restore credibility.

Don't Be Discouraged

There is usually little indication given in the meeting about the ultimate buying decision by the investor. Meetings that appear to be disasters can end up with the investor placing a large order. Conversely, other meetings that seem to be great successes are often not followed by an order.

Get Ready

Road shows are exhausting. Management teams have been known to refer to them as "the Bataan Death March." While the comparison is a disservice to U.S. veterans, what is true is that some managements love them and some hate them. Three

EXHIBIT 23-4

Representative Subsidiary IPO Road Show Schedule

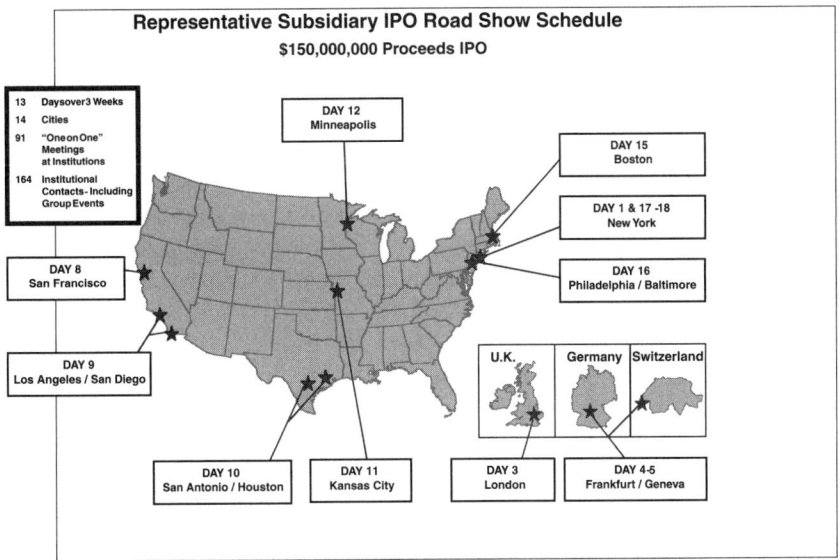

weeks of nonstop meetings and presentations is exhausting. The geographic reach of a representative carve-out IPO road show is illustrated in Exhibit 23–4.

A Final Point

Always carry a spare computer with the presentation loaded, a spare projector and cables, spare batteries, and backup hard copy. Anything that can go wrong generally will, at least once during the road show.

THE ROLE OF THE ROAD SHOW IN CREATING EFFECTIVE IPO PRICING

The price range placed on the cover of the printed preliminary prospectus and discussed with potential investors is set based on a valuation analysis but tempered by the lead and comanagers' views on current market conditions. The objective is to set a price that will create sufficient demand for the stock in the IPO so that it trades to a modest premium in the aftermarket and then grows stronger. Some companies push for an unrealistically high price range. This is almost always counterproductive. These IPOs are either not successful and are withdrawn, or they are only sold at a reduced price, reflecting a "distress" discount. Buyers have a limited attention span and limited time to devote to appraising potential investments. When confronted with an overpriced offering, they tend to move on and spend time on other, more realistic deals. Regaining investor attention often requires pricing the stock considerably lower to clear the market. Lowering the price creates an aura of failure about an IPO that deters investors.

The formal pricing meeting between the shareholders, the subsidiary, and the lead and comanagers takes place at the end of the road show. The issuing price depends on a number of factors. Foremost among these factors is the state of the book. The book indicates interest from each investor and the price limits of each investor, if given. This will help set the price. It is simply an issue of supply and demand.

From the time of the filing to the time of the pricing of the IPO, much may have changed. The subsidiary's story has been tested with real investors and found strong or wanting. The markets overall may have changed and the market for IPOs will have likely changed even more than the overall market. This will usually result in some change in the offering price or in the size of the offering, or both. In a strong market with an issuer with a story that had traction, the price and the size of the IPO may be increased from that estimated at the time of filing (an increase of up to 20 percent in dollar size is permitted by the SEC without recirculating the prospectus).

However, should market conditions have deteriorated since the filing date, and if the story did not catch fire with investors, the price may be reduced from the estimate at the time of the filing or the size of the offering decreased, or both. If there is a weak order book, the managers will not be willing to go ahead with the IPO, and it will be postponed. A reduction in size and/or price is always a bitter blow to all involved. A smaller and lower-priced IPO is disappointing, but it still provides a base for the subsidiary to build a public following and fulfill many of the other objectives of the IPO. Some of the finest-performing public companies went public with distressed offerings in difficult markets with offerings sharply reduced in size and price. Two examples are Novellus Systems and Solectron Corporation, both of which went on to fame and fortune.

At the conclusion of the pricing meeting the lead and comanagers will tell the parent and subsidiary and any large selling shareholders the price and number of shares that they are willing to purchase from each of these parties to resell in the IPO. If there is agreement on price, the underwriting documents will then be signed. The lead manager's and comanagers' sales forces will then call the larger investors and confirm the allocations. The issuer should take another step and ensure that it carefully reviews the allocation of shares in the IPO to various institutions and to any syndicate members that it wants to ensure get paid.

As the offering date approaches, the lead manager will request indications of buying interest from investors. The objective is to ensure that demand for the IPO is well in excess of the size of the offering. With sufficient excess demand, the lead manager is in a position to allocate stock to investors in quantities below their expressed levels of interest. Given reasonable market conditions, the resulting perception and reality of excess demand will help support the issuers' stock in the aftermarket. A lead manager will want to see an IPO oversubscribed by at

EXHIBIT 23–5

IPO Median Gain on First-Day Trading

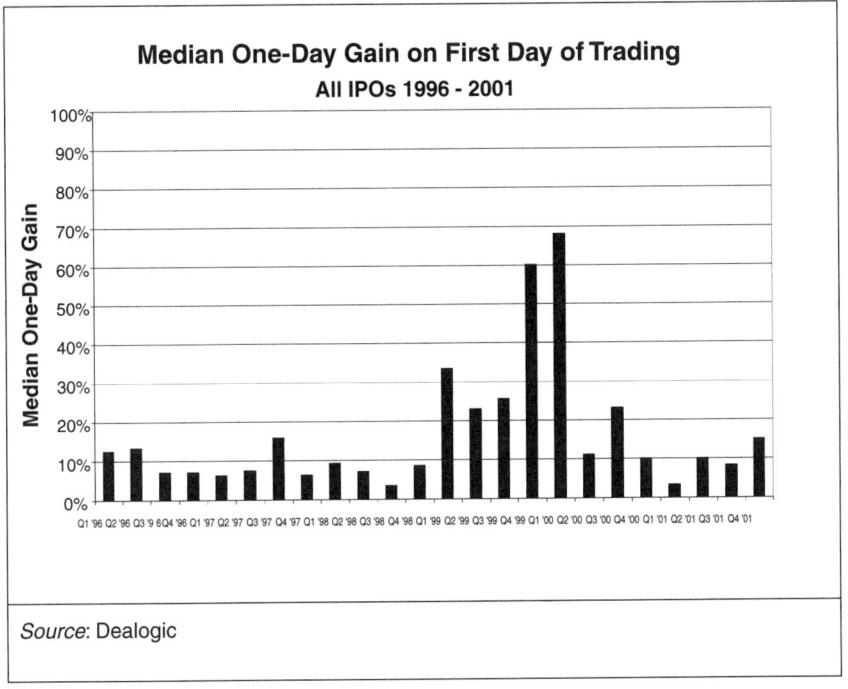

Source: Dealogic

least a factor of three—there should be orders for three times as many shares are being offered. This unmet demand is needed for a successful aftermarket following the IPO.

In normal times (meaning an average strong market), a well-priced IPO will trade to a 10 to 15 percent premium and hold its value in the aftermarket. The investors in the IPO will have done well and the subsidiary will not face either the gyrations of a steep spike in the share price followed by a drop or the disappointment of an IPO that goes down in price from the offering and disappoints investors. Exhibit 23–5 illustrates the first-day gain on IPOs. It shows that in normal markets, an IPO should be priced to appreciate 10 to 15 percent when first traded.

UNDERWRITING SPREADS

At the pricing meeting there will also be a discussion about the appropriate underwriting spread for the IPO.

The underwriting spread is the fee to the investment banks for selling the IPO. It is defined as the difference between the price at which the IPO is sold to

EXHIBIT   23–6

Gross Spreads on IPOs in 2001

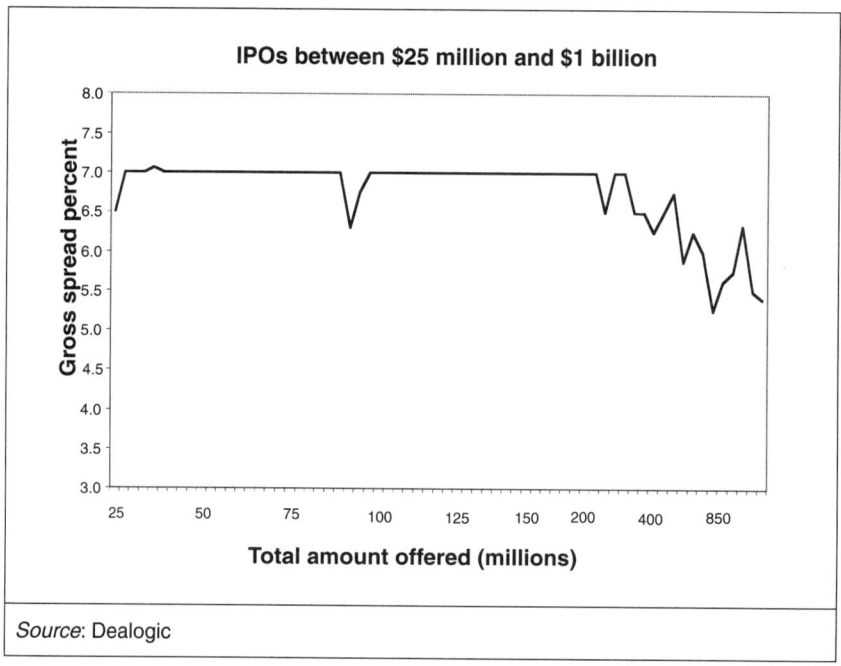

Source: Dealogic

investors and the price at which the shares are purchased from the subsidiary, parent, or selling shareholders by the lead manager on behalf of the underwriters. For example, an IPO is set at a price of $20 per share. This is the price at which shares are sold to the public investors. The spread is agreed on at 7 percent. The lead manager then purchases the shares from the subsidiary for $18.60 per share.

The lead manager should have already had discussions with the parent and subsidiary and any large selling shareholders on the range of potential spreads. This is narrowed to a single percentage at the pricing meeting, and the relevant discount at which the underwriters will purchase the shares from the issuer (and selling shareholders, if any) is agreed on. A largely retail-placed IPO will tend to be at the higher end of the range of spreads for comparably sized IPOs. The underwriting discount is, by far, the largest expense to the subsidiary or parent on most IPOs.

As Exhibit 23–6 indicates, the spread on IPOs tends to be fairly consistent at 7 percent for most IPOs except very small ones or very large ones. While there are the odd exceptions, these few imply special circumstances. For an IPO under $150 million in proceeds, assume 7 percent will be the spread.

Even the exceptions on deals under $200 million in Exhibit 23–6 do not contradict the rule. For example, one is the 6.5 percent spread on the $26 million

Peet's Coffee & Tea Inc. IPO in January 2001 that was sold in an experimental sale of shares in a Dutch auction IPO lead-managed by a small firm. Another is the 6.3 percent spread on the $84 million Stelmer Shipping Ltd. IPO in March 2001, an IPO for an Athens-based operator of oil tankers by nonmainstream managers.

ONCE PRICING HAS BEEN SET, IMPORTANT STEPS ARE SET IN MOTION

After pricing has been agreed to by all of the necessary parties, an underwriting agreement will be signed obligating the underwriters to purchase the agreed shares and obligating the issuer to sell them. Next, the pricing amendment to the registration statement is filed with the SEC. The pricing amendment sets out the offering price of the shares to the public, the underwriting spread, the net proceeds to the company, and the net proceeds of any shares sold by the parent or other shareholders. At the same time, the SEC is asked to declare the registration statement "effective." Once the registration statement is declared effective, customer orders can be confirmed by the lead manager's and comanager's sales forces, and the sales syndicate is updated about its shares allocation. Alternatively, a 430A procedure may be used where the pricing disclosure follows the SEC declaring the registration statement effective.

After the registration statement becomes effective, the final prospectus is printed and distributed to everyone who received a copy of the red herring and to others who expressed an interest in purchasing the stock.

MARKET STABILIZATION: MANAGING THE AFTERMARKET

The Overallotment Option, or Green Shoe

Immediately following the IPO, the lead manager is permitted by the SEC to engage in *stabilization* of the offering. This is intervention in the market by the lead manager to ensure an orderly market. Stabilization involves considerable risk for the lead manager. If it is goes short the stock to supply the market and the price then goes up after the IPO, it will incur a large loss. If it goes long the stock by purchasing shares in the open market to support the IPO and the price then goes down, it will also incur a large loss. These losses can easily erase any profit from the IPO. One way for the lead manager to mitigate the risk of a large loss is through the use of an overallotment option, also known as the Green Shoe—named after the Green Shoe Company on whose offering this practice was first initiated. Most investment banks will not undertake an IPO unless there is a Green Shoe. The Green Shoe permits the lead manager to purchase up to a specified number of additional shares from the subsidiary at the offering price for up to 30 days following the IPO. The Green Shoe is usually for 15 percent of the offering (the limit imposed by the NASD).

The Green Shoe enables the lead manager to establish a short position in the stock by selling more shares in the IPO than the offering amount. The purpose of this short position is to allow the lead manager to then purchase shares in the open market should the IPO weaken. Should the price of the stock be under pressure, the lead manager purchases shares in the open market to support the IPO and thereby cover the short position. Should the IPO be strong and the stock price go up after the offering, the lead manager will turn to the Green Shoe and purchase the shares to cover the short position from the subsidiary (or selling shareholders). The Green Shoe protects the lead manager from having to purchase shares in the open market to cover the short at a loss and also, through these purchases, give more fuel to a rising price. Because the shares in the Green Shoe must be sold at the IPO price, the underwriters do not make a profit on them (other than the additional underwriting spread), but they avoid a loss. Despite the Green Shoe, the lead manager may still make losses, stabilizing the IPO in the aftermarket. Losses incurred in stabilizing an IPO are paid for by all the underwriters of the IPO pro rata to their underwriting commitment.

The shares for the Green Shoe may come from the subsidiary or from the sale of stock by the parent or selling shareholders. Providing the shares for the Green Shoe is also often a way for the parent or selling shareholders of the subsidiary to sell stock in the IPO. It is much more palatable when the subsidiary is less established and presents greater risk to IPO investors to have the parent or selling shareholders sell stock in the Green Shoe than in the IPO itself, as the Green Shoe is only exercised should the IPO be a success and have a strong aftermarket.

In cases where the subsidiary is only partially owned by the parent and its current management has shares it desires to sell in the IPO, investors will definitely prefer to see any sales by the current management in the Green Shoe rather than the IPO itself. The negative for all the parties providing the shares for the Green Shoe is the uncertainty over whether the Green Shoe will be exercised and the number of shares that will ultimately be sold, as the Green Shoe will not be exercised should the IPO be weak.

The existence of the Green Shoe is disclosed on the cover of the prospectus. In addition to stabilization, there are other methods used by the lead manager to ensure a good aftermarket immediately following the IPO, such as not paying a sales commission to the salesperson on any shares sold in the IPO that are immediately resold by the buyers following the IPO.

SUMMARY

Smart marketing and pricing of an IPO are critically important components of the IPO process, as the former creates demand, and the latter ensures that buyers will act on their buying interest. This chapter examined these concepts and also looked at how a marketing road show can help determine IPO pricing. It also discussed the importance of creating—and sustaining—interest in the aftermarket because this impacts the ongoing success of a newly public company. Chapter 24 will look at the factors that help a newly public company succeed in a very challenging business environment.

CHAPTER **24**

SUCCEEDING AS A
PUBLIC COMPANY

INTRODUCTION

For IPOs, mergers, and spin-offs to be viewed as successful SER transactions, the subsidiary needs to become a successful public company. The parent or, in the case of a spin-off, its shareholders benefit from this success through the appreciation in the value of the subsidiary's shares that they own. If the parent continues as a majority or minority shareholder, the success of the subsidiary in the public markets is necessary for the parent to obtain the economic benefit of its ownership interest.

The company benefits from a successful SER transaction as well, because it is able to use its stock for acquisitions, raise additional capital and equity-related capital such as convertible debt, repay debt, and use its stock to attract and retain employees. Note that this chapter uses the term *company* to refer to the subsidiary, as the subsidiary may actually be an independent company after specific SER transactions.

However, most public companies do not perform well after going public. For example, as noted in Chapter 4, 82 percent of the companies that went public in 2000 through IPOs were trading, at year-end 2001, below their IPO price. This is sobering. As a result, the public companies, its employees, the parent, and the public shareholders all suffer.

Therefore, the purpose of this chapter is to detail the steps that should be followed immediately after a company becomes public. We will pay particular attention to creating and maintaining trust with investors and research analysts, as this will have a large impact on determining the value of the newly public company's stock. The company's management should view public stock investors and the community that supports them as important and valuable customers. Specifically, investor demand for the subsidiary's stock allows the subsidiary to use the public markets to raise capital and gives value to its stock for use in acquisitions and employee equity compensation.

However, there are thousands of public companies competing for investor time and money. As in all very competitive markets, securing investor support requires that the company understand the different investors and their requirements and that it deliver a quality product that meets the demands of the investors.

KEY STEPS TO CREATING A SUCCESSFUL PUBLIC COMPANY

There are many factors that contribute to the creation of a successful public company. The purpose of this discussion is to list some steps that should be followed to ensure that there is a greater chance that a newly public company will succeed in the public markets. These steps include the following:

- Building and maintaining the trust and support of investors
- Building and maintaining the trust and support of investment bank research analysts
- Steering a course between executing a long-term business strategy and meeting investor demands for short-term earnings growth
- Using the public markets as a strategic tool to help grow the company
- Complying with securities laws
- Managing employee expectations in a volatile stock market

The first part of this discussion is devoted to building and maintaining the support of investors and investment bank research analysts. After that we will examine the balance of the steps listed here.

Building and Maintaining the Support of Investors and Research Analysts

Investors

While some institutional investor segments may turn over their portfolios up to 10 times a year and are constantly moving on to the next hot company, other institutional investors prefer to have long-term holdings in quality companies and low portfolio turnover. In many cases, these are the investors that the management of the company should seek out and cultivate.

Research Analysts

An important relationship for any company is with the investment bank equity research analysts covering the industry and the company. Analysts have a key role as intermediaries with investors. As with investors, credibility is the underlying basis for a strong relationship with research analysts. However, analysts and smart investors always want an edge. Their job is to trade in information.

Good analysts are skeptical, ask tough questions, and develop a wealth of industry sources. The company should be prepared for questions arising from many directions. Research analysts are wary today of being perceived as cheerleaders for companies that they cover and are trying to maintain more objectivity than in the past. Certainly, too cozy a relationship between companies and analysts during the stock market bubble led to a loss of analyst credibility with investors, which must be rebuilt.

Relations with research analysts are less close than they were a few years ago. As well, the requirements of SEC Regulation FD for nonselective disclosure have caused many companies to be less open and less willing to share confidential information with analysts than in the past. As a consequence, companies are less able or willing to provide detailed forecasts to analysts. However, the analysts are important to the communication strategy of the company.

Although the research analysts and investor constituencies are different, many of their demands are the same. In order to build and maintain the trust of both communities, do the following:

- *Report quarterly earnings promptly and accurately.* Delays cause apprehension, and a long reporting cycle does not look sharp to investors.

- *Create realistic earnings expectations.* Repeatedly missing forecasts is a sign that the subsidiary's management does not understand its business or industry and results in a loss of management credibility and the loss of investor and analyst interest in the subsidiary, neither of which is easily restored. Very few companies that lose credibility ever regain analyst or investor interest while being led by the same management team. These companies must change management, be acquired, or face a future languishing as an underperforming "orphan" in the public market, with a low stock price and no following. Conversely, a company that has obtained the trust of public investors and research analysts by consistently meeting or exceeding its commitments will have considerable latitude to execute a long-term strategy that may adversely affect short-term earnings.

- *Disclose any negative news fully.* It is important to always promptly disclose, even when the news is unfavorable. Especially when management has been blindsided and embarrassed by an unanticipated deterioration in the business, there is a natural temptation to want to hide and not face angry investors; few managers enjoy being abused. However, investors often cite the openness and availability of management when there is bad news as a reason to have confidence in the company and its management team.

- *Make senior managers available for questions on a regular basis, either over the phone or in person at conferences.* The CEO should expect to spend one day a week on investor and analyst relations. These responsibilities are necessary for the success of the company and will include time spent at investor conferences and on investor road shows. The CEO must also find time to supervise public accounting and legal compliance.

After the IPO, an investor relations firm may play a constructive role in introducing the management to potential investors by sponsoring investor meetings and exposing the subsidiary's story to a wider audience. The role may also include organizing financial press relations and investor communications, including quarterly conference calls and assistance in preparing the annual report and website.

* *Keep investors informed about key corporate developments.* The company should keep investors informed on corporate developments through annual and quarterly reports, proxy statements, press releases, direct mailings, conferences, a website, and shareholders' meetings. In all but the largest companies, investor communications should be led by the CEO and should not be delegated because that may result in the creation of an inconsistent message. A true test of the ability of management to communicate effectively with investors is when the newly public company is having difficulty. When there are difficulties, some management teams hide, while others are proactive and reach out to analysts, investors, and the press before the competition has a chance to get to them with its own, much less flattering, interpretation of events.

FOLLOWING A PUBLIC SER

The success of any IPO, spin-off, or other public SER for the subsidiary and for the parent if it has not sold all its shares in the SER is dependent on investor interest in a stock in the aftermarket. This section will briefly look at how a company can help create—and sustain—investor interest in the stock of the newly public company.

About three months after the public SER, the lead manager of the IPO or the advisor on a spin-off should sponsor follow-on group and individual meetings for the subsidiary's management with institutional investors in major cities. The objective of these meetings is to communicate important updates to existing investors and to interest new investors. These meetings should be scheduled to coincide with important company announcements, although care must be taken to meet all fair disclosure rules and regulations Protocol calls for the subsidiary to allow the lead manager or advisor to set up the first set of institutional visits, as a debut tour with another firm will embarrass the sales force of the lead manager or advisor— investors assume that the issuer is unhappy with its performance. Even if that is actually the case, nothing is gained by deliberately alienating the lead manager's or advisor's sales force. Once a quarter, the subsidiary should consider going on a similar investor tour. On these later visits, it is a good idea to also engage the sales forces of the other managers and other firms providing research coverage by allocating specific cities to each firm to organize.

Most investment banks have periodic conferences to bring together institutional investors and sponsored companies. The subsidiary should expect that the managers or spin-off advisor will invite the subsidiary to relevant events. There are also other investor conferences of every type and description sponsored by industry groups, PR and consulting firms, and others. Some conferences are large multi-industry events with hundreds of companies presenting, and other conferences are short and industry specific or focus on a particular subject or theme. The management of a successful public company could easily spend much of the year doing little but attending investor conferences. Instead, choose a limited number to go to each year. Ensure that Regulation FD, which prohibits selective disclosure of material information, is adhered to and that there is no selective disclosure at these events. Many companies either webcast their presentation at an investor conference or put hard copy of the presentation on their website to ensure compliance with SEC Regulation FD.

OVERCOMING THE CHALLENGES

While these steps seem fairly straightforward, the challenge is to balance the tasks of building and maintaining investor and analyst trust with meeting short-term projections and creating long-term growth opportunities concurrently.

One reason this dual responsibility can be so daunting is that the CEO or board of directors focuses too much on the stock price, placing great pressure on the organization, which may be excessive and not grounded in realistic expectations of what can be achieved. At best, such pressure leads to a focus on short-term results at the expense of the future. At worst, excessive pressure can lead to the adoption of questionable practices and even fraud. The consequences of efforts to keep the stock price up, despite deteriorating fundamentals, do eventually catch up with the company and its management, as recent examples ranging from Xerox to Enron prove. Yet there are many public companies that implement long-term strategies but nevertheless have fine experiences as public companies. The two are not necessarily a contradiction. The key is to communicate regularly, honestly, and effectively with investors and analysts who may be more than willing to sacrifice short-term gains for long-term growth and profitability.

Factors Influencing Pressure on the Company for Short-Term Results

The pressure on quarterly earnings will vary depending on a number of factors including the composition of the actual shareholder base, which the company can control to some degree. Let's take a look at this factor in more detail.

Composition of the Shareholder Base

There is a wide spectrum of potential investors in a public company, ranging from momentum investors focused entirely on quarterly earnings to very long-term investors who hold portfolio companies for years. Long-term investors are not typically concerned with quarter-to-quarter events if they are convinced of the underlying soundness of the corporate strategy. Generally, however, short-term investors have been the most willing to pay high price multiples for stocks. Exhibit 24–1 illustrates the relationship between type of investor, time horizon as reflected in portfolio turnover, and willingness to pay a high multiple for a stock. The actual multiples that different types of investors will pay change dramatically with market conditions. All multiples come down in bear markets and go up in bull markets. However, the relative spread generally remains.

EXHIBIT 24–1

Attributes of Investment Styles in a "Normal" Public Market

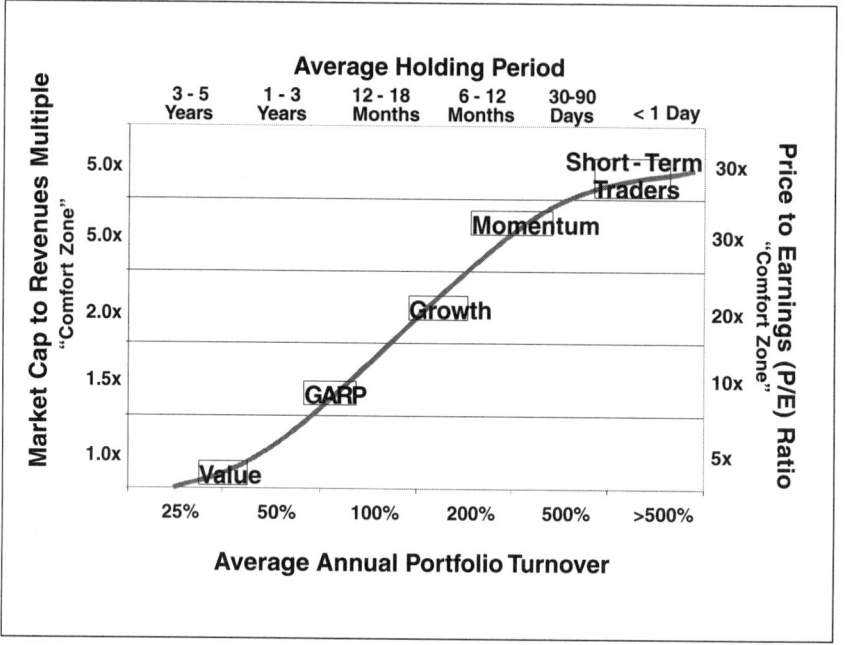

Here are some additional details about the different types of investors.

Short-Term Traders   Short-term traders are found primarily at the trading desks of institutional funds and at investment bank trading desks. They may employ large sums of capital. Retail investors were also active as online day traders from 1996 to 2001. Not much is heard of these folks anymore. As their name implies, traders hold stocks for very short periods of time. They are often short one stock to hedge another position. Traders do help make liquid markets.

Momentum Investors   Momentum investors formed the backbone of the investors group in many high-multiple stocks in the late 1990s and 2000. During that period, they played a significant role in what are known as the "nosebleed" (i.e., irrationally high) valuations of favored companies. These investors are primarily institutional fund managers, mutual funds, and hedge funds. They turn over their portfolio up to 10 times a year. As a result, they make a significant contribution to the brokerage revenues of investment banks, and they tend to receive a disproportionate allocation of shares in hot IPOs.

Momentum investors are far from ideal investors for a company trying to build long-term value and a solid shareholder group. While momentum investors do take stocks to very high prices, this can be a double-edged sword. When momentum investors decide that a company no longer has earnings and revenue momentum, they sell quickly or short the stock. Even the most favored momentum stock (and there was no more of a darling than Cisco Systems) sooner or later falls out of favor when its growth slows, it stumbles, or market sentiment simply turns negative toward its sector. Many former darlings of momentum investors end up as broken stocks or orphans without market support. These companies usually have great difficulty building a new shareholder base after such a crash, and doing so may take years. Momentum investing is no longer nearly as dynamic as it was in the late 1990s. Many momentum funds lost 50 percent of their value in 2000 and 2001. For example, the Janus Twenty Fund, an aggressive momentum fund investor and part of the Denver-based Janus Funds group, went from a high of $93.80 per share of net asset value in March 2000 to a low of $32.52 in September 2001, a loss of 65 percent. Many of the more aggressive momentum investors lost more than this. Janus Fund's small-cap fund, the Janus Venture Fund, fell sharply in the dot-com debacle. Its net asset value per share reached $166.66 in March 2000 and fell to a low of $33.36 in September 2001, a decline of 80 percent. Not to single out Janus, the once high-flying Amerindo Technology Fund went from a high of $44.40 per share of net asset value in March 2000 to a low of $3.49 in September 2001, a loss of over 92 percent of its value. However, some momentum investors called the market right and are still thriving and active.

Growth Investors   Growth investors focus on longer-term investments in companies with good growth rates. They will hold the stock as long as they are convinced that the company will continue to grow. However, they are also attuned to momentum factors and quarterly earnings.

GARP (Growth at a Reasonable Price) Investors   These are longer-term investors. They buy and hold good growth companies. These funds have strict valuation criteria, but they are good supporters of quality growth companies.

Value Investors   Value investors look for stocks of companies that are sound but trading at relatively low multiples. They buy orphan stocks abandoned by the momentum investors. They require a long time horizon for the stock to come to reflect its fundamental value. The masters at this style of investment include the State of Wisconsin Investment Board, Baron Capital, and Central Securities. They are patient investors and will not reach for a stock outside their strict valuation criteria. They often have exceedingly low portfolio turnover—and are, therefore, the bane of brokers. They are great investors for a company out to build long-term value. Often, they do not sell when the stock of a quality company recovers and finds its footing.

INFLUENCING THE COMPOSITION OF THE SHAREHOLDER BASE

While the composition of the investor base is not entirely within the subsidiary's control, the company may greatly influence the composition of the investor base through the following factors:

• *The choice of investment banks to sponsor the company.* Some investment banks are associated more with momentum investors and others more with longer-term investors.

• *The investor conferences the company attends after it is public.* Some conferences attract momentum investors and others long-term investors.

• *The projections given to the market on future earnings and revenue growth.* Consistently downplaying expectations will have two beneficial results: the company is less likely to miss its forecasts and it is less likely to attract momentum investors.

FACTORS BEYOND THE CONTROL OF THE COMPANY THAT AFFECT ITS STOCK PRICE

There are many factors beyond the control of the company that affect its stock price, including:

• *Investor sentiment toward the industry sector.* With most companies, regrettably, sentiment toward the industry sector will be more important to the stock price in the short term than will the actual performance of the company. When an industry is favored, even mediocre companies in that industry will receive high valuations. In times of industry disfavor, even companies that are performing flawlessly will be punished.

• *Overall market conditions.* The stock market consistently overvalues stocks in times of a buoyant economy and undervalues them in times of recession or slower growth.

• *Supply and demand for the company's stock.* Stocks sold in markets are subject to the same volatile short-term supply-and-demand factors as in any other market. This is especially true for the less efficient markets in smaller- and mid-capitalization stocks. There may be temporary imbalances resulting from a large institution that wants to sell a significant block, or the parent may be making significant sales of stock in the market. This supply may drive the price down considerably, as the market makers or specialists reduce the price to find buyers and protect their position and take advantage of the opportunity. If faced with this situation, all that the management of the company can do is attempt to provide support for sellers through a campaign of institutional visits prior to the large block coming on the market to create buying interest in the stock, or encourage large sellers to join together and offer their shares in an organized follow-on offering of secondary shares. Alternatively, a large buyer wishing to purchase a significant position may drive the price up.

- *Investor games.* Even some well-known investors may play games with stocks. With purchases and subtle promotion, investors can, for a time, drive up the price of the stock of a company—especially one with a limited public float or with short sales and well-placed rumors—and drive it down. The company can do very little in this circumstance other than refraining from encouraging or supporting the activity.

Stop Worrying About the Stock Price— Go Build a Great Company

Many of the factors determining the stock price are beyond the company's control. However, creating real value for investors is within its control. This can be accomplished by building great businesses that generate shareholder value. In the long term, markets reward performance.

OTHER STEPS TO CREATING A SUCCESSFUL PUBLIC COMPANY

Having spent quite a bit of time examining how to build and maintain relationships with investors and analysts, we will now turn our attention to other steps that should be taken following a successful IPO to help create a successful public company.

Use the Public Stock Market to Enhance Growth

As with most markets, the public stock market is often not efficient in the short term. Insightful management teams exploit overly optimistic valuations in the public market to create shareholder value through raising capital and using stock in acquisitions. There is no better example of exploiting a short-term market opportunity than that of America Online (AOL), which brilliantly used its absurdly overvalued stock to buy control of a major company, Time Warner. In contrast, Yahoo! did not use its similarly overvalued stock effectively and gave away most of its value when the Internet bubble burst. Similarly, when the stock is genuinely undervalued and the company has excess cash, it may consider repurchasing stock. However, most managements firmly believe their stock is undervalued—whatever the price. A good reality check is not to repurchase shares unless the stock price is below book value.

Manage Employee Expectations

One of the most important jobs of a public company's senior management is ensuring that employees stay focused on the business and not on daily swings in the stock price. There is no secret formula for this. It certainly helps from the perspective of managing employees if the company becomes public in a less than buoyant market; then it will not have wild swings in the stock price to worry about and can focus everyone on building value. The stock then may build gradually in value over time. Microsoft went public in the terrible technology market of 1986 and never looked back. The most difficult challenge is maintaining employee enthusiasm in a depressed stock market. It seems for years that no matter how well the company does, the stock market does not reward progress. Take heart—it does eventually.

SUMMARY

Unfortunately, many companies assume that becoming public through a spin-off, merger, or IPO is the end objective in itself or that being public guarantees future success. Yet, in most cases, creating value for the parent requires that the subsidiary not just become a public company but also succeed in the public markets. Unfortunately, the reality is that many newly public companies fail to create shareholder value. They set unrealistic expectations or they fail to communicate with analysts and investors in a smart and proactive manner. As the creation of a public company is often only the start of a successful SER process, it is important that companies put as much effort into succeeding as a public company as they put into structuring an SER transaction, for the maximum benefit of the parent, the subsidiary, and, ultimately, both sets of shareholders.

SCHEDULE OF SELECTED PUBLIC EQUITY REDEPLOYMENT TRANSACTIONS 1995–2002

EXHIBIT APPENDIX A-1

Selected Carve-out Public Offerings

Selected Carve-Out Public Offerings
January 1, 1995–March 31, 2002

Issue date	Issuer	Ticker	Business description	Principal amount (mm)	Parent	Ticker of parent	Business description of parent
03/21/02	Travelers Property Casualty	TAPa	Ppty, casualty ins svcs	3,885	Citigroup Inc	C	Global financial svcs
03/20/02	Alcon Inc	ACL	Dvlp eye care prod & equip	2,301	Nestle SA	NSRGY	Produce chocolate, other foods
02/12/02	GameStop Corp	GME	Own, op video game stores	325	Barnes & Noble Inc	BKS	Op retail book stores
02/04/02	Sunoco Logistics Partners LP	SXL	Op refined prod & oil pipeline	101	Sunoco Inc	SUN	Mnfr, whl petroleum prod
10/29/01	Anthem Inc	ATH	Managed health care plans	1,728	Anthem Insurance Companies, Inc.	Private	Insurance co
10/25/01	Penn Va Resources Partners LP	PVR	Coal mining	136	Penn Virginia Corp	PVA	Oil & gas exploration, prodn
08/09/01	Mykrolis Corporation	MYK	Dvlp liquid delivery systems	105	Millipore Corp	MIL	Mnfr analytical prod
06/13/01	FMC Technologies Inc	FTI	Mnfr oil & gas machinery	221	FMC Corp	FMC	Mnfr chem,auto process equip
06/12/01	Kraft Foods Inc	KFT	Brand food & beverages	8,680	Philip Morris Cos Inc	MO	Mnfr cigarettes
05/17/01	Instinet Group Inc	INET	Electronic trading svcs	464	Reuters Group PLC	RTRS	Intl news svcs
05/14/01	Kinder Morgan Mgmt LLC	KMR	Own & op prod pipeline system	1,047	Kinder Morgan Energy Partners	KMP	Operate natural gas pipelines
04/30/01	Reliant Resources Inc	RRI	Electricity & energy svcs	1,560	Reliant Energy Inc	REI	Electric utility;holding co
04/09/01	Valero LP	UDL	Operate crude oil pipeline	110	Ultramar Diamond Shamrock Corp	UDS	Mnfr,whl petroleum prod
3/27/01	Agere Systems Inc	AGR.A	Mnfr communications semiconductors	6480	Lucent Technologies Inc	LU	Mnfr telecom equip, software
2/5/01	Williams Energy Partners LP	WEG	Dist refined petroleum prod	75	Williams Cos Inc	WMB	Gas utility
11/9/00	Luminent Inc	LMNE	Fiber-optic prod	168	MRV Communications Inc	MRVC	Mnfr semiconductors
8/16/00	Teledyne Technologies Inc	TDY	Electronic, communications prod	72	Allegheny Teledyne Inc	ALT	Mnfr specialty materials, metal
8/10/00	Orient-Express Hotels Ltd	OEH	Own, and op hotels	172	Sea Containers Ltd	SCR.B	Passenger transport svcs
8/7/00	America Online Latin America	AOLA	Internet service provider (ISP)	400	AOL Time Warner Inc	AOL	Telecom svcs
7/26/00	TyCom Ltd (Tyco Intl Ltd)	TCM	Fiber-optic networks, svcs	900	Tyco International Ltd	TYC	Mnfr, whl elelctric components
7/10/00	Axcelis Technologies	ACLS	Mnfr ion implantation equip	325	Eaton Corp	ETN	Mnfr automotive parts
6/26/00	eFunds Corp	EFDS	Electronic payment svcs	93	Deluxe Corp	DLX	Mnfr bank checks, comp forms
6/26/00	Stratos Lightwave Inc	STLW	Mnfr optical transceivers	148	Methode Electronics Inc	METHB	Mnfr electronic devices
6/23/00	Genuity, Inc.	GENU	Internet svcs	1,913	Verizon communications	VZ	Communications svcs

Selected Carve-Out Public Offerings
January 1, 1995–March 31, 2002

Issue date				Parent	Principal amount (mm)	Ticker of parent	Business description of parent
6/14/00	Osca Inc	OSCA	Specialized oil & gas	Great Lakes Chemical Corp	84	GLK	Mnfr chemicals, pesticides
5/30/00	NRG Energy Inc	NRG	Electric & gas utility svc	Northern States Power Co	478	NSP	Electric & gas utility
4/26/00	AT&T Wireless Group	AWE	Wireless voice, data svcs	AT&T Corp	8,874	T	Own, op telecom sys
4/4/00	Cabot Microelectronics Corp	CCMP	Develop abrasive chemicals	Cabot Corp	64	CBT	Mnfr carbon black
3/30/00	PetroChina Co Ltd	PTR	Oil & gas exploration, prodn	China National Petroleum Corp	776	CNPZ CH	Crude oil & natural gas in China
3/22/00	inSilicon Corp	INSN	Mnfr semiconductors	Phoenix Technologies	35	PTEC	Develop systems software
3/1/00	Palm Inc	PALM	Develop applications software	3Com Corp	345	COMS	Mnfr, whl networking systems
2/25/00	Hotel Reservations Network Inc	ROOM	Online hotel reservations	USA Network (Seagram Co)	64	VO	Music entertainment svcs
2/16/00	Choice One Communications	CWON	Telecom svcs	ACC Corp	80	ACCC	Telecom svcs
11/30/99	NBCi	NBCI	Internet media content	General Electric Corp	1,529	GE	Diversified
12/15/99	Xpedior Inc	XPDR	Computer consulting svcs	PSINet Inc	119	PSIX	Internet service provider (ISP)
12/1/99	McAfee.com Corp	MCAF	PC management solutions	Network Associates Inc	43	NETA	Dvlp network software
11/17/99	Agilent Technologies Inc	A	Mnfr test, measurement equip	Hewlett-Packard Co	1168	HWP	Mnfr computers, testing equip
11/17/99	Retek Inc	RETK	Bus software solution	HNC Software Inc	55	HNCS	Develop neural network systems
11/9/99	Expedia Inc	EXPE	Online travel svcs	Microsoft Corp	45	MSFT	Dvlp, whl computer software
11/9/99	Next Level Communications	NXTV	Mnfr broadband comm equip	General Instrument Corp	93	SEM	Mnfr discrete semiconductors
11/2/99	Thomson Multimedia	TMS	Mnfr, whl audio, video prod	Thomson SA (France)	375	TOMS FP	Mnfr audio & video equip
10/7/99	Homeservices Com Inc	HMSV	Online real estate svcs	MidAmerican Energy Holdings Co	60	MEC	Electric utility
10/1/99	BlackRock Inc	BLK	Investment management svcs	PNC Bank Corp	122	PNC	Bank holding co
10/1/99	Williams Communications Group	WCG	Fiber-optic communications svcs	Williams Cos Inc	651	WMB	Gas utility
9/15/99	NETsilicon Inc	NSIL	Mnfr networking silicon chips	Osicom Technologies Inc	14	FIBR	Mnfr communications equip
7/29/99	Digex Inc	DIGX	Managed web hosting svcs	Intermedia Communications Inc	160	ICIX	Telecom svcs
7/20/99	Engage Technologies Inc	ENGA	Internet mktg software	CMGI Inc	60	CMGI	Dir mail advertising svcs
7/20/99	Genentech Inc	DNA	Manufacture pharmaceuticals	Roche Holding AG	1800	RO	Mnfr pharmaceuticals
7/13/99	TIBCO Software Inc	TIBX	Develop Internet software	Reuters Holdings PLC	73	RTRS	Intl news svcs
6/25/99	US Search Corp.com	SRCH	Info about individuals	Kushner-Locke Co	60	KLOC	Motion picture prodn svcs
6/23/99	TD Waterhouse Group Inc	TWE	Online brokerage svcs	Toronto-Dominion Bank	457	TD	Commercial bank holding co
6/15/99	CareInsite Inc	CARI	Health e-commerce network	Medical Manager Corp	84	MMGR	Mnfr plastic components
6/9/99	Azurix Corp	AZX	Water svcs	Enron Corp	600	ENE	Whl petroleum, petroleum prods
5/25/99	barnesandnoble.com Inc	BNBN	Online book retail market	Barnes & Noble, Inc.	300	BNBN	Online book retail market

Continued

Selected Carve-Out Public Offerings
January 1, 1995–March 31, 2002

Issue date	Issuer	Ticker	Business description	Principal amount (mm)	Parent	Ticker of parent	Business description of parent
5/13/99	MIPS Technologies Inc	MIPS	Mnfr electronic computer	242	Silicon Graphics Inc	SGI	Mnfr computer systems
5/7/99	NetObjects Inc	NETO	Internet software	72	IBM Corp	IBM	Mnfr computers, office equip
4/30/99	Consol Energy Inc	CNX	Coal mining	44	Rheinbraun AG	RWEG	Mnfr petro; pvds electric svcs
4/13/99	MIH Ltd	MIHL	Pay-television svcs	70	MIH Holdings	MHH SJ	Mnfr digital decoder
4/9/99	iTurf Inc	TURF	E-commerce retail svcs	40	Delia's Inc	DLIA	Own, op catalog houses
4/8/99	Hugoton Royalty Trust	HGT	Oil & gas trust	150	Cross Timbers Oil Co	XTO	Oil & gas exploration, prodn
4/6/99	Evercel Inc	EVCL	Mnfr storage batteries	8	Energy Research Corp	ERCC	Dev carbonate fuel cell tech
3/10/99	Du Pont Photomasks Inc	DPMI	Mnfr photomasks	91	El du Pont de Nemours and Co	DD	Mnfr indl chemicals, fibers
2/11/99	United Pan-Europe Comm NV	UPC	Telecom svcs	519	United International Holdings	UIHIA	Prd cable television svcs
2/4/99	Delphi Automotive Systems Corp	DPH	Mnfr automotive components	1360	General Motors Corp	GM	Motor vehicles, accessories
2/4/99	Modem Media. Poppe Tyson Inc	MMPT	Internet professional svcs	31	TN Technologies	TNO	Pvds advertising, PR svcs
1/15/99	MarketWatch.com Inc	MKTW	Internet search engine svc	30	CBS MarketWatch	DBCC	Financial data, quotation svcs
12/9/98	Infinity Broadcasting Corp	INF	Own, op radio broadcasting stns	2352	CBS Corp	CBS	Own, op broadcasting stations
11/19/98	Banco Santander de Puerto Rico	SBP	Commercial bank	140	Banco de Santander SA	STD	Bank holding co
10/21/98	Conoco	COCA	Mnfr petroleum products	2970	El du Pont de Nemours and Co	DD	Mnfr industrial chemicals, fibers
8/12/98	Convergys	CVG	Billing, mgmt solution svcs	259	Cincinnati Bell Inc	CSN	Telecom svcs
7/30/98	Maxtor Corp	MXO	Mnfr computer disk drives	361	Hyundai Electronics Industries Co.	HYECF	Electronics co
7/27/98	IDG Books Worldwide Inc	IDGB	Publish books	49	International Data Group Inc	5331Z	Publishing group
6/29/98	MIPS Technologies Inc	MIPS	Mnfr electronic computer	71	Silicon Graphics Inc	SGI	Mnfr computer systems
6/24/98	Rhodia SA	RHA	Mnfr specialty, ind chemicals	235	Rhone-Poulenc SA	RP	Mnfr chemicals & cosmetics
6/17/98	Unigraphics Solutions Inc	UGS	CAD, CAE, CAM, PDM software	64	Electronic Data Systems Corp	EDS	Information tech svcs
4/30/98	Heller Financial Inc	HF	Business finance svcs	723	Mizuho Holdings Inc	MZHO JP	Investment holding co
4/28/98	Ziff-Davis Inc	ZD	Pub computing-related products	319	Softbank Corp	SFT GR	Investment mgmt svcs
4/2/98	Omega Protein Corporation	OME	Produce prod derived from fish	90	Zapata Corp	ZAP	Mnfr animal & marine fats
3/25/98	ONIX Systems Inc	ONX	Mnfr process control device	43	Thermo Instrument Systems Inc	TMO	Mnfr scientific tech, equip
3/4/98	Waddell & Reed Financial Inc	WDR	Investment mgmt holding co	364	Torchmark Corp	TMK	Insurance co; holding co
12/10/97	Thermo Vision	VIZ	Mnfr medical monitoring equip	17	Thermo Instrument Systems Inc	TMO	Mnfr scientific tech, equip
11/24/97	Electric Lightwave Inc	ELIX	Telecommunication svcs	140	Citizens Communications Co	CZN	Telecom svcs
11/21/97	Teligent Inc	TGNT	Telecom svcs	90	Teligent LLC (Associated Group)	AGRPA	Telecom svcs

Selected Carve-Out Public Offerings
January 1, 1995–March 31, 2002

Issue date	Issuer	Ticker	Business description	Principal amount (mm)	Parent	Ticker of parent	Business description of parent
11/13/97	Magyar Tavkozlesi	MTA	Telecom svcs	62	Magyar Com GmbH	AIT	Telecom svcs
11/12/97	CIT Group Inc	CIT	Misc bus finance svcs	834	Dai-Ichi Kangyo Bank Ltd	DAIKY	Investment holding co
11/11/97	Novacare Employee Services Inc	NCES	Help supply svcs	54	NovaCare Inc	NOV	Physical rehab svcs
10/24/97	Priority Healthcare Corp	PHCC	Whl pharmaceuticals	28	Bindley Western Industries Inc	BDY	Wholesale pharmaceuticals
10/7/97	Logility Inc	LGTY	Internet software	26	American Software	AMSWA	Software holding co
9/30/97	Engel General Developers Ltd	ENGEF	Dvlp single-family housing	30	Yaakov Engel Construction	ENGY IT	Own, op construction co; hldg co
9/15/97	NewCom Inc	NWCM	Mnfr computer equipment	15	Aura Systems Inc	AURA	Pvds R&D. testing svcs
7/14/97	SulzerMedica	SM	Mnfr medical implants	47	Sulzer AG	SULZ	Mnfr industrial machinery
6/20/97	Metrika Systems Corp	MKA	Mnfr measurement technologies	25	Thermo Instrument Systems Inc	TMO	Mnfr scientific tech, equip
6/5/97	ASE Test Ltd	ASTSF	Chip tests for semiconductors	68	Advanced Semiconductor	ASX	Mnfr semiconductors
5/21/97	Hartford Life	HLI	Insurance, financial svcs	469	ITT Hartford Group Inc	ITT	Own, op hotels, casinos
5/15/97	Westfield America Inc	WEA	Own, op shopping centers	256	Westfield Holdings Ltd	WSFA	Real estate development firm
4/24/97	Hertz Corp	HRZ	Auto, truck rental svcs	352	Ford Motor Co	F	Mnfr autos, trucks, auto parts
4/8/97	Nexar Technologies Inc	NEXR	Mnfr customizable computers	30	Palomar Medical Technologies	PMTI	Mnfr, whl laser med devices
4/3/97	Commodore Separation Tech	CXOT	Mnfr separation technology	35	Commodore Applied Technologies	COES	Environmental treatment svcs
3/26/97	Chicago Bridge & Iron Co	CBI	Mnfr steel tanks	180	Praxair Inc	PX	Mnfr industrial gases
3/7/97	ATL Products Inc	ATLPA	Mnfr computer storage devices	18	Odetics Inc	ODETA	Mnfr info processing prod
2/26/97	NACT Telecommunications	NACT	Whl, pvds telecom equip,svcs	33	GST Telecommunications Inc	GTE	Telecommunication svcs
2/6/97	Knightsbridge Tankers Ltd	VLCCF	Water transportation svcs	240	ICB Shipping	ICBS	Shipping co
2/4/97	CarMax Group	KMX	Retail new & used cars	241	Circuit City Stores Inc	KMX	Own, op electronics stores
12/18/96	BA Merchant Svcs	BPI	Payment processing svcs	244	BankAmerica Corp	BAC	Bank holding co
12/4/96	TTI Team Telecom International	TTIL	Communications software svcs	20	Team Computers and Systems	TEAM IT	Whl computers, printing mach
11/26/96	Biacore International AB	BCORY	Mnfr analytical instruments	48	Upjohn Co	PNU	Mnfr pharmaceutical prod
11/13/96	Monterey Resources Inc	MRC	Oil & gas exploration, prodn	88	Santa Fe Energy Resources	SFR	Oil & gas exploration, prodn
11/11/96	ProSource Inc	PSOS	Wholesale groceries	51	Onex Corp	OCX	Mnfr packaging prod
10/31/96	New Holland	NH	Mnfr, whl agricultural equip	749	Fiat SpA	FIA	Mnfr motor vehicles
10/30/96	Depuy Inc	DPU	Mnfr orthopedic devices	206	Corange Ltd	N/A	Mnfr pharmaceuticals
10/30/96	Midway Games Inc	MWY	Mnfr video games	107	WMS Industries Inc	WMS	Mnfr, whl amusement games
10/25/96	Metris Companies Inc	MTRS	Personal credit svcs	42	Fingerhut Cos Inc	FHT	Retail prods via catalogs

Continued

Selected Carve-Out Public Offerings
January 1, 1995–March 31, 2002

Issue date	Issuer	Ticker	Business description	Principal amount (mm)	Parent	Ticker of parent	Business description of parent
10/17/96	XLConnect Solutions Inc	XLCT	Integrated sys design svcs	29	Intelligent Electronics Inc	INEL	Whl, ret computer systems
10/11/96	Sabre Group Holdings	TSG	Travel info dist svcs	347	AMR Corp	AMR	Passenger airline; holding co
9/25/96	Abercrombie & Fitch Co	ANF	Own, op clothing stores	84	Limited Inc	LTD	Own, op women's apparel stores
9/19/96	Houston Exploration Co	THX	Oil & gas exploration, prodn	85	THEC Holdings Corp (Brooklyn)	KSE	Gas utility
9/13/96	Thermo Fibergen Inc	TFGU	Mnfr paper inds machinery	39	Thermo Fibertek Inc	TMO	Mnfr scientific tech, equip
8/22/96	TransAct Technologies Inc	TACT	Mnfr transaction-based printers	11	Tridex Corp	TDX	Mnfr printheads & printers
8/20/96	Atria Communities Inc	ATRC	Residential care svcs	70	Vencor Inc	VC	Pvds health care svcs
8/8/96	National Processing Inc	NAP	Data processing svcs	90	National City, Cleveland, Ohio	NCC	Commercial bank holding co
7/10/96	Capital Factors Holdings Inc	CAPF	Short-term bus credit svcs	22	Capital Bank, Miami, FL	CAPL	Bank holding co
7/3/96	Elbit Vision Systems Ltd	EVSNF	Mnfr process control instrmnts	20	Elbit Ltd (Elron Electronic)	ELRNF	Technology holding co
6/27/96	Trex Medical Corp	TXM	Mnfr mammography, x-ray equip	26	ThermoTrex Corp	TMO	Mnfr scientific tech, equip
6/20/96	Ryerson Tull Inc	RT	Wholesale steel	73	Inland Steel Industries Inc	IAD	Mnfr steel; holding co
6/13/96	Du Pont Photomasks Inc	DPMI	Mnfr photomasks	60	El du Pont de Nemours and Co	DD	Mnfr indl chemicals, fibers
6/4/96	CanWest Global Communications	CGS.A	Own, op television stations	112	CanWest Global Communications	CGS.A	Own, op television stations
6/4/96	SGL Carbon AG	SGLC	Mnfr carbon brushes, electrodes	37	Hoechst AG	HFAG	Mnfr chemicals & fibers
5/22/96	American States Financial Corp	ASX	Fire & marine insurance co	192	Lincoln National Corp	LNC	Insurance holding co
5/7/96	Associates First Capital Corp	AFS	Finance, leasing svcs	1351	Ford Motor Co	F	Mnfr autos, trucks, auto parts
4/25/96	American Portable Telecom Inc	APTI	Cellular telephone svcs	145	Telephone & Data Systems Inc	TDS	Telecom svcs
4/22/96	Travelers/Aetna Ppty Casualty	TAP	Property, casualty ins svcs	708	Travelers Insurance Group Inc	TRV	Insurance co
4/18/96	CompuServe Inc	CSRV	Internet service provider (ISP)	364	H&R Block Inc	HRB	Income tax preparation svcs
4/3/96	Lucent Technologies Inc	LU	Mnfr telecom equip, software	2279	AT&T Corp	T	Own, op telecom sys
4/2/96	Sipex Corp	SIPX	Mnfr semiconductors	25	Tractebel SA	TREB	Electric & gas utility
4/1/96	Lycos Inc	LCOS	Pvds Internet svcs	39	CMGI	CMGI	Direct mail advertising svcs
4/1/96	Scania AB	SCV.A	Mnfr, whl trucks, buses	313	Investor AB	INVS	Investment holding co
3/28/96	Tadiran Telecommunications	TTELF	Mnfr communications equipment	52	Tadiran Ltd (Koor Industries)	KOR	Holding co
3/27/96	Thermo Sentron Inc	TSR	Mnfr packaging machinery	37	Thermedics (Thermo Electron)	TMO	Mnfr scientific tech, equip
3/21/96	First USA Paymentech Inc	PTI	Payment processing svcs	61	First USA Financial	FUS	Pvds credit card svcs
3/19/96	ThermoQuest Corp	TMQ	Mnfr mass spectrometers	42	Thermo Instrument Systems Inc	TMO	Mnfr scientific tech, equip
3/8/96	Sterling Commerce	SE	E-commerce software	210	Sterling Software Inc	SSW	Dvlp sys, applications software

Selected Carve-Out Public Offerings
January 1, 1995–March 31, 2002

Issue date	Issuer	Ticker	Business description	Principal amount (mm)	Parent	Ticker of parent	Business description of parent
2/8/96	ContiFinancial Corp	CFN	Finance business svcs	94	Continental Grain Co	Private	Produce grains, poultry prod
2/1/96	Intercardia Inc	ITRC	Mnfr pharmaceuticals	28	Interneuron Pharmaceuticals	IPIC	Mnfr biopharmaceuticals
12/12/95	Ascent Entertainment Group Inc	GOAL	Entertainment svcs	80	COMSAT Corp	CQ	Pvds satelite communications svcs
11/21/95	Buckeye Cellulose Corp	BKI	Mnfr specialty cellulose pulps	64	Buckeye Technologies Inc	BKI	Mnfr specialty cellulose pulps
11/6/95	ROSS Technology Inc	RTEC	Computer-aided design sys svcs	35	Fujitsu Ltd	FJTSY	Mnfr semiconductors, computers
10/25/95	Donaldson Lufkin & Jenrette	DLJ	Investment bank	191	Equitable Companies Inc	EQ	Life insurance co
10/23/95	Intimate Brands Inc	IBI	Own, op women's accessory store	52	Limited Inc	LTD	Own, op women's apparel stores
10/11/95	Diamond Offshore Drilling Inc	DO	Oil & gas well drilling svcs	260	Loews Corp	LTR	Insurance holding co
10/10/95	Union Pacific Resources Group	UPR	Oil & gas exploration prodn	562	Union Pacific Corp	UNP	Railroad transport svcs
9/21/95	Midwest Express Holdings Inc	MEH	Investment holding company	63	Kimberly-Clark Corp	KMB	Mnfr sanitary paper prod
8/14/95	AVX Corp	AVX	Mnfr ceramic capacitors	357	Kyocera Corp	KYR GR	Mnfr semiconductor prod
8/8/95	WFS Financial	WFSI	Personal credit svcs	49	Western Financial Savings Bank	WES	Automobile leasing svcs
8/3/95	ThermoSpectra	THS	Mnfr precision imaging equip	19	Thermo Instrument Systems Inc	TMO	Mnfr scientific tech, equip
7/27/95	Forcenergy Gas Exploration Inc	FGAS	Oil & gas exploration, prodn	60	Forcenergy AB	FORC	Oil & gas exploration, prodn
7/26/95	Red Lions Hotels	RCX	Own, op hotels	117	Red Lion Inns LP	RED	Own, op hotels
7/18/95	BT Office Products Intl Inc	BTF	Whl office stationary, supplies	108	Buhrmann-Tetterode NV	KPPN	Mnfr folding paperboard boxes
7/13/95	MEMC Electronic Materials Inc	WFR	Mnfr silicon wafers	345	Huels AG	VEBG	Electric utility
7/12/95	Tele-Communications Intl	TINTA	Cable TV svcs	252	Tele-Communications Inc	TCOMA	Cable television svcs
6/1/95	US Order Inc	USOR	Equip rental, leasing svcs	42	InteliData Technologies Corp	INTD	Pvds computer, telecom svcs
4/20/95	General Cable PLC	GCAB	Cable communication svcs	152	General Utilities Holdings Ltd	EAUG	Real estate development firm
4/6/95	Boise Cascade Office Products	BOP	Whl stationary, office supplies	87	Boise Cascade Corp	BCC	Mnfr paper, paper prod

Sources: Dealogic, Thomson Financial, and the SEC

EXHIBIT A-2

Selected Public Spin-Offs

Selected Public Spin-Offs
January 1, 1995–March 31, 2002

Issue Date	Spun-off Company	Ticker	Business Description	Immediate Parent	Ticker	Business Description
02/27/02	Mykrolis Corporation	MYK	Dvlp liquid delivery systems	Millipore Corp	MIL	Mnfr analytical prod
01/11/02	Adelphia Business Solutions	ABIZ	Telecom svcs	Adelphia Communications Corp.	ADLAC	Own, op cable TV systems
1/02/02	United States Steel Corp	X	Mnfr steel products	Marathon Oil Corp	MRO	Own, op oil & gas operations
12/03/01	Imagistics International Inc	IGI	Mnfr, whl copy and fax machines	Pitney Bowes Inc	PBI	Mnfr office equip
12/03/01	Acuity Brands, Inc	AYI	Mnfr lighting equip	National Service Industries	NSI	Ops textile rental, & envelope indus.
11/29/01	Unitrin, Inc	UTR	Mnfr motion control units	Curtiss-Wright Corp	CW	Mnfr aircraft control systems
11/16/01	Viasys Healthcare Inc	VAS	Mnfr medical devices	Thermo Electron Corp	TMO	Mnfr scientific tech, equip
11/09/01	CBNY Investment Services Corp	CIVS	Securities brokerage firm	Commercial Bank of New York	CBNY	Commercial bank
08/23/01	Vialta, Inc	VLTAV	Mnfr DVD players	ESS Technology Inc	ESST	Mnfr semiconductors
08/10/01	Liberty Media Group	LMC.A	Cable TV svcs	AT&T Corp	T	Own, op telecom system
08/09/01	Kadant Inc	KAI	Mnfr paper industry machinery	Thermo Electron Corp	TMO	Mnfr scientific tech, equipment
08/06/01	Zimmer Holdings Inc	ZMH	Mnfr, whl orthopedic implants	Bristol-Myers Squibb Co	BMY	Mnfr drugs, cosmetics
08/06/01	Riverstone Networks Inc	RSTN	Internet infrastructure	Cabletron Systems Inc	CS	Mnfr, whl install LAN, WAN
07/09/01	Certegy Inc	CEY	Payment svcs	Equifax Inc	EFX	Info, data processing svcs
07/09/01	AT&T Wireless Services Inc	AWE	Cellular telecom svcs	AT&T Corp	T	Own, op telecom system
06/29/01	Rockwell Collins, Inc	COL	Mnfr aviation electronics prod	Rockwell International Corp	ROK	Mnfr avionics; automation system
06/29/01	Kaneb Services LLC	KSL	Industrial field svcs	Xanser Corp	KAB	Industrial field svcs
05/14/01	Roxio Inc	ROXI	Dvlp digital mgmt software	Adaptec Inc	ADPT	Bandwidth mgmt solutions
04/28/01	Stratos Lightwave Inc	STLW	Mnfr optical transceivers	Methode Electronics Inc	METHB	Mnfr electronic devices
04/23/01	Williams Communications Group	WCG	Pvds fiber-optic telecom svcs	Williams Cos Inc	WMB	Gas utility
3/30/01	Rainbow Media Holdings Inc	RMG	Holding company	Cablevision Systems Corp.	CVC	Cable TV svcs
3/23/01	Flowers Foods Inc	FLO	Mnfr bakery prod	Flowers Industries, Inc.	FWI	Produces, markets line of food
3/5/01	PracticeWorks Inc	PRW	Dvlp dental mgmt software	Infocure Corp	INCX	Medical info system
3/2/01	Inter.net Global Ltd	Private	Internet service provider (ISP)	PSINet, Inc	PSIX	Internet solutions
2/28/01	Marine Products Corp	MPX	Shipbuilding svcs	RPC, Inc	RES	Oilfield svcs
2/8/01	McData Corp	MCDT	Enterprise switches, software	EMC Corporation	EMC	Enterprise storage system
2/1/01	Global Payments Inc	GPN	E-commerce svcs	National Data Corp	NDC	Info svcs, data processing
1/30/01	Bowlin Travel Centers Inc	BWTL.OB	Travel agency	Bowlin Outdoor Advertising and Travel Centers Inc	BWN	Advertising & travel svcs

Selected Public Spin-Offs
January 1, 1995–March 31, 2002

Issue Date	Spun-off Company	Ticker	Business Description	Immediate Parent	Ticker	Business Description
12/29/00	eFunds Corp	EFDS	Elecronic payment svcs	Deluxe Corporation	DLX	Commercial svcs
12/29/00	Axcelis Technologies	ACLS	Mnfr ion implantation equip	Eaton Corporation	ETN	Mnfr engineered prod
12/11/00	Sybron Dental Specialties Inc	SYD	Mnfr dental equip, supplies	Apogent Technologies	AOT	Laboratory & life science prod
12/1/00	Fluor Corp	FLR	Engineering, construction svcs	Massey Energy Co	MME	Prdcs, processes, sells coal prod, svcs
11/13/00	Vast Solutions	Private	Dvlp wireless prod	Paging Network, Inc	PAGEQ	Wireless messaging svcs
11/13/00	BAB Holdings-Food Industry Bus	INCU	Own, op food court franchise	BAB, Inc	BABB	Prdces, retail food prod, svcs
10/25/00	Harbor Global Co Ltd	HRBGV	Venture capital firm	The Pioneer Group, Inc	PIOG	Pvds investment mgmt, advis svcs
10/10/00	Florida East Coast Inds Inc	FLA	Investment holding company	The St. Joe Company	JOE	Real estate operating co
10/3/00	Moody's Investors Ice	MSCI	Dvlp instructional software	Dun & Bradstreet Corporation	DNB	Financial information
10/2/00	Retek Inc	RETK	Business software solution	HNC Software Inc	HNCS	Dvlp, mrkt, supports application software
10/2/00	Avaya Inc	AV	Mnfr communications systems	Lucent Technologies Inc	LU	Designs, builds, delivers networking prod
10/2/00	Cabot Microelectronics Corp	CCMP	Develop abrasive chemicals	Cabot Corp.	CBT	Mnfr, sells chemicals & other materials
8/18/00	Key3Media Group Inc	KME	Pvds trade show svcs	Ziff-Davis Inc	ZD	Media, marketing, publishing co
8/16/00	VelocityHSI Inc	VHSI.OB	Pvds Internet svcs	BRE Properties, Inc	BRE	REIT; own, op apartments
7/27/00	Palm Inc	PALM	Develop applications software	3Com Corp	COMS	Pvds networking products & solutions
7/24/00	APW Ltd	APW	Mnfr computer, electronic equip	Actuant Corporation	ATU	Mnfr, mrkt industrial prod, svcs
7/13/00	Stilwell Financial Inc	SV	Financial mgmt svcs	Kansas City Southern Industries, Inc	KSU	Holding co for transportation subsidiaries
7/7/00	PFSweb Inc	PFSW	Transaction management	Daisytek International Corporation	DZTK	Distributes computer, office automation supplies, accessories
7/6/00	SeraNova Inc	SERA	Info tech svcs	Intelligroup, Inc	ITIG	Global application svcs provider
6/30/00	ANC Rental Corp	ANCX	Passenger rental svcs	Autonation, Inc	AN	Retails, finances, svcs new/used vehicles
6/30/00	Delta Apparel	DLA	Mnfr t-shirts, sweatshirts	Delta Woodside Industries, Inc	DLW	Prdcs, sells textiles & apparel
6/30/00	Duck Head Apparel Co	DHA	Mnfr men's pants	Delta Woodside Industries, Inc	DLW	Prdcs, sells textiles & apparel
6/28/00	Visteon Corp	VC	Mnfr, whl automotive parts	Ford Motor Company	F	Design, mnfr, svc cars & trucks
6/20/00	MIPS Technologies Inc	MIPS	Mnfr electronic computer	Silicon Graphics, Inc	SGI	Variety of visual computing systems
6/2/00	Agilent Technologies Inc	A	Mnfr test, measurement equip	Hewlett-Packard Company	HWP	Imaging/printing sys, computing sys & info tech svcs
5/9/00	Redband Broadcasting	Private	Pvds audio programming svcs	Looksmart	LOOK	Internet search infrastructure co
5/3/00	C- Cube Semiconductor Inc	CUBED	Design, sell semiconductors	C- Cube Microsystems Inc	CUBE	Pvds electronic components & semiconductors
4/3/00	Energizer Holdings Inc	ENR	Mnfr batteries and flashlights	Ralston Purina Company	RAL	Prdcs dry dog & soft-moist cat foods, prod
4/3/00	Three Rivers Bank & Trust Co	TRBC	Bank holding company	US Bancorp	USB	Pvds various banking svcs

Continued

E X H I B I T A–2

Continued

Selected Public Spin-Offs
January 1, 1995–March 31, 2002

Issue Date	Spun-off Company	Ticker	Business Description	Immediate Parent	Ticker	Business Description
3/31/00	Edwards Lifesciences Corp	EW	Mnfr cardiovascular prods	Baxter International Inc	BAX	Dvlp, mnfr, mrktsmedical prod & technologies
3/28/00	Anatel Communications Corp	N/A	Mnfr, whl software	Analogic Corp	ALOG	Internet communication svcs
3/23/00	Grant PrideCo Inc	GRP	Mnfr engineered tubular prod	Weatherford International, Inc	WFT	Equipment & svcs for oil & gas industries
3/16/00	Gentiva Health Services Inc	GTVHV	Home health care svcs	Olsten Corporation	OLS	Human resource svcs & computer sys svcs
3/15/00	Sabre Holding Corp	TSG	Travel info svcs	AMR Corporation	AMR	Op airline & pvds connecting svcs
3/13/00	MI Entertainment Corp	MIEC	Own, op horse racetracks	Magna International Inc	MGA	Mnfr automotive parts
2/15/00	eLoyalty Corp	ELOY	Management consulting svcs	Technology Solutions Company	TSCC	Information technology solutions
1/24/00	Logix Communications Entrp Inc	1373IZ	Telecom svcs	Dobson Communications	DCEL	Wireless telephone svcs
1/4/00	CoorsTek Inc	CRTK	Mnfr ceramic prod	Arguss Communications, Inc	ACX	Telecom infrastructure svcs
12/31/99	Sedona Worldwide Inc	SDWWW.OB	Retail personal hygiene prod	ILX Resorts Incorporated	ILX	Dvlp, op, mrkt upscale vacation ownership resorts
12/16/99	Huttig Building Products Inc	HBP	Whl doors, windows, millwork	Crane Co	CR	Mnfr engineered industrial prod
11/30/99	Teledyne Technologies Inc	TDY	Electronic, communications prod	Allegheny Technologies Inc	ATI	Metals producer
11/30/99	Water Pik Technologies Inc	PIK	Mnfr electric housewares	Allegheny Technologies Inc	ATI	Metals producer
11/5/99	Lanier Worldwide Inc	LR	Whl, retail office equip	Harris Corporation	HRS	Range of products, svcs for telecom
11/4/99	Tenneco Packaging Inc	PTV	Pvds corrugated packaging svcs	Tenneco Automotive Inc	TEN	Mnfr, distribute auto/truck prod & equip
11/1/99	Circle.com	CIRC	Online business svcs	Snyder Communication	SNC	Direct marketing, advertising, communications
10/22/99	Neiman-Marcus Grp	NMG	Own, op department stores	Harcourt General Inc	H	Multiple-media publisher
10/20/99	Tender Loving Care Health Svcs	TLCI	Pvds temporary help svcs	Staff Builders, Inc	SBLI	Human resource svcs
10/19/99	CIRCOR International Inc	CIR	Mnfr, whl fluid regulation prod	Watts Industries, Inc	WTS	Designs, mnfrs, sells line of valves
10/4/99	Omnova Solutions Inc	OMN	Mnfr emulsion prod	Gencorp Inc	GY	Prdcs value-added sys for aerospace & defense industries
9/24/99	Consolidated-Tomoka Land Co	CTO	Prod, whl fruits; own, op hotels	BKF Capital Group, Inc	BKF	Investments mgmt & advisory svcs
9/23/99	Ventiv Health Inc	VTIV	Health care marketing svcs	Snyder Communication	SNC	Direct marketing, advertising, communications
9/1/99	Lynch Interactive Corp	LIC	Software	Lynch Corporation	LGL	Diversified manufacturing co
8/24/99	Too Inc	TOO	Mnfr, ret girls clothing	The Limited, Inc	LTD	Specialty retailer, op multiple retail stores
8/12/99	Conoco Inc	COC	Explores, dvlps, prdc crude oil, natural gas	El du Pont de Nemours and Co	DD	Mnfr industrial chemicals, fibers
8/10/99	Anthony & Sylvan Pools Corp	SWIM	Pool installation svcs	Essel Corporation	ESSF	Swimming pool & spa equip, other swimming prod
7/27/99	Gartner Group Inc	IT	IT research, analysis svcs	IMS Health Incorporated	RX	Medical info sys

Selected Public Spin-Offs
January 1, 1995–March 31, 2002

Issue Date	Spun-off Company	Ticker	Business Description	Immediate Parent	Ticker	Business Description
6/28/99	Genzyme Surgical Products	GZSP	Mnfr, whl surgical instruments	Genzyme Corporation	GENZ	Dvlp, mkt medical/biomedical prod
6/18/99	Interstate Hotels Co	IHC	Own, op hotels & motels	Patriot American Hospitality, Inc	PAH	Hotel REIT
6/15/99	RJ Reynolds Tobacco Holdings	RJR	Mnfr cigarettes, tobacco prod	Nabisco Group Holdings Corp	NGH	Mnfr, mkt misc food prod
5/28/99	Delphi Automotive Systems Corp	DPH	Mnfr automotive components	General Motors Corp	GM	Motor vehicles, accessories
5/10/99	Triad Hospitals Inc	TRI	Own, operate hospitals	HCA Inc	HCA	Op hospitals & other health care facilities
5/10/99	Lifepoint Hospitals Inc	LPNT	Own, operate hospitals	HCA Inc	HCA	Op hospitals & other health care facilities
5/3/99	Gentek Inc	GK	Mnfr motor vehicle parts	The General Chemical Group Inc	GCG	Prdcs chemicals, e.g., soda ash & calcium chloride
5/3/99	VoiceStream Wireless Corp	VSTR	Cellular communications svcs	Western Wireless Corporation	WWCA	Wireless communications svcs
4/27/99	Investment Technology Group	ITG	Securities brokerage firm	Jefferies Group, Inc	JEF	Brokerage & investment banking svcs
4/27/99	Celera Genomics Corp	CRA	Research, dvlp svcs	PE Corp	PKN	Genomic info & mnfr instruments
4/7/99	Evercel Inc	EVRC	Mnfr storage batteries	Energy Research Corp	ERC	Alternative energy sources
3/24/99	Varian Associates-Semiconductor	VSEA	Mnfr, whl semiconductor equip	Varian Medical Systems, Inc	VAR	Supplier of medical prod
3/24/99	Varian Inc	VARI	Mnfr, whl scientific equip	Varian Medical Systems, Inc	VAR	Supplier of medical prod
3/18/99	Pulitzer Inc	PTZ	Publish newspapers	Pulitzer Publishing	PTZ	Publish newspapers
2/22/99	Arch Chemicals Inc	ARJ	Mnfr hi-performance chemicals	Olin Corp	OLN	Mnfr chemicals
1/19/99	Momentum Business Applications	MMTM				
1/4/99	Lakes Gaming Inc	LACO	Own, op casinos	Grand Casinos, Inc	GND	Dvlp, construct, manage casino hotels
1/4/99	Priority Healthcare Corp	PHCC	Whl pharmaceuticals	Bindley Western Industries, Inc	BDY	Wholesale dist pharmaceuticals/related health care prod
12/31/98	Pennzoil-Quaker State Co	PZL	Oil & gas exploration, prodn	PennzEnergy Company	PNZL	Oil & gas production
12/31/98	Convergys	CVG	Billing, mgmt solution svcs	Broadwing Inc	BRW	Integrated telephone products & solutions
12/31/98	Conexant Systems Inc	CNXT	Mnfr semiconductors	Rockwell International Corporation	ROK	Mnfr industrial automation/robots
12/31/98	Park Place Entertainment	PPE	Own, op casinos	Hilton Hotels Corp	HLT	Own, op hotels
12/31/98	Specialty Products &Insulation	SPIE	Whl mech insulation, prod	Irex Corporation	IREX	Mnfr, sell prod for building & construction
12/29/98	Crestline Capital Corp	CLJ	Own, op hotels	Host Marriott Corporation	HMT	Op REITS, hotels
12/15/98	Hi/fn Inc	HIFN	Integrated software svcs	STAC Software, Inc	STAC	Application software
11/24/98	Sprint PCS	PCS	Wireless telecom svcs	Sprint Corp	FON	Telecom svcs
11/18/98	Excel Legacy	XLG	Real estate investment trust	New Plan Excel Realty Trust	NXL	REITS, shopping center

Continued

Selected Public Spin-Offs
January 1, 1995–March 31, 2002

Issue Date	Spun-off Company	Ticker	Business Description	Immediate Parent	Ticker	Business Description
11/6/98	Waddell & Reed Financial Inc	WDR	Investment mgmt holding co	Torchmark Corporation	TMK	Life/health insurance, financial svcs
10/19/98	Vornado Operating Inc	VOO	Real estate development firm	Vornado Realty Trust	VNO	REITS, diversified
9/30/98	LTC Healthcare Inc	LTI	Health svcs	LTC Properties, Inc	LTC	REITS, health care
9/24/98	Metris Companies Inc	MTRS	Personal credit svcs	Fingerhut Companies, Inc	FHT	Database marketing, retail stores
9/23/98	Leap Wireless International	LWIN	Telecom svcs	QUALCOMM Inc	QCOM	Dvlp, deliver digital wireless comm prod/equip
9/22/98	Insignia ESG Holdings Inc	IEG	Housing mgmt svcs	Insignia Financial Group, Inc	IFS	Real estate mgmt & svcs
9/11/98	American Med Security-HMO Bus	AMZ	Own, op HMO	United Wisconsin Services	UWZ	Medical HMO
8/31/98	Hungarian Broadcasting-Adult	HBCO	Adult TV broadcasting svcs	Hungarian Broadcasting Corp	HBCOP	Broadcasting television
8/20/98	Penwest Pharmaceuticals Co Inc	PENX	Manufacture pharmaceuticals	Penford Corp	PPCO	Researches, develops, commercializes drug delivery system
8/11/98	Penton Media Inc	PME	Publish bus, trade magazines	Pittway Corporation	PRY	Mnfr, dist electronic security devices
7/1/98	RH Donnelley Corp	RHD	Publish yellow pages	Dun & Bradstreet Corporation	DNB	B2B & commercial svcs
6/19/98	OMI Corp-International Div	OMM	Own, op deep sea transport	Marine Transport Corporation	MTLX	Marine transportation svcs
6/16/98	Avalon Holdings	AWX	Waste transport svcs	American Waste Services, Inc	AWS	Waste mgmt & disposal
6/12/98	US West Media Group	UMG	Cable television svcs	US West Communications	USW	Telecom svcs
6/10/98	Chicago Title Corp	CTZ	Title insurance, trust svcs	Alleghany Corporation	Y	Property & casualty reinsurance & insurance
6/10/98	Aztec Technology Partners Inc	AZTC	Technology consulting svcs	US Office Products Company	OFIS	Retail office supplies
6/10/98	Navigant International Inc	FLYR	Travel agencies	US Office Products Company	OFIS	Retail office supplies
6/10/98	School Specialty Inc	SCHS	Whl school supplies	US Office Products Company	OFIS	Retail office supplies
5/14/98	Abercrombie & Fitch Co	ANF	Clothing stores	The Limited, Inc	LTD	Specialty retailer, op multiple retail stores
5/5/98	Omni Doors Inc	OMDO	Mnfr doors & cabinets	Millennia, Inc	MENA	Diversified mgmt c
5/5/98	ITT Educational Services Inc	ESI	Secondary degree svcs	Starwood Hotels & Resorts	HOT	Own, manage hotel franchises
5/1/98	Vencor Inc	VCRIQ	Health care svcs	Ventas Inc	VTR	Real estate investment trust
4/7/98	Associates First Capital Corp	AFS	Finance, leasing svcs	Ford Motor Company	F	Design, mnfr cars & trucks
4/7/98	SonoSite Inc	SONO	Diagnostic medical equip	American IR Technologies, Inc	ATLI	Develops, markets consumer electronics
4/6/98	Midway Games Inc	MWY	Manufacture video games	WMS Industries	WMS	Design, mnfr, sale of gaming devices
4/1/98	Ralston Purina-Intl Animal	AGX	Produce animal feed	Ralston Purina Company	RAL	Produces dry & moist pet food
3/30/98	Vlasic Foods International Inc	VLFIQ.OB	Produce, whl frozen foods	Campbell Soup Co	CPB	Mnfr convenience food prod
3/23/98	Marriot International Inc	MAR	Own, op lodging facilities	Marriot International	SDH	Own, op hotels
3/11/98	Bolle Inc	BLE	Whl eyeglass lenses, frames	PerkinElmer, Inc	PKI	Global technology prod
3/10/98	Allergan Specialty	ASTI	Whl pharmaceuticals	Allergan, Inc.	AGN	Eye care & specialty pharmaceutical prod

Selected Public Spin-Offs
January 1, 1995–March 31, 2002

Issue Date	Spun-off Company	Ticker	Business Description	Immediate Parent	Ticker	Business Description
2/24/98	NSC Corp	NSCC	Asbestos abatement svcs	Waste Management, Inc	WMI	Waste management. svcs
1/30/98	Hussmann International Corp	HSM	Refrigeration equip	PepsiAmericas, Inc	PAS	Package, sell, dist soft drink prod
1/30/98	Midas Inc	MDS	Automotive repair svcs	Whitman Corporation	WH	Beverages
12/31/97	Emerging Communications Inc	ECM	Local telephone svcs	Atlantic Tele-Network, Inc	ANK	Local, long distance, intl. telephone svcs
12/20/97	Agritope Inc	AGTO	Biotechnology prod	Epitope INC	EPTO	Mnfr diagnostic kits
12/16/97	Georgia-Pacific-Timber Company	TGP	Own, op timber tracts	Georgia-Pacific Corp	GP	Prdc, dist pulp, paper, consumer prod
12/11/97	Corn Products Intl	CPO	Prdcs processed corn prod	Bestfoods	BFO	Intl food co
12/10/97	Thermo Vision Corporation	VIZ	Medical monitoring equip	Thermo Optek Corp	TOC	Designs, mnfr photonics prod
12/3/97	AmSurg	AMSGA	Pvds physician mgmt svcs	American Healthways, Inc	AMHC	Specialized disease mgmt svcs
11/3/97	UNOVA Inc	UNA	Whl data collection sys	Western Atlas, Inc	WAI	Supplies oilfield reservoir info technology
10/31/97	LNR Property Corp	LNR	Own, op real estate properties	Lennar Corporation	LEN	Homebuilder & provider of residential financial svcs
10/15/97	Choice Hotels Intl	CHH	Own, op hotels	Sunburst Hospitality Corp	SNB	Own, op extended-stay hotels
10/7/97	Tricon Global Restaurants	YUM	Own, op fast-food restaurants	PepsiCo, Inc	PEP	Op worldwide soft drink, juice, & snack food businesses
10/7/97	BEI Technologies Inc	BEIQ	Electronic devices	BEI Medical Systems Company, Inc	BMED	Dvlp, mnfr variety of gynecology prod
10/2/97	Meritor Automotive Inc	MRA	Whl car, truck equip & parts	Rockwell International Corp	ROK	Mnfr industrial automation/robots
10/1/97	RCN Corp	RCNC	Telecom svcs	Commonwealth Telephone Enterprises, Inc	CTCO	Wireless telecom co
9/30/97	Crescendo Pharmaceuticals Corp	CNDO	Mnfr pharma preparations	ALZA Corporation	AZA	Pharmaceutical prod co
9/19/97	Cable Michigan Inc	CABL	Cable TV svcs	Commonwealth Telephone Enterprises, Inc	CTCO	Wireless telecom co
9/1/97	Solutia Inc	SOI	Mnfr industrial chemicals	Monsanto Co	MON	Technology-based agricultural solutions
8/8/97	ChoicePoint	CPS	Insurance agency	Equifax	EFX	Financial info & processing solutions
7/29/97	Marcam Solutions Inc		Pvds prepackaged software	MAPICS, Inc	MAPX	Dvlp global enterprise software
7/28/97	BJ's Wholesale Club Inc	BJ	Own, op misc merchandise store	HomeBase, Inc	HBI	Op home improvement warehouse stores
7/28/97	NextLevel Systems Inc	GIC	Mnfr communications systems	General Semiconductor, Inc	SEM	Dvlp power semiconductor
7/25/97	Monterey Resources Inc	MRC	Oil & gas exploration, prodn	Santa Fe Energy Resources	SFR	Energy resources
7/23/97	CommScope	CTV	Mnfr coaxial cable	General Semiconductor, Inc	SEM	Dvlp power semiconductor
7/15/97	Unique Casual Restaurants Inc	CMPP	Own, op eating places	Daka International, Inc	DAKA	Op retail restaurants

Continued

451

Selected Public Spin-Offs
January 1, 1995–March 31, 2002

Issue Date	Spun-off Company	Ticker	Business Description	Immediate Parent	Ticker	Business Description
7/7/97	Griffin Land & Nurseries Inc	GRIF	Own, op landscape, nurseries	Culbro Corporation	CBO	Prdc, dist cigars & tobacco
6/14/97	Crescent Operating	COPIOB	Own, op health care facilities	Crescent Operating, Inc	COPI	Own, op portfolio of assets
5/14/97	Vital Images Inc	VTAL	Dvlp data imaging software	Bio-Vascular, Inc	BVAS	Dvlp, mnfr variety of surgical prod
3/31/97	Halter Marine Group Inc	HLX	Mnfr offshore support vessels	Trinity Industries, Inc	TRN	Mnfr transportation & construction prod
3/21/97	Getty Petroleum Mktg	GPM	Oil & gas exploration, prodn	Getty Realty Corp	GTY	Real estate investment trust
3/3/97	SLH Corp	SLHO	Real estate agency	Labone Inc	LABS	Laboratory testing svcs
1/2/97	Unisource Worldwide Inc	UWW	Wholesale printing paper	IKON Office Solutions, Inc	IKN	Broad range of copying & imaging solutions
12/31/96	NCR Corp	NCR	Mnfr business machines	AT&T Corp	T	Telecom svcs
12/31/96	Primex Technologies Inc	PRMX	Mnfr defense-related equip	Olin Corp	OLN	Mnfr chemicals
12/31/96	Covance Inc	CVD	Operate clinical laboratory	Corning, Inc	GLW	Optical networking prod
12/31/96	Quest Diagnostics Inc	DGX	Medical research svcs	Corning, Inc	GLW	Optical networking prod
12/31/96	Deltic Timber Corp	DEL	Mnfr timber products	Murphy Oil Corporation	MUR	Worldwide gas & oil exploration
12/19/96	Echelon International Corp	EIN	Real estate development firm	Florida Progress Corporation	FPC	Electric utility svcs
12/12/96	Newport News Shipbuilding	NNS	Mnfr/repair aircraft carriers	Tenneco, Inc	TEN	Diversified manufacturing co
12/4/96	TCI Satellite Entertainment	LSATA	Pay TV svcs	Tele-Communications Inc	TCOM	Telecom
12/3/96	Consolidated Freightways Corp	CFWY	Trucking company	Consolidated Freightways Inc	CNF	Freight svcs
11/25/96	BlowOut Entertainment	BLWTQ	Videotape rental svcs	Rentrak Corporation	RENT	Distributes prerecorded videocassettes
11/18/96	Access Beyond Inc	ACCB	Mnfr modems	Penn DataComm Networks, Inc	PNRL	Telecom equip
11/1/96	ACNielsen Corp	ART	TV viewers estimation svcs	Dun & Bradstreet Corporation	DNB	B2B svcs & commercial svcs
11/1/96	Cognizant	CTSH	Information svcs	Dun & Bradstreet Corporation	DNB	B2B svcs & commercial svcs
10/21/96	Martin Marietta Materials	MLM	Mnfr products for steel industry	Lockheed Martin Corp	LMT	Mnfr aerospace systems, prod
10/17/96	Advanced Digital Information	ADIC	Mnfr automated tape libraries for data storage	Interpoint Corp	INTP	Design, mnfr standard high-density converters
10/16/96	Union Pacific Resources Group	UPR	Oil & gas exploration, prodn	Union Pacific Corporation	UNP	Op rail transportation & trucking business
10/14/96	Footstar Inc	FTS	Ret shoe store holding co	Melville Corporation	MES	Retail
10/7/96	Sterling Commerce	SLG GR	E-commerce software	Sterling Software	SSW	Various software programs
10/2/96	Millennium Chemicals Inc	MCH	Mnfr industrial chemicals	Hanson plc	HNS	Prdce, supply building materials
10/1/96	Allegiance Corp	AEH	Health care svcs	Baxter International Inc	BAX	Dvlp, mnfr, mrkt medical prod & technologies
9/30/96	Lucent Technologies Inc	LU	Mnfr telecom equip, software	AT&T Corp	T	Telecom svcs
9/9/96	Cuno Inc	CUNO	Mnfr fluid power pumps, motors	Commercial Intertech	TEC	Designs, mnfr machinery for construction & mining
8/15/96	Dial	DL	Mnfr ret, whl, mkt consumer prod	Viad Corp	VVI	Pvds prod and svcs for payment & marketing svc industry

Selected Public Spin-Offs
January 1, 1995–March 31, 2002

Issue Date	Spun-off Company	Ticker	Business Description	Immediate Parent	Ticker	Business Description
8/2/96	Billing Information Concepts	BILL	Direct billing svcs	USLD Communications Corp	USLD	Telecom svcs
7/1/96	Imation	IMN	Mnfr data storage devices	Minnesota Mining & Mfg Co. (3M)	MMM	Diversified manufacturing co
6/12/96	PolyMedica Biomaterials Inc	PLMD	Mnfr surgical supplies	CardioTech Instruments Inter Inc	CTE	Dvlp, mnfr health care devices, prod
6/10/96	Electronic Data Systems Corp	EDS	Integrated systems svcs	General Motors Corporation	GM	Motor vehicles, accessories
5/31/96	Tupperware	TUP	Mnfr plastic consumer prod	Premark International, Inc	PRM	Design, mnfr, dist food equip & other housewares
5/9/96	Bone Care International	BCII	Bone research svcs	Lunar Corporation	LUNR	Dvlp medical instrument prod
5/9/96	Payless ShoeSource Inc	PSS	Shoe stores	The May Department Store Company	MAY	Retail department stores
3/27/96	Earthgrains Co	EGR	Mnfr whl bread, baked goods	Anheuser-Busch Companies	BUD	Brewery
3/11/96	Morrison Fresh Cooking Inc	MFC	Eating places	Morrison Restaurants Inc	MRN	Retail restaurants
3/11/96	Morrison Health Care Inc	MHI	Cafeterias	Morrison Restaurants Inc	MRN	Retail restaurants
3/1/96	Endocare Inc	ENDO	Mnfr surgical equip	Medstone International, Inc	MEDS	Mnfr, mkt, maintains medical prod
2/23/96	Sprint Cellular Co	PCS	Telecom svcs	Sprint Corp	FON	Telecom svcs
1/26/96	KSW Inc	KSWW.OB	Heating sys installation	Helionetics, Inc	HLXC	Prdc electronic components
1/24/96	Highlands Insurance Group Inc	HIC	Insurance co	Halliburton Company	HAL	Energy svcs & engineering & construction svcs
1/4/96	Bally's Health & Tennis	BFT	Fitness centers	Bally Entertainment Group	BLY	Own, op casinos & resorts
1/4/96	Pittston Svcs Grp-Pittston Bur	PZB	Security svc, freight transportation	Pittston Co	PZS	Conglomerate
1/2/96	Roadway Express	ROAD	Trucking co	Caliber System, Inc	CBB	Transport svcs
12/28/95	Castle & Cooke Inc	CCS	Real estate development firm	Dole Food Company	DOL	Diversified food co
12/26/95	Host Marriott Services	HMS	Own, op concession stands	Host Marriott Corporation	HMT	Hotel operator
12/20/95	ITT Corp	ITT	Own, op hotels, casinos	ITT Corp	ITT (IIN)	Op hotels, gaming, & info svcs
12/20/95	ITT Hartford Grp Inc	HIG	Pvds insurance svcs	ITT Corp	ITT (IIN)	Op hotels, gaming, & info svcs
12/15/95	Culligan Water Technologies	CUL	Mnfr whl purification prod	Samsonite Corporation	SAMC	Design, mnfr luggage
12/12/95	Clean Diesel Tech	CDTI	Mnfr emission control tech	Fuel-Tech NV	FTEK	Dvlp, sell air pollution control tech
11/30/95	Schweitzer-Mauduit	SWM	Mnfr cigarette papers	Kimberly-Clark Corporation	KMB	Mnfr tissue, personal care, & health care prod
11/10/95	Investors Financial Services	IFIN	Investment management svcs	Eaton Vance Corp	EV	Mkt, manage mutual funds
11/7/95	Healthdyne Info Enterprises	HDIE	Info retrieval svcs	Healthdyne, Inc	HDYN	Home health care svcs & prod
10/3/95	Ben Franklin Retail Stores Inc	BFRS	Variety stores	Avatex Corporation	AVAT	Own interests in hotels & office buildings

Continued

Continued

Selected Public Spin-Offs
January 1, 1995–March 31, 2002

Issue Date	Spun-off Company	Ticker	Business Description	Immediate Parent	Ticker	Business Description
10/2/95	MFS Communications	MFST	Telecom svcs	Level 3 Communications, Inc	LVLT	Telecom svcs
10/2/95	Transport Holdings	TLIC	Insurance holding company	Citigroup Inc	C	Various financial svcs
9/29/95	TransPro Inc	TPR	Mnfr whl heat transfer systems	Allen Group	ALN	Mnfr industrial & consumer prod
9/13/95	EVEREN Capital Corp	EVR	Securities brokerage firm	Kemper Corp	KFC	Life insurance svcs
9/7/95	Airways Corp	AAIR	Passenger airline	Mesaba Holdings Inc	MAIR	Holding co
8/31/95	Crown Vantage	CVANQ	Mnfr paper prod	Fort James Corporation	FJ	Mnfr paper prod
7/3/95	Promus Hotel Corp	PRH	Own, op hotels	Promus Companies Inc	PRI	Owns properties
6/29/95	Dave and Buster's	DAB	Own, op restaurants	Edison Brothers Stores, Inc	EDBT	Retailer of apparel & footwear
6/14/95	PolyVision Corp	PLI	Mnfr flat display panels	The Alpine Group, Inc	AGI	Mnfr, sell wire & cable prod
6/1/95	US Industries Inc	USI	Mnfr whl consumer prod	Hanson plc	HAN	Produces, supplies building materials
5/22/95	Healthdyne Technologies Inc	HDTC	Mnfr specialized med devices	Healthdyne, Inc	HDYN	Home health care svcs & prod
2/13/95	MAI Systems Corp	MBF	Mnfr mini- and microcomputers	Vector Group Ltd	VGR	Mnfr, sell consumer prod

Sources: Dealogic, Thomson Financial, and the SEC.

Selected Tracking Stock Public Offerings and Spin-Offs
January 1, 1995–March 31, 2002

Issue Date	Tracking Stock	Ticker	Business Description	Amount Filed (mm)		
01/31/02	Carolina Group	CG	Mnfr cigarettes, tobacco prod	1,127	Loews Corp	LTR	Diversified
12/12/01	Rainbow Media Group	RMG	Cable operators	267	Cablevision Systems Corp	CVC	Cable svcs provider
08/09/01	Sprint PCS	PCS	Wireless telecom svcs	1,715	Sprint Corp	SDE	Telecom svcs
07/27/01	CarMax Group	KMX	Car dealerships	137	Circuit City Stores Inc	CC	Electronics stores
06/07/01	MCI Group	MCIT	Communications svcs	2,042	Worldcom, Inc	WCOM	Telecom svcs
06/07/01	Worldcom Group	WCOM	Communications svcs	51,060	Worldcom, Inc	WCOM	Telecom svcs
01/04/01	Liberty Media Conv debentures	LCM.D	TV programming/broadcasting	600	AT&T Corp	T	Telecom svcs
01/04/01	Liberty Media Conv notes	LCM.N	TV programming/broadcasting	817	AT&T Corp	T	Telecom svcs
10/20/00	Alcatel OED	ALAO (ADR)	Mfg optoelectronics for telecom	1,070	Alcatel	ALA	Mnfr telecom equip
09/27/00	University of Phoenix Online	UOPX	Online education	70	Apollo Group	APOL	Educational svcs
04/26/00	AT&T Wireless Group	AWE	Wireless voice, data svcs	8,874	AT&T Corp	T	Telecom svcs
02/29/00	PE Biosystems Group	PEB	Mnfr analytical instruments	423	PE Corp	ABI	Mnfr genomic info & mnfr instruments
02/29/00	Celera Genomics Group	CRA	Prvd. genetic information	983	PE Corp	ABI	Mnfr genomic info & mnfr instruments
11/18/99	Go.com	GO	Internet svcs and software prod	1,536	The Walt Disney Co	DIS	Entertainment
11/10/99	Liberty Media	LMG/A	TV programming/broadcasting	855	AT&T Corp	T	Telecom svcs
11/10/99	Liberty Media Conv debentures	LCM.D	TV programming/broadcasting	750	AT&T Corp	T	Telecom svcs
10/29/99	Circle.com	CIRC	Internet customer mgmt svcs	260	Snyder Communication	SNC	Direct mkting, advertising, communic
8/4/99	Quantum Hard Disk Drive Group	HDD	Mnfr hard disk drives for data storage	552	Quantum Corporation	QNTM	Mnfr data storage

Continued

455

Continued

Date	Name	Ticker	Description	Proceeds	Company	Ticker	Description
8/4/99	Quantum Storage Systems Group	DSS	Storage prod	2,290	Quantum Corporation	QNTM	Mnfr data storage
6/18/99	Cybear Group IPO	CYBA	Electronic svcs for health care	48	Andrx Corp	ADRX	Mnfr pharmaceuticals
5/25/99	DLJdirect IPO	DIR	Investment banking svcs	320	Donaldson Lufkin & Jenrette	DLJ	Integrated investment & merchant bank
5/25/99	Barnesandnoble.com IPO	BNBN	Online books	450	Barnes & Noble	BKS	Retail book stores
3/30/99	ZDNet	ZDZ	Online news, entertainment svcs	190	Ziff-Davis Inc	ZD	Media for computing & tech
2/4/99	Sprint PCS	PCS	Wireless telecom svcs	399	Sprint Corp	FON	Telecom svcs
12/17/97	Georgia-Pacific Group (Timber Group)	TGP	Grows timber & mnfr wood fiber	238	Georgia-Pacific Corp	GP	Mnfr pulp, paper, consumer prod
11/3/97	Genzyme Corp (Tissue Repair)	GZTR	Mnfr biological prod	40	Genzyme Corp	GENZ	Dvlp prod, svcs for medical needs
4/24/97	Hertz Corp., The	HRZ	Auto rental svcs	480	Ford Motor Company	F	Mnfr motor vehicles, accessories
2/4/97	CarMax Group	KMX	Retail new & used cars	241	Circuit City Stores Inc	CC	National retailer of electronics
3/26/96	Fletcher Challenge Building	FRCEF	Mnfr building materials	N/A	Fletcher Challenge	N/A	Diversified (New Zealand)
3/25/96	Fletcher Challenge Paper	FLP	Mnfr paper	N/A	Fletcher Challenge	N/A	Diversified
3/25/96	Fletcher Challenge Energy	FEG	Oil & gas production	N/A	Fletcher Challenge	N/A	Diversified
1/3/96	Pittston Brinks's Group	PZB	Security svc, freight transportation	N/A	Pittston Co	PZS	Diversified
10/12/95	Genzyme Corp (General Division)	GENZ	Mnfr therapeutic & surgical prod	150	Genzyme Corp	GENZ	Dvlp prod,svcs for medical needs
9/22/95	Genzyme Corp (Tissue Repair)	GZTR	Mnfr biological prod	48	Genzyme Corp	GENZ	Dvlp prod, svcs for medical needs
7/21/95	Consumers Gas Group	CPG	Gas utility	200.0	CMS Energy Corp	CMS	Energy svcs, facilities
6/8/95	Electronic Data Systems Corp	EDS	Sys & tech svcs	1,147	General Motors Corp	GM	Mnfr motor vehicles, accessories

IPO proceeds do not include overallotment.

Sources: Dealogic, Thomson Financial, and the SEC

NOTES

INTRODUCTION

1. In fact, SERs have dominated the IPO market for several years, as Exhibit N–1 shows.
2. *Business Week,* April 15, 2002.
3. R. Frank, "Mergers of the '90s Become Today's Spinoffs," *The Wall Street Journal,* February 6, 2002.

    See also R. Barker, "Deal Mania Sandy Weill–Style," *Business Week,* April 1, 2002; T. K. Grose, "Bloated by Diverse Acquisitions, Many Firms Are Using Spin-offs to Slim Down to Their Core Businesses," *Time Europe,* April 1, 2002.

CHAPTER 1

1. See discussion of the C-Cube example in Chapter 8.
2. The Hughes Institute also wanted a mechanism to protect its downside and ensure liquidity and received serial puts to GM.
3. However, this may not be a sufficient reason to justify a tax-free spin-off under IRC Section 355. The test is benefit to the parent, not benefit to the parent's shareholders. This is an important distinction.
4. See discussion of the Goodrich spin-off in Chapter 8. However, also see the discussion of the Sealed Air/W.R. Grace transaction in Chapter 8.

Improved Focus

5. On the benefits of focus, see C. Christensen, *The Innovator's Dilemma: When New Technologies Cause Great Firms to Fail,* Harvard Business School Press, 1997. R. Comment and G. Jarrell, ("Corporate Focus and Stock Returns," *Journal of Financial Economics,* vol. 37, 1995, pp. 67–87) find that improved corporate focus leads to stock valuation gains. These authors conclude that performance improvement follows focus-increasing events.

    P. Berger and E. Olfek ("Diversification's Effect on Firm Value," *Journal of Financial Economics,* vol. 51, 1995, pp. 1175–1200) conducted a study of the returns from refocusing by diversified parents and the reasons for such refocusing compared to a comparable control group that did not undertake a refocusing program. The conclusions include that multisegment companies are valued at a discount compared to pure plays and that diversified parents undertaking focus-increasing programs had

NOTES

EXHIBIT N-1

Five Largest U.S. IPOs by Year

Rank	Type of Transaction	Issuer	Industry	Principal Amount ($ millions)
		2001		
1	Carve-out SER	Kraft Foods Inc.	Food & Beverage	8,680
2	Carve-out SER	Agere Systems Inc.	Computers & Electronics	4,140
3	IPO	Prudential Financial Inc.	Finance	3,025
5	Carve-out SER	KPMG Consulting	Consulting	2,328
4	IPO	Principal Financial Group	Investment services	2,127
		2000		
1	Tracking Stock SER	AT&T Wireless Services Inc.	Telecommunications—Wireless	10,620
2	IPO	MetLife Inc.	Insurance—Life	3,310
3	Carve-out SER	TyCom Ltd.	Telecommunications—Services	2,249
4	Carve-out SER	Genuity Inc.	Computers & electronics	1,913
5	IPO	John Hancock Financial Services Inc.	Finance—Business Services	1,734

Includes underwriters' overallotment.

Source: Dealogic

significantly higher returns relative to a control group, following the announcement of the program. The excess return averaged 7.3 percent, and higher returns were closely correlated with the extent of the parent's diversification prior to the refocusing announcement.

Equity carve-outs and spin-offs are used in several studies to test the corporate focus hypothesis because cross-industry carve-outs and spin-offs create an increase in focus. L. Daley, V. Mehrotra, and R. Sivakumar ("Corporate Focus and Value Creation: Evidence from Spinoffs," *Journal of Financial Economics,* vol. 45, 1997, pp. 257–281) discusses spin-offs and corporate focus, and A. Boone ("Can Focus Explain Carve-out Gains?," Pennsylvania State University, working paper, 2001) discusses equity carve-outs and corporate focus. Both find support for the positive effect of increased focus.

Improved Operating Performance

According to Randall Woolridge, a finance professor at the Smeal College of Business Administration at Pennsylvania State University, "There is a sense of urgency for the newly spun-off company to bring products to market, cut costs, and curtail losses because there is no longer a parent to rely on" (M. Vickers, "Pick Your Moment," *Business Week*, May 13, 1996). L. Deley and R. Sivakumar ("Corporate Focus and Value Creation," *Journal of Financial Economics*, vol. 45, 1997, pp. 257–281) also find significant improvements in operating performance following spin-offs. H. Desai and P. Jain ("Firm Performance and Focus: Long-Run Stock Market Performance Following Spin-Offs," *Journal of Financial Economics*, vol. 54, pp. 75–101) confirmed significant post-spin-off improvement in operating performance following a spin-off. However, they find that the improvements are confined to focus-improving spin-offs. They also found that spin-offs that improve the focus of the parent and the subsidiary result in significant improved operating performance for both the parent and the subsidiary.

See also J. Bower and C. Christensen, "Disruptive Technologies: Catching the Wave," *Harvard Business Review*, January-February 1995, pp. 43–53; J. Day, P. Mang, A. Richter, and J. Roberts, "The Innovative Organization," *The McKinsey Quarterly*, no. 2, 2001; P. Zarowin, "What Determines Earnings-Price Ratios: Revisited," *Journal of Accounting Auditing and Finance*, Summer 1990. Professor Zarowin concludes that differences in P/E ratios are attributable to differences in expected growth rates.

CHAPTER 2

Empirical Studies on the Overall Performance of Public Equity SERs

1. R. Hennessey, "IPOs Also Raise Visibility," *Dow Jones Newswire*, June 10, 2002.
2. A 1999 study of the performance of 168 public SERs from 1988 to 1998 with over $200 million in revenues at the time of the SER found that "Such restructurings can indeed increase shareholder value if properly carried out" (*The McKinsey Quarterly*, 1999; sources: SDC, Compustat, Bloomberg, McKinsey internal). See Exhibits N–2 and N–3.

   The SERs and parents in these studies are not compared to peer company performance, a more meaningful measure than the overall indices, but they do indicate a

E X H I B I T   N–2

Value Creation by Public Equity SERs for Subsidiary Shareholders

Total return to shareholders*	Equity SER	Russell 2000 Index	S&P 500 Index
Minority carve-out	23.9	11.0	(‡)
Spin-off	25.9	19.1	17.2
Tracking stocks†	19.1	(‡)	21.2

*Two year compound annual growth rate in percent.

†The sample on tracking stocks is too small to be statistically significant in this study.

‡A comparison against this index was not included.

EXHIBIT N–3

Value Creation by Public Equity SERs for Parent Shareholders

Total return to shareholders*	Sample size	Parent	S&P 500 Index
Minority carve-out	46	22.1	22.1
Spin-off	79	18.2	17.5
Tracking stocks†	16	21.4	21.5

*Two year compound annual growth rate in percent.

†The sample on tracking stocks is too small to be statistically significant in this study.

Source: A. Anslinger, S. Bonini, and M. Patsalos-Fox, *The McKinsey Quarterly,* no. 1, 2000, pp. 98–105.

reasonable return, even for tracking stocks. Interestingly, P. Finegan ("A Closer Look at the Value of Split-Ups," *Corporate Finance Review,* 1998) finds that while both deconglomerate and deintegration SERs result in positive announcement returns, deintegration transactions result in higher positive announcement returns than deconglomerating transactions. An example of a deintegration transaction is General Motors Corporation's SER of its parts-making subsidiary Delphi Automotive Systems. An example of deconglomerating transactions is the SERS by Sears Roebuck & Company of its insurance operation, Allstate Insurance, and its stock brokerage operation, Dean Witter Discovery. Finegan speculates that the SER information is reflected more in the stock of the conglomerate at the time of the announcement. The study suggests that vertically integrated companies benefit from reexamining their belief that they need to control the entire value chain. Finegan studied only large public market SERs between January 1992 and January 1996. The study only looked at transactions that were significant for the parent and included announced transactions that were not completed due to a sale of the subsidiary.

As noted, a number of studies have shown that the announcements of equity carve-outs produce positive stock returns for the stock of the parent: K. Schipper, and A. Smith, "A Comparison of Equity Carve-outs and Seasoned Equity Offerings," *Journal of Financial Economics,* vol. 15, 1986, pp. 153–186; A. Klein, J. Rosenfeld, and W. Beranek, "The Two Stages of an Equity Carve-out and the Price Response of Parent and Subsidiary Stock," *Managerial and Decision Economics,* vol. 12, 1991, pp. 449–460.; and H. Mulherin and A. Boone, Comparing Acquisitions and Divestitures," *Journal of Corporate Finance,* vol. 6, 2000, pp. 117–139. Two general explanations are given in the studies for these parent stock gains. The first explanation is that equity carve-outs result in divestiture gains due to separate financing for the subsidiary's investment projects, the creation of pure-play stocks (Schipper and Smith, 1986), and that parents and their carved-out subsidiaries become more competitive in their industries through increased focus.

A second and somewhat conflicting explanation is that parents raise capital through equity carve-outs when the parent's shares are relatively undervalued and the subsidiary's shares are relatively overvalued. The carve-out announcement signals to the market this parent undervaluation (V. Nanda, "On the Good News in Equity Carve-Outs," *Journal of Finance,* vol. 46, pp. 1717–1736; S. C. Myers and

N. Majluf, "Corporate Financing and Investment Decisions When Firms Have Information Investors Do Not Have," *Journal of Financial Economics,* vol. 13, 1984, pp. 187–221).

This asymmetric information hypothesis predicts that the stock of the parent will react positively to carve-out announcements, that the stock of the parent's competitors will react positively to carve-out announcements, and that the stocks of the subsidiary's competitors will react negatively to carve-out announcements. While the asymmetric information hypothesis makes no explicit predictions about changes in operating performance, improvements in subsidiary operating performance would not seem to be consistent with subsidiaries being overvalued. Subsequent decreases in operating performance might be consistent with overvaluation. Empirical evidence supports both these explanations. One study (J. Allen, and J. McConnell, "Equity Carve-outs and Managerial Discretion," *Journal of Finance,* vol. 53, 1998, pp. 163–186) examines the use of the carve-out stock offering proceeds for a sample of 188 equity carve-outs from 1978 to 1993 and finds that announcement-period gains for parents are higher if the proceeds are paid out than if they are retained. This result provides support for the divestiture gains hypothesis. Another study (Allen and McConnell, 1998), using a sample of 336 equity carve-outs from 1980 to 1997, evaluates three-year returns of parent and subsidiary stocks after the carve-out and concludes that the long-term returns are related to the number of the parent's business segments before the carve-out. The authors conclude that divestiture gains arise from increasing the focus of the parent and the subsidiary. Other studies have shown performance improvements from focus.

A recent study also finds divestiture gains in equity carve-outs. This study (Mulherin and Boone, 2000) looked at 25 equity carve-outs from 1990 to 1999 and concludes that the positive effects associated with equity carve-out announcements are due to synergistic gains. A 2002 study (A. Vijh, "The Positive Announcement-Period Returns of Equity Carveouts: Asymmetric Information or Divestiture Gains?," *Journal of Business,* vol. 75, 2002) finds a direct relation between announcement-period returns and the ratio of subsidiary assets to nonsubsidiary assets, supporting the divestiture gains explanation. This study concludes that the evidence shows that the market reacts positively to the announcement of carve-outs due to divestiture gains. Another 2002 study (J. R. Woolridge, H. M. Hulburt, and J. A. Miles, "Value Creation Through Equity Carve-outs," *Financial Management,* 2002), using a large sample of equity carve-out events during the 1980s and 1990s, finds operating performance improvements for both parents and carved-out subsidiaries. The authors conclude that equity carve-outs accompany significant improvements in operating performance. However, a previous study (M. Slovin, M. Sushka, and Steven R. Ferraro, "A Comparison of the Information Conveyed by Equity Carve-Outs," *Journal of Financial Economics,* 1995), using a sample of 36 equity carve-outs over the period from 1980 to 1991, finds that share prices of equity carve-out rival firms react negatively to carve-out announcements. The authors of this study interpret this finding as evidence that carve-out announcement signals to investors that managers believe the subsidiary, and therefore its competitors, are overvalued.

The evidence supports the view that relative industry valuation affects the parent's decision to issue new stocks. Industries in which the underlying business of the new stock operates have higher market-to-book, higher price-to-sales, lower earnings-to-price, and lower intrinsic value-to-price ratios than the other industries, and median earnings-to-price, market-to-book, price-to-sales, and intrinsic value-to-price for the equity.

The evidence supports the view that that equity restructurings are able to create new stocks that have different risk-return characteristics to the parent stock and so are expected to attract a different type of investor. The risk-return characteristics of the parent stock differ before and after the equity restructuring transactions. The beta of the parent stock decreases significantly after equity restructuring transactions. Returns of new stocks are significantly more volatile relative to those of their parents.

See also R. Comment and G. Jarrell, "Corporate Focus and Stock Returns," *Journal of Financial Economics,* vol. 37, 1995, pp. 67–87; L. Daley, V. Mehrotra, and R. Sivakumar, "Corporate Focus and Value Creation: Evidence from Spinoffs," *Journal of Financial Economics,* vol. 45, 1997, pp. 257–281; G. Hite, and J. Owers, "Security Price Reactions Around Corporate Spin-Off Announcements," *Journal of Financial Economics,* vol. 12, 1983, pp. 409–436; A. Klein, J. Rosenfeld, and W. Beranek, "The Two Stages of an Equity Carve-out and the Price Response of Parent and Subsidiary Stock," *Managerial and Decision Economics,* vol. 12, 1991, pp. 449–460; D. Logue, J. Seward, and J. Walsh, "Rearranging Residual Claims: A Case for Targeted Stock," *Financial Management,* vol. 25, 1996, pp. 43–61; J. Miles and J. Rosenfeld, "The Effect of Voluntary Spin-off Announcements on Shareholder Wealth," *Journal of Finance,* vol. 38, 1983, pp. 1597–1606; K. Schipper and A. Smith, "Effects of Recontracting on Shareholder Wealth: The Case of Voluntary Spin-Offs," *Journal of Financial Economics,* vol. 12, 1983, pp. 437–467; A. Vijh, "Long Term Returns from Equity Carveouts," *Journal of Financial Economics,* vol. 51, 1999, pp. 273–308.

Greater Combined Research Coverage

By increasing focus, more total Wall Street following is often obtained. S. Gibson, P. Healy, C. Noe, and K. Palepureport, in a 1998 paper presented at the American Accounting Association annual meeting, showed that the results of a study of 146 equity carve-outs, spin-offs, and tracking stock offerings between 1990 and 1995 find significantly increased total levels of analyst coverage following a public equity SER. T. Chemmanur and I. Paeglis ("Why Issue Tracking Stocks?," Boston College, Carroll School of Management, 2000) also find a significant increase in the number of analysts following the parent and subsidiary combined following a carve-out, spin-off, or tracking stock issue compared with peer firms matched in industry and size that did not undertake SERs. See Exhibit N–4.

Dissenting Opinion

In contrast with these studies, a study by the consulting firm Booz, Allen & Hamilton (S. Scherreik, "Spin-Offs: Gems Among the Trash?," *Business Week,* April 15, 2002) of 232 spin-offs (the term *spin-offs* in this article also includes carve-outs, judging by the examples cited) by companies in the Standard & Poor's 500 index during the 1990s confirms the outperformance of parent's stock. It finds that, on average, the parent company's shares outperformed the S&P index by 3.8 percent. However, it also finds that, on average, the subsidiary's shares underperformed the index by 0.5 percent. The reasons cited for this include the fact that parents tend to spin off underperforming operations, take advantage of stock market overpricing in utilizing a spin-off instead of a sale, and overload subsidiaries in spin-offs with debt or dump other liabilities on them.

See also M. Hellerman and B. Jones, "The 'Would'ves, Could'ves, and Should'ves' of Spin-Offs," *Journal of Business Strategy,* July 2000; I. Springsteel, "Engineering Run Amok: Have Spin-offs, Carve-outs and Tracking Stocks Lost Touch with Reality?," *Investment Dealers Digest,* November 13, 2000.

EXHIBIT N–4

Impact of Public Equity SERs on Analyst Coverage

Number of Analysts Covering the Combined Companies			
	Before the SER	After the SER	Difference
Spin-offs	18.2	22.3	4.1
Carve-outs	16.2	19.1	2.9
Tracking stocks	19.3	24.4	5.1
Matched firms	20.5	19.5	(1.0)

Source: T. Chemmanur and I. Paeglis, "Why Issue Tracking Stocks?," Boston College, Carroll School of Management, 2000.

CHAPTER 4

1. For a good discussion of the steps to prepare for an SER, see M. D. Lord, S. W. Mandel, and J. D. Wager, "Spinning out a Star," *Harvard Business Review,* June 2002.
2. K. Ryan, "Manager's Journal: From Spinoff to Success," *The Wall Street Journal,* September 8, 1997.
3. C. Terhune, "Georgia-Pacific Will Set IPO for Consumer-Products Unit," *The Wall Street Journal,* May 7, 2002.
4. The IRS and SEC, if the subsidiary will be public, require that the subsidiary be financially viable. After that requirement is met, the allocation of liabilities is settled by negotiation. An early version of this discussion of the tax consequence of SERs was published in an article on spin-offs in 1995 in *Financier* magazine, written by the author and Robin Graham.
5. FAS 144, issued in 2001, requires that the parent recognize a loss if the book value of the subsidiary is greater than its FMV at the date of the spin-off.

CHAPTER 5

1. At least outside my beloved wife's home state of Louisiana.
2. R. Brealey and S. Myers, *Principles of Corporate Finance,* Chapter 5, McGraw-Hill, 6th ed., 1999.

   My great thanks to my partner, Professor Charles Wolf, for his review and additions to this chapter.

CHAPTER 6

1. Minority carve-outs are not only a U.S. activity. In Japan, NEC Corp announced in July 2002 that it intended to conduct a minority carve-out IPO stock offering of its semiconductor business, NEC Electronics. The new semiconductor company will have annual sales of $6 billion.

2. A. Annema, W. Fallon, and M. Goedhart, "Do Carve-outs Make Sense?," *McKinsey on Finance,* 2001; A. Annema, W. Fallon, and M. Goedhart, "When Carve-outs Make Sense," *The McKinsey Quarterly,* 2002.

3. A study conducted by J.P. Morgan (R. Escherich, "U.S. Commentary on the M&A Markets," J.P. Morgan Securities, Inc., 1997) examined 101 carve-outs between 1986 and 1997. It found that, on average, the share price of the parent rose between 3 and 4 percent in the 90 days following the announcement of a carve-out. In the case of 12 carve-out companies in which the parent announced there would be a later spin-off, the share price of the carve-out performed 11 percent above the market 18 months after the initial public offering. Professors Jeffrey W. Allen of SMU and John McConnell of Purdue looked at 188 equity carve-out transactions between 1978 and 1993 ("Equity Carve-outs and Managerial Discretion," *Journal of Finance,* vol. 53, 1998, pp. 163–186; Professor Allen is Corrigan Research Fellow and Associate Professor at SMU). This study finds that the average excess return for the parent associated with carve-outs for the full sample is +2.12 percent over the three-day interval surrounding the carve-out announcement. In the 54 carve-outs in which the parent announced that the funds would be used wholly or primarily to repay debt or to pay a dividend to shareholders, the average excess return for the parent is +6.63 percent.

4. A study that looked at 83 carve-outs between 1981 and 1990 found that carved-out companies had significantly higher revenue, asset growth, and earnings than the industry peers during the first three years following a carve-out (J. A. Miles, J. R. Woolridge, and H. M. Hulbert, "Value Creation from Equity Carve-Outs," Pennsylvania State University, 1998). Another study that looked at 628 carve-outs (minority and majority) from 1981 to 1995 found that, on certain tests, the subsidiaries outperformed benchmarks (A. Vijh, "Long-Term Returns from Equity Carve-Outs," *Journal of Financial Economics,* vol. 51, 1999, pp. 273–308). Vijh's universe of minority and majority carve-outs had the following characteristics: median percent of subsidiary offered, 32.2 percent; median parent ownership after the carve-out, 58.6 percent; median offering value, $100 million (in 1995 dollars).

5. McKinsey, 2000.

6. K. Schipper and A. Smith report that 98 percent of carve-outs have a parent officer on the board ("A Comparison of Equity Carve-outs and Seasoned Equity Offerings," *Journal of Financial Economics,* vol. 15, 1985, pp. 153–186.

7. Note that the tests for tax consolidation differ somewhat from the tests for a tax-free spin-off. This difference is most relevant where two classes of stock are used, as explained in Chapter 9.

8. CEO George Hatsopoulos quoted in "Spinning It Out at Thermo Electron," *The Economist,* April 10, 1997.

9. For a study of the returns from Thermo's first 11 carve-outs, see J. Allen "Capital Markets and Corporate Structure: The Equity Carve-outs of Thermo Electron," *Journal of Financial Economics,* vol. 48, 1998, pp. 99–124.
   See also CFO Magazine, March 1999, pp. 97–98.

CHAPTER 7

1. In Cooper-Beldon, the subsidiary entered into a tax-sharing agreement with the parent requiring the subsidiary to pay to the parent the cash value of the step-up.

2. Needham & Company acted as advisor to General Signal in the divestiture of its semi-conductor equipment operations and was a comanager of the Electroglas carve-out IPO.
3. Needham & Company was a comanager of the Du Pont Photomask IPO and subsequent follow-on offerings.

CHAPTER 8

1. T. K. Grose, "Bloated by Diverse Acquisitions, Many Firms Are Now Using Spin-offs to Slim Down to Their Core Business," *Time Europe,* April 1, 2002.
2. Professors Cusatis and Woodridge (P. Cusatis, J. Miles, and R. Woodridge, "Restructuring Through Spin-Offs: The Stock Market Evidence," *Journal of Financial Economics,* vol. 33, 1993, pp. 293–311) find that parents and subsidiaries of spin-offs earn positive returns over three years compared with comparable companies. Professors D. Desai and P. Jain ("Firm Performance and Focus: Long-Term Stock Market Returns Following Spinoffs," *Journal of Financial Economics,* vol. 54, 1999, pp. 75–101) find that long-term gains are significantly positive when comparing spin-offs against comparable companies. According to Desai and Jain, superior stock market performance by the subsidiary is associated with improved operating performance following the spin-off. In the three years following those spin-offs, there was an increased business focus (defined as operating in fewer SIC codes), and spin-offs earn a positive return of 33.4 percent over benchmarks.
3. Professors J. Miles and J. Rosenfeld ("The Effect of Voluntary Spin-off Announcements," *Journal of Financial Economics,* vol. 38, 1983, pp. 1597–1606) find a positive return for the parent of approximately 3 percent after a spin-off transaction has been announced.
4. A. Dittmar,, "Capital Structure in Corporate Spin-Offs" Kelley School of Business, Indiana University, working paper, 2002.
5. A study by V. Mehrotra, W. Mikkelson, and M. Partch ("The Design of Financial Policies in Corporate Spinoffs," Lundquist College of Business, University of Oregon, working paper, 2002) of one-step spin-offs from 1979 to 1997, where the parent distributed a substantial portion of its assets in the spin-off, finds that the parent chooses a target capital structure for the subsidiary that takes into consideration the ability of the subsidiary to cover interest payments and the risks of financial distress. The study finds that liabilities are distributed consistent with the traditional theory of capital structure—the entity with a higher ratio of property, plant, and equipment to total assets is allocated greater financial leverage and differences in financial leverage are positively related to differences in profitability, and are negatively related to difference in the variability of industry operating income.

   The study also finds that differences in managerial incentives and oversight, such as managers' and directors' ownership stakes, board composition, and board size, do not account for differences in financial leverage allocations. In addition, pre-spin-off chief executive officers do not appear to transfer an unusually low or high level of financial leverage onto the firms they will manage following a spin-off. The study found no evidence for theories that managers' private interests determine capital structure choices in spin-offs.
6. The next step for U S West was sad. Qwest Communications bought the remainder of U S West for $35 billion in 1999 in a hostile takeover fueled by Wall Street's infatuation with Qwest and its grand strategy to wire the world with fiber-optic cable. The

E X H I B I T   N–5

Debt and Dividends in Spin-Offs

Total spin-offs reviewed in the study	129
Total spin-offs without debt allocation or funds transfer	39
Total spin-offs where the parent allocates debt to the subsidiary or the subsidiary transfers funds to the parent	90
Parent allocates debt to the subsidiary	56
Subsidiary pays the parent dividend	32
Subsidiary repays intercompany indebtedness to the parent	19
Parent forgives intercompany indebtedness from the subsidiary	2
Subsidiary pays parent a dividend	32
The categories are not mutually exclusive.	
Source: A. Dittmar	

     regional Bell had revenues of $13 billion in 1999 compared with Qwest's $3.9 billion. U S West also earned a profit of $1.3 billion, while Qwest lost money on operations. Qwest took on billions of dollars in debt to build out its nationwide fiber-optic network. Demand failed to materialize and Qwest soon ran into financial difficulties, exacerbated by the discovery of some highly questionable and aggressive accounting practices. See Exhibit N–5.

7. One mechanism to reduce the tax impact of a taxable spin-off is for the subsidiary to issue to the parent before the spin-off preferred stock having a liquidation preference equal to some or all of the likely fair market value of the subsidiary at the time of the distribution to the parent's shareholders. The stock of the subsidiary that is distributed in the taxable spin-off to the parent's shareholders represents at the time of the spin-off only a claim on the future appreciation in the value of the subsidiary. The transaction is still taxable, but taxes are minimized. Value to the shareholders of the subsidiary only occurs after the spin-off, when its value increases over that of the preferred stock.

8. For a description of the Agere carve-out, see N. Alster, "Spinning in Circles?," *Electronic Business,* July 2002.

9. The head of the PGBC is Steve Kandarian, a successful entrepreneur who has stated that he will look carefully at all transactions affecting pension benefits.

10. K. Brown and B. Brooke ("Institutional Demand and Security Price Pressure: The Case of Corporate Spin-Offs," *Financial Analysts Journal,* September/October 1993) conducted a study of 74 publicly traded spin-offs highlighting the tendency for institutional investors of parents to sell their newly dividend holdings in the spun-off subsidiaries.

11. In *Pope & Talbot v. Commissioner of Internal Revenue,* the IRS's position was upheld by the U.S Circuit Court for the 9th District in 1999 (9771359).

12. The requirement for more than 50 percent continuing ownership by the parent's share-holders counts only historic shareholders before the spin-off. However, all historic shareholders are not equal. Some shareholders of the parent at the time of the spin-off may not count toward the 50 percent requirement. This was an issue in the tax-free spin-off of Agere to Lucent's shareholders. Before the spin-off, Lucent used its stock to make many acquisitions. The IRS determined that the Agere transaction was tax free but cautioned that shareholders of any company acquired by Lucent for stock prior to the spin-off of Agere would not count as historic Lucent shareholders toward the 50 percent test if the acquisitions were made after Lucent had begun to "seriously consider" the Agere spin-off.
13. R. Bonte-Friedheim and J. Guyon, "Long Division: Hanson Reveals Plans for Breakup," *The Wall Street Journal Europe,* January 31, 1996.
14. P. Dwyer and H. Dawley, "The Urge to Demerge Hits Hanson," *Business Week,* February 12, 1996.
15. Needham & Company was a comanager of the DII Group follow-on public offering.
    See also P. Colon, "Should You Give These Orphaned Stocks a Home?," *Business Week,* October 15, 1990; R. Lowenstein, "Confessions of a Corporate Spin-off Junkie," *The Wall Street Journal,* March 28, 1996; J. Rehak, "3 Years On, the Sum of Hanson's Parts Exceeds the Whole," *International Herald Tribune,* July 10, 1999; R. Willens, "Liability Assumption in a Spin-Off," Lehman Brothers research report, September 21, 2001.

CHAPTER 9

1. S. Lacey, "Public Markets Leave Side Door Open: There Is an Alternative, Less Flashy Route to Going Public: The One-Step Spin-Off," *Red Herring,* June 15, 2001.
2. For a description of the earlier days of Palm, albeit one definitely from the singular viewpoint of the Palm founders, see Andrea Butter and David Pogue, *Piloting Palm: The Inside Story of Palm,* John Wiley & Sons, 2002.
3. The Palm carve-out also illustrates how the stock market may not function efficiently in pricing the subsidiary's shares in the post-IPO and pre-spin-off period. Prior to the IPO, 3Com fixed the distribution ratio of Palm shares to 3Com shareholders at 1.52 shares of Palm for every share of 3Com. Therefore, one share of 3Com should have been worth at least 1.52 times the Palm share price plus some value for 3Com's other business. Yet at the end of the first day of trading following the IPO, Palm closed at $95.06 per share and 3Com at $81.81. Based on the 1.52 ratio, the price of 3Com's shares should not have been less than $145. At $81.81 per share, the remaining businesses of 3Com had a negative value of $63 (or minus $22 billion). An investor at that time could have bought the same dollar value of 3Com shares in the market rather than buying Palm shares and received not only more Palm shares in the spin-off but also an interest in the rest of 3Com for free. This extreme mispricing continued for over two months.
    The Palm carve-out/pending spin-off relative valuations appear to violate a basic premise of financial theory: identical assets should have identical prices (i.e., with good information, the same asset should not trade at the same time at different prices). This premise is based on the assumption that arbitrageurs will step in and remove any mispricing in return for a profit. With a spin-off, if there is a significant mispricing of the relative value of the subsidiary's stock, arbitrageurs should sell short the stock of the subsidiary and buy the stock of the parent (arbitrageurs sell short by

borrowing shares from an existing holder, selling those shares in the market, and later buying back the shares in the market to return to the lender; arbitrageurs make a profit if the price of the shares falls in the interim). Arbitrageurs would close a relative valuation gap by driving down the price of the subsidiary's shares and increasing the price of the shares of the parent.

O. A. Lamont and R. H. Thaler discuss the Palm spin-off in a 2002 research report draft for the Graduate School of Business, University of Chicago and the National Bureau of Economic Research, titled "Can the Market Add and Subtract: Mispricing of Tech Stock Carve-Outs." One possible explanation that Lamont and Thaler offer is that there is a risk that the spin-off is not consummated. However, they conclude that the risk in Palm seemed out of proportion to the mispricing. Lamont and Thaler ask why arbitrageurs didn't step in to correct this mispricing by selling short shares of Palm and buying shares of the parent. The chief explanation they offer is that there were restraints on short selling by arbitrageurs that prevented them from closing the relative valuation gap. In order to sell a stock short, an arbitrageur has to find stock to borrow. This is not always possible.

This explanation is repeated in a 2002 research paper by J. D. Duffie, James Irvin Miller Professor of Finance, Stanford Graduate School of Business, titled "Short Selling May Affect Stock and Bond Prices." Professor Duffie writes that in the Palm case, traders found it difficult to find stock to borrow. "Following its IPO, Palm was ripe for shorting, but would-be short-sellers were thwarted by a sluggish securities-lending market," he concluded.

Palm's mispricing is not unique. Lamont and Thaler found five other cases between April 1996 and August 2000 in which parent companies were valued unambiguously lower than the firms they had just carved out and were going to spin off. In each case, the market eventually corrected itself—but only gradually.
4. Needham & Company is advising Palm on the PalmSource spin-off.

CHAPTER 10

1. M. Tonkawa, "Enthralled Japan Sony's Embrace Encourages Others to Adopt American Tool," *International Herald Tribune,* April 14, 2001, p. 13.
2. "Are Two Stocks Better Than One?," *Business Week,* June 28, 1999.
3. *Forbes,* December 13, 1999.
4. *U.S. News & World Report,* December 20, 1999.
5. There have been a number of academic studies of tracking stocks that are favorable on their value creation: S. Zuta, "Diversification Discount and Targeted Stock: Theory and Empirical Evidence," University of Maryland, working paper, 2000; J. D'Souza and J. Jacob, "Why Firms Issue Targeted Stock," *Journal of Financial Economics,* vol. 56, 2000, pp. 459–483; M. Billett and D. Mauer, "Diversification and the Value of Internal Capital Markets: The Case of Tracking Stock," *Journal of Banking and Finance,* vol. 24, 2000, pp. 1457–1490; D. Logue, J. Seward, and J. Walsh, "Rearranging Residual Claims: A Case for Targeted Stock," *Financial Management,* vol. 25, 1996, pp. 43–46; T. Chemmanur and I. Paeglis, "Why Issue Tracking Stocks?," Boston College, Carroll School of Management, 2000; and J. Elder and P. Westra, "The Reaction of Security Prices to Tracking Stock Announcements," *Journal of Economics and Finance,* vol. 24, no. 1, Spring 2000, pp. 36–55.
6. J. Elder and P. Westra, "The Reaction of Security Prices to Tracking Stock Announcements," *Journal of Economics and Finance,* vol. 24, no. 1, Spring 2000, pp. 36–55.

7. J.P. Morgan Securities, 1995.

8. T. Chemmanur and I. Paeglis, "Why Issue Tracking Stocks?," Boston College, Carroll School of Management, 2000.

9. P. Anslinger, S. Klepper, and S. Subramaniam, "Breaking Up Is Good to Do," *The McKinsey Quarterly*, no. 1, pp. 16–27.

10. M. Billett and A. Vijh, "The Market Performance of Tracking Stocks," University of Iowa Business School, working paper, 2001.

11. The evidence supports the view that business divisions that generate tax benefits are more likely to be tracked than carved out or spun off. Business divisions that underlie tracking stocks generate more net operating losses than those that are carved out or spun off.

12. David Thomas, Esq., of Kirkpatrick and Lockhart, LLP, brought to my attention the use of a tracking stock to separate out venture or investment operations.

13. J. Hass, "Directorial Fiduciary Duties in a Tracking Stock Equity Structure: The Need for a Duty of Fairness," *Michigan Law Review*, June 1996, pp. 2089–2177. Professor Hass was also quoted in *Business Week* (March 6, 2000) as saying. "It's a duty-of-loyalty bear trap . . . you have one servant, the board, serving two or more masters."

14. For a further discussion of the unwinding terms of tracking stocks, see E. Tuna, "Determinants and Consequences of Equity Restructurings: How Are Tracking Stocks Different to Equity Carve-outs and Spin-Offs?," University of Michigan Business School, research paper, 2002. See also Exhibit N–6.

15. G. Miles, "Why USX Isn't Afraid," *Business Week*, May 14, 1990.

    See also Tracking Stocks: Do They Create Value?, Securities Data Publishing, Inc., 2000; C. Quintanilla, "Interstate Bakeries Set to Buy Ralston's," *Wall Street Journal*, January 9, 1995; S. Scherreik, "Tread Carefully When You Buy Tracking Stocks," *Business Week*, March 6, 2000.

CHAPTER 12

1. See Exhibit N–7.

2. J. Lim and A. Saunders, "Initial Public Offerings: The Role of Venture Capitalists," The Research Foundation of the Institute of Chartered Financial Analysts, 1990.

3. A. Brav and P. Gompers, "Myth or Reality? The Long-Run Underperformance of Initial Public Offerings: Evidence from Venture and Non-Venture Capital-Backed Companies," *Journal of Finance*, vol. 52, no. 5, December 1997, pp. 1791–1821.

4. T. Hellmann and M. Puri, Stanford University, GSB research paper no. 1561, May 1999.

5. My thanks to my partner, Laura Black, for her assistance with the Corsair example. Needham & Company acted as financial advisor to TRW in forming the Corsair partnership.

CHAPTER 13

1. Professor Ranjay Gulati suggested some of the criteria for a successful strategic partnership referred to here in a 2001 presentation, "Why Alliances Fail." Professor Gulati is Michael L. Nemmers Associate Professor of Technology and E-Commerce at the Kellogg Graduate School of Management, Northwestern University.

2. Needham & Company acted as advisor to TRW in the RFMD transaction.

3. The structure of the barnesandnoble.com partnership was highlighted in a paper by Craig Wasserman. Mitchell Presser, Lawrence Makow, and Jared Rusman, published in 2000 by W. R. Hambrecht & Company.

EXHIBIT N–6

Representative Unwinding Terms for Tracking Stocks

Parent	Subsidiary	Treatment of the tracking stock in an exchange for parent stock at the option of the parent	Treatment of the tracking stock in the event of a sale of the subsidiary
Apollo Group	University of Phoenix Online	The parent stock is exchanged for the tracking stock at an initial 25% premium. The premium declines by 5% per year to 10%. There is no premium paid if the market capitalization of the tracking stock exceeds 60% of the combined parent and subsidiary market capitalization for 20 trading days or if there would be adverse tax consequences.	The sale proceeds are distributed as a special dividend to the tracking stockholders.
The Walt Disney Co.	Go.com	The parent stock is exchanged for the tracking stock at a 20% premium in year one, 15% in year two, 10% in years three to nine, and 5% thereafter.	The sale proceeds are distributed as a special dividend to the tracking stockholders.
General Motors Corp.	Electronic Data Systems Corp.	The parent stock is exchanged for the tracking stock at a 15% premium. No optional exchange is allowed if the dividends on the tracking stock are less than a set amount.	The tracking stock is exchanged for parent stock at a 20% premium.
Quantum Corp	Quantum Hard Disk Drive Group	The parent stock is exchanged for the tracking stock at a 10% premium for the first five years and then at no premium.	The sale proceeds are distributed as a special dividend to the tracking stockholders; or the tracking stock is exchanged for parent stock at a 10% premium for the first five years and then at no premium.
Ziff-Davis	ZDNet	The parent stock is exchanged for the tracking stock at an initial 25% premium that declines to 15% in year three.	The sale proceeds are distributed as a special dividend to the tracking stockholders; or the tracking stock is redeemed; or the tracking stock is exchanged for parent stock at a 10% premium.

Sources: Needham & Company, SEC filings, Tuna

See also S. Chan, J. Kensinger, A. Keown, and J. Martin, "Do Strategic Alliances Create Value," *Journal of Financial Economics,* vol. 46, no. 2, 1997.

CHAPTER 14

1. This is an example of an exchange premium on non-zero-coupon exchangeable debt. The market price of the public stock is $20 per share at the time the debt is issued, and the price of the debt is $1000. With no premium, the investor holding the debt would have the right to exchange the debt for 50 shares of the public stock. With a 20 percent exchange premium, the exchange price would be $25 per share. The investor would receive only 40 shares upon the exchange. The premium is usually expressed in a percentage of the stock price of the public stock at the time of the issue of the exchangeable debt.

2. A news story on Bloomberg at the time of the offering stated the following: " 'AT&T can get their money right away, but it doesn't hit the stock (of Cablevision) as hard,' said Donna Jaegers, an analyst at Invesco Funds Group Inc. in Denver, which owns shares of both companies. 'If they tried to throw that all on the market at once, that

E X H I B I T   N–7

Equity into Venture-Backed Companies

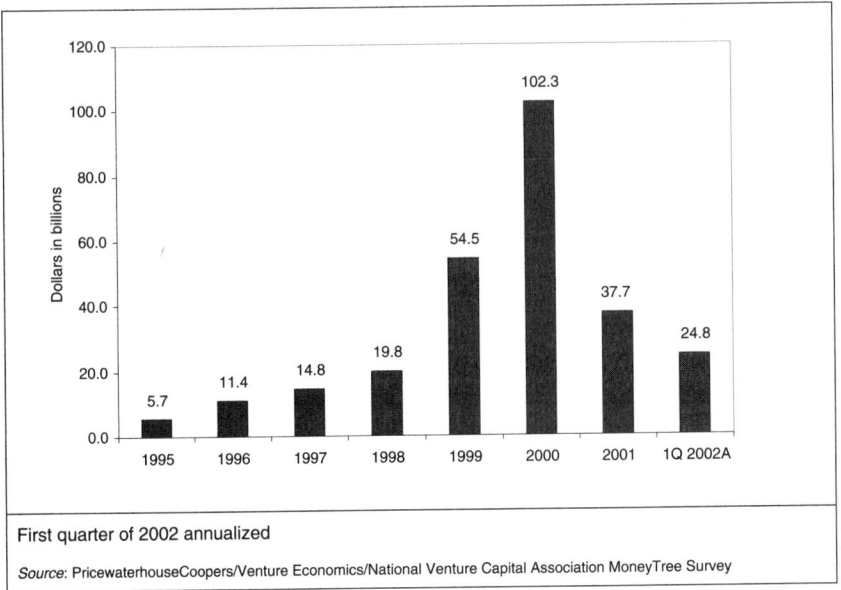

First quarter of 2002 annualized

Source: PricewaterhouseCoopers/Venture Economics/National Venture Capital Association MoneyTree Survey

would depress the price even further.' At that time, the price of the Cablevision stock had fallen 37 percent since May 31, 2001."

CHAPTER 15

1. Needham & Company advised FEI in these mergers.
2. S. McCartney, "AMR's Sabre to Acquire Preview Travel," *The Wall Street Journal,* November 5, 1999.
3. See also T. Burton and S. Lipin, "Grace, Fresenius in Dialysis Pact," *The Wall Street Journal,* February 5, 1996.
4. Needham & Company advised Micro General in this merger.

CHAPTER 16

1. Adapted from John C. Michaelson, "Exit Strategies," Chapter 8 in *Starting Up and Advising an Emerging Massachusetts Business,* Massachusetts Continuing Legal Education, 2002.

CHAPTER 17

1. Needham & Company advised ESS in the spin-off of Vialta and was the lead manager of the subsequent follow-on ESS public offering. It also advised Vialta on the partnership with Artisan Home Entertainment.

The management of ESS, and in particular the CFO, Jim Boyd, was of great help in reviewing this case study.

2. Treatment of parent stock options in a spin-off:

One issue with structuring the Vialta spin-off was that Vialta employees held nonqualified ESS stock options at the time of the spin-off. Until recently there was uncertainty over the how the IRS would treat unexercised parent nonqualified stock options and unvested parent restricted stock that had been issued to subsidiary employees prior to a spin-off but were exercised or vested only after the spin-off. IRC Section 1032 states that there is no recognized gain or loss when nonqualified stock options are exercised or restricted stock vests and that the employee only has taxable compensation income at that time. However, IRC 1032 applies to options and restricted stock issued by a company to its employees. After a spin-off, the subsidiary is an independent company separate from the parent and its employees are no longer parent employees.

If Section 1032 still applied, the tax consequences would be much more favorable to the parent, the subsidiary, and subsidiary employees in a spin-off. In this case, after a spin-off there would be no recognized gain or loss to the parent or the subsidiary when the parent's nonqualified stock options or restricted stock grants to subsidiary employees issued prior to the spin-off were exercised or vested. As well, employees of the subsidiary would continued to delay incurring taxable compensation income until they exercised nonqualified stock options or the restricted stock vested rather than incur the tax at the time of the spin-off. However, the validity of this approach was unknown. In a recent revenue ruling, 2002-1, the IRS agreed that the treatment of parent nonqualified stock options and unvested restricted stock held by subsidiary employees would not change with a spin-off. The parent and the subsidiary would continue to not recognize any gain or loss on exercise or vesting of the parent nonqualified stock options and unvested restricted stock granted prior to the spin-off, and employees of the subsidiary would still delay incurring compensation income until they exercised their nonqualified stock options or the restricted stock vested.

This ruling was brought to my attention by an article by K. L. Lester in *The Business Review,* May 31, 2002.

3. A parent shareholder must allocate the tax cost basis of all parent shares held on the spin-off record date and the subsidiary shares received in the spin-off. This allocation requires knowing (a) the market value of the subsidiary and parent shares on the day of the distribution (for parent shares, the market value is based on prices for shares trading ex- the spin-off dividend), and (b) the distribution ratio of subsidiary shares for parent shares. The holding period for the parent shares will carry over to the subsidiary shares.

The parent usually provides its shareholders with the necessary tax information for preparing tax filings in relation to parent shares held at the time of the spin-off and subsidiary shares received in the spin-off. To determine tax liability on any parent or subsidiary shares that are sold by the parent shareholder, the parent shareholder must allocate the tax cost basis of all the parent shares that the shareholder owns to which the distribution of spin-off shares is made (generally all the parent shares unless there are different classes of parent stock that receive differing ratios of subsidiary shares in the distribution) between the parent shares held on the spin-off record date and the subsidiary shares received in the spin-off. This allocation requires the shareholder to know the market value of the subsidiary and parent shares on the day of the distribution (for parent shares, the market value is based on prices for shares trading ex- the spin-off dividend); and the distribution ratio of subsidiary shares for parent shares. The tax holding period for the parent shares is carried over to the subsidiary shares.

CHAPTER 18

1. Professor Ritter is cited in N. Alster, "Initial Offerings Take a Turn to the Traditional," *The New York Times,* May 19, 2002.

CHAPTER 19

1. R. Comment and G. W. Schwert, "Poison or Placebo?," *Journal of Financial Economics,* vol. 39, 1995.
2. G. W. Schwert, "Poison or Placebo," University of Rochester, discussion paper, Spring 2002.
3. J.P. Morgan Chase M&A Research.
4. L. Bebchuk, J. Coates. IV, and G. Subramanian, "The Powerful Antitakeover Force of Staggered Boards: Theory, Evidence and Policy," *Stanford Law Review,* vol. 54, 2002.
5. The Ohio takeover laws received considerable attention during the hostile bid for TRW by Northrop. They appear to have been effective in obtaining a higher price for the TRW shareholders.

CHAPTER 20

1. An excellent detailed guide to the IPO process is Stephen Blowers, Peter Griffith, and Thomas Milan, *The Ernst & Young Guide to the IPO Value Journey,* John Wiley & Sons, 1999. See also *Going Public—What the CEO Needs to Know,* a handbook published by Peat Marwick Main & Co. (1998).
2. Some law firms that are closely identified with quality IPOs are Akin, Gump, Choate Hall; Cooley Godward; Dorsey & Whitney; Gadsby & Hannah; Gray, Cary; Gunderson Dettmer; Hale & Dorr; Heller Ehrman; Kaye, Scholer; Morrison & Foerster; Pillsbury Winthrop; Stoel Rives; Testa Hurwitz; and Wilson, Sonsini.
3. *Fortune,* June 24, 2002.
4. *The Wall Street Journal,* September 3, 2002.
5. R. Hennessey, "More IPOs Choose to List on NYSE in a Sign That Times Have Changed," *The Wall Street Journal,* April 29, 2002.

INDEX